Women

writing culture

Women writing culture

Edited by

Ruth Behar

and

Deborah A. Gordon

University of

California

Press

Berkeley

Los Angeles

London

University of California Press
Berkeley and Los Angeles, California

University of California Press, Ltd.
London, England

© 1995 by The Regents of the University of California

Library of Congress Cataloging-in-Publication Data

Women writing culture / edited by Ruth Behar and Deborah A. Gordon.
    p.   cm.
    Includes bibliographical references and index.
    ISBN 0-520-20207-4 (alk. paper). — ISBN 0-520-20208-2 (pbk. alk.
paper)
       1. Women anthropologists—Attitudes. 2. Ethnology—Authorship.
3. Ethnology—Philosophy. 4. Feminist anthropology. 5. Women's
writings. 6. Feminist literary criticism. I. Behar, Ruth, 1956– .
II. Gordon, Deborah A., 1956– .
GN27.W66 1995
305.42—dc20   95-36791
                                                  CIP

The ornamental motif is from the woodcut "Exchange Value" by
Pamela Terry.

Printed in the United States of America

9 8 7 6 5 4 3 2 1

The paper used in this publication meets the minimum requirements of
American National Standard for Information Sciences—Permanence of
Paper for Printed Library Materials, ANSI Z39.48-1984.

Ruth Behar dedicates this book to her teachers
Hildred Geertz and James W. Fernandez

Deborah Gordon dedicates this book to her teachers
Donna Haraway and James Clifford

Contents

Part III: Does Anthropology Have a Sex?

Part IV: Traveling Feminists

Coeditors Deborah A. Gordon and Ruth Behar. (Photograph by Coco Fusco, 1994)

Preface and Acknowledgments

THIS COLLECTION of essays is the product of a sustained and intense dialogue between us about the meaning of the three words of our title, *women, writing,* and *culture.* Although we are scholars and teachers of quite different training and sensibilities, we have carried on a long-distance friendship and collegial relationship for the past four years that was born out of curiosity over questions relating to feminism, writing, and anthropology. What does it mean to be a woman writer in anthropology, a discipline deeply rooted in the narrative of the male quest? How does it change the history of anthropology to truly take seriously the writing of women anthropologists? Is there an ethnographic practice that is uniquely feminist? If there is, how is this feminist ethnography distinct from both the "anthropology of women" of the 1970s and the analysis of gender of the 1980s?

Ruth Behar initially came up with the idea for a book on these issues as a result of her planning and teaching a graduate seminar at the University of Michigan in 1991 titled "Women Writing Culture: Twentieth-Century American Women Anthropologists." Out of the course, Behar organized a highly successful conference, "Women Writing Culture: Anthropology and Its Other Voices," in which Deborah Gordon was one of the keynote speakers. So much enthusiasm was generated by the conference at Michigan that Behar decided to move forward on plans for a book.

Feeling how profound was her intellectual debt to Deborah Gordon's pioneering work "Writing Culture, Writing Feminism," an early feminist critique of the anthology *Writing Culture,* Behar invited Gordon to coedit this volume. Traveling, phoning, faxing between Ann Arbor and Wichita we continued our conversation, clarifying for ourselves and each other our different stakes in this project. Ours was a unique and unprecedented editorial collaboration between a feminist ethnographer (Behar) and a feminist historian of anthropology (Gordon). *Women Writing Culture,* the product of our dialogue, indeed offers both another history of the story of anthropology and another vision of the anthropology waiting to be built out of our creative writing about the past and the present.

Working with the contributors, we began to see the shape of the collection emerge around anthropology's new location between feminism and multiculturalism. All of the essays, even those that are about crossing international cultural borders, bear some relationship to the vexed debates currently taking place in the United States over identification and difference. *Women Writing Culture* offers a response to the controversy surrounding the Western canon and the worthiness of women's studies as an intellectual pursuit and suggests anthropology's relevance to these discussions.

Our general call for contributions concerning the theme of women's writing of culture brought us a range of works, from biographical and historical essays to fiction, theater, memoirs, travelogues, theoretical reflections, and literary criticism. By going beyond the conventions of the academic essay to explore more daring forms of expression, *Women Writing Culture* provides a range of feminist visions of the dilemmas of writing culture in the twentieth century. At the same time, rather than feeling paradigm exhaustion, the contributors to this book assert their confidence in the possibility of constructing other models for ways to write creatively that are sensitive to the racial history, sexual politics, and moral predicaments of anthropology. We think this book will make it impossible to ever again think about the predicaments of cultural representation without seeing the central role of women in its theory and practice. With chutzpah and pathos, we mean to push anthropology over the edge, into that stormy sea of arguments about the fate of multiculturalism in an America that is still profoundly uncertain about how far it wants to let feminism go.

§

As editors we would like most of all to thank the contributors for their cooperation, patience, and hard work in the process of writing and revising their essays. At the University of California Press, Naomi Schneider provided sensitive editorial guidance and encouragement with the volume. We wish to express our sincere gratitude to the anonymous reviewer at University of California Press and to Benjamin Orlove, of the Editorial Committee, for their helpful suggestions and enthusiastic support of our project.

Deborah Gordon would like to acknowledge the Center for Women's Studies at Wichita State University for support for this project. The Marian Chuzy faculty research funds at the center provided financial support. Colleagues in women's studies Gayle Davis, Carol Konek, and Dorothy Miller provided a supportive working environment during the book's genesis. Sue Wilcox gave administrative help with the editorial process, faxing and mailing copies of essays. Her humor helped with some of the more stressful moments in editing a book as substantial as this one. In addition, colleagues in the theory writing and reading group Roger Berger, Stephen Moore, Harold Veeser, and Nancy West provided an intellectually stimulating context in which to discuss ideas in this book. All of them read drafts of my essays here and, more importantly, made me feel that the work mattered. Students in the seminar "Gender, Race and Knowledge," taught at Wichita State University in spring

1994 and 1995, responded to ideas about feminist ethnography that I presented in class. I would like to thank Tom De Lillo for support and advice during the final editing process. Finally, thanks to Ruth. For faith, trust, emotional and intellectual sustenance.

Ruth Behar would like to thank all of the graduate students in her University of Michigan class on "Women Writing Culture," where the idea for this book was first articulated. At the "Women Writing Culture" conference, my colleague Carol Karlsen was an especially nurturing presence. She kindly connected me to Willem de Blecourt of the Editorial Board at *Critique of Anthropology,* where a dress rehearsal for this book was tried out in the December 1993 special issue of the journal. Among many colleagues at the University of Michigan who encouraged this project, I want to particularly thank Bruce Mannheim, Gracia Clark, Abby Stewart, Sherry Ortner, and the members of my writing group, Joanne Leonard, Julie Ellison, Patsy Yaeger, and Anne Gere. It took enormous organizational skills to turn an unwieldy stack of essays into a manuscript, and I am indebted to Rachael Cohen, Kim Gaines, and Amy McDonald for their generous secretarial and editorial assistance. I am grateful, as ever, to David Frye, who helped in various ways and tried in vain to bring order to my chaotic computer files. I am grateful, too, to my dear son, Gabriel, for his compassion and understanding. My thanks to the MacArthur Foundation for a fellowship that saved my life more than once and allowed me to take time off from teaching to dedicate myself to writing and editing this book. Finally, thanks to Debbie, for her faith, trust, sustenance. And for sisterhood, such as I could never have imagined.

Ruth Behar & Deborah A. Gordon
Ann Arbor and Wichita, December 12, 1994

In Yolanda Fundora's pencil drawing Autoretrato-Autocrítico, *the breasts brush up against the arm and hand clutching the pencil. (Drawing courtesy of Yolanda V. Fundora)*

Introduction: Out of Exile

The Bare-Breasted Woman with the Eyes at Her Back

WHAT FIRST attracted me to Yolanda Fundora's drawing were the bare breasts of the woman clutching the pencil. In anthropology it is always the other woman, the native woman somewhere else, the woman who doesn't write, the !Kung woman, the Balinese woman, the *National Geographic* woman, who has breasts. Breasts that can be seen, exposed, pictured, brought home, and put into books.

The woman anthropologist, the woman who writes culture, also has breasts, but she is given permission to conceal them behind her pencil and pad of paper. Yet it is at her own peril that she deludes herself into thinking her breasts do not matter, are invisible, cancer won't catch up with them, the male gaze does not take them into

Ruth Behar

account. Remember what the Guerrilla Girls once told the Western art world? Only bare-breasted women make it into the Metropolitan Museum of Art. In Yolanda Fundora's drawing, the breasts brush up against the arm and hand clutching the pencil.

The woman in the drawing regards the world with the direct and steady gaze of a keen observer. But behind her is a sea of eyes. When a woman sits down to write, all eyes are on her. The woman who is turning others into the object of her gaze is herself already an object of the gaze. Woman, the original Other, is always being looked at and looked over. A woman sees herself being seen. Clutching her pencil, she wonders how "the discipline" will view the writing she wants to do. Will it be seen as too derivative of male work? Or too feminine? Too safe? Or too risky? Too serious? Or not serious enough? Many eyes bore in on her, looking to see if she will do better or worse than men, or at least as well as other women.

The eyes on a woman's back are also her own eyes. They are everything she has seen in her travels and in her return home. They represent the different roles a woman assumes in the various places where she sojourns, each eye seeing her at a slightly different angle. Sitting down to write, a woman sheds the clothes of each of the different roles she has played and lets all the eyes of her experiences come forth as she contemplates her life and begins to put pencil to paper.

Yolanda Fundora intended her drawing to be a self-portrait. She wanted to find a way both to define and to undefine herself as a Cuban-born artist who has shuttled between Puerto Rico and New York City. She wanted, she says, not to always have to categorize herself, so she decided to make the woman a color that does not exist in real life. A twilight blue, purple woman. Her hair, suggesting a rainbow of indecision, a flowering androgynous peacock, is multicolored—blue, pink, purple, yellow, white, black. Behind the woman the sun has set, the moon has risen, and the tip of an island, an unknown country, beckons from afar.

The picture is also a group self-portrait, Yolanda Fundora says. She drew it a few years ago when she was part of a women's art collective in Puerto Rico. Controversies and debates surfaced all the time among the members of the collective about their role as women artists. The sea of eyes acknowledges the different ways in which women look at the world as well as the willingness of women to accept, rather than to annihilate, such a confusing diversity of visions. When women look out for one another, the sea of eyes on our backs is no longer anything to fear.

Yolanda Fundora's artistic vision encapsulates the spirit of this book, which is all about seeing anthropology through other eyes. The eyes are those of women who do their writing as anthropologists, aware of how their own identity is constructed as female within a discipline rooted in male musing about foreign lands. In focusing on the legacy of women's anthropological writings and on the dilemmas women anthropologists encounter as writers, this book is both unique and long overdue. All eyes, indeed, are on us. But we are not afraid to look back—and to offer a vision of a different anthropology that places women's writing center stage in the debate about how, for whom, and to what end anthropologists embark on journeys that bring them home again to their desks and, nowadays, to their computers. To computers, let us not forget, assembled by the delicate hands of a native woman somewhere else.

A Fork in the Road Where *Writing Culture* Meets *This Bridge Called My Back*

This book was born of a double crisis—the crisis in anthropology and the crisis in feminism.[1] It is a 1990s response to two critical projects of the 1980s that emerged separately, like parallel lines destined never to meet, but which this book has set about to join together. One project, emerging within anthropology, was the postmodernist or textualist critique, best exemplified by the anthology *Writing Culture: The Poetics and Politics of Ethnography*, edited by James Clifford, a historian of anthropology, and George Marcus, an anthropologist and critic of "realist" traditions in ethnographic writing. Their book was the product of a limited-seating "advanced seminar" at the School of American Research in Santa Fe.[2]

The other project, stemming from critiques of white middle-class feminism by lesbians and women of color, emerged from outside the academy and yet entered the women's studies mainstream through the anthology *This Bridge Called My Back*, edited by Cherríe Moraga and Gloria Anzaldúa, a pair of Chicana lesbian poet-critics.[3] Without academic tenure, Moraga and Anzaldúa worried about paying the rent while producing their book, in which they encouraged women of color who had not thought of themselves as writers to participate. The *Writing Culture* project fell squarely within academic territory; the project of *This Bridge Called My Back* was a challenge to the closed borders of that territory.

I was warned both by our concerned female editor and by a kindly male anthropologist who cares deeply about this project (and contributed to *Writing Culture*) to emphasize that *Women Writing Culture* is a new and distinctive enterprise, something totally original, with no kinship to *Writing Culture*. Otherwise, I was told, we would run the risk of having our book dismissed (by men) as derivative—"And now we hear from the women about the same old thing." While I appreciate this sensible advice, I prefer to be bold and fearless and claim *Writing Culture* as a key precursor to our feminist project.

The publication of that anthology in 1986 set off a debate about the predicaments of cultural representation that shook up North American anthropology and brought a new self-awareness to the discipline. Even those who criticized *Writing Culture* acknowledged its importance by giving it their serious attention.[4] The book's purpose was to make an incredibly obvious point: that anthropologists write. And, further, that what they write, namely ethnographies—a strange cross between the realist novel, the travel account, the memoir, and the scientific report—had to be understood in terms of poetics and politics. In a discipline notoriously overcrowded with literary wannabes like the famed Ruth Benedict and Edward Sapir, who hid their poems from the watchful eyes of Papa Franz Boas, the "father" of American anthropology, this revelation was not earthshaking.[5] But never before had the power of anthropological rhetoric been subjected to such keen and sophisticated textual analysis, extinguishing any remaining sparks of the presumption that ethnographies were transparent mirrors of culture. Its contributors questioned the politics of a poetics that depends on the words of (frequently less privileged) others for its existence and yet offers none of the benefits of authorship to those others who participate with the anthropologist in the writing of culture.[6]

Only Mary Louise Pratt, the lone woman contributor to the anthology, and a literary critic no less, dared to wonder aloud whether it truly was such a great honor to be scripted into the books anthropologists write. How was it, she asked mischievously, with the liberty of someone from outside the discipline, that anthropologists, who are such interesting people doing such interesting things, produce such dull books?[7]

In his introduction to *Writing Culture,* James Clifford sought to answer Pratt's devilish but important question by asserting that anthropology needed to encourage more innovative, dialogic, reflexive, and experimental writing. At the same time, the "new ethnography" was also expected to reflect a more profound self-consciousness of the workings of power and the partialness of all truth, both in the text and in the world. The "new ethnography" would not resolve the profoundly troubling issues of inequality in a world fueled by global capitalism, but at least it would seek to decolonize the power relations inherent in the representation of the Other.[8] The *Writing Culture* agenda promised to renew anthropology's faltering sense of purpose.

Yet women anthropologists and women's anthropological writings were decidedly absent from that agenda. Like a miniature version of the great twentieth-century revolutionary plans that promised one day to solve the "woman question," the *Writing Culture* project asked women "to be patient, to understand . . . [that] their needs—what with Ideology, Politics, and Economics—were nowhere near the top."[9] In an act of sanctioned ignorance, the category of the new ethnography failed to take into account that throughout the twentieth century women had crossed the border between anthropology and literature—but usually "illegally," as aliens who produced works that tended to be viewed in the profession as "confessional" and "popular" or, in the words of Virginia Woolf, as "little notes." The *Writing Culture* agenda, conceived in homoerotic terms by male academics for other male academics, provided the official credentials, and the cachet, that women had lacked for crossing the border. Even the personal voice, undermined when used by women, was given the seal of approval in men's ethnographic accounts, reclassified in more academically favorable terms as "reflexive" and "experimental."[10]

Writing Culture, not surprisingly, both saddened and infuriated many women anthropologists. No two pages in the history of anthropological writing have ever created as much anguish among feminist readers as did James Clifford's uneasy statements justifying the absence of women anthropologists from the project of *Writing Culture.* Pushed to account for this gap by the criticism of a feminist reader who reviewed the book in manuscript, Clifford made the now infamous claim that women anthropologists were excluded because their writings failed to fit the requirement of being feminist *and* textually innovative.[11] To be a woman writing culture became a contradiction in terms: women who write experimentally are not feminist enough, while women who write as feminists write in ignorance of the textual theory that underpins their own texts.

The first major feminist response to these ideas was offered by Deborah Gordon, the coeditor of this book, who argued that "an important problem with 'experimental' ethnographic authority is its grounding in a masculine subjectivity which encourages feminists to identify with new modes of ethnography, claiming to be decolonial, while simultaneously relegating feminism to a strained position of servitude." Yet Gordon insisted that the essays in *Writing Culture* were not malicious; they were simply emblematic of the "ineffective management of men's negotiation of feminism."[12] Following Gordon's insight, Judith Newton and Judith Stacey have chosen to explore in their essay for this volume precisely the difficulties men experience in locating themselves within feminism, as they try to avoid being tourists or, worse, interlopers in womanist terrain.

Certainly it is not our aim in this book to argue for a simple male-female opposition between *Writing Culture* and *Women Writing Culture*. Feminist revision is always inclusive of those men who, as Joseph Boone and Michael Cadden put it, want to abjure the "male gaze" and to learn to "resee" reality in engendered terms rather than through an "I/eye" that imagines itself as transcendent.[13] But the fact is that *Writing Culture* took a stab at the heart of feminist anthropology, which was devalued as a dreary, hopelessly tautological, fact-finding mission—so, tell us, my dear, are women among the Bongo-Bongo indeed so terribly different? As Catherine Lutz notes in her essay for this volume, the constant pressure on us as women to work on our bodies and our fashions now shifted to our writing, which needed more work if its "style" was ever going to measure up.

Afterwards, those of us who had gone into anthropology with the dream of writing and had had our wings clipped for not being analytical enough took hold of the pen with a fervor that would never again permit us to stash our flashes of insight under our beds as Emily Dickinson did with her poetry. In truth, the *Writing Culture* project was a sullen liberation. For we could not miss the irony: As women we were being "liberated" to write culture more creatively, more self-consciously, more engagingly by male colleagues who continued to operate within a gendered hierarchy that reproduced the usual structure of power relations within anthropology, the academy, and society in general.

And thus the irony of this book—which might never have come about if not for the absence of women in *Writing Culture*. Just as the anthology *Woman, Culture and Society,* the landmark text of our 1970s feminist predecessors, appropriated and thereby transformed the anthropological classic, *Man, Culture and Society,* so too we have reclaimed the project of *Writing Culture.*[14] More than twenty years ago Adrienne Rich asserted that male writers do not write for women, or with a sense of women's criticism, when choosing their materials, themes, and language. But women writers, even when they are supposed to be addressing women, write for men; or at least they write with the haunting sense of being overheard by men, and certainly with the inescapable knowledge of having already been defined in men's words. That is why "re-vision," the act of "entering an old text from a new critical direction," is for women "an act of survival. . . . We need to know the writing of the past . . . not to pass on a tradition but to break its hold over us." [15]

But it is tiring to always have to be responsive; that is so often the role women play in our society. Fortunately, although this book began as a feminist response to *Writing Culture,* it grew into something much larger. Our book initiates another agenda that goes beyond *Writing Culture* in its inclusiveness, its creative process, its need to combine history and practice, its humor, its pathos, its democratizing politics, its attention to race and ethnicity as well as to culture, its engendered self-consciousness, its awareness of the academy as a knowledge factory, its dreams. Feminist revision is always about a new way of looking at all categories, not just at "woman." The essays collected here envision another history as well as another future for anthropology, an intellectual pursuit which not too long ago was (and even now often is) still defined as the study of "man."

If *Writing Culture*'s effect on feminist anthropologists was to inspire an empowering rage, the effect of *This Bridge Called My Back,* on the other hand, was to humble us, to stop us in our tracks. We read *This Bridge,* many of us, as graduate students or beginning assistant professors, belatedly educating ourselves in the issues affecting women of color in our country, which our education in anthropology had neglected. Many of us, too, became conscious of our own identities as "women of color," even if our anthropological training made us skeptical about the limitations of the term. As Paulla Ebron and Anna Lowenhaupt Tsing note in their essay in this volume, reading *This Bridge* brought new energy to those of us in the academy searching for ways to understand how our politics of knowledge could be reshaped by the women's movement, the African American civil rights movement, and the Chicano/Chicana cultural movements. And yet *This Bridge* thrust a different kind of arrow into the heart of feminist anthropology—it made us rethink the ways in which First World women had unself-consciously created a cultural other in their images of "Third World" or "minority" women. [16] And it forced feminist anthropology to come home. [17] *This Bridge* not only called attention to white feminist oversights but also signaled the importance of creating new coalitions among women that would acknowledge differences of race, class, sexual orientation, educational privilege, and nationality. That the divisions between women could be as strong as the ties binding them was a sobering, and necessary, lesson for feminism. Indeed, *This Bridge* was a product of the most severe and painful crisis the North American feminist movement had ever faced—its need to come to terms with the fact that Other Women had been excluded from (or sometimes, just as matronizingly, unquestioningly included within) its universal project of liberation. Placing *This Bridge Called My Back* side by side on the bookshelf with *Writing Culture,* feminist anthropologists felt the inadequacy of the dichotomies between Subject and Object, Self and Other, the West and the Rest.

There was also a deep concern in *This Bridge* with the politics of authorship. The contributors, women of Native American, African American, Latin American, and Asian American background, wrote in full consciousness of the fact that they were once the colonized, the native informants, the objects of the ethnographic gaze, and they pondered the question of who has the right to write culture for whom. Anthropologists and similar specialists, they asserted, were no longer the unique purveyors of knowledge about cultural meanings and understandings. Questioning anthropology's often static, unpoliticized, comfortably-somewhere-else concept of culture, they challenged anthropologists to take into account the discriminations of racism, homophobia, sexism, and classism in the America to which we continually returned after pursuing our research in faraway places. Aware of the privileges of authorship, they wrote to challenge the distancing and alienating forms of self-expression that academic elitism encouraged. As Gloria Anzaldúa expressed it, "They convince us that we must cultivate art for art's sake. Bow down to the sacred bull, form. Put frames and metaframes around the writing."[18] Breaking open the notion of "form" in order to democratize access to writing, *This Bridge Called My Back* included poems, essays, stories, speeches, manifestos, dialogues, and letters.

Audre Lorde wrote an open letter to Mary Daly, asking if she viewed her as a native informant: "Have you read my work, and the work of other black women, for what it could give you? Or did you hunt through only to find words that would legitimize your chapter on African genital mutilation?" Gloria Anzaldúa wrote a letter to Third World women writers in which she recalled the pain of coming to writing: "The schools we attended or didn't attend did not give us the skills for writing nor the confidence that we were correct in using our class and ethnic languages. I, for one, became adept at, and majored in English to spite, to show up, the arrogant racist teachers who thought all Chicano children were dumb and dirty." And Nellie Wong, in a letter to herself, spoke of the need to write in many voices and forms while realizing the futility of simply writing: "Your poems and stories alone aren't enough. Nothing for you is ever enough and so you challenge yourselves, again and again, to try something new, to help build a movement, to organize for the rights of working people, to write a novel, a play, to create a living theater that will embody your dreams and vision, energy in print."[19]

Women Writing Culture follows in the spirit of *This Bridge Called My Back* by refusing to separate creative writing from critical writing. Our book is multivoiced and includes biographical, historical, and literary essays, fiction, autobiography, theater, poetry, life stories, travelogues, social criticism, fieldwork accounts, and blended texts of various kinds. We do not simply cite the work of women of color or recite the mantra of gender, race, and class and go on with academic business as usual, handing difference over with one hand and taking it away with the other.[20] For we have become all too aware that not only were women anthropologists excluded from the project of *Writing Culture* but so too were "native" and "minority" anthropologists.[21] In the words of the African American critic bell hooks, the cover of *Writing Culture* hid "the face of the brown/black woman" beneath its title, graphically representing the concealment that marks much of the writing inside.[22] That concealment was based on an odd assumption: that experiments in writing were not likely to flow from the pens of those less privileged, such as people of color or those without tenure.[23] But as Audre Lorde once fiercely asserted, poetry is not a luxury for women and people of color; it is a vital necessity, "the skeleton architecture of our lives."[24]

Many of the contributors to this book are themselves women of color or immigrants or people of hybrid identity who know what it is like to be othered and so bring to anthropology a rebellious undoing of the classical boundary between observer and observed. Many are the first generation of women in their families to have attained a university education and so bring to anthropology a sharp sense of unease with the hierarchies embedded in educational institutions. Some are lesbians. Some are married with children. Some have chosen to be wives but not mothers, or mothers but not wives. Some are happily single and childfree. Some are tenured and comfortable but kept by administrative burdens from doing the writing that matters. Some are untenured and struggling to do the writing that matters while juggling heavy teaching loads and the burdens of being "junior" faculty. Three are students struggling to do the writing that matters while trying to earn a doctorate. We even have a male voice, that of a young graduate student searching for another location between the history of men's musing about foreign lands and the impact of feminist awakenings. Our individual trajectories are certainly as diverse as our contributions to this book. If there is a single thing, a common land that all of us are seeking, it is an anthropology without exiles.

The Question of the Canon, or Do Alice Walker and Margaret Mead Pose a Threat to Shakespeare and Evans-Pritchard?

Anthropology, in this country, bears the shape of a woman—Margaret Mead, the most famous anthropologist of our century. As anthropologists, we ought to be proud of this robust woman and want to claim her, but in reality many of us are embarrassed by her. Only now and then, if she is ruthlessly attacked, do we rise to her defense. Usually we do not take her very seriously. So we are not likely to pay attention when James Clifford remarks in the first page of his introduction that the cover photograph of *Writing Culture*, depicting a white male ethnographer scribbling in a notepad under the gaze of a few local people, "is not the usual portrait of anthropological fieldwork." And he goes on: "We are more accustomed to pictures of Margaret Mead exuberantly playing with children in Manus or questioning villagers in Bali."[25]

This is an interesting slip. Margaret Mead was a prolific writer who outwrote her male colleagues and used her pen to explore genres ranging from ethnography to social criticism to autobiography. As Nancy Lutkehaus points out in her essay in this volume, between 1925 and 1975 Mead published more than 1,300 books, biographies, articles, and reviews. She also wrote short pieces for publications ranging from *The Nation* to *Redbook* magazine, to which she contributed a monthly column. Mead was a public intellectual immersed in the issues of her time; she appeared frequently on television talk shows, and when *Rap on Race* was published she insisted that it keep the dialogical form out of which it had emerged in her conversations with James Baldwin. Yet Mead's reputation as a serious scholar has been damaged by her image in the discipline as a "popularizer." Edward E. Evans-Pritchard, a male contemporary who was an exemplar of the professional model of ethnographic writing that became dominant in the discipline, branded Mead's writing as belonging to the "Rustling-of-the-Wind-in-the-Palm-Trees School." The erasure of Mead as a scholar, writer, and public intellectual, Clifford's slip of the pen, attests to the fact that it is the image of the woman anthropologist as the one who plays with the children and questions the villagers, not the one who writes the texts, that lives on, despite the mythic conception of American anthropology as a profession that is especially receptive to the contributions of women.

Sadly, Clifford is not alone in failing to recognize women's theoretical and literary contributions to anthropology. Nor is it simply men in the discipline who are to blame for overlooking women's work. In her study of citation practices in anthropology, Catherine Lutz underscored how both female and male authors tend to cite more often the presumably "theoretical" writing of men, while women's writing, which often focuses on gender issues, is cited less frequently and usually in circumscribed contexts. In much the same way that the traces of women's labor go unseen in the larger society, Lutz suggests that women's labor in anthropology is quietly erased by the maintenance of a prestige hierarchy within the discipline that has fixed a (male) canon of what counts as important knowledge.[26]

In the United States we have grown accustomed to hearing of debates about the "canon" in departments of English. In recent years several major universities have been revising the traditional curriculum to include writings by women and minorities, the two "groups" who are being called upon to diversify the standard white male reading list of "great books."[27] Even the media have jumped into the debate by offering gloomy science fiction visions of a world where the treasures of high Western culture, perennials dusted and passed on through the generations and the centuries, have been replaced by the faddish writings of black women and ethnic writers, taught by their intolerant and radical supporters in the academy.[28]

One symbol for the perceived threat posed by the canon wars was the media's claim (which is totally bogus) that books by Alice Walker are now assigned more frequently than Shakespeare in English departments.[29] As a hysterical article in *Time* put it, "Imagine a literature class that equates Shakespeare and the novelist Alice Walker, not as artists but as fragments of sociology. Shakespeare is deemed to represent the outlook of a racist, sexist and classist 16th century England, while Walker allegedly embodies a better but still oppressive 20th century America. . . . Where is this upside-down world? . . . It is to be found on many U.S. college campuses." [30]

In fact, a key conclusion of the debate has been the need not simply to add the work of excluded writers to standardized reading lists but also to examine how the process of marginalization has shaped the works produced within the dominant culture. As Toni Morrison has put it, "Looking at the scope of American literature, I can't help thinking that the question should never have been 'Why am I, an Afro-American, absent from it?' It is not a particularly interesting query anyway. The spectacularly interesting question is 'What intellectual feats had to be performed by the author or his critic to erase me from a society seething with my presence, and what effect has that performance had on the work?'" [31] Hazel Carby, commenting on Morrison's text, adds, "Preserving a gendered analysis for texts by women or about women and an analysis of racial domination for texts by or directly about black people will not by itself transform our understanding of dominant cultural forms." [32]

Strangely, anthropologists stayed silent at a time when these debates about the literary canon, which were really about negotiating the meaning of Western culture, formed part of everyday public discourse in the United States. Yet anthropologists have much to learn from these debates as well as much to contribute. Although the debates have been reduced, by their detractors, to a battle over the relative merits of the work of Shakespeare and Alice Walker, the key question at stake is what kind of writing will live on in the minds of the coming generation of readers and writers and what kind of writing will perish from neglect and thereby lose its chance to shape and transform the world. Lamenting the "race for theory" that has overtaken the academic literary world, the African American critic Barbara Christian has astutely remarked, "I know, from literary history, that writing disappears unless there is a response to it." [33]

For many anthropologists, who enter the profession out of a desire to engage with real people in real (and usually forgotten) places, the literary critic, with "his" reading list of the great books of Western civilization, is a symbolic antithesis. At least in its classical form, anthropology was a discipline that was "rough and ready." [34] Even today, we do not totally believe in books and archives; we believe somehow (still!) in the redemptive possibilities of displacement, of travel, even if, as happens lately, our voyages only return us to our own abandoned hometown or our high-school graduating class. [35] We go in search of life experience, the stuff that, in a profound way, makes books disturbingly ridiculous. Yet ironically we make books out of the things we did not think we could find in books. We end up, as the poet Marianne Moore would say, planting real people and places in the imaginary gardens of our books.

But as academic anthropologists we do not simply write books, we teach books, just as our colleagues do in departments of English. If our fieldwork goes well, if our dissertation is approved, eventually most of us end up—or at least hope to—in the classroom, teaching neophytes what anthropology is all about. We may tell a few anecdotes, but it is our reading lists that communicate to students what constitutes legitimate and worthwhile anthropological knowledge. Anthropologists have belatedly begun to realize that we, too, have a canon, a set of "great books" that we continue to teach to our students, as dutifully as they were once taught to us in graduate school. That these books just happen to be the writings of white men is an idea that can never be brought up. It seems somehow impolite, given anthropology's virtue as the first academic discipline even to give a damn about all those remote and often vanquished cultures. So we habitually assign the writing of Evans-Pritchard because his work on the Azande and the Nuer has been enshrined as part of our "core" reading list. Yet we rarely ask students to engage with the writing of Alice Walker, even though, as Faye Harrison persuasively shows in her essay for this volume, she has long seen herself as an active interlocutor with anthropology.

The professional management of anthropology exercises power not just by fixing the value of certain texts in an ahistorical, acultural realm of the classics but by determining which emerging ethnographic writings will be inscribed into the discipline and which will be written off. As Lorraine Nencel and Peter Pels state, "To be taken seriously in the academy, we also have to write ourselves *in* the history of the discipline and, consequently, write *off* rival academic currents." [36] That is, of course, how canons are constructed. As Joan Vincent puts it, "When we find ourselves holding in our hands 'classical' ethnographies, we know that we are about to read the victors in struggles for past and present recognition and the attribution of significance." The textualist critique in *Writing Culture* did not go far enough, Vincent notes, because beyond analyzing specific texts it is also necessary "to address the politics around the writing of the text, the politics of reading the text, and the politics of its reproduction." [37]

Recently, American anthropologists have bemoaned the fact that their colleagues in literature leave them out of their discussions about the canon and the possibilities of multicultural teaching. [38] But the continued lack of critical reflection about our own canon suggests that anthropology has yet to carry out the radical kind of self-examination that would bring its multicultural quest home. We assume that because we have always studied "the other," we have somehow, in the animist fashion we used to attribute to primitive mentality, incorporated the insights of multiculturalism into the academic settings in which we work. American anthropology under the direction of Franz Boas, a German Jew, made an early contribution to undermining racism and to bringing to the national consciousness an awareness of the destruction wreaked upon Native Americans. But repeatedly invoking Boas and resting on those laurels will not build an anthropology of the present. Our anthropology department faculties and student bodies have a long way to go before they become ethnically diverse, while in our teaching we continue to reproduce the theoretical knowledge of Euro-American males.

Why is it that the legacy of what counts as social theory is traced back only to Lewis Henry Morgan, Karl Marx, Emile Durkheim, Max Weber, Michel Foucault, and Pierre Bourdieu? Why is there not a parallel matrilineal genealogy taking off from, say, the turn-of-the-century work of Charlotte Perkins Gilman? She wrote not only a major treatise, *Women and Economics,* but also the short story "The Yellow Wallpaper," a brilliant allegory about the madness of a woman who was prevented from reading and writing.[39] Why is the culture concept in anthropology only traced through Sir Edward Tylor, Franz Boas, Bronislaw Malinowski, Claude Lévi-Strauss, and Clifford Geertz? Could the writing of culture not be traced, as the essays in this volume suggest, through Elsie Clews Parsons, Ruth Benedict, Margaret Mead, Ella Deloria, Zora Neale Hurston, Ruth Landes, and Barbara Myerhoff to Alice Walker? Could we not follow this trajectory down to the contemporary oral history and literacy work, analyzed by Deborah Gordon in her essay in this volume, of Rina Benmayor and other Hunter College researchers in the El Barrio Project on Puerto Rican women living in Harlem? At the same time, shouldn't we approach our canon more androgynously and attempt to understand the interplay of male and female theorizing of society and culture? Not only do we need to take a bilateral approach, we need also to question our assumption that, in anthropology, "issues and isms develop unlineally and from within" and turn our attention to "constellations of expatriates, emigrés, professionals, and amateurs engaged in dislocated writing and performance."[40] And do we not need to explore fully, as Toni Morrison and Hazel Carby suggest, the gendered and racial erasures buttressing the canon as we have come to know it? Why is it that anthropology—the discipline whose legitimacy is so wrapped up in the multiplicity of languages and worlds—continues to be conceived in such resolutely patrilineal and Eurocentric terms?

It is high time for a debate about our canon. As Faye Harrison argues, anthropology has tended to relegate the contributions of minorities and women "to the status of special interest trivia . . . the authorized curricular menu of expendable 'add and stir' electives. . . . A socially responsible and genuinely critical anthropology should challenge this iniquitous reaction, and, furthermore, set a positive example by promoting cultural diversity where it counts, at its very core."[41] The essays in this volume offer one entrance into that debate, retelling the story of American anthropology in ways that allow us to imagine what Alice Walker might say, not only to Shakespeare but also to Evans-Pritchard and Mead.

Women Writing Culture is rooted in pedagogical concerns, which are also political, epistemological, and historical concerns. This book grew out of my own, often frustrating, efforts to rethink the anthropological canon. In 1991, inspired by Gordon's critique of *Writing Culture,* I taught a graduate seminar at the University of Michigan on "Women Writing Culture: Twentieth-Century American Women Anthropologists."[42] Seventeen women graduate students with diverse interests in anthropology took the course, and together we tried to understand the particular challenges that ethnographic writing has posed for women authors. Our discussions generated tremendous excitement. For the anthropology students in the group, the course filled a lacuna and served as a challenge to the core course program, a yearlong exploration of the history and theory of the discipline that in the year I was teaching included Ruth Benedict as the sole woman author on the reading list. For me, teaching for the first time in my career a course with the word "Women" in the title, I learned firsthand what it meant to teach a course so dangerous—or merely so irrelevant—to the other sex that no men dared sign up for it. Had I called the course simply "Writing Culture," I am certain the enrollment pattern would have been different. Of course, the more subversive act would have been to have called the course "Writing Culture" and still only have taught the writings of women ethnographers!

Teaching "Women Writing Culture" it became clear to me that, to avoid erasing myself as a woman professor of anthropology, I needed to refigure the canon of anthropological knowledge as it is defined and passed on from one generation to the next in the academy. I needed another past, another history. So I looked for models in the texts of those women ethnographers who came before us. Alice Walker has written that "the absence of models in literature as in life . . . is an occupational hazard for the artist, simply because models in art, in behavior, in growth of spirit and intellect—even if rejected—enrich and enlarge one's view of existence." Possibly, in that search for models, my hand would be blistered by the sacred wax of "pure theory"—as Adrienne Rich puts it in a poem that imagines "a woman sitting between the stove and the stars."[43] But I needed to forge ahead in order to learn how I, as a woman, am scripted into the discipline that gives me permission to script others into my writings.

However, I found it depressing to undertake this search alone. There were too many histories to recover, too many dilemmas to resolve, too many silences to break. To challenge all those excuses for politely shunting aside women's work in anthropology, *Women Writing Culture* needed many of us speaking at once.

Madwomen in the Exotic

The women's movement divided up intellectual labor in such a way that feminist anthropologists set out in search of the "origins" of gender inequality and feminist literary critics set out in search of "lost" female literary traditions.[44] While feminist literary critics went about unearthing the literary women missing from the Western tradition, feminist anthropologists were expected to journey beyond the West, through either the Human Relations Area Files or actual fieldwork, in order to bring back deep truths about womanhood that Western women could use in achieving their own liberation.[45]

Perhaps because origins seemed closer to fundamental truths, feminist literary critics often borrowed theoretical concepts from feminist anthropologists, especially ideas about the nature/culture split and the sex-gender system. Feminist anthropologists were much less influenced by the new readings of sexual/textual politics that quickly became the trademark of feminist literary criticism. On the whole, they preferred to pursue links with classical social theory and political economy and to write carefully argued yet confident texts, studded with cross-cultural examples, that persuasively made the case for women's universal subordination while often also revealing the myths of male power. As Deborah Gordon suggests in her conclusion, we need to let go of the reductionist dichotomy of "conventional" versus "experimental" ethnography to fully understand the complex historical moment out of which early feminist anthropological writing arose. Indeed, the classical texts of that historical moment—*Woman, Culture and Society* and *Toward an Anthropology of Women*—were perceived as original and ground breaking, offering a major paradigm shift in the theorizing of anthropology as an intellectual, political, and cultural practice. But the *Writing Culture* critique showed that the mark of theory, as Lutz argues, is ultimately male controlled. Feminist anthropologists may have carried the theoretical day, but by the standard of the avant-garde textual theory promoted by *Writing Culture* they wrote in terms of a notion of grand theory that was outdated, even conservative. No matter how hard they try, women's work is never quite theoretical enough.

Unlike feminist literary criticism, which had an important impact on the reading, teaching, and writing of literature, there was always, as Marilyn Strathern sagely noted, an awkwardness about the conjunction of anthropology and feminism. The awkwardness arose from the difficulty of maintaining the premise of anthropology as a Self in relation to an Other in a context where the feminist researcher is herself an Other to patriarchy's Self.[46] In a case of curious serendipity, two American feminists, Lila Abu-Lughod, located on the East Coast, and Judith Stacey, located on the West Coast, published essays at around the same time with exactly the same title: "Can There Be a Feminist Ethnography?" For Stacey, a fully feminist ethnography can never be achieved, for feminist politics, rooted in sensitivity to all contexts of domination, is incompatible with the basic premise of ethnography, which is that "the research product is ultimately that of the researcher, however modified or influenced by informants." Abu-Lughod was more optimistic about the possibility of a feminist ethnography grounded in the particularities of women's lives and stories. Yet she accepted Clifford's assessment that feminist anthropologists who hold academic credentials rarely experiment with form. Abu-Lughod suggested that the alternative "women's tradition" of ethnographic writing, which is both literary and popular, is associated with the "untrained" wives of anthropologists, from whom feminist anthropologists need to detach themselves in order to assert their professional status.[47]

Stacey and Abu-Lughod addressed themselves to an emerging notion of feminist ethnography distinct from both the anthropology of women (an effort to understand the lives of women across cultures) and feminist anthropology (an effort to understand the social and political ramifications of women as the second sex). At the same time, Kamala Visweswaran offered an early definition of feminist ethnography as a project bridging the gap—to which *Writing Culture* had so bluntly drawn attention—between feminist commitment and textual innovation.[48] Indeed, since the publication of *Writing Culture*, there has been an explosion of creative works of feminist ethnography that seek to close this gap while staying attuned—as suggested by *This Bridge Called My Back*—to the relationships between women across differences of race, class, and privilege.[49] Our book is situated within this emerging feminist ethnography and its predicaments.

The development of a corpus of feminist ethnographic works that are post–*Writing Culture* and post–*This Bridge Called My Back* has led to a new self-awareness about what it means to be women writing culture. With the pioneering work of Deborah Gordon, we now have our first sophisticated and ambitious history of the awkward relationship between feminist and experimental ethnography, revealing how gender and genre are interwoven in anthropology's canonical texts.[50] *Women Writing Culture* tries to suggest answers to some primary questions: Have ethnographic authority and the burden of authorship figured differently in the works of women anthropologists? What is the cultural logic by which authorship is coded as "feminine" or "masculine," and what are the consequences of those markings? What kind of writing is possible for feminist anthropologists now, if to write unconventionally puts a woman in the category of untrained wife, while writing according to the conventions of the academy situates her as a textual conservative?

One of the major contributions of feminist literary criticism is its assertion that writing matters tremendously for women; that how we plot ourselves into our fictions has everything to do with how we plot ourselves into our lives. From this perspective, some of the criticisms of *Writing Culture* go too far in their skepticism about the crucial importance of texts.[51] As Rachel Blau DuPlessis puts it, "To compose a work is to negotiate with these questions: What stories can be told? How can plots be resolved? What is felt to be narratable by both literary and social conventions?" Literary texts, rather than being mimetic, can provide "emancipatory strategies" for "writing beyond the ending," beyond the narratives of romance or death that have been, for women, the cultural legacy from nineteenth-century life and letters.[52]

Anxiety is the other inheritance that trails women who write. Not the "anxiety of influence" described by Harold Bloom as the quintessential drama of the male writer's Oedipal slaying of powerful male literary precursors but a more basic anxiety, the anxiety of authorship itself. Interestingly, in order to respond to Bloom's trim yet highly influential volume, Sandra Gilbert and Susan Gubar produced a bible-sized tome, *The Madwoman in the Attic*, in which they suggested that women writers in the nineteenth century wrote in the face of deep fears—about being unable to create, unable to become precursors, unable to overcome their distrust of authority. As "daughters" receiving the tradition from stern literary "fathers" who viewed them as inferiors, women attempting the pen "struggled in isolation that felt like illness, alienation that felt like madness." Yet in writing their agoraphobia and hysteria into literature, they created a female literary subculture that empowered other women writers. Unlike the revisionism of male writing in Bloom's anxiety of influence, which imagined "a threatening force to be denied or killed," women's search for female literary precursors "proves by example that a revolt against patriarchal literary authority is possible."[53]

Fifteen years later, the image of last century's woman writer (a privileged white woman, to be sure) as a "madwoman in the attic" remains persuasive, despite its limitations.[54] At the least, the idea of women's anxiety of authorship offers a frame within which to begin to engender the notion of ethnographic authority. Of course, there is a vivid contrast between the entrapped women of nineteenth-century Western literature and the roaming, restless women anthropologists of the twentieth century. But even today, after feminist awakenings, we struggle to make our voices heard and to convince ourselves that our writing, in a time of increasing poverty, racism, inequality, xenophobia, and warfare, still somehow matters. We struggle to believe that our writing is not a cushion against the madness, or worse, a form of madness itself. When the essays for this volume arrived in unwieldy numbers, I relished the idea of producing a book as formidable, as imperative, as wildly desirous of space on the bookshelf as *The Madwoman in the Attic*. Our own *Madwomen in the Exotic*.

Mary Morris notes in her introduction to an anthology of the travel writings of women that going on a journey or awaiting the stranger have been the two plots of Western literature. Women have usually been those who wait. But, Morris adds, when women grow weary of waiting, they can go on a journey; they "can be the stranger who comes to town." Yet women necessarily travel differently, aware of their bodies, their sex, fearing catcalls and rape, seeking freedom of movement, many times in the disguise of men's clothes.[55]

If, indeed, the only narrative traditionally available to women is the love or marriage plot, to try to live out the quest plot, as men's stories allow, is a radical act— even an ungendering, as attested to by the many stories of women anthropologists who have played the role of "honorary male" in the field or have suffered the consequences of being improper "daughters."[56] Anthropology, as the male quest plot turned institution, is by its very nature a paradoxical pursuit for women. Susan Sontag went so far as to claim that being an anthropologist "is one of the rare intellectual vocations which do not demand a sacrifice of one's manhood."[57]

Anthropology makes heroes of men, allowing, even insisting, that they exploit their alienation, their intrepid homelessness, their desire "to make a life out of running" for the sake of science, as Laurent Dubois puts it in his essay in this volume. Dubois, a white male student entering the profession, asks himself, "Has my story already been written?" Situating himself within the male quest narrative inherited, not invented, by anthropology, he interrogates his own desire to run from home in search of the same long horizons sought by his literary hero Bruce Chatwin; and he pays attention, as his own feminist consciousness takes shape, to Chatwin's wife, who was always there, waiting in the suburbs for her husband to return.

In its identification with manhood, anthropology has always been ambivalent about the anthropologist's wife. Barbara Tedlock's essay offers a fascinating perspective on the sexual division of textual labor between anthropologist husbands and incorporated wives. With wit and passion, Tedlock shows how the works of wives, which have often reached wide reading audiences, were treated as unauthorized and illicit within anthropology. Yet throughout the history of the profession, and even in some contemporary situations, male anthropologists have depended on the unpaid and often unrecognized labor of their wives. Tedlock even tells of an anthropologist who tried to persuade his wife to have a baby in the field so he could obtain information from her for his research! Most importantly, Tedlock suggests that the image of the devalued wife looms over those women who do become anthropologists in their own right. Even as they seek professional credibility, women anthropologists continually undermine their own ethnographic authority by revealing their uncertainty about fieldwork and ethnographic writing.

Anxiety of authorship is the legacy of our terror at having to become (honorary) males.

In Search of a Women's Literary Tradition in Anthropology

For a woman to be able to travel in the early days of anthropology, she had to have not a room of her own but plenty of spunk and money of her own. This was certainly true of the "mother" of American anthropology, Elsie Clews Parsons, who financed not only her own research but also the research of many other women anthropologists. It was Parsons who introduced Ruth Benedict to feminist anthropology at the New School for Social Research and persuaded her to go further in her studies with Franz Boas at Columbia University. And yet despite her wealth and prominence, as Louise Lamphere notes in her essay in this volume, Parsons never attained a permanent position within the academy. Because she could not train graduate students herself, it was not her name but, rather, that of Boas that became associated with the school of early American anthropology. Women who pursued the quest plot in the early days of the profession did not come home to chairs of anthropology; they had only their writing by which to stand or fall. And so their writing needed to have its own sources of resiliency.

Ruth Benedict, we learn from Barbara Babcock's essay in this volume, always recognized that ethnographic description occurs as writing. In fact, Benedict was often chided for writing too well, for writing anthropology too much like a poet. She frequently turned to literary models, reading Virginia Woolf's *The Waves* as she wrote her own *Patterns of Culture*. Ruth Benedict had come to anthropology, like Elsie Clews Parsons, fascinated with the "New Woman" of the interwar years, the woman "not yet classified, perhaps not classifiable." But in becoming an anthropologist she tucked her feminism away, letting it surface mainly in her use of irony and giving voice to her lesbianism only in her obsession with the "abnormal." Before she turned to anthropology a publisher rejected her manuscript about the "restless and highly enslaved women of past generations," and Benedict never again returned to those feminist concerns explicitly. It was left to Margaret Mead, Ruth Benedict's student, to reopen the bridge between feminism and anthropology, but in ways bristling with excessive assurance about women's possibilities that went against the grain of her teacher's more somber vision.

Like Benedict and Mead, Zora Neale Hurston and Ella Cara Deloria were student-daughters of Papa Franz. Yet Hurston, an African American woman, and Deloria, a Native American woman, were treated more as "native informants" than as scholars in their own right.[58] Neither attained an academic position or, until recently, had much of an impact on anthropology. Their white sisters fared better in getting a foot in the door of the academy, but even Benedict was denied the Chair in Anthropology at Columbia University, becoming a full professor only in the year that she died, and Mead was shunted off to the American Museum of Natural History.

What these four women shared (besides their common infantilization as "daughters" of Papa Franz) was an impatience with the flat impersonal voice that was becoming the norm in the ethnographies of their time. They sought, instead, perhaps because of their inability to reproduce themselves in the academy, to reach a popular audience with their own creatively storied writings. Since that time, as Narayan has noted, two poles have emerged in anthropological writing: on the one hand, we have "accessible ethnographies laden with stories" (assigned to introductory anthropology students to whet their appetite) and, on the other, "refereed journal articles, dense with theoretical analyses" (assigned to graduate students and privileged in core courses). But Narayan asks, "Need the two categories, compelling narrative and rigorous analysis, be impermeable?" As she suggests, they are seeping into each other in increasingly hybrid ethnographic texts.[59] A key contribution of the essays in this book is the revelation of how women, past and present, fruitfully resolve the tension between these two poles of writing.

As Janet Finn points out in her essay in this volume, Deloria was uncomfortable with the distancing forms of fieldwork and writing recommended by her mentor. Deloria told Boas in a letter that "to go at it like a whiteman, for me, an Indian, is to throw up an immediate barrier between myself and the people." Unable to earn wages in academic arenas, Deloria worked as a research assistant and informant for Boas and other scholars in the anthropological equivalent of piecework. The patronage of white scholars was crucial for Deloria, as it was for another contemporary Native American writer, Mourning Dove, whose novels explored the pressures of being a half-blood Indian woman. Deloria herself, eager to find a way of representing a Sioux woman's life that did not use typifications, wrote a novel, *Waterlily,* which she dedicated to Benedict, who encouraged her efforts. But *Waterlily,* which today reads like a model of how to blend ethnography and fiction, was rejected in Deloria's lifetime by publishers who claimed there was no audience for such writing.

By undertaking a nuanced reading of Hurston's *Mules and Men,* Graciela Hernández reveals how the multiple voices of Hurston as ethnographer, writer, and community member are subtly mediated by the use of a storytelling style that gives power to the spoken words of her informants over the written words of her own text. Hurston's return to her home community in Eatonville, Florida, with the "spyglass of Anthropology" obtained in Morningside Heights forced her to negotiate the relationship between ethnographic authority and personal authenticity. Out of that negotiation came a text about African American folk culture that was postmodern before its time in enacting an exemplary hybridity that combined engaged scholarship with a nuanced portrait of Hurston's own intellectual process. As bell hooks notes, "An essay on Hurston would have been a valuable addition to the collection *Writing Culture*. . . . In many ways Hurston was at the cutting edge of a new movement in ethnography and anthropology that has only recently been actualized." [60]

The essays on Deloria and Hurston are an important first step to recovering the as yet unwritten history of minority women who struggled to find their voice in anthropology. There are other equally important precursors, such as the Mexican American folklorist Jovita Gonzalez, whose paradoxical embrace of male power complicates our image of ethnic-feminist consciousness. [61] As "native anthropologists" writing at a moment when the border between self and other was sharply demarcated, Deloria and Hurston, as well as Gonzalez, were put in the position of needing to rethink the cultural politics of being an insider. The legacy of their writing is of crucial significance to the current challenge to the role of the "detached observer" and to anthropology's shift toward the study of borderlands. [62]

For Ruth Landes, another Boasian daughter, it was not the concept of culture that attracted her to anthropology but, rather, the antiracism that had initially been at the core of its intellectual practice. Sally Cole reveals that Landes continued to theorize about the ethnography of race in her writings on Brazilian and American society, even as the establishment of professional anthropology in postwar universities led anthropologists to abandon the debate on race in favor of the less-politicized notion of the "science of culture." She held firm, too, in the face of pressure from her more powerful male colleague Melville Herskovits, who criticized her for focusing on race and not on "Afro-American culture." Landes wrote "against culture"— a concept recently elaborated by Lila Abu-Lughod—long before it was fashionable to do so in anthropology.

Barbara Myerhoff, in turn, was a writer with a wide popular following as well as a pioneer in the reflexive study of ethnicity and of Jewish studies in anthropology. As Gelya Frank remarks, had Myerhoff not died prematurely of lung cancer, she might have become the Jewish Margaret Mead. Myerhoff's final work as an anthropologist was not a text but an innovative film, *In Her Own Time*, that mixed autobiography and ethnography to express in unusual depth the experience of her own dying. Frank explores the contradictory ways in which Myerhoff turned to the Orthodox and Lubavitcher Jews for spiritual meaning in her final days, acting out the role of an anthropologist "in a trance of deep play," an anthropologist facing her own limitations in achieving a coherent Jewish identity. To bring Myerhoff's work into the canon is to undo another erasure—the Jewish awareness of difference that has been a central, yet closeted, part of anthropology since Franz Boas. [63]

Faye Harrison proclaims that if ethnography is often a kind of fiction, then the converse, that fiction is often a kind of ethnography, is also true. Alice Walker, as Harrison shows, has long written fiction that is a dialogue with anthropology. It is Walker who, in writing about her own own search for Hurston in the 1970s, restored her to anthropology, which had cast her into oblivion, revitalizing interest in her work not just as a fiction writer but also as an anthropologist and a folklorist. Aware that Hurston's precarious position in anthropology has as much to do with her being black as with her writing in creative ways that go against the grain of conventional anthropological reporting, Walker has chosen to stay out of academic anthropology and to enact a corpus of fictional works that embody and expand upon anthropological concerns. Harrison's thoughtful reading of Walker's *The Temple of My Familiar* demonstrates how this text offers a complement and critique to such globalizing works of anthropological theorizing as Eric Wolf's *Europe and the People without History,* which omit gender and race perspectives. Yet Harrison also wisely points out that Walker is only one among many black women and minority intellectuals whose work ought to occupy a central place in the anthropological discussion of the poetics and politics of writing culture.

In their essay on reading across minority discourses, Paulla Ebron and Anna Tsing take on, precisely, the new fictional literature by African American and Asian American writers. As they note, it is no longer social scientists (like Margaret Mead) who are shaping U.S. public understandings of culture, race, and ethnicity but novelists such as Toni Morrison and Amy Tan. Although the literary turn in anthropology is often dismissed as an exercise in self-indulgence, Ebron and Tsing offer a fresh reading of minority discourse as a way of forming alliances among the once colonized. That reading is subtle and crosses many borders simultaneously, showing how representational authority is differently achieved by women and men of color in the United States. "People of color," as they note, names a tension as well as a hope, embedded in their own project, which unfolded in the context of the Los Angeles uprising and Black-Asian hostilities.

Working ethnographically with living writers rather than with literary sources, Smadar Lavie likewise engages in a reading across minority discourses. Her essay focuses on the displacement of language, identity, and homeland in the lives and writings of border poets living in Israel. These border poets are cast into minority status because their Mizrahi and Palestinian backgrounds make them exiles within the Ashkenazi definition of the nation of Israel. Lavie's essay offers a crucial, and necessary, counterpoint to Gelya Frank's treatment of Jewish identity in the work of Barbara Myerhoff. More poignantly, Lavie reflects on the way she herself, as a woman of color within the Israeli system, had to choose migration to the United States in order "to keep her voice," though that, ironically, has meant ceasing to write in Hebrew, her native language.

Dorinne Kondo enacts another kind of reading across minority discourses in her own playwriting, inventing the unforgettable character of Janice Ito, an Asian American film professor who dreams of becoming the African American disco diva Grace Jones. Seeking to subvert dominant conceptions of race, Kondo says she turned to theater because it was a space where Asian Americans could be something other than model minorities. Theater also allowed her to make the shift from the textual to the performative and to carry out engaged collaborative work. It opened a space for her to be a "bad girl," not a "sad girl."

Fiction, as both Kondo and Narayan show, can be an ideal genre for putting flesh back both on the anthropological subject and on ourselves as women of the academy. Fiction also reaches a broad audience because it entertains as well as educates, enabling anthropological insights to travel further. In our age, when borders rather than closed communities prevail, readership is no longer homogenous. Ethnography should not be like "those first class lounges behind hidden doors in the airport, which only certain people, having paid their dues, get to walk through."[64] For ethnography to matter in a multicultural world it needs to reach a wider range of audiences both in and beyond the academy.

Along with fiction, a variety of creative nonfiction genres now exist to widen anthropology's reach. Yearning for an anthropology that will be written not just by and for other academics, Deborah Gordon takes a close look at how new kinds of collaborative texts can be created when ethnographic research takes place within community agendas. Sharing privilege, sharing literacy, sharing information—which in our world is power—is one way for feminist relationships in postcolonial conditions of inequality to bridge the gaps between women in the academy and women in ethnic communities. The El Barrio project (of the Center for Puerto Rican Studies at Hunter College in New York City) focuses on oral history work as a way to empower women to revise the scripts of their lives. Women teaching other women the writing skills they need offers a model, Gordon suggests, for expanding the focus on writing culture beyond the purely aesthetic dimensions of the individual text to a truer opening of the doors of anthropological writing to all who wish to enter.

Collaborative work has always been a key part of feminist practice. *Women Writing Culture* emerges from a collaboration between myself and Deborah Gordon and from our affectionate agreement to disagree. Whereas I, as a feminist ethnographer, place the accent on how women write culture, Gordon, as a feminist historian of anthropology, places the accent on how women are written by culture. Our introduction and conclusion are meant to be in tension with each other. Similarly, we have already seen how Ebron and Tsing together explore minority discourse from African American and Asian American vantage points. Judith Newton and Judith Stacey, in turn, join forces to examine how the feminist desire for multiple alliances might reach out to male cultural critics searching for ways to locate themselves within feminism. Studying "up," they hope to bring back new feminist lessons, learning what men (and white women) gain by adopting "traitorous identities" that challenge their own privilege but help to build a nonsexist and nonracist society.

Working collaboratively in a different way to explore diasporic identity, Aihwa Ong, who views herself not as Asian American but as an expatriate Chinese, seeks out the stories of newly immigrant Chinese women as they come into their own sense of agency in the United States. At the same time, she questions the notion of privileged nativism and notes that being positioned as some kind of insider to the culture does not predispose one to produce a politically correct ethnography of the Other. Indeed, she reminds us that Third World women in the Anglophone academic world are privileged in comparison with women from their ancestral cultures. Feminist ethnographers need to develop a "deterritorialized" critical practice that deals with inequities not only in that "other place" but also in one's "own" community.

In her tale of two pregnancies, Lila Abu-Lughod offers a keen example of how to deterritorialize ethnography, tacking back and forth between her own technological experience of pregnancy and the experiences of her Bedouin and Egyptian friends. Abu-Lughod's focus on her impending motherhood also breaks a taboo. The first generation of feminist anthropologists, who viewed motherhood as one of the central institutions that kept women from attaining power in the public sphere, never wrote about their own conflicts between reproduction and anthropology. In the last decade, as feminism has come under increasing attack and abortion rights have been challenged, motherhood has become a public goal for women. Articles are continually appearing in the mainstream press about women who endanger their fetuses or regret having chosen a career over motherhood.[65] Feminist ethnographers in this country are not immune to these cultural pressures, and Abu-Lughod is brave to speak of them, opening a space for others to tell their stories. Abu-Lughod herself felt equally vulnerable to the pressures of her Bedouin and Egyptian friends who pitied her childlessness.

Ellen Lewin's essay offers a counterpoint to these concerns. With verve and insight, Lewin reflects on the heterosexual assumption that undergirds anthropology, which until recently has seemed not to require explanation or theorizing. Indeed, anthropology does have a sex, as I suggested earlier, being virtually synonymous with manhood. Yet doing lesbian ethnography leads Lewin to the conclusion that identity is always in flux among ethnic, racial, age, professional, and other markers. A lesbian is never only a lesbian. Lewin's desire to feel identified with her lesbian subjects backfires among those women who, unlike her, have chosen to become mothers without husbands. By focusing on differences among lesbians, Lewin adds an unusual level of complexity to our understanding of the dilemmas of working ethnographically on one's "own culture."

The vast majority of the essays in this book follow the current trend in American anthropology of focusing on writing culture here, in the United States, where we make our living as anthropologists of the academy. Our aim, ultimately, has been to examine the poetics and politics of feminist ethnography as a way of rethinking anthropology's purpose in a multicultural America. One limitation of this approach is that it could not be more international in its focus.[66] Yet by working in those spaces we think of as "home," which in turn are crosscut by multiple intersecting spaces of identification and difference, our book makes an important theoretical contribution: we move away from the "West" versus the "Rest" and the "Self" versus "Other" dichotomies that uncritically informed *Writing Culture* and still remain central to the quest narrative of anthropology. Even whiteness, as Kirin Narayan shows in her story, is not a monolithic identity but is layered with shades of difference that blur the boundaries between "inside" and "outside." As Anna Tsing notes, "Participant-observation begins at home—and not only because we are studying 'ourselves'; part of every 'us' is 'other' too." [67]

Indeed, as I relate in my essay "Writing in My Father's Name," I had to engage with the most profound predicaments I had ever faced as an anthropologist when I brought struggles from home into my ethnography, *Translated Woman.* It pained me to discover that I had alienated my parents by writing about them in ways they found disturbing. Anguished about my "wickedness," I returned to Mexico, hoping to be vindicated by giving the book I had written about her to my *comadre* Esperanza. But there was no redemption; my *comadre* told me she did not want to keep a text she would never be able to read.

Writing hurts.

Because writing hurts, Kirin Narayan's Charity—a white woman on the outside but with a heart lost in India—is an endearing creation of the feminist anthropological imagination. For Charity enacts the romance of being loved, even adored, for her writing. Her anthropological account of an Indian village is read passionately, consumed from head to toe, by a male anthropologist, about whom Charity only knows that he is a "Weberian." The letters from her admiring reader fill her with hope and nostalgia, as she faces the fact that she is no longer the confident graduate student writing the exemplary dissertation, but a marginal person in the academy, trying to maintain a tenuous grip on reality by summoning up her memories of those theories in the texts of Radcliffe-Brown and Malinowski and *Writing Culture* that she once studied with such devotion.

What will happen to Charity? Will her writing bring success, fulfillment, a move from the margins to the center? Let us try to imagine a bright future for this ambivalent heroine—and for all women writing culture as this century rushes to a close.

Notes

I am deeply grateful to Deborah Gordon, Rachael Cohen, Lila Abu-Lughod, Kirin Narayan, Anna Tsing, Benjamin Orlove, an anonymous reviewer for the University of California Press, and our editor, Naomi Schneider, for their thoughtful and encouraging comments on this text. My thanks to Laura Kunreuther for the epigraph from Virginia Woolf. An earlier version of these ideas appeared in my "Introduction," special issue on "Women Writing Culture: Another Telling of the Story of American Anthropology," Ruth Behar, ed., *Critique of Anthropology* 13, no. 4 (1993): 307–26.

1. This double crisis had earlier inspired feminist anthropologists to think about our purpose. See, in particular, Lila Abu-Lughod, "Can There Be a Feminist Ethnography?" *Women and Performance: A Journal of Feminist Theory* 5 (1990): 7–27.

2. James Clifford and George Marcus, eds., *Writing Culture: The Poetics and Politics of Ethnography* (Berkeley: University of California Press, 1986). The emphasis put on the fact that the book emerged from an "advanced seminar" is striking; the word "advanced" appears three times on the first page of the preface. For further background, see George E. Marcus and Dick Cushman, "Ethnographies as Texts," *Annual Review of Anthropology* 11 (1982): 25–69.

3. Cherríe Moraga and Gloria Anzaldúa, eds., *This Bridge Called My Back: Writings by Radical Women of Color* (New York: Kitchen Table, Women of Color Press, 1983).

4. See, for example, Clifford Geertz, *Works and Lives: The Anthropologist as Author* (Stanford: Stanford University Press, 1988); Richard Fox, ed., *Recapturing Anthropology: Working in the Present* (Santa Fe, N. Mex.: School of American Research Press, 1991). At 25,000 copies, *Writing Culture* has also sold well, a rare feat for an academic collection of essays published by a university press.

5. On the intellectual and poetic exchanges and conflicts of Sapir and Benedict, see Richard Handler, "Vigorous Male and Aspiring Female: Poetry, Personality, and Culture in Edward Sapir and Ruth Benedict," in *Malinowski, Rivers, Benedict and Others: Essays on Culture and Personality,* ed. George W. Stocking, Jr. (Madison: University of Wisconsin Press, 1986), 127–155.

6. I recognize that in this capsule summary I am offering an image of *Writing Culture* as a monolithic text. As many readers have pointed out, there were key differences among the authors in the book. For example, Talal Asad's essay does not concern textual theory; Michael Fischer's essay focuses on ethnic autobiography rather than on ethnography; and Paul Rabinow's essay criticizes the preoccupation with textual form and also seeks an uneasy alliance between anthropology and feminism that stands in opposition to James Clifford's stance. Yet, despite these differences, the book has been read not as a collection of essays that are in conversation with each other but, indeed, as a programmatic treatise calling for anthropologists to be more aware of the literary foundations of what they do. The book continues to be read through the filter of Clifford's introduction, which emphasizes textual form and theory, and so, in reader-response fashion, this is the perspective I too emphasize.

7. Mary Louise Pratt, "Fieldwork in Common Places," in *Writing Culture,* 33.

8. For further discussion, see George E. Marcus and Michael M. J. Fischer, *Anthropology as Cultural Critique: An Experimental Moment in the Human Sciences* (Chicago: University of Chicago Press, 1986). Richard Fox, in his introduction to *Recapturing Anthropology* (p. 9), criticizes the textualist approach for misunderstanding the nature of power and for subscribing to a myth of anthropological writing as artisanship rather than as "industrial discipline."

9. Slavenka Drakulič, *How We Survived Communism and Even Laughed* (New York: Harper Perennial, 1993), 46–47.

10. For example, Paul Rabinow's *Fieldwork in Morocco* (Berkeley: University of California Press, 1977) and Vincent Crapanzano's *Tuhami: Portrait of a Moroccan* (Chicago: University of Chicago Press, 1980) were viewed as original examples of experimental ethnography, even though they clearly built on a tradition of women's writing that included Laura Bohannan's *Return to Laughter* (New York: Doubleday, 1964; orig. 1954) and Jean Briggs's *Never in Anger* (Cambridge, Mass.: Harvard University Press, 1970). Curiously, the only text by a woman ethnographer that was discussed in any detail in *Writing Culture* was Marjorie Shostak's *Nisa: The Life and Words of a !Kung Woman* (New York: Vintage Books, 1981), a life history written by the wife of an anthropologist involved in the Harvard Kalahari Project, whose vivid personal account of fieldwork has secured it a favored place in introductory anthropology courses.

11. See James Clifford, "Introduction," in *Writing Culture,* 21–22, where he claims that those women anthropologists who had made textual innovations "had not done so on feminist grounds," while, on the other hand, those who, as feminists, were "actively rewriting the masculinist canon" had not "produced either unconventional forms of writing or a developed reflection on ethnographic textuality as such."

12. Deborah A. Gordon, "Writing Culture, Writing Feminism: The Poetics and Politics of Experimental Ethnography," *Inscriptions* 3/4 (1988): 8, 21. Other responses followed,

including Frances Mascia-Lees, Patricia Sharpe, and Colleen Ballerino Cohen, "The Postmodernist Turn in Anthropology: Cautions from a Feminist Perspective," *Signs* 15 (1989): 7–33; Margery Wolf, *A Thrice-Told Tale: Feminism, Postmodernism, and Ethnographic Responsibility* (Stanford: Stanford University Press, 1992); Barbara Babcock, "Feminism/Pretexts: Fragments, Questions, and Reflections," *Anthropological Quarterly* 66, no. 2 (1993): 59–66.

13. Joseph A. Boone and Michael Cadden, eds., *Engendering Men: The Question of Male Feminist Criticism* (New York: Routledge, 1990), 3.

14. Michelle Zimbalist Rosaldo and Louise Lamphere, eds., *Woman, Culture and Society* (Stanford: Stanford University Press, 1974); Harry Lionel Shapiro, *Man, Culture and Society* (New York: Oxford University Press, 1956). *Writing Culture* can be seen as a masculinist response to *Woman, Culture and Society.* The fascinating complexities of this politics and history are more fully explored in Deborah Gordon's conclusion to this book.

15. Adrienne Rich, "When We Dead Awaken: Writing as Re-Vision," in her *On Lies, Secrets, and Silence: Selected Prose 1966–1978* (New York: Norton, 1979), 35–38.

16. Moraga and Anzaldúa, *This Bridge Called My Back.* Also see Chandra Talpade Mohanty, "Under Western Eyes: Feminist Scholarship and Colonial Discourses," in *Third World Women and the Politics of Feminism,* ed. Chandra Talpade Mohanty, Ann Russo, and Lourdes Torres (Bloomington: Indiana University Press, 1991), 1–80. In this context we should also note the importance of the work of "native" women anthropologists outside the United States. See, for example, Soraya Altorki and Camillia El Solh, eds., *Studying Your Own Society: Arab Women in the Field* (Syracuse, N.Y.: Syracuse University Press, 1988).

17. The impact of *This Bridge Called My Back* on feminist anthropology can be seen in Faye Ginsburg and Anna Lowenhaupt Tsing, eds., *Uncertain Terms: Negotiating Gender in American Culture* (Boston: Beacon Press, 1990).

18. Gloria Anzaldúa, "Speaking in Tongues: A Letter to Third World Women Writers," in *This Bridge Called My Back,* 167. Also see her anthology, *Making Face, Making Soul: Haciendo Caras: Creative and Critical Perspectives by Women of Color* (San Francisco: Aunt Lute Foundation, 1990).

19. Audre Lorde, "An Open Letter to Mary Daly," Gloria Anzaldúa, "Speaking in Tongues," Nellie Wong, "In Search of the Self as Hero: Confetti of Voices on New Year's Night," in *This Bridge Called My Back,* 96, 165–66, 180–81.

20. Norma Alarcón, "The Theoretical Subjects of *This Bridge Called My Back* and Anglo-American Feminism," in *Criticism in the Borderlands: Studies in Chicano Literature, Culture, and Ideology,* ed. Héctor Calderón and José David Saldívar (Durham, N.C.: Duke University Press, 1991), 37.

21. See the important minority critiques of Lila Abu-Lughod, "Writing against Culture," 137–62, and José Limón, "Representation, Ethnicity, and the Precursory Ethnography: Notes of a Native Anthropologist," 115–35, in *Recapturing Anthropology*; Angie C. Chabram, "Chicana/o Studies as Oppositional Ethnography," *Cultural Studies* 4, no. 3 (1990): 228–47; Christine Obbo, "Adventures with Fieldnotes," in *Fieldnotes: The Makings of Anthropology,* ed. Roger Sanjek (Ithaca, N.Y.: Cornell University Press, 1990), 290–302. For a rethinking of minority positioning, see Virginia R. Dominguez, "A Taste for 'the Other': Intellectual Complicity in Racializing Practices" and "Comments," *Current Anthropology* 35, no. 4 (1994): 338–48.

22. bell hooks, *Yearning: Race, Gender, and Cultural Politics* (Boston: South End Press, 1990), 130–31.

23. James Clifford, "Introduction," in *Writing Culture,* 21, n. 11; Paul Rabinow, "Representations Are Social Facts: Modernity and Post-Modernity in Anthropology," in *Writing Culture,* 234–61.

24. Audre Lorde, "Poetry Is Not a Luxury," in her *Sister Outsider: Essays and Speeches* (Trumansburg, N.Y.: The Crossing Press, 1984), 36–39.

25. Clifford, "Introduction," 1.

26. Catherine Lutz, "The Erasure of Women's Writing in Sociocultural Anthropology," *American Ethnologist* 17, no. 4 (1990): 611–27. It would be worthwhile to expand Lutz's analysis to see to what extent the contributions of anthropologists of color are likewise, or perhaps more irrevocably, erased through standard citation patterns. On counteracting the erasure of women's labor in the history of anthropology, see Nancy J. Parezo, ed., *Hidden Scholars: Women Anthropologists and the Native American Southwest* (Albuquerque: University of New Mexico Press, 1993); and Barbara A. Babcock and Nancy J. Parezo, *Daughters of the Desert: Women Anthropologists and the Native American Southwest, 1880–1980* (Albuquerque: University of New Mexico Press, 1988). As Barbara Babcock pointed out to me, it is significant that the History of Anthropology series at the University of Wisconsin Press has studiously avoided gender, feminism, and women anthropologists. Certainly, George W. Stocking, Jr., the editor of the series, has written the most thorough and thoughtful historical account of our anthropological canon. See his *The Ethnographer's Magic and Other Essays in the History of Anthropology* (Madison: University of Wisconsin Press, 1992).

27. Renato Rosaldo, *Culture and Truth: The Remaking of Social Analysis* (Boston: Beacon Press, 1990); Mary Louise Pratt, "Humanities for the Future: Reflections on the Western Culture Debate at Stanford," *South Atlantic Quarterly* 89 (1990): 7–25. Renato Rosaldo is one of the few anthropologists who has engaged with the debates around multiculturalism. He also has been a key exception to the trend to write off women's work in anthropology. In *Culture and Truth,* he criticizes the Weberian "manly" ethic and instead identifies with feminist thinking. Rosaldo not only tries to write anthropology that is rooted in the emotions of grief, sorrow, and rage, but he consciously reclaims subjective forms of social analysis used by women anthropologists (see pp. 1–21 and 168–95).

28. The American media, for the most part, represented the debate as being about "The Rising Hegemony of the Politically Correct," as one article was titled (Richard Bernstein, *New York Times,* October 20, 1990, sec. 4, p. 1). A huge outpouring of articles and reviews on the subject appeared during 1990 and 1991.

29. Hazel Carby, "The Canon: Civil War and Reconstruction," *Michigan Quarterly Review* 28, no. 1 (1989): 36.

30. William A. Henry III, "Upside Down in the Grove of Academe," *Time,* April 1, 1991, 66.

31. Toni Morrison, "Unspeakable Things Unspoken: The Afro-American Presence in American Literature," *Michigan Quarterly Review* 28, no. 1 (1989): 11–12.

32. Carby, "The Canon," 40.

33. Barbara Christian, "The Race for Theory," *Feminist Studies* 14, no. 1 (1988): 78.

34. Geertz, *Works and Lives,* 137.

35. See, for example, Limón, "Representation, Ethnicity, and the Precursory Ethnography"; and Sherry Ortner, "Reading America: Preliminary Notes on Class and Culture," in *Recapturing Anthropology,* 163–89.

36. Lorraine Nencel and Peter Pels, "Introduction: Critique and the Deconstruction of Anthropological Authority," in *Constructing Knowledge: Authority and Critique in Social Science,* ed. Lorraine Nencel and Peter Pels (London: Sage Publications, 1992), 17.

37. Joan Vincent, "Engaging Historicism," in *Recapturing Anthropology,* 49.

38. Annette Weiner, "Anthropology's Lessons for Cultural Diversity," *Chronicle of Higher Education,* July 22, 1992, 31–32. In response, the 1992 annual meeting of the American

Anthropological Association made multiculturalism its central theme, but the relevance of the canon debates to anthropology was not the main subject of discussion.

39. Charlotte Perkins Gilman, *The Yellow Wallpaper and Other Writings* (New York: Bantam Books, 1982).

40. James A. Boon, "Between-the-Wars Bali: Rereading the Relics," in *Malinowski, Rivers, Benedict and Others,* 243. Also see James A. Boon, *Other Tribes, Other Scribes: Symbolic Anthropology in the Comparative Study of Cultures, Histories, Religions, and Texts* (New York: Cambridge University Press, 1982). An exemplary reading across genres can be found in James Clifford, "On Ethnographic Self-Fashioning: Conrad and Malinowski," in his *The Predicament of Culture: Twentieth-Century Ethnography, Literature, and Art* (Cambridge, Mass.: Harvard University Press, 1988), 92–113. More readings across genders and ethnicities are needed, as suggested by Ebron and Tsing in their essay in this volume.

41. Faye V. Harrison, "Anthropology as an Agent of Transformation: Introductory Comments and Queries," in *Decolonizing Anthropology: Moving Further Toward an Anthropology for Liberation,* ed. Faye V. Harrison (Washington, D.C.: American Anthropological Association, 1991), 6–7. Also see Michel-Rolph Trouillot, "Anthropology and the Savage Slot: The Poetics and Politics of Otherness," in *Recapturing Anthropology,* 17–44.

42. In my seminar, as in this collection of essays, I decided to keep the focus on the role of women in American cultural anthropology to maintain historical continuity. While this perspective may seem limited, there is still much missing here about women's contributions just to American cultural anthropology. Clearly, it would be worthwhile to expand this feminist reading of the history of women in anthropology to other national traditions and eventually to develop an international perspective. Within the British tradition, for example, one might ask why Edmund Leach's *Political Systems of Highland Burma* (Boston: Beacon Press, 1964) was hailed as a ground-breaking departure from classical functionalism while Audrey Richards's *Chisungu: A Girl's Initiation Ceremony Among the Bemba of Northern Rhodesia* (London: Faber and Faber, 1956) was not (Peter Pels, personal communication). On women in British social anthropology, see Nancy Lutkehaus, "'She Was Very Cambridge': Camilla Wedgwood and the History of Women in British Social Anthropology," *American Ethnologist* 13, no. 4 (1986): 776–98.

43. Alice Walker, *In Search of Our Mothers' Gardens* (New York: Harcourt Brace Jovanovich, 1983), 4; Adrienne Rich, "Divisions of Labor," in her *Time's Power: Poems 1985–1988* (New York: Norton, 1989).

44. See Rosaldo and Lamphere, *Woman, Culture and Society;* Rayna Reiter (Rapp), ed., *Toward an Anthropology of Women* (New York: Monthly Review Press, 1975); Peggy Reeves Sanday, *Female Power and Male Dominance: On the Origins of Sexual Inequality* (Cambridge, England: Cambridge University Press, 1981); Henrietta Moore, *Feminism and Anthropology* (Minneapolis: University of Minnesota Press, 1988); Micaela di Leonardo, ed., *Gender at the Crossroads of Knowledge: Feminist Anthropology in the Postmodern Era* (Berkeley: University of California Press, 1991); Elaine Showalter, *A Literature of Their Own: British Women Novelists from Brontë to Lessing* (Princeton, N.J.: Princeton University Press, 1977); Ellen Moers, *Literary Women: The Great Writers* (New York: Oxford University Press, 1977); Nancy K. Miller, *Subject to Change: Reading Feminist Writing* (New York: Columbia University Press, 1988); Carolyn G. Heilbrun, *Hamlet's Mother and Other Women* (New York: Ballantine, 1990).

45. A classical example is Shostak's *Nisa*. See Deborah A. Gordon's insightful analysis of this text in *A Troubled Border: Feminism and the Textual Turn in Anthropology* (Ann Arbor: University of Michigan Press, forthcoming).

46. Marilyn Strathern, "An Awkward Relationship: The Case of Feminism and Anthropology," *Signs* 12, no. 2 (1987): 276–92. Recently, the awkwardness has been recast in terms

of the relationship between postmodernism and feminism. See Mascia-Lees, Sharpe, and Cohen, "Postmodernist Turn"; Linda J. Nicholson, ed., *Feminism/Postmodernism* (New York: Routledge, 1990); Deborah Gordon, "The Unhappy Relationship of Feminism and Postmodernism in Anthropology," *Anthropological Quarterly* 66, no. 3 (1993): 109–17.

47. Judith Stacey, "Can There Be a Feminist Ethnography?" *Women's Studies International Forum* 11, no. 1 (1988): 22–23; Abu-Lughod, "Can There Be a Feminist Ethnography?" 18–19.

48. Kamala Visweswaran, "Defining Feminist Ethnography," *Inscriptions* 3/4 (1988): 36–39. Also see Visweswaran's *Fictions of Feminist Ethnography* (Minneapolis: University of Minnesota Press, 1994).

49. Judith Stacey, *Brave New Families* (New York: Basic Books, 1990); Dorinne Kondo, *Crafting Selves: Power, Gender, and Discourses of Identity in a Japanese Workplace* (Chicago: University of Chicago Press, 1990); Karen McCarthy Brown, *Mama Lola: A Vodou Priestess in Brooklyn* (Berkeley: University of California Press, 1991); Lila Abu-Lughod, *Writing Women's Worlds: Bedouin Stories* (Berkeley: University of California Press, 1992); Ruth Behar, *Translated Woman: Crossing the Border with Esperanza's Story* (Boston: Beacon Press, 1993); Anna Lowenhaupt Tsing, *In the Realm of the Diamond Queen* (Princeton, N.J.: Princeton University Press, 1993).

50. Gordon, *Troubled Border*.

51. I think this is the case with the feminist critique of Mascia-Lees, Sharpe, and Cohen, "The Postmodernist Turn," and to some extent with the volume edited by Fox, *Recapturing Anthropology*.

52. Rachel Blau DuPlessis, *Writing beyond the Ending: Narrative Strategies of Twentieth-Century Women Writers* (Bloomington: Indiana University Press, 1985), 3; Patricia Yaeger, *Honey-Mad Women: Emancipatory Strategies in Women's Writing* (New York: Columbia University Press, 1988); Carolyn Heilbrun, *Writing a Woman's Life* (New York: Norton, 1988).

53. Harold Bloom, *The Anxiety of Influence: A Theory of Poetry* (New York: Oxford University Press, 1973); Sandra M. Gilbert and Susan Gubar, *The Madwoman in the Attic: The Woman Writer and the Nineteenth-Century Literary Imagination* (New Haven: Yale University Press, 1979), 48–51. Limón, in "Representation, Ethnicity, and the Precursory Ethnography," is the only anthropologist who, to the best of my knowledge, draws on the idea of the anxiety of influence. On the ambivalence academic women feel toward the authority they do hold, see Nadya Aisenberg and Mona Harrington, *Women of Academe: Outsiders in the Sacred Grove* (Amherst: University of Massachusetts Press, 1988).

54. On the complexities of recent feminist literary criticism, see Marianne Hirsch and Evelyn Fox Keller, eds., *Conflicts in Feminism* (New York: Routledge, 1990); Gayle Greene and Coppélia Kahn, eds., *Changing Subjects: The Making of Feminist Literary Criticism* (New York: Routledge, 1993).

55. Mary Morris, ed., *Maiden Voyages: Writings of Women Travelers* (New York: Vintage Books, 1993), xv–xxii.

56. For discussion of these issues, see Peggy Golde, ed., *Women in the Field: Anthropological Experiences* (Berkeley: University of California Press, 1986); Diane Bell, Pat Caplan, and Wazir Jahan Karim, eds., *Gendered Fields: Women, Men and Ethnography* (New York: Routledge, 1993); Diane Wolf, ed., "Feminist Dilemmas in Fieldwork," special issue of *Frontiers: A Journal of Women's Studies* 13, no. 3 (1993): 1–103.

57. Susan Sontag, "The Anthropologist as Hero," in her *Against Interpretation* (New York: Doubleday 1986; orig. 1966), 74.

58. This view of the "native scholar" is, unfortunately, not yet obsolete; see Obbo, "Adventures with Fieldnotes." Also see the comparative essay by Deborah A. Gordon, "The Poli-

tics of Ethnographic Authority: Race and Writing in the Ethnography of Margaret Mead and Zora Neale Hurston," in *Modernist Anthropology: From Fieldwork to Text,* ed. Marc Manganaro (Princeton, N.J.: Princeton University Press, 1990), 146–162.

59. Kirin Narayan, "How Native Is a 'Native' Anthropologist?" *American Anthropologist* 95, no. 3 (1993): 28–29.

60. hooks, *Yearning,* 143.

61. José Limón, "Folklore, Gendered Repression, and Cultural Critique: The Case of Jovita Gonzalez," *Texas Studies in Literature and Language* 35, no. 4 (1993): 453–73.

62. On borderlands in anthropology, see Rosaldo, *Culture and Truth.*

63. For an important discussion of how anthropology's discomfort with assertive Jewishness has created an "epistemology of the Jewish closet," see Virginia Dominguez, "Questioning Jews," *American Ethnologist* 20, no. 3 (1993): 618–24.

64. Laurent Dubois, "Namings" (unpublished essay written for a seminar taught by Ruth Behar, "Ethnography Writing Workshop," 1994).

65. Faye D. Ginsburg, *Contested Lives: The Abortion Debate in an American Community* (Berkeley: University of California Press, 1989); Anna Lowenhaupt Tsing, "Monster Stories: Women Charged with Perinatal Endangerment," in *Uncertain Terms,* 282–99; Anne Taylor Fleming, *Motherhood Deferred: A Woman's Journey* (New York: G. P. Putnam's Sons, 1994).

66. Even staying focused on the tradition of American cultural anthropology, many important figures are absent, including Gladys Reichard, Hortense Powdermaker, Gene Weltfish, Jean Briggs, and Eleanor Leacock. To fill in gaps, see the excellent volume by Ute Gacs, Aisha Khan, Jerrie McIntyre, and Ruth Weinberg, eds., *Women Anthropologists: Selected Biographies* (Urbana: University of Illinois Press, 1989).

67. Anna Tsing, letter to Ruth Behar, October 13, 1994. My sincere thanks to Anna for the lucid reflections in her letter to me, on which I have drawn for the ideas in this paragraph.

I

Beyond Self
and
Other

1

Kirin Narayan

NO MATTER how often Charity looked up at the world map above the department secretary's desk, it still struck her as strange. Tilting inward, continents elongated as El Greco figures, the map simply did not have the right shape. The Americas claimed the center, knocking Europe and Africa off to the right. At each side were partial Indias: one with Punjab severed, the other missing several northeastern states. Scattered across all these realigned continents were pins with colored knobs, each pin locating a culture described in a senior thesis written recently by an anthropology major. Charity had been responsible for guiding a few of these projects.

She was looking at the map now because there was nothing else to do as Wendy, the department secretary, sorted through the mail. If Wendy was openly watched, she slowed down: sighing, examining stamps, turning over each piece of mail before she relinquished it to one of the cubbyholes she faced.

Just standing in the department office, Charity knew, could delay Wendy too. But Charity had arrived at the same moment as the plump man from the college post office who each afternoon bore in the plastic tray of mail. She had glimpsed the red and blue chevrons of an airmail envelope and couldn't draw herself away. Stretching out the moments, she stamped her boots, hung up her down coat, ran a hand through her cap-flattened hair. Nothing had reached her box yet. With the key to her office cold between thumb and forefinger, she inspected the map. She wondered whether the thesis about religious practices among Trinidadian Hindus who'd emigrated to Britain would be represented by one pin or three.

At a university with a graduate school, such pins in primary colors marked students off in faraway places. In this small liberal arts college, though, a pin puncturing paper meant nothing more than an attachment to certain shelves of books in the library. And the Whitney College library was so close that Charity could see the snowdrifts gathering on the steps and at the base of the twin pillars donated by the class of 1836. The map and the library in the same frame of vision mixed a claustrophobia so mean that Charity turned for a better look at Wendy's stack. Manila interoffice envelopes lined with names of professors and administrators were making their weary rounds within the campus. But there were also publishers' catalogues, letters machine-stamped from other institutional addresses in the United States, and what promised to be a few airmail envelopes or aerograms: paper that had traveled far.

It was Wendy of anthropology—not Jane of economics, Betty of English, or Christine of religion—who handled Third World grained envelopes of nonstandard sizes carrying bright boxed scenes related to development, tourism, or political figures with unpronounceable names. Recently when Wendy had been honored for twenty-five years of service to the college, she had brought along a stamp collection culled from countless afternoons of sorting mail. The Whitney College newspaper had carried a photograph of her—a plump, bespectacled woman given to wearing bows and ribbons—posing with a page of rare stamps from New Guinea, Togo, and Bhutan.

"One for you," Wendy finally turned to say.

"Ah," said Charity. Had her loitering been that obvious?

"It's that ant-track writing again," Wendy waved an envelope in Charity's direction. "Every mailman between here and India must have needed a magnifying glass."

Charity reached out a hand with the same sensation as having just downed an espresso. She let herself into her office and locked the door. She lit up a cigarette and pushed aside the latest pile of blue books on her desk. Ever since smoking behind the bathrooms at boarding school she did this furtively, a stolen pleasure now reinforced by campus laws against smoking in offices. She ran her fingers over the tiny writing on the envelope and the hard ridges of the reglued stamps. Wendy would expect these stamps.

Then, with a sandalwood cutter that still gave off a fragrance, she slit the envelope and unfolded the bundle inside. There they were, the ant tracks released: scurrying across the page, pressing deep into the paper to leave impressions on the other side, spilling into margins in after-the-fact elaborations. He always covered both sides of every page, and the pages went on: three, five, sometimes even ten.

§

. . . *Thanks for the xerox of the relevant pages from the 1918 Trigarta District Gazetteer. Ironic, isn't it, that these key volumes are in libraries in Berkeley, Chicago, and wherever else, but you can't get your hands on them anywhere in Trigarta? That information really helps me out.*

Well, there went the electricity. Now I'm writing by lantern and if these pages have a stench of kerosene you'll know why. It's one of those clear nights, starlight clotting the sky and trickling down over the mountains in their winter white. I spent the day recording midwinter children's games, not because it's my research topic but maybe because I have some sort of unexamined nostalgia for the days when anthropologists were responsible for documenting everything. (Incidentally, do you have any idea whether Bhargava included any of these games in that book you mention in the dissertation? No, I ain't angling for more xeroxes, I'm just curious about whether anyone has written about the games, the symbolism of the walnuts used, etc., etc.).

Have been trying to act on your request for more slides of the tulsi *plant — sorry you hadn't alerted me at the time when the plant was to be married in November. (This is my first experience with plants that have weddings.) At the moment, the plants are looking fairly withered, and the women's paintings on the plant's platform are fading fast. Following your tip about Prakash Singh's courtyard I went over there with my camera. Was received warmly and sat down to drink tea in one of the kitchens off the courtyard, though all the relatives from across the way crowded in for entertainment. As usual, every interaction with me as a foreigner was framed by comedy. Some of the kids were giggling so that they were thwacked by their mothers (also smothering smiles into their gauze scarves) and then there were loud bawls. Just mention America and the next question is whether I know you, though once in a while someone will bring up a relative who works in New Jersey or even Kuwait and ask if I know them. I told this set of inquisitors that I'd never met you, which disappointed the women mightily. When I added that you sometimes wrote to help me out with my research, I was quizzed on your health.* Suksanth? *Any children?* Mundu? *None that I know of, I said. I am deputed to send you greetings, to tell you to come soon, and to remind you that Raju's sister would like a watch with a little face just like the one you wear.*

Anyhow, to get back to the tulsi *plant. As usual, this courtyard also had the stick-figure divine bride and groom borne in the palanquins escorted by players from the band, and surrounded by trunks and brass pots of dowry. But the dowry also unmistakably included a sofa set, a bicycle, and a television painted in that same spare folk style! I guess times they are a-changing for the Gods too. I'll have the slides developed next time I get down to Delhi. Maybe I'll be able to locate some peripatetic scholar who could mail them from the U.S.*

Late in the day I was ushered into a darkened room where the men sat with a bottle of whisky. I was settled down under portraits of turbaned ancestors, rows of group photographs from graduating classes and army regiments, and cross-stitched deities with many arms. After the Hindi news on television, we watched "I Love Lucy" reruns: in English, without subtitles. . . .

§

"Boy, it'll be great to have this tenure thing behind me," said Isaac, depositing a quick but delicious kiss on the nape of Charity's neck. She was washing spinach in the sink, and Isaac had just taken over the tap to fill a large pot with water for pasta.

"Just a few weeks to go," said Charity, turning. Despite the three years she'd looked upon his face uncountable times a day, she still enjoyed the swoop of his nose, the set of his chin, and his black eyes as they focused in on hers, softening from their usual watchfulness. He was happy today because he'd had advance news from his chairman that the Department of Mathematics would probably vote unanimously to recommend him for tenure. A department meeting still lay ahead, and approval was needed at several rungs of the college administration. So far, though, the prognosis was excellent.

Isaac set the pot on the stove, the burner clicking as it came to life. With his back to her, he asked, "So, is it too soon to start?"

"Start what?" Charity responded. She knew perfectly well what he meant.

"You know, toss them out. Those pills."

Charity concentrated on the crinkled wetness of spinach leaves. "Maybe we should see if I'm reappointed for next year first," she said. She had originally been hired at the college to replace someone who was off for a year's fieldwork in Kathmandu; the following year, having just married Isaac, she had stepped in again for someone who had a fellowship in North Carolina. With shrinking funds available for academic research, no one had been on leave this past year, but Charity had been filling in with a joint appointment in anthropology and English, taking over a folklore course that had been lying dormant on the books since her friend Gita Das had left.

"Charity," said Isaac, "you know that that money from my grandmother . . ."

"I know," said Charity. They had had this conversation before. "But look, I just don't want to be unemployed if I can help it. I've got to keep a toehold in the profession until my book gets written."

"It'll get written," said Isaac. She felt his hand on her shoulder, giving it a squeeze. "You know it will."

Ever since Isaac had begun to put together his tenure file, he had been buying paperbacks on conception, childbirth, and parenting that he left in obvious places: in the basket filled with magazines beside the toilet, under the clock radio by their bedside, on the coffee table among library books and a cube of photographs. He also had been buying books on Judaism and befriending people from the Department of Religion. He said that one had to think through the background you gave a child.

Charity didn't have much to say. She had no interest in passing along her own Baptist missionary upbringing. When she and Isaac first began seeing each other, a distrust of organized religion was one of the many intersections they uncovered with hesitation followed by delight. There had been a certain glee in disappointing—maybe even horrifying—both sets of parents by marrying into an alien faith. Isaac had not had a particularly religious upbringing in the suburbia where he grew up. Charity realized it was a privilege to be able to shed a background. Even as she identified less and less with Christianity, Isaac was increasingly haunted by reports of swastikas spray-painted on houses in Montana, car bombs leveling Argentinian synagogues, ancient cemeteries vandalized in Eastern Europe.

Since it was a Friday night, when dinner was cooked, Isaac pinned a yarmulke to his hair. He brought out a book of Hebrew prayers transliterated and translated into English. He lit candles and began to chant. Charity watched from the sidelines, her mind wandering.

As Isaac started to pour the red wine, he shot Charity a wary look. She wondered if by not participating she was reflecting back an image in which his solemnity had something laughable about it—a thought vaguely connected to how people in Trigarta found Joel hilarious. But she was standing apart where she could (should?) have joined in, and Joel was joining in where nobody expected him to—it wasn't quite the same. After all her years of singing hymns around off-tune pianos followed by years of convincing herself it was fine not to, wouldn't it be a farce to now take up another set of prayers? Wouldn't participating be laughable?

As Isaac broke the bread, Charity conjured up the company of Radcliffe-Brown and Malinowski. What exactly had that debate between those anthropological forefathers been about? One said that ritual relieved anxiety, the other said that not doing the right rituals made for anxiety. There was an article about this in the faded gray *Reader in Comparative Religion*. Maybe it was reprinted in the new paperback edition with the shiny brown cover. Where was that book anyway? On campus, or in her study upstairs?

They sat down to eat. Charity filled the tension that had opened up between them by reconstructing the debate about rituals and anxiety. She usually enjoyed telling Isaac about anthropology: it was her way of linking up the world of ideas to which she was now professionally tied with the nitty-gritty of her daily life. Isaac twirled his spaghetti as she told him about Radcliffe-Brown's development of Durkheim's points about group solidarity generated through ritual. He was very quiet when she started in on Mary Douglas and how things that didn't quite fit clear cultural categories were threatening. He started to line up the salt and pepper shakers, the wine bottle, his wine glass, and his water glass in a phalanx across the table.

"Those people are just theorizing." Isaac nudged the water glass a millimeter to the right, then finally looked up. "How can you say anything about someone else's practice unless you know it from inside?"

Charity could see he was hurt. Was it the baby, the Shabbat, or the place inside her where the two joined? She chose to answer Isaac's question as a professional. "I guess that's an old problem in anthropology," she said. "How much can bystanders, what we call participant observers, really understand? Do you have to dress up in feathers to say what's going on in a war dance? Do you have to know grief from inside to understand mortuary rites?"

"It's complicated," Isaac said, chewing at his bread. "Take two people, even within the same society. If they don't have the same backgrounds, what do they really share?"

"There's got to be some way to understand different points of view through dialogue," Charity said. "You know, talking sympathetically." She wished Isaac would look at her and not at the burnished lemons on the framed poster by her head. Standing up to fetch the salad dressing they'd left on the counter, what she'd really been meaning to say came out in a rush: "Isaac, *really*, I just don't see why you're so hell-bent on rushing into sleepless nights and smelly diapers. How will I ever finish my book with a kid howling to be picked up and burped and fed all the time?"

Isaac focused on her. His face was flushed, almost shy; his black eyes were very bright. Charity realized at once that she shouldn't have described a baby in quite such tangible terms. Lately Isaac had developed the alarming habit of accosting mothers wheeling strollers in malls, of staring wistfully out into the snow when yet another friend called to say they were having a baby. He stood up too and stepped toward her.

"Charity, honey," he said into her hair. "It takes time to get pregnant. It takes time to be pregnant. If you're not reappointed, you could spend the time working on your book. You could be done before . . . it. I promise you what I said before: halftime child care." His arms were warm and comforting, his hands gentle as he stroked her cheek. "Halftime," he repeated. Her forehead fitted precisely into the niche at his neck.

Even as Charity clutched Isaac tighter, she wished desperately that she could fly off from this farmhouse in the falling snow. She wished she could toss away the stack of blue books she had to grade by Monday, erase the deadline for her paper in an edited volume, have not agreed to address the local Amnesty International chapter on human rights in India. She wished the winter would end. She wished she could slip under a mosquito net with one of her sisters and talk all through the night.

§

Faith, Hope, and Charity: all three sisters had been called "Baby" by the servants. Their missionary parents had run a hospital in western India, the father a doctor, the mother a nurse. There was a never-ending stream of sick or injured village and tribal people to their bougainvillea-draped bungalow. While the parents worked, the girls rolled out mats under the mango trees or played badminton. Sometimes they would sneak out and play with the local children who lived beyond the bungalow gates. There was a game Charity especially enjoyed called *paggadi*, in which you and a partner both extended arms, crossing them at the wrist, and then leaned back, balanced by each other's weight, to take mincing steps that whirled you round, round, breathless, laughing around. If the girls were discovered, their mother would pull a lice comb through their hair and check between their fingers for signs of scabies. Charity never understood why, if her parents worked with these people all day, their daughters were to keep a supposed distance.

When each sister turned five she was sent off to a boarding school up north, returning home only for the long winter vacations. At boarding school there were other children of missionaries, diplomats, or development experts, and all their textbooks were from America. Though the family occasionally visited grandparents in Colorado and Wisconsin on home leave through the years, until Charity entered college in New York, she thought of America in glossy, slightly fantastic terms. It was the home of Jane, Dick, and Spot; a place where milk did not need to be boiled and gave no cream; where prayer circles made for miraculous cancer cures; where underwear had elastic that did not grow limp after a few washes.

In America, Charity always found it difficult to feel American. Visually, she passed perfectly, with her green eyes and fine hair that was almost blonde in summer. She could wear the products she had stared at in magazines—already old by the time they reached India—and reclaim, for a moment, the wonder of this other way of life. Yet it seemed that even when she was living as an American, she was watching from outside, seeing the strangeness of that way of life. Also, the clip and intonation of her upbringing had remained in her voice. She could never say more than a few sentences without someone interrupting in a voice that seemed unnaturally hearty and flat, "Where are you from?"

Where? This was a hard question. With her first cultural anthropology class in college there seemed a glimmer of hope that there might be an answer. She also took every class on India she possibly could, finding new identities for the people who had shifted so uncomfortably between Them and Us as they unknowingly awaited redemption. She studied Indian religion and did a field project at a Hindu immigrants' temple where at last she accepted *prasad,* food offerings, of the sort her parents had so strictly warned the girls against (as though, she thought in retrospect, its sweet flavors spilled both amoebas and heresy). In graduate school she wrote long papers about missionaries in South Asia and enlarged her Hindi beyond imperatives. She had decided on a project about gender and religion. It had simply been chance that her advisor, leaning back in his chair and eyeing his bookshelf, had said, "Trigarta: by the way, there hasn't been much done up there."

She had used anthropology to move away from America, constructing and reclaiming a more foreign self through eighteen months of fieldwork in Trigarta. Yet it was Isaac's Americanness that had drawn her to him. From that first day they met standing in line for lunch at the faculty orientation—each new to town, each new to teaching—she had been intrigued. She liked his Brooks Brothers' shirts, knowledge of sixties children's television, memories of his father throwing a ball after work. It was reassuring that he had never been outside America and that she could reinvent India for him through herself: not as a place that made her marginal but that was somewhere central to her past. When the companionship of someone to grade papers with through big empty weekends unwrapped into the gift of intertwined nights, she was overwhelmed. She loved how bright his eyes were, the softness of his hands in her hair. She reveled in how their conversations flowed, cutting through layer upon layer of intimacy without ever running dry. It also didn't hurt that at the time he was a Jewish agnostic and that her parents—now retired to Wisconsin—would recoil.

As the red and gold fall turned to a monochrome winter, Isaac and she had taken increasing refuge in each other's company. Requests that he give her a ride to faculty dinners were gradually replaced by outright joint invitations. Yet Charity's sisters had not been enthusiastic when they learned she was dating the only single, heterosexual, and attractive man on the entire faculty in this remote campus. "Loneliness is not love," wrote Hope from Tanzania, where she was carrying on a fourth-generation tradition of mission work. "Don't make decisions in drought conditions," said Faith, the New York photographer, over the phone. "Heavens, Charity, don't you have any girlfriends around to set you straight?" But the few other young women of her age were either engrossed in raising small children or just weren't her type. Charity had never lived through a New England winter before, had never felt so shiveringly stripped of all that was familiar: friends, routines, locales. It was only under Isaac's down comforter, his body hot against hers, that she could shake off the chill.

In March—when it should have been spring but resolutely remained winter—they had gone for a drive one afternoon along the snowy back roads that bore one away from campus. They had seen an old stone farmhouse for sale. It was a house with broad porches and a view of forests on one side. They agreed that they would both like to live there, hanging out baskets of fuchsia and tending an herb garden when summer arrived. And yet to do this together—those mortgage forms, those insurance applications, those monthly payments—it really would help to be a unit that was legitimately, socially defined. Isaac's mother was on a senior citizens' tour of China. Charity's parents were off visiting Hope in Africa. It had been a civil ceremony, without any family present from either side, to beat the closing date on the house. Charity knew they should have waited, should have lived together first, should at least have had a few almost unresolvable fights. Yet this marriage was an act of affirmation—of heat and high color—in the coldest, longest, gray-and-white winter of her life.

§

What Isaac had said about not practicing and building theories clung to Charity through the following weeks. It haunted her as she stared at the screen of her computer. It sprang center stage in her wandering thoughts during all-college faculty meetings in an overheated room full of overheated opinions. There seemed such a huge gulf between the Vermont winter and life in Trigarta, on which her job depended; a yawning ravine between the confident graduate student she had been when she did fieldwork and the professionally marginal person she had become. Even with field notes, the dissertation, boxes and boxes of tapes and slides, her memory was becoming blurred. What could she really say that was new and also true about these lives she had made it her business to describe?

Trigarta. The word brought a haze of green sunshine to her eyes: terraced fields, clumps of bamboo, slate roofs glinting, a bus wheezing by. A flycatcher swooped, tail looping, streaming, white. Her friend Padma would be squatting by the stream, thumping out clothes on the rocks as detergent bubbled on toward the next village. Their best conversations had always been out there, away from Padma's husband and children, the sun warm on their backs. Padma's close-set eyes shot mischief as she described for Charity the skits that women performed, dressed in their husbands' clothes, when all the men of the settlement set off in a groom's party to fetch a new bride. How could Padma, with her quick mind and vigorous opinions, ever be stuffed into the word "informant"?

They were less informants than indulgent friends, these women she spent months with: participating in their lives. They had sunned together on rope cots in courtyards during the winter, had ridden the bus into town squeezed so tight it was hard to be sure where one body ended and another began. They had fanned flies away from children's sleeping faces on hot afternoons, had sat all night in smoky rooms for weddings, had commiserated over the government's inability to contain soaring prices.

She had been physically present with the women, but internally, where was she as she connected their opinions to theories? Even when she didn't have a notebook in hand, she was always posting messages to herself about what to record later. A small part of what she had learned in that year and a half was gathered up, amber fossils, in her dissertation. If she had not been teaching and working on a new marriage over these last two years, they might be set in a university press book that anyone could pick up and enter inside.

Joel had ordered her dissertation from Ann Arbor microfilms, reading it minutely, laboriously, appropriating each experience and insight. This was, after all, the very same field site, and though his project was very different, he took up every piece of information she had. Charity had no idea whether he brought the same intensity to the works of the others who had researched Trigarta—Barry, Varma, McBell. She wondered if he wrote to them too.

She had pieced together this much about him: he had grown up in U.S. consulates across the world; he had been a journalist before he went to graduate school; he first learned of Trigarta when his father brought back a set of snapshots taken on a trip up north with Galbraith. Charity guessed that Joel must be older than the usual graduate student. He appeared to be alone in the field. There was never a mention of a woman in the letters, no mention of children. But who knew? A lot could be hidden in the penumbra of life around a professional exchange. How much did vivid stories, though, really count as "professional"?

In Charity's replies to Joel's letters she argued about interpretations, suggested readings, elaborated on scenes that hadn't been in the dissertation and that she'd almost forgotten she remembered. The exchange of ideas had begun to lure her back into rewriting her book for a few hours each weekend in between preparations for class, household chores, and the ever-renewing piles of student papers. Like him, she kept Trigarta central to her side of the interchange. If the rhythms and responsibilities of her present life pushed into this correspondence at all, it was only in hints from the margins.

§

Maybe it was the complacency on this campus that was getting to her, Charity thought one weekday night as she was preparing for class. She would send each one of her students out to collect a piece of folklore used by or about a culturally different group. The assignment (typed, double-spaced, proofread) would be due in her office the following Monday.

Whitney College tried hard to recruit minority and foreign students, but most of its students were still overwhelmingly American, privileged, and white. They seemed to have stepped out of a glossy skiing catalogue, and they drove Saabs and Volvos their parents had bought in the event of a drunk-driving accident. On their way from wealth to more wealth, they looked down on the faculty, in their rusting Japanese cars, with disdain. Charity sometimes got trouble from tall boys in her classes who were destined to be corporate chairmen or at least senators: they seemed unable to believe that a young woman with a strange accent might actually make a fair input to their grade point average.

After Charity had issued her assignment she began to wonder where cultural difference would actually be located and made real in a place like this. Among the scholarship students whose clothes and part-time jobs suggested they were of a different class? In pockets in the dorms: Pakistani boys who were all on the soccer team and ate their meals speaking Urdu, the circle of aristocratic Italians who had graduated from the same school and radiated incestuous exclusivity? In the films brought in by the French Club each Saturday for free campus viewing? At the Shabbat services Isaac had begun to attend, and from which he came home humming tunes very unlike the hymns that Charity could not forget? Some of the faculty were from foreign countries, yet at any gathering their difference was erased by the shared denominator of college gossip.

Charity arrived midmorning on Monday to find a paper pinned on her office door without an envelope to shield its contents. Wendy was in a huff. Mr. Henderson, the department chairman, cornered Charity as he dashed off to class. "I'd like to talk to you when I get back," he said, brusque and redfaced. Charity went into her office and looked more closely at the paper.

There's this guy who loves his girlfriend so much that he tattoos her name on his penis. When it's erect, it reads WENDY and otherwise, it's just WY. Well, one day this guy is in New York City, and he goes into a public urinal. There's this big black man peeing beside him, and he just can't help noticing that he has a

WY on his penis too. "This is really a coincidence!" he tells the big guy. "So your girlfriend's name is also Wendy?" "What do you mean?" the big guy asks. "I mean, what's that WY?" The big guy laughs. "That's no WENDY, man. It says, WELCOME TO JAMAICA, HAVE A NICE DAY."

Soo Chen, the student—one of Charity's best—went on to point out that this was part of a larger cycle of "black dick jokes." She used theories from the class to interpret this joke in terms of gender relations, male hierarchies, the grotesque and carnivalesque, and sexual anxiety about the Other. It was an excellent interpretation.

When the next bell pierced through the morning, Charity went into Mr. Henderson's office. He offered her a seat and nudged a box of Kleenex and a jar of candy toward her (he had once explained that these were helpful with girls after exams). After some preliminary remarks about the weather—always a safe topic in the Northeast—he fixed her with cold blue eyes and asked some pointed questions: Were dirty jokes a course requirement? Were students not aware that those who served the college should be respected? Might not assignments that insulted particular minority groups involve the college in lawsuits?

Charity tried to explain that Soo did not mean to be impertinent but no manila envelopes had been on hand. Stereotypes, she said, could only be deconstructed through close examination. She agreed to bring Soo in for a formal apology to Wendy. All through the interview, Charity prayed to herself that this incident would not cost her her reappointment. It was a relief to get into the car with Isaac that evening, to drive away into the open snowfields, to transform the story from trauma to comedy through retelling. She stopped short, though, of writing about it to Joel. He had no place in the day-to-day details of her life.

§

It was yet another Monday in the relentless, gray progression of weeks. Charity opened the window when there was a knock on her door. Winter air swirled sharp into the radiator-dried interior. She hid her ashtray and folded up the letter. It was probably a student in search of counsel: hand-holding duties spilled beyond office hours, especially when midterms were at hand. But it was Wendy.

"Oh, excuse me, umm." Wendy said. Male professors were universally "Mr." at this college, but somehow the female professors ended up being referred to by their first names. In the clash between what people called these women behind their backs and how they ought to be addressed, most ended up stripped of names that could be used to their faces. "I want to talk to you about those letters you get," said Wendy. "You know, the ant tracks from India."

"Certainly," said Charity, tensed. Was Wendy going to lecture her about the propriety of married women receiving such thick tracts? Why did everyone on this campus feel they had a right to observe and interfere in each other's lives?

"I've noticed," Wendy continued, "that you've been receiving a lot of those letters."

"It's common in professional correspondences," said Charity. "We happen to be colleagues." Jesus! This was reminiscent of boarding school, hanging one's head before the Anglo-Indian matron, extending a hand for a whack. Was Wendy still on the rampage because of that folklore item?

"Well, I just wondered," Wendy said.

"Yes?"

"I don't want to interfere . . . but I wondered if you could tell this person that they're sending the same stamps pretty often. If you look at what you got today it's the same as last week and the week before."

Charity examined the envelope on her desk. Tiny scenes formed a jagged patchwork around the address. Five navy-blue women in saris balanced pots on their heads, striding out in matched precision worth fifty paise each time. The cows they'd just milked stood patiently in the background, enclosed in a different world from the hairy, glaring, barbed-wire-fence-nudging cows Isaac and Charity confronted on their daily drives. For a rupee apiece, cotton blossoms burst out from a sepia background: cotton, snowball white. The ten-paise fillers were farmers hoeing beside irrigation canals. The fields, stretching out in an inner horizon, were as green as the faraway summer.

"Sure, I'll write to . . . the person," Charity said, looking up from the envelope to give Wendy an ungrudged smile. "The only problem might be if the village post office doesn't have others in stock. When I was there I sometimes had to go to a main post office a long bus ride away to find anything in the denomination for airmail. Sure, I'll mention it."

"If you don't mind," said Wendy.

When Wendy left, Charity lit another cigarette and returned to where she had left off, on page 6:

Thanks for the reference from C.I.S. . . . I tracked it down in the library when I got to Delhi and think that what he's arguing about egalitarianism mingling with hierarchy does fit. By now Dumont-bashing is passé (I'd better figure out how this fits in with subalterns). I'm actually quite intrigued by the idea of friendship as a subversion of social structure. You had some of that in your dissertation on the groups of girls that gather for Goddess worship from a cross-section of castes. I'm trying to get a handle on it among men. Is it an outgrowth of education in schools, or was it there all along within a village setting? I'm not quite sure, maybe the oral histories will help. Among women, I'm handicapped by being a strange and foreign man. Children cry when they see me, they really do, giving mothers an excuse to withdraw to inner rooms. I try to be amused by the mirror that incredulity and suspicion holds up for me, but on a daily basis it can get disorienting. I don't know that I can really help you with those questions you sent, but I'll try.

I agree that an anthropological sensibility is important at this moment in time, as interactions between different taken-for-granted perspectives are speeded up by the global media, trade, travel, migration. I guess that what we call an anthropological sensibility really boils down to accepting that there aren't any ultimate solu-

tions—each is somehow tempered by culture and circumstance. And more and more, everything is jumbled. . . .

Just as she was about to turn the page, the telephone rang and there was an impatient sequence of knocks at her door. Charity put the letter away and returned, for the moment, to the round of duties that fenced in her energies.

§

"Judaism is a family religion," Isaac softly said. It was his birthday, and his parents had sent him a Torah. After dinner he showed Charity how each page was arranged. Hebrew was a beautiful script, to Charity a mix of Sanskrit and Japanese. She ran her fingers over the black patterns, seeing how it could be alluring to enter this gilded, complex world that Isaac had spread out before them. She could even understand why Isaac now sat in on intermediate Hebrew. Yet she felt no tug toward this world herself.

"I want to pass this on to our children," said Isaac.

"Sure," said Charity.

"This really matters to me," Isaac continued, tensing against the shrug in her voice. "I want you to participate."

"I guess they'd have to be formally converted," Charity said, examining her nails. This was stalling for time. "Look, I always stand beside you as you light the candles. If you want to read a page of the Torah each morning I really don't object."

"You watch," Isaac looked at her with troubled eyes. "You don't join."

"At least I don't interfere." Charity leaned away. She blurted, "Isaac, I can't participate more and be true to who I am."

Isaac pressed a palm on the open page, as though drawing in its strength. "We'll confuse the children if we give them two different messages," he said. "They'll grow up without being sure of who they are or just what's right. In this mixed-up world people need strong roots. If we're raising children, it's our responsibility to give them all the security we can."

Charity stopped herself from shooting: "What children?" She was still staunchly punching out birth control pills, though a new wariness had made its way into their bed. To press down sharp words, she thought about an article she had once read on ethnicity. It must have been in that *Writing Culture* collection. Maybe she should put together a course on ethnic identity to figure out what Isaac was after. She quoted someone, she wasn't quite sure who, aloud: "In the postmodern world all identity is hybrid."

"Charity," said Isaac, placing the book on the coffee table and fitting his arm around her. "This isn't some sort of fancy theory, this is our life. I want it to be a Jewish life and not leave you out of it. I want us do this together."

"What about India?" said Charity, feeling bleached, as if she might cry.

"What about it?" asked Isaac. "I'm not talking about your research, I'm talking about our family life."

When they held each other, Charity felt a barrier between their chests: a mingling of vulnerability, distance, disappointment. She thought of the time at the end of the semester when they had been invited over by well-meaning colleagues for a party that turned out to have a Christmas theme. "Happy Hannukah," the hostess had said to Isaac. Later, the hostess had steered him toward the piano so he could lead them in Christmas carols, and she was upset that he had demurred. "Her attitude was that if she recognized Hannukah, I should join in for Christmas," Isaac had fumed on the ride home. "Couldn't she see that as a Jew I might not want to participate, that this is a choice?"

If Isaac could understand this about a group, Charity wondered, why couldn't he see the analogy in their household? Could dialogue really build bridges across differences: planks laid down with agreement, swaying suspensions hung through persuasion, girders tempered in hot argument and cemented with affection? What exactly did one need to build a bridge with at least two broad highways that would stand up to many daily commutes?

§

It wasn't just the Trigarta crew that huddled around Charity's desk. Fellow professionals clustered also in her classroom, weaving around her head, fragments of their words rising to her lips. Some of these people had been dead for many decades; others were still alive. She'd glimpsed some of their names on tags at conferences, looking swiftly up to take in the face, and she'd heard some of them speak from behind podiums. She'd even been introduced to a few, standing in hotel lobbies. And some were old friends. Scholarship, Charity reflected, was fellowship too, ideas arrayed around vivid personalities. After noticing at a plenary session that a man whose work she admired combed his hair over a bald spot, she had never felt quite the same about his ideas. Or running into a distantly recognized name and seeing the woman's smile, her audacious earrings, her handwoven jacket, Charity had sought out her book with all the intensity of a fan. These fellows who inhabited other anthropologists—what impact, Charity wondered, did they carry as people shaping not just ideas but lives? Participating in the common profession, they observed each other too; observing, they grew and changed.

Marina Alvares, who had invited Charity to be on a panel at the last American Anthropology Association meetings, was now editing a volume of the papers. Charity knew that Marina had gone to the same graduate school as Joel. The next time Marina called to announce deadlines, Charity slipped the conversation around to him: "Tell me, what is this Joel Powell like?"

"Oh, he's a Weberian," Marina said, ever the resolute Marxist.

"I mean, as a person: what is he like?"

"He's a good colleague," said Marina. "Real good with references."

Charity saw it was inappropriate to press this further.

§

Wendy had distributed an application form for summer research support from the college. This year, because of some new bequest by the Class of 1935, it was a spring rather than a fall deadline. She looked up from her typewriter as Charity drew out the sheet of paper from her mailbox.

"If you want me to type that thing be sure to get it in a few days ahead," Wendy instructed. "These days with those word processors, everyone ends up giving me their forms with blank spaces to fill. The last minute, too. I'll be all backed up the day they're due."

Charity was turning the form over and over. "Yes, Wendy," she said absently.

Charity studied the form some more in her office. For once, this was something that visiting faculty could apply for. She actually did need to get more information and check back with people before the dissertation could be published, and a summer grant would help her do it. But Isaac? He wanted her to work on the house this summer, now that his tenure had been approved. He pleaded that she quit those occasional stealthy cigarettes he could always catch with a kiss. He was dropping hints about using the leisure time for baby-making. It could be a summer of mornings in their futon bed, opening herself at last to his domestic plans. Or else she could spend the summer on rope cots at the edges of other peoples' lives, observing them, her own future on hold.

Looking around her office, she did not see the messy piles of papers, the books lined up on the shelves, the framed photograph of Isaac. She saw parrots swooping after ripe leeches, greens of many shades and textures overlapped and intertwined. She heard women singing as they stood ankle deep in muddy water, transplanting young rice, as buses wheezed past in clouds of blue smoke. She smelled clothes dried dankly indoors as rain poured unrelentingly, day after day, night after night.

Just where did her responsibility lie?

Hope would most certainly not lavish good-wife advice. Married and with four children, she would urge, "Stick to your career, don't compromise. If you go have a baby, you might as well forget being anything more than a faculty wife who's hired now and then for a course." Faith, still single, would insist that Charity hold on to a man who loved her and wanted to have her children: at all costs, she should hug him, stroke him, hold him tight. "Heck," Faith had recently said over the phone, "if we put up with evening prayers every day for years, what's the problem with sticking it out through one evening a week and in holiday seasons a few extra?"

Charity sat with her elbows on her desk, eyes open in the darkness of her palms. She listened to her older sisters' voices, wondering if her own would ever join in, calm, firm, certain of being right. Living with someone, sleeping beside him night after night, even her breath was intertwined with his. How could she separate herself enough to diverge from his desires?

After a while, Charity slid open a drawer and pulled out a file marked TRIGARTA—CORRESPONDENCE. She sniffed the paper, smelling Indian stationery stores, mold, and kerosene. Then she shuffled through the sheets, not to read, but to ponder the patterns of those tiny trails. Anthropologists had written about divining from poisoned chickens, cowrie shells, kangaroo droppings, yarrow sticks. They wrote about how other people made sense of their lives, not about their own quests for certainty. Where, Charity wondered, would she find a divinatory system for the way a pen tracked across blank paper? If only she could gain a revelation, a clear vision, of the larger realities these squiggles of ink emerged out of and pointed into: self-directed, hurrying ants.

2

Bad Girls: Theater, Women of Color, and the Politics of Representation

Dorinne Kondo

"WHY A PLAY?" Ruth Behar asked me as we were discussing ideas for this contribution. The question set me to musing, reawakening the reasons I became involved in, then captivated by, Asian American theater, first as an academic critic, later as fledgling playwright, and now as a dramaturge in productions both Asian American and multicultural. Theater specifically has come to possess me—not film, not visual art, not poetry or novels—though I also love those genres and though theater does not exclude any of them. What, then, is the genealogy of that joy, pleasure, and excitement, and how did theater "choose me" as a subject of investigation and co-creation?

Cultural production in any register, for those of us "on the margins," is a process of representing our emergent, always historically mediated identities, creating a space for us to "write our faces," to paraphrase the playwright/performance artist/novelist Han Ong.[1] Like so many people on the margins, Asian Americans are generally erased from realms of cultural representation. Perhaps worse, when we are depicted it is only to be stereotyped yet again, a kind of symbolic violence that influences not only how we are treated by others but also how we think of ourselves. In that light, plays, films, poetry, and novels written by Asian Americans can constitute a stunningly powerful affirmation that we exist.

Here the live aspect of theater is critical. Live

performance not only constitutes a site where our identities can be enacted, it also opens up entire realms of cultural possibility, enlarging our senses of ourselves in ways that have been, for me, especially powerful. Theater shows us that Asian Americans can be other than model minorities or gangsters, lotus blossoms or dragon ladies, scientists or gardeners. We can write plays; we can perform, act, design, direct. Theater helps to widen the possibilities of how one can imagine one-self as a racialized subject at this moment in history. I remember, for instance, how central Asian American theater was in keeping alive my sense of Asian American, and specifically Japanese American, identity. Going to the theater became part of a ritual of returning "home," a performative production of racial and ethnic identity. Similarly, prose can scarcely capture how transfixed I was at the Broadway produc-tion of M. Butterfly. Here—on Broadway!—was a lavish, thoroughly professional production, written by an Asian American, featuring stunningly adept Asian Ameri-can actors, designers, and musicians. "Thunderstruck," trite though it may seem, is the only word that can describe my shock at seeing such an incisive, multilayered political critique of Orientalism and essentialized gender and racial identities played out with such powerful emotional impact on a mainstream stage. Searingly moving, M. Butterfly spoke eloquently to me as a woman of color and an Asian American woman, despite the inevitably complicated politics of representation involved in the piece. It is the only time I have ever felt I had to write about something—again to put it melodramatically, but I think not untruthfully—as though my life depended on it. My essay on M. Butterfly[2] and the book I am currently writing on Asian American theater constitute in part a tribute and a documenting of an important moment in American cultural production, as people on the margins come to voice. My scholarly work then becomes a way of trying to "write our faces" in an aca-demic register and of helping to explore the possibilities offered to us by the vexed identity of "Asian American."

The sense of empowerment and possibility fostered by Asian American theater led me to enroll in the David Henry Hwang Writers Institute at East West Players in Los Angeles, the oldest extant Asian American theater troupe in the country. Origi-nally my rationale was ethnographic: I would learn about the craft of playwriting through participant observation for my book on Asian American theater. Moreover, I hoped the class would provide entrée into the larger Asian American theater world, especially given that the course was to be taught by playwright Rick Shiomi, best known for his off-Broadway hit, the detective spoof Yellow Fever, and that Hwang himself would be coming to class from time to time. My hopes for transfer-ring from academic prose to creative writing were much more modest. Since my for-ays into such realms had been limited to bad high-school poetry and grade-school fairy tales, my decision seemed on the one hand outrageous and audacious. On the other hand, performance artist Chloe Webb's refrain from a recent piece came to mind: "Why not?"

My hopes for the class were fulfilled beyond my wildest expectations. Actually trying to write creatively in the context of the course provided innumerable insights into theater; it was revelatory, a kind of paradigm shift. The insights—though seemingly mundane as I describe them now—were so exciting that I could hardly sleep, so absorbing that a usually brutal 45-minute freeway commute seemed only minutes long. Most amazing was the way theater illuminated the truth of the post-structuralist dictum of "no fixed text," for even subtle changes in acting, intonation, lighting, blocking (the movements of the actors on stage), stage business, or design, among other factors, shaped, even totally changed, meaning. Indeed, one of the functions of a play-writing class like that of the Writers Institute is to give writers the opportunity to *hear* their work, first in class, read by classmates, and then at the end of the session, read by professional actors. Only when one has heard one's script read well can one know if the scene works. Even then, it is often difficult to sift out the influence of various factors: the writing, the directing, the venue, the casting, and so on. Never has the intentional fallacy been so obvious, for these extra-textual forms of making meaning can utterly transform the playwright's intent. This is the most rewarding, as well as the most frustrating, aspect of collective creative endeavor. When acting, directing, writing, and design all come together, the result is something wonderful that far exceeds the intention of the author. When one or another is found wanting, it can be an experience of utter frustration. Such are the risk and the thrill of the theater.

In short, theater signals for me a kind of paradigm shift away from the purely textual toward the performative, the evanescent, the nondiscursive, the collaborative. It can attempt to make political/intellectual/aesthetic interventions in another register, enabling playwright and audiences to confront dilemmas and situations that are "good to think" in powerfully engaging modes quite different from conventional academic prose.

§

Theater, for me, has been a vehicle for empowerment, so perhaps it is not surprising that the theme of my first play is, precisely, the process of empowerment. The premise—which I hope is amusing and, inevitably, problematic—concerns Janice Ito, a young Asian American film professor who dreams of becoming Grace Jones, the tall, androgynous African American actress, singer, disco diva. Through alliances with other women of color, Ito exacts revenge on the structures of power that oppress her.

I began parts of this piece during the fall of 1991 in play-writing class, the fall of the Anita Hill–Clarence Thomas hearings. Sexual harassment and courtroom drama were much on everyone's mind. Over the years I have been collecting mental files of incidents of sexual and racial harassment in the academy, both mine and others', from the little—and often breathtakingly offensive—things said at cocktail parties and meetings to physical harassment of various kinds. A monologue I wrote in class about an Asian American woman who was constantly treated with disrespect ("dissed") and who dreamed of becoming Grace Jones was paired with a short dialogue between an Asian American woman faculty member and an Orientalist, eventually becoming the nucleus for my play-in-progress, *Dis(graceful)l Conduct*. The tone was to be "Brecht meets music video," political commentary underlying a wacky, ridiculous, funny comedy/musical to a disco beat—just in time for seventies retro. The title is meant to be polysemous: Grace Jones of course gave me the opportunity to play with the many meanings of "grace." At one level, "grace-full" can be seen as a synonym for empowered; "dis," the hip-hop term for "disrespect," that is, a putdown. At another level, there are constant conflicts of interpretation in the play about what counts as disgraceful conduct. Is it the Orientalist professor and his harassment? The actions of the women of color, seen by the white men as threatening the canon and the foundations of power—indeed, Western civilization? Grace's outrageous behavior? Ito's stereotyping of Grace?

As the play engages common struggles against harassment, it also thematizes the identifications people of color have across racial lines with other people of color, whether it be Dan Kuramoto, the leader of the jazz fusion group Hiroshima growing up in East Los Angeles and wanting to be a *cholo*; African American musician Patrice Rushen, appearing on various album covers in Native American or Chinese garb; the Motown parody *The Last Dragon*, a kung fu movie with Tai-Mak, an African American overly identified with "Oriental wisdom"; or the ways in which rap has become a multiracial medium. These identifications I see as potentially utopian, in their gesture of solidarity and coalition, but potentially equally problematic.

This dilemma in cultural representation lies at the heart of the play's premise. However amusing the sight gag of the imposing Grace Jones and the smaller Janice Ito, however earnest my intention to say something about cross-racial identifications and forms of coalition among people of color, the Grace Jones character inevitably reinscribes the stereotype of the phallic black woman who never experiences pain or vulnerability and who therefore is never endowed with a complex subjectivity. In its readings, some African American women have taken issue with this stereotype; others see it as trying to come to terms with and problematizing that very stereotyping. Scene Ten is an attempt to thematize that issue; I hope to grapple with that dilemma more effectively in subsequent revisions. Mindful of these dilemmas, *Dis(Graceful)l Conduct* nonetheless attempts to say something about alliances among women of color to fight the gender and racial stereotyping/oppressions that manifest themselves in the harassment so many of us encounter on a regular basis and to suggest that alliance and coalition are possible. It is my hope that women of color in the academy, above all others, will find something in the play that speaks to their/our experiences.

§

The first scene opens with Janice Ito, a young assistant professor who is thrilled with her new job at the Mount Olympus of scholarship, Ivy University. Naive and idealistic, she sees Ivy as a place that represents the life of the mind, the finest of

DORINNE KONDO

human endeavor. Six months later, she is the Invisible Asian Woman as she dodges students hurling racial insults and is forced to socialize with colleagues who first ignore her, then proceed to drop casual racial and sexual insults at a cocktail party. At the end of Scene One, as the colleagues freeze, she speaks her fantasies of becoming Grace Jones, Ito's icon of female strength.

Scene Two introduces an anomaly, a Sansei (third-generation Japanese American) cleaning woman, Nancy Kawano, who bemusedly observes Ito in her Grace Jones fantasy. Nancy is meant to be a kind of omniscient narrator-in-training, a wise-cracking, no-nonsense woman who has a tense relationship with the more privileged Ito. She is also meant to break stereotype, as a domestic/manual worker rather than as a member of the model minority. After Nancy leaves, refusing Ito's conversational gambits and attempts at friendship, Cabot—one of the senior colleagues from Scene One—knocks on the door and issues an insinuating invitation. It is creepy, and Ito shivers as she refuses his advances and leaves her office.

Scene Three introduces us to Justin Nakagawa, a figure drawn from some of the men I have known in Asian American political movements. Charismatic and sexy, he also tries to be a man of the nineties, cooking for his girlfriend Janice and genuinely attempting to be supportive. Justin and Janice first make passionate love, then Justin makes her dinner. They begin to argue about politics, as he pressures her to attend a trial and help out at the coalition by decorating for the Halloween party rather than going to her out-of-town speaking engagement. Their mutual physical attraction—though it wins out in this scene—cannot transcend the real differences in their philosophies: his, that only grass-roots activism really matters; hers, that the academy is also an important site of intervention. The scene also engages the well-documented sexism of many race-based political movements of the sixties, in which women were supposed to type and get the coffee, not make speeches or shape policy. Justin also represents a type of Asian American activist labeled "one of those Black Japanese" by a play-writing classmate of mine. That is, Justin identifies with African Americans and uses African American speech patterns, a common urban phenomenon that may be even more pronounced among activists of the left. The identification of both Justin and Ito with African Americans speaks eloquently of the persistence of the black-white binary in the dominant imagery and of the in-the-middle position of Asian Americans and Latinos on that unidimensional hierarchy. If you are Asian American or Latino, especially on the East Coast, white and black are the poles, and if you don't identify with one, you identify with the other. This phenomenon simultaneously highlights the critically important historical legacy of the civil rights movement, as the efforts of African Americans became important sources of inspiration and support for other peoples of color.

Scene Four reintroduces Cabot and his active libidinal energies. He makes suggestive remarks to a student, which Nancy interrupts, and we get some inkling in this scene of the insecurities and fears that feed his sense of diminished potency and shape his crazily logical rationale for harassing women. On the following day he calls Ito away from her preparations for a talk in order to advise her about the renewal of her contract, a pretext for his physical advances. To what extent he succeeds is left ambiguous.

Scene Five, reproduced here, is Ito's paranoid fantasy/worst nightmare/heightened reality. All of the forces impinging on her life come together to overwhelm her. The intended effect is musical, a kind of rapid chorus of successive oppressions, if you will. The scene should be funny, as well as pathetic and poignant, with a humorous touch at the end as Grace Jones providentially appears and Act One comes to a close.

SCENE FIVE

[Nancy surveys the scene from a platform upstage.]

NANCY: The pace grew ever more vertiginous.

[Lights come up stage right. Justin stands in a space that represents the office of the coalition. Lights come up stage left. Cabot stands in his office. A spot illuminates Ito, who stands center stage, still with long hair and clothed in appropriate academic drag.]

JUSTIN: Where were you at the trial, baby? We were counting on you. I thought you were down with the people.

[Ito runs over to Justin.]

ITO: I am, Justin. I am down with the people. I'm so sorry I wasn't there. I'll never do it again. Where are the phones? Hello? This is the Asian American Coalition. I'm calling to ask you to donate to our Justice Fund. Oh, thank you, thank you.

Hello? This is the Asian American Coalition. We'll be sending you a press release soon. What's your fax number?

Hello? This is the Asian American Coalition. Could you tell me the next deadline for grant proposals?

Justin, Justin, how'm I doing? Shit, I forgot about the Halloween party. What did I do with the streamers? And the coffee. . . . Do you have enough coffee?

JUSTIN: There's never enough, baby.

ITO: I've tried so hard . . . to give to the movement. And to you.

JUSTIN: You have to give more, baby.

[The lights on Justin change color.]

CABOT: Ito, Ito, where are you?

[Ito runs over, frantically.]

ITO: Here, Professor Cabot.

CABOT: That lecture series. How's it coming?

ITO: Oh, fine, fine. Three speakers lined up.

CABOT: Only three? The department was hoping for at least five.

ITO: Five? Five. . . . Well, I'll see what I can do.

CABOT: Ito, while you're here . . . how about a massage? Maybe you can walk on my back, like those Japanese girls do in *Sayonara*.

ITO: I'm not very good at it . . . but I'll try.

CABOT: And afterwards . . . the position on page 52.

ITO: That one. I don't like that one.

CABOT: Remember, our first meeting about contract renewal is next week.

ITO: Yes, OK, 52. . . .

[An alarm clock rings.]

    Oh, Professor Cabot, it's time for my class. I have to run.

CABOT: I expect to see you the minute class is over.

ITO: Yes, of course, of course.

[Ito runs to center stage, where a podium has appeared. Clips from a Godard film are projected on a screen.]

    And the scopophilic male gaze permeates New Wave cinema as it permeates the popular imagination. That's all for today. Don't forget to pick up your final exams.

[She holds out a huge stack of blue books. Students come to get their exams.]

STUDENT: A C? God, I can't believe it. What a bitch. *[To Ito:]* I think you should change the grade. I deserve at least a B.

ITO: This loosely connected string of words is virtually incomprehensible.

STUDENT: You mean you're not going to change my grade?

ITO: I'm sorry. You were lucky to pass.

STUDENT: Okay, Professor Ito.

[He stands in front of her, tears up the exam, and runs off.]

ITO: Hey, you spoiled little bastard! Just try that again! I'll show you.

[Ito yanks off her long-haired wig to reveal a crew-cut. She turns around and strides upstage, facing Nancy.]

NANCY: What happened to your hair?

ITO *[proudly]*: I cut it. To look like Grace Jones.

NANCY: I don't know. I kinda liked it when it was long . . . you know, flapping around in the breeze.

ITO: It's just easier this way.

NANCY: Like I said, some people have it easier than others.

ITO *[abashed]*: Yeah, I guess so.

[Chimes sound out six o'clock.]

ITO: Shit, the dry cleaners are going to close. And it was my turn to go to the grocery store.

[She turns around and runs downstage. A group of students walks in front of her.]

STUDENT: Ching chong, ching chong.

[They run off. Ito whirls around.]

ITO: You racist motherfuckers! Where are you? Come here! *[Her voice trails off as she realizes they have disappeared.]* Come here. . . .

[An alarm clock rings.]

ANNOUNCEMENT: Flight 122 is departing for Baltimore from Gate 17. All ticketed passengers should be on board.

ITO: Wait, wait!

[She runs to podium center stage.]

OLD BOY 1: Professor Ito, wouldn't you say that this work is extremely reductive? Politics passing for scholarship?

ITO: Well, no. I would argue that meaning and power are coextensive.

OLD BOY 2: But there you are. A totally subjective view. Ridiculous.

OLD BOY 1: More than ridiculous. Preposterous.

OLD BOY 2: Offensive.

OLD BOY 1: Politically correct.

[They begin throwing things at her.]

ITO: But . . . no, please stop!

[Lights flash on and off on Justin and Cabot as they speak. Ito runs back and forth between them.]

JUSTIN: Hey, baby, where were you? Aren't you down with the people?

CABOT: Ito, where are you? I want my massage.

JUSTIN: The telephones are ringing.

CABOT: Position 52, don't forget.

JUSTIN: Another streamer, over there.

CABOT: Your contract comes up next week.

NANCY: Some people just have it easier than others.

JUSTIN: Baby.

CABOT: Ito.

STUDENT: Yoko Ono.

JUSTIN: Baby.

CABOT: Ito.

[Ito, who has been running back and forth, collapses center stage. The song, "Use Me," is heard softly in the background.]

NANCY: "Use Me," a mildly funky tune originally recorded by Bill Withers, perhaps best known for the plaintive "Ain't No Sunshine When She's Gone." It achieved new and ironic shades of meaning with the Grace Jones rendition. Ms. Jones brought out the playful, yet ominous, sadomasochistic subtext, signaled by the sound that follows each invocation of "use me." Perhaps it is the crack of a whip. Perhaps it is a slap.

[The song is amplified full blast.]

> Well, I'm gonna spread the news
> That if it feels this good getting used,
> Keep on using me
> Till you use me up [whack]
> Till you use me up [whack]
> Come on and use me up [whack][3]

[Ito begins to rise, and during the first chorus of "Use Me" she staggers with each "crack of the whip." As the song continues, she struggles up to the rhythms

DORINNE KONDO

of the music and begins to take off her academic power jacket. She gets tangled in the sleeves. She continues her attempts to stand, struggling in time with the music. By the end she is upright, though teetering precariously.]

[A dazzling spotlight and clouds of smoke on the upstage ramp. Grace Jones descends, following a pathway of light, and ceremoniously gives Ito an Uzi and an Issey Miyake[4] designer dress in a plastic dry-cleaning bag.]

GRACE JONES: You might need these.

ITO: Oh, Grace. Thanks. *[Pause.]* But isn't this a bit much?

GRACE JONES: They're very you.

[A cloud of smoke. Grace Jones disappears, as lights go to black.]

END OF ACT ONE

Act One marks the end of naturalistic representation and realist convention, presaged in Scene Five. The following scene, which opens Act Two, is, so far, my favorite—an encounter between Grace Jones and Ito, as Ivy is slowly beginning to show signs of auto-destruction. Is apocalyptic change in the air? Act Two is animated by a spirit of fantasy and play, even if the fantasies concern revenge and revolution. Evident in the scene are themes that animate my academic work as well: reclaiming the conventionally feminine as sites of power (Ito's fixation on Issey Miyake clothes, the fashion show with Grace Jones and Ito); refiguring the conventionally masculine in other terms (the Uzi as an accessory). This is the watershed, as Ito begins to believe in her own empowerment.

SCENE SIX

[The stage is awash in a new light; it has an eerie warmth. Bricks are scattered on the ground, rubble from a wall and a bombed-out Georgian building that seem to be on the verge of crumbling. Ivy is beginning to resemble a war zone. The Uzi and the dress are on the ground in front of Ito, who stands center stage.]

ITO: Holy fuck. *[She turns around and looks at her surroundings.]* What the hell happened here? All this rubble . . . at Ivy? I mean really, it's just a little too apocalyptic, don't you think? Shades of L.A.

[She assumes a declamatory mode.]

Although Ivy remained unassailed through it all. "Minorities" never existed in sufficient numbers to cause the slightest concern, much less a "riot."

[As she looks down at the dress, her eyes light up. She grabs the dress and frantically tears it out of the dry-cleaning bag, trying it on as she continues to talk.]

My god my god my god. It really is an Issey Miyake. I mean vintage, the real deal. Space-age samurai retro polyurethane coated jersey with rattan bustier. Spring summer 1981. A collection so avant-garde it was said to transcend the vicissitudes of fashion. Shit, this university has a billion-dollar endowment. . . . You'd think a girl could at least find a full-length mirror. . . .

[Ito continues to fuss with the outfit, attempting to catch her reflection in bits of broken glass.]

[Suddenly, the audience is blasted by the opening angelic chorus and the funky riffs from "Slave to the Rhythm." Grace Jones enters. The music ends abruptly.]

GRACE JONES: Hey there, Ito girl. I was right. You're looking more and more like yourself.

ITO: Grace! I thought you were gone. Or a residual effect of the sake I had at Justin's. So you really do exist.

GRACE JONES: My ontological status is . . . Let me just say that for the moment I prefer to remain inscrutable.

ITO: Better you than me, honey.

GRACE JONES: Well, your mood seems to have improved considerably.

ITO: I don't know, Grace . . . this light, and this dress. . . . It's the power suit of my dreams. I won't ever need to buy shoulder pads.

GRACE JONES: There is that look of Japanese armor, yes. But you have forgotten the other key element of the ensemble. You must remember—the perfect power suit needs the perfect accessory. Something simple. That makes a statement.
[Picks up the Uzi and strikes a pose.]
    Comme ça.

ITO: Wow. Too much.

GRACE JONES: Now you try.

ITO: Oh, I'm terrible with anything resembling a mechanical object.

GRACE JONES: Not a mechanical object. An accessory.

ITO *[tentatively]*: OK. Since you put it that way.
[Ito takes up the Uzi awkwardly and emulates Grace's movements.]
    Oh. That wasn't too bad.

GRACE JONES: Ma chère, tout à fait formidable. Encore une fois, and you'll have it down.

ITO: But I still feel so awkward. . . .

GRACE JONES: Let's go, girlfriend.

ITO: But it's daunting, this thing. So . . . phallic.

GRACE JONES: Just think seventies high disco.

[Grace grabs her own Uzi and begins to execute a series of movements, which Ito copies awkwardly at first, then with increasing skill, so that by the end the two women are beautifully synchronized. They strike poses, sometimes pointing at the audience, in a dazzling dance sequence that resembles Kabuki, vogueing, and target practice. Grace Jones's "Warm Leatherette" would be ideal accompaniment. After a few minutes they stop, breathless.]

GRACE JONES: There. I knew you had potential. Underneath those tweeds.

ITO: It's unbelievable. . . . They seem so boring now.

GRACE JONES: Camouflage. But the signs were unmistakable. The passion in your eyes . . . luminous, unquenchable, riveting. I recognized it right away.

DORINNE KONDO

ITO: You mean. . . .

GRACE JONES AND ITO [in unison]: Object lust.

[Lights appear down a mock runway center stage. The two emulate models in a fashion show, sashaying up and down the runway. Grace Jones's "The Fashion Show" would be appropriate accompaniment.]

GRACE JONES: The heat.

ITO: Of the chase.

GRACE JONES: The rush.

ITO: Of discovery.

GRACE JONES: The fire.

ITO: In the loins.

GRACE JONES: The satisfaction.

ITO: When you find.

GRACE JONES: The perfect.

ITO: Outfit.

GRACE JONES: Object.

ITO: Of desire.

GRACE JONES: Languid elegance.

ITO: Exquisite tailoring.

GRACE JONES: Draping fabric.

ITO: Defining space.

GRACE JONES: Around the body.

ITO: The chance.

GRACE JONES: To refigure the self.

ITO: To appropriate.

GRACE JONES: The accoutrements of power.

ITO: To articulate.

GRACE JONES: A new identity.

[Lights come down on the runway. The two stop their fashion show.]

ITO: Oh, Grace, I knew you'd understand.

GRACE JONES: Just remember, high disco. And when in doubt, accessorize.

ITO: You're not leaving again?

GRACE JONES: In one sense.

ITO: So, that means. . . .

GRACE JONES: You're the academic. Hermeneutics 101.

[She exits with a flourish, to the accompaniment of the chattering, reverberating voices from "Operattack." Ito starts to run after her, then stops, looking puzzled. Suddenly realization strikes her.]

ITO [to the audience]: Freud. "Mourning and Melancholia." The subject introjects the lost object.

[Ito calls to Grace.]

I take you wherever I go.

[Ito strides around the stage with confidence.]

You know, the rubble. . . . It's such a mess. But there's something oddly
hopeful about it.

The rest of the play is highly open to revision, but suffice it to say that the fantastic, playful quality continues. Ito is visited by other figures from history, film, and literature, including Lady Murasaki, author of *The Tale of Genji,* Madame Butterfly, and film director Akira Kurosawa, and she finds herself able to form alliances with some of these characters and with the other women in the play. They reveal Cabot and his colleagues in a nefarious plot to dominate the academy and—who knows?—the world, with mannequins—clones of white people who seem "of color" on the surface. However, the women also discover Cabot's collection of stereotypes, mannequins useful in the cause of upholding Western civilization. Among these is Grace Jones herself, dressed as her primitive character from *Conan the Barbarian.* Here is the most direct problematizing of the Grace Jones stereotype. Ito finds herself crestfallen that her heroine, Grace, is also a white man's invention. Grace Jones herself refuses to be confined by Ito's expectations or by those of the white men, and she, along with the other awakened stereotype, Butterfly, takes Ito to task for her shortsightedness and her own unexamined prejudices.

SCENE TEN

[Ito is still on the floor, despondent, looking almost as though she is asleep, in
half-light. Lights come up on Grace Jones, who begins to stir from her man-
nequin's position. She wears a leopard-skin suit and brandishes a spear, after her
character in Conan the Barbarian. The Butterfly mannequin stands frozen.
Grace begins a series of exercises with her spear.]

GRACE JONES: Un, deux, trois, quatre. Un, deux, trois. . . .

ITO: Grace?

GRACE JONES: You interrupted me. . . . Trois, quatre.

ITO: Grace.

GRACE JONES: Un, deux. . . .

ITO: Grace.

GRACE JONES: You know, chérie, sometimes you are a nuisance.

ITO: Well, excuse me. I just have to ask you something.

GRACE JONES: Must you interrupt me? I'm trying to get the circulation going
again, a very painful and time-consuming process after standing in such a ridiculous position for so long.

ITO: Grace, . . . how could you do it?

GRACE JONES: Do what?

ITO: You know . . . the mannequin. The mold. The white man's invention.

GRACE JONES: Yes, Little Miss Politically Correct Holier Than Thou? What are
you saying?

ITO: I worshipped you. And . . . to see you here. . . . It's just shattering.

GRACE JONES: Ma petite idiote. That is the last straw.

ITO: But look at you . . . that leopard-skin suit. It's disgraceful.

GRACE JONES: Chérie. It may be true that the Jean-Pauls and Arnolds and Dolphs of the world . . . not to mention the multitudes of my fans, INCLUDING YOU . . . have been of use in cultivating my outrageous persona. Some may consider my cinematic exploits to be, shall we say, politically incorrect. But frankly, ma petite, I love being outrageous. I loved that gorilla suit. I loved looking like a caged panther. I loved driving that chariot, whipping those white boys. And the choice to be outrageous is mine. All mine.

ITO: Yes, but don't you worry about. . . .

GRACE JONES: What, Ms. Political Puritan? Ideological fallout? Setting a bad example for generations of African American children?

ITO: Well, now that you mention it. . . .

GRACE JONES [sighing]: To be honest, from time to time it crosses my mind. The exotic Africa business. [Pause.] But Ito, honey, you didn't seem to mind. Ever consider that you are part of the problem?

ITO: Who, me? I . . . I don't see how. I mean, you've been such a source of comfort during all my terrible travails at Ivy. . . .

GRACE JONES: I know, I know. [To the audience:] Now girlfriend is going to go into that tiresome litany about how no one listens to her, how she's invisible, how everyone treats her like a servant . . . uh, the whining. As though she's the only one who ever suffered.

ITO: No one listens to me, I'm invisible, everyone treats me like a servant.

[Grace mouths the words with Ito, who catches her. They exchange dirty looks.]

ITO: OK, OK. I know I sound like a broken record. But I just need someone to look up to. To inspire me, to give me strength.

[Butterfly begins to stir.]

GRACE JONES: But why me?

BUTTERFLY: Yeah, why her?

ITO: Oh, my.

BUTTERFLY: What's she got that I don't have? Why can't I, an ASIAN woman, be your inspiration?

ITO: I hate to say this, but. . . .

GRACE JONES: Go ahead, girl.

ITO: You're such a wimp. And a ho. [To Grace:] And you're so strong. And so powerful.

GRACE JONES: But you see.

BUTTERFLY: You're doing it.

GRACE JONES: Playing into it.

BUTTERFLY: Creating the mold.

GRACE JONES: Dressing the mannequin.

ITO: Yes, but . . . I didn't think. . . .

GRACE JONES: Precisely.

BUTTERFLY: You didn't think.

[The two women imitate each other.]

GRACE JONES: Neither of us could exist without the other. Butterfly–lotus blossom, the ultrafeminine, the flip side of. . . .

BUTTERFLY: The phallic Black Amazon.

ITO: Oh, my God. . . .

GRACE JONES: A little food for thought.

BUTTERFLY: We have to go, darling.

GRACE JONES: Films to do.

BUTTERFLY: Miniseries on tap.

ITO: Does this mean you won't be coming on my mission? I have a plan.

GRACE JONES: I've already told you.

ITO: I know. High disco. Accessories. Thanks a lot.

BUTTERFLY: My. No need to be testy.

[The women assume each other's stereotyped voices and mannerisms.]

GRACE JONES: Sayonara, Ito-san.

BUTTERFLY: Au revoir, chérie.

ITO: Ciao, girls.

GRACE JONES AND BUTTERFLY: WOMEN.

ITO: OK already. *[Pause.]* Will I ever see you again?

[The women smile enigmatically. Donna Summer's "Bad Girls" blasts, and they dance out to the disco beat.]

This scene, in particular, raises the question of risk and accountability in introducing the issues of cross-racial identification and coalition. Art forms, including theater, produce a kind of politics of accountability very different from that of conventional academic discourse, arising from a different kind of authority and a different stake the audience might have in what it sees. That is, theater—or most theater—presumes no cult of expertise or arcane jargon, no credentials necessary to respond or evaluate. Moreover, its impact can occur on multiple levels, engaging multiple senses, producing a more visceral impact than does textual prose and hence eliciting greater intellectual/emotional response. Consequently and rightfully, everyone can claim to own the representation, because everyone can be affected by it and authorized to respond.

The issues of accountability and the complicated politics of representation across racial lines were never clearer to me than with my work as a dramaturge for Anna Deavere Smith's production, *Twilight: Los Angeles 1992,* heralded by *Time, Newsweek,* and *The New Yorker* as an historic event in Asian American theater. Smith's theatrical method depends on characterizing a place by interviewing its inhabitants, and she courageously took on the complex events surrounding the riots/rebellion/unrest of April 1992 in the complex city of Los Angeles. Unusual for a theatrical production, there were four dramaturges on *Twilight:* myself; Héctor Tobar, a reporter for the *Los Angeles Times* and of Guatemalan descent; African American poet/critic Elizabeth Alexander; and Oskar Eustis, the resident director at the Mark Taper Forum, where *Twilight* was staged. Conventional theatrical dramaturgy—research, acting as in-house critics for the production as the writing was being shaped from, literally, night to night—was only part of our duty. Obviously, we were also to represent our essentialized racial "communities," to see what the unintended effects of particular choices might be in terms of the politics of representation. Our dramaturgical sessions were often impassioned, argumentative, contentious, painful—and wonderful. As a politically committed artist, Smith remained open and did her best to listen and be accountable to multiple constituencies, multiple communities, which often had contradictory agendas. How much easier and more elegant, in a conventional sense, it would have been if Smith had decided to stage only African Americans—itself a perfectly legitimate strategy. Surely then she would have left herself open to less criticism, but ultimately she would have failed to address the larger conflicts and possibilities presented by the racial mix in Los Angeles and by the complexity of the events of April 1992. She would, in short, have risked too little. However, I cannot equate my position with Smith's. Third-generation Japanese Americans are economically and ideologically positioned in a site of relative privilege vis-à-vis most African Americans. Though I desire to write solidarity among women of color, my play also reinscribes a problematic stereotype of African American women and thus reinforces my own privilege. As I continue to revise *Dis(graceful)l Conduct,* I intend to problematize this positioning more fully.

In short, cross-racial representation is a risky business. It is never innocent; it can reinscribe stereotypes, subvert good intentions, reenact forms of oppression. It can also open the way toward coalition, toward thematizing the urgent dilemmas that now animate our lives. It can be one step toward subverting dominant conceptions of race in the American imaginary: monolithic racial groups neatly arranged along some unilinear scale, whites at the top, Asian Americans and Latinos in the middle, African Americans at the bottom, Native Americans erased or off the scale. The complex and multiple positionings, the strategic assertion of essentialist identities, the diversity within categories, the inability of categories to figure complexity—these are some of the hopes for oppositional creation and representation in artistic and academic registers, even as the dangers of reinscription can never be entirely avoided.

Despite these dangers, theater still offers a critically important site where new cultural possibilities are being explored, performed, and suggested, with utopian impact. In avant-garde/performance art forms, theater allows for exploration, outrageousness, and flights of fancy that would be censored in more popular media such as television. Of course, this can draw the predictable charges of elitism—as do the relatively higher ticket prices (quadruple the price of a film, easily, for mainstream/regional theater; twice the price for many smaller venues; the same or less for community-based groups). Yet, for an artist, theater can be an accessible medium, especially varieties of performance art that require little more than the human voice and body. And, as I have argued, for audiences who are positioned on the margins, the live aspects of theater, seeing performers palpably there, can in fact have a profound impact that goes beyond that of mechanically reproduced media. Consequently, though this may be an age of mechanical reproduction, critics of theater who dismiss it as merely the nostalgia for presence fail to see the ways in which theater can empower artists and audiences on the margins. Mindful of the problems of elitism and more restricted audiences, I continue my passion and pleasure in theater as a site for the production of identities and as a potential site of contestation. Creating theater can in a sense re-create the world as one would like to see it, and my experiences with *Dis(Graceful)l Conduct* and *Twilight* have offered opportunities to imagine the always problematic, but potentially hopeful, moments of alliance and coalition among peoples of color. The stage is a place where we can be "bad girls," to invoke Donna Summer, not as "sad girls" but as women of color daring to be outspoken and outrageous, uniting to fight the sources of our common oppression.

Notes

1. See Christian Huygen, "Han Ong Writes Himself," *Outlook* 17 (1992): 35–40.

2. Dorinne Kondo, "*M. Butterfly:* Orientalism, Gender, and a Critique of Essentialist Identity," *Cultural Critique* 16 (1990): 5–29.

3. Grace Jones, "Use Me," *Nightclubbing* (Island Records, 1981).

4. Issey Miyake is among the avant-garde of international high fashion and one of the preeminent Japanese designers, along with Yohji Yamamoto and Rei Kawakubo of Comme des Garçons. He is known for his innovative use of materials and the architectural shapes of his clothing. My book *Crafting Selves* features a cover photo of a mannequin dressed in Miyake's rattan bustier and polyurethane-coated jersey skirt that is mentioned in the play. Grace Jones modeled for Miyake in Paris before her international success as a disco diva and actress in the late seventies and the eighties.

Ruth Behar

December 18, 1992

AS USUAL, my mother is monopolizing our phone conversation. We've been talking for close to an hour, she in New York and I in Miami Beach. I am waiting at my grandmother's house for a visa for Cuba, a visa that will never arrive. Suddenly my mother calls out to my father, *"¿Quieres decirle algo a tu hija?"* Whenever she asks him if there's anything he wants to say to *his* daughter, my heart skips a beat. Since my teenage years, my relationship with my father has been tense and uneasy, perched on a faultline. Sometimes he calls back that he has nothing to say to me. That hurts. But at times he's cheery. *"Oye,"* he says, switching the phone to the speaker mode, "How can I get twenty copies of your book, *Translated Woman?"* He can't be serious, I think. I ask why he wants so many copies. "For my business associates," he replies in his best no-nonsense voice. And then, with the melodramatic sizzle of a Latin American soap-opera star, he says, "Even though you've dragged my name into infamy." We both laugh. It's one of our good nights.

"My name is coming out in all kinds of places," my father continues. That morning a fellow salesman had left a copy of my *New York Times* op-ed essay, "Bridges to Cuba," on my father's desk. Mr. Schaeffer, or La Cerveza, as my father has nicknamed his colleague, had written across the photocopy, "Not bad for a textile salesman's daughter."

My parents, like the larger Cuban American community of which they form a part, burned the bridge back to Cuba after Fidel Castro took power, and they want nothing to do with the island until his regime has ended, unabsolved by history. By writing in such a public place about my longing for a bridge between the Cubans who left and those who stayed behind, I have flaunted the fact that I am an ungrateful, disobedient daughter, not only of my parents but also of the community. Although the op-ed piece has still not made it any easier for a *gusana* like me to return to Cuba, I have declared my exile from the exiles, and I expect to get a scolding for it.

Still in a joking mood, my father says, "I'm seeing my name everywhere. What are you doing to *my* name?" He's referring to our common last name, what he considers *his* last name. The last name his father gave to him. The last name he gave to me. The last name that identifies me as his daughter. It's a name I should have lost long ago, after getting married. But how could I let go of that Sephardic name, so resonant with histories of expulsion, loss, and desire for memory? How could I paste on my husband's prosaic cowboy-boot name? And yet, maybe if I had taken my husband's name, I'd finally be able to leave my father's house.

"Take care," my father says. He's never on the phone for more than five minutes. He clicks off the speaker and my mother gets back on the line. She proceeds to tell me how much the last chapter of my book has upset her. She's more upset, even, than my father. "I thought your book was going to be about the life of that Mexican woman. I didn't think you were going to say those things about your father." My mother's role in the family has always been to defend my father's honor. "He doesn't even remember doing what you said he did with your letters."

I call the last chapter of my book a shadow biography. There, I tell the story of how I attained the privilege of writing down the story of another, less privileged woman's life, the life of Esperanza Hernández, a street peddler. To emphasize the wrenching nature of my relationship to the written word, which is the currency of power in the academic world, I reflect on a traumatic event in my life that took place shortly after I left home for college, against my father's will. One day, out of anger about my increasing distance from the family, my father picked up a pile of letters I had written home, sarcastically read aloud the parts in which I claimed to love him and my mother, and then proceeded to tear them up before my eyes.

"*Mira*, I'm going to tell you something, Rutie," my mother announces. "*La mierda no se revuelve, porque apesta.*" Don't stir up the shit, because it will stink. "You know, Rutie, I'm not a typist. *Ya es la segunda vez que lo dices.*" It's true, I've twice described my mother in my writing as a typist rather than by her title, Diploma Aide. I try to apologize, but my mother is not done with me yet. "And why did you have to tell everybody your father was ashamed that his father was a peddler in Cuba? That wasn't nice." I wish I could get my mother to understand the poetic logic of my storytelling. "Mami, don't you see? My book is about the life story of a peddler in Mexico. And my own grandfather was a peddler in Cuba, but Papi was always so ashamed of his origins that he couldn't even talk about it. Don't you think that's interesting?" But I can't convince her. Writing about the shame seems only to compound the shame of the shame.

In my training to become an anthropologist I was taught to worry about how I represented "the other" in my writing. I became attuned to the ethical, cultural, and political implications of using the life stories of faraway people to provide anthropological insights back home. But what do you do when your parents are "the other"? And, unlike those faraway "others," those "primitives" somewhere else who have no idea they're ending up in the anthropologist's book, they actually read what you write? And phone you up to tell you what they think? Does it give you permission to be less charitable? To write stinky stories?

I say good-bye, and my grandmother gets on the phone to talk to my mother. Hanging up, she looks at me accusingly and asks why I haven't shown her my book yet. How can I not have shared such a major accomplishment with her? In the flurry of continual phone calls to the Cuban Interest Section in Washington to check on the status of my visa, there hadn't been a chance, somehow, to show my grandmother the book.

As soon as I put the book in my grandmother's hands, I regret not having shown it to her earlier. She holds the book up very close to her nearly blind eyes and declares it beautiful. "I'm going to keep this book as my Hanukkah gift, even if you won't give it to me," she announces in her Yiddishized Spanish. I immediately tell her that, of course, the book is for her to keep, but I realize those words have come too late.

It is getting close to midnight and my grandmother, who grew old selling cloth in Havana and New York, puts on her pajamas, takes out her teeth, and gets into bed with *Translated Woman*. From the adjoining living room, as I stay up writing late into the night, I hear her reading the dedication and acknowledgments aloud. My grandmother starts books from the beginning, like you're supposed to. Reading slowly, loudly, my grandmother, who is eighty-five and an insomniac, keeps the book glued to her face for more than an hour. When I tell her to try to get some rest, she refuses, saying she wants to read further. With her one good eye that isn't even that good, clouded as it is with a cataract and glaucoma, my grandmother searches out my every word, hurling each noun, preposition, and verb into the thick tropical night. The words I catch dissolve in my hands like snow, or tears.

§

December 31, 1992

"Are you sure you still want to have it?" I am asking my mother long distance. She had said she would throw a book party for me when *Translated Woman* was published, but I don't want her to feel obligated, especially if the book is so upsetting to her and my father. For some reason, we both feel we need to resolve this matter before the new year begins.

"*Yo soy fiel a mi palabra,*" she replies. True to her word. . . .

§

True to her word, my mother licks two thousand stamps for the mailing list of the Latino cultural arts center in Queens, New York, that is sponsoring the book party for *Translated Woman.* The center doesn't even provide the stamps. My mother has to buy them. She tells all her officemates at New York University about the party. She enlarges the postcard invitation on her office photocopier and tacks it up on the wall by her desk. She telephones, more than once, everyone in El Grupo, the group of Jewish-Cuban friends who for thirty years have watched each other forge new lives in the America on this side of the border. She prepares miniature *borekas,* filled with cheese and mashed potatoes, like my father's Sephardic mother used to make, and *enrolladitos,* swirled tuna hors d'oeuvres with a pimiento-stuffed green olive in the center. She mixes up a spinach dip with water chestnuts. She finds Mexican chips flavored with avocado and strange chilis. She chooses white wine and ginger ale and diet Coke and champagne and cranberry juice for the children. She orders flowers and corsages. She clears a space in the dining room of the Fresh Meadows house, which she is always saying is too small, for the book boxes containing one hundred copies of *Translated Woman.*

At the party in the basement of a local branch of the Queens Public Library I am introduced three times with great fanfare, and then I do a dramatic reading from the book while the trunk of our car is being broken into just outside the front door. From the wobbly stage, as I tell the story of Esperanza the peddler and Ruth the anthropologist who wrote down her words, I stare out at my brother, who my mother has insisted come from Philadelphia for the event, my Uncle Bill and Aunt Sylvia, El Grupo members Nina, Emilio, Miriam, Enrique, Fanny, and Zelmi, my mother's handsome, young, gay officemate, my father's cousin Rubén, my kindly editor, Deb Chasman, who has flown in from Boston, my friend Teo, who, as always, will have to leave early to pick someone up at the airport, my father, my mother, my husband David, my six-year-old son Gabriel, impatient to start selling the books, and a handful of strangers. When I'm done, I sign copies of the book, writing long, involved, personal messages to each buyer that my mother will later tell me her friends Nina and Zelmi declared absolutely unreadable. I meet again, for the first time in years, my high school history teacher, Mrs. Weinstein, whom my mother has managed to invite without telling me. The past and the present and the future, my girlhood and my womanhood, Cuba, Mexico, and New York, are all scrambled up. Before the party ends someone yells out, "Aren't you going to take any pictures?" and my mother runs for her camera, calling my father and brother over. The four of us come together, posing with the book, with Esperanza, the happy family.

Later that evening we count up the small pile of twenty dollar bills. Seventy-five translated women, like glum orphans, are sent back to their corner in the dining room of my parents' too-small Fresh Meadows house to await proper resettlement on someone's bookshelf. The all-important *New York Times* book review that we have been awaiting with growing desperation for the last six months has not yet appeared, and there's a good chance, my editor tells me, that bookstores will soon be returning their unsold stock. Under the circumstances, the hapless women are left to make themselves at home, stacked up like sardines in boxes that will be moved down to the basement before the summer ends.

§

July 2, 1993

I am at the Wesleyan Writers Conference for a week, thinking it will be good for me to return to the place where I once lost confidence in myself as a writer and to try again. They've given me a scholarship. And put me in an industrial brick dorm room with a smelly hallway carpet and greasy pay phone. Meals are to be had cafeteria-style in a noisy, crowded dining room that unnerves and terrifies. In the classroom, just another humble student in the audience, not a teacher authoritatively in the front, I again become my old, fade-into-the-background, shy self. I have brought five translated women with me on this trip, but I don't say a word about them. At the end of the week, someone, maybe me, finally presses our teacher, the author of a well-regarded memoir, to answer a question we've not been able to stop asking: Should we, as writers, be worried about hurting those about whom we write? "Look," she says, bored. "People aren't emotional hemophiliacs who you prick and they bleed to death in front of you. They can take it better than you think."

§

July 4, 1993

It all started harmlessly enough. On July 3 my father donned his USA T-shirt, put out his two American flags, a small one and a large one, and taught my son, Gabriel, how to salute them. Then Gabriel tried to get me to salute the flags. I said I wouldn't, not even as a joke. And my mother said, laughing, "*Oye,* come on, why don't you salute the flag? This is the country that gave you the Macartí. Let's see if they take it away from you!"

Usually, by July 4, I'm not in New York with my parents. I'm in Mexico or Spain, being an anthropologist. Usually, this is a holiday my parents celebrate triumphantly with El Grupo, no liberal, college-educated daughter there to question their patriotism. But this year they've not made any plans. It's a hot, hot day, the kind in which murders so often take place in movies. About a hundred degrees. Steamy. Sultry. Pavement like hot coals.

Late in the morning, to draw Gabriel away from the television, we decide to take a walk to the park. The sprinklers are on at full intensity, and Gabriel is soon running in and out of the water, enjoying getting his clothes totally drenched. After a while my father tires of watching and says he's going home. My mother tries to get him to stay for the sake of family unity, but when he starts to bristle with impatience, she relents and lets him go.

There are several ideal fathers at the park. One is with a toddler in diapers, who keeps returning to him to clear the mud from her sandals. Another is with his preschool son and daughter, helping them to understand the principles of aerodynamics that govern the proper use of the monkey bars. My mother says the guy must be divorced and this must be his day with the kids because of the amount of attention he's giving them. But my husband says, no, the guy's a weekend dad. During the week, David adds, it's all mothers at the park; he knows, he's been one of them.

We return home to discover my father asleep with the newspaper on his lap. My mother prepares lunch, wakes up my father, and we sit down to eat. "Tell me about the period in your life when you did all those paintings," I say to my father to make conversation, noticing how the walls of their Fresh Meadows house are filled with brightly colored canvases he painted when I was in my teens. I've been thinking that I want to do more justice to my father in my future writing, that I've been too harsh on him.

Snarling, he replies, "I don't want to talk. Don't put me in your memoirs anymore, okay?"

"But I really want to know," I say.

"I don't want to tell you anything. I'm the *tirano* with the whip, remember?"

Trying to keep my cool, I reply, "In anthropology, you're what they call a 'reluctant subject.'"

"Then what are you?" my father says, his tone growing angry.

"I guess I'm an overly inquisitive anthropologist."

"Oh, no, you're more than that. *Hay dos o tres cosas que te he querido decir pero no me he atrevido.*"

"What have you been wanting to say to me?" I shoot back. "Go ahead and tell me."

"That you wrote those things about me in your book *para mortificar,* to bother me. That's the only reason."

"That's not true!"

"Oh, yes, it is. You think I don't know you? I don't want you to write about me again. I prohibit you from writing about me, now or ever. *Te prohibo.*"

"I'll write whatever I please."

"*Si estás tan acabada,* if I've harmed you so much, then how can you write books and win prizes? You need to go see a psychiatrist if you think I've done you so much harm."

My father is threatening me in the oddest way—become a madwoman in the attic, he's saying, if you want me to believe I wasn't a perfect father.

RUTH BEHAR

"You want to make yourself a martyr. They told you that in the *Chronicle*, right there, *te lo dijeron allí*. You like to be a victim."

It is indescribable, the ache you feel when your own father quotes what your critics say about you in print. Yet my father is suggesting that I am the one who has turned *him* into a victim in my writing. The pen, he's saying, is mighty mean in the hands of a wicked daughter.

Hoping it will amuse him and defuse his anger, I tell my father about the case of Sara Levi Calderón, the pseudonym of a Jewish Mexican writer. Her book *Dos Mujeres*, or *Two Women*, a thinly disguised memoir about her lesbian experiences, quickly became a bestseller after her infuriated father bought out the first edition of 1,500 books and burned them.

But my father is not amused. "I'd do the same as that woman's father if I had the resources," he says. "And I'd tear those letters up again if I had the chance," he adds, admitting for the first time that he remembers.

I can no longer hold back my rage. "You know, you're very destructive. All you want is to destroy me!"

Dropping his fork, my father stalks out of the room. After that I am put in solitary confinement. I get total silence, broken only for telegraphic messages on the Jewish New Year and on Thanksgiving. Echoes from the labyrinth.

A nightmare: Seventy-five translated women are burning in the flames. And there my name, the name I took from my father, is burning too.

§

July 5, 1993

Everyone has gone to sleep, except my mother and me. As we sit at the glass-and-chrome kitchen table, she tells me she's never seen my father cry the way she saw him cry last night. Had he really been such a terrible father? She says he wants to know how long he has to keep paying for what he did to me in the past.

I do not see my father's tears. I do not hear his questions. My mother, as always, is our messenger. She tells me my father has been depressed, *muy* down, that he worries he's not functioning as well as he should.

"*Y la gente es mala*," my mother continues. "People are nasty. They come up to your father and ask him, 'How did you tear up your daughter's letters, like this, like that?' And your father says, 'No, I just tore them up, ripped them to pieces. I was very cruel. A real tyrant.'" And my mother adds, "*Y él se lo traga*. He just takes it. Swallows it."

Could my words be destroying my father? Didn't the teacher say people aren't emotional hemophiliacs?

I try to explain to my mother why I wrote about the tearing up of the letters. I tell her that in the book I analyze the event and even partly blame myself, saying it had to do with my assimilation and my father's inability to understand that I was growing up and away from them. My mother doesn't hear it. I still wrote about something I shouldn't have written about. Something cruel. Why did I do it? she asks. Because it hurt me, I reply.

Crossing the border with Esperanza's book, I've crossed into some dangerous family territory, too. That is *trapos sucios,* dirty linen you've exposed, my mother says. Why didn't you go find someone else's *trapos* to write about? Isn't that what you're supposed to do as an anthropologist? Admit you used Esperanza's story to get vengeance on your father. Admit, admit, admit. . . . Could I have been so wicked? So horribly and terribly wicked?

"Didn't you have to ask Esperanza for permission to write down her story?" my mother is asking.

"Yes."

"If you had to ask Esperanza for permission to write about her, why don't you have to ask permission to write about us?"

"But you and Papi are part of my life," I say. "It's different." I don't admit it to her, but I know my mother is asking a good question. When Esperanza began to talk to me, she was concerned that her story not get out to her immediate neighbors. Initially she wanted the story to be translated into English, to be known only to the gringos on the other side of the border.

My mother says, "So you write all those terrible things about us . . . well, about your father, but it also hurts me. And then we have to have a book party to celebrate. 'Look, everyone, see how terrible we are, now buy the book.'"

"Mami, you were the one who wanted to have the book party, remember?"

It dawns on me that I include my parents too much in my professional life. But how could I not? I'm still my father's daughter. I carry his name. And I allow my parents to have a claim on my work. I not only send them reviews of my book, which my mother promptly photocopies and sends to everyone in the family and El Grupo, I can't stop writing about them. Immigrants succeed through their children; they sacrifice, they invest, so their children will succeed. And the immigrant daughter, who worries about surpassing her parents, keeps trying to include them in her work, to throw a raft their way, so they can sail together on the choppy seas of the academy.

In writing about my parents, I also seem to be trying to mark the distance I've traveled, the distance that separates me from them and gives me the power to describe our relationship. In his memoir *Hunger of Memory,* Richard Rodriguez declares, "I am writing about those very things my mother has asked me not to reveal." He says he often felt paralyzed by the image of his parents' eyes moving across the pages of his text. But this, he says, didn't weaken his resolve. There is a place, he feels, "for the deeply personal in public life."[1] On this, if not on most other things, I agree with Rodriguez. Where I differ from him is that, as a daughter, I keep longing for my parents to approve of my writing, even when, perhaps especially when, I'm being "bad."

"Your father comes home and says, '*Que yo, Alberto Behar, tenga todo esto—*

una casa, muebles, dinero en el banco, vacaciones' [That I, Alberto Behar, have all this—a house, furniture, money in the bank, vacations]. He's come far, very far, from where he started, your father."

My mother pauses. "You know what your father says is the best thing you've given us?"

"What?"

"Gabriel, our first grandson."

Better the daughter's womb than her books.

§

July 12, 1993

In Texas we stop at the AAA to buy car insurance to go to Mexico. The car has to be put in the name of "the owner." I bought the car, but David, we've decided, is going to be the primary driver on this trip, so we're going to put the car in his name. That means he won't be able to leave Mexico without the car. I need to know that if my son and I have to fly out of Mexico suddenly, for any emergency, we can do it. What this scenario would be like in reality, I have no idea. I imagine an absurd cartoon: David at the wheel of the car, racing to catch up with our airplane. Reluctantly, as happens every time we go to Mexico, I have to acknowledge I feel safer giving David the responsibility for the car that is supposed to be mine.

We fill out the forms. David signs his name. Then we are asked for a credit card. I put mine down on the desk. No, can't be mine. Has to be in his name. Don't you see it's his car, lady? As a point of feminist honor I want to tell the clerk that in case she has assumed I'm my husband's dependent she should know she's terribly mistaken. But I keep quiet. David fishes out his credit card. I'm the one who got him his card, I almost want to announce. I pay, I pay, not him, not him. . . .

My father was always reminding my mother (and my brother and me) of how he was the breadwinner and therefore deserved the most respect. We never could give him enough, no matter how hard we tried. In my relationship with David, I've needed to assert to the world that I, Ruth Behar, yes, the woman, am the head of our household. When I bought our house, I asked to have my name listed first on the title, just like a man. Of course, the title arrived with my name second. I became furious, and I accused David of being secretly pleased that patriarchy had worked in his favor. David, not me, went to the title office to have the deed changed. They told him that the computers are set up to name the man first, the woman second. That's how it is; anything else is a lot of trouble.

Now, as we wait for the paperwork on the car to be finished, I remind David of how terrible it is to be forced into the position of The Wife. Again I start accusing him of not really caring, of enjoying his male power. I'm so riled up I'm virtually demanding he announce to the torpid AAA clerk that he's *my* dependent. He doesn't respond. He just looks at me, sad.

§

July 16, 1993

I am driving to Saltillo. After crossing the border, we normally stop for the night in Monterrey, but the AAA guide has lured us on, promising a mountain view and a pool if we can just drive for another hour and a half. I'm anxious to keep moving forward, to get to Mexquitic quickly, so I can finally place *Translated Woman* in Esperanza's hands. I've brought ten copies, imagining she may want more than one, imagining she may want to give copies away to her friends.

Moments before, as I sat behind David watching the back of his head as he drove, I thought of how I hated being driven around by a man. And yet I also know that I would never take this long car trip across the border alone. Now, as I drive, drive, drive, on the new two-lane highway, the argument with my father running through my head, the car, suddenly, I don't know how, seems to be spinning, zigzagging, and I can't control it. Eleven bottles of distilled water we just bought in Laredo for Gabriel, all piled into the front seat, are falling onto my lap, and David is yelling, "Ruth, be careful, you've gone too far to the right!" and I'm certain we'll end up upside down, smashed, our blood in a river on the highway.

I don't know how, but I keep my hands on the steering wheel and slow the car down until it stops at the side of the road. Then David says, "I'd better drive," but as I'm pulling off my seat belt I notice the car dying on us. It's dead. And we're stuck. It's gotten dark so fast. Lightning up ahead. The three of us, with all our things piled into the car and on the roof, stuck. Gabriel wants to cry and I say to him, "Don't cry, it'll be worse if you cry." And then I want to cry and he says, "Mami, don't cry. You'll only make it worse." The night falls like a shadow over my life.

David pulls up the hood of the car. While trying to see what went wrong, he manages to hail a huge tow truck. The man promises to come back for us after picking up another car. We wait. I try to get out, but my legs are shaking so hard I can barely stand up. Gabriel puts his little hands together and tries to invent a prayer. Finally the man returns, attaches our car to the back of his truck, and drags it all the way back to Monterrey. In payment I give him four crisp twenty-dollar bills, the value of four discounted translated women, all the leftover money from my book party.

That night we stay at a dejected hotel near the Volkswagen dealership. All night I am trembling. I can't get off the road. I keep feeling the wheels of the car under me, rolling, rolling. All night I am being suddenly awakened by David, yelling out, "Ruth, be careful. . . ." All night, that sense of falling asleep and needing to wake up, quick, before it's too late.

They fix the car the next morning, a Saturday, and we are back on the road again by afternoon. For the rest of our stay in Mexico I keep to the passenger seat.

§

RUTH BEHAR

The car is unpacked, except for the color television, an almost-new Sony. David and I drive up the hill, now paved, to Esperanza's house. Sitting with Esperanza in her bedroom, where she keeps her religious altar with the image of Pancho Villa, she brings us up-to-date on the events of her life during the three years since we last saw each other. "Ay, *comadre*," she exclaims, "the little television you gave me broke and I went to three repairmen and none of them could fix it and they all still managed to get money out of me. Except the last guy was the smartest: He told me to buy another one. So I did, *comadre*. I bought a cheap television on the street. Here it is. It's not working very well, either."

"Oh, you have a new television, *comadre*, so maybe you don't need another one?" I say.

"*Comadre, yo acepto todas las que me traigan*. All the televisions, just bring them here to me!" And she laughs.

From the car we bring out the Sony, and Esperanza nearly jumps for joy. David sets it up, and when he's through Esperanza covers it with a white crocheted cloth. Then I dig into my camera bag and tentatively place *Translated Woman* in her hands. She holds the book carefully, tenderly, like you hold a newborn for the first time. Staring at the cover, she tells me she cut out the snake from the photocopy I sent her. The snake should not have been over her head, it should have been under her feet, to show that she dominates it, she says to me, and she puts the book back in my hands.[2]

"*Comadre*, you can keep the book," I say to her.

"Oh, thank you, *comadre*, I'll show it to my clients. They've been asking me when they're going to see the book you've written about my *historias*." She drops the book into a plastic shopping bag and turns back to admire the television. "What a nice television you've given me, *comadre*. Just what I needed, *comadre*. How can I thank you?"

§

We're not around a kitchen table anymore. The house with the mint-green walls is no longer available for rent. We're in a different house now, a better house, as it turns out, where there's always hot water and a proper living room with two sofas and an armchair. We sit opposite one another on the sofas, farther apart than in the past. I've set out, for Esperanza and her younger daughter Norberta, a plate of pink-and-white marshmallow cookies and *galletas Marías* that were given to Gabriel as gifts at his birthday party the day before. It is ten in the evening, and David and Gabriel are already asleep.

Esperanza is asking what she should do with a money order I sent her in April at the request of her son Mario, who wrote saying they needed the funds to buy an irrigation motor. They hadn't needed to cash the check, after all, because they had enough with the money I'd sent before. Although it would be nice to be able to keep the check in case any emergency occurs, Esperanza tells me she feels she ought to return it to me.

"*Comadre, usted me ha dado mucho,*" she begins. "You've given me so many things. The tape recorder. The first television. It lasted for three years before it broke. Now you have brought me another one. And you sent me those sheets. With whom did you send them? With Rocío, right? And you've given me all those blouses. And I bought myself a stove, secondhand, but a good one. It was filthy, but we got it clean after scrubbing it for a whole day. And I bought myself some blankets. There I am, keeping warm under my *comadre*'s blankets. *Yo tengo orgullo de mi comadre. Si no, yo no soy nadie.* I'm proud of my *comadre*. Without you, I'm no one."

I tell Esperanza that it's fine, that she should keep the money order in case they need it later on. And then, in words I will forever regret, I follow the advice of a friend, who has told me to be firm and to say that I won't always be able to send her money whenever her son writes requesting it. I explain that I've given her half of my advance, and that so far the book has not earned any money, but that I hope it soon will, so I can give her more.

"No, *comadre*, don't be worrying about that. *No vamos a estar a pide y pide.* We're not going to be asking and asking all the time. *No tenga cuidado.* Don't worry. For my part, I won't be asking you for anything more. You've been very generous and I'm embarrassed, *comadre*. No one here gives like you do. No one at all. I'm going to give you back that piece of paper, *comadre*. Tomorrow I'm bringing it back."

"*Comadre*, please, I want you to keep it. I know you need reading glasses. Please, keep that check and buy the glasses with it."

"I'm giving it back, so we won't be in your debt. We're so sold out to you that the best we can do is give you one of us to take back with you. No, *comadre*, don't be worrying about that. I won't ask for anything else, even if I'm dead and dying. I've already told my son Mario that when I'm breathing my last, if they need money for my wake and burial, to get it from our piece of land. And if they can't do that, then to find a box my size at least, and leave me at the cemetery."

"But won't you want music, *comadre*?" I ask, trying to lighten the mood.

"Oh, yes, of course! *Con mi buena música. ¿Pues para qué lloran? Al cabo ya no va a revivir el muerto. Pues mejor que bailen* [With good music. Why do they bother crying? The dead aren't going to awaken again. It's better if they dance]."

Serious again, I say, "But if anything happens, *comadre*, you know you can count on me."

"Let's see how our cucumbers do this year. And let's see if our beans and corn help us. I'm grateful for everything you've given me, *comadre*, and I won't be asking you for anything else."

In the morning Esperanza stops by to take us to her field, where we will see their new irrigation motor, hidden in an underground ditch, and eat a delicious variety of prickly pears that she will give to David and me straight from her knife. From a yellow plastic bucket she pulls out the money order. "Here, *comadre*," she says. "We don't want to be in your debt." Then she pulls out *Translated Woman*. "Please, take this back, too. We can't read it, anyway."

§

August 20, 1993

As I say good-bye, I try one last time to persuade Esperanza to keep the copy of *Translated Woman* she has given back to me.

"I already know my *historia*," she says. "And besides, this is in English. My children can't read it."

I try to insist she keep the book as a souvenir.

"No, *comadre*, you take it back. Sell it. So it won't be sitting there gathering dust. You worked hard on it. You should make some money."

I assure her there are many, many copies of The Book in circulation. But I can't convince her to keep the book about her life that I've spent six years writing. All I can do is get her to sign her name on the copy she has returned to me. And then I ask: If I come back next time with the book in Spanish, will she accept it? Yes, she says, she will. And she'll know how to handle any criticisms, from her husband, from her neighbors, from anyone. She's not afraid anymore of being called a witch.

It pains me to pack the book away. But I understand that not accepting the book is my *comadre*'s way of refusing to be the translated woman. Looking back as I walk away from her house, I see her two long braids meeting at the center of her back and regret, again, my harsh words to her about money.

I have come to Mexico, as usual, with a project, this time to document Esperanza's response to the book I've written about her life story. What can I say? That I wrote the book, brought it back, and my *comadre* didn't want it? That I almost killed myself and David and Gabriel on the highway getting here? That my father is no longer speaking to me? Foolish, foolish is the anthropologist who mixes up the field with her life.

§

September 1, 1993

The visa for Cuba arrives as I am leaving Mexico. We speed all the way back to Ann Arbor, where I have left behind my Cuban passport, and the next day I leave for Miami and then for Cuba. I spend five whirlwind days in Havana, where an old friend of my mother's breaks my heart by giving me her collection of swizzle sticks she has been saving since New Year's of 1959, which she and her husband celebrated at the Hotel Riviera with my parents. "That's all I have, the memories of those times," she tells me.

A few hours later, back at the Miami airport, I call David. "Are you ready?" he asks. "The *New York Times* book review is out." Titled "The Academic and the Witch," the review celebrates my ethnography while castigating my venture into autobiography: "The lesson is clear, the lives of anthropologists are rarely as rich and fascinating as those of their subjects."

It doesn't matter if my life is boring, if I'm not a sufficiently exotic Other. By the end of the month, just by virtue of a *New York Times* review, the book sells out.

§

My mother and I are comparing how our Yom Kippur fasts went this year. She tells me that my father, who is still not speaking to me, went up to the altar during the Torah reading and gave a donation of eighteen dollars, which stands for Life in Hebrew, to mark the forthcoming paperback edition of my book. It's not the book he would have liked his daughter to have written, but a book it is, nonetheless, his daughter did write it, and he has no choice but to be proud of it—even if it causes him pain.

§

At a Vietnamese restaurant in Wichita I am recalling with Debbie Gordon how wounded I felt at the end of the conference on "Women Writing Culture" I organized two years earlier with the women graduate students who had taken my course on the same subject. A couple of the students, with whom I had worked hard to make their papers presentable, suddenly forgot about my presence as soon as the event was over. To my dismay, they filled their plates from the lavish Middle Eastern buffet I had arranged for the occasion and formed a closed circle around one of my male colleagues. He refused to eat anything, saying he had to get back to work. Then, like a guru, he plopped himself in the center of the circle of women and began to lead a discussion about the possibilities for feminist mainstreaming of the year-long core course in the anthropology department. At the time the only female author on the reading list for the course was Ruth Benedict. That absence had been the subject of my course as well as of our conference.

How could the students so swiftly forget their education and enact such a typical family romance? How could they rush into the arms of the absent father, who had not shown much concern before for feminist issues, and abandon their intellectual mother, who had empowered them to speak in the first place? The ridiculously sad ending to our feminist conference had cast a shadow, for me, on the "Women Writing Culture" project. Feminist bridges, I realized, are easily broken. But could I write about what happened without seeming jealous or vindictive?

Debbie tells me I ought to write about the incident. But she also asks if I now understand my parents better, how they too felt betrayed but celebrated the publication of my book anyway. Her question forces me to confront the bitter irony of my longings. After all, my parents can't get me to thank them for leaving Cuba to give me a better future, so why should I expect gratitude from my students?

"Teaching women is a lot like raising daughters," Debbie suddenly says. "You raise them and then they leave you, even turn against you."

"It occurs to me that it's our mothers who raise us, but we're always writing in our father's names," I say, or want to imagine myself saying.

"In anthropology we have the legacy of Papa Franz and his daughters," Debbie continues.

"Right, and it's a strange legacy," I reply, warming to the subject. "You know, when I went to graduate school at Princeton, everyone wanted to know if I'd be working with Clifford Geertz. But Cliff was the archetypal absent father, off at the Institute for Advanced Study and inaccessible to students. All we had was his aura. The person who taught us anthropology, who generously gave us her time, was Hilly Geertz, his ex-wife. She and Cliff divorced while I was a student, and I remember my loyalties were with Hilly. I identified with her pain and loss and betrayal. And I remember thinking that, from then on, I would resist citing Cliff's work, resist accepting him as an intellectual father. Everyone cited *his* writing, not *hers*. There was more of it to cite, of course, in those days. Now Hilly has come into her own as an anthropologist, writer, and art critic, and she's producing beautiful and thoughtful books on Balinese aesthetics. I can't tell you what joy that gives me."

The two of us become quiet, watching as our dinner of rice and vegetables and shrimp, topped with fresh cilantro, is gracefully set on the table. "That's what interests me so much about the first generation of feminist anthropologists," Debbie says, passing me the rice. "They wanted to figure out the origins of sexual inequality in order to see what it would take to change men and thus raise the status of women. Hunter-gatherers, who seemed to have sexual harmony, were especially important to those early feminist theories. Marjorie Shostak's life story about Nisa is a perfect example of the feminist utopian storytelling of that era.[3] Despite the evidence of wife battering in Nisa's story, Shostak can't let go of the allegory that heterosexuality functions perfectly among the !Kung, or at least that it functions better than in our own society. That's the sense in which she's not simply writing culture but being written *by* the culture."

"And what would you say is the allegory of *Translated Woman*?" I ask cautiously, as if asking to have my palm read.

"I think your book is a story of deep, deep gender conflict. There is wife battering, there is a dysfunctional marriage, there is child abuse. Your allegory is the end of heterosexuality. The gender conflict that is only nascent in Shostak's book emerges in all its ambivalence in your book."

"That's interesting. As a matter of fact, I took Shostak's book with me to Mexico, and I had it in mind as I wrote *Translated Woman*. It seems odd to me now that my book appears to be about the encounter of two women, meeting and forming a relationship against all odds, against the barriers of race, class, and nationality, but what obsesses us is our relationships with the central men in our lives, especially our fathers. And I've come to see a vivid contradiction in my work with Esperanza. While she's telling me about how she's given up on men as unredeemable, I'm being accompanied by a man who has bent over backward so I can live a feminist life."

"What you bring home now is so different. Complicated tales of complicity and power. Of weeping, as you do in your last chapter, for your own naïveté about the academy and the way it commodifies people. Of fearing that you, in turn, are commodifying Esperanza even before you've written about her. Your book seems to mark the end of something else—maybe it's the end of feminist utopias in anthropology."

§

November 30, 1993

I'm on the mythical island I had always heard of as I was growing up but had never been able to visit—Long Island, in New York. *Translated Woman* has become a Traveling Woman. Peddling my *comadre*'s story as she asked me to, here on this side of the border, has taken me far and wide, from airports to colleges to hotels and home again. I keep feeling that—like my father, who traveled throughout Latin America on business trips when I was a teenager—I'm trying to run away from something. Everywhere I go my head hangs in shame because I don't forget that I owe Esperanza more than I will ever be able to pay her and that even so I will always have more money than her.

On the island I present an early version of this paper, and afterward, over a mixed Japanese-Chinese dinner of sushi, tofu balls, slinky noodles, and spicy shrimp with steamed rice, I'm told by a women's studies professor that she felt embarrassed by the sections of the paper that were so intensely focused on my conflicts with my family. But then she told herself that if I were saying these things about Esperanza they wouldn't bother her at all. They'd just be ethnography. I'm reminded of Nancy Miller's point that personal writing creates an unsettling awareness of the cost of writing. As she says, "The embarrassment produced in readers is a sign that it is working. At the same time, the embarrassment blows the cover of the impersonal as a masquerade of self-effacement."[4]

§

December 22, 1993

I return from a two-week trip to Cuba on the same day that Fidel Castro's estranged daughter, Alina Fernández Revuelta, arrives in the United States after eluding the Cuban authorities by sporting the musty wild-haired wig of tourist drag. Fidel's daughter leaves Cuba to defy the power of the Patriarch, whom she denounces as a tyrant. I, on the other hand, must keep returning to Cuba to search for the Papi who used to take me on walks along the Malecón seawall, my dress puffing up in the breeze, nothing yet needing to be forgiven.

§

I am in Iowa City, sitting in a hotel room overlooking a river whose name I have forgotten to ask. Yesterday afternoon, for the fifth and final time, I presented this essay to a university audience under the auspices of the Ida Beam distinguished lectureship. (I've also forgotten to ask who was Ida Beam.) This time, preparing to let the essay go, I felt myself plagued with doubts as I read aloud. I felt certain I was boring my audience, that I sounded like I was whining, that I was proving my father right by presenting myself as beleaguered by him, my mother, my critics, even Esperanza. It is one thing to embarrass the audience to make a point about the masquerade of self-effacement, but what about my own embarrassment? Is it an inevitable consequence of having my intellectual work also be personal work?

The audience stunned me by being incredibly friendly—more than that, people were nurturing, protective, even intimate in their empathy—and so I decided to share my worries with them: Is this essay really okay? Can I let this go to press? Please, I begged, playing a strange devil's advocate, tell me, save me, before it's too late, before I regret what I've confessed to. Having completely scattered any semblance of authority and power to the winds, people rushed to my defense, telling me I'd raised exactly the kind of issues that needed to be raised about how the pangs of love and the concern for ethics cross paths in surprisingly similar ways in writing about both family relationships and fieldwork relationships. The audience, significantly, was made up largely of women faculty and graduate students—I counted four males in an audience of about thirty-five people. Had I opened up, asked for advice so candidly, because I was in a roomful of women? Although my essay, on this rereading, had struck me as being an uncomfortably melodramatic cultural tale, I'd pulled on my audience's heartstrings and made them actually *care* about Esperanza and me. No matter how much I urged the audience to criticize me, there did not seem to be a single positivist in that room. Unbelievable, I thought, could the academy have changed so much? Why was no one scolding me for being too self-indulgent? Was the unwillingness to criticize me the ultimate sign that I'd made it in the academy? No, it must be that people in Iowa are too polite. Only when I asked if I should add a postscript did they tell me it would be a good idea. They were willing to admit, at least, that the essay needed a more satisfying resolution, another ending, a happier ending.

Indeed, much has changed since *Translated Woman*'s first year. Esperanza's story is now widely read by students in women's studies, anthropology, history, rhetoric, and Latin American and Latina/Latino studies. As Esperanza wished, her story is passing from ear to ear on this side of the border. She worried that "eyes that don't see" are "hearts that don't feel" (*ojos que no ven, corazón que no siente*), but the truth is the gringos and gringas are greatly moved by her story. The book is selling. Esperanza's story has become a successful export just as the Mexican economic crisis has touched bottom and the mask of progress represented by free trade has been torn away. And I, not Esperanza, am reaping the greater benefits, even though I share the royalties with her.

Meanwhile, I've adopted the strategy of silence, exile, and cunning with regard to my writing, keeping every word hidden from my father and mother, withholding from them the knowledge that I am flying around the country inscribing the story of our dissolution as a family ever more irrevocably into the academy. Eyes that don't see, heart that doesn't feel, I hope. This story I can't resolve happily either. Without my parents' eyes moving across these pages, I move from hotel to hotel, searching for oceans in rivers with no names, an orphan.

Notes

I am grateful to the various audiences who listened to this essay and responded generously and honestly: the Women's Studies Program and Anthropology Department at State University of New York at Stonybrook, the Anthropology Department at Duke University, the Chicano Studies Program at University of California at Santa Barbara, the Women's Studies Program at Wellesley College, and the Anthropology Department, Women's Studies Program, and the Center for International and Comparative Studies at the University of Iowa. Warm thanks to Deborah Gordon, Deb Chasman, and Teofilo Ruiz for their encouragement and wisdom.

1. Richard Rodriguez, *Hunger of Memory* (New York: Bantam, 1983), 184–85.

2. In the original cloth edition of *Translated Woman,* there is a snake motif over the cover photograph of Esperanza. In deference to Esperanza's wishes, the snake motif was removed from the cover of the subsequent paperback edition.

3. Marjorie Shostak, *Nisa: The Life and Words of a !Kung Woman* (New York: Vintage Books, 1981).

4. Nancy K. Miller, *Getting Personal: Feminist Occasions and Other Autobiographical Acts* (New York: Routledge, 1991), 24.

Another History, Another Canon

4

Feminist
Anthro-
pology:
The Legacy
of Elsie Clews
Parsons

Louise
Lamphere

SEVENTY YEARS ago, in 1923, Elsie Clews Parsons became president of the American Ethnological Society for a two-year term. During the 1910s, in her late thirties and early forties, she had distinguished herself as a social psychologist and feminist, writing several important books during the period Nancy Cott has associated with the birth of modern feminism.[1] By the age of forty-nine, when she assumed the AES presidency, Parsons had become part of Boasian anthropology at Columbia University, immersing herself in ethnological research among the Pueblos and funding the work of countless southwestern researchers, including many women. All told, Parsons, who died in 1941, wrote more than ninety-five articles on the Southwest, culminating in her two-volume grand synthesis, *Pueblo Indian Religion*.[2] In the 1960s and 1970s the AES honored Parsons by awarding a prize each year to the best graduate-student essay in a national competition. When the prize was discontinued the last medal was given to the president and handed down from president to president as a symbol of office. Thus the 1989 AES meetings in Santa Fe, a few miles from Española and Clara True's ranch, where Parsons stayed during her first trip to the Southwest in 1910, seemed an appropriate time to commemorate the work of Elsie Clews Parsons. I particularly wanted to make a connection between Parsons's feminist writing and the

*Elsie Clews Parsons at the San Gabriel Ranch in Alcalde, New Mexico, ca. 1923.
(Photograph courtesy of the American Philosophical Society)*

reemergence of feminism in anthropology in the 1970s and 1980s. Michelle Rosaldo and I were ignorant of Elsie Clews Parsons when we edited *Woman, Culture and
Society*[3] in the early 1970s. Instead, we turned to Margaret Mead for the quotation
that begins our book. We might have written a different introduction had we read
Parsons's books.

My own interest in Parsons I owe to Barbara Babcock and Nancy Parezo, who
invited me to participate in a conference on "Daughters of the Desert"—a retro-
spective on women anthropologists who conducted research on Native American

　　　　　　　　　LOUISE LAMPHERE

cultures in the Southwest—held at the University of Arizona in 1986. Parsons's contributions were explored in a paper by Louis Hieb and have been detailed in the conference catalogue by Babcock and Parezo.[4] Parsons's key financial support for the research of Ester Goldfrank, Ruth Bunzel, Ruth Benedict, and others emerged from many papers, and her role as a mentor to Gladys Reichard was covered very minimally in my own contribution.[5] In both writing and revising this paper I became indebted to Babcock's more recent and insightful research, which uncovers and underscores the feminist sensibility in Parsons's work.[6]

Throughout this paper I shall compare Parsons's scholarship of the teens and 1920s to the feminist anthropology that emerged during the 1970s and 1980s. I see important similarities in the focus on cultural universals in both Parsons's writing in the teens and the feminist anthropology some of us wrote in the 1970s. This universalizing tendency was followed by a transition to more detailed ethnographic research for Parsons in the 1920s and for feminists in the 1980s. On the other hand, there are crucial differences. The more muted feminism in Parsons's ethnological work in the 1920s and 1930s contrasts with its more explicit and continued presence in the writings of women anthropologists today. This relates, I argue, to complex differences between the state of anthropological theory in the late Boasian period and that of the present, as well as differences between the social and political context of feminism of the 1920s and 1980s.

The Making of a Feminist

Before exploring this comparison further, a few details of Parsons's life are in order. Elsie Clews grew up in a wealthy New York City family. Her father, Henry Clews, was a Wall Street broker, and her mother was a distant relative of President James Madison. The family summered at a mansion ("The Rocks") in Newport, and Elsie's mother put aside $10,000 each year for "mistakes in clothes."[7] Elsie managed to talk her father into letting her attend newly opened Barnard College, from which she graduated in 1896. She went on to earn her M.A. and Ph.D. at Barnard, studying under Franklin H. Giddings, an evolutionary sociologist. She taught briefly at Barnard before marrying Herbert Parsons in 1900, at the age of twenty-four. Parsons's feminism grew out of her independent spirit and was a rejection of the confining life of a wealthy Victorian debutante and socialite. She scandalized her mother by going for an unchaperoned swim with a young man on a secluded Newport beach when she was a teenager.[8]

Herbert Parsons tolerated his wife's independence and feminism, even though it threatened to disrupt his political career as a reform Republican congressman, a post he held between 1905 and 1911. The publication of her book *The Family*[9] created headlines in New York in 1906. The book was an outline of her lectures at Barnard, which took an evolutionary view of marriage and family patterns using ethnological data. It created a furor because it advocated trial marriage. Elsie sent a copy to Theodore Roosevelt, Herbert's patron in the Republican party, hoping to reassure the president that the book was really "very dry reading." Roosevelt seemed pleased to receive a copy and in a teasing manner promised to read the famous book and discuss it over lunch.[10]

During the first ten years of her marriage Parsons bore six children, four of whom lived to adulthood. Her wealth allowed her to raise her children with a full staff of housekeepers and child nurses and gave her the freedom to travel. She spent several years in Washington, D.C., but returned to New York in 1911 after her husband finished his third term as a congressman. Between 1913 and 1916 she wrote five feminist books, interconnected studies that focused on how marriage, the family, religion, and social etiquette constrain women. In several she emphasized the need for individual freedom and choice.

At the same time she began to abandon her brand of sociological feminism for ethnology. As Peter Hare, her grandnephew, writes in his biography, "She moved slowly from a generalizing style to rigorous empirical methods."[11] During those years she came under the influence of Franz Boas and his graduate students, Alfred Kroeber, Robert Lowie, and Pliny Goddard. Goddard wrote to Parsons, characterizing the dual nature of her life in this transitional period when she was attracted to anthropology yet still writing feminist books: "Your winter activities are propaganda and your summer ones research."[12] By 1916 (at forty-two) she talked about giving up generalizing. In an oft-quoted passage to Lowie, she wrote, "You [Lowie], Kroeber and Hocart make the life of a psychologist not worth living. I see plainly I shall have to keep to the straight and narrow path of kinship nomenclature and folktale collecting." By the 1920s, when Parsons was president of the AES, her publications were almost completely ethnological.

A closer examination of these two crucial decades in Parsons's life—the teens and the 1920s—reveals the social and intellectual forces that first shaped Parsons's feminism and that then propelled her into an anthropological setting with little room for such concerns in an era of political quiescence and a more private feminism.

Parsons's Early Writings and the Feminism of the Teens

The teens, particularly the years of World War I, were a time of social ferment and protest in which socialist, feminist, and other radical ideas were common in New York City, especially among the middle-class and upper-class avant-garde in Greenwich Village. Nancy Cott contrasts the Greenwich Village feminists with earlier suffragists. These college-educated, bourgeois women rejected the image of service and motherhood associated with the women's movement of the nineteenth century. They were women who welcomed irreverent and radical behavior in art, politics, and the labor movement. According to Cott, "They considered themselves socialists or progressives leaning toward socialism and had, unlike most of the American population, a tolerance for 'isms.' They embedded their critique of gender hierarchy in a critique of the social system."[13] They wanted to break with dichotomized categories of "Man" and "Woman" and to equate womanhood with humanity. As Charlotte Perkins Gilman described the "Feminist": "Here she comes, running, out of prison and off pedestal; chains off, crown off, halo off, just a live woman."[14]

During the teens, after her return from Washington, Parsons was part of this new feminism, but her relationships were broader and included three intellectual circles in New York City. The first was that of Boas and his male graduate students. Parsons met Boas as early as 1907, and she was the first woman whom he interested in anthropology. In 1913 Boas helped Parsons arrange a trip to the Yucatán,[15] but they had a relatively formal relationship during this period. She became closer to Lowie, Goddard, and Kroeber, inviting the latter two to her home in Lenox, Massachusetts. Robert Lowie recalled that her door was open to the younger graduate students, whom she fed and sent off to enjoy her box at the opera.[16] While Goddard was primarily an admirer, her relationship with Kroeber was a much more challenging and complex one.[17] Their friendship was at first warm and playful and then, after a month of joint fieldwork at Zuni in September 1917, difficult and more distant.[18] In later years they resumed a respectful professional relationship and, after her death, Kroeber wrote that he admired her "rigorous honesty and courage of mind."[19]

Parsons made her first trips to the Southwest between 1910 and 1913. These increased in frequency as she became more attracted to anthropology, with its "insistence on a rigorously empirical approach" and "a consciousness of problem and method."[20] In 1915 she observed a Navajo Enemy War ceremony and went on to visit Zuni.[21] She made additional trips to Zuni and Laguna over the next four years, including the month with Kroeber at Zuni in 1917 and fieldwork with Boas in Laguna in 1919.[22] These short excursions provided the material for her ethnographic articles on Zuni and Laguna that were published in the late teens.[23]

The second circle was that of the Greenwich Village radicals. In Mable Dodge's salon she met Walter Lippmann, with whom she helped found the *New Republic*.[24] She also came to know Max Eastman and wrote several articles for his monthly *The Masses*. The magazine, a well-regarded "underground" journal of the time, provoked censorship by the post office in 1917 and a conspiracy trial of the editors in 1918 for antiwar views. *The Masses* was dominated by such male "heavies" as Max Eastman, Floyd Dell (a sexual radical who wrote *Love in the Machine Age*), and John Reed (whose later commitment to the Russian Revolution was chronicled in the movie *Reds*). It was full of antiwar cartoons, accounts of strikes, avant-garde drawings, and poetry. Nevertheless, it had an important feminist component, with many cartoon critiques of male dominance, poems by Amy Lowell, fiction by Mable Dodge, and articles on birth control, Emma Goldman's trial, and women's role in the garment trade.

Parsons's third circle included Heterodoxy, a club of sixty-five radical feminists who met for Saturday lunches every two weeks in Greenwich Village beginning in 1912. Founded by Marie Jennie Howe, it included heterosexual and lesbian women, activists and professionals. Among its famous members were Crystal Eastman, Stella Coman Ballantine (Emma Goldman's niece), Charlotte Perkins Gilman,

Agnes deMille, and Elizabeth Gurley Flynn. At their lunches members discussed women's rights, political issues of the day, and a whole host of other topics—from how women were raising their children to revelations about their own upbringing.[25] One of the members used Parsons's classification of family types from her book *The Family* in a published spoof on mating patterns found among the members of Heterodoxy entitled, "Marriage Customs and Taboo among the Early Heterodities."[26]

Parsons's writing during this period (1912–1919) was prolific—and her most explicitly feminist. She published five books and a number of scholarly articles in the *American Anthropologist*, the *Journal of American Folklore*, and the *American Journal of Sociology*. She also wrote popular pieces for *The Masses*, the *New Republic*, and *Harper's Weekly*. In her book *Beyond Separate Spheres*, Rosalind Rosenberg argues that by the teens Parsons had given up the evolutionary approach espoused by her teacher Franklin Giddings and evident in her book *The Family*. She rejected a "slavish devotion to evolutionary theory" and a set of cultural stages. Instead, she became a "de facto functionalist," arguing that the principle motives of human behavior are unconscious and that civilized and primitive peoples are no different in their behavior.[27]

Parsons's books of this period focus on the theme of social restraint, and they juxtapose cross-cultural examples with ones from her own society. There is a generalizing tone here—a search for universals and a focus on women's social roles. *The Old-Fashioned Woman* and *Religious Chastity*, both published in 1913, and *Fear and Conventionality, Social Freedom,* and *Social Rule* all reflect a concern for the universal in women's experience that is parallel to the themes emphasized by those of us who wrote for *Woman, Culture and Society* in 1974.[28]

The Old-Fashioned Woman, to cite the best example, uses ethnographic evidence to demonstrate how women's lives are constrained from birth to widowhood by taboos, confinement, and exclusion from male affairs. Digging through the available ethnography of the day (for example, Spencer and Gillen on the Aborigines, Frazer's *The Golden Bough*, and George Dorsey on the Wichita), Parsons juxtaposes the experience of women in tribal groups with that of women in ancient state societies and in our own "modern time." Each page is a pastiche of examples.

For instance, in the chapter "In Quarantine," about menstrual taboos, she says, "But it is during menstruation that a woman is most generally considered dangerous. . . . The Bushmen think that at a glance from a menstruous woman, a man becomes at once transfixed and turned into a tree which talks. . . . If a Pueblo Indian touches a menstruous woman, or if a Chippeway uses her fire, he is bound to fall ill."[29] And the list continues. So-called civilized societies, she notes, also harbor such beliefs and often restrict women's behavior. Women are banned from sugar refineries in the north of France (because a menstruous woman would blacken the sugar), and in England people believe that meat cured by a menstruous woman is tainted.[30]

In a discussion of marriage entitled "Her Market Price," Parsons announces that "Women are an important item in primitive trade." In this chapter she discusses various forms of bride-price before turning her attention to prostitution and slavery, other examples of the exchange of women for goods. In the chapter on "The Exclusive Sex" Parsons tells us that "Women are quite generally excluded from a share in public affairs. The Nagas have a war stone no woman may look upon and live. In anti-suffrage argument a voting booth seems to be nearly as dangerous a spot for women." Women are often frightened away from men's exclusive activities or they are given "minor parts," thus securing feminine devotion and becoming what Parsons called "The Ladies' Gallery." [31]

In these and other chapters we see the overarching shadow of male dominance, the confinement and constriction of women, and their lack of value. Example after example is cited (meticulously footnoted), but the point is the universality of women's condition. European examples (of so-called civilized peoples) are juxtaposed with those from tribal peoples as diverse as the Australian Aborigines, the American Indians, and the Samoans. Women's positions in archaic states and African kingdoms help to amplify Parsons's commentary on constraint, taboo, and exclusion. [32]

Parsons's contributions to *The Masses* take on these same themes of social control and constraint. Her article on marriage cites customs among the Tlingit, the Arabs, and the Koreans that mark a change in status, conferring "a new life." A Tlingit woman changes the silver pin in her lip for a wooden one, a Javanese woman burns her dolls, a Spartan bride had to give up going to public games, but in Korea, it is the man, not the bride, who does up his hair. Why all these changes? "Society," Parsons writes, "modern and primitive, stamps marriage with extraneous features, insists on making of it a novelty, because society thereby controls it, or rather, through marriage thus artificialized, it controls sex." [33]

In two of her later books Parsons begins to explore why women are divided from men, developing a theory grounded in the universality of social convention and social categories. In *Fear and Conventionality* she argues that social conventions are a way of erecting barriers because of a universal fear of change, dread of novelty, and dislike of the unusual. "Sex is one of the two greatest sources of difference between its members society has to apprehend. It deals with the disturbing factor in its characteristically simple, unconscious way. It separates men and women as much as possible." Thus "No Vedda may come in contact with any woman of his own age except his wife. . . . Corean boys were taught that it was shameful to set foot at all in the women's part of the house." [34] And in New York a woman has her escort ride with the cab driver since there is no chaperone to watch over them if they share the same seat.

The possibility of breaking through rigid social categories is explored in *Social Freedom*, published in 1915. Sex, along with age, kinship, and caste, is the major social classification that sets up rigid divisions, against which, with a "maturing culture," there is some attempt to struggle. "Freedom from the domination of personality by sex is the gift *par excellence* of feminism, a gift it brings to men as well as women." Parsons believed that sex relationships were beginning to change. Under increased freedom from rigid social categories, "Sex becomes a factor in the enrichment of personality. . . . It is a factor, not an obsession. . . . No longer a source of distress or annoyance, it is not kept separate from life nor repressed into the obscene. It is free to express itself, developing its own tests, standards and ideas. According to these ideals, relations between men and women will be primarily personal relations, secondarily sexual."[35]

Parsons was also a pacifist, and she opposed U.S. participation in World War I. She was against her husband's enlistment and refused to let anyone wearing a uniform into her home—including Herbert. She was disillusioned when many of the intellectuals associated with the *New Republic* began to support the war in 1917. Rosenberg argues that Parsons's hopes for progress and reform were dashed by World War I: "At the war's end, Parsons made a final break with public life and her own brand of feminism and escaped into anthropological fieldwork. Her friend Kroeber later suggested that she burned out on reform and that her growing understanding of culture's power over the individual made her even less optimistic about individual action."[36]

The Twenties: Parsons's Presidency of the AES and the Boasian Legacy

The twenties, as James Clifford has shown, were the years in which classic ethnography was formulated, as exemplified by Malinowski's *Argonauts of the Western Pacific* and Margaret Mead's *Coming of Age in Samoa*.[37] However, Parsons's fieldwork was much different from that of Malinowski and Mead. In the 1920s Parsons stayed with the Boasian tradition, which represented a more polyphonic description, but she framed that description in terms of culture elements, diffusion, and culture history. She remained aligned with Boas and Goddard and became a mentor to Gladys Reichard, who was almost a "daughter to Boas" and who, intellectually, remained a Boasian throughout her life. Parsons was never close to Mead, Benedict, or Sapir, the anthropologists in the Columbia milieu who were theorizing about the relationship between culture and the individual and were writing from a more humanistic point of view.[38]

During the 1920s Parsons continued to make short trips to the Southwest, expanding her research outward from Zuni, visiting Laguna in 1919 and 1920, Hopi in 1920, Jemez in 1921, and Taos in 1922.[39] In the mid 1920s, when she was president of AES, she conducted research on the Tewa, working out of the Spanish village of Alcalde and having informants visit her there.[40]

Given Pueblo resistance to researchers, especially those who wanted to know about religion, information was always obtained piecemeal. Anthropologists were never able to present a "seamless whole"; nor could they have "pitched their tents among the natives." Parsons, like others of the period, relied primarily on information from one family (the host) and from a small circle of paid informants. In more secretive pueblos like Isleta, notes were made during interviews in a hotel room or at a nearby Spanish village.[41] This relatively clandestine research (although Parsons took care never to reveal the names of her informants) gives us (in the 1990s) the sense that anthropologists were almost "prying information, often secret, out of the natives."

Few southwestern researchers engaged in writing with the kind of ethnographic authority which claimed that "I was there, so you are there." Instead, a scholarly article was often a blend of different voices—the anthropologist as observer, the native as co-observer answering the anthropologist's questions "on the spot," the notes of previous anthropological observations, and a narrative of a "prototypical" ceremony by a native informant. Although male anthropologists used this style, Parsons, along with Gladys Reichard and Ruth Underhill, were at the forefront in adding women's voices, along with their own observations, to their texts.

During the 1920s Parsons continued to be interested in women, but she was committed to collecting ethnographic detail that was written up in this polyphonic Boasian mode. We see this style of writing, one that recognizes the position of the ethnographer and gives voice to her informants, most vividly in Parsons's important series of articles on mothers and children published in *Man* between 1919 and 1924. These essays are a compendium of beliefs and practices—offerings women make in order to get pregnant, taboos surrounding birth (to avoid deformities in the child), postpartum practices and naming ceremonies—and Parsons concretizes these beliefs by including the accounts of individual women. For example, in the article on "Mothers and Children at Laguna," Parsons gives her hostess Wana's narrative of the naming ceremony used for her two-week-old baby (performed ten days before her visit). It includes Wana's drawing of the altar and a text of the medicine man's prayer in both Keres and English.[42] The Hopi article tells what Parsons's hostess did to have a boy child and gives a verbatim account from her Tewa informant.[43] In contrast to these articles in which native voices emerge, several of the articles on Zuni and the Tewa are more a list of taboos or sayings that describe a range of behavior: the disciplining of children, or what a mother says when a child loses its first tooth. There are fewer personal experiences here (either as narrated by informants or as observed by Elsie) and more individual bits of information gathered from various informants at unstated times and places.[44]

These articles contrast markedly with Parsons's use of ethnography in *The Old-Fashioned Woman* and *Fear and Conventionality*. They do not focus on the separation of the sexes, on the exclusion of women, or even on the constraints of convention. Gone from these texts are attempts to moralize or point out a generalization about human nature or even an implicit contrast with our own culture. Convention and custom are recorded, but there is little commentary on their constraining nature and no theory accounting for adherence to tradition. In one article, on the Zuni masked figures that are used to terrorize and control children, the theme of constraint and the control of behavior is still present in the selection of the topic. But comparisons are limited to childrearing practices at other pueblos. Parsons's own observations of an *a'Doshle* "haranguing" a little boy are described in order to convey a vivid sense that the boy was frightened, but there is no attempt to comment on the ways in which behavior is constrained by the custom. No implicit subtext judges Zuni practice or compares it to our own. The importance of individual freedom and the artificiality of social conventions are no longer issues in this "ethnographic" description.

When she was president of the AES, Parsons published two "landmark" essays, "Tewa Kin, Clan, and Moiety" and "The Religion of the Pueblo Indians."[45] The works arrange data on the Pueblo cultures from west to east, contrasting the matrilineal orientation of the Hopis with the weak clans at Keres and among the Tewa and the presence of the kachina cult and prayer-feather offerings in the western pueblos—complexes that "diminish steadily" to the east and north.[46] These essays mark her commitment to Boasian issues about cultural variation and diffusion and had a lasting impact on the field. The contrast between western and eastern pueblo social organization, for example, was more fully developed in the work of Fred Eggan.[47]

After Parsons's last field trip to the Southwest, in 1932, she began to turn her attention elsewhere—to Mexico, the Caribbean, and Peru. In *Mitla: Town of the Souls* Parsons retains the polyphonic style she utilized in her articles during the 1920s as well as her interest in the position of women. Her chapter on family and personal life documents women's experiences in pregnancy and childbirth. In it we read about the town's midwives, Isadora and Señora Be'ta, their birthing techniques, the baths they give women after their children are born, and their remedies for delayed deliveries.[48] There is an account of one of the many marriage ceremonies Parsons attended, plus a lengthy discussion of sicknesses, cures, and difficulties with witchcraft. Here and in the remainder of the book we come to recognize a "cast of characters," many of whom recount stories of witchcraft or suggest cures that have been successful. Some are subjects of the portraits or participants in the narratives detailed in the chapter on town gossip. In that chapter Parsons relates her own experience in the earthquake of January 14, 1931, when she escaped from her room only moments before the ceiling collapsed.[49] This volume, like the ethnographies, fictionalized accounts, and life histories of Reichard and Underhill, constitutes the growing body of ethnography from a woman's point of view that blossomed during the 1930s, only to be forgotten in subsequent decades.[50]

During this period Parsons's interest in the Southwest continued through her editing of Stephen's *Hopi Journal* and her most important southwestern book, *Pueblo Indian Religion,* published in 1939.[51] In the latter the informants and observations of the earlier articles have disappeared, supplanted by a homogenous "ethnographic present" and an overriding concern with Boasian issues, particularly cultural innovation and borrowing. Each group—the Hopi, the Zuni, the Tewa—becomes an "absolute subject," to use Clifford's phrase. Parsons's voice becomes marginalized, relegated primarily to the footnotes. In this transformation of observation, narratives by informants, and the dialogues between ethnographer and native—in other words, data constituted in discursive, dialogical conditions—become textualized. "The data thus reformulated need no longer be understood as the communication of specific persons. An informant's explanation or description of custom need not be cast in a form that includes the message 'so and so said this.' A textualized ritual or event is no longer closely linked to the production of that event by specific actors. Instead, these texts become evidences of an englobing context, a 'cultural reality.'"[52] In *Pueblo Indian Religion* the multiple voices and the person of Parsons as observer disappear, and the historical specificity of differing accounts is even more difficult to find in the footnotes.

We have come to the end of a long process. First, Parsons's writing embodied a feminism that sought to generalize about women's situations based on a juxtaposition of ethnographic example with Western custom. During the 1920s and into the 1930s her prose, in which Babcock sees the prefiguring of "poststructuralist" ethnography, focused on ethnographic particulars and incorporated a pastiche of contextualized observation, informant narration, descriptive vignettes concerning individuals, and the question/answer interrogation of consultants.[53] And finally, many of her later publications exemplified a synthetic ethnology—one in which variability and culture contact are the theme but in which the dialogue between observer and informant is erased and the framework of Boasian culture history dominates.

This assessment would be incomplete if it did not emphasize Parsons's important financial contributions. Without Parsons's support, American anthropology and Southwest research would have been a much more piecemeal endeavor. For example, she paid Ester Goldfrank's and Ruth Bunzel's salaries as Boas's secretaries in the early 1920s. She financed the research of Benedict, Bunzel, Reichard, Leslie White, and many others through the Southwest Society. She kept the *Journal of American Folklore* afloat and funded numerous other publications. Our sense of cultural variability and of the influence of the Spanish Conquest among the Pueblos owes much to Parsons's research.

However, Parsons, like almost all of the other women in anthropology in the 1920s, never held a position within academe. Her wealth allowed her to travel and do fieldwork and fund the research of others; she remained a patron of anthropology rather than one who could shape its future through the direct training of students. Yet Parsons was hardly alone in her peripheral institutional position within anthropology. Gladys Reichard had a full-time position—but at an undergraduate college. Ruth Benedict was denied the position of chair of the Columbia University Anthropology Department and did not become a full professor until the year she died; Margaret Mead was peripheral at Columbia, shunted off to her tower office in the American Museum of Natural History. Even in the West, where there were a number of women in archaeology and in museum positions, only Florence Hawley Ellis held a full-time position in the 1920s or 1930s in the anthropology department at the University of New Mexico.

Parsons touched the lives of most of the women around Boas, whether by providing funds for their jobs or field research or by mentoring their anthropological work. Her role as a source of intellectual energy and financial support has been hidden behind that of Boas, whose leadership and institutional place have been continually affirmed by historians of anthropology. Only recently has Parsons's role reemerged, through the work of women scholars.[54] Though there were cleavages (between those who remained more in the Boasian mold and those whose work fostered the emergence of the study of culture and personality), Parsons was key to the maintenance of the strong network of relations among women anthropologists at Columbia that flourished in the 1920s and 1930s. Yet for the most part Parsons's feminism remained a muted part of her ethnological writing, and the marginal positions of these women within anthropology limited their impact on the next generation of anthropologists.

The Reemergence of Feminism in the 1970s

When feminism reemerged in the 1970s as a political movement, it contained a critique of women's domestic roles that was reminiscent of the issues about which Parsons wrote: sexuality, marriage, motherhood, and the exclusion of women from the wider political sphere. Like Parsons in the teens, many of us were participating in several overlapping intellectual circles: consciousness-raising groups that probed the sexual politics of our personal lives and the history of the women's movement in America, antiwar-movement activities ranging from marches to study groups and conferences, and intellectual inquiry within the context of traditional departments and professional meetings. Many of these activities and the groups associated with them were centered on universities, but some feminists participated in women's health collectives and political organizations that had a community base.

For those of us who were instructors and assistant professors in universities it seemed important to put together our feminism and our academic interests. We set out to correct the "relative invisibility" of women and their treatment as "passive sexual objects, devoted mothers, and dutiful wives" by constructing courses on women in each of our disciplines.

Shelly Rosaldo, Jane Collier, and others taught one such course in anthropology at Stanford University in early 1971, and I taught one at Brown University in 1973. Simultaneously, women anthropologists were beginning to give scholarly papers on women's roles in areas of their own research. Our book, *Woman, Culture and Society,* emerged from the Stanford course, from papers delivered at the 1971 meeting of the American Anthropological Association in New York, and from our own network of female anthropologists.

My correspondence with Shelly Rosaldo between 1971 and 1973 reflects the way in which the framework and tone of *Woman, Culture and Society* evolved. Our initial impulse was to correct the male bias in anthropological writing by analyzing the viewpoint of women, to define the position of women in our own and other cultures, and to delineate the ways in which women are actors even in situations of subordination. The outline of our book we presented to publishers was one that examined women using a variety of topics: socialization and the family; women in the economy; women in society; politics and kinship; and beliefs, ideology, and symbolic culture.

Not until Rosaldo drafted the introduction did the theme of universal subordination begin to shape the collection. Placing Nancy Chodorow's and Sherry Ortner's articles at the front of the book, immediately after her own article, was part of an attempt to give the book a theoretical coherence. Chodorow's article "Family Structure and Feminine Personality" had initially been in the "Socialization and Family" section, and Ortner's article "Is Female to Male as Nature Is to Culture?" had been in the "Beliefs, Ideology and Symbolic Culture" portion, at the end of the book. Ortner's piece was moved forward partly because other articles in that section were never completed. In the end we gave up the idea of organizing the book into topical sections; instead, we grouped papers that complemented each other.

Pushing forward with the universal asymmetry theme and becoming committed to a book that would make a theoretical contribution meant that the introductory three essays made broad ethnographic comparisons. They echo the generalizing tone of *The Old-Fashioned Woman, Fear and Conventionality,* and *Social Rule.* In documenting subordination, both Rosaldo and Ortner focused on many issues cited by Parsons—exclusion, the taboos surrounding menstruation and childbirth, and sexual separation. They often juxtaposed examples from their society and cross-cultural examples.

Several passages written by Rosaldo contain the same emphasis on exclusion and constraint as Parsons's passages quoted above. For example, in discussing cultural expressions of sexual asymmetry, Rosaldo contrasted the Arapesh and the Tchambuli (both studied by Margaret Mead) with the Yoruba and the Iroquois. Among the Arapesh, she said,

> A wife was felt to be a "daughter" to her husband, and at the time of the dominant male ritual . . . she was required to act like an ignorant child. . . . Yoruba women may control a good part of the food supply, accumulate cash and trade in distant and important markets, yet when approaching their husbands, wives must feign ignorance and obedience, kneeling to serve the men as they sit. . . . Even the Iroquois . . . were not ruled by women; there, powerful women might instate and depose their rulers, but Iroquois chiefs were men.[55]

In Rosaldo's view this asymmetry could best be explained by a social-structural opposition between a domestic sphere associated with women and a public sphere associated with men. This had consequences for the establishment of male authority and the association of men with achieved status. In making her point about authority Rosaldo drew parallels between Tuareg and American men in the ways in which they distance themselves from women and hence create authority:

> Tuareg men have adopted the practice of wearing a veil across the nose and mouth. . . . high status men wear their veils more strictly than do slaves or vassals; women have no veils; and to assure his distance, no man is supposed to permit his lover to see his mouth. (In parts of American society, it would seem that men wear their veil of a newspaper in the subways and at breakfast with their wives).[56]

Ortner's argument for universal asymmetry resorted less often to ethnographic example, but she detailed the case of the Crow to support her three criteria for subordination: explicit devaluing of women; implicit statements of inferiority, such as the attribution of defilement through symbolic devices; and social-structural arrangements that excluded women from contact with the highest powers of society.

> In sum, the Crow are probably a fairly typical case. Yes, women have certain powers and rights, in this case some that place them in fairly high positions. Yet ultimately the line is drawn: menstruation is a threat to warfare, one of the most valued institutions of the tribe, one that is central to their self-definition; and the most sacred object of the tribe [the Sun Dance doll] is taboo to the direct sight and touch of women.[57]

Ortner's explanation for women's subordination was rooted in the association of men with culture that is highly valued, while women are universally seen as closer to nature and hence to be devalued.

Parsons's writing echoes clearly in these articles. Not only am I struck by the same generalizing tone and the use of ethnographic example to bolster an argument about human universals, but Rosaldo and Ortner focus on many of the same issues—taboos, constraints, and exclusionary practices—often centering on women's bodies, their sexuality, and their reproductive roles as mothers.

Although the first three articles of *Woman, Culture and Society* generated a great deal of controversy, they did represent a coherent theoretical position. Unlike Elsie Clews Parsons's eclectic ethnological examples, underlain by a gesture toward a human propensity for boundaries, conventions, and constraints, our earlier theories assumed a framework that differentiated cultural, sociological, and psychological levels of explanation. For Rosaldo, Ortner, and Chodorow, woman's role as mother played a central role in the explanation of universal asymmetry. Theoretical dichotomies like domestic/public and nature/culture helped to make sense of women's roles at an analytical level absent from Parsons's work. Those who were influenced by materialism had a clear sense of how to build a framework that suggested an economic explanation for social and cultural phenomena. Here Karen Sacks's reworking of Engels's theory and Rayna Reiter's analysis of the historical creation of domestic and public spheres in France are the best examples.[58] We were the inheritors of the integration of the work of Durkheim, Weber, and Marx into sociology and anthropology—an integration that had not yet shaped the sociology and anthropology of Parsons's day.

Conclusions

The contrast between Parsons's feminism and her ethnology and that of recent feminist anthropologists is partly an intellectual one. Boasian ethnography allowed a pastiche of observation, interrogation, and native accounts. Yet the framework

LOUISE LAMPHERE

into which Parsons put her data was one that gave primacy to the culture element and to processes of diffusion and borrowing. While Mead and Benedict—the younger generation of anthropologists—were differentiating the individual from culture, Parsons remained in the Boasian mold.

The 1960s generation of female anthropologists learned an anthropology that had incorporated sociology—the intellectual heritage of Marx, Weber, and Durkheim. Culture, social structure, and psychology were differentiated levels of analysis in Talcott Parsons's synthesis, which influenced Clifford Geertz, David Schneider, and those who taught social theory at Harvard University. British anthropology, in which social structure (derived from Durkheim) was the organizing tool, was widely read. And the implicit impact of Marx was filtered through Leslie White's work, which shaped the training of graduate students at the University of Michigan. More recently, postmodernism, particularly the work of Michel Foucault, Jacques Lacan, and Jacques Derrida, has taken us to a new stage, one in which French male theorists set the tone for a synthesis of cultural, social, and political-economy approaches.

But feminist anthropology in the 1970s was also shaped by social movements, just as Parsons's views had been shaped by progressive reform, feminism, and pacifism in the teens. Women did make inroads into the major universities as graduate students and had an impact on the way in which the social sciences dealt with some issues. However, suffrage and feminist progressive reform were peripheral to the academy, especially during the pre–World War I years. Feminist debates over the proper education of women never reformed the curriculum or focused on the need for more research on women per se. As I have emphasized, women themselves did not have a secure place in coeducational institutions, and they were not granted tenured professorships in the elite universities.

In contrast, the 1960s brought a refeminization of anthropology graduate programs, and the number of young female Ph.D.'s on the job market had increased by the early 1970s. We were in a better position to take jobs at elite institutions, though knocking down these barriers has been a struggle, as I know from my own Title VII suit against Brown University.

Equally, if not more important, are the differences between World War I and the Vietnam War in shaping feminist anthropology. The antiwar movement during World War I was broken through suppression of the Industrial Workers of the World, the Communist scare, and restrictions on immigration. The radicals who contributed to *The Masses* retired to private life and abandoned social-reform movements in the 1920s. Finally, the United States won World War I, contributing to a postwar era very different from the one that followed the Vietnam War. Vietnam had relatively little popular support and spawned a radical student movement which grew at the same time as participation in the minority-rights, feminist, and gay- and lesbian-rights movements increased. These movements had important support from students and some academics, who pushed to reform curricula to include material on these disenfranchised groups.

Despite the rightward movement of the United States in the 1980s, universities, much to dismay of the right wing, have remained havens for diverse scholarship. Even though students have turned to computer sciences, accounting, and engineering in many schools, women's studies and ethnic studies have survived, now with the support of sympathetic minority and female administrators.

These differences, both intellectual and political, have allowed feminist anthropology to establish a more central position within anthropology in general, as the Gender and Curriculum Project and the growing Association for Feminist Anthropology as a section within the American Anthropological Association indicate.[59] The outpouring of scholarship on women will continue to bring feminism to the center of anthropology in a way in which Elsie Clews Parsons—given the intellectual and political constraints of her time—could not. This would reclaim the feminist heritage of Elsie Clews Parsons for anthropology—a fitting task for the next few decades of scholarship and research.

Notes

This is a revised version of the 1989 AES Distinguished Lecture (originally published in the *American Ethnologist* 16 [1989]: 518–33). I would like to thank Henry Rutz, organizer of the 1989 AES Meetings, held in Santa Fe April 5–9, and the AES Board for inviting me to speak. In making the revisions for this book, I have taken advantage of a wealth of new scholarship on Parsons by Barbara Babcock, Rosemary Levy Zumwalt, and Desley Deacon. I have been particularly influenced by Barbara Babcock's introduction to *Pueblo Mothers and Children,* which explores the feminist aspects of Parsons's work during the 1920s in the Southwest and argues that throughout Parsons's life there was an interest in understanding "the relation between social formations and *female* subjectivity—in particular the cultural construction of gender and sexuality and reproduction, the sexual division of labor and the subjugation of women" (Introduction to *Pueblo Mothers and Children: Essays by Elsie Clews Parsons, 1915–1924* [Santa Fe, N.M.: Ancient City Press, 1991], 18). I would also like to thank my colleague Marta Weigle for her helpful comments on an early draft of this paper.

1. Nancy Cott, *The Grounding of Modern Feminism* (New Haven, Conn.: Yale University Press, 1987).

2. Elsie Clews Parsons, *Pueblo Indian Religion,* 2 vols. (Chicago: University of Chicago Publications in Anthropology, 1939).

3. Michelle Zimbalist Rosaldo and Louise Lamphere, eds., *Woman, Culture and Society* (Stanford: Stanford University Press, 1974).

4. Louis A. Hieb, "Elsie Clews Parsons in the Southwest," in *Hidden Scholars: Women Anthropologists and the Native American Southwest,* ed. Nancy J. Parezo (Albuquerque: University of New Mexico Press, 1993), 63–75; Barbara A. Babcock and Nancy J. Parezo, *Daughters of the Desert: Women Anthropologists and the Native American Southwest, 1880–1980* (Albuquerque: University of New Mexico Press, 1988).

5. Louise Lamphere, "Gladys Reichard among the Navajo," in *Hidden Scholars,* 157–88.

6. Barbara A. Babcock, "Not Yet Classified, Perhaps Unclassifiable: Elsie Clews Parsons, Feminist/Anthropologist" (Paper presented at the American Anthropological Association Meeting, Phoenix, Ariz., November 1988), and "Elsie Clews Parsons and the Pueblo Construction of Gender," in *Pueblo Mothers and Children,* 1–23.

7. Peter Hare, *A Woman's Quest for Science: Portrait of Anthropologist Elsie Clews Parsons* (Buffalo, N.Y.: Prometheus Books, 1985), 27.

8. Elsie Clews Parsons, *The Family* (New York: G. P. Putnam's Sons, 1906).

9. Hare, *A Woman's Quest for Science*, 33–34.

10. Ibid., 14.

11. Ibid., 135.

12. Ibid.

13. Cott, *Grounding of Modern Feminism*, 35.

14. Ibid., 37.

15. Rosalind Rosenberg, *Beyond Separate Spheres: Intellectual Roots of Modern Feminism* (New Haven, Conn.: Yale University Press, 1982), 166.

16. Ibid., 168.

17. Desley Deacon, "The Republic of Spirit: Fieldwork in Elsie Clews Parsons's Turn to Anthropology," *Frontiers* 12, no. 3 (1991): 24.

18. Rosemary Levy Zumwalt, *Wealth and Rebellion: Elsie Clews Parsons, Anthropologist and Folklorist* (Urbana and Chicago: University of Illinois Press, 1992), 172.

19. Alfred Kroeber, "Elsie Clews Parsons," *American Anthropologist* 45 (1943): 253.

20. Ibid.

21. Elsie Clews Parsons, "Note on Navajo War Dance," *American Anthropologist* 21 (1919): 465–67.

22. Zumwalt, *Wealth and Rebellion*, 176–79, 236–38.

23. Elsie Clews Parsons, "A Few Zuni Death Beliefs and Practices," *American Anthropologist* 18 (1916): 245–56; "The Zuñi A'Doshlei and Suuke," *American Anthropologist* 18 (1916): 338–47; "The Zuñi La'mana," *American Anthropologist* 18 (1916): 521–28; "Mothers and Children at Laguna," *Man* 19 (1919): 34–38; and "Mothers and Children at Zuñi," *Man* 19 (1919): 168–73.

24. Rosenberg, *Beyond Separate Spheres*, 168.

25. Judy Schwarz, *Radical Feminists of Heterodoxy* (Lebanon, N.H.: New Victoria Publishers, 1982).

26. Florence Guy Woolston, "Marriage Customs and Taboo among the Early Heterodities," *Scientific Monthly*, November 1919.

27. Rosenberg, *Beyond Separate Spheres*, 170–71.

28. Elsie Clews Parsons, *The Old-Fashioned Woman: Primitive Fancies about the Sex* (New York: G. P. Putnam's Sons, 1913); *Religious Chastity: An Ethnological Study* (New York: Macauley, 1913); *Fear and Conventionality* (New York: G. P. Putnam's Sons, 1914); *Social Freedom: A Study of the Conflicts between Social Classifications and Personality* (New York: G. P. Putnam's Sons, 1916); *Social Rule: A Study of the Will to Power* (New York: G. P. Putnam's Sons, 1916).

29. Parsons, *The Old-Fashioned Woman*, 91–92.

30. Ibid., 97.

31. Ibid., 192–202, 275, 296–97.

32. Barbara Babcock argues that Parsons's writing in this period constitutes a feminist cultural critique and is "neither as evolutionary nor as universalizing as many of her critics and biographers have implied. Her early feminist sociology texts bear rereading not only for their challenge to the idea of cultural evolution and insistence on cultural relativism but also for her repeated questioning of 'the social need for women's subordination'" (Babcock, "Elsie Clews Parsons," 19).

33. Elsie Clews Parsons, "Marriage: A New Life," *Masses* 8 (September 1916): 27.

34. Parsons, *Fear and Conventionality,* 119–20.

35. Parsons, *Social Freedom,* 36.

36. Rosenberg, *Beyond Separate Spheres,* 176.

37. Bronislaw Malinowski, *Argonauts of the Western Pacific* (Prospect Heights, Ill.: Waveland Press, 1984, originally published 1921); Margaret Mead, *Coming of Age in Samoa* (New York: Morrow, 1928).

38. Although Benedict took her first anthropology course from Parsons at the New School in 1919, Margaret M. Caffrey (*Ruth Benedict: Stranger in This Land* [Austin: University of Texas Press, 1989], 96) suggests that Parsons's inductive approach to anthropology was different from the deductive thinking that came much more naturally to Benedict. She was Parsons's research assistant for several years during the 1920s, working on a concordance of Southwest mythology, but Caffrey (pp. 156, 226–27) concluded that although Parsons was a supporter of Benedict, she was not a close personal friend, not someone who admired and supported Benedict's work on the Pueblos as it developed during the 1920s and 1930s.

39. Zumwalt, *Wealth and Rebellion,* 233–40.

40. Hieb, "Elsie Clews Parsons," 9–13.

41. Zumwalt, *Wealth and Rebellion,* 240–43.

42. Parsons, "Mothers and Children at Laguna."

43. Elsie Clews Parsons, "Hopi Mothers and Children," *Man* 21 (1921): 98–104.

44. Parsons, "Mothers and Children at Zuñi"; and "Tewa Kin, Clan, and Moiety," *American Anthropologist* 26 (1924): 333–39.

45. Parsons, "Tewa Kin, Clan, and Moiety"; "The Religion of the Pueblo Indians," *Proceedings, Twenty-First International Congress of Americanists,* 1925.

46. Parsons, "Tewa Kin, Clan, and Moiety," 339; and "Religion of the Pueblo Indians," 140.

47. Fred Eggan, *The Social Organization of the Western Pueblos* (Chicago: University of Chicago Press, 1950).

48. Elsie Clews Parsons, *Mitla, Town of the Souls and Other Zapoteco-Speaking Pueblos of Oaxaca, Mexico* (Chicago: University of Chicago Press, 1936), 74–79.

49. Ibid., 463.

50. Gladys Reichard, *Spider Woman: A Story of Navajo Weavers and Chanters* (New York: MacMillan, 1934) and *Dezba: Woman of the Desert* (New York: J. J. Augustin, 1938); Ruth M. Underhill, *Papago Woman* (American Anthropological Association Memoir 46; New York: Holt, Rinehart and Winston, 1936).

51. Elsie Clews Parsons, ed., *Hopi Journal of Alexander M. Stephen* (Columbia University Contributions in Anthropology 23; New York: Columbia University Press, 1936).

52. James Clifford, *The Predicament of Culture: Twentieth-Century Ethnography, Literature, and Art* (Cambridge, Mass.: Harvard University Press, 1988), 39.

53. Babcock, "Elsie Clews Parsons," 16.

54. Rosenberg, *Beyond Separate Spheres;* Judith Friedlander, "Elsie Clews Parsons," in *Women Anthropologists: A Biographical Dictionary,* ed. Ute Gacs, Aisha Khan, Jerrie McIntyre, and Ruth Weinberg (Westport, Conn.: Greenwood Press, 1988), 282–90; Babcock, "Not Yet Classified" and "Elsie Clews Parsons"; Deacon, "Republic of Spirit"; Zumwalt, *Wealth and Rebellion.*

55. Michelle Zimbalist Rosaldo, "Woman, Culture, and Society: A Theoretical Overview," in *Woman, Culture and Society,* 19–20.

56. Ibid., 27.

57. Sherry Ortner, "Is Female to Male as Nature Is to Culture?" in *Woman, Culture and Society,* 70.

58. Karen Brodkin Sacks, "Engels Revisited: Women, the Organization of Production and Private Property," in *Woman, Culture and Society,* 207–22; Rayna Reiter, "Women and Men in the South of France," in *Toward an Anthropology of Women,* ed. Rayna Reiter (New York: Monthly Review Press, 1975), 252–82.

59. Sandra Morgen, ed., *Gender and Anthropology: Critical Reviews for Research and Teaching* (Washington, D.C.: American Anthropological Association, 1989).

5

"Not in the Absolute Singular": Rereading Ruth Benedict

Barbara A. Babcock

We accept without any ado the equivalence of human nature and of our own cultural standards. But many primitives have a different experience. They have seen their religion go down before the white man's. Their economic system, their marriage prohibitions. They have laid down the one and taken up the other, and are quite clear and sophisticated about variant arrangements of human life. If they do talk about human nature, they do it in plurals, not in the absolute singular *(my emphasis).*

— RUTH BENEDICT,
"The Science of Custom," 1929

POET, FEMINIST, and anthropologist, Ruth Benedict (1887–1948) began her study of custom by steeping herself "in the lives of restless and highly enslaved women of past generations."[1] "Slowly and painfully, over many years of frequent depression and perplexity, [she] found a path away from the traditional set of social expectations for women to her own distinctive identity and creativity."[2] She was thirty-two years old when she discovered anthropology and began one of the profession's most distinguished careers, while often describing herself as "not having the strength of mind not to need a career."[3] Within fifteen years she had written the most influential book in twentieth-century anthropology, *Patterns*

Ruth Fulton Benedict in her Columbia University office, ca. 1940. (Photograph by Helen Codere; courtesy of Special Collections, Vassar College Libraries)

of Culture, and had been starred as a "leading scientist" in *American Men of Science.*

Like her friend and colleague Edward Sapir, Benedict found in cultural anthropology "the healthiest of all skepticisms." Adamantly resisting "the absolute singular," Benedict developed an interpretive anthropological practice that has been aptly described as "one great effort in behalf of the idea of cultural relativity."[4] In "The Science of Custom" essay, from which I have taken not only the title but the epigraph and the conclusion of my essay, Benedict outlines the "epistemology of the oppressed" and the attendant "double-voiced discourse" that all of her anthropology embodies.[5] Benedict's distinctive contribution to "the science of man" anticipates many of today's postmodern concerns with anthropology and colonialism, with cultural texts, with the rhetoric of ethnography and the intersection of anthropology and the humanities, with anthropology as cultural critique, and with feminism and anthropology.

As a poet and a woman as well as an anthropologist, Benedict was committed to talking about human nature "in plurals," to seeing discourse and knowledge as "situated," as "perspectivist."[6] Given not only her sensitivity to the complexity, mediatedness, and multideterminancies of cultures, of texts, and of the interpretation thereof, but also her sense of style, Benedict always wrote with what Victor Barnouw calls "a lyrical awareness of balance and phrase which went far above and beyond the normal call of academic duty."[7] The lyricism as well as the irony of her prose also went very much against the contemporary conventions of anthropological discourse, leading her critics to dismiss her work as poetic and popular, and even her admirers to foreground her as "a tall and slender Platonic ideal of a poetess" rather than as a significant social scientist.[8] While Benedict's irony makes her our contemporary and allies her to feminists such as Donna Haraway, its liability is that it enables misreading. Nonetheless, as I reread not only Benedict but misreadings of her, I do not doubt that she would assert with Haraway that "single vision produces worse illusions than double vision or many-headed monsters."[9]

§

I wanted so desperately to know how other women had saved their souls alive.

— RUTH BENEDICT,

quoted in Margaret Mead, *An Anthropologist at Work*, 1973

Ruth Benedict's life was characterized by a failure to fit into roles appropriate to her sex and her time. As she herself described, and as her biographers, Margaret Mead, Judith Schachter Modell, and Margaret M. Caffrey, have amply documented, hers was a traumatic, unhappy childhood. Her father, a physician, died when she was two years old, and her mother, subject to fits of weeping and paroxysms of grief, supported the family by teaching. In contrast to her younger sister, Margery, Ruth disliked domestic duties in the Shattuck household in upstate New York and escaped as often as she could with her grandfather to the barn and the fields and into a world of her own imagining. If she did not want to hear her mother, at times she literally could not, for a childhood attack of measles left her partially deaf and exacerbated her sense of alienation.

Despite the difficulties of her deafness, Benedict excelled in school and found in reading and writing a legitimate escape from family relationships and duties. She received a scholarship to Vassar College, where she studied English literature. By the time she graduated—Phi Beta Kappa—in 1909, she had already published poetry and prize-winning critical essays on such subjects as "Literature and Democracy" and "The Racial Traits of Shakespeare's Heroes." In the fall of 1910 she joined two Vassar classmates for a year abroad. Although the trip exceeded her expectations, she returned to an empty and disappointing job as a caseworker for the Charity Organization Society in Buffalo and once again had to battle the "blue devils" of depression. In 1911 Ruth and her mother moved to Pasadena, California, to join Margery and her family. Still in search of meaningful work, Ruth took a teaching job at the Westlake School for Girls.

Living in these circumstances and working with "old maids" who shared their experiences and regrets with her prompted some gloomy reflections on the role and fate of women in our society. As Margaret Caffrey points out, "She had discovered, within three years of leaving college, the limited possibilities open to women. The two most favored areas for women, teaching and social work, were female ghettos,

BARBARA A. BABCOCK

limited in scope, salary, and status. She could not reconcile herself to a life in either area."[10] In October 1912 Benedict wrote in her journal: "I've just come through a year in which I have not dared to think . . . not dared to be honest, not even with myself." But, as the following remarks in her journal suggest, she was not only thoughtful but brutally honest:

> So much of the trouble is because I am a woman. To me it seems a very terrible thing to be a woman. There is one crown which perhaps is worth it all — a great love, a quiet home, and children. . . . A great love is given to very few. Perhaps this make-shift time filler of a job is our life work after all. It is all so cruelly wasteful. There are so few ways in which we can compete with men — surely not in teaching or in social work. If we are not to have the chance to fulfill our one potentiality — the power of loving — why were we not born men? At least we could have had an occupation then.[11]

In June 1914, thinking she had found her "great love," she married Stanley Benedict, a research chemist at Cornell Medical College, and settled into the life of a housewife in suburban New York City. In November of that year, after noting how happy, satisfying, and transforming her relationship with Stanley was, she outlined her plans for the winter. She hoped to study Shakespeare and Goethe, but her "pet scheme" was "to steep myself in the lives of restless and highly enslaved women of past generations and write a series of biographical papers from the standpoint of the 'new woman.' My conclusion so far as I see it now is that there is nothing 'new' about the whole thing . . . that the restlessness and groping are inherent in the nature of women."[12] The hoped-for children did not come, and Ruth was increasingly preoccupied with her "own ambitions" and her "sense of futility." "Surely," she wrote in December 1915, "the world has need of my vision as well as of charity committees."[13]

Ruth dealt with her unhappy marriage as she had with her childhood, by writing: "Expression is the only justification of life that I can feel without prodding. The greatest relief I know is to have put something in words."[14] In addition to her journal, she poured her frustrations and her passions into poems, which she later published under the pseudonym Anne Singleton. And, believing that "the feminist movement needs heroines," Benedict devoted much of her writing in this period of her life to "New Women of Three Centuries," her "empirical biography" of three different lives in three different times and places: Mary Wollstonecraft, Margaret Fuller, and Olive Schreiner. As Modell remarked, "One cannot read the drafts of 'Mary Wollstonecraft' without realizing the extent to which the eighteenth-century woman's life became a model and a challenge for Ruth's life . . . that the attraction of her subject's 'lavish expense of spirit' threatened her aimed-for equilibrium . . . [and that she] did not wholly anticipate the quandary she got into by sharing, even vicariously, these 'enacted principles.'"[15]

The more involved she became with Mary's "superb ego," the more her feminism became a "passionate attitude" and, as she wrote in 1916, "more and more I realize I want publication."[16] After completing a draft of the Wollstonecraft essay, Benedict sent it and a prospectus for the book, now titled "Adventures in Woman-hood," to Houghton Mifflin. As Modell observed, "She needed the recognition represented by publisher approval to bolster her sense of worth and possibly to 'prove' her case to Stanley, . . . [who] doubted her ability to stick to the project." When Houghton Mifflin rejected the essay, "she jammed drafts, notes, and sketches into a carton . . . [and] sent away for the course catalog from the recently established New School for Social Research."[17]

§

I haven't strength of mind not to need a career.

— RUTH BENEDICT,
quoted in Margaret Mead, *An Anthropologist at Work*, 1973

In the fall of 1919 Benedict enrolled in a course very much related to her personal concerns: "Sex in Ethnology," which consisted of "surveys of a number of societies presenting a distinctive distribution of functions between the sexes, and of topical analysis of the division of labor between men and women."[18] The course was taught by Elsie Clews Parsons, wealthy feminist sociologist turned ethnographer, who had been instrumental in founding the New School. This nonconformist woman believed not only that the mind seeks escape from classification as it matures but that a "maturing culture struggles against its categories";[19] she also asserted that "the more thoroughly a woman is classified the more easily is she controlled. . . . The new woman is the woman not yet classified, perhaps not classifiable."[20] In this "new woman" Benedict found a kindred spirit and a courageous role model who "fearlessly rejected all conventions that constrained the free development of personality."[21]

Parsons had turned to ethnography after a trip to the Southwest in 1910 and had come to believe that empirical anthropology, with "its techniques for studying the ways in which self-expression is checked by social forces," was a more effective way of promoting her convictions than was direct propaganda.[22] Of Benedict, as of Parsons, it could be said that "she studied the science of society the better to fight back against society."[23] Without question, Parsons's preoccupation with the relationship between individual creativity and sociocultural constraints was to inform all of Benedict's anthropology. If their feminist motivations were similar, their intellectual styles and their anthropological methods were very different. Parsons was the more inductive, given to careful ethnographic description and compendia of empirical data. Benedict was deductive in her approach and subsequently trafficked less in description than in a "distinctive sort of redescription: the sort that startles."[24]

During the next two years Benedict took several more courses at the New School with the brilliant and erratic Alexander Goldenweiser. She was deeply influenced by this generous and enthusiastic teacher, who "could smell a totalitarian under any disguise" and who was "eager to build bridges over positions separated by an

BARBARA A. BABCOCK

infinite abyss."[25] "The most philosophical of anthropologists," Goldenweiser was very much concerned with psychological and psychoanalytical questions relevant to the study of culture and was responsible for "giving Benedict an early awareness of the possibility of psychological patterning at the base of culture."[26] After two and a half years, Parsons and Goldenweiser decided that Benedict should work toward a Ph.D. in anthropology, and Parsons went uptown to Columbia University to recommend her to Franz Boas. "Quickly sensing the vigorously imaginative mind veiled by her painfully shy demeanor, Boas waived credit requirements," and, after just three semesters, Benedict received her Ph.D. in 1923.[27] Her dissertation, "The Concept of the Guardian Spirit in North America," was a library study that not only reflected Boas's interest in the diffusion of culture traits but also expressed Benedict's interest in the power of religious awe and in the "patterns" into which the vision-complex was "formalized" in a given culture.[28] Anticipating Lévi-Strauss's concept of *bricolage,* she concluded this study with the statement that "It is, so far as we can see, an ultimate fact of human nature that man builds up his culture out of disparate elements, combining and recombining them; and until we have abandoned the superstition that the result is an organism functionally interrelated, we shall be unable to see our cultural life objectively, or to control its manifestations."[29] Many years later, in one of several obituary essays she wrote for Boas, she argued that the sort of diffusion study he had encouraged "was not an end in itself nor did it by itself furnish the key to the understanding of culture."[30]

Between this man who was stimulated to action "because the conditions of our culture ran counter to my ideals" and whose whole outlook on social life was determined by the question "How can we recognize the shackles that tradition has laid upon us? For when we recognize them, we are also able to break them,"[31] and the quiet, questing woman who admired his energy, his principles, and his stern devotion to his discipline, there developed "a mutual dependency and intellectual exchange that lasted until his death in 1942."[32] As a German Jew, Boas experienced racism firsthand; as an anthropologist, he believed that "it is pertinent to ask whether any group has a rational basis for a claim to rights not accorded to others";[33] as professor and chairman of anthropology at Columbia, he was especially "hospitable" to women, remarking in 1920 that "all my best students are women."[34] Presumably he regarded Benedict as the best of the best, for she stayed on at Columbia, first as a teaching assistant, then as a lecturer on a series of one-year appointments after receiving her Ph.D. Although she became "indispensable" to Boas, he did not give her the position of teaching his Barnard College class when he gave it up in 1923. He had persuaded the Barnard administration to replace him with a full-time instructor, and since Gladys Reichard, another favorite student, was thirty years old and single, he felt she needed the job more. Benedict was sorely disappointed, and this was no doubt one of the several factors that contributed to strained and distant relations between these two women over the next twenty-five years. Boas did, however, conspire with Elsie Clews Parsons to provide funding for Benedict, especially after her application to the National Research Council was turned down because of her age, despite Parsons's intervention. In their experience, Frank Lillie wrote, "a person who has not already become established in University work [by age thirty-five] is not very promising material for development." [35]

Whether teaching at Columbia or working on a concordance of Southwest mythology and folklore funded by Elsie Clews Parsons, Benedict lived in a New York City apartment and commuted on weekends to Bedford Hills to see Stanley and sustain a disintegrating marriage. Although she had realized in 1920 that "the more I control myself to his requirements, the greater violence I shall do my own— kill them in the end," she did not separate from Stanley completely until 1930. [36] Boas finally recognized that Benedict needed a "real" job to support herself, and he secured her appointment as an assistant professor in 1931. It was, as Edward Sapir wrote in congratulating her, "a modest and criminally belated acknowledgment of [her] services." [37]

In 1922 Benedict had made the acquaintance of two individuals with whom she developed deep and mutually influential relationships. One was linguist and anthropologist Edward Sapir, whose letter to her praising and commenting at length on her dissertation initiated a lively and voluminous correspondence in which they shared their interests in anthropology, psychology, and poetry and a friendship that lasted until his death in 1939. The other was Margaret Mead, a student in Boas's Barnard anthropology course, who was to become her colleague, confidante, lover, and literary executor. Mead also shared and stimulated Benedict's interests in poetry and psychology, but, unlike Sapir, she took from more than she gave to the brilliant yet unassuming woman who had encouraged her to study anthropology and had interceded with Boas to allow her to go to Samoa.

Because of her generosity of spirit and her own search for meaning as a woman, Benedict mediated between many Columbia students and "Papa Franz," edited and rewrote countless dissertations, and in later years, if neither Boas nor Parsons could come up with funds for research and publication, gave them "no-strings-attached" grants out of her own pocket. As Ruth Underhill remarked in an interview shortly before she died, "Boas and Benedict opened a door through which a light shined on me." She was not alone in this experience: during the years (1921–1940) when Benedict was most active in the Columbia department, nineteen women and twenty men received Ph.D.'s.

Benedict preferred dealing with texts and other scholars' data, which Mead referred to as her "fondness for scrappy ethnography," for her deafness made fieldwork difficult. Nonetheless, because of the fetishism of fieldwork in anthropology and because of her precarious professional position at Columbia, she pragmatically enacted this rite of passage. [38] Her first fieldwork, in 1922 under Alfred Kroeber's guidance, was with the Serrano, Southern California Shoshoneans. She never returned to these people but later published "A Brief Sketch of Serrano Culture" and the moving "Cups of Clay" vignette in chapter 2 of *Patterns of Culture*.

In 1923 she accepted a Southwest Society fellowship to collect material for Parsons's concordance of Pueblo myths and folktales, and more than a year later she finally followed Boas, Parsons, Kroeber, and Goldfrank to the Southwest. "Still relatively whole and functioning, sharply differentiated in psychological tone from its neighbors in the same environment, Zuni culture seems to have had a great attraction for Benedict—as indeed Pueblo culture in general had for a number of alienated intellectuals."[39] Benedict was profoundly moved by the Zuni landscape as well as the culture. She wrote to Mead in 1925 that she had "discovered in myself a great fondness for this place,"[40] and, as she prepared to leave several weeks later: "This is the last morning in Zuni. . . . Ruth Bunzel came by Friday's mail wagon. Yesterday we went up under the sacred mesa along stunning trails where the great wall towers above you always in new magnificence. . . . When I'm God I'm going to build my city there."[41]

§

Peoples' folk tales are their autobiography.

— RUTH BENEDICT,
Encyclopedia of the Social Sciences, 1931

Although hampered by her deafness and forced to work through interpreters, Benedict collected hundreds of pages of myths and tales at Zuni in 1924 and 1925 and at Cochiti in 1925, subsequently published as *Tales of the Cochiti Indians* and *Zuni Mythology*. Many years later one of her Zuni interpreters recalled that she "spoke gently," was "polite" and "generous," and "generally worked with old men."[42] Her principal informant was Nick Tumaka, whom Kroeber described as "the outstanding intellectual of Zuni."[43] Tumaka appeared in Benedict's *Patterns of Culture* as one of the "most striking individuals" and in *Zuni Mythology* as "Informant 7," "a person of great ability, of commanding presence, and with a great personal need for achieving eminence, which he sought primarily in the medicine societies."[44]

When she left Zuni to work at Cochiti Pueblo in the summer of 1925, Benedict planned to stay in Peña Blanca, a nearby Hispanic village, and to have informants come to work with her there. Both Boas and Parsons had advised her "not to set foot in Cochiti" if she wanted to work intensively with informants. Within days, however, she was living in the pueblo and writing to Mead, "I never do get this sense of the spiked dangerous fence that Elsie, and Dr. Boas in this case, make so much of."[45] Probably not, because the Cochitis that I know recall the same gentle, generous lady that the Zuni do, and because since the 1880s, when Adolph Bandelier was thrown out of Santo Domingo and "welcomed with open arms at Cochiti," this pueblo has been more hospitable to outsiders than have other Rio Grande Keres villages. Here, too, her favorite "old man" was the outstanding intellectual, widely referred to in the village as "mucho sabio." Described both in letters to Mead and in the introduction to *Tales of the Cochiti Indians* as "Informant 4," this "great old character" was Santiago Quintana, the grandfather of Cochiti potter Helen Cordero and the storyteller whom she has represented in her world famous clay figures. He was very much concerned that those who wrote about Cochiti "got the old ways right," and he was the valued friend and informant of several generations of anthropologists and interpreters of Cochiti life: Bandelier, Starr, Saunders, Curtis, Parsons, and finally Benedict. His son, Pablo, and daughter-in-law, Caroline, were Esther Goldfrank's hosts and helpers; his granddaughter, Helen, has changed my life by sharing her art and experience with me.

Both *Cochiti Tales* and *Zuni Mythology* are careful, competent collections arranged in the scholarly fashion of the day into Anglo folktale categories—Hero Tales, Animal Tales, and so forth—and identifying narrators only by numbers. One can presume, however, that had Benedict not been deaf and had she been able to do more fieldwork, very different texts, presentations, and interpretations would have resulted. There is much in the introductions to these collections and in her entries on "Folklore" and "Myth" in the *Encyclopedia of the Social Sciences* that bears rereading and is quite relevant to contemporary folk-narrative scholarship and to analysis of cultural texts.[46] In his 1937 review of *Zuni Mythology,* Stith Thompson urged all folklorists and anthropologists to read Benedict's introduction, and they should be so urged today. Her statements that "peoples' folk tales are . . . their autobiography and the clearest mirror of their life," that myths are "a native comment on native life," that novelistic tales are "fictionalized versions of native life," and that folklore "tends to crystallize and perpetuate the forms of culture that it has made articulate"[47] sound very like much more recent reflexive formulations of cultural texts such as cockfights as "stor[ies] that [the Balinese] tell themselves about themselves,"[48] formulations in which, except for those of James Boon, Benedict's name is noticeably absent. Yet it was she who wrote in a 1924 research proposal to study Pueblo mythology: "The advantage of mythological material over any other, for the characterization of tribal life, consists in the fact that here alone we have these things recorded wholly *as they themselves figure them to themselves.*"[49]

Given the assumptions and practices of folklore scholarship in the 1930s, which unfortunately persisted long afterward, Benedict's introduction to *Zuni Mythology* is particularly important in several respects: in emphasizing the value of intensive studies of the narratives of a single culture rather than a comparison of disparate elements from several cultures and a study of incident distribution; in relating narrative themes to cultural values and behavior; in debunking folklorists' myth of "communal authorship" and pointing out that "what is communal about the process is the social acceptance by which the trait becomes a part of the teaching handed down to the next generation"; in calling attention to individual creativity "within traditional limits" and pointing out "the possibility of the study of the native narrator, that is, the literary materials which he has at his disposal and his handling of them"; in describing sex differences in both the tales and the telling; and in foregrounding the aesthetic and literary qualities of such "primitive" narratives—"mythology is a highly developed and serious art in Zuni."[50] Here, as in "Folklore," Benedict modified Boas's culture-reflection view not only by regarding folk tales themselves as a "living, functioning" cultural trait but also by emphasizing the importance of studying "local literary conventions"—"folklore is literature and like any art it has traditional regional stylistic forms which may be studied like any other art form." [51] Perhaps most importantly, she eloquently evoked the power of the human imagination to make, remake, and reflect upon reality, anticipating Lévi-Strauss by several decades. Instead of treating tales as "survivals," as primitive expressions with no aesthetic or awareness thereof on the part of their tellers, Benedict argued that "man in all his mythologies has expressed his discomfort at a mechanistic universe. . . . He has recast the universe into human terms. The world man actually lives in . . . always bulks very small in relation to the world he makes for himself." [52]

These same values and concerns informed Benedict's editorship of the *Journal of American Folklore*. During her fifteen years (1925–1940) as editor she did much to professionalize the field of folklore and to move it beyond motif collections and folk-narrative distributions. In contrast to Stith Thompson, she was an early supporter of "applied folklore," encouraging folk festivals and the work of the Federal Writers' Project. In the 1920s, at Elsie Clews Parsons's behest, Benedict was also involved not only with collecting and editing tales but also with compiling a concordance to Southwest Indian mythology. Two Columbia students, Gene Weltfish and Erna Gunther, assisted on this project. Benedict found this work boring and tedious, so she turned the project over to Gunther in 1926.

If Mead was the more powerful and intimate influence in Benedict's life and work, Sapir was the much more profound and intellectual one. Shortly after she returned from the Southwest in 1925, he chastised her for not "sending verses" and for spending more time on Zuni myths than on her poetry. A year later he sent her a poem entitled "Zuni," in which he urged her to "keep the flowing of [her] spirit in many branching ways / Through the dry glitter of the desert sea and the sharpness of the mesa." [53] Such communications not only kept "Anne Singleton" writing poetry but also heightened Ruth Benedict's awareness of the literary qualities of the Zuni materials. Sapir was mistaken, however, in his assertion that her "poems [were] infinitely more important than anything, no matter how brilliant, you are fated to contribute to anthropology." [54] As Benedict herself realized when Harcourt turned down her book of poems in 1928, "They aren't good enough to give one's life to." [55]

In the introduction to *Zuni Mythology*, Sapir's influence is also evident in Benedict's exploration of the mechanisms of compensation and displacement that operated in the translation of inhibited materials into socially acceptable terms and images to explain striking divergences between some stories and Zuni values and behavior. From his very first letter to Benedict in 1922 concerning her dissertation, Sapir had urged her to look for psychological patterns underlying the differences in cultures and had lamented the gulf between anthropologists who studied culture as a set of institutions without reference to the individual and psychologists who analyzed the mental processes of individuals without reference to the cultural context in which they occurred.

§

A culture, like an individual, is a more or less consistent pattern of thought and action.

— RUTH BENEDICT,
Patterns of Culture, 1934

The year 1927 is frequently singled out as the theoretical beginning of culture and personality studies in anthropology. Sapir's pioneer paper "The Unconscious Patterning of Behavior in Society," in which he argued that "all cultural behavior is patterned" and that "it is futile to classify human acts as such as having an inherently individual or social significance," set the frame of reference for later work in this area.[56] This essay also established the linguistic model for culture and personality studies that David Aberle, in particular, was later to criticize.

In September 1928 Benedict presented a paper, "Psychological Types in the Cultures of the Southwest," which not only manifests Sapir's influence but also was clearly the product of ten years of study with Parsons, Goldenweiser, Boas, and Kroeber. Because of Boas's openly expressed distaste for psychoanalysis, "it has never been sufficiently realized how consistently throughout his life [he] defined the task of ethnology as the study of 'man's mental life,' of 'fundamental psychic attitudes of cultural groups,' and of man's 'subjective worlds.'"[57] To cite two examples that surely influenced Benedict's approach to culture and personality and to patterns of culture, in 1888 Boas argued that "the first aim of ethnological inquiry must be critical analysis of the characteristics of each people,"[58] and in 1928 he asserted that "wherever there is a strong, dominant trend of mind that pervades the whole cultural life it may persist over long periods and survive changes in mode of life."[59] Four years later, in "Configurations of Culture in North America," Benedict was to write: "Such configurations of culture, built around certain selected human traits and working toward the obliteration of others, are of first-rate importance in the understanding of culture.... Cultural configurations stand to the understanding of group behavior in the relation that personality types stand to the understanding of individual behavior."[60]

In assessing the influence of psychiatry on anthropology and the role played by Sapir and Benedict, Clyde Kluckhohn observed of "Psychological Types" and "Configurations of Culture" that "every page is colored by an attitude that can only be called 'psychiatric' and which must be traced eventually from the influence of psychiatry."[61] If Benedict was influenced by psychology and psychoanalysis, psychoanalysis was also influenced by her anthropology. For example, in *The Neurotic Personality of Our Time,* Karen Horney "emphasized cultural conditions at the expense of the orthodox (Freudian) libidinal drives and infantile experiences" and was openly indebted to Benedict's relativism and anti-essentialism.[62]

BARBARA A. BABCOCK

One of the historical factors that contributed to the sudden interdisciplinary growth and influence of culture and personality studies was the arrival from Nazi Europe of refugees with Freudian and Gestalt perspectives. In the 1930s eminent intellectuals such as Karen Horney, Erich Fromm, Franz Alexander, and Erik Erikson participated along with Benedict in Abram Kardiner's seminars, first at the New York Psychoanalytic Institute and then at Columbia, as a joint effort with Ralph Linton. Benedict and Horney spent a great deal of time together during the summer of 1935, and that fall Horney taught her first course, "Culture and Neurosis," at the New School for Social Research. That course and her subsequent essay of the same title were, like Benedict's "Anthropology and the Abnormal," concerned with the extent to which neuroses were "moulded by cultural processes" and normal-abnormal categories were "culturally determined." [63]

Given Benedict's history and temperament, it should come as no surprise that she became as preoccupied as she did with understanding and writing about the deviant personality and the relativity of the definitions of normal and abnormal. In a contemporaneous essay, "The Emergence of the Concept of Personality in the Study of Cultures," Sapir reflexively suggested that "the discovery of the world of personality is apparently dependent upon the ability of the individual to become aware of and to attach value to his resistance to authority" and that "temperamental radicals tend to be impatient with a purely cultural analysis of human behavior." [64] In that same essay he asserted that "culture is not something given but something to be gradually and gropingly discovered," and he suggested that "studies in the field of child development" would be a test of "the fruitfulness of the study of culture in close conjunction with a study of personality." [65] Not surprisingly, studies of child development became central to subsequent government-funded work that was done in the Indian Education and Research Project (1941–1947), directed by Laura Thompson, and to Benedict and Mead's "national character" study (1947–1949), which grew out of their war work.

Culture and personality study as developed by Benedict emphasized not only child development and acculturation but also the collection and analysis of life histories, for she believed, as did Sapir, that "there is a very real hurt done our understanding of culture when we systematically ignore the individual." [66] In contrast to Boas, who regarded life histories as being of "limited value," Benedict argued that "life histories are important because from them one can study special cases of the kind of impact this culture has on individuals." [67] She encouraged and enabled the publication of Underhill's *The Autobiography of a Papago Woman*, the first and for many years "only substantial document on a Southwestern Indian woman," [68] and she wrote a foreword for it that was finally published with the 1979 edition. In the 1930s and 1940s hundreds of life histories were collected—many of them in the Southwest—but very little was done with most of them, except to mine them for ethnographic data. In Benedict's presidential address to the American Anthropological Association the year before she died, life histories figure prominently in her plea for science tempered with humanism: "If we are to make our collected life histories count in anthropological theory and understanding, we . . . must be willing to study them according to the best tradition of the humanities." [69]

With regard to the development of culture and personality studies and Benedict's contribution thereto, a 1926 letter from that other "temperamental radical," Sapir, contains a very revealing and consequential postscript: "I nearly forgot the purpose of my note, which was to tip you off to apply for a research fellowship to the Social Science Research Council. . . . Don't make it as technical as last year. Pueblo mythology doesn't excite people any more than Athabaskan verbs would. . . . Can't you devise some general subject in the American Indian field that outsiders can warm up to?" [70]

The project presumably was "Project 35" (later "Project 126"), "The Culture and Personality of North American Indians," which began in 1931, involved research with twenty tribes, and supported countless graduate students. Dissatisfied with "'the highly formal accounts of primitive cultures which had been customarily given by ethnologists,' Benedict proposed through longer periods of residence among the respective tribes and greater attention to detail in the description of their behavior to improve upon earlier work and to study the psychological patterns as well as the overt manifestations of culture." [71] The impact of this project was considerable. By 1935, when she wrote her four-year report, a bill had been presented in Congress through cooperation with the Bureau of Indian Affairs (BIA) to provide for ethnologists to aid in Indian tribal administration; by 1941 the BIA had, under John Collier's leadership, instituted an interdisciplinary study designed "to investigate the problems of personality development in relation to cultural patterning in the situational context of several Indian tribes . . . and to apply the results to the problem of Indian administration and education." [72]

One of the largest programs in applied anthropology, this seven-year project, directed by Laura Thompson and focused on southwestern tribes—Papago, Navajo, Hopi, and Zuni—would have been inconceivable without Benedict's earlier work. In Thompson's "Outline for Use in the Pilot Study, Research on the Development of Indian Personality," presenting purpose, rationale, and methods, Benedict's influence is clearly evident but never officially acknowledged. [73] The more serious appropriation and erasure, however, was Ralph Linton's editing and publishing the book based on the fieldwork that Benedict had directed on "The Culture and Personality of North American Indians." Linton, who was named chair of the Columbia department in 1937, resented and competed with Benedict at every turn, and in 1940 he published her students' work as *Acculturation in Seven American Indian Tribes.*

Benedict also took Sapir's advice to heart in writing another book on culture and personality that "outsiders can warm up to." *Patterns of Culture,* which described culture as "personality writ large," made anthropology "available to the man on the street," was translated into fourteen languages, became the best-selling and most influential book in twentieth-century anthropology, and engendered considerable disciplinary debate. For all that this text too was subsequently misread or appropriated, it was unmistakably Benedict's own.

§

Long before I knew anything at all about anthropology, I had learned from Shakespearean criticism — and from Santayana — habits of mind which at length made me an anthropologist.

— RUTH BENEDICT,
"Anthropology and the Humanities," 1947

Much has been written about *Patterns of Culture* in relation to culture and personality studies, many regarding the book as little more than a rendering of those ideas with regrettable generalization and overstatement into readable and accessible terms—"Psychological Types" and "Configurations of Culture" writ large. Much less has been said about the literary and philosophical pre-texts of *Patterns* or about the fact that this is the book of a poet, a philosopher, and a feminist as well as of an anthropologist. Most of what has been said in this regard is negative, many anthropologists finding *Pattern*'s literary qualities and philosophical framework "unfortunate," "distorting," or proof positive that it isn't "scientific." Benedict herself repeatedly rejected such dualisms as "art vs. science," and her vision was, as Boon and Geertz have pointed out, much more paradoxical and self-ironic.[74]

Melville Herskovits was one of very few anthropologists who saw *Patterns* as a welcome return to the distinguished writing tradition of early anthropological literature. Even Margaret Mead, who had urged Benedict to write it "all in your own style" and who, with Bateson during that fateful Christmas on the Sepik, was much influenced by the manuscript, felt that such an artful delineation of cultures as personalities would have only been possible for a scholar who had not "really" lived among the "buzzing, blooming confusion" of actual tribal situations and who had, of necessity, relied on the interpretations of native informants and other anthropologists.[75]

Ever the positivist, Mead made a very revealing remark in a 1933 letter to Benedict from Tchambuli in which she criticized Radcliffe-Brown and Malinowski: "I am more and more convinced that there is no room in anthropology for philosophical concepts and deductive thinking."[76] Benedict was not convinced, for in sharp contrast to Mead's unquestioning positivism and American penchant for empiricist simplification, Benedict believed that "data were meaningless without abstraction from them of a higher order of meaning" which informed them.[77] Twelve years earlier, one of the men Mead was criticizing had written what reads like a charter for *Patterns of Culture*: "The details and technicalities of the Kula acquire their meaning in so far only as they express some central attitude of mind of the natives . . . his *Weltanschauung*."[78]

"Malinowski, somewhat disappointingly, [did] not go on to the examination of these cultural wholes,"[79] but Benedict did. And the same European tradition of "philosophical anthropology" that had influenced both Boas and Malinowski shaped *Patterns of Culture*. While Benedict herself and several of her commentators have acknowledged this heritage, Mead tried to dispel "the ghosts of German theoreticians," denying that Dilthey and Spengler had provided an intellectual framework for Benedict's work and claiming, in at least two publications, that Boas had "insisted" she discuss them and that neither writer "had shaped her ideas."[80] Perhaps to ensure acceptance of her interpretation, Mead suppressed at least a page and a half about Dilthey and Spengler when she reprinted "Configurations of Culture" in 1974 in her "anthological biography," *Ruth Benedict*. This was not an isolated instance: Kardiner's influence on Benedict's work in culture and personality was similarly denied. More seriously, Mead pruned and edited Benedict's papers before turning them over to Vassar.

Both in "Configurations" and in *Patterns of Culture*, Benedict remarked that Dilthey had put forward the proposition that cultures must be studied as configurations around dominant ideas. For Dilthey, whom "anthropologists of experience" such as Victor Turner have rediscovered in recent decades, *Weltanschauung* was not a permanent fixed structure but a dynamic living pattern that expresses itself in religious, aesthetic, and philosophic forms.[81] As Benedict pointed out and emulated in *Patterns of Culture*, Dilthey's analysis of great philosophical configurations sees them as "great expressions of the variety of life," exposes their "relativity," and "argues vigorously against the assumption that any one of them can be final."[82] And, while Benedict criticized Spengler's thesis in *Decline of the West*, she credited him for popularizing Dilthey's insights and endorsed his notion of "destiny ideas" that "evolve within a culture and give it individuality."[83]

We may never know what Mead's motives were, but these statements and actions, in conjunction with her urging of Benedict to delete the "miscellaneous source materials" and the words of Boas, Lowie, and Malinowski in *Patterns*, reveal an egotism and a preoccupation with originality and authority to which Benedict was constitutionally opposed.[84] Like Boas, Benedict repeatedly resisted all forms of authority, including her own. Fortunately, Mead did not have her way in this case, for the strength of *Patterns* is its intertextuality, its *bricolage*. *Patterns* enacts what it describes—the organization of the "rags and tatters of cultures" into a pattern through an integrating principle. It is a book made like a quilt about cultures made like quilts. Piecing and quilting, recent feminist critics and writers suggest, are a trope for women's art in general and their writing in particular. The quilting analogy is valid, for the radicalness of this book, which "strikes off integration against diversity to vitalize both,"[85] lies in its awareness of the mediatedness of cultural interpretations and in its own nonabsolutist interpretation of "the inventions of cultures,"[86] whether by native, by anthropologist, or by poststructuralist feminist.

Just as surely as did Sapir, Benedict questioned "whether a completely impersonal anthropological description . . . is truly possible for a social discipline," and she recognized, as did he, that culture is an "abstraction."[87] Few of her critics have realized that in the process of writing for "the Macy shopper" she deconstructed anthropological discourse *avant la lettre*[88] and exposed its "rhetoric of violence"— that "anthropology as a Western science of man studies man as *the* human species."[89] From the kind of anthropology that Benedict practiced and wrote—and she did not make that distinction in the way most anthropologists do—Sapir ventured to predict that "the concept of culture which will then emerge, fragmentary and confused as it will undoubtedly be, will turn out to have a tougher, more vital, importance for social thinking than the tidy tables of contents attached to this or that group which we have been in the habit of calling 'cultures.'"[90]

With regard to this "fragmentary and confused" concept of culture, there is much more that is Nietzschean about *Patterns* than his "fine phrases" describing contrasting types as Apollonian and Dionysian. Despite Nietzsche's explicit misogyny, Benedict was, like other feminists then and now, attracted to his "gay science" and his ironic, deconstructive perspectivism.[91] While Victor Barnouw, like Mead, asserts that Benedict "turned to Nietzsche, Spengler, and Dilthey" under Boas's "somewhat jaundiced eye,"[92] she had in fact read Pater and Nietzsche as a Vassar undergraduate. In 1926 Benedict sent her marked copy of *Zarathustra* to Mead in Samoa. Mead was later to remark that "Nietzsche had been an old favorite of hers,"[93] again acknowledging but dismissing the theoretical underpinnings which, like those of Dilthey, merit further consideration.

Trained in literary criticism, Benedict read cultures and personalities as "writ," as "texts" organized around tropes, such as the "idea of fertilization" in Pueblo culture that Hermann Haeberlin first formulated in 1916.[94] Long before anthropologists were talking about "key symbols," "root metaphors," "master tropes," and cultural "texts" and the semiotics of culture, she was writing it, teaching us not only to read cultures as texts but also to read texts as cultural documents. Unlike many anthropologists, Benedict recognized that ethnographic description and ethnological comparison occurs as writing. I can easily imagine her asking herself privately, as James Boon has done publicly: "How can ethnography and literature shirk each other as long as ethnographers write?"[95] More than forty years ago, in one of her last public addresses, "Anthropology and the Humanities," Benedict made this "heretical statement": "To my mind the very nature of the problems posed and discussed in the humanities is closer, chapter by chapter, to those in anthropology than are the investigations carried on in most of the social sciences. . . . Once anthropologists include the mind of man in their subject matter, the methods of science and the methods of the humanities complement each other. Any commitment to methods which exclude either approach is self-defeating."[96]

Benedict never "shirked" literature, and at the time she was writing *Patterns of Culture* she was reading Virginia Woolf's novel *The Waves*. Woolf's method of evoking essential spirit rather than realistically describing character appealed to her and clearly influenced her own book, "in which the complexity of human society is conveyed through the juxtaposition of distinct, particular types."[97] Instead of Woolf's six characters and six different versions of a person, Benedict inscribed three cultures and three different versions of "reality." In *The Waves* a central, absent character is created through the reflections of six others; in *Patterns* American culture is portrayed through the images and reflections of three other cultures. Rather than writing biographies of three women, as she had once planned in "Adventures in Womanhood," she wrote biographies of three cultures and, by implication, a fourth. And, like the poet she was, Benedict constructed her argument through images— images juxtaposed in such a way that, as Geertz pointed out, "the all-too-familiar and the wildly exotic . . . change places."[98]

In contrast to Parsons's lengthy "labor of description" (*Pueblo Indian Religion*), Benedict took a "poetic" approach to inscribing the essential patterns of Pueblo experience in what was to become the most criticized section of *Patterns of Culture*.[99] She selected and exaggerated those Pueblo culture traits that supported her conception of their Apollonian genius and overlooked those that seemed to reflect a conflicting drive, underplaying the tension and factionalism in Pueblo society. Many of the criticisms center on her minimizing Dionysian excess in the form of alcoholism and violence. From her realist perspective, Esther Goldfrank in particular criticized Benedict's idealist rendering of Pueblo culture. Goldfrank's characterization is apt, for, as John Bennett and others have remarked, interpretations of Pueblo culture differ markedly depending on the values of the interpreter and on whether one focuses on ideology or on praxis.[100] Those cultural descriptions, such as Benedict's and Thompson's, that are elaborated on the basis of ideology, which Bennett calls "organic," see Pueblo culture and society as essentially integrated and harmonious.[101] Those, such as Goldfrank's and Dorothy Eggan's, that focus on praxis, which Bennett terms "repressive," emphasize the tension, conflict, and fear in Pueblo life and the extent to which the individual is suppressed and repressed.[102]

Kluckhohn once remarked to E. Adamson Hoebel that "Benedict did not report Pueblo society as is but Pueblo culture as conceived by the old men in particular."[103] But does anyone, can anyone, "report Pueblo society as is"? Are not the old men's textualizations of their culture as valid, as important, as the constructions of Pueblo life that the ethnographer "writes up" on the basis of his or her observations of behavior? I suspect that the "truth" about Pueblo culture is somewhere in between the ideal and the real, between ideology and praxis, and I know that many of those who criticize *Patterns* fail to read Benedict's own qualifications, self-criticisms, and cautionary notes.[104] Hoebel was not alone in thinking it "paradoxical" that "in spite of her highly questionable techniques of observation she was able to contribute theory and methodological devices of such great import and lasting value."[105] But, as Boon has pointed out and as much southwestern anthropology demonstrates, it is all too easy for ethnographers to run aground in the sands of their data, losing both their sense of irony and their sight of the larger picture.[106] Deafness, training, and temperament forced Benedict to "read over the shoulder of the natives," the old men "anthropologists" of Pueblo society, and enabled her to go beyond or behind minutiae to the integrating principles that held the "rags and tatters" together.

Neither do I think it an accident that *Patterns of Culture* was written by a woman, for who better to describe, as Elsie Clews Parsons did before her, the constraints of custom and the power of patriarchal institutions. Thanks to Mead, Modell, and Caffrey, we now know much more than we did about the feminist Benedict behind the anthropologist Benedict, but there is still much to be said, beyond what I have suggested in this essay, about the extent to which these concerns informed her anthropology. In practicing and writing an anthropology in which the superiority, detachment, and objectivity characteristic of "scientific colonialism" were both implicitly and explicitly deconstructed, Benedict anticipated many of the issues now being discussed in feminist and postmodernist anthropology.[107] We are just beginning to understand what she meant by "necessary researches," when she remarked in 1940 that "women in the field of anthropology have contributed to its development not only as trained anthropologists, but as women."[108] One of the obvious things that rereading Benedict reveals is the feminist subtext that most of us have missed. Perhaps the most serious and most ignored of all is the conclusion of *Patterns of Culture,* in which she builds up (down?) to a plea for cultural relativism and tolerance by toppling images of male dominance in our own society, noting that neither the Puritan divines of the eighteenth century nor the male egoists of the 1930s are "described in our manuals of psychiatry because they are supported by every tenet of our civilization."[109] Although not quite so witty, acerbic, and explicit as Virginia Woolf in *Three Guineas,* written in the same decade—this was after all "anthropology for the common man"—Benedict just as surely drew a parallel between the development of fascism and the patriarchal family.[110]

§

Liberty is the one thing no man can have unless he grants it to others.
— RUTH BENEDICT,
"Primitive Freedom," 1942

Although in 1934 Benedict feared that Boas had "given up science for good works"[111] and lamented the time lost to research and writing, world events forced her to realize that anthropologists could no longer do pure science, and after Boas fell ill in 1936 she followed him into the arena of public struggle against racism and intolerance. In 1939–1940 she finally took a sabbatical leave and used it to write *Race: Science and Politics,* published in 1940. This text is, as Mead remarked in her 1958 foreword to the Compass Books Edition, "the core of Ruth Benedict's approach to the question of the human consequences of racial discrimination."[112] The book was followed by a variety of public education activities, including lectures, a film, numerous articles in popular journals, and the popular and controversial pamphlet coauthored with Gene Weltfish, *The Races of Mankind,* of which more than 750,000 copies were distributed.[113] While Benedict was widely criticized for popularizing and simply compiling anthropological clichés about race and cultural relativism, her role in educating the "common man" as to the facts of race versus the claims of racism cannot be underestimated.

The discourse of *Race* is, however, more than "good works" and simplified scholarship, for this, like Benedict's writing in general, is coded and double voiced. And, as in the work and writing of many feminists of her own and earlier generations, issues of race and ethnicity stand in for gender. Not only is she talking about science and politics, she is talking about race and gender, about differences, about Otherness and oppression. "To state a difference," she says in her introduction to the 1943 edition, "is not by that token to label it 'bad.' "[114] If, as Sander Gilman argued, Freud transmuted the rhetoric of race into the construction of gender, Benedict did the opposite.[115] *Race* is replete with the ironic strategies, the "re-readings by juxtaposition" used by contemporary feminist and cultural critics to denaturalize and antiessentialize. This is particularly obvious in her discussion of mixed blood and racial purity, in which, for example, she concludes a paragraph on "hybrid vigor" with the following sentence: "Nature apparently does not condemn the half-caste to physiological inferiority"; in chapter titles such as "A Natural History of Racism"; and in the postmodern assemblages of quotations, "What They Say," with which she concludes each chapter.[116]

In 1943 Benedict went to Washington, D.C., as head of the Basic Analysis Section, Bureau of Overseas Intelligence, Office of War Information. Here, "with Mead and other anthropologists, she pioneered in the application of anthropological methods to complex societies and the study of culture 'at a distance,' working through documentary and literary materials and interviews with émigré informants in a series of 'national character' studies."[117] Benedict was particularly adept at reading cultural texts; she had, as Mead remarked, "a disciplined and highly sophisticated approach to published materials . . . and [a] penchant for building up a picture from fragmentary data."[118] Her war work produced her most elegant and eloquent book, *The Chrysanthemum and the Sword,* a thematic analysis of Japanese culture based entirely on written materials and interviews with Japanese Americans.[119]

Several commentators have seen in this book, which "she cared more about than any other she had written,"[120] both an integration of scraps and fragments into a complex portrait of Japanese culture that is also a critique of American culture and an integration of her different selves, the poet and the scientist, in a book that combined "a sense of the strength and integrity of cultural pattern with the 'special poignancy of the human spirit trapped always in ways which limit its full expression.' "[121] If anything, *The Chrysanthemum and the Sword* was, in addition to being popular, "almost too well written." Once again Benedict was more blamed than praised for writing anthropology "like a poet," for "linguistic pleasure (literary language) is placed on the side of the feminine; banned, like female desire."[122] In a discipline dominated by male reason and rededicated in the postwar years to being "the science of man," the contributions of this "anything but right-minded woman" to writing culture and to "sensibility" and the aesthetic dimension of life have been simultaneously disparaged, ignored, and widely appropriated.[123]

While Modell asserts in the introduction to her biography of Benedict that "inevitably social scientists today must acknowledge her point of view," unfortunately, many do not.[124] Not those who describe themselves as interpretive anthropologists and analyze cultural texts and tropes; not postmodern, deconstructive cultural critics; and notably not feminist anthropologists, all of whom are indebted to the textual and disciplinary boundaries that Benedict crossed, to her insistence on writing about human nature "in plurals," and to her determination to live "fearlessly with and within difference(s)."[125] Benedict's dignity and courage "lay in the fact that she went after important issues" and in her recognition that anthropological, like feminist, practice "can be a fundamentally deconstructive strategy which questions the possibility of universals or absolute meaning and exposes the constitution of power at stake in their assertion."[126] "What," she asked in "The Science of Custom" and all of her subsequent cultural criticism, is the meaning of life except that by the discipline of thought and emotion, by living life to its fullest, we shall make of it always a more flexible instrument, accepting new relativities, divesting ourselves of traditional absolutes?[127]

Notes

1. Margaret Mead, *An Anthropologist at Work: Writings of Ruth Benedict* (New York: Avon Books, 1973), 132. Throughout this essay, words and phrases in quotation marks are, unless indicated otherwise, taken from Ruth Benedict's unpublished and published writings, many of which were collected and reprinted by Margaret Mead in *An Anthropologist at Work*. The phrase "writ large," which I use several times, is also Benedict's. In her classic formulation in *Patterns of Culture* (Boston: Houghton Mifflin, 1934), Benedict describes culture as "personality writ large" (p. 46). Portions of this essay were previously published under the same title in *Frontiers* 12, no. 3 (1992): 39–77; and in *Hidden Scholars: Women Anthropologists and the Native American Southwest*, ed. Nancy J. Parezo (Albuquerque: University of New Mexico Press, 1993), 107–28; and are reprinted here with their permission.

2. Mary Catherine Bateson, *With a Daughter's Eye: A Memoir of Margaret Mead and Gregory Bateson* (New York: William Morrow, 1984), 118.

3. Mead, *Anthropologist at Work*, 3.

4. Abram Kardiner and Edward Preble, *They Studied Man* (New York: World Publishing, 1961), 208. More recently, Richard Handler has described her method as "fundamentally comparative and hermeneutic" ("Ruth Benedict and the Modernist Sensibility," in *Modernist Anthropology: From Fieldwork to Text*, ed. Marc Manganaro [Princeton, N.J.: Princeton University Press, 1990], 175).

5. I am indebted to an anonymous reader of an earlier version of this essay for the very apt description of Benedict's work as embodying an "epistemology of the oppressed," a concept articulated by feminist sociologists Liz Stanley and Sue Wise in *Breaking Out Again: Feminist Ontology and Epistemology* (London: Routledge, 1993). The phrase "double-voiced discourse," which has become a given in feminist literary criticism, was initially used by Elaine Showalter.

6. For further discussion of "situated knowledge" and "perspectivist knowledge," see Donna Haraway, "Situated Knowledges: The Science Question in Feminism and the Privilege of Partial Perspective," in her *Simians, Cyborgs, and Women* (New York: Routledge, 1991), 183–201; and Diane Lewis, "Anthropology and Colonialism," *Current Anthropology* 14 (December 1973): 581–602.

7. Victor Barnouw, "Ruth Benedict: Apollonian and Dionysian," *University of Toronto Quarterly* 18 (1949): 242.

8. Ibid.

9. Haraway, "Situated Knowledges," 154. For further discussion of Benedict's ironies and her Swiftean mode of social critique, see Clifford Geertz, who points out (in *Works and Lives: The Anthropologist as Author* [Stanford: Stanford University Press, 1988], 106) that her repeated rhetorical strategy is "the juxtaposition of the all-too-familiar and the wildly exotic in such a way that they change places." And, for a discussion of irony in anthropology in the work of Benedict's mentor, Franz Boas, see Arnold Krupat, "Irony in Anthropology: The Work of Franz Boas," in *Modernist Anthropology*, 133–45.

10. Margaret M. Caffrey, *Ruth Benedict: Stranger in This Land* (Austin: University of Texas Press, 1989), 68.

11. Mead, *Anthropologist at Work*, 119–20.

12. Ibid., 132.

13. Ibid., 135.

14. Ibid., 143.

15. Judith Schachter Modell, *Ruth Benedict: Patterns of a Life* (Philadelphia: University of Pennsylvania Press, 1983), 103, 106.

16. Mead, *Anthropologist at Work*, 135.

17. Modell, *Ruth Benedict*, 107–8.

18. *New School Bulletin* (1919): 14.

19. Elsie Clews Parsons, *Social Freedom: A Study of the Conflicts between Social Classifications and Personality* (New York: G. P. Putnam's Sons, 1915), 105.

20. Elsie Clews Parsons, *Social Rule: A Study of the Will to Power* (New York: G. P. Putnam's Sons, 1916), 56–57. For more on the relationship between feminism and anthropology in Parsons's work, see Barbara A. Babcock, "'Not Yet Classified, Perhaps Not Classifiable': Elsie Clews Parsons, Feminist/Anthropologist" (unpublished manuscript, 1988) and "Elsie Clews Parsons and the Pueblo Construction of Gender," in *Pueblo Mothers and Children: Essays by Elsie Clews Parsons*, ed. Barbara A. Babcock (Santa Fe, N. Mex.: Ancient City Press, 1991), 1–27.

21. Peter H. Hare, *A Woman's Quest for Science: Portrait of Anthropologist Elsie Clews Parsons* (Buffalo, N.Y.: Prometheus Books, 1985), 7.

22. Ibid., 135.

23. Alfred Kroeber, "Elsie Clews Parsons," *American Anthropologist* 45, no. 2 (1943): 252.

24. Geertz, *Works and Lives*, 112.

25. Sidney Hook, Ruth Benedict, and Margaret Mead, "Alexander Goldenweiser: Three Tributes," *Modern Quarterly* 11, no. 6 (1940): 31.

26. Virginia Wolf Briscoe, "Ruth Benedict, Anthropological Folklorist," *Journal of American Folklore* 92 (1979): 452.

27. George Stocking, "Ruth Fulton Benedict," in *Dictionary of American Biography: Supplement for 1946–50*, ed. John A. Garraty and Edward T. James (New York: Scribner's, 1974), 71.

28. At this time, most of Boas's students did library dissertations and only did fieldwork after receiving their Ph.D.'s. Kroeber and Lowie, among others, also followed this pattern. It did not, however, become grounds for criticism of their work, as it did of Benedict's.

29. Ruth Fulton Benedict, "The Concept of the Guardian Spirit in North America," *Memoirs of the American Anthropological Association* 29 (1923): 84–85.

30. Ruth Fulton Benedict, "Franz Boas as an Ethnologist," in "Franz Boas, 1858–1942," *Memoirs of the American Anthropological Association* 61 (1943): 29.

31. Franz Boas, "An Anthropologist's Credo," *The Nation* 147, no. 9 (1938): 202, 204.

32. Judith Schachter Modell, "Ruth Benedict, Anthropologist: The Reconciliation of Science and Humanism," in *Toward a Science of Man: Essays in the History of Anthropology*, ed. Timothy H. H. Thoresen (The Hague: Mouton, 1975), 195.

33. Boas, "Anthropologist's Credo," 203.

34. Esther Goldfrank, *Notes on an Undirected Life: As One Anthropologist Tells It* (Flushing, N.Y.: Queens College Press, 1978), 18. See also Mead, "Apprenticeship under Boas" in *The Anthropology of Franz Boas: Essays on the Centennial of His Birth*, ed. Walter Goldschmidt, *Memoirs of the American Anthropological Association* no. 89 (Washington, D.C.: American Anthropological Association, 1960), 29–45.

35. Letter to Elsie Clews Parsons from Frank Lillie, May 23, 1924, Ruth Fulton Benedict Papers, Vassar College Library, Poughkeepsie, N.Y.

36. Mead, *Anthropologist at Work*, 143.

37. Letter to Benedict from Edward Sapir, March 16, 1931, Benedict Papers, Vassar College.

38. For further provocative discussion of the fetishism and conventions of fieldwork in anthropology, see James A. Boon, *Other Tribes, Other Scribes: Symbolic Anthropology in the Comparative Study of Cultures, Histories, Religions, and Texts* (Cambridge, England: Cambridge University Press, 1982) and "Functionalists Write, Too: Frazer/Malinowski and the Semiotics of the Monograph," *Semiotica* 46, no. 2/4 (1983): 131–49.

39. Stocking, "Ruth Fulton Benedict," 71.

40. Mead, *Anthropologist at Work*, 291.

41. Ibid., 293.

42. Triloki Pandey, "Anthropologists at Zuni," *Proceedings of the American Philosophical Society* 116, no. 4 (1972): 333–34.

43. Elsie Clews Parsons, *Pueblo Indian Religion*, vol. 1 (Chicago: University of Chicago Press, 1939), 64.

44. Benedict, *Patterns of Culture*, 260–61, and *Zuni Mythology*, vol. 1, Columbia University Contributions to Anthropology, vol. 21 (New York, 1935), xxxix.

45. Mead, *Anthropologist at Work*, 299.

46. Ruth Fulton Benedict, "Folklore" and "Myth," *Encyclopedia of the Social Sciences*, vol. 11 (New York: Macmillan, 1931, 1933), 288–93 and 178–81.

47. Benedict, "Folklore," 291, and *Tales of the Cochiti Indians*, Bulletin of the Bureau of American Ethnology, no. 98 (Washington, D.C.: U.S. Government Printing Office, 1931), xiii, 221 (reprinted 1981, University of New Mexico Press, Albuquerque).

48. Clifford Geertz, *The Interpretation of Cultures* (New York: Basic Books, 1973), 448.

49. Benedict, research proposal, Benedict Papers, Vassar College. My emphasis.

50. Benedict, *Zuni Mythology,* xxix, xii.

51. Benedict, "Folklore," 291.

52. Ruth Fulton Benedict, "Magic," *Encyclopedia of the Social Sciences,* vol. 11 (New York: Macmillan, 1933), 44.

53. Mead, *Anthropologist at Work,* 181, 188.

54. Ibid., 182.

55. Ibid., 91.

56. Reprinted in David G. Mandelbaum, ed., *Selected Writings of Edward Sapir* (Berkeley: University of California Press, 1968), 546–48. For further discussion of poetry, personality, and culture in the work of Edward Sapir and Ruth Benedict, which emphasizes their different points of view, see Richard Handler, "Vigorous Male and Aspiring Female: Poetry, Personality, and Culture in Edward Sapir and Ruth Benedict," in *Malinowski, Rivers, Benedict and Others: Essays on Culture and Personality,* History of Anthropology, vol. 4, ed. George W. Stocking, Jr. (Madison: University of Wisconsin Press, 1987), 127–55. Handler overstates the case, however, in claiming that Benedict never accepted or understood Sapir's critique of reification. Like most of Benedict's commentators, he ignores her concern with the deviant, the dialectical, and the paradoxical and seems to miss her irony altogether. And, again, in "Ruth Benedict and the Modernist Sensibility," I think Handler overstates the contrast between Sapir and Benedict and misreads her concept of culture.

57. Benedict, "Franz Boas," 31.

58. Franz Boas, *Race, Language, and Culture* (New York: Macmillan, 1940), 629.

59. Franz Boas, *Anthropology and Modern Life* (New York: W. W. Norton, 1928), 151.

60. Ruth Fulton Benedict, "Configurations of Culture in North America," *American Anthropologist* 34, no. 6 (1932): 23–24, 26, 27.

61. Clyde Kluckhohn, "The Influence of Psychiatry on Anthropology in America during the Past One Hundred Years," in *One Hundred Years of American Psychiatry,* ed. J. K. Hall et al. (New York: Columbia University Press, 1944), 597.

62. Barnouw, "Ruth Benedict," 248; Karen Horney, "Culture and Neurosis," *American Sociological Review* 1 (1936): 221–35, and *The Neurotic Personality of Our Time* (New York: W. W. Norton, 1937).

63. Ruth Fulton Benedict, "Anthropology and the Abnormal," *Journal of General Psychology* 10 (1934): 59–82.

64. Reprinted in Mandelbaum, *Selected Writings,* 592.

65. Ibid., 595–96.

66. Ibid., 593.

67. Abraham H. Maslow and John J. Honigmann, "Synergy: Some Notes of Ruth Benedict," *American Anthropologist* 72, no. 2 (1970): 321.

68. Clyde Kluckhohn, "Southwestern Studies of Culture and Personality," *American Anthropologist* 56, no. 4 (1954): 686; Ruth Underhill, *The Autobiography of a Papago Woman, Memoirs of the American Anthropological Association,* no. 46 (Menasha, Wis.: American Anthropological Association, 1934) (reprinted 1979 as *Papago Woman,* Holt Rinehart, & Winston, New York).

69. Ruth Fulton Benedict, "Anthropology and the Humanities," in *Ruth Benedict,* ed. Margaret Mead (New York: Columbia University Press, 1974), 175.

70. Mead, *Anthropologist at Work,* 184–85.

71. Briscoe, "Ruth Benedict," 458.

72. Laura Thompson, "Exploring American Indian Communities in Depth," in *Women in the Field: Anthropological Experiences,* ed. Peggy Golde (Chicago: Aldine, 1970), 50.

73. Laura Thompson, "Outline for Use in the Pilot Study, Research on the Development of Indian Personality," Papers of the Indian Education and Research Project, National Anthropological Archives (Washington, D.C.: Smithsonian Institution, 1941–1947).

74. Boon, *Other Tribes,* 44; Geertz, *Works and Lives,* 102–28.

75. Mead spent Christmas 1932 in the field at Ambunti, the government station on the Sepik River, with her anthropologist husband, Reo Fortune, as well as Gregory Bateson, with whom she fell in love and whom she subsequently married. The threesome read and discussed the manuscript of *Patterns of Culture.* For a fascinating and revealing discussion of the mediations among Mead, Fortune, Bateson, Benedict, the Sepik and Bali, and the critical role played by the manuscript of *Patterns of Culture* therein, see James A. Boon, "Mead's Mediations: Some Semiotics from the Sepik, by Way of Bateson, on to Bali," in *Semiotic Mediations: Sociocultural and Psychological Perspectives,* ed. Elizabeth Mintz and Richard J. Parmentier (New York: Academic Press, 1985), 333–57, and "Folly, Bali, and Anthropology or Satire across Cultures," in *Text, Play, and Story: The Construction and Reconstruction of Self and Society,* ed. Edward M. Bruner (Washington, D.C.: American Ethnological Society, 1984), 156–77.

76. Mead, *Anthropologist at Work,* 334.

77. Briscoe, "Ruth Benedict," 461.

78. Bronislaw Malinowski, *Argonauts of the Western Pacific* (New York: Dutton, 1921), 517.

79. Benedict, "Configurations of Culture," 2.

80. Mead, *Anthropologist at Work,* 210–11, and *Ruth Benedict,* 47.

81. See Edward Bruner and Victor Turner, *The Anthropology of Experience* (Urbana: University of Illinois Press, 1986).

82. Benedict, *Patterns of Culture,* 52.

83. Benedict, "Configurations of Culture," 3.

84. For further discussion of *Patterns of Culture* and the significance of the intertexts and concepts that Benedict retained and that Mead would have weeded out, see Boon, *Other Tribes,* 105–8.

85. Ibid., 107. For further discussion of women's discourse as piecing, see Barbara A. Babcock, "Taking Liberties, Writing from the Margins, and Doing It with a Difference," *Journal of American Folklore* 100 (1987): 398, and "Mud, Mirrors, and Making Up: Liminality and Reflexivity in *Between the Acts,*" in *Victor Turner and the Construction of Cultural Criticism,* ed. Kathleen M. Ashley (Bloomington: Indiana University Press, 1990), 86–116.

86. See Roy Wagner, *The Invention of Culture* (Chicago: University of Chicago Press, 1975), for an enlightening discussion of the invention of culture by man in general and by the anthropologist in particular.

87. Mandelbaum, *Selected Writings,* 593.

88. I first used this concept and the phrase *avant la lettre* in the original Wenner-Gren conference version of this essay in 1986. In *Works and Lives* Geertz uses the same concept and phrase, without attribution, regarding Ruth Fulton Benedict, *The Chrysanthemum and the Sword* (Boston: Houghton Mifflin, 1946).

89. Trinh T. Minh-ha, *Woman, Native, Other: Writing Postcoloniality and Feminism* (Bloomington: Indiana University Press, 1989), 56. For more on the rhetorical violence of the sciences of man, see Teresa deLauretis, *Technologies of Gender: Essays on Theory, Film, and Fiction* (Bloomington: Indiana University Press, 1987). For more on scientific discourse and "the problem of woman" in general and of Benedict in particular for contemporary feminist anthropologists, see Babcock, "Feminisms/Pretexts: Fragments, Questions, and Reflections," *Anthropological Quarterly* 66 (1993): 59–66.

90. Mandelbaum, *Selected Writings*, 597.

91. In a recent collection of essays on Nietzsche, feminism, and political theory, Daniel Conway argues that "if the project of feminist epistemology is to incorporate the radically situated knowledges of women and other subjugated agents, then its practitioners must take the 'postmodern' turn outlined by Nietzsche and implemented by Haraway" (*"Das Weib an sich*: The Slave Revolt in Epistemology," in *Nietzsche, Feminism and Political Theory*, ed. Paul Patton [New York: Routledge, 1993], 111).

92. Barnouw, "Ruth Benedict," 243.

93. Mead, *Anthropologist at Work*, 210.

94. H. K. Haeberlin, "The Idea of Fertilization in the Culture of the Pueblo Indians," *Memoirs of the American Anthropological Association* 3, no. 1 (1916): 1–55.

95. Boon, *Other Tribes*, 20.

96. Benedict, "Anthropology and the Humanities," 165–66, 175–76.

97. Virginia Woolf, *The Waves* (New York: Harcourt, Brace, 1931); Modell, *Ruth Benedict*, 192.

98. Geertz, *Works and Lives*, 106.

99. See Benedict's review of *Pueblo Indian Religion* in *Review of Religion* 4 (1940): 438–40.

100. Esther Goldfrank, "Socialization, Personality, and the Structure of Pueblo Society (with particular reference to Hopi and Zuni)," *American Anthropologist* 47 (1945): 516–39; John W. Bennett, "The Interpretation of Pueblo Culture: A Question of Values," *Southwestern Journal of Anthropology* 4, no. 2 (1946): 361–74.

101. Laura Thompson, "Logico-Aesthetic Integration in Hopi Culture," *American Anthropologist* 47 (1945): 540–53. Despite her obvious indebtedness and her repeated use of the words "pattern" and "configuration" in this essay, Thompson does not cite Benedict, as she did not in other publications and proposals associated with the Indian Education and Research Project.

102. Dorothy Eggan, "The General Problem of Hopi Adjustment," *American Anthropologist* 45 (1943): 357–73.

103. E. Adamson Hoebel, "Major Contributions of Southwestern Studies to Anthropological Theory," *American Anthropologist* 56, no. 4 (1954): 720–27. For a critique of Apollonian anthropology and discussion of Benedict's idealization of Zuni in terms of both personal psychology and the attraction of 1920s intellectuals to the Puebloan Southwest as well as their romantic primitivism, see George Stocking, "The Ethnographic Sensibility of the 1920s and the Dualism of the Anthropological Tradition," in *Romantic Motives: Essays on Anthropological Sensibility*, History of Anthropology, vol. 6, ed. George W. Stocking, Jr. (Madison: University of Wisconsin Press, 1989), 208–76.

104. This is notably the case in Li An-Che, "Zuni: Some Observations and Queries" (*American Anthropologist* 39 [1937]: 62–76), despite the valid criticisms that he makes of her interpretation of Pueblo leadership. For Benedict's self-criticism and qualifications, see *Patterns of Culture*, esp. 228–29.

105. Hoebel, "Major Contributions," 724.

106. For a critique of the fetishism of fieldwork, the biases of empiricism, and the conventions of the functionalist monograph, see Boon, "Functionalists Write, Too"; and James Clifford, "Dada Data," *Sulfur* 10 (1984): 162–64, and *The Predicament of Culture: Twentieth-Century Ethnography, Literature, and Art* (Cambridge, Mass.: Harvard University Press, 1988), esp. chap. 1, "On Ethnographic Authority," and chap. 4, "On Ethnographic Surrealism."

107. For further discussion of scientific colonialism, see Lewis, "Anthropology and Colonialism." Regarding recent debate on these and other issues at the intersection of feminism, postmodernism, and anthropology, see "Constructing Meaningful Dialogue on Difference: Feminism and Postmodernism in Anthropology and the Academy," ed. Frances E. Mascia-Lees and Patricia Sharpe, a special issue of *Anthropological Quarterly* 66, nos. 2–3 (1993); Diane Bell, Pat Caplan and Wazir Jahan Karim, eds., *Gendered Fields: Women, Men and Ethnography* (New York: Routledge, 1993); and "Special Issue on Women Writing Culture," ed. Ruth Behar, *Critique of Anthropology* 13, no. 4 (1993).

108. Ruth Fulton Benedict, "Women and Anthropology," in *The Education of Women* (New York: The Institute of Professional Relations, for the Women's Centennial Congress, 1940).

109. Benedict, *Patterns of Culture*, 277–78.

110. Virginia Woolf, *Three Guineas* (New York: Harcourt, Brace, 1931). The phrase "anthropology for the common man" was the title of Elgin Williams's critical essay in *American Anthropologist* 49, no. 1 (1947): 84–90, occasioned by the publication of a 25-cent edition of *Patterns of Culture*.

111. Mead, *Anthropologist at Work*, 348. For more on Boas and race, see Franz Boas, *Race, Language, and Culture* (New York: Macmillan, 1940); *A Franz Boas Reader: The Shaping of American Anthropology*, ed. George W. Stocking, Jr. (Chicago: University of Chicago Press, 1974); and George W. Stocking, Jr., *Race, Culture, and Evolution: Essays in the History of Anthropology* (Chicago: University of Chicago Press, 1982). For more on Boas and the mobilization of scientists against racialism in the 1930s, see Elazar Barkan, "Mobilizing Scientists against Nazi Racism, 1933–1939," in *Bones, Bodies, Behavior: Essays on Biological Anthropology*, History of Anthropology, vol. 5, ed. George W. Stocking, Jr. (Madison: University of Wisconsin Press, 1988), 180–205.

112. Ruth Fulton Benedict, *Race: Science and Politics* (New York: Viking Press, 1959), Compass Books edition, with a foreword by Margaret Mead, viii.

113. Ruth Fulton Benedict and Gene Weltfish, *The Races of Mankind* (New York: Public Affairs Committee, 1943).

114. Benedict, *Race: Science and Politics*, rev. ed. (New York: Viking, 1943), viii.

115. Sander L. Gilman, *Freud, Race, and Gender* (Princeton, N.J.: Princeton University Press, 1993), chap. 1.

116. Benedict, *Race* (1959), 52.

117. Stocking, "Ruth Fulton Benedict," 72. For further discussion of the war work of Benedict, Mead, and Bateson, see Virginia Yans-McLaughlin, "Science, Democracy, and Ethics: Mobilizing Culture and Personality for World War II," in *Malinowski, Rivers, Benedict and Others*, 184–217.

118. Mead, *Ruth Benedict,* 59.

119. Benedict, *Chrysanthemum and the Sword.*

120. Mead, *Ruth Benedict,* 64.

121. Stocking, "Ruth Fulton Benedict," 72.

122. Mary Jacobus, ed., *Women Writing and Writing About Women* (London: Croom Helm, 1979), 14.

123. Geertz (*Works and Lives,* 124) describes Benedict as "anything but right-minded." For more on Benedict and the dualism of science and sensibility in anthropology, see Stocking, "Ethnographic Sensibility." Stocking does not, however, remark on the gendered nature of this opposition.

124. Modell, *Ruth Benedict,* 13.

125. Minh-ha, *Woman, Native, Other,* 84. For more on the exclusion of Benedict's work, see Babcock, "Feminism/Pretexts."

126. Barnouw, "Ruth Benedict," 252. After making this statement, Barnouw goes on to remark:

> *Anthropologists who classified potsherds or measured skulls could afford to criticize her methodology. Their procedures, no doubt, were impeccable in comparison to hers, but the final value of their work still remains to be discovered. Too many of Boas's students got bogged down among the intricate details of kinship-systems or basket-weaves without having much understanding of why they worked so hard. When Franz Boas published page after page of blueberry-pie recipes in Kwakiutl, the old man probably knew what he was after; but when his students did the same kind of thing, they often lacked the driving central purpose which animated Boas. They mastered techniques and methods within their special fields, but often accomplished little more than that. It requires courage to stick to the important issues, and Ruth Benedict had that courage.*

The latter statement and other observations about feminist practice that provide insight into anthropology as written, deconstructed by Benedict were made by Biddy Martin in "Feminism, Criticism, and Foucault," *New German Critique* 27 (1982): 3–30.

127. Ruth Benedict, "The Science of Custom," *Century Magazine* 117, no. 6 (1929): 649. In a letter of January 16, 1929, to Margaret Mead in New Guinea, Benedict wrote: "I finished my *Century* article—on time too—and even had time to show it to Papa Franz. . . . I trembled when he said he wanted to see me about a point. I'd told him that I thought he'd hate the *Century* article. But no, 'he thought an article like that would do more good than his book. He wished he could write in that way, but he couldn't'" (Mead, *Anthropologist at Work,* 311).

6

Janet L. Finn

FIRST — *The anomalous position heretofore occupied by the Indians in this country can not much longer be maintained. The reservation system belongs to a "vanishing state of things" and must soon cease to exist.*

SECOND — *The logic of events demands the absorption of the Indians into our national life, not as Indians, but as American citizens.*

THIRD — *As soon as a wise conservatism will warrant it, the relations of the Indians to the Government must rest solely upon the full recognition of their individuality. Each Indian must be treated as a man, be allowed a man's rights and privileges, and be held to the performance of a man's obligations. Each Indian is entitled to his proper share of inherited wealth of the tribe, and to the protection of the courts in his "life, liberty, and pursuit of happiness." He is not entitled to be supported in idleness.*

FOURTH — *The Indians must conform to "white man's ways" peaceably if they will, forcibly if they must. They must adjust themselves to their environment, and conform their mode of living substantially to our civilization. This civilization may not be the best possible, but it is the best the Indians can get. They can not escape it, and must either conform to it or be crushed by it.*

FIFTH — *The paramount duty of the hour is to prepare the rising generation of Indians for the new order of things thus forced upon them. A comprehensive system of education modeled after the American public school system, but adopted to the special exigencies of the Indian youth, embracing all persons of school age, compulsory in its demands and uniformly administered should be developed as rapidly as possible.*

SIXTH — *The tribal relations should be broken up, socialism destroyed, and the family and the autonomy of the individual substituted. The allotment of lands in severalty, the establishment of local courts and police, the development of a personal sense of independence, and the universal adoption of the English language are means to this end.*

— THOMAS J. MORGAN,
Report of the Commissioner of Indian Affairs, 1889

This may sound a little naive . . . but I actually feel that I have a mission: To make the Dakota people understandable, as human beings, to the white people who have to deal with them.

— ELLA DELORIA,
letter to H. E. Beebe, 1952

It is all wrong, this saying that Indians do not feel as deeply as whites. We do feel, and by and by some of us are going to be able to make our feelings appreciated, and then will the true Indian character be revealed.

MOURNING DOVE,
quoted in the *Spokesman Review,* 1916

THE STARK WORDS of Commissioner Morgan encapsulate the direction of official U.S. Indian policy of the late 1800s. These words set the historical stage for understanding the personal and political concerns to which two Native American women writing culture, Ella Deloria and Mourning Dove, respond. Deloria and Mourning Dove came of age during the height of the U.S. government civilizing mission for American Indians. The mission of these women was to write for cross-cultural understanding by writing against the grain of dominant representations of Native Americans.

Ella Deloria, a member of the Yankton Sioux of South Dakota, was an ethnographer and educator whose contributions to anthropology were rich and varied. Her professional career lasted from the 1920s to the 1970s. She produced texts on Dakota language, public policy documents, ethnographic accounts of the Sioux for a popular audience, and a novel, *Waterlily,* the evocative story of Dakota life drawn from women's experience.[1]

Mourning Dove was the literary name chosen by Christine Quintasket, an Interior Salish woman and member of the Colville Confederated Tribes of Northeastern Washington state.[2] She is credited with being the first Native American woman to

JANET L. FINN

publish a novel. Her novel, *Co-ge-we-a, the Half-Blood,* was published in 1927, nearly eleven years after she finished writing it. Although Mourning Dove identified herself primarily as a novelist, she also produced a variety of texts, including *Coyote Stories,* a collection of Okanogan folk tales, and an autobiography, edited and published posthumously in 1990.[3]

I became acquainted with Mourning Dove's novel through previous research on representations of American Indian women. Then, when I began to read the work of Ella Deloria, I became intrigued by the common themes in the experiences of the two women. In this paper I explore the parallels and contrasts in their works and lives as writers, activists and "cultural mediators."[4] In the first part of the exploration I summarize Deloria's and Mourning Dove's early experiences of melding cross-cultural knowledge and their commitment to education. Next I examine the dilemmas they faced as women of color fulfilling multiple roles as scholars, laborers, and caregivers, paying particular attention to the relationships they negotiated with their white, male mentors. In the third part I consider the creative resistance in their works and lives, and I explore their choice of the novel as a vehicle for voicing Native American women's experiences.

The works of Ella Deloria and Mourning Dove raise questions about the "truth" value of the novel and the ethnographic text in representing cultural experience. By calling a work fiction, does one remove it from the realm of argumentation? Does that diminish its power to contest the history and practices to which it responds? In what forms can knowledge be packaged to best challenge the histories of misrepresentation by dominant groups? Recent critical writings have addressed the fictional character and inherent partiality of ethnographic truths. James Clifford writes that "culture is always relational, an inscription of communicative processes that exist, historically, *between* subjects in relations of power."[5] Lacking in this understanding of culture is a sense of urgency and struggle on the part of less powerful subjects to inscribe their own stories in this "politics of identification."[6] Deloria's and Mourning Dove's works and lives are grounded in a time in which federal policy sought to erase complex pasts and to inscribe a simplistic future for American Indians. While both women challenged this inscription by writing and telling stories of personal and cultural histories, there are important differences in their approaches. I characterize Deloria as the teacher, enlightening her white audience about "a way of life that worked."[7] In contrast, Mourning Dove plays the trickster who mocks and plays with the boundaries of truth and fiction.

Incorporation

Ella Deloria was born in 1888 to Sioux parents and grew up on the Standing Rock Reservation in South Dakota.[8] Her father, a convert to Christianity, was an ordained Episcopal minister who served the reservation. Deloria was educated in mission boarding schools. She professed a deep Christian faith and an enduring respect for the inseparable spiritual and cultural values of the Dakota people.

She attended Oberlin College and Teachers College, Columbia University, and she held teaching positions at Indian boarding schools, colleges, and adult education programs. Deloria was keenly aware of the power of the written word. She devoted much of her scholarship to transcribing Dakota language and history. She was not content with the fixed image on the page as the final product of her scholarship. She was a gifted lecturer and storyteller who engaged in the exchange of cultural knowledge with diverse audiences. In addition to her numerous teaching positions, Deloria chaired a Commission on Indian Education in 1961 and later served as assistant director of the Over Museum at the University of South Dakota. Late in her career she returned to teaching at a private Episcopal girls' school, funded largely by the Daughters of the American Revolution (DAR). Through this arrangement Deloria became a popular speaker on the DAR lecture circuit. She valued the power of performance and used storytelling to preserve cultural knowledge, build cross-cultural understanding, and give voice to Native American women's experiences.[9]

Mourning Dove begins her autobiography with the story of her birth in 1888:

> I was born near the present site of Bonner's Ferry, Idaho, while my mother and grandmother were in a canoe crossing the Kootenay River. . . . My father had helped to swim the horses, and my mother and her mother started over in a canoe with a Kootenay named Swansen, a name given to him by the fur traders. He paddled hard, but I came into the world before he could beach the canoe. They had brought clothing for a newborn, but it was left on a packhorse on the other side of the river, with our other gear. The Kootenay man kindly pulled off his plaid shirt and lent it to my grandmother to swaddle me. Thus my first clothing was a man's shirt, and my parents always felt that this led me to act more like a boy, a tomboy, who liked to play more with the boys than with the girls.[10]

Mourning Dove uses her birth story to introduce her audience to the world she experienced and created.[11] The story depicts her entry into a world that was not quite ready for her, foreshadowing her many struggles as a woman challenging gendered "traditions" in both Anglo and Salishan societies. And it is in a man's shirt, not the constricted trappings of womanhood, that Mourning Dove metaphorically finds comfort. She places herself from birth in the crosscurrents of cultural boundary waters, with no guarantees of safe passage.

Mourning Dove shares with Deloria the experience of being and becoming Indian in the context of Christian missionary influence.[12] She describes how her parents, like many Salish, accepted a spiritual dualism of deeply held Catholic and Salishan beliefs.[13] However, her narrative accounts of the missions and boarding schools also speak to the powerful presence of the Jesuits and the control wielded by the Catholic church on the reservation. For example, in her autobiography she recalls an encounter between her mother and Father De Rouge of the Goodwin Mission:

> The good (Jesuit) priest came forward and shook hands with Mother, spying me behind her wide skirts. He looked right at me and asked if I had made my first

communion. He had a way of jumbling up words from several Indian languages he had learned so that his words sounded childish, but I dared not chuckle at his comment. Instead, I shook my head in answer to his question. He looked at mother reproachfully and, shaking his head, said, "Tut, Tut, Lucy. You must let your child go to school with the good sisters to learn her religion so that she can make her first communion like other children of her age." Mother tried to make a protest, saying she needed me at home to care for the babies. But Father De Rouge could seldom be enticed to change his mind. He always had a very strict, ruling hand with the Indians. His word was much respected by the natives of the Colville Reservation.

He shook his finger at Mother and said, "Tut, tut, Lucy, I command you." Then, pointing at the cross atop the bell tower of the church, he continued, "Your church commands that your child must go to school to learn her religion and the laws of the church." In obedience, Mother promised to send me to the mission for the fall term of 1898.[14]

Mourning Dove's education was often fragmented and frustrating. As a young child she was traumatically isolated from her family and placed in the unfamiliar world of the mission boarding school. Although health problems and family concerns interrupted her formal education, Mourning Dove was determined to read and write. She credits a young Irish boy, Jimmy Ryan, who shared her childhood home, with helping her learn to read:

My father came back from one of these [freight hauling] trips with an orphan white lad, about thirteen, named Jimmy Ryan. He had previously lived with his uncle in Butte, Montana. . . . Jimmy was a great reader of yellowback novels. It was from one of his books that I learned the alphabet. I could spell the word Kentucky before I ever had a primer because it occurred frequently in the novel Jimmy taught me from. One day Mother papered our cabin with Jimmy's novels. When he got home, he made no protest, but he got busy and continued to read from the wall, with me helping to find the next page.[15]

The "penny dreadfuls" Mourning Dove read with Jimmy Ryan inspired her love of romantic fiction and her own choice of literary genre as a writer.

Mourning Dove was determined to master reading and writing in English, her second language. She attended the Fort Shaw Indian School in Montana, serving as a matron in exchange for her schooling. She went on to secretarial school and later took a teaching post on the Okanogan reservation. She made strategic use of Anglo education in her efforts to develop her writing and teaching skills, but she remained critical of those systems as well. Perhaps Mourning Dove is offering her own sentiments when she writes that her protagonist, Co-ge-we-a, was an apt student who "seemed to imbibe knowledge and not content" at the mission boarding school.[16] Mourning Dove took her personal experiences and political concerns to public forums. She stood before civic groups advocating tribal fishing rights and sat with

Camp Fire Girls telling stories of Okanogan life. In 1935 she became the first woman elected to the Colville Tribal Council.

I have touched lightly on the role of the boarding school in Deloria's and Mourning Dove's experiences as students and teachers. An examination of the central place of the boarding school in federal assimilationist policy is beyond the scope of this paper.[17] Suffice it to say that the experiences of Mourning Dove and Deloria present a complex incorporation of cultural knowledge that challenges the educational assumptions of the boarding school project (that is, that children can be simply stripped of their "Indianness" and cloaked with patriotism, individualism, and the fear of God). Practically speaking, boarding schools were some of the few places where Native American women had access to "respectable" jobs. Deloria's long-time teaching career suggests an optimism about boarding school education, while Mourning Dove may have swallowed her skepticism for the sake of economic survival while working as a matron and teacher. Through contrasting personal experiences, both women recognized schools as key sites of cultural inscription and as important arenas in which to situate themselves in their practice of cultural mediation.

Negotiation

The personal labor histories of Ella Deloria and Mourning Dove are statements about the material struggles and emotional demands these women faced. Their labors exemplify the multiple jeopardies of many American Indian women in the United States, for their commitment to writing was realized only at great personal expense. Their fieldwork and writing were tucked around the edges of their paid labor for others and their long-term commitments to the unpaid labors of love practiced by many women—family caregiving. Deloria was devoted to caring for her father, sister, nieces, and nephews. Mourning Dove, the oldest of five children, took on many family responsibilities as her mother's health failed. Mourning Dove lost her only child, born during her marriage to Hector McCloud. However, she was seldom without children in her life, because she helped to raise her nieces and nephews.[18]

Both women experienced the chronic vulnerability of their low economic status. While Deloria was able to earn wages translating Dakota texts and conducting ethnographic fieldwork, her labor was the anthropological equivalent of piecework, managing from contract to contract and depending on the patronage of established white scholars.[19] The preeminent American anthropologist Franz Boas occasionally employed Deloria to verify previous accounts of social organization, ceremonies, and vision quests among the Sioux. She spent the summer of 1929 as a research assistant to a Columbia University psychologist, testing the "motor skills and social habits" of girls living on the Standing Rock Reservation.[20] Deloria's lack of formal credentials left her on the professional margins. Her status as a native scholar was appropriated at times to give legitimacy to the work of others. For example, as a team member in a public policy study of Navajo land use, Deloria was placed in the awkward political position of representing the "Indian View," suggesting that inter-tribal diversity was reducible to a single voice.[21] Ironically, it was this very process of homogenization of image that Deloria was struggling to challenge in her work.[22]

Christine Quintasket's manual labors in domestic service and migrant farm work left little time for the creative labors of her literary persona, Mourning Dove. She worked as a housekeeper, picked apples and hops, cooked meals for the field-workers, and, when time allowed, collected "folklores."[23] And at the end of the day, she wrote down her stories. Her life was punctuated by chronic illness, her health status a commentary on harsh living conditions. Although Christine married twice, her marriages did not bolster her vulnerable economic position, because her spouses were also dependent on the vagaries of the migrant labor market. Mourning Dove and Deloria shared a determination to inscribe their stories both because of and in spite of the obligations that shaped their lives.

Perhaps the most intriguing parallels and contrasts in Ella Deloria's and Mourn-ing Dove's practices of negotiation are exemplified in their relationships with their male mentors. The politics of gender, race, and class were subtly but powerfully artic-ulated through these relationships. Deloria maintained a long-time relationship as a research assistant and informant to Franz Boas. Mourning Dove's patron was Lucul-lus McWhorter, a homesteader, historian, and self-styled Indian rights activist in Washington state, whom she met at a Frontier Days celebration in about 1915.[24] These relationships were key conduits through which Deloria and Mourning Dove could channel their knowledge and experience; the relationships were also sources of frustration for both women as they struggled to make their views of the world understandable to their mentors. The paradoxical nature of these relationships that simultaneously supported and distorted the voices of Deloria and Mourning Dove is palpable in the correspondence between the women and their mentors. Both women exchanged letters over the years with their patrons. My access to their letters is lim-ited to selected correspondence published in secondary sources, where processes of extraction and interpretation have already taken place.[25] I hesitate to interpret too much from these selections; I explore them instead as another textual layer in which to consider the complexity of life experience to which these women respond.[26]

Ella Deloria's relationship with Franz Boas is fraught with the complexities and contradictions expressed by many "native" women anthropologists.[27] Boas was committed to the comprehensive documentation of North American Indian cul-tures. While Deloria's labor supported Boas's ethnographic agenda, her role as informant seemed to be valued more than her role as a scholar. Reports of her rela-tionship with Boas and the tone of their correspondence also reflect a strong mutual respect.[28] While Boas cultivated a paternal persona and was often referred to as "Papa Franz," Deloria transformed that title of kinship to "Father Franz,"[29] a reflection of her respect and her sense of kinship obligation.[30] It is this expression of a kinship bond with Boas that renders Deloria's relationship with him especially poignant. For Deloria, kinship obligations were intimately tied to her ways of knowing the world. Her knowledge of the power and centrality of kinship ties among the Dakota people was an experiential knowledge, one which she lived as she documented its diverse forms. Boas, however, saw personal relationships as separate from the objective rigors of his anthropological project. In her correspondence with Boas, Deloria sought to sensitize him to their epistemological differences and to educate him about the dilemmas of fieldwork for the native anthropologist.[31]

For example, in 1928 Boas had enlisted her skills in verifying previous accounts of the Sun Dance ceremony. Deloria wrote to him describing the dilemmas she faced because one of the key informants was also a relative of hers with a strong resistance to Anglo influences:

> He is my uncle — my father's half brother. My father is the only son of my grandfather's real wife, the one he bought with horses. This man is the son of my grandmother's cousin. Her people gave her to my grandfather to take as a second wife. This uncle hates my father because he considers him disloyal to the teachings and practices of his father. Some say he will not tell me anything. Others that he might because of my relationship to him. I am, you see, his daughter (according to the Dakota kinship system).[32]

Deloria anticipated the reluctance of her informants to speak about the ceremony and to share knowledge with outsiders. She noted, however, they might also feel obligated to share their stories because of their kinship ties to her. Their continuing dialogue about the Sun Dance ceremony and other cultural practices points to Boas's concern with verification and documentation of an "objective" truth, while Deloria could not separate the veracity of her informants' accounts from the significance of their relationship to her.

The differing meaning of kinship obligations exemplifies the epistemological chasm that resonates through the works of many indigenous scholars and the "Western" counterparts who peer into their worlds. Deloria could not extricate herself from this crisscross of relationships for the sake of scholarly scrutiny. She not only reported on and documented kinship systems and social organization, she was also obligated by those ties to a lifetime of caregiving responsibilities. While Boas valued the knowledge Deloria gained from her intimate connection to her informants, he presumed that as an objective researcher she could detach herself from the world she documented to fulfill her scholarly obligations. Deloria's correspondence with Boas posed an ongoing challenge to that belief. Her poignant letter to Boas dated November 6, 1928, illustrates the complex web of responsibilities in which her scholarship was enmeshed:

> My father was in such a critical state and there was nobody else to care for him and give him his medicines correctly so I was both occupied and on a fence about writing till things should seem to be a bit brighter. The only danger now is to guard against pneumonia, while he is still in bed. He can not speak, and writes all his wants, but it is an effort to do that. Only I can decipher his writing.

JANET L. FINN

I can not say at the present writing that he will be all right. But in a few days, say a week, if he continues to improve, I will make some arrangements for his care, and come back. There are plenty of women willing and glad to do the cooking, washing, etc., but there is nobody right here to take charge and carry out the doctor's orders.

Just about every old-time Indian from this, Rosebud, and the other reservations has been here to see him, some staying in tents for a week, so I have been writing down all I have got hold of. I am eager to come in and will certainly do so as soon as I can get away, but today I can not tell just how soon that may be. I thought many times that he was going, but he rallied each time and has been picking up the last three days.

I will only be too glad to continue after my term is up, and give, without pay, next fall what time I am losing now.[33]

Financial struggles were an ongoing concern for Deloria as she negotiated small research contracts with Boas and other established white scholars. The impact of this concern is voiced in her letter to Boas of February 7, 1936:

Now, as regards my returning to New York. I have never told this, but besides my nieces and nephews for whom I am guardian, I am responsible for providing the roof for my sister as well as for me. She has never had the advantages I've had; and though she has a small income to feed and clothe her, I can not just leave her and go off. That would not be right; besides we have no home at all. I live in my car, virtually; all our things are in it. And if I go anywhere, I find it cheapest to go in my car; and take my sister with me. I love her. I can not do otherwise than give her a home of sorts. . . . If I were alone in the world, I might risk it; but with things as they stand, I am afraid to return to New York, so far from the reservation, for so little money.[34]

I am struck more by the context than the content of this letter. When Deloria wrote it, she was a forty-seven-year-old woman living on an isolated, economically depressed reservation in South Dakota. She was invested in a profession that valued the documentation and preservation of historic life ways over the dynamics of domination and resistance that defined the cultural present in which she lived.

The relationship of Mourning Dove to her patron Lucullus McWhorter echoes similar themes of obligation, illness, and financial struggle. Writing to McWhorter amid a measles outbreak in 1917, she reports:

No. I do not expect to go hop picking this year. I cannot possible go any where[.] I have to much to look after. I have a little niece that is with me now. her papa has enlisted and gone to war and there are two children so. I took the baby which is 4 years old and left the boy who is 7 years of age. he will likely attend the mission school this year. My sister is not strong and she is not able to take care of her little ones.[35]

In language very telling of the power dynamics of their relationship, biographer Dexter Fisher describes McWhorter as charging Mourning Dove with the task of preserving the cultural history of her people.[36] Mourning Dove saw in McWhorter a sponsor for her lifelong desire to write novels informed by and incorporating Native Americans' experiences. McWhorter recognized her literary ability and saw in her the ideal informant capable of documenting the "primitive folk ways" of the Okonogan peoples. Mourning Dove agreed to assist McWhorter in his salvage ethnography project in exchange for his support in the editing and publishing of her fictional work. For McWhorter, editorial control over Mourning Dove's writing offered him a means for voicing his political views through her text.[37]

Mourning Dove's correspondence with McWhorter reveals a style reminiscent of Zora Neale Hurston.[38] Mourning Dove at times played on the native image her patron held of her, employing colloquial self-references such as Injun and squaw.[39] Her style, however, is dramatic, and the letters themselves are stories in which she constructed herself as a character and melded her identity with Co-ge-we-a, her main protagonist. For example, while awaiting word on the publication of *Co-ge-we-a* she writes:

> I am very sorry that "Cogeawea" has taken some more of your valuable time.
> I hope she can be able to repay you a little on Christmas day. You never hinted
> what you wish from that "squaw." she has taken so much of your time and is
> still delayed of being published. I am beganing to think she is an unlucky 13.
> Or she has caused this war, so as to save herself from getting into book form.[40]

These multiple characters experimented with identities as she variously signed herself as Mourning Dove, Christal, Christine, or Catherine.[41] Like Boas, McWhorter was obsessed with determining the veracity of his key informant's accounts. McWhorter's search for ethnographic facts was mediated by a woman who challenged the very premises of his notion of truth. I suggest that both Mourning Dove and Deloria understood that ethnographic truth was partial, perspectival, and embedded in social and material relations of power and obligation. Their letters offer glimpses into the struggles that shaped their cultural understanding and into the complex fusions of meaning and power through which their knowledge was extracted in the process of ethnographic production.

Against the Grain

At times Mourning Dove and Deloria voiced strong challenges to their mentors and to the stance of the Anglo ethnographer. Mourning Dove writes, "No foreigner could possibly penetrate or research these [the legends, religion, customs and theories of my people] because of the effort needed to overcome the shy reluctance of the Indian when it comes to giving information to whites."[42] And Deloria, in a letter to Boas, more bluntly states, "To go at it like a white man, for me, an Indian, is to throw up an immediate barrier between myself and the people."[43] These words suggest a theme of resistance that plays out in multiple and complex ways throughout these women's works and lives. I am still grappling with my own construction of this theme and its place in my reading of Deloria's work. Much of her writing conveys a sense of a cultural whole, set apart from struggle and contest. In reading her nonfiction work *Speaking of Indians*, I found myself uncomfortable at times with the conciliatory tone Deloria uses to engage a white readership.[44] She seems to avoid any hint of recrimination for the repressive history of U.S. public policy toward American Indian peoples. However, there are stories within the text that offer strategic and subtle commentaries on resistance. For example, she describes the Sioux use of government issue muslin to line the inside of their new domiciles—log homes—in the postallotment era: "On these [wall coverings] they painted beautiful designs and made lovely . . . drawings of historical scenes . . . and courtship scenes."[45] She described the incorporation and refashioning of the material culture of white society to create a context of familiarity within the foreign walls of the log home. Deloria's story merges incorporation and creativity as the muslin is taken in and made over. The story suggests resistance as the outside walls of the log home stand stoic and silent, not divulging the activity within. The very materials of the white system become the walls of resistance and the symbols of creativity.

In contrast to Deloria, Mourning Dove's writings strain with her resistance to the constraints of gender roles she experienced within both Salishan and white societies. In her autobiography she openly voiced her resistance to men and marriage as a young woman. She refused the esoteric knowledge of love medicine offered her by a Salish medicine woman, resisting what she saw as obligations that would bind her to traditional tribal roles.[46] In the 1930s she expressed her resistance through direct political action in the effort to preserve Indian rights and resources on the Colville Reservation.[47] A painful statement on the toll her struggle extracted from her appears in that ironic textual summary of one's life, her death certificate. Her death is attributed to "exhaustion from manic depressive psychosis."[48] In a single label the years of political resistance were reduced to personal pathology encoded in a permanent text that she is unable to challenge.

Through their novels, both Deloria and Mourning Dove wrote against the dominant grain of Indian image making. Their novels challenged the capacity of impersonal ethnographic accounts to "capture" Native American experience; they countered popular stereotypes of Indian people; and they posed an alternative form for elucidating cultural knowledge. Deloria's novel, *Waterlily*, follows the life of a young Dakota woman growing up on the plains in the late nineteenth century. Waterlily's day-to-day experiences reveal Dakota values and cultural practices. As Waterlily learns the complexities of kinship systems and their obligations, so does the reader. Deloria pays careful attention to the central place of children in Dakota life. Perhaps this serves as her own subtle commentary on Anglo practices of removing Indian children from family and culture and placing them in adoptive homes and boarding schools.

Deloria tells stories at many levels in *Waterlily*. Through the character of a tribal elder she describes the cultural sanctity of storytelling: "Speech is holy; it was not intended to be set free only to be wasted. It is for hearing and remembering." [49] Here Deloria poses the relational and emotive context of storytelling such that the story is inseparable from the act of telling. She uses stories throughout the novel both to educate her readers about cultural practices and to demonstrate a process of learning that contrasts sharply with the Anglo educational system.

Deloria also portrays the respect for personal dignity that shapes relations between women. She describes the hesitance of Dakota women to share their intimate secrets, pleasant or unpleasant, with other women, noting that "she could live and die with her own secrets and she did so. Her one concern was to maintain her dignity." [50] Ironically, it seems as if the very dignity Deloria finds to be so intimate to Dakota women's experience is violated in efforts to come to terms with women's struggles. I remain torn by my own participation in this process as I probe Deloria's private world. I am reminded of my first reading of *Waterlily* as Deloria drew me into the centrality of Dakota women's experience, then abruptly confronted me with my whiteness and separateness from her world. Swiftly and silently, the violence of white presence penetrated the core of Dakota life with the arrival of smallpox-infested blankets. My intimacy with Waterlily was suddenly polluted by a sense of complicity. I wanted to set myself apart from this history and to claim my place among the circle of women I had come to know. I felt a flush of shame, reminded that I cannot erase my history and its privileges. And what conditions of history and privilege allow me now to pull aside the muslin walls of dignity covering Deloria's private struggles? I find I must rethink the "personal as political" and situate that maxim of feminism within a context of critical inquiry that asks: Which person? Whose politics?

Mourning Dove crafts a very different story of Native American women's experience in her western romance novel, *Co-ge-we-a, the Half-Blood*, the story of a mixed-blood young woman coming of age in the rural West in the early 1900s. Co-ge-we-a is caught between the pull of her roots to Okanogan culture and the pressure to assimilate into the encroaching white world. In contrast to the sense of cultural integrity that Deloria creates, Mourning Dove writes of fractures and tensions. Co-ge-we-a's identity as "half blood" locates the conflicts and contradictions of social position in the body of the woman.

Mourning Dove takes the reader into Co-ge-we-a's private world of thought and feeling. Co-ge-we-a is a spirited woman, who, like her creator, chafes against the constraints of her gender, race, and class identities. Mourning Dove uses Co-ge-we-a's private thoughts for her own social commentary. She addresses the diversity of Indian women's experience and the particular nature of her own struggles by placing Co-ge-we-a in a position of uncertainty vis-à-vis her two sisters, one enacting a stereotypically "traditional" Native American woman's role, the other "passing" in her marriage to a white rancher.

A central plot develops around Co-ge-we-a's growing affections for a white suitor. Densmore, the suitor, is up to no good; he has self-interest in mind as he seeks to marry Co-ge-we-a. Mourning Dove articulates gender and race conflict through this relationship. She also uses the themes of trust and betrayal in the relationship as a metaphor for the larger struggle for preservation of native kinship, land, and resources.

Mourning Dove weaves features central to Salishan culture, such as spirit power and the sweat lodge, into her text.[51] She develops the character of Stemteema, Co-ge-we-a's grandmother, as the storyteller. Stemteema provides a voice for Salish history and beliefs, creating a cultural pattern counter to the events unfolding in the story. Through Stemteema, Mourning Dove is able to incorporate Okanogan stories and storytelling style into a text reminiscent of a Harlequin romance. Her popular literary genre becomes a tool for popular education.

The novels of Mourning Dove and Deloria placed women center stage and challenged both scholarly and popular representations of Native Americans. Their novels were integral parts of their broader commitment to cultural mediation. But this brings us back to the earlier questions of genre, authenticity, audience, and impact. Deloria seems to accept the distinction between ethnography and fiction. Confronted with the limits of ethnographic authority, she turned to the novel as a way of knowing the complex and cohesive world of the Dakota Sioux. Mourning Dove challenges the very distinction between truth and fiction that forms the premise for these questions. She was an experimental writer ahead of her time, the trickster who paid a heavy price for her deep play at the boundaries of gender, culture, and truth.

In ironic contrast to the urgency of these women's missions, years passed before their novels appeared in print. Mourning Dove's novel was published after eleven years of effort. Deloria completed *Waterlily* in 1944, but it was not published until 1988. The erasures of these works may stand as a statement to the relative powerlessness of the women's inscriptions in the political moment in which they wrote. And what of the current rekindled interest in their works? Have they finally "come to voice" only to become subjects in another politics of identification through academic scrutiny?[52]

Deloria and Mourning Dove are part of a legacy of women who have recognized the value of what anthropologist Faye Harrison has termed "anthroperformance."[53] Harrison speaks to the pedagogical power in communicating the social and cultural processes of lived experience through fiction, drama, and performance. She points to the pioneering work of folklorist and novelist Zora Neale Hurston and of dancer and anthropologist Katherine Dunham in creatively integrating performance as pedagogy.[54] Similarly, Deloria and Mourning Dove creatively melded cultural knowledge and lived experience into expressive forms that offer new ways of knowing. Both women had a keen awareness of the politics of popular knowledge. They were concerned not so much with knowledge about the world as with knowledge for transformation of their worlds.

They sought truth in emotive experience and used their positions in the borderlands to translate those truths across cultural boundaries. Their works echo the themes of feminist and postmodern anthropologists who call for consciousness of one's own multiple and at times conflicting subject positions.[55] They acknowledged their political missions, self-consciously explored avenues of textual expression, and turned to the novel to reach audiences they hoped to transform.

The politics and poetics of the Native American women's voices, represented in the lives and works of Deloria and Mourning Dove, anticipate many of the conflicts and struggles being addressed today by feminist anthropologists.[56] The politics of ethnographic fieldwork and the dilemmas inherent in writing texts are issues that resonate through the living and telling of these women's lives over the past century. Trust and betrayal, the authority of the written word, and the politics of knowledge production and appropriation are meaningful themes for Deloria and Mourning Dove. There are many lessons to learn from those who have rejected the powerful constraints of convention and have played with ways of knowing the world. In the folk wisdom of country music, we are "walking contradictions, partly truth and partly fiction." The challenge for women writing culture is to grasp the truth value of our contradictions.

Notes

An earlier version of the essay appeared in "Women Writing Culture," Ruth Behar, ed., *Critique of Anthropology* 13, no. 4 (1993): 335–49.

1. Ella Deloria, "The Sun Dance of the Oglala Sioux," *Journal of American Folklore* 42, no. 166 (1929): 354–413; *Dakota Texts* (New York: G. E. Stechert, 1932); *Speaking of Indians* (Vermillion, S. Dak.: State Publishing, [1944] 1983); and *Waterlily* (Lincoln and London: University of Nebraska Press, 1988); Franz Boas and Ella Deloria, *Dakota Grammar* (Memoirs of the National Academy of Sciences 23, Second Memoir; Washington, D.C.: Government Printing Office, 1941); Thomas Jones, Harold Allen, Charles Loran, and Ella Deloria, *The Navajo Indian Problem: An Inquiry* (New York: Phelps-Stokes, 1939).

2. See Jay Miller, "Mourning Dove: The Author as Cultural Mediator," in *Being and Becoming Indian: Biographical Studies of North American Frontiers*, ed. James Clifton (Chicago: Dorsey Press, 1989), 160–82; and Alanna Brown, "Mourning Dove's Canadian Recovery Years, 1917–1919," *Canadian Literature* 124/125 (Spring/Summer 1990): 113–23, for a more thorough discussion of Mourning Dove's family and cultural heritage. Brown writes that Mourning Dove "may be Okanogan, Colville, and/or Lake, and Irish in descent" (Brown, "Mourning Dove's Canadian Recovery Years," 113–14). She suggests that Mourning Dove's treatment of "the half-breed question" in *Cogewea* may stem from the contradictions of her own experience (Mourning Dove, *Co-ge-we-a, the Half-Blood: A Depiction of the Great Montana Cattle Range* [Boston: Four Seas, 1927; reprinted 1981 as *Cogewea*, University of Nebraska Press, Lincoln]). Mourning Dove, in her introduction to *Coyote Stories*, writes, "My people are the Okanogan and the Swhyayl'-puh (Colville), closely related Salishan tribes, and I also have relatives in the En-koh-tu-me-whoh, or Nicola, band of the Thompson River Indians in British Columbia. My father's mother was a Nicola, and his father was a Hudson's Bay Company man, a hardy, adventurous Celt" (Mourning Dove, *Coyote Stories*, ed. and illus. Heister Dean Guie (Caldwell, Idaho: Caxton, 1933), 8–9.

3. Mourning Dove, *Coyote Stories, Cogewea,* and *Mourning Dove: A Salishan Autobiography* (Lincoln and London: University of Nebraska Press, 1990). *Coyote Stories* underwent editorial revision by her mentor, Lucullus McWhorter, and his colleague Heister Dean Guie, a news editor. Clifford Trafzer and Richard Scheuerman (*Mourning Dove's*

Stories [San Diego, Calif.: San Diego State University Press, 1991], 8) argue that the stories were "rewritten and altered by McWhorter and Guie to fit their ideas about what should be presented." Similarly, the chapter titles and organization of her autobiography resemble a classic ethnographic format that may reflect the literary style of the editor more than that of the author.

4. The term *cultural mediator* is used by Beatrice Medicine in "Ella Deloria: The Emic Voice" (*MELUS* 7, no. 4 [1980]: 23–30) and by Jay Miller in "Mourning Dove," 161, 174–76, 180.

5. James Clifford, "Introduction: Partial Truths," in *Writing Culture: The Poetics and Politics of Ethnography,* ed. James Clifford and George E. Marcus (Berkeley: University of California Press, 1986), 15. Numerous critical writings in anthropology have challenged the authority and "truth" of ethnographic texts. See, for example, George E. Marcus and Dick Cushman, "Ethnographies as Texts," *Annual Review of Anthropology* 11 (1982): 25–69; and Renato Rosaldo, *Culture and Truth: The Remaking of Social Analysis* (Boston: Beacon Press, 1989). Feminist writers have addressed questions of gender politics embedded in current discussions of representation, truth, and ethnographic authority. See, for example, Deborah Gordon, "Writing Culture, Writing Feminism: The Poetics and Politics of Experimental Ethnography," *Inscriptions* 3/4 (1988): 7–24; Judith Stacey, *Brave New Families: Stories of Domestic Upheaval in Late Twentieth Century America* (New York: Basic Books, 1990); and Kamala Visweswaran, "Defining Feminist Ethnography," *Inscriptions* 3/4 (1988): 26–57.

6. Visweswaran, "Defining Feminist Ethnography," 39.

7. Deloria, *Speaking of Indians* and *Waterlily.*

8. I draw from Janette Murray, "Ella Deloria: A Biographical Sketch and Literary Analysis" (Ph.D. diss., University of North Dakota, 1974); Medicine, "Ella Deloria"; and from Agnes Picotte, "A Biographical Sketch of the Author," in Deloria, *Waterlily,* 229–31. See these works for more detailed accounts. Picotte notes that Dakota refers to all divisions of Sioux people. Dakota and Sioux are used interchangeably in these texts, and I employ both terms here. Medicine gives Deloria's birthdate as January 30, 1888; Picotte lists the date as January 31, 1889. Biographical information on Mourning Dove is drawn largely from her autobiography, *Mourning Dove;* from Alice Poindexter (Dexter) Fisher, "Introduction," in *Cogewea,* i–xxvi; from Brown, "Mourning Dove's Canadian Recovery Years"; and from Miller, "Mourning Dove," and "Introduction," in *Mourning Dove.*

9. Medicine, "Ella Deloria"; Murray, "Ella Deloria."

10. Mourning Dove, *Mourning Dove,* 10.

11. Miller describes Mourning Dove's birth story as foreshadowing her life of "constant motion and independent activity," and he challenges the truth of Mourning Dove's claims that her paternal grandfather was of Scottish descent (ibid., xii, xvi).

12. I have borrowed the expression "being and becoming Indian" from Clifton's work of the same name.

13. Mourning Dove, *Mourning Dove,* 24, 142.

14. Ibid., 25–26.

15. Ibid., 186.

16. Mourning Dove, *Cogewea,* 16.

17. The literature on the role of boarding schools in the history of American Indian education is extensive. In an important analysis David Wallace Adams ("Fundamental Considerations: The Deep Meaning of Native American Schooling, 1880–1900," *Harvard Educational Review* 58, no. 1 [1988]: 1–28) contextualizes Indian education from 1880 to 1900 in terms of Protestant ideology, capitalism, and Republicanism. Carolyn Attneave

and Agnes Dill ("Indian Boarding School and Indian Women: Blessing or Curse?" in *National Institute of Education Conference on the Education and Occupation of American Indian Women* [Washington, D.C.: Government Printing Office, 1976], 211–31) address boarding schools in terms of women's experiences. Margaret Szasz ("Listening to the Native Voice: American Indian Schooling in the Twentieth Century," *Montana: The Magazine of Western History* [Summer 1989]: 42–54) explores personal accounts of student experiences in boarding schools. Robert Trennert ("Educating Indian Girls at Non-Reservation Boarding Schools, 1878–1920," *Western Historical Quarterly* 13 [July 1982]: 271–90; *The Phoenix Indian School: Forced Assimilation in Arizona, 1891–1935* [Norman: University of Oklahoma Press, 1988]; and "Selling Indian Education at World's Fairs and Expositions, 1893–1904," *American Indian Quarterly* 11, no. 3 (1989): 203–20) presents an excellent series of case studies that place the cultural politics of particular boarding school histories in a larger economic context.

18. Brown, "Mourning Dove's Canadian Recovery Years."

19. Murray, "Ella Deloria"; Medicine, "Ella Deloria."

20. Murray, "Ella Deloria."

21. Jones et al., *Navajo Indian Problem.*

22. Deloria, *Speaking of Indians*, 212.

23. Fisher, "Introduction."

24. Miller, "Mourning Dove," 166.

25. Brown, "Mourning Dove's Canadian Recovery Years"; Murray, "Ella Deloria"; Miller, "Mourning Dove"; Fisher, "Introduction"; Mourning Dove, *Mourning Dove.*

26. I have used both "mentor" and "patron" here. I am still uncertain as to which term best portrays the nature of the relationship. The term mentor suggests that these men were grooming the women to take over their roles, which was certainly not the case. "Sponsorship" suggests a level of financial support that was not in evidence here. It seems that the relationships may have more parallels to a client/patron relationship, though that may suggest a more particular type of arrangement than I read here.

27. Beatrice Medicine, "Learning to Be an Anthropologist and Remaining 'Native,'" in *Applied Anthropology in America*, ed. Elizabeth Eddy and William Partridge (New York: Columbia University Press, 1978), 182–96; Gwendolyn Mikell, "Zora Neale Hurston (1903–1960)," in *Women Anthropologists: Selected Biographies*, ed. Ute Gacs, Aisha Khan, Jerrie McIntyre and Ruth Weinberg (Urbana: University of Illinois Press, 1989), 160–66; Christine Obbo, *African Women: Their Struggle for Economic Independence* (London: Zed Press, 1990).

28. Medicine, "Ella Deloria"; Murray, "Ella Deloria."

29. Raymond DeMallie, "Afterword," in *Waterlily*, 233–44.

30. Medicine, "Ella Deloria."

31. Murray, "Ella Deloria"; Medicine, "Learning to Be an Anthropologist."

32. Ella Deloria, letter to Franz Boas, August 21, 1928, in Murray, "Ella Deloria," 103. I am particularly indebted to Janette Murray for publishing generous excerpts from Deloria's letters to Boas. She allowed Deloria to "speak for herself" and provided rich insights into the relationship between Deloria and Boas.

33. Ella Deloria, letter to Franz Boas, November 6, 1928, in ibid., 104.

34. Ella Deloria, letter to Franz Boas, February 7, 1936, in ibid., 122–23.

35. Mourning Dove, letter to Lucullus McWhorter, September 1, 1917, in Brown, "Mourning Dove's Canadian Recovery Years," 115.

36. Fisher, "Introduction."

37. Fisher, "Introduction"; Miller, "Mourning Dove."

38. Mikell, "Zora Neale Hurston"; Graciela Hernández, "Multiple Subjectivities and Strategic Positionality: Zora Neale Hurston's Experimental Ethnographies," this volume.

39. Miller, "Mourning Dove," 169; Mourning Dove, *Cogewea,* xii.

40. Mourning Dove, letter to Lucullus McWhorter, October 8, 1917, in Brown, "Mourning Dove's Canadian Recovery Years," 117.

41. Miller, "Mourning Dove"; Mourning Dove, *Mourning Dove.*

42. Mourning Dove, *Mourning Dove,* 12.

43. Ella Deloria, letter to Franz Boas, July 11, 1932, in Murray, "Ella Deloria," 114.

44. *Speaking of Indians* was originally published by Friendship Press, under the sponsorship of the Missionary Education Movement, which may account for its conciliatory tone (Murray, "Ella Deloria," 140).

45. Deloria, *Speaking of Indians,* 60–61.

46. Mourning Dove, *Mourning Dove,* 81.

47. Miller, "Mourning Dove"; Mourning Dove, *Mourning Dove.*

48. Miller, "Mourning Dove," 180.

49. Deloria, *Waterlily,* 50.

50. Ibid., 179.

51. Fisher, "Introduction," xi.

52. Visweswaran, "Defining Feminist Ethnography."

53. Faye Harrison, "Three Women, One Struggle: Anthropology, Performance and Pedagogy," *Transforming Anthropology* 1, no. 1 (1990): 3.

54. Ibid., 2.

55. James Clifford, "Introduction: Partial Truths," in *Writing Culture,* 1–26; Patricia Caplan, "Engendering Knowledge: The Politics of Ethnography," *Anthropology Today* 4, no. 5 (1988): 8–12, and no. 6 (1988): 14–17; Gordon, "Writing Culture."

56. Faye Harrison, "Anthropology as an Agent of Transformation: Introductory Comments and Queries," in *Decolonizing Anthropology: Moving Further Toward an Anthropology for Liberation* (Washington, D.C.: American Anthropological Association, 1991), 1–14; Gordon, "Writing Culture"; Judith Stacey, "Can There Be a Feminist Ethnography?" *Women's Studies International Forum* 11, no. 1 (1988): 21–27; Obbo, *African Women.*

Multiple Subjectivities and Strategic Positionality: Zora Neale Hurston's Experimental Ethnographies

Graciela Hernández

[Mother Catherine] laid her hand upon my head.

"Daughter, why have you come here?"

"Mother, I come seeking knowledge."

ZORA NEALE HURSTON,
The Sanctified Church, 1981

LIKE HURSTON, I came to this project seeking knowledge and with the intent of contributing to the debates on feminist contributions to experimental ethnographies. In my interpretations of Hurston, I want to place her unequivocally within a tradition that has been effaced by masculinist bias in both the theory and the practice of anthropology.[1] However, this desire is mediated by an evaluation of Hurston that recognizes the nexus of historical forces circumscribing her scholarship. My work on Hurston is an attempt to move beyond polar categorizations that either lionize or disparage her as a cultural figure.[2] Instead, I hope my work serves to suggest Hurston's historical significance during the early to mid-twentieth century and her relevance in contemporary literary and anthropological debates. Rather than embracing a sense of closure, my work attempts to attribute meaning while remaining open to negotiations of these meanings.

While reflecting on Hurston's scholarship constitutes the main analysis of this paper, I must also recognize my relationship to the work I under-

Zora Neale Hurston on a folklore-collecting trip, late 1930s. (Photograph courtesy of Jane Belo Papers, Margaret Mead Collection, container P94)

take. Not only must I locate Hurston in the particular sociopolitical moments in which she wrote and is now being widely read, I must address my own position within these debates. As Carol B. Stack has recently written, feminists must call our own writing practices into question: "The goal is to explore and experiment—to learn and write as much about our own understanding of how we locate our voice in our writing as possible."[3] My concerns are provoked by voices of African American feminist scholars whose commitment to a discourse inflected with race and gender analysis have brought attention to works frequently overlooked. The most

glaring example of such erasure is Zora Neale Hurston. Recently, challenges to literary and anthropological canons have served to reverse the historic erasure of
Hurston, yet displacements of gender, "race," class, and sexuality remain a problem
in some interpretations of her work.

The displacement of the crucial social categories that inform Hurston's work
troubles cultural critic Michelle Wallace. Wallace points to the alarming example of
Harold Bloom, editor of *Zora Neale Hurston*. She claims that Bloom's practices
erase the interpretive frameworks used by the very scholars he anthologizes and
thus constitute a cosmic blunder: "Bloom's introduction . . . supersedes the text that
follows. He morbidly objectifies Hurston in a sexually charged image of Western
culture's embedded anti-feminism. Hurston's silent black body floats to the surface
of a systemic dilemma."[4] Bloom's approach, then, lends further urgency to "sexual/
textual" acts that do little, if anything, to interrogate the historical conditions that
account for Hurston's past erasure or her current cult status in feminist and African
American scholarly communities. Other black feminist critics, such as bell hooks,
maintain the necessity of claiming black women's cultural traditions and, more
importantly, recognizing their intellectual traditions, even while admitting that
the construction of such a tradition is due to urgent political demands.[5] After all,
P. Gabrielle Foreman writes, "The lack of a discernible tradition has been a silencing
agent in the history of Blacks, of women, of Black women, of indeed marginalized
groupings. Without a 'tradition' into which to fit us, we have been misunderstood,
misinterpreted, and finally, often quickly dismissed."[6]

While Wallace asks valid questions about the appropriation of African American
women's cultural contributions as well as their intellectual insights, these questions
are structured along binary oppositions. As a result, Wallace counterposes the work
done by men against the scholarship undertaken by women, as well as the contributions (or not) made by whites against those made by African Americans. It is here
that I wish to complicate such a cartography by asking what a Chicana feminist
scholar can contribute to an analysis of Hurston and to the ongoing construction of
African American feminist interpretive schemes.[7] Foregrounding questions about
my relationship to African American feminist criticism and the responsibilities I
take on when I represent Hurston as a historical subject answers Hazel Carby's call
that "black feminist criticism be regarded critically as a problem, not a solution, as
a sign that should be interrogated, a locus of contradictions." Black feminist critical
theory should yield a vantage point from which to regard "racisms and sexisms . . .
as particular historical practices articulated with each other and with other practices in social formation."[8] I would like to meld Carby's historical approach with
the contemporary warnings by social scientists. For example, Diane L. Wolf writes
that scholars should "consider how we as feminist researchers are constituted as
culturally, socially, and historically specific subjects in particular global configurations of economic and political powers."[9] Moving back and forth between a
method that scrutinizes social practices and one that interrogates contemporary

structures of power is one way of grasping those aspects of Zora Neale Hurston's life that continue to elude understanding.

Considering Hurston's life and cultural production from the perspectives developed by social scientists and by black feminist literary critics is also appropriate because Hurston's texts defy disciplinary frameworks. The literary tradition advocated by Foreman, for example, reveals the problems that occur when one clings to narrow definitions of literature and, I would add in the case of Zora Neale Hurston, to narrow definitions of ethnography. Foreman argues for a more expansive vision of textual production, suggesting that black women's cultural artifacts exceed and challenge the boundaries enacted by traditional approaches to scholarly studies.[10] In a similar vein, Kamala Visweswaran urges the reconstruction of ethnographic canons in a way that explores the place of literary forms such as the novel and the short story and underscores the intertwining of race and gender with questions of genre.[11]

My interpretation of Hurston follows a similar line of thinking. While Hurston's ethnographies may draw on traditional ethnographic strategies, it is imperative to ask what other traditions inform her work. I will argue that Hurston's ethnographies are experimental in the sense that they extend ethnographic convention to what have been bracketed, until recently, as literary strategies.[12] Furthermore, Hurston introduces an authorial presence into her work, eschewing the assumption that the ethnographer stands outside the social relations of the field and subsequent representations of fieldwork. The subjective accounts found in *Mules and Men* (1935) and *Tell My Horse* (1938), two of Hurston's ethnographies, anticipate current dilemmas and scholarly trajectories. The use of the subjective destablizes Hurston's ethnographic authority, yet it also provides a vantage point from which to view her shifting allegiances. Hurston's ethnographies demonstrate that self-reflexivity, in and of itself, does not necessarily ameliorate disparate power relations. Rather, Hurston shows the potential for the self-reflexive mode to unmask the asymmetrical relationships that exist between researchers and the communities they study.

Finally, one must remember that in spite of these strategies, Hurston does participate in the codification of knowledge and the consolidation of anthropology as a discipline. It is my goal to explore the ambiguity produced as Hurston participates in the institutionalization of anthropology while she simultaneously undermines a project that deems the ethnography a final repository of knowledge.

Biographical and Historical Considerations

Understanding Zora Neale Hurston's life requires a biographical inquiry, though such a narrative has proved difficult to reconstruct. Robert E. Hemenway's text *Zora Neale Hurston: A Literary Biography* continues to remain the most thorough reckoning of Hurston's life and work. Hurston was the daughter of an encouraging mother and sobering father who lived in a Florida town populated and governed by

African Americans.[13] Hemenway notes that the representation of Hurston "as a barefoot girl standing before a ramshackle dwelling" on the front cover of her auto-biography, *Dust Tracks on a Road,* belies the relatively comfortable childhood Hurston had known. Soon after the death of her mother and her father's subsequent remarriage, Hurston broke away from her family and developed an independence that sustained her throughout most of her difficult life.[14] The privilege she had known as a young girl would never be hers again, and she would later become dependent on a variety of unstable sources of economic support.

Zora Hurston's intermittent encounters with institutions of higher education began with her enrollment at Morgan Academy in Baltimore. By 1920 she had obtained an associate degree from Howard Academy in Washington, D.C. She quickly began to cultivate the literary connections made possible by her award-winning writing. It was Hurston's ambition as a fiction writer that led her to pursue her dreams in New York City, where she soon partook of the urban cultural scene and enrolled in Barnard College.[15] Hemenway offers a poignant image of Hurston as she arrived in New York City:

> She carried most of her belongings in her bag, including a number of manu-scripts that she hoped would impress. Even if they did not, she was confident of her ability to survive in the big city; she had been on her own since the age of fourteen. Brown skinned, big boned, with freckles and high cheekbones, she was a striking woman; her dark brown eyes were both impish and intelligent, her voice was rich and black — with the map of Florida on her tongue.[16]

Little did Hurston know that she stood poised at a crossroad. Nor did she realize that soon the "belongings in her bag" would be transformed by a variety of person-alities and agendas.

Originally encouraged by leading intellectuals of the time, including Charles S. Johnson, W. E. B. Du Bois, and Alain Locke, Hurston and other "New Negroes" quickly attempted to establish their own cultural sensibility. Acting in tandem with Wallace Thurman and Langston Hughes, this group of young artists worked to disseminate their theoretical perspectives on the relationship between art, culture, and politics. The culmination of their views was embodied in the publication of *Fire!!,* a literary magazine that rejected a bourgeois conception of art in favor of a proletarian-based approach to it.[17] Hemenway concludes that Hurston's involve-ment in this cultural movement, known as the Harlem Renaissance, provided her with a space in which to forge her perspectives on representation: "She . . . struggled with the dangers of surveying the masses from the mountaintop, treating the folk material of the race as a landscape to be strip-mined in order to fuel the creative force."[18] The bulk of Hurston's cultural contributions attest to this struggle. Thus, her work is marked by the blurring of boundaries across genres, disciplinary con-cerns, and theoretical impulses.

As the vortex that was the Harlem Renaissance subsided and the completion of Hurston's collection of folktales approached, Hurston began to consider the possibilities of completing a Ph.D. in anthropology and folklore under the tutelage of Franz Boas.[19] As early as 1930 she entertained the idea of working toward a doctorate. However, material restraints, a constant in Hurston's adult life, and lack of support from her powerful patron, Mrs. Rufus Osgood Mason, thwarted such a goal.[20] By 1935 Hurston shrugged off her patron's control and won a fellowship from the Rosenwald Foundation to pursue her course of study. Shortly after determining the terms of the fellowship, however, foundation officials expressed doubts about Hurston's commitment to scholarship. As a consequence, instead of offering her two years of support, the foundation guaranteed only one semester of funding.[21] About the doctorate, Hurston would later write, "[I am] working like a slave and liking it. But I have lost all my zest for a doctorate. I have definitely decided that I never want to teach, so what is the use of the degree. It seems that I am wasting two good years of my life when I should be working."[22] Her response to the foundation president, Edwin Embree, reveals the economic realities Hurston faced as she pondered the direction of her academic career:

> You would understand that I would not be able to do anything important towards a doctorate with a single semester of work. So I did what could amount to something. I wrote two plays, . . . I wrote the first draft of my next novel [Their Eyes Were Watching God] which has already been accepted by my publishers. It was six months of most intensive labor, because I considered it simply must count constructively. . . . Please accept my profound thanks. . . . It [the fellowship funding] was short but important in my career.[23]

These epistolary excerpts reveal much about Hurston's ambition and savvy. The disjunction between her responses—the cavalier rejection of the academy and the spirited rejoinder to Embree—captures Hurston's refusal to passively accept the negative assessments of herself and the narrow definitions of her scholarship. Yet the traces of false bravado lurking in the margins of her letter also expose her vulnerability as a gendered, classed, and racialized subject whose livelihood depended on other people's interpretations of her research.

In spite of Hemenway's exhaustive scholarship and sensitive rendering of Hurston's biography, such an account cannot adequately contextualize Hurston's accomplishments and failures. A broader assessment of the intellectual and sociopolitical milieus that inform Hurston's life and work provides for a complex evaluation that looks beyond Hurston's enigmatic personality to the historical forces that structured the world in which she lived. The critical studies undertaken by scholars Gwendolyn Mikell and Deborah Gordon have contributed much to the debates about representational strategies in Hurston's research and writing. According to Mikell and Gordon, the popular interest in race relations, the theoretical shifts in anthropology, and the institutionalization of anthropology within the academy were three of the significant developments that had an impact on Hurston's intellectual trajectory.

One of the first scholars to situate Hurston within a history of anthropology was

Gwendolyn Mikell. "Seldom discussed in relationship to Zora Neale Hurston," Mikell writes, "are the anthropological traditions which she inherited and to which she contributed by virtue of her background and commitment to the study of black life."[24] Moving away from diffusionist theories and evolutionist approaches, American anthropologists during the 1920s were busy revising nineteenth-century approaches to social analysis. The stress on cultural relativity at Columbia University was a reflection of Franz Boas's impact on the field of anthropology. Mikell also identifies the importance of psychological analysis to Hurston's thinking. Ruth Benedict, in particular, was one of the scholars at Columbia University whose work was deeply informed by the contemporary interest in Freud and Jung.[25]

The theoretical trajectory of anthropology as a discipline was not the only cultural current that shaped Hurston intellectually. Mikell argues that

> *Hurston's reference point is her experience within the Afro-American environment. From rural southern Black roots, she begins a process of transformation which moved her into the cultural dynamism of the Harlem Renaissance writers, and further into the rarefied atmosphere of the Columbia intellectual world. Hurston belonged to all three worlds, each of which exerted pressures moving her in one direction or the other at various moments. In reading her ethnography, one must remember that she was the contradictory product of the class and race-conscious American society of the 1930s.*[26]

Mikell explores Hurston's place in the ethnographic canon by positioning her work in the context of a broad range of cultural developments and theoretical innovations. By conveying the simultaneity of Hurston's experiences, Mikell persuasively begins the process of historicizing her intellectual formation.

Such an early critical intervention into debates about Hurston's place in both ethnographic and literary canons allows Deborah Gordon to flesh out the demands of those "three worlds" alluded to by Mikell. In particular, Gordon carefully attends to the ways in which multiple demands and complex mentoring situations forced Hurston to mediate between competing theoretical traditions and methodological approaches. In New York City she entered into an ongoing cultural debate concerning the relationship between art and black culture. Hurston's involvement in these debates brought her to the attention of scholars such as Alain Locke. Locke sought to articulate the aesthetic experience of black culture that had the potential to recreate an African American culture. By widely disseminating African American art, Locke sought to increase racial self-awareness in the black community. His vision and his role as a cultural leader positioned him as mentor to a number of young artists, including Hurston.[27] Hemenway writes that while "Hurston thought of [Locke] as a mother hen . . . she also sought his approval. Locke sometimes disapproved of Zora . . . [and] although he respected her talent, he was not hesitant to offer counsel."[28]

A second mentor who explicitly controlled aspects of Hurston's cultural production was Mrs. Rufus Osgood Mason, a white woman who was Hurston's patron from 1927 to 1933. Not only did Mrs. Mason exercise editorial discretion over Hurston's writing, she in effect owned the rights to much of Hurston's early collections of folklore.[29] As Hurston's often sole means of financial support, Mrs. Mason used her access to material resources to influence African American scholarly and artistic endeavors. Her approach was clearly at odds with the theory and methodology taught by Franz Boas at Barnard College and Columbia University.[30] Gordon identifies Boas as Hurston's third mentor. Unlike her other tutors, he stressed the need to explore the wider cultural implications of the work she undertook. Describing the clash inherent between those differing representational styles, Gordon states that "Boas had urged Hurston in her early fieldwork trips to focus on the behavioral or stylistic aspects of the story-telling sessions that she saw in the South. Because Mason had collected folklore materials during an earlier period, she 'knew' folklore as a different kind of object than Boas." Thus the disparate mentoring situation affected Hurston's writing so that it "look[ed] like a negotiation of these distinctions, a compromise between competing writing styles for the representation of African-Americans—one that was scholarly, objective, and attentive to designating larger meanings, and the other more 'popular,' laying out of objects as if in an art museum."[31] While Gordon neglects to note the termination of the relationship between Hurston and Mrs. Mason after 1933 and before the publication of Hurston's primary pieces, surely the legacy of those early years of training under her patron left their mark on Hurston's consciousness.

The Texture of Zora Neale Hurston's *Mules and Men*

More nuanced readings of Hurston's contributions to anthropology are possible as a result of the recent scrutinization of traditional canons. I will focus my reading on *Mules and Men,* one of Hurston's monographs that is often praised for its ability to capture the southern Negro "folk" sensibility. Overlooked in this characterization is the comparative nature of the text that vitiates any sense of a monolithic African American "folk" community. Rather, Hurston provides ethnographic details of three distinct communities and their claims to differing folk traditions, songs, community tensions, work ethics, and spiritual expressions. Hurston emphasizes her insight into the dynamism of southern culture, stating that "Negro folklore is not a thing of the past. It is still in the making. Its great variety shows the adaptability of the black man: nothing is too old or too new, domestic or foreign, high or low, for his use."[32] The accounts of social and cultural life in Eatonville and Loughman, Florida, and New Orleans defy static portrayals that reify "the folk" and prove Hurston an adept interlocutor as she shuttles among these three separate communities.

Crucial to my interpretation of Hurston is an understanding of how subjective analysis and literary strategies inform her attempts to seize interpretive power.[33] Hurston's presentation of herself as an actor in her ethnographic accounts is perhaps the most outstanding feature of her work. She most eloquently summarizes her guiding logic in her autobiography, *Dust Tracks on a Road:* "Nothing that God ever made is the same thing to more than one person. That is natural. There is no single face in nature because every eye that looks upon it, sees it from its own angle. So every man's spice-box seasons his own food. Naturally, I picked up the reflections of life around me with my own instruments, and absorbed what I gathered according to my inside juices."[34] Departing from standard ethnographic conventions that demand the use of a distant voice, Hurston readily admits she is a part of the cultural scene she observes.[35] This development is significant because she challenges and debunks a social science paradigm that prizes objectivity as an indicator of "social truth." Within this historical context, she chooses to imbue her research with another kind of truth-value, one laden with her subjective interpretations.

A less widely acknowledged feature of Hurston's ethnographic writing is those conventions currently recognized as literary strategies.[36] I propose that Hurston's style in *Mules and Men* produces what I loosely term a literary harmonic.[37] Originally I conceptualized the emergence of such an harmonic from Hurston's attempts to cultivate subjective and objective voices throughout her work. Rethinking this concept has led me to suggest more strongly that Hurston heavily implicates her audience in the creative act by calling on a reader's subjective interpretations of the text. Hurston seems to self-consciously realize that the creation of meaning is as much a matter of a reading strategy as it is about her own writing strategy. Indeed, she provides the key by which to unlock the polyvalent meanings in her work when she quotes Larkins's advice about "them kinda by-words": "They all got a hidden meanin', just like de Bible. Everybody can't understand what they mean. Most people is thin-brained. They's born wid they feet under de moon. Some folks is born wid they feet on de sun and they kin seek out de inside meanin' of words."[38] Hurston mockingly challenges her readers to actively engage her words and to carefully construct their own interpretations of her highly subjective accounts.

The consequences of such a highly experimental technique were unknown, and the early reviews are indicative of a limited cultural vision on issues of race, class, and gender. For example, Lewis Gannett, writing for the *New York Herald Tribune Weekly Book Review,* offered his assessment that "They [Hurston's informants] all lied, as only a black man can lie, and only to a dark girl whom he trusts."[39] H. I. Brock, in a review in the *New York Times Book Review,* stated that "The writer has gone back to her native racial quality entirely unspoiled by her Northern college education. She has plunged into the social pleasures of the black community and made a record of what is said and done when Negroes are having a good gregarious time, dancing, singing, fishing, and above all, and incessantly, talking."[40]

By overestimating the importance of "social pleasures" in these African American communities, Brock makes the role of cultural expression in African American communities exotic. Both of these reviewers ultimately reduce the differences between Hurston and her subjects and trivialize the complexity of African American community life. These patronizing and racist responses betray the assumptions on which dominant culture was predicated and against which Hurston tried to write.

Hurston does not, as these reviewers do, rely on an essentialist vision of race;

nor does she easily elide class differences or gender hierarchies.[41] By accounting for her own experiences, Hurston accomplishes at least two things. First, she points to the socially constructed nature of race and gender, as well as to the variability of these constructions across time and place. Second, her status as an interlocutor in these three southern communities gives her the latitude to describe the different ways race, gender, and class manifest themselves in the South. The contents of these social beliefs and practices are given concrete articulation in Hurston's powerful descriptions of African American cultural life.

From the beginning of her account, Hurston introduces herself and her racial experience. She says that collecting Negro folklore "would not be a new experience for me. When I pitched headforemost into the world I landed in the crib of negroism."[42] The crib to which she refers is Eatonville, the first incorporated "all-black town" in Florida. Hurston's knowledge of the townspeople in Eatonville is vital to this collection of folklore. Continuing to describe her arrival in Eatonville, she writes:

> I didn't go back there so that the home folks could make admiration over me because I had been up North to college and come back with a diploma and a Chevrolet. I knew they were not going to pay either one of these items too much mind. I was just Lucy Hurston's daughter, Zora, and even if I had — to use one of our down-home expressions — had a Kaiser baby, . . . I'd still be just Zora to the neighbors.[43]

In these two passages Hurston reveals the ways in which she is inscribed into the Eatonville setting. Not only does she illuminate herself in racial terms, she also reveals the particular gender implications of her membership in the Eatonville community as a "native daughter." The position as a daughter, it should be noted, circumscribes her challenge to this community based on class differentials. Therefore, according to Hurston, ownership of a car and a college diploma do not substantially threaten to distance her from the Eatonville inhabitants.

The time Hurston spends in Eatonville is best described in terms of a metaphoric neutrality. As Hurston pulls her car into Eatonville, she states that "I hailed them [the townsmen] *as I went into neutral.*"[44] While it is the automobile that moves into neutral, Hurston may indicate that her social position as a daughter sanctions her presence in Eatonville. Conflicts that could be actualized on other levels, such as race and class, are therefore neutralized.[45] Thus she begins to collect "lies" during an initial interaction with a group of townsmen seated on the store porch. Hurston, responding to their queries in black English vernacular, declares that she has come to collect folklore. Answering their incredulous question as to why she would want to do that, Hurston replies, " 'We want to set them [folktales] down before it's too late.' " " 'Too late for what?' " they ask. " 'Before everybody forgets all of 'em,' " Hurston responds.[46] Hurston alerts the townsmen that their words will be the subject of academic scrutiny, yet because she appeals to them openly, they are ready to contribute to her project.

Hurston's portrayal of herself shifts as she narrates her movement from one set-ting to another. Accordingly, the movement out of Eatonville and into Polk County complicates the race, class, and gender dynamics. With the movement to Polk County, Hurston must establish credibility in order to gain the trust of a community unfamiliar with her. When she first presents herself to her new informants, she is rejected because she appears to be of relatively high socioeconomic standing vis-à-vis the workers she encounters. Hurston curses the fact that she is wearing a $12.74 dress purchased at Macy's, while all the other townswomen are wearing $1.98 dresses purchased by mail order. In order to overcome this barrier Hurston enacts her own series of lies and tells them she is a bootlegger's woman.

In the initial narrative of her arrival in Polk County, Hurston is profoundly aware of herself as a woman. The concern with her physical appearance and the self-declaration of herself as a bootlegger's woman charge her with a sexual energy. This sexually charged image contrasts boldly with the unassuming image of an Eatonville daughter. When Hurston admits that she "got confidential and told them all what I wanted," she seems to imply that she can simply disregard the particu-lar way in which she has identified her presence.[47] However, as I will show later, Hurston is forced to confront the consequences of her self-positioning. Given her need for access to the men, whom she perceives to be the keepers of a folkloric tra-dition, Hurston must sacrifice her physical integrity in order to dispel suspicion based on perceptions of her social standing. Ironically, her perceived sexual accessi-bility leaves her vulnerable to the attacks of Ella and Lucy, two women in the Polk County community.

At the height of her experiences in Polk County, Hurston continues to comb the cultural landscape in search of spiritual traditions. Not coincidentally, Hurston's dilemma, that of the charged relationships between men and women, is highlighted in her collections of Christian religious expression in Polk County. One day at dusk, she records the sermon of an itinerant preacher, or a "stump-knocker," delivering the word to the lumber-camp inhabitants. The content of his sermon concerns God's dictates about the creation of woman and about the relationship between men and women. After praising God's creation of the natural world, the preacher relays his message about the creation of woman:

> Then he took of de dust of de earth
> And made man in his own image.
> And man was alone,
> Even de lion had a mate
>
> . . . .
>
> So God put Adam into a deep sleep
> And took out a bone, ah hah!
> And it is said that it was a rib.
> Behold de rib!
>
> . . . .

> Brothers, if God
> Had taken dat bone out of man's head
> He would have meant for woman to rule, hah
> If he had taken a bone out of his foot,
> He would have meant for us to dominize and rule.
> He could have made her out of back-bone
> And then she would have been behind us.
> But, no, God Almighty, he took de bone out of his side
> So dat places de woman beside us;
> Hah! God knowed his own mind.
> Behold de rib![48]

The place of a woman in these black communities, this sermon suggests, is one in which she is intimately bound to the side of a man. Purportedly about the mutuality that should exist between men and women, the most deep-seated assumption embedded in this creation story is that of the heterosexual union. The passage takes on added significance in that it sheds light on Hurston's position within the Polk County community. She highlights the limited number of social roles available to women and demonstrates that she cannot easily escape the threads that bind her to the social fabric.

Hurston's concerns with spirituality, the body, and gender forcefully emerge from the subtext and assume primary importance in the third section of *Mules and Men*. In this section Hurston narrates her departure from Florida and documents her attempts to become an initiate of hoodoo, a spiritual practice with roots in West African beliefs and practices. Hurston first relays her attempts to locate a hoodoo doctor. Encountering "women reading cards and doing mail order business in names and insinuations," she quickly determines that "[n]othing [was] worth putting on paper."[49] After she locates a reputable mentor, ceremonial preparations begin. During these ritual practices designed to placate the spirit world, Hurston's body and psychic state become the central focus of her narrative.

The first initiation ceremony completed by Hurston requires three days of solitude. Under the guidance of hoodoo doctor Luke Turner, Hurston testifies that she "had five psychic experiences and awoke at last with no feeling of hunger, only one of exaltation."[50] The most curious aspect of these ceremonies is the way in which Hurston entrusts her naked body to the hands of the mostly male practitioners. As she is preparing for this first ceremony, for example, we are told that she wears nothing more than snakeskins for three days. Moreover, many men witness such preparation. When Hurston studies with Anatol Pierre, she is bathed and dried by him before she begins her period of meditation.

This last section further complicates our understanding of social dynamics in the South. In an ethnography that often overflows with the conflictual nature of race, class, and gender, this section is relatively conflict free. Although she potentially places her body in harm's way, Hurston never recounts any experiences that smack of the highly charged sexual imagery characterizing her Polk County experience. One reason for this could be the nature of the spiritual community she encounters. Hoodoo may offer women a place outside conventional social roles. Thus the meaning of Hurston's body is not overdetermined by prevailing gender and racial norms. Featuring her body so prominently in the ethnographic venture is yet another methodological innovation and experimental aspect of this highly subjective narrative.

Anthropology and the Subversion of Authority

Zora Neale Hurston not only uses a highly experimental discursive style, she also invokes standard ethnographic tropes. Of these tropes, the most outstanding example is the invocation of the spyglass. Hurston tells the reader that the discipline of anthropology gave her the "spyglass" she needed in order to "stand off and look at my garment."[51] It imbues the narrative with a sense of authority and credibility. Claiming anthropological method as a useful tool with which to evaluate her culture also serves to instill Hurston with a certain amount of power. She will not simply be listening to and recording folkloric accounts in a haphazard manner. Instead, she implies that these accounts will be systematically obtained and translated within a theoretical framework. By invoking the theory and methodology of an academic discipline, Hurston legitimizes her final written product.

The spyglass is a revealing image that bears critical discussion because of its far-reaching implications both for anthropology as a discipline and for ethnography as a practice. Furthermore, in the case of Hurston it is a less discernible marker of difference. This spyglass serves not only as an image that neatly positions Hurston as the objective observer but also as an instrument with the theoretical and literal potential to inflict violence on the observed. With spyglass in hand, Hurston has the potential to bring that which is far from view into sharp and static focus; once that view becomes apprehensible, those subjects become open to objectification. Because of her spyglass, Hurston, like other ethnographers with glasses in hand, has the potential power to define and fix meaning, to rarefy the complexity of the lives around her.

I stress that Hurston has the potential to occupy space in a totalizing manner because even as she tightly weaves an authoritative persona, she also debunks her own interpretive power. An examination of her narrative voices in chapters 9 and 10 reveals the growing relationship between Big Sweet and Hurston and the escalating conflict between Lucy, Ella, Big Sweet, and Hurston. In the last few pages of *Mules and Men*, Ella and Lucy collude to kill Hurston at a public gathering, a dance. An in-depth quotation provides a sense of the confusion and violence that characterize Hurston's and the reader's exit from the field:

> *Just about that time Lucy hopped up in the doorway with an open knife in her hands. She saw me first thing. . . . One door in the place and Lucy standing in it.*

GRACIELA HERNÁNDEZ

So she started walking hippily straight at me. She knew I couldn't get out easily because she had me barred and she knew not many people will risk running into a knife blade to stop a fight. So she didn't have to run. I didn't move but I was running in my skin. I could hear the blade already crying in my flesh. . . . But a flash from the corner and Lucy had something else to think about besides me. Big Sweet was flying at her with an open blade and now it was Lucy's time to try to make it to the door. . . . Jim Presley punched me violently and said, "Run you chile! Run and ride! Dis is gointer be uh nasty ditch." [52]

While this scene brilliantly captures conflict and confusion, it is a scene that cannot be read strictly as text. Rather, it begs to be read as a statement about the relationship between informants and ethnographer, between text and voice, and between authority denied and authority seized. In other words, the text cannot be separated from a complex web of social relationships.

One of the implications that can be immediately suggested in this aftermath is that in Hurston's quest to find acceptance among the Polk County residents, her sexualized identity works against her. Another ironic point is that the community accepts Zora Neale Hurston as so much a part of itself that it tacitly sanctions the violence directed at her by Lucy. As a member of the community Hurston has to deal with acts of violence, as do all of its other members. Yet these conclusions posit that the violence enacted against the ethnographer is of the same caliber as the discursive violence enacted against their informants. These conclusions elide the fact that Hurston escapes relatively unscathed, while those trapped in the dance hall experience the bloodshed and chaos precipitated by her presence. I propose, as does John Dorst, that Hurston portrays "the demise of Authority" in her text. [53] Specifically, Hurston moves on the symbolic level in this last section of the text. As the women in the Polk County community move to kill Zora, so Hurston moves to destabilize her own interpretive authority.

Rather than suggest a vacuum where space exists without power and authority, Hurston provides compelling clues as to the movement and location of power. In the last few paragraphs, Lucy states "Ah got de law in mah mouf." [54] Lucy takes the "law," in this case the authority and power to define meaning, away from Hurston and into her own hands, or "mouf." Perhaps one of the most significant consequences of Lucy's actions is her assertion of the primacy of the spoken word over the written text. Hurston has gone to collect the folklore and folktales from different African American communities to "set them down before it's too late," yet Lucy strategically moves to disrupt Hurston's unproblematic exit of the field situation with folk knowledge in hand. The epistemic privilege of the written text is debunked in favor of the oral. In the final scenes of Part I, the power to define the terms on which an ethnographer works, records, and leaves the field lies not with the interlocutor but with the informants. Hurston casts doubt on the ethnographer's ability to adequately represent these different communities and criticizes a discipline that offers people up for view through the lenses of the spyglass.

Conclusion

I began this essay by suggesting the relevance of Zora Neale Hurston's intellectual contributions to contemporary feminist debates over race, representation, and the politics of ethnography. The bulk of Hurston's work on southern rural communities provides important historical information about the beliefs, values, and practices of an essential segment of the African American population. Her research begins to disentangle the colliding vectors of race, gender, and class in American culture by pointing to the specific meanings of those social markers across time and space. In her ethnographic journeys and the representations of them, Hurston demonstrates how race, gender, and class influence her position within the communities she studies. She offers a model by which to gauge our efforts as we grapple with our own subjective presence in our writings and our practices in the field. By calling her own interpretive power into question, Hurston insists that researchers and cultural workers alike recognize the limitations of their representational strategies. In doing so, she urges us to become more cognizant of the politics of representation. As her work was once left to languish unheard and unread, she demands that we become more attuned to both the polyphony and cacophony resounding in the world around us and that we commit ourselves to the call of those voices, as well.

Notes

I would like to thank Ruth Behar for the tremendous amount of support and encouragement she gave me as this paper underwent numerous revisions. I am also deeply indebted to Deborah Gordon and the anonymous reviewer at the University of California Press for their insights. The transformation of my ideas would not have been possible without their critiques. Finally, I dedicate this essay to all of my friends and family who supported me during a prolonged illness. An earlier version of this essay, titled "Multiple Mediations in Zora Neale Hurston's *Mules and Men*," appeared in "Women Writing Culture," Ruth Behar, ed., *Critique of Anthropology* 13, no. 4 (1993): 351–362.

1. Two accounts that attempt to map the impact of feminist and gendered analysis on anthropology are found in Micaela di Leonardo, "Introduction: Gender, Culture, and Political Economy: Feminist Anthropology in Historical Perspective," in *Gender at the Crossroads of Knowledge: Feminist Anthropology in the Postmodern Era*, ed. Micaela di Leonardo (Berkeley: University of California Press, 1991), 1–48, and Diane Bell, "Introduction I: The Context," in *Gendered Fields: Women, Men, and Ethnography*, ed. Diane Bell, Pat Caplin, and Wazir Jahan Karim (New York: Routledge, 1993), 1–18. Of the two, only Bell's introduction mentions Hurston's collections.

2. For examples that fall into such polar interpretations, see Alice Walker's pathbreaking essay that championed Hurston as a role model for African American women (Alice Walker, "In Search of Zora Neale Hurston," *Ms. Magazine*, March 1975, 74–79, 85–89). Hazel Carby's recent publication reverses this trend. Not only does Carby argue that Hurston's attempts at cultural representation amount to "a discursive displacement of the historical and cultural transformation of [the Great M]igration," she also reiterates the traditional divide in African American literary studies that forces one to choose between embracing Richard Wright or Zora Neale Hurston: "The antagonism between them [Hurston and Wright] reveals Wright to be a modernist and leaves Hurston embedded in the politics of Negro identity." See Hazel Carby, "The Politics of Fiction, Anthropology,

and the Folk: Zora Neale Hurston," in *New Essays on "Their Eyes Were Watching God,"* ed. Michael Awkward (New York: Cambridge University Press, 1990), 77, 79.

3. Carol B. Stack, "Writing Ethnography: Feminist Critical Practice," *Frontiers: A Journal of Women's Studies* 8, no. 3 (1993): 81.

4. Michele Wallace, "Who Owns Zora Neale Hurston?: Critics Carve Up the Legend," in her *Invisibility Blues: From Pop to Theory* (New York: Verso, 1990), 176; Harold Bloom, ed., *Zora Neale Hurston* (New York: Chelsea House Publishers, 1986). For an alternative contextualization of Hurston's work, see Henry Louis Gates, Jr., and K. A. Appiah, eds., *Zora Neale Hurston: Critical Perspectives Past and Present* (New York: Amistad, 1993).

5. bell hooks, "Saving Black Folk Culture: Zora Neale Hurston as Anthropologist and Writer," in her *Yearning: Race, Gender, and Cultural Politics* (Boston: South End Press, 1990), 135–43.

6. P. Gabrielle Foreman, "Looking Back from Zora, or Talking out Both Sides of My Mouth for Those Who Have Two Ears," *Black Literature Forum* 24 (Winter 1990): 662.

7. Similarly, Barbara Johnson asks questions about her identity, her audience, and the impact of both on her scholarship (Barbara Johnson, "Thresholds of Difference: Structures of Address in Zora Neale Hurston," in her *A World of Difference* [Baltimore: Johns Hopkins University Press, 1987], 172–83). In my case, thinking through my identity has become important because of a remark made by a conference participant after I delivered my initial observations on Hurston's ethnography. The participant suggested that my identity as an "authentic Chicana" authorized me to speak, vis-à-vis the other women on the Hurston panel, without equivocation or self-referentiality. That characterization caught me off guard, yet it also pushed me to reconceptualize the terms on which I discussed Hurston's scholarship. See Graciela Hernández, "Multiple Mediations in Zora Neale Hurston's *Mules and Men*, Part I," in "Women Writing Culture," Ruth Behar, ed., *Critique of Anthropology* 13 (December 1993): 351–62. For a discussion of the problematic distinctions between the "native" and the "nativized," see Wazir Jahan Karim, "Epilogue: The 'Nativized Self' and the 'Native,'" in *Gendered Fields*, 248–51. Certainly, as the editors of the recent special issue of *Frontiers* point out, the "dichotomies [between insiders and outsiders] seemed more and more simplistic and unable to capture the complexities of both kinds of relations women developed and the differences among women in the communities they studied" ("From the Editors," *Frontiers* 13, no. 3 [1993]: xi). Finally, see Patricia Zavella, "Feminist Insider Dilemmas: Constructing Ethnic Identity with 'Chicana' Informants," *Frontiers* 13, no. 3 (1993): 53–76.

8. Hazel Carby, *Reconstructing Black Womanhood: The Emergence of the Afro-American Woman Novelist* (New York: Oxford University Press, 1987), 15, 18.

9. Diane L. Wolf, "Introduction: Feminist Dilemmas in Fieldwork," *Frontiers* 13, no. 3 (1993): 6. See also Deborah Gordon, "Writing Culture, Writing Feminism: The Poetics and Politics of Experimental Ethnography," *Inscriptions* 3/4 (1988), esp. 19.

10. Foreman, "Looking Back from Zora," 651.

11. Kamala Visweswaran, "Defining Feminist Ethnography," *Inscriptions* 3/4 (1988): 39.

12. See Deborah Gordon, "The Politics of Ethnographic Authority: Race and Writing in the Ethnography of Margaret Mead and Zora Neale Hurston," in *Modernist Anthropology: From Fieldwork to Text*, ed. Marc Manganaro (Princeton, N.J.: Princeton University Press, 1990), 146–62. See also James Clifford, "Introduction: Partial Truths," in *Writing Culture: The Poetics and Politics of Ethnography*, ed. James Clifford and George E. Marcus (Berkeley: University of California Press, 1986), 1–26.

13. Robert E. Hemenway, *Zora Neale Hurston: A Literary Biography* (Urbana: University of Illinois Press, 1977), 12, 13–15. Some scholars have interpreted Hurston's first novel, *Jonah's Gourd Vine* (1934; New York: Harper Perennial, 1990), as a biographical fiction-

alization of the relationship between Hurston's parents. Certainly, Hurston mythologizes her mother in her autobiographical account, *Dust Tracks on a Road* (1942; New York: Harper Perennial, 1991), esp. 7–17, and 61–69. It is widely acknowledged that the final published version of *Dust Tracks* is the result of heavy-handed editing. For an exemplary examination of original and edited manuscripts of *Dust Tracks,* see Claudine Raynaud, "'Rubbing a Paragraph with a Soft Cloth'? Muted Voices and Edited Constraints in *Dust Tracks on a Road,*" in *De/Colonizing the Subject: The Politics of Gender in Women's Autobiography,* ed. Sidonie Smith and Julia Watson (Minneapolis: University of Minnesota Press, 1992), 24–64.

14. Hemenway, *Zora Neale Hurston,* 14–15, 17.

15. Ibid., 17–19, 45.

16. Ibid., 10.

17. Ibid., 43, 45, 47.

18. Ibid., 50.

19. For an argument that Hurston's first academic interest was geography, not anthropology, see Michelle S. Johnson "Juju Leaves in the Center of a Whirlwind: African American Nature/Culture Mediation," Ph.D. dissertation, University of Michigan, 1994.

20. Hemenway, *Zora Neale Hurston,* 205–12; Gwendolyn Mikell, "The Anthropological Imagination of Zora Neale Hurston," *Western Journal of Black Studies* 7, no. 1 (1983): 27–35.

21. Hemenway, *Zora Neale Hurston,* 206–7.

22. Zora Neale Hurston, May 14, 1935, quoted in ibid., 210. It is unclear with whom Hurston is corresponding.

23. Zora Neale Hurston, letter to Edwin Embree, June 28, 1935, in ibid., 210–11.

24. Mikell, "Anthropological Imagination," 29.

25. Ibid. For an example of a psychoanalytic explanation of culture, see Ruth Benedict, *Patterns of Culture* (Boston and New York: Houghton Mifflin, 1934). Mikell's analysis suggests that Ruth Benedict significantly influenced Hurston's scholarship on both African American and Caribbean culture. This issue deserves in-depth exploration. One of Hurston's documented references concerning Benedict is found in a letter directed to Franz Boas. When she asked Boas to write the introduction to *Mules and Men,* Hurston requested that Benedict review the manuscript. See Mikell, "Anthropological Imagination," 30; Hemenway, *Zora Neale Hurston,* 63, 163–64. Mikell's research is promising because she anticipates questions concerning the relationships among a group of women working with Boas at Columbia University during the 1920s and 1930s, including Margaret Mead, Ruth Benedict, and Zora Neale Hurston. Deborah Gordon ("Politics of Ethnographic Authority") directly compares and contrasts Mead's and Hurston's scholarship and historical contexts. In her essay in this volume, Janet Finn explores the relationship between Boas and yet another female student, Native American Ella Deloria.

26. Mikell, "Anthropological Imagination," 33.

27. Gordon, "Politics of Ethnographic Authority," 160–61; Hemenway, *Zora Neale Hurston,* 38–42.

28. Hemenway, *Zora Neale Hurston,* 40.

29. Ibid., 110.

30. Gordon, "Politics of Ethnographic Authority"; Mikell, "Anthropological Imagination."

31. Gordon, "Politics of Ethnographic Authority," 160.

32. Zora Neale Hurston, "Characteristics of Negro Expression," in her *The Sanctified Church* (Berkeley: Turtle Island, 1981), 56.

33. I borrow the term "interpretive power" from Jean Franco, *Plotting Women: Gender and Representation in Mexico* (New York: Columbia University Press, 1989).

34. Hurston, *Dust Tracks.*

35. For a standard ethnographic monograph about African American culture that contrasts sharply with Hurston's ethnography, see Hortense Powdermaker, *After Freedom: A Cultural Study in the Deep South* (New York: Viking, 1939).

36. Visweswaran, "Defining Feminist Anthropology," 39.

37. This analogy seems appropriate, given Hurston's musical interests. For example, for her documentation of and interest in music, see the appendices of her ethnographies *Mules and Men* (New York: Perennial Library, 1990; originally published 1935) and *Tell My Horse* (New York: Perennial Library, 1990; originally published 1938).

38. Hurston, *Mules and Men,* 125.

39. Lewis Gannett, *New York Herald Tribune* Weekly Book Review, October 11, 1935 (reprinted in Gates and Appiah, *Zora Neale Hurston,* 11).

40. H. I. Brock, *New York Times Book Review,* November 10, 1935 (reprinted in ibid., 14).

41. For an historical overview of racial formation in the United States, see Michael Omi and Howard Winant, *Racial Formation in the United States: From the 1960s to the 1980s* (New York: Routledge, 1986).

42. Hurston, *Mules and Men,* 1.

43. Ibid., 2.

44. Ibid., 7, my emphasis.

45. The place of the automobile in other early- to mid-twentieth-century ethnographies also seems to be significant. For some ethnographers it operates as a neutral domain wherein they elicit unwitting responses from their informants. See Powdermaker, *After Freedom;* John Howard Griffin, *Black Like Me* (Boston: Houghton Mifflin, 1961).

46. Hurston, *Mules and Men,* 8.

47. Ibid., 65.

48. Ibid., 141.

49. Ibid., 191. For a discussion of Hurston's interest in hoodoo, see Johnson, "Juju Leaves in a Whirlwind."

50. Ibid., 199.

51. Ibid., 1.

52. Ibid., 178–79.

53. John Dorst, "Reading *Mules and Men:* Toward the Death of the Ethnographer," *Cultural Anthropology* 2 (1987): 316.

54. Hurston, *Mules and Men,* 179. I am indebted to both June Howard and Michael Awkward for calling my attention to this point.

Ruth Landes and the Early Ethnography of Race and Gender

Sally Cole

IN 1991, when Ruth Behar asked me to contribute to this volume, I was a postdoctoral fellow at McMaster University in Hamilton, Canada, and Dr. Ruth Landes, professor emerita of its department of anthropology, had died the previous month. Shortly thereafter, her friends, colleagues, and former students gathered at a memorial service to share their memories and to acknowledge her contribution to anthropology. That was my first year at the university, and I had never met Landes. Throughout that spring, as people at the department shared with me their memories and knowledge of her, I began to wonder why I knew almost nothing about her work. I had recently completed a book about women and work in rural Portugal in which I had incorporated women's stories. More than half a century earlier Landes had written *The Ojibwa Woman,* in which she had relied on women's stories in her ethnographic representation of Ojibwa society.[1] I was situating my current research on Portuguese immigrant workers in Canada in the area of ethnic studies which Ruth Landes had pursued in writings on race and ethnicity in America and Brazil, and I had just written a paper urging that feminist anthropologists begin to reclaim the heritage of women's writing in anthropology. Ruth Behar's invitation thus offered me a perfect opportunity. I began to interview Landes's former

Ruth Landes at age fifty-five in Los Angeles, 1963. (Photograph courtesy of Ellen Wall, personal friend)

students and colleagues and to read her extensive writings and correspondence. The project has since led me to undertake a biography of Ruth Landes. This essay is a first look at that larger project.

Recent critical debates in anthropology have defined ethnography as writing culture and have tended to focus on writing as it produces texts. Noting that the anthropological concept of culture has served to maintain intact self-other racial hierarchies in ethnographic writing, Lila Abu-Lughod urges instead that we begin to write against culture. That, she suggests, involves not only the writing process (and, perhaps, textual innovations) but also the research process, including the generation of basic research questions and theorizing about those questions.[2] Working with this expanded definition of what it is that anthropologists do—research and writing—I discuss Ruth Landes's writings on race, gender, and culture in her book *City of Women,* based on her 1938–1939 fieldwork in Bahia, Brazil. I argue that the research questions, theoretical frameworks, and writing styles Landes explores in *City of Women* can be understood today as early forms of writing against culture or, as Landes might have viewed it, writing against writing culture. In Landes's day, however, the scientific concept of culture was key to canon-making in the discipline, which was seeking to secure its institutional and authoritative foundations. As a result, *City of Women* was dismissed by contemporaries as an unscientific travelogue and a personal memoir. For Landes continued to theorize race when culture was displacing race as American anthropology's central paradigm. She tells us that she went to Brazil to study "race relationships," that after several weeks of immersion in the race, class, and gender politics of 1930s Brazil she realized that her "training in pure science had left [her] unprepared for such events" and thus decided to let Bahians "speak to [her] on their own terms." In addition, pursuing her personal and theoretical interests in gender and sexuality, Landes chose as her ethnographic focus the woman-centered Afro-Brazilian spirit-possession religion, *candomblé*, and began participant observation that contextualized candomblé in local history and politics. This theoretical and methodological approach ran counter to peer efforts within American anthropology that employed the concept of culture as static, internally consistent, and outside history and that interpreted Afro-American culture in terms of African survivals. Landes's theorizing of gender and sexuality, particularly as it yielded descriptions of women ritual leaders and male homosexuality, intensified the controversies surrounding her work. My purpose in reviving these controversies is twofold: to suggest that writing against culture has a history as a subtext in anthropology but that writing was, during the professionalization of the discipline and until recently, marginalized; and, secondly, to show that documenting the processes and strategies of marginalization reveals that they continue to the present.

In this chapter, then, I suggest that the reasons it is important to know about Landes's work today are the very reasons she did not receive recognition in her lifetime and that they explain why I knew so little about her. Although Landes did not escape the exoticization of cultural difference of her day, she did resist the methods of "othering" that were then becoming current. She rejected the scientific writing style of "ethnographic naturalism" to assert textual authority;[3] she resisted the cataloguing of cultural traits and the removal of culture from its social, political, and economic contexts; and she did not write "unruly experience" out of her texts but, instead, reproduced her subjects' contesting interpretations of what was happening.[4] She defined race and gender as topics for scientific research, and she insisted on situating herself as a Jew and a woman in her writing—a practice that, although increasingly current in present-day anthropology, was anathema to the rhetorical assertions of ethnographic authority that prevailed in the anthropology of her day. Rereading *City of Women* and analyzing its reception in the discipline compels us to acknowledge that, even though we need "systematic, sharply new methods or epistemologies," we also need to examine critically how anthropology handled epistemological crises in the past.[5] Recent movements in ethnographic canon-making are not as novel as they appear when we document some of the historical casualties of the process of disciplinary professionalization.

Ruth Landes in Brazil, 1938–1939

When I left Rio for the United States, Brazilian friends escorted me to the boat, and one of them said, half teasing but with a certain defiant patriotism, "Now you can tell them that no tigers walk in our streets."

I nodded, and added: "I'll tell them also about the women. I think they help make Brazil great. Will Americans believe that there is a country where women like men, feel secure and at ease with them, and do not fear them?" [6]

So Landes ends *City of Women*, an ethnography of candomblé. Written in descriptive prose and dialogue, the book is a testament to the vitality and dignity of the women ritual specialists who, through candomblé, help give meaning to the lives of women living in poverty in black Bahia. It is also a personal memoir of Landes's year in Brazil.

Candomblé merges African beliefs and practices associated with Yoruban spirits and those associated with Catholic saints. In the 1930s there were an estimated 100 to 150 candomblé temples in Bahia alone. Each was led by a priestess called Mother (*mãe de santo*) and was composed of her community of women initiates and followers, called daughters (*filhas de santo*). Each temple had its own rituals, teachings, and regalia; intense rivalries existed among the temples. The priestesses were so named because of their ability to be possessed by African spirits. They were also known to be seers, diviners, and healers. The women supported themselves and their children through the payments they received for their ritual expertise, and most were also involved in street marketing and other activities in the informal sector. Candomblé was thus also an economic system—a means of livelihood—and a mutual support system for women living in extreme poverty.

Landes records her first meeting with one of the candomblé leaders, "a big impressive woman named Luzía," at a temple and in the company of other women:

Her manner was tired as she acknowledged the women by extending her hand in a most indifferent fashion for their kiss of salutation. "A blessing, my mother?" each asked.

"Be blessed, my daughter," she granted in a deep, hoarse voice, not the voice of a man or of a woman but the voice of a sibyl.

She talked and moved majestically, strolling over to a low curved bench which was painted white and encircled a white pillar in the center of the room. . . . She sat down on the bench, spreading her thighs like an eastern potentate and leaning her elbows on them. Her flowing skirts made a huge circle on the floor. She began to intone the chants, and the old women near her got up and danced in bare feet. She intoned further, and they lifted up offerings of oil, rum and pop-

corn, offerings which were to buy the good will of Exu and compensate for
sending him out of the house. . . .

   Watching Luzía, I would have said she was not the least interested in this
routine, for her deep monotone pulled the songs lazily and her sad eyes were
shut. But I cannot know, for they had roused her from her nap, and after all she
knew her gods so well, as had her mother and aunt and sisters before her. How
many numberless times had she chanted the Padê, bargaining with the docile
demon to leave the gods in peace and carry mischief to the crossroads?[7]

And, meeting Menininha, considered by Brazilian ethnologists the greatest living
priestess, Landes writes:

   I wondered if any outsider could have suspected her position. She sat in the
shaded entrance to her house, a black shawl wrapped about her head and
bosom despite the heat, and a tray of sweets on a little stand beside her. . . .

   Menininha led me indoors. She handed her shawl and tray to a young girl
and walked into the front room where Cleoza lolled at the window.

   "Come in, my lady," the priestess urged listlessly, "let us sit down and have
a little visit." She lowered herself heavily into a flimsy chair, placing her palms
on her thighs. Suddenly she was remote and obscure as a Stone Age Venus. Her
shawl gone, sitting in a loose cotton dress, her great breasts flowed over a great
stomach which bulged over tremendous thighs supported by powerful legs
tapering to small ankles and feet. Her brief sleeves exposed large arms, masses
of firm smooth flesh that dimpled hugely at the elbows and ended in seemingly
fragile wrists and hands.

   "My lady," she said quietly, unlike the usual Brazilian woman, "you wanted
to see me?"[8]

Landes replied carefully that she wanted to learn about Menininha's temple and to
see her dance. She writes:

   Months later, after I had met many priestesses and ogans (an African word that
is truly anachronistic in these matriarchal surroundings, since it means lord or
master), after I had seen many ceremonies and experienced something of the
emotions to which they gave rise, after I had begun to take their logic for granted,
I realized the enormity of my request to Menininha. She was a great leader, her
life was passed on a priestly pedestal. One could no more ask her to perform
than one could ask a minister to give a casual demonstration of the mysteries
of his creed.[9]

   Landes's narrative focuses on her encounters with individuals and her participation in the calendar of ritual events. Her description is personal: She is not a distanced observer but is very much present as a figure in the text; she uses the first
person and describes her own feelings and reactions; and she uses dialogue to report

her conversations with candomblé practitioners and with other observers, including Brazilian journalists, scholars, medical specialists, and expatriates. Landes is conscious of and open about her positionality: She continually reminds us that she is a woman and that, as a woman in Brazil, she was constrained or defined in specific ways that also effectively defined her access and methods in the field. Only after she met and began to collaborate with black folklorist and journalist Edison Carneiro—also a scholar of candomblé—was she able, with his escort, to escape the constraints of life as a white woman and to begin intensive participant observation in the candomblé temples of the black neighborhoods of Bahia. As an intellectual, a visitor, an interviewer, and an analyst, she was comfortable with Carneiro and the local group of poets and journalists with whom she spent a great deal of time and who were, like her, sympathetic observers of candomblé. She felt isolated from the Brazilian elite that included some academics and government officials. This sense of isolation came, she tells us, not only from her observation of the social boundaries the elite maintained between themselves and the black underclass who were the subjects of Landes's ethnographic research but also from her identification as a Jew and her sensitivity to and horror at the apparent acceptance of Nazis in elite Brazilian society in the 1930s. She was to pay dearly, however, for distancing herself from the local elite. She also separated herself from the community of British and American expatriates in Brazil whom she describes as racist and insular. She recalls her experiences the previous year (1937–1938), when she had taught in the segregated American South at the black university, Fisk, in Nashville. She was attracted to the apparently greater flexibility in relations of color in Brazil but observed at the same time how these were nuanced by relations of class, gender, region, and occupation.

In the passages quoted above, Landes may appear to late-twentieth-century readers to exoticize her women subjects, especially through her focus on the body, but such an interpretation would be a limited reading. Some knowledge of Ruth Landes will lead to a better understanding of her point of view: Her focus on women and possession and her keen observations of expressions of sexuality in the candomblés derives from her fusing of the personal and the intellectual—a strategy she used consistently throughout her life.

Landes was strongly influenced by her teacher Ruth Benedict. In 1934 Benedict had published an article entitled "Anthropology and the Abnormal," in which she argued that behavior considered abnormal in America at the time—such as spirit possession and trance, homosexuality, paranoia, and megalomania—could be the foundation of authority and leadership in other cultures and in which she stressed the need for ethnographic research on these subjects. Although it had not been her original purpose in coming to Brazil, Landes soon identified candomblé as an ethnographic focus that would allow her to explore trance and possession and homosexuality in Afro-Brazilian culture, and her consciousness of gender and sexuality made her ideally suited to this research. Candomblé had been the subject of extensive research by both Brazilian and American scholars since the late nineteenth century, but Landes was the first to acknowledge the central role and the experience of women and the first to identify sexuality as an important motivation for both male and female participants in candomblé temple life.[10]

Landes's new insights derived from her personal and intellectual fascination with the body (male and female) and with lived sexuality in all its representations. She was born in 1908 and had come of age during the sexual freedom of the 1920s, so sexuality was an important part of her identity and of her presentation of self. Moreover, she admired people who were open about their sexuality. She always took immaculate care of and pride in her own body, swimming almost daily and even dying peacefully on her bed while doing her morning sit-ups. Until her death, at the age of eighty-two, Landes was a familiar sight in the women's locker room at the McMaster University pool. Nude, legs apart and firmly planted in what was for her a characteristic stance, she would engage in intense conversation with a student who, more often than not, was seeking to cover her own body with a towel. Landes saw the body as an expressive instrument capable of asserting authority and power, and she frankly admired the bodies of the Bahian women, as well as the women's control over their sexuality. In *City of Women* she frequently mentions the women's common-law husbands, who "visited" them at the temples but did not live with them. Landes herself had married young (in 1929), in part to legitimize sex, but the marriage had ended within a few years, due to what Landes described as the "confines of domesticity" prescribed for a middle-class wife in America. According to Landes, the women of the candomblés understood that legal marriage would undermine their economic and sexual independence and that "Marriage means another world, something like being a white person, it brings prestige but not necessarily joy in living."[11] She clearly envied and perhaps longed for the women's apparent freedom of movement, of body, and of sexuality.

Also central to Landes's theoretical framework and writing was the contextualization of candomblé in the larger social currents of 1930s Brazil. She offers vivid descriptions of the expatriate American colony, the pockets of nazism, the anticommunist political intrigues, and the Brazilian bourgeoisie and its views of candomblé (as murder, poisonings, and sex orgies). She reports conversations she had with Brazilian poets, scholars, and journalists in which she was impressed by how they viewed candomblé and the life and culture of black Bahia as integral to Brazilian culture and society: "Afro-Brazilian" was then the widely accepted term. She reflects on her conversation at a street festa with a Brazilian poet who reminded her:

> *"African traditions are now Brazilian — and we call them Afro-Brazilian."*
> *I remembered white friends in Nashville and New Orleans and I had an acute physical awareness at the moment of the opposition between the convictions I had left at home and the convictions I was encountering here. The difference between them was terrible. And, thinking only this, I sighed: "My Southern acquaintances would be horrified. They would think you had lost*

SALLY COLE

your 'pride.' Even I, because I am used to them, have to strain myself to fol-
low you."

"Really?" demanded Edison, and the others slowed up to listen. "What can
be so difficult?"

"Well, North Americans think in terms of race. A black man is inferior to a
white man because of his race."

"What about the black man's culture?"

"That doesn't matter. A black man isn't supposed to have any of his own,
only what he gets from white; and that he is supposed to hide."

It was very embarrassing to explain these matters, especially in the face of
their incredulity.[12]

In her ethnography of candomblé, Landes thus inserts her subject into history and into a larger political complexity. She refuses to reproduce the theoretical and rhetorical assertions of her peers and of senior scholars who interpreted candomblé as a static syncretic product and who unproblematically catalogued African "survivals." Instead, she offers conflicting local and subjective interpretations of the meaning of candomblé. Of her contemporaries, however, Roger Bastide appears to have been alone in acknowledging the theoretical difference and value of Landes's ethnography. In *African Religions of Brazil* Bastide wrote that, unlike prevailing studies of the period that too often treated candomblés as "museum specimens," Ruth Landes's *City of Women* began "to give an adequate idea of their dense, teeming vitality."[13]

Finally, throughout the book Landes interweaves her description and analysis of black social and historical experience in Brazil with her reflections and introspection about race relations in the United States. This subtext—the comparative study of race and ethnic relations—was central to her anthropology, as was the comparative ethnography of gender. It was her ethnographic theorizing about race and gender, however, that was the target of criticism and the basis on which her work was marginalized from the emergent anthropological canon.

Silencing the Ethnography of Race and Gender

In her 1970 reflexive essay "A Woman Anthropologist in Brazil," Landes writes that she went to Brazil to study "race relationships" and specifically to describe a society in which, unlike the United States, blacks freed from slavery were also freed from racism. Landes, like many liberal Americans in the 1930s, was attracted by Gilberto Freyre's portrait of Brazil as a "racial democracy" in his books *The Master and the Slaves* and *The Mansions and the Shanties*. Landes had met Chicago sociologist Robert Park, who was similarly influenced by Freyre and whose student Donald Pierson was at the time writing his book *Negroes in Brazil,* based on fieldwork in Bahia between 1935 and 1937. Park arranged for Landes to spend a year teaching at Fisk University prior to going to Brazil in order to learn, she says, "something at first hand of American 'racial etiquette.'"[14] This may appear to be an unusual preparation for fieldwork in Brazil, but teaching at Fisk and living in the segregated South was one of the most important and formative experiences of Landes's life, one she returned to in memory again and again throughout her life, and one that very much influenced how she went on to conduct fieldwork in Bahia. Landes was one of only a handful of white northerners teaching at Fisk and living on campus. She was shocked and repelled by the color barrier that ruled daily life for both whites and blacks. She fell in love with and carried on a necessarily clandestine love affair with a black physics professor several years her senior. Although he died a few years later, this relationship remained important to her for the rest of her life. She explored her experiences of interracial intimacy in an unpublished novel which she described as a "lightly fictionalized" account of her year at Fisk and which she revised and resubmitted to publishers several times—for the last time just a few years before she died. When Landes later began an open love affair with Edison Carneiro in Bahia she was absolutely conscious of and theoretically reflexive about the different conditions for interracial intimacy in Brazil and in the United States.

The daughter of socialist labor organizer Joseph Schlossberg, Ruth Landes grew up among liberal Jews in New York City. Through her father she had met black intellectuals and writers of the Harlem Renaissance, including Alain Locke, W. E. B. Du Bois, James Weldon Johnson, Walter White, and Zora Neale Hurston. She received her M.S.W. from the New York School of Social Work in 1929 based on thesis research on the storefront churches of the followers of Marcus Garvey, the so-called Negro Jews, in Harlem.[15] About this time and also through her father she met anthropologist Alfred Goldenweiser, who introduced her to Franz Boas. Boas was looking for students to conduct research on African Americans; Ruth Landes was looking for an escape from her marriage. Boas's vision of anthropology as an antiracist science very much attracted her, and she began to work toward a doctorate in anthropology.

Boas's vision of American anthropology was, however, a lone voice in the discipline and one very much localized in New York—which, not incidentally, was also the focus of the increasing racial and ethnic diversity in U.S. society in the 1920s. The majority opinion in the discipline—as it then existed at Yale and Harvard universities and at the Smithsonian Institution, for example—held that Native American societies were the primary focus of ethnological research, while research in physical anthropology perpetuated the views of nineteenth-century Social Darwinism that linked race and culture in a single hierarchical and evolutionary sequence. The period was one of massive immigration (especially of Jews and Italians), and scientific views about race fed public pressure to pass anti-immigration laws. In a forty-volume scientific report commissioned by the U.S. Congress in 1911 to document the "deterioration" of the "American stock" due to immigration, Franz Boas's contribution was the only one that argued against racial determinism and that focused instead on the role of environmental influences. In succeeding decades Boas engaged students in a series of studies that sought to document how environment modified the features of migrant populations, including southern blacks who had migrated to the northern states.

Elazar Barkan has recently argued that the consistent theme of antiracism in Boas's work and teaching can be traced directly to his personal experiences as a Jew in Germany and as a Jewish immigrant in America. Boas, Barkan says, never saw himself as an American, always as an "other." Barkan considers it significant that many of the anthropologists who later identified themselves as Boasians were German and/or Jewish immigrants and that antiracist anthropology was localized among Boasians and at Columbia University. Barkan's argument is that ethnic background and personal experience intimately influenced the research questions individual anthropologists asked and the theories they developed.[16] Reflecting on the relative positions of individual anthropologists—both those who define the canon and those who define its margins—is a necessary and important part of a revisionist history. The experience of Ruth Landes (who also positioned herself as a woman) offers an example of the process at work.

Landes's vision of anthropology was nurtured by Boas, and she retained a Boasian approach throughout her life, even after the scientific critique of racism had all but disappeared from the discipline's agenda after World War II. For, as Johnetta Cole has noted, very few of Boas's students (or at least of those well placed to define the anthropological canon in the postwar period) continued with the Boasian antiracist project for anthropology. And research on African Americans retained a lower priority than research on Native Americans.[17]

In "American Anthropologists and American Society" Eric Wolf attempted to explain the retreat of anthropology from the scientific debate on race. He describes Boasian anthropology as a kind of Liberal Reformism that was a critical response both to nineteenth-century Social Darwinism and to twentieth-century experiences of immigration. Wolf sees the development by Boasians of theories of acculturation, cultural pluralism, cultural relativism, and culture and personality as the intellectualizing of the increasing cultural diversity in American society. But, according to Wolf, the realities of World War II shattered the Boasian vision. The postwar period was a time of "moral confusion." Anthropology's response, Wolf says, was "one of retreat"; as Margaret Mead put it, anthropologists "took their marbles and went home."[18] The postwar period was also a time of expansion for universities, in which professional anthropology, seeking to secure its institutional base, presented itself as the science of culture. Although academic anthropologists did not reopen the debate over race, Landes continued to offer theories of race in her writings on both Brazilian and American society. Because such discourse was silent in anthropology, her work remained outside the disciplinary canon.

Landes's first publications on her field research in Brazil were two articles that appeared in 1940. "Fetish Worship in Brazil" was a "scientific" report in which Landes catalogued the cultural traits, beliefs, and practices of candomblé; "A Cult Matriarchate and Male Homosexuality" was a description of the transvestite and homosexual practices of the men who attached themselves to female-headed candomblé temples. The latter article stirred such a hostile reaction among established Brazilian and American scholars that, as readers of her manuscript (*City of Women*) on the same material, they advised academic presses not to publish the book.[19] *City of Women* was finally published in 1947, but it was sold as a trade book and, more often than not, was reviewed as a "very intelligent travel work" or as a "tourist account."[20]

The reception of *City of Women* by the discipline offers an illustration of canon-making and of marginalizing the ethnography of race and gender. Melville Herskovits reviewed the book for the discipline's flagship journal, the *American Anthropologist*. His review is critical and is based on three perceived problems: Landes's theoretical focus on race and not culture, specifically the new area of Afro-American culture that Herskovits himself was establishing within anthropology; her gender-conscious and sexualized analysis of candomblé; and her field methods and conduct.

The Herskovits Hat: Interpreting African American Culture

Herskovits, like Landes, had been a student of Franz Boas (although of the preceding generation), was the son of German Jewish immigrants to the Midwest, and, also like Landes, had conducted his first research in Harlem in the 1920s. His initial theoretical perspective had been to take an assimilationist view, but by the late 1920s he was arguing the essentially opposing view and documenting African cultural survivals in the music, art, language, family structure, and religion of African Americans. He conducted fieldwork in West Africa and in Surinam, Haiti, and the southern United States and began to develop Afro-American culture as a research area within anthropology. According to Walter Jackson, Herskovits "began to see himself as an interpreter of Africa to Afro-Americans."[21] Gertrude Fraser suggested that research on African American culture in the 1930s and 1940s envisioned only two possible analytical frameworks: one was to measure assimilation into white American society; the other was to look to Africa for explanations for the cultural differences of African Americans. "[I]n either case, African-American culture was largely examined in terms of something or somewhere else."[22] Herskovits had begun his career pursuing the first approach and later established his position as an advocate of the second. Landes, however, appears to have been working within a third and alternative theoretical framework that Fraser does not note: Landes observed Afro-Brazilian religion on its own terms. She believed she was studying a new religion, one that was an integral part of the contemporary way of life of the urban poor whose lives she understood to be structured and situated by larger political and economic complexities in Brazil. Furthermore, she did not portray candomblé as a homogeneous phenomenon; rather, she described diversity in ritual knowledge and practices among the candomblés that generated rivalries and conflict.

Herskovits's critique of Landes's work in Brazil had a permanent effect on her career and effectively excluded her from participation in African American culture studies in anthropology. He asserted that she had been "ill prepared" to conduct research in Bahia because "she knew so little of the African background of the material she was to study that she had no perspective." [23] He maintained that it was because Landes had not been adequately trained "in the Africanist field" that she had developed "the false perspective on the role of men and women in the culture that gives the book its misleading title." [24] He continued:

> *What Miss Landes does not realize is that men have places that are quite as important as those of the women; that the African counterparts of the Bahian cults have priestesses as well as priests. . . .*
>
> *The basic thesis is wrong, also, because of the misreading of an economic cause—that is, few men are initiates, in Bahia no less than in Africa, because they cannot afford the time it takes, because in Africa it is easier to support a woman in the culthouse than to withdraw a man from productive labor for months on end. Miss Landes overstresses the homosexuality of male priests— there are many "orthodox" as well as* caboclo *priests in Bahia who have no tendency toward inversion.*[25]

Unlike Ruth Benedict, Landes's teacher, Herskovits appears to have accepted current Freudian ideas that labeled homosexuality as "deviant"; his critique was further flawed by ethnocentrism and by the lack of ethnographic knowledge at the time about women's economic and religious roles not only in Bahia but also in West Africa.[26] However, his status as department chair at Northwestern University and Landes's status as an unemployed woman with a recent doctorate established his greater authority to define appropriate subjects, methods, and interpretations of anthropological research and were not incidental to the difficulty Landes subsequently had in finding employment as an anthropologist—for she did not obtain a permanent academic appointment until she was fifty-seven, thirty-five years after she received her Ph.D. Landes understood the situation acutely and did not hesitate to confront Herskovits at a conference a few years after the review appeared. Throughout her career she delighted in telling students about this meeting. She was a strikingly attractive woman, and Herskovits reportedly began to flirt with her in a patronizing manner. When she said, "You don't know who I am do you? I am Dr. Landes," he became uncomfortable, suddenly remembered a previous appointment, and quickly excused himself. Shortly before she died Landes bequeathed to a favorite student what she called "The Herskovits Hat"—the hat she had worn that day.

Not a Daughter in the Field: The Sexuality of Women Anthropologists

Herskovits's main criticism of *City of Women* derived from unstated yet prevailing assumptions about the personal comportment of anthropologists in the field. Under the guise of a more general discussion of what he called "the proper training of students going into the field," he questioned Landes's field methods in Brazil. He noted that, like most American anthropologists, Landes had received training for fieldwork on Indian reserves but that she had not been trained in "what might be called the diplomatic aspects of field-work." In particular, "students of acculturated societies must be . . . taught how to conduct themselves in the capital as well as in the bush, told how to turn the corners of calling cards, when to leave them, and how to 'sign the book.'"[27] What Herskovits was indirectly referring to was that Landes had slighted a major Brazilian scholar, Artur Ramos, and had disregarded race, class, and gender boundaries in Brazilian society. Instead of depending on the patronage and endorsement of a senior (white) scholar like Ramos, she had allied herself with a junior (black) folklorist and journalist, Edison Carneiro.[28] With Carneiro, Landes pursued a level of participant observation and obtained data on candomblé in Bahia that Ramos's armchair methods could not yield. Fueling Herskovits's criticism was the knowledge that Landes and Carneiro were lovers during their year of collaborative research. This relationship challenged assumptions about what constituted scientific comportment in the field and about what methods could yield authoritative ethnography.

Through participant observation anthropologists are expected to establish relationships based on rapport and trust, but students usually receive only vague instruction on how to develop these relationships. At the same time, it is assumed that a boundary must be preserved between the anthropological self (the scientist) and the native self (the subject). There has also been an implicit assumption of celibacy in the field, an assumption that maintaining the boundary between the scientific self of the anthropologist and the sexual self of the anthropologist is a necessary and fundamental condition for preserving the desired objectivity of the scientist from the subjectivity of the native. Only recently have some anthropologists begun to be frank about having acted as sexual selves in the field—and not always to the critical acclaim of colleagues.[29] The relationship between any of this behavior and the ethnographic product has not been systematically investigated; the assumption has only been made that the product would necessarily be an unscientific one—as, indeed, Herskovits argued in the case of Landes.

In a recent essay entitled "Lovers in the Field: Sex, Dominance and the Female Anthropologist," Jill Dubisch explains that the idea of women anthropologists having lovers in the field has been almost unthinkable because such behavior not only would break the unwritten code that prescribes celibacy for the lone field-worker but also would undermine what has been an accepted hierarchy of relations between a Western researcher (assumed to be male) and an exotic Other. Furthermore, a woman anthropologist having sexual relations in the field overturned Western conceptions of male dominance and female subordinance (for, being Western, she would also, it was assumed, be dominant). This was less true, Dubisch argues, for male anthropologists because Western conceptions of Others have often intertwined the exotic and the erotic and have usually portrayed the Other as female. Male sexual Others have less frequently been portrayed or examined.[30]

Instead of being trained or even encouraged to develop a self-concept as an adult anthropologist, anthropological women have been socialized to position themselves as daughters in the field and as "daughterly ethnographers" in their texts.[31] Although the role of daughter can vary across and even within cultures, daughterliness in different societies has been found to prescribe subservience, intimacy, respect, and/or dependence. Female graduate students continue to be told that their best strategy for acceptance and integration into a community may be to present themselves as neophytes, not only in the culture but also in the female gender role. The experience of Ruth Landes (who was thirty years old, was married, held a Ph.D., and had two published books when she went to Brazil) further illustrates that not only have women anthropologists been expected to assume the role of daughter in the field but that this was to be their role throughout their professional lives in the discipline. Although Landes adored Franz Boas and considered him and Ruth Benedict to be her mentors, all her life she (like his other women students) referred to him as "Papa Boas." In a 1980 essay entitled "Women in Anthropology" she stated that while he had a high regard for the intellect of his women students, he did not see a need to assist them in securing academic appointments. This infantilization of women anthropologists was never disputed. Nowadays the fallout following Landes's Brazilian fieldwork would be entirely predictable; indeed, most of us now receive the kind of training Herskovits advocated, in that we are told of the importance of cultivating relations with national scholars in our ethnographic areas. For women students and professional anthropologists, this often means daughterly deference to established male scholars in our fields. While male students may experience similar socialization, their student role as son is considered temporary and transitional to their potential role as heir. Even now, no such future adult roles are assumed for women.

In her essay "Sex and Violence in Academic Life or You Can Keep a Good Woman Down," Caroline Ramazanoglu describes how academic women who assume an adult status are viewed: "Women who resist the male domination of higher education . . . will be seen as unnatural, sexually undesirable, aggressive women whose personal peculiarities must account for their deviant behavior."[32] While writing this essay, I began to remember that, as a student, I had in fact heard of Ruth Landes, who was invariably described in negative terms and dismissed as "a difficult woman," "disagreeable," and "eccentric." I now understand that Landes—who was the first to describe herself as stubborn (she delights in telling us that in Brazil she received letters addressed to "Mrs. R. Mallet-Head Landes") and who was beautiful, attracted to men as lovers, and an original and uncompromised thinker—was constructed by the profession in this way because she did not assume a respectful, subordinate, daughterly role with her male colleagues. Never a daughter in the profession, until the end of her life she insisted that all but her close friends refer to her as "Dr. Landes."

Feminist Readings of Ruth Landes Writing Culture

Ruth Landes was one of the first anthropologists to focus on gender, sexuality, and women's experiences in her texts. To illustrate how subtle and pervasive are the mechanisms of silencing and marginalization in the academy, I consider how her ethnography has been read not by her male contemporaries but by second-generation feminist scholars. *City of Women* was out of print for many years, but *Ojibwa Woman* was reprinted in 1971 and so has come under recent critical scrutiny in the discipline.

Rayna Green, in a review essay on Native American women in the influential feminist journal *Signs,* recognizes Landes as a pioneer but in the same breath dismisses her work without documentation or discussion: "The thirties initiated trends that later became important areas of study. The first major work on Native American women was published, Ruth Landes's flawed and male-centered *The Ojibwa Woman,* which introduced to anthropologists the possibility of writing important works on tribal women." [33] This widely read review had the effect of discouraging a new generation of students and scholars from taking Ruth Landes seriously.

Similarly, in an important article entitled "Women's Status in Egalitarian Society: Implications for Social Evolution," Eleanor Leacock discusses *Ojibwa Woman* and acknowledges that "Landes deserves credit for making available such full material on women that explicit criticism of her work is possible." But then Leacock proceeds to expose and itemize what she perceives to be contradictions in Landes's ethnography: Ojibwa women are described, for example, in some places in the text as self-sufficient and autonomous and in other instances as inferior to men. [34] These contradictions emerge, Leacock says, in part because of "changes taking place in women's socioeconomic position and in part from [Landes's] lack of a critical and historical orientation toward her material." [35] They can be explained, she argues, by adopting an historical materialist theoretical framework. Leacock was committed to a social evolutionary perspective on gender relations that viewed the increasing subordination of women to men as a product of changing economic relations (including the development of agriculture, private property, and the state). As hunter-gatherers, then, the Ojibwa were to Leacock an example of a society in which egalitarian gender relations had prevailed prior to the intensification of trade and state relations with the larger Canadian society. Leacock was a pioneer in her efforts to introduce a gender consciousness to anthropology, but in developing her increasingly sophisticated theoretical argument she devalued the work of a pioneer from a previous generation when she took Landes's book out of historical context to use as fodder in an academic debate with her primarily male Marxist colleagues.

Leacock's critique had the effect of denying Landes a reading by a new generation of students, like myself, who were undertaking fieldwork on women and development (which in the 1980s replaced women's status as the urgent research question) and who had turned to Leacock's writing for theoretical perspective. As a graduate student in the early 1980s at the time of these rereadings and as a member of the feminist caucus in my department, I remember deciding, based on critiques like Green's and Leacock's, that there were real problems with *Ojibwa Woman* and that there was no need to read it. Thus women (including feminists) have also contributed to what Catherine Lutz has called the "disciplining of women's voices" and the "erasure of women's writing" in sociocultural anthropology.[36]

Conclusion

There is a real need to read the writing of early anthropologists and to understand the relationship between their experiences in the field and in their professional careers and the location of their writing in the anthropological canon. When we recover the history of ethnographic writing we discover that there has long been experimentation (by both women and men) that includes many of the "textual innovations" to which "new" ethnographers in the 1980s laid claim: first-person narration, multivocality, transcription of dialogue, reflection on the impact of the ethnographer's feelings and relations with subjects and interlocutors, and so on. Anthropologists have also long experimented with the recording of subjective experiences in their published and unpublished letters, diaries, memoirs, biographies, autobiographies, novels, poems, and prefaces—all of which need to be understood as ethnographic writing.[37]

In addition, as the work of Ruth Landes shows, the history of women ethnographers reveals not only or exclusively innovative and noncanonical styles of writing but also substantive and theoretical contributions. Landes's theoretical focus and empirical research on race and gender constituted in her day "writing against culture," in Abu-Lughod's terms. Recovering the history of the ethnography of race and gender is an important and necessary complement to Abu-Lughod's argument that we begin to write against culture. An historical consciousness reveals that unsettling the concept of culture or, as I have termed it, writing against writing culture has long been a subtext in anthropology. It was a part of the antiracist work of pre–World War II Boasians; it was part of the critique of colonialism that began in the 1960s;[38] it was central to the work of historical materialists (like Eleanor Leacock); and it is the project of contemporary feminists and ethnographers.

Finally, just as important as recognizing the continuities in textual practices in anthropology is recognizing the continuities in the politics of canon-setting and in the interrelated practices of marginalizing theoretical paradigms and rhetorical styles of writing. For rereading Ruth Landes also reveals the hegemonic practices at work in the discipline that operated to marginalize her and her work. And, as the writings of contemporary feminist and African American anthropologists reveal, processes not dissimilar to those Landes experienced continue to effectively erase much current theoretical work on race and gender.[39]

Notes

Ruth Landes arranged for her papers to be deposited in the National Anthropological Archives at the Smithsonian Institution upon her death. The Ruth Landes Papers comprise seventy-eight boxes of letters, fieldnotes, and unpublished articles, lectures, and manuscripts.

This chapter is based on preliminary research with the Landes Papers, on published materials, and on interviews with faculty and former students of the Department of Anthropology at McMaster University, as well as with Landes's former colleagues and students from her years (1959–1962) at the Claremont Graduate School in California.

I would like to thank the Social Sciences and Humanities Research Council of Canada for funding. I would also like to express my appreciation to Victoria Burbank for her comments on earlier drafts of this paper, written while I was a visiting scholar in the Department of Anthropology at the University of California at Davis (1991–1992), and to the editors and readers of this book for their comments and encouragement. In employing a biographical approach to the history of anthropology I follow Barbara Laslett's argument for the theoretical importance of and need for biography in the social sciences ("Biography as Historical Sociology: The Case of William Fielding Ogburn," *Theory and Society* 20 [1991]: 511–38). I also follow Sydel Silverman in viewing biography or individual case studies of anthropological careers as sources of data necessary for developing an accurate understanding of the history of theory in anthropology—in Landes's case, the theorizing of race and gender. In her introduction to *Totems and Teachers* ([New York: Columbia University Press, 1981], ix), Silverman writes, "The development of theory is a social process, a product of life histories embedded in time and place."

1. Ruth Landes, *The Ojibwa Woman* (New York: Columbia University Press, 1938). Landes's writings on race and ethnicity include: "A Northerner Views the South," *Social Forces* 23 (1945): 275–79; *The City of Women* (New York: Macmillan, 1947; reprinted in 1995 by the University of New Mexico Press with a new introduction by Sally Cole entitled "Ruth Landes in Brazil: Writing, Race, and Gender in 1930s American Anthropology"); "Biracialism in American Society: A Comparative View," *American Anthropologist* 57 (1955): 1253–64; *Culture in American Education* (New York: John Wiley & Sons, 1965); *Latin Americans of the Southwest* (St. Louis: McGraw-Hill, 1965); and "Negro Jews in Harlem," *Jewish Journal of Sociology* 9 (1967): 175–89. The ways in which my interests parallel those of Ruth Landes can be seen in Sally Cole, *Women of the Praia: Work and Lives in a Portuguese Coastal Community* (Princeton, N.J.: Princeton University Press, 1991); "Is Feminist Ethnography 'New' Ethnography?" in *Ethnographic Feminisms: Essays in Anthropology,* ed. Sally Cole and Lynne Phillips (Ottawa: Carleton University Press, 1995); and "'We're Both Portuguese but Don't Confuse the Two': Farm, Factory and Fisheries Workers in Southwestern Ontario," in *Two Generations: The Portuguese in Ontario,* ed. Manuela Marujo (Toronto: Multicultural History Society of Ontario, forthcoming).

2. James Clifford and George Marcus, eds., *Writing Culture: The Politics and Poetics of Ethnography* (Berkeley: University of California Press, 1986); Lila Abu-Lughod, "Writing against Culture," in *Recapturing Anthropology: Working in the Present,* ed. Richard Fox (Santa Fe, N. Mex.: School of American Research, 1991).

3. The phrase "ethnographic naturalism" comes from Jonathan Spencer, "Anthropology as a Kind of Writing," *Man* 24 (1989): 145–64.

4. The phrase "unruly experience" is used by James Clifford in *The Predicament of Culture: Twentieth Century Ethnography* (Cambridge, Mass.: Harvard University Press, 1988), 25.

5. Ibid., 23.

6. Landes, *City of Women* (1995), 248.

7. Ibid., 44.

8. Ibid., 79–80.

9. Ibid., 81.

10. As early as 1896, physician and professor of forensic medicine Raymundo Nina Rodrigues of Bahia (1862–1906) was studying spirit possession in the candomblés. After

his premature death, scholars at the Instituto Nina Rodrigues continued his work. Of those scholars Artur Ramos, a physician who specialized in forensic medicine, became the most well known in America. See Raymundo Nina Rodrigues, *O animismo fetichista dos negros bahianos* (Rio de Janeiro: Civilização Brasileira, 1935) and *Os africanos no Brasil*, 4th ed. (São Paulo: Companhia Editora Nacional, 1976; orig. 1932); Artur Ramos, *O folk-lore negro do Brasil* (Rio de Janeiro: Civilização Brasileira, 1935). See also Edison Carneiro, "The Structure of African Cults in Bahia," *Journal of American Folklore* 53 (1940): 271–78; *Candomblés da Bahia*, 6th ed. (Rio de Janeiro: Civilização Brasileira, 1978); *Religiões negras. Negros Bantus,* 2d ed. (Rio de Janeiro: Civilização Brasileira, 1981; orig. published separately in 1936 and 1937). For American scholars writing on candomblé in the 1930s and 1940s, see Donald Pierson, *Negros in Brazil: A Study of Race Contact in Brazil* (Chicago: Chicago University Press, 1942); Melville Herskovits, "African Gods and Catholic Saints in New World Negro Belief," *American Anthropologist* 39 (1937): 635–43; "The Social Organization of the Candomblé," in *The New World Negro*, ed. Frances Herskovits (Bloomington: Indiana University Press, 1969), 226–47; and Melville and Frances Herskovits, "The Negroes of Brazil," *Yale Review* 32 (1943): 263–79.

11. Landes, *City of Women*, 148.

12. Ibid., 101–102.

13. Roger Bastide, *The African Religions of Brazil*, trans. Helen Sebba (Baltimore, Md.: Johns Hopkins University Press, 1978), 210.

14. Ruth Landes, "A Woman Anthropologist in Brazil," in *Women in the Field: Anthropological Experiences,* ed. Peggy Golde (Chicago: Aldine, 1970), 120.

15. Landes's M.S.W. thesis was later published as "Negro Jews in Harlem," *Jewish Journal of Sociology* 9 (1967): 175–89.

16. Elazar Barkan, *The Retreat of Scientific Racism: Changing Concepts of Race in Britain and the United States between the World Wars* (Cambridge, England: Cambridge University Press, 1992). On Boas as the single most important force shaping American anthropology in the twentieth century, see George W. Stocking, Jr., ed., *The Shaping of American Anthropology 1883–1911: A Franz Boas Reader* (New York: Basic Books, 1974).

17. Johnetta Cole, "Foreword: The South in US and US in the South," in *Americans in the South: Issues of Race, Class and Gender,* ed. Hans A. Baer and Yvonne Jones (Athens: University of Georgia Press, 1992), xii. Sidney Mintz has noted that research on African Americans was considered secondary to research on Native Americans; see his "Introduction" to a re-edition of Melville J. Herskovits, *The Myth of the Negro Past* (Boston: Beacon Press, 1990; orig. 1941), ix–xxi. There were anthropological studies of African Americans, but they were considered marginal at the time. See, for example, Zora Neale Hurston, *Mules and Men* (Bloomington: Indiana University Press, 1978; orig. 1935) and *Tell My Horse* (Berkeley: Turtle Island Press, 1981; orig. 1938); Hortense Powdermaker, *After Freedom: A Cultural Study of the Deep South* (New York: Viking, 1939). In Brazil the situation was similar. Of the five students Columbia sent to Brazil in the late 1930s, Landes was the only one to do fieldwork among blacks and in an urban setting; the others (Jules Henry, Buell Quain, William Lipkind, and Charles Wagley) conducted research with Indians in the Amazon Basin.

18. Eric Wolf, "American Anthropologists and American Society," in *Reinventing Anthropology,* ed. Dell Hymes (New York: Pantheon, 1974), 259–60; Margaret Mead, as quoted in Virginia Yans-McLaughlin, "Science, Democracy, and Ethics: Mobilizing Culture and Personality for World War II," in *Malinowski, Rivers, Benedict and Others: Essays on Culture and Personality,* ed. George Stocking (Madison: University of Wisconsin Press, 1986), 214.

19. Ruth Landes, "Fetish Worship in Brazil," *Journal of American Folklore* 53 (1940): 261–70; "A Cult Matriarchate and Male Homosexuality," *Journal of Abnormal and*

Social Psychology 35 (1940): 306–97; Edison Carneiro, "Uma 'falseta' de Artur Ramos," in *Ladinos e crioulos: estudos sobre o Negro no Brasil,* ed. Edison Carneiro (Rio de Janeiro: Civilização Brasileira, 1964), 223–27.

20. See, for example, reviews by John Honigman in *Social Forces* 26 (1947): 227; and Virginia Mishnun in *The Nation* 165 (1947): 128.

21. Walter Jackson, "Melville Herskovits and the Search for Afro-American Culture," in *Malinowski, Rivers, Benedict and Others,* 109.

22. Gertrude Fraser, "Race, Class, and Difference in Hortense Powdermaker's *After Freedom: A Cultural Study of the Deep South,*" *Journal of Anthropological Research* 47 (1991): 407.

23. Melville Herskovits, review of *The City of Women, American Anthropologist* 50 (1948): 124.

24. Ibid.

25. Ibid.

26. Abundant research has since documented the social and economic autonomy, and often dominance, of West African women. For a review of this literature, see Betty Potash, "Gender Relations in Sub-Saharan Africa," in *Gender and Anthropology: Critical Reviews for Teaching,* ed. Sandra Morgen (Washington, D.C.: American Anthropological Association, 1989), 189–227. For a recent study documenting male homosexuality in Bahian candomblés, see Jim Wafer, *The Taste of Blood: Spirit Possession in Brazilian Candomblé* (Philadelphia: University of Pennsylvania Press, 1991).

27. Herskovits, review of *City of Women,* 282. Ruth Landes, like the majority of her contemporaries under Boas and Benedict, had received her training in anthropology through fieldwork in North American Indian societies. She had conducted her doctoral research among the Ojibwa of Emo, Ontario, Canada in 1932–1933 and had undertaken further research in 1934–1935 with the neighboring Chippewa of Red Lake, Minnesota, later in 1935 on the Santee Dakota Indian Reservation at Red Wing, Minnesota, and in 1935–1936 with the Potawatomi at Mayetta, Kansas. This work resulted in five books and numerous articles.

28. In "Uma 'falseta' de Artur Ramos," Carneiro describes how Ramos, throughout his career, made "vulgar insinuations" about Landes's saying she was inordinately interested in "the sexual life of Negroes," charges that, Carneiro says, emerged "solely from [Ramos's] pride and vanity." In her essay "A Woman Anthropologist in Brazil," Landes reports that Ramos recruited the allegiance of Melville Herskovits, who in 1939 cosigned a letter containing these charges to Gunnar Myrdal, then director of "The Negro in America" project and for whom Landes was working when she returned from Brazil. I have not yet been able to locate a copy of this letter. In *City of Women* Landes also describes how, for months, her activities in Bahia were monitored by undercover police and how she was required to leave Brazil in June 1939 because of a supposed "passport irregularity."

29. See, for example, Manda Cesara, *Reflections of a Woman Anthropologist* (Toronto: Academic Press, 1982); Esther Newton, "My Best Informant's Dress: The Erotic Equation in Fieldwork," *Cultural Anthropology* 8 (1993): 3–23; Paul Rabinow, *Reflections on Fieldwork in Morocco* (Berkeley: University of California Press, 1977); Wafer, *Taste of Blood.*

30. Jill Dubisch, "Lovers in the Field: Sex, Dominance and the Female Anthropologist" (paper presented at the American Anthropological Association annual meeting, Chicago, 1991). On the feminization of the "Other," see also Barbara Babcock, "A New Mexican Rebecca: Imaging Pueblo Women," *Journal of the Southwest* 34 (1992): 400–437.

31. Jean Briggs, *Never in Anger: Portrait of an Eskimo Family* (Cambridge, Mass.: Harvard University Press, 1970), and "Kapluna Daughter," in *Women in the Field,* 19–44; Dorinne Kondo, *Crafting Selves: Power, Gender, and Discourses of Identity in a Japanese Workplace* (Chicago: University of Chicago Press, 1990).

32. Caroline Ramazanoglu, "Sex and Violence in Academic Life or You Can Keep a Good Woman Down," in *Women, Violence and Social Control*, ed. Jalna Hanmer and Mary Maynard (Basingstoke, England: Macmillan Press, 1987), 62.

33. Rayna Green, "Review Essay: Native American Women," *Signs* 6 (1980): 248.

34. Elenore Leacock, "Women's Status in Egalitarian Society: Implications for Social Evolution," *Current Anthropology* 19 (1978): 212. For an alternate reading of *The Ojibwa Woman*, see Sally Cole, "Women's Stories and Boasian Texts: The Ojibwa Ethnography of Ruth Landes and Maggie Wilson," *Anthropoligica*, forthcoming. I argue that contradiction in the texts is the result of tensions between three storytelling practices that mediate Landes's Ojibwa ethnography: the Boasian textual tradition, Ojibwa women's storytelling, and the gendered script for American daughters of Russian Jewish immigrants like Landes.

35. Ibid., 252.

36. Catherine Lutz, "The Erasure of Women's Writing in Sociocultural Anthropology," *American Ethnologist* 17 (1990): 612.

37. See, for example, Eleanor Smith Bowen, *Return to Laughter: An Anthropological Novel* (New York: Anchor Books, 1954); Briggs, *Never in Anger;* Frederica de Laguna, *Voyage to Greenland: A Personal Initiation into Anthropology* (New York: Norton, 1977); Elizabeth Fernea, *Guests of the Sheik: An Ethnography of an Iraqi Village* (New York: Anchor Books, 1965); Landes, *City of Women;* Margaret Mead, *Letters from the Field 1925–75* (New York: Harper and Row, 1977); Bronislaw Malinowski, *A Diary in the Strict Sense of the Term* (New York: Harcourt, Brace & World, 1967); Robert Maybury-Lewis, *The Savage and the Innocent* (Boston: Beacon Press, [1965] 1988); Hortense Powdermaker, *Stranger and Friend: The Way of an Anthropologist* (New York: W. W. Norton, 1966); Marjorie Shostak, *Nisa: The Life and Words of a !Kung Woman* (New York: Vintage Books, 1981); Mary Smith, *Baba of Karo: A Woman of the Muslim Hausa* (London: Faber and Faber, 1954); Margery Wolf, *The House of Lim: A Study of a Chinese Farm Family* (Englewood Cliffs, N.J.: Prentice-Hall, 1968).

38. See, for example, Talal Asad, *Anthropology and the Colonial Encounter* (London: Ithaca Press, 1973).

39. See Faye Harrison, "Anthropology as an Agent of Transformation: Introductory Comments and Queries," in *Decolonizing Anthropology: Moving Further Toward an Anthropology for Liberation* (Washington, D.C.: American Anthropological Association, 1991), and "The DuBoisian Legacy in Anthropology," *Critique of Anthropology* 12 (1992): 239–60; Lutz, "Erasure of Women's Writing"; Frances Mascia-Lees, Patricia Sharpe, and Colleen Ballerino Cohen, "The Postmodernist Turn in Anthropology: Cautions from a Feminist Perspective," *Signs* 15 (1989): 7–33; Sandra Morgen, "Introduction," in *Gender and Anthropology;* Margery Wolf, *A Thrice-Told Tale: Feminism, Postmodernism and Ethnographic Responsibility* (Stanford: Stanford University Press, 1992).

9

Margaret Mead and the "Rustling-of-the-Wind-in-the-Palm-Trees School" of Ethnographic Writing

Nancy C. Lutkehaus

ALTHOUGH Margaret Mead is seldom credited these days with having written feminist, let alone experimental, ethnography, perhaps more than any other anthropologist—male or female—Mead consciously experimented with the writing of ethnography and explored other modes of presentation—visual, audio, and electronic. Given our current interest in the anthropologist as author, as well as feminist scholars' interest in women writers, Mead's distinct authorial style and her public role as an American intellectual and writer make it imperative that we take a second look at her contributions to the writing of culture.[1]

One of the twentieth century's most prolific anthropologists and writers, between 1925 and 1975 Mead published more than 1,300 articles, essays, books, biographies, autobiographies, book reviews, and prefaces in both scholarly and popular publications.[2] The latter ranged from *The Nation* and the *New York Times* to *Parent's* and *Redbook* magazines. Her public success was based to a large extent on her concern for writing and speaking vividly and without academic jargon. It was also a result of her interest in experimenting with new technologies in research and communication.

During the 1930s and 1940s Mead, along with her husband, Gregory Bateson, developed innovative uses of still photographs and film as research

As a scientist Margaret Mead was often interviewed on radio and television. (Photograph courtesy of Department of Library Services, American Museum of Natural History, negative #337425; date of photograph unknown)

tools. Mead herself saw a connection between the pageants she used to write and produce as a child and her later interest in directing and constructing ethnographic films in the field.[3] The use she and Bateson made of film and photographs remained focused for the most part on the role that visual images could play as tools for the comparative analysis of form over time and place.[4]

Beginning in the 1950s Mead pioneered the use of the television talk-show interview as a forum for the presentation of anthropological insights and findings. While Mead had been known to the American public before the advent of television, by the 1960s her appearances on talk shows with hosts such as Johnny Carson made her name almost a household word. She was acutely aware of the power of the mass media as a cultural and educational tool and of the relationship between the written and spoken word and the power of the visual image. As her colleague Rhoda Metraux cogently observed, Mead's "most winning gift was surely her capacity for immediate, zestful response." Asked a question, she made a point of answering thoughtfully and concisely, "sometimes with a single word, sometimes sharply, and most often with humor."[5] With such performance skills, she was an interviewer's, and audience's, delight.

Mead, committed to the legacy of the open-air chautauquas that had developed in nineteenth-century rural America, believed that democracy was based on engaged public conversation. She embraced television talk shows as a form of "electronic chautauqua," a powerful medium for her message, strategically broadcasting her ideas about social reform, race, marriage, the family, childhood, male-female relations, and the perpetuation of liberal democracy in America. Ironically, as Mead's popular success increased, she was simultaneously marginalized in academic anthropology, highlighting the ambivalent relationship American intellectuals have historically had with the media and popular culture.[6]

As a result of her career as a popularizer of anthropology Margaret Mead walked a tightrope, balancing her image as scientist with that of media star and writer of "science fiction" rather than positivist science. When A. C. Haddon, one of the founders of British social anthropology, dismissed Mead's work by insinuating that it was little more than the observations of a lady novelist, and when several decades later another doyen of British anthropology, E. E. Evans-Pritchard, derisively referred to her work as "feminine" and exemplary of the "rustling-of-the-wind-in-the-palm-trees" kind of anthropological writing, they scarcely could have anticipated a time when Mead's skill as a writer of ethnography would come to be seen in a different light.[7]

Rather than analyze the criticisms that have been waged past and present about the content of Mead's work, I want to look at the innovative aspects of her writing, those dimensions that went against the grain of the dominant modernist style of ethnography.[8] I also want to highlight the integral relationship for Mead between the process of writing and the development of anthropological theory and method. I begin with Mead's best-known work, her first book, *Coming of Age in Samoa,* in which she used her Samoan findings to reflect on education in America, and her letters from the field. I then consider lesser-known works, such as the monthly column of short essays she published for many years in *Redbook* magazine and her dialogue with author James Baldwin in *A Rap on Race.*[9] Finally, I discuss the ways in which gender, race, and class played important roles in her choice of issues and topics and the modes and venues in which she presented her findings. The fact that Mead was a woman not only allowed, but also actively helped to shape, her experiments in writing culture.

The Scientist as Writer

More than many anthropologists, Mead consciously valued the practice of writing as integral to the practice of science—the writing, as she put it, of "literate English," rather than "the heavy German style which dominated the American university dissertation field."[10] Her conviction about the importance of writing was rooted in her family background. In her autobiography, *Blackberry Winter,* Mead recollects that "[w]riting was what my parents did, and writing was as much a part of my life as gardening and canning were in the life of a farmer's daughter of that day. Yet it was something much more special—something other people around us did not do." [11] From an early age writing was something she associated with both of her parents—one a sociologist, the other an economist—as well as something that made her, and her family, special. By the age of ten she had embarked on writing her first novel. She also wrote poetry, pageants, articles for school newspapers, and numerous letters to friends.

At Barnard College in New York City, Mead continued her interest in writing by editing the college newspaper and discussing and sharing poetry and literature with a group of fellow students who called themselves the Ash Can Cats. Among this group was one young woman, Leonie Adams, who as an undergraduate was already a published poet. Leonie's genius as a poet, Mead recounts, caused her to abandon any serious thought of becoming a writer herself. Nevertheless, her interest in literature and in writing poetry continued in her graduate-student days and was cultivated by her professional and personal friendships with the anthropologist Ruth Fulton Benedict at Columbia University and the linguist Edward Sapir, both of whom also wrote poetry. Fearing their mentor Franz Boas's approbation, Mead and Benedict kept their poetry writing clandestine, segregating their "artistic" or literary expression from their scholarly work. [12]

Mead's realization that she was not a talented poet seems to have freed her to find another format in which to integrate the two seemingly contradictory demands of scientist and artist. Reflecting on her decision to write ethnography rather than fiction, in later years Mead interpreted her changing notion of herself as a writer in the following terms: "Once I had satisfied myself that human cultures were far more complex and interesting than anything I could create and that in my attempts to write fiction I had actually been trying to understand real situations that I had encountered as a child, I had no further desire to write fiction." [13]

Although Mead abandoned any intention of becoming a serious poet or novelist, she never abandoned her desire—some say addiction—to writing. As Bateson remarked, "It was almost a principle of pure energy. . . . She was like a tugboat. She could sit down and write three thousand words by eleven o'clock in the morning and spend the rest of the day working at the museum." [14] But for Mead it appears that her compulsion to write was motivated not by displaced energy but by a sense of "the scientific vocation as she understood it." [15] For she saw the task of the anthropologist as one in which science—as a tool for the gathering of insights—and art—as a means for the expression of these insights—combined to communicate truths about the human condition. In a letter from the field written to friends and colleagues Mead contemplated the similarities and differences between the anthropologist and the novelist:

> So the fieldworker must choose, shape, prune, discard this and collect finer detail on that, much as a novelist works who finds some minor character is

threatening to swallow the major theme or that the hero is fast taking him out of his depth. But unlike the novelist . . . the fieldworker is wholly and helplessly dependent on what happens — on the births, deaths, marriages, quarrels, entanglements, and reconciliations, depressions and elations of the one small community. . . . One must be continually prepared for anything, everything — and perhaps most devastating — for nothing.[16]

Here we see a clear expression of Mead's sense that an anthropologist is also quite fundamentally a writer, not only in the sense of crafting finely honed ethnographic texts but also in the thick of the fieldwork process. The latter point is one that anthropologists have only lately realized as they have come to reflect on the epistemological status of fieldnotes—the written documents that anthropologists produce while in the field, the "raw" makings of the final "cooked" ethnography concocted sometime later, away from the immediacy of the field.[17]

Mead's "Coming of Age" in Samoa

"A Day in Samoa," the second chapter of *Coming of Age in Samoa,* opens in a lyrical—albeit clichéd—manner: "As the dawn begins to fall among the soft brown roofs and the slender palm trees stand out against a colourless, gleaming sea, lovers slip home from trysts beneath the palm trees or in the shadow of beached canoes, that light may find each sleeper in his appointed place."[18]

The lush prose of this wordscape contrasts with the book's closing exhortations on behalf of reform in education. The two modes exemplify how Mead oscillated, as Clifford Geertz says most ethnographers do, between different rhetorical intentions. These include the subjective stylist, or anthropologist as author, and those of privileged expert, the anthropologist as social scientist. Mead was criticized for the emphasis she placed on the authorial or artistic, more feminine dimensions of her writing, at the expense of the scientific, or masculine.[19]

Moreover, Mead's decision to conclude her first book with two chapters about the relevance of her Samoan findings to the lives of contemporary Americans was another deviation from the scholarly format anthropologists usually followed. She had written these concluding chapters, "Our Educational Problems" and "Education For Choice," at the suggestion of her publisher, William Morrow. Based on a series of public lectures she had given in New York City to a working girls' club, Mead gave answers to such questions as "What are the rewards of the tiny, ingrown biological family opposing its closed circle of affection to a forbidding world, of the strong ties between parents and children, ties which imply an active personal relationship from birth until death?" in which she suggested that a larger family community "seems to ensure the child against the development of the crippling attitudes which have been labeled Oedipus complexes, Electra complexes, and so on."[20]

Thus from the very beginning Mead's ethnographic writing was shaped by the dialogic of her interaction with public audiences. Mead had not specifically written *Coming of Age* for a popular audience, but she did "take what was then a very

NANCY C. LUTKEHAUS

unusual course. I was trying to write a book on a technical subject, in which ethnological and psychological jargon would have been expected, and to make it intelligible to specially concerned groups of people, particularly those who had to work with adolescents in our own society."[21] She did not realize then that "if a book were written in English, stripped of technical jargon—which in the ethnographic literature of those days meant the use of an enormous number of words in the native language—it would automatically become accessible to the educated world, be easy reading for beginners in college and easily translatable into other languages."[22] Of course, Mead downplays the fact that she had provocative and timely things to say about topics such as education, adolescence, and the family that were of great interest to laymen and specialists alike.

Mead realized that her closing exhortations in *Coming of Age in Samoa*, though based on scholarly research and comparison between Samoa and America, were at best scientifically informed opinions. But she stated with conviction such thoughts as

> *Chief among our gains must be reckoned the possibility of choice, the recognition of many possible ways of life, where other civilizations have recognized only one. Where other civilizations give a satisfactory outlet to only one temperamental type, be he mystic or soldier, business man or artist, a civilization in which there are many standards offers a possibility of satisfactory adjustment to individuals of many different temperamental types, of diverse gifts and varying interests.*[23]

Mead's voice changes here from its opening lyrical register to one in which she uses Samoa as an allegory, a story of difference from which Americans can deduce lessons for themselves. The tone has changed from a softly feminine to a more sternly masculine voice of authority, that of the expert telling people "Look, we must take stock of our assets and make the best of them." Mead was twenty-seven years old when she wrote these words. Some negative reactions to her work may have been motivated as much by her presumption in assuming this male voice of authority as by her feminine or novelistic voice. The fact that Mead was willing to make such generalizations and to spell out their implications for American society contributed to the denigration of Mead's professional reputation among fellow anthropologists. Paradoxically, it simultaneously endeared her to the general public, for its conclusions presented a utopian vision of a liberal democratic society that generations of Americans read about with enthusiasm. A reevaluation of Mead's so-called limitations shows us that much of her work prefigured what anthropologists such as George E. Marcus and Michael Fischer have recently identified as the mission of anthropological discourse, to serve as a form of "cultural critique."[24]

Mead's Rhetoric and the Popularization of Anthropology

By the time the reviews of *Coming of Age in Samoa* had been published, with their intimation that the book would become a public success (a rare phenomenon for any ethnography, either in the 1920s or at present), Mead had already embarked on another field project, this time to New Guinea. In the books she wrote based on this and subsequent New Guinea research—*Growing Up in New Guinea, Sex and Temperament in Three Primitive Societies,* and *Male and Female*—Mead continued to strive to present her findings and their implications for Western society in clear prose, unencumbered by the use of foreign words and anthropological jargon.[25]

The last of these volumes, *Male and Female,* subtitled *A Study of the Sexes in a Changing World,* was a logical extension of her previous New Guinea ethnographies. Rather than writing about only one or two societies, in this book she decided to write about men and women across the spectrum of cultural variation from the position of an omniscient anthropologist, basing her statements about sex and gender on a synthesis of her observations of both primitive and Western societies.[26] In order to guide her readers through the text, Mead included an introductory chapter, "How an Anthropologist Writes." She begins by discussing the meaning of the idiom "from where I sit," significant because it is "an admission that no person ever sees more than part of the truth, that the contribution of one sex, or one culture, or one scientific discipline that may itself cross both sex and cultural lines, is always partial, and must always wait upon the contribution of others for a fuller truth."[27] The prescience of this statement is startling, because it has been lost to recent critics of modernist anthropology such as Clifford, who cite understanding of the partial and contested nature of truth as one of the hallmarks of postmodernist, male anthropology. Mead continues by identifying her authorial position: "This book is being written from the standpoint of a woman of middle age, of an American, and of an anthropologist." Feminists would later take Mead and other white, middle-class women writers / social scientists to task for not having included their racial and class identities as important aspects of their subjectivities.[28] However, the reason advocates of both experimental anthropology and feminist anthropology have overlooked this insight in recounting the history of challenges to the modernist canon is Mead's apolitical, culturally relativist position that skirts the issue of power and domination. Her argument for the inclusion of women's points of view along with those of men was that doing so would "help [us] to see the human race completely." The notion that certain points of view are associated with dominant positions of power and authority, while others are deemed subordinate, was not part of Mead's problematic. In this instance, she was a victim of her own theoretical blindness.

Nonetheless, by midcentury, for better or for worse, the name Margaret Mead was widely associated with the popularization of anthropology. Her public reputation was not simply fortuitous, it was the result of a conscious decision. She worked hard at the creation of her popular acclaim, but her decision was not based merely on a desire for fame.[29] It had scholarly roots in her association at Columbia University with Boas and his intellectual agenda for the promotion of a scientific theory of cultural relativism—whereby the constructed nature of our own Western beliefs and values was revealed through comparison with the institutions, values, and beliefs of non-Western societies.[30] It was also part of her job mandate when she was originally hired by the American Museum of Natural History to help disseminate the findings of anthropology to a broad public. Public education has long been the stated goal of museums, and Mead took seriously the challenge the curator of ethnology, Pliny E. Goddard, presented to her when she joined the staff in 1925: "to make ethnology as familiar to a wide and supportive audience as previous curators had made the subject of archeology."[31]

But perhaps most fundamentally, it was the result of her skill as a writer and her pleasure in the written (and by extension, the spoken) word. It was quite clear to her as a student, she later said, "that writing was a very valuable tool and that the anthropologist who could write like Malinowski, who was already reaching a wide audience, had a tremendous edge over his less gifted contemporaries."[32] Significantly, both Malinowski and Mead, who intentionally worked at cultivating their "gifts" of writing, were criticized by fellow anthropologists for their popular success.

Why did the public find Mead's ideas and prose so appealing, while academic anthropologists found them so reprehensible? In an article entitled "Margaret Mead: Science or Science Fiction?" the British social scientist Peter M. Worsley analyzed Mead's rhetorical style.[33] Writing more than twenty-five years before Clifford, Marcus, and others brought to our attention the rhetorical aspects of ethnographic writing that create ethnographic authority, Worsley critiques what he and others saw to be Mead's strengths and simultaneously provides an explanation of why they also were her weaknesses. As the title of his article implies, the debate focused on the practice of objective science as opposed to the art or craft of science fiction.

Worsley said that Mead "writes with considerable vividness in a style which, though not to everyone's taste, enables her to bring a scene, a quarrel, a landscape, a whole society, before the reader's eyes."[34] It is obvious, of course, that this is not to his taste. Next, he says, Mead "conveys a sense of excited participation in a research problem that many a detective-story writer might envy. 'You and I,' she says, 'are going to see if we can sort this problem out.'" Worsley's allusion to a detective-story writer underscores the "science fiction" dimension in Mead's writing. Then, "she tells the reader, 'this problem is of enormous, immediate, urgent, theoretical and practical importance.' To solve it, too, the reader will have to leave stuffy Boston or Tunbridge Wells and fly with Margaret Mead to the romantic 'South Seas.'"[35] Worsley's own rhetorical style implies that this was the stuff of fantasy and science fiction again, not the stolid prose of serious science. Presenting a lyrical passage from *Sex and Temperament in Three Primitive Societies,* Worsley concludes by saying that "the ration of romance is quite high" and refers to Evans-Pritchard's snide characterization of Mead's work as exemplary of the "rustling-of-the-wind-in-the-palm-trees" style of ethnography.[36]

After dismissing Mead's writing style as flamboyant and filled with flights of fancy, Worsley moves on to discuss her subject matter. "Mead," he says, "deals with very important themes in a serious way."[37] Here he refers to her cross-cultural research on the effects of cultural determinism on crucial aspects of human behavior such as child development and gender and their lasting contributions to the anthropological attack on ethnocentrism.

Appearing to give Mead credit for the seriousness of her research topics, Worsley goes on to undercut any praise she might deserve by implying that she more or less prostitutes her scientific principles by pandering to her readers' more prurient interests: "Above all, she deals with sex. Though she tackles serious questions, there is little doubt that she has played upon the fact that many of her readers have a less than scientific interest in sex and in her work, aroused by titles and headings suggesting all sorts of salacious possibilities—'Fathers, Mothers and Budding Impulses' (*Male and Female*), 'Experiences of the Average Girl' (*Coming of Age in Samoa*) [Salacious in *whose* mind?, one is tempted to ask here!] . . . or, in the work under review, the delightfully simple chapter-heading 'Women, Sex and Sin' [*New Lives for Old: Cultural Transformation, Manus, 1928–1953*]." [38]

In an attempt to explain why Mead's work appeals to a broad audience that also includes more sophisticated readers, Worsley suggests that "[m]ore serious readers are attracted not merely because she deals with sex, but because she relates her 'primitive' findings to civilized society. . . . Running through the bulk of her work is a warm liberal-humanist appeal which elicits a ready response from progressive and open-hearted readers. . . . All of this is put over with optimism and confidence. She reassures, strengthens and encourages her readers." [39]

Not only does Worsley express no sympathy with Mead's plea for greater freedom in society's view of the potential and gifts of each sex—and here we need to remember that Worsley wrote his words well before the second wave of feminism arose in England and the United States and resensitized men to women's liberation—he reveals a rather jaundiced view of the general reading public and disdain for the liberal sentiments of an educated but nonetheless weak-minded (primarily female?) readership. [40]

The reductionism of Worsley's analysis tempts the reader to see his critique of Mead's literary style as a continuation of a lengthy tradition in English letters of criticism of feminine writing. [41] Indeed, Haddon's allusion to Mead as little more than a lady novelist and Evans-Pritchard's characterization of her style as feminine add to this assessment. Lest we think that this line of argument about Mead's writing is a product of the prefeminist past, we need only take a closer look at the rhetoric of Mead's most recent, and most vehement, critic, Derek Freeman, which again attempts to discredit Mead's work by associating it with fiction rather than with science. [42]

The books to which Worsley refers actually dealt more with issues of childhood, adolescence, parent-child relations, the family, the generation gap, marriage, and male-female relations than with sex and sexuality per se. Although Mead considered the latter subjects as well, they were handled within the context of the broader range of issues regarding male-female relations, children, and the family. These topics have been of quintessential concern to both academic and activist feminists, but until recently they were denigrated by male anthropologists as less worthy of scientific study than topics such as political and economic organization.[43]

Mead came to these issues through her sense of herself as a gendered person, as a woman. Her form of "experiential authority" is not simply a matter of the distanced, authorial "I was there"—that has been noted as a fundamental rhetorical strategy in the male modernist ethnography—but a more immediate conveying of the sensual dimensions of the experience that characterizes her work as feminine. Thus, for example, in *Male and Female* she approaches her discussion of gender similarities and differences through a focus on the body: "Living in the modern world, clothed and muffled, forced to convey our sense of our bodies in terms of remote symbols like walking-sticks and umbrellas and hand-bags, it is easy to lose sight of the immediacy of the human body plan."[44]

Mead then goes on to describe aspects of pregnancy, childbirth, and infancy among various societies, concluding her chapter on "First Learnings" with the statement: "Through the body, the ways of the body are learned." This is yet another example of Mead's prefiguring a theoretical orientation that was developed by later scholars.[45]

With the passage of time and changes in style of ethnographic writing, some of the very "excesses" in Mead's writing that Worsley pointed out have come to be seen not only as fundamental ploys in the establishment of ethnographic authority but also as fundamental to the role of anthropology as engaged cultural critique. It was Mead's early books—the canonical works *Coming of Age in Samoa, Sex and Temperament in Three Primitive Societies,* and *Male and Female* that contributed to the establishment of her reputation as a public figure and a popularizer of anthropology—that exemplify these characteristics. But lesser-known examples of Mead's writing, such as correspondence composed while doing fieldwork, reveal the breadth of her experimentation in writing culture.

Letters from the Field

For Mead, writing letters from the field to friends and family back home about a typical epistolary topic such as the weather provided her with the opportunity to launch into a detailed description of local beliefs and to end with a minianalysis of indigenous symbolism and supernaturalism. (Mead was perhaps the original practitioner of what Geertz later labeled "thick description.") Writing from the village of Alitoa, a mountain Arapesh settlement in New Guinea, Mead noted that

> *The weather has continued glorious, although now that the northwest monsoon is dying there are bad storms which make the thatch stand up like fur on the back of an angry cat and knock down the more superannuated houses of the village. All wind and rain come from supernatural creatures called* walin *who inflict storms on the entire community whenever unwanted people from another clan invade their domain, or when members of the proper clan come and do not*

speak politely, reminding them of the relationship. . . . These people have made the man-o-bush into the devil, the man who traffics in the temporary angers of his nice neighbors, the professional sorcerer. The ghosts they have localized under the care of the walin *of each clan and you do not have to encounter them if you go hunting elsewhere and are careful where you get your firewood.*[46]

Her words are not the language of scientific reportage but the demonstration of her pleasure in writing and in conveying her experience to others. She conceived of her letters as being circulated among a network of friends and colleagues. The letters were more than a venue for her preliminary analysis of ethnographic data; they provided her with the opportunity to reflect "publicly" on the very methodology of anthropology. In her introduction to the collection of letters from the field, Mead wrote that when she first went to Samoa and New Guinea in the 1920s

We did not yet recognize that every detail of reaching the field and of interchange with those who tried to bar or facilitated our way to our field site were also part of our total field experience and so of our field work. . . . We have learned that every part of the field experience becomes part of our evolving consciousness — the impressions gained on the journey, our interchanges with government personnel at many levels, with missionaries and teachers and businessmen . . . the books we read, the chills and fevers that accompany work in hot jungles or high, cold mountains.

As she notes about the practice of fieldwork: "Only in this century have we attempted systematically to explore and comprehend the nature of the relationship between the observer and that which is observed."[47]

When Mead began to send letters from the field, she had no sense, she later wrote, that "I was discussing the making of a method, that in making what I was doing intelligible to myself and to my family and friends I was recording steps in the development of a new kind of holistic approach."[48] And yet, just as Mead developed her particular style of writing and her view of ethnography as a tool of cultural critique in part through her experience of writing public lectures, her understanding of anthropological method also developed organically and experientially out of her practice of writing. Moreover, her letters remain a rich source of reflexivity on the practice of fieldwork. Given the contemporary critique of earlier anthropologists' attempts at objectivity, Mead's letters stand as testimony to her prescience in understanding the subjective role of the observer. As such they are not only of interest because they reveal valuable insights into the epistemological bases of the data Mead and her fellow researchers gathered, they are also important as historical documents that record the development of anthropology as an empirical science.

Aspects of the Present / Visions of the Future: *Redbook* Magazine

As the anthropologist Marshall Sahlins sardonically notes, Mead "made parenthood, menopause, and other experiences of her adult life into *Redbook* magazine articles that taught middle-class white American women how to live theirs."[49] Inspired by the model of Eleanor Roosevelt's newspaper column, for seventeen years Mead, in collaboration with her colleague Dr. Rhoda Metraux, wrote a monthly column for *Redbook*, a popular women's magazine. According to Metraux the essays represented "a continuing dialogue about American culture and the concerns of anthropology in the contemporary world that had its origins long ago in the exigencies of World War II," the period when Mead worked in Washington, D.C., on the application of anthropological insights to various aspects of the American war effort.[50]

Mead's major source of inspiration for these articles was her extensive schedule of public lectures and participation in scholarly seminars, conferences, and symposia. Crisscrossing the United States, Mead would gather questions, absorb impressions, and record the pulse of various sectors of American society on a wide variety of topics that she and Metraux then fashioned into pithy essays that addressed contemporary concerns. Subjects such as "American Families Today—and Tomorrow," "Children—Our Future," "Women in Today's World," and "New Directions" included essays on abortion, adoption, bisexuality, and divorce. For example, in a 1974 article about divorce Mead suggested that "marriage insurance" should be created to protect children and ex-spouses from the exigencies of broken marriages. Insurance, Mead said, is a peculiarly American institution. "It fits both our ideas of responsibility and our basic optimism":

> *Similarly, marriage insurance could remove some of the anxiety, the fear, that haunts every mother of young children, and increasingly, every responsible father, that a break down of the family will prevent parents from doing what they have every good intention of doing: caring for each other and for their children. . . .*
>
> *Marriage insurance is not the only possibility, but it indicates the direction in which we should be moving in our search for ways to give marriage greater stability and make divorce, which we accept, a responsible relationship that we can honor—not simply the severance of a relationship.*[51]

It is easy to see articles such as this as an example of the tradition of "experts' advice to women," in which doctors, social workers, psychologists, and psychiatrists offered advice on "the woman question"—what women wanted, how women could deal with their changing roles in a changing world.[52] They were unique, however, in that the expert was also a woman, and therefore they were more widely appealing to women. Mead wrote from her own experiences as a woman. Thus she could write insightfully "On Being a Grandmother": "Curious! Through no immediate act of my own, my status was altered irreversibly and for all time. It is always so, of course. The birth of a child, an extraordinarily small and fragile creature, changes one's own place in the world and that of every member of a family in ways that cannot be completely foreseen."[53] Mead's words not only reflect her training as an anthropologist—in which the researcher learns to think about kinship relationships from varying perspectives—but also express the experience of a particular kinship role in an immediately accessible, because personal, prose.

Despite, or perhaps because of, their grounding in her personal experiences, Mead's *Redbook* articles may be likened to forms of "mass-produced fantasy" for women such as romance novels and soap operas. More pragmatic, of course, than these genres, yet like them, Mead's essays presented alternative visions of what women's lives could be like in the future.[54] Thus they are more than simply expert advice or self-help manuals. There is also a utopian dimension to them, for they conveyed novel suggestions for imagining ways the present could be transformed into a better future.

The "Dialogical" Mode: Benedict's Biography and Baldwin's "Rap on Race"

One of the signposts of postmodernist anthropology has been the notion of dialogism—the incorporation of multiple voices into the anthropological text. The virtue of dialogism, according to critics of traditional modernist texts, is its ability to convey conflicting or diverging points of view and thus to present a more accurate representation of the heterogeneous nature of social life than does the artfully constructed, seamless text of the omnipotent voice of authorial authority.

Not surprisingly, Mead had experimented with forms of dialogism before other anthropologists championed it as a textual strategy. Having agreed to write a biography of her mentor and longtime friend at Columbia, the anthropologist Ruth Fulton Benedict, Mead said that she conceived of the work as a four-way conversation among Benedict, Mead, the linguist Sapir, and Boas at Columbia, individuals who had been of great importance to Benedict's intellectual development.[55] Different sections of the book incorporated historical and biographical material from these other individuals as well, providing information about the social and intellectual context in which Benedict produced her own work. Rather than following the normal practice of using bits and pieces of quotations, Mead said that "[w]hile working on the book I became interested in an anthropological style of biography which would present materials in large, cohesive chunks. Ruth Benedict's diaries from 1923 to 1926, her unpublished poems, letters from Sapir to Benedict were all presented as material whose internal integrity was not violated by the usual biographical style."[56] This format also reflects an anthropological concern with the presentation of an informant's complete texts as well as the desire to situate them within their cultural and historical context.[57]

The notion of dialogue was carried to its logical extreme in *A Rap on Race*. In the summer of 1970, when much of America's attention was focused on the war in Vietnam, Mead and James Baldwin met on several consecutive evenings in a New York City apartment to conduct an informal conversation—to rap, as they chose to call it, reflecting then-current black slang—about race. The resulting dialogue was edited and published in conversational format.

The book received highly mixed reviews. These varied not only according to the reviewers' race but also according to their evaluation of the book's format. One cynical reviewer (a writer himself, of course) decried the use of a tape-recorded conversation, calling it a degradation of the art of writing.[58] Another reviewer, Anatole Broyard, saw the format as part of its inherent value. It not only allowed for the presentation of "the black man's rhetoric," it also gave "one white a chance to speak for all those who may be baffled, a chance to get inside black rhetoric with James Baldwin, the most publicized black writer of our time."[59] But Mead, of course, was no ordinary "white." Broyard praised her for her insightful "interrogation." He saw Baldwin as a "native informant" whom Mead the anthropologist, trained in the translation of cultural differences, attempted to understand in order to communicate her findings to the rest of (white) America. It would perhaps be more apt to characterize the discussion as an attempt by a black poet and a white social scientist to find some common ground on which to understand Baldwin's experience of racial prejudice in America. For example:

BALDWIN: What I am trying to say—and I know we don't really disagree on this—is that now in the 20th century we are going to find only two terrible facts: the fact of prose, on every single level from television to the White House, and the fact of the hope of poetry, without which nobody can live. I use poetry now in its most serious sense. . . .[60]

MEAD: I acknowledge the commitment and I think also we have mainly communicated in poetry. You see, all the conversation that we've been having is primarily this poetic communication. It's not prose, it's poetry.

BALDWIN: But that's very important, isn't it?

MEAD: Sure, it's poetry and not prose. But I'm not a good poet.

BALDWIN: Neither am I, but I am a poet. . . . I don't mean anything about my talent, whatever it may be. That has nothing to do with it. . . . I'm talking about a certain kind of responsibility . . . and that is really toward the future, however mystical that may sound.

MEAD: No, I agree.

BALDWIN: One is a commitment to generations unborn. That is what it is all about. And I don't care what word one uses, poetry or prose. But I'm a poet.

MEAD: Yes, but I'm not.

BALDWIN: Oh, I don't agree with you. I don't think that's true. I think that you and I, for example have met and understand each other and are committed to each other because we really, no matter what the terms might be, have the same commitment. And that commitment is to the human race.

MEAD: But I don't think that makes one a poet.

BALDWIN: That is what makes you a poet.[61]

In this conversation race, not gender, is the salient dimension of identity. The misperceptions and failed communication the dialogue records are emblematic both of the gaps in experience between blacks and whites in America and of the different mentalities of poet and anthropologist. As Deborah Gordon has pointed out in her comparison of Mead's ethnography with that of African American writer/ethnographer Zora Neale Hurston, race as well as gender was inscribed in the professionalization of anthropology and the writing of ethnography.[62] Although Mead may have once written poetry, when she spoke with Baldwin she spoke as a social scientist.

While Broyard saw the virtue of the dialogue as lying in Mead's ability to pull apart a fine metaphor "to see what it's made of" and then to return Baldwin's rhetoric to him, "translated into plain English," Mead, more perceptively, defended the format as an accurate record: "The tape recorder makes possible the kind of interchange which is rarely possible in discussion of race, and when the discussion is printed, the reader cannot help but read both sides of the issues involved."[63] Mead was right. With the passage of time *A Rap on Race* can now profitably be analyzed as an historical document, valuable for the insights it reveals about the two speakers' "subject positions" on race precisely because we have Mead's questions and interactions along with those of Baldwin.

The Impact of Gender on Mead's Work

After surveying the variety of genres of the written and spoken word which Margaret Mead utilized and with which she experimented, one is hard put to find another anthropologist who has demonstrated such breadth and versatility, or one who had such public acclaim as a scientist. Why is it, then, that from the publication of *Coming of Age in Samoa* to the present, some anthropologists have either dismissed her work as that of a lady novelist or completely ignored it when reviewing the history of experimentation in the writing of culture?

The very fact of Mead's experimentation—and the public success she enjoyed as a result of it—undermined her standing within male-dominated academia and damaged her reputation as a serious scholar. Thus, paradoxically, as Mead's popularity grew, her academic reputation suffered. There have always been individuals who were jealous of Mead's success. However, it is too easy to conclude, as some academics do nowadays, that most negative responses to Mead were simply due to jealousy. It is more likely—and more discomforting to some—that they were based on far more complex and far-reaching prejudices and concerns. The two that were most strongly, but unconsciously, felt were academic biases against popular culture and "female" topics.

On the one hand, anthropologists have not been immune from the intellectual tradition of a scholarly antipathy to the popular ("low" versus "high") culture, of which the popularization of anthropology seems to have been considered by some to be a glaring example—hence the fact that individuals like Malinowski were also sometimes looked down on by fellow scholars[64]—as has Mead's association with

NANCY C. LUTKEHAUS

television.[65] On the other hand, we have seen how the criticisms of Mead's writing by male anthropologists such as Worsley contain a latent denigration of, if not an outright aversion to, the female topics Mead chose to focus on—subjects such as childhood, adolescence, marriage, and the family. These topics traditionally have not been held in high repute by the male-dominated field of social anthropology and thus were devalued as unworthy of serious scientific and anthropological concern.[66]

However, both Mead's gender and the gendered topics she chose to focus on undoubtedly contributed to her popular success. For many of her female contemporaries, Margaret Mead was an exemplar of the New Woman of the 1920s and 1930s, the "ultimate liberated woman," a model for young women who were eager to live full lives as mothers and were also committed social, political, or intellectual actors.[67] The advice she prescribed in her *Redbook* articles carried the imprimatur not only of an expert but, and more significantly, of an expert who was also a woman.

In conclusion, I suggest that Mead's success was based largely on two things: her ability to write lucid and compelling prose, and the timeliness and broad appeal of the topics she chose to write about. Mead cultivated the capacity to conduct research and to write on topics she considered relevant to her own life and experience and, by extension, to other women—and men.[68] There is additional salience to Sahlin's comment that Mead took the experiences of her adult life and translated them into magazine articles that taught middle-class white American women how to live theirs. More than merely a passing observation, his statement, perhaps unintentionally, is also a comment on her method. A common theme runs through the corpus of Mead's work, whether written for the anthropologist, the educated layman, or the general public: her authorial subjectivity. Male authors like Geertz have criticized Mead's style as undisciplined, loose-limbed, and improvisational, "saying seventeen things at once and marvelously adaptable to the passing thought, white-line curlicuing if ever there was such."[69] It is just this improvisational, diffuse style of writing that, according to French feminist critics, characterizes *l'écriture féminine,* in contrast to the "phallic single-mindedness" of male writing.[70]

In contrast to most male writers, Mead grounded her writing in the immediacy of her own sensate experience. This is more than merely a form of autobiography or egocentrism. It is the result of a phenomenological approach to ethnographic research. However, Mead's ultimate appeal was not simply that it was feminine but, paradoxically, that she combined masculine and feminine capacities.[71] For Mead also addressed a range of issues that were not commonly gendered as feminine, such as nuclear disarmament, the environment, American democracy, and the state of the world.[72] Thus, as Sahlins reminds us, the reasons for Mead's success "seem to lie in deeper contradictions of the American consciousness, which she as a woman was uniquely able to express, and as a manly woman was uniquely able to synthesize. . . . Synthesizing the masculine and the feminine, she acquired a sort of mythic perfection."[73] As anthropologists have told us, anomalous beings, mythological or human, are often either venerated or abused, or both. They are venerated as powerful because of their extraordinary features—and abused for their difference.

Although I have emphasized the feminine quality of Mead's writing, which is undoubtedly one of its most salient characteristics, she in fact combined her form of "writing through the body" with a strong masculine pragmatism. This element of her style comes through most strongly in her conversations with James Baldwin, in which Mead the social scientist, who believes in facts and the ability to discover the truth of an event, confronts Baldwin the poet, who believes in the power of the imagination and the truth of the emotions. Here Mead is the masculine voice; Baldwin, the feminine other. This discussion of Mead's writing is thus not an origin story; it has not simply uncovered the neglected roots of a contemporary feminist ethnography, for Mead is a far more complex exemplar than that story would allow, and perhaps is therefore all the more informative and compelling.

Notes

1. See Betty Friedan's critique of Margaret Mead and her book *Male and Female: A Study of the Sexes in a Changing World* (New York: Morrow, 1949) in *The Feminine Mystique* (New York: Norton, 1974). George E. Marcus and Michael M.J. Fischer (*Anthropology as Cultural Critique* [Chicago: University of Chicago Press, 1986]), Clifford Geertz (*Works and Lives* [Stanford: Stanford University Press, 1988]), Deborah Gordon ("Writing Culture, Writing Feminism: The Poetics and Politics of Experimental Ethnography," *Inscriptions* 3/4 [1988]: 7–24), and Ruth Behar ("Introduction: Women Writing Culture: Another Telling of the Story of American Anthropology," *Critique of Anthropology* 13, no. 4 [1993]: 307–25) are among the contemporary anthropologists discussing the writing of culture who do specifically mention Mead.

2. Mead, *The Complete Bibliography: 1925–1975*, ed. Joan Gordan (The Hague: Mouton Press, 1976).

3. Ibid., 3.

4. See Margaret Mead and Gregory Bateson, *Balinese Character: A Photographic Analysis* (New York: New York Academy of Sciences, 1942); and Margaret Mead and Frances Cooke MacGregor, *Growth and Culture: A Photographic Study of Balinese Childhood* (New York: Putnam, 1951). See also Ira Jacknis, "Margaret Mead and Gregory Bateson in Bali: Their Use of Photography and Film," *Cultural Anthropology* 3, no. 2 (1988): 160–77; and Andrew Lakoff, "Freezing Time: Anthropological Photography and the Development Narrative," *Visual Anthropology Review* (forthcoming).

5. Rhoda Metraux, *Aspects of the Present* (New York: William Morrow, 1980), 9.

6. A focus on Mead's career and her relationship to the mass media can give us insights into anthropology's historically ambivalent relationship with the popularization of our discipline and its engagement with the public. It also points out the changing nature of anthropology's attitude toward the mass media and its public audience today. See Nancy Lutkehaus, "Margaret Mead as Media Icon" (paper presented at the American Anthropological Association annual meeting, Washington D.C., 1993).

7. A. C. Haddon, quoted in Aliston Hingston-Quiggen, *Haddon, the Head Hunter* (Cambridge, England: Cambridge University Press, 1948); E. E. Evans-Pritchard, *Social Anthropology* (Glencoe, Ill.: Free Press, 1954), 96.

8. These came to the fore most recently with Derek Freeman's critique, *Margaret Mead and Samoa: The Making and Unmaking of an Anthropological Myth* (Cambridge, Mass.: Harvard University Press, 1983). Freeman's book caused a spate of responses pro and con

regarding Mead and her work. See James Clifford and George E. Marcus, eds., *Writing Culture: The Poetics and Politics of Ethnography* (Berkeley: University of California Press, 1986) for one of the first statements defining modernist ethnography. See also Marc Manganaro, ed., *Modernist Anthropology* (Princeton, N.J.: Princeton University Press, 1990).

9. Margaret Mead, *Coming of Age in Samoa* (New York: Morrow, [1928] 1961); Margaret Mead and James Baldwin, *A Rap on Race* (Philadelphia: Lippincott, 1971).

10. Mead, *Complete Bibliography*, 3.

11. Margaret Mead, *Blackberry Winter* (New York: Morrow, 1972), 81.

12. Benedict went so far as to publish her poetry under a pseudonym. See Barbara Babcock's discussion of Benedict in this volume. See also Mead's biography of Benedict, *An Anthropologist at Work* (Boston: Houghton Mifflin, 1959); and Regna Darnell, *Edward Sapir: Linguist, Anthropologist, Humanist* (Berkeley: University of California Press, 1990).

13. Mead, *Complete Bibliography*, 4.

14. Jane Howard, *Margaret Mead: A Life* (New York: Simon and Schuster, 1984), 253.

15. Steven Weiland, *Intellectual Craftsmen: Ways and Works in American Scholarship* (New Brunswick, N.J.: Transaction Press, 1991), 176.

16. Margaret Mead, *Letters from the Field: 1925–1975* (New York: Harper and Row, 1977), 181.

17. The notion of "raw" versus "cooked" field materials come from James Clifford, "Notes on (Field)notes," in *Fieldnotes: The Makings of Anthropology,* ed. Roger Sanjek (Ithaca: Cornell University Press, 1990), 47–70. See also Geertz, *Works and Lives,* and the other authors in Sanjek, *Fieldnotes.*

18. Mead, *Coming of Age in Samoa,* 14.

19. Either implicit or explicit in these critiques is the contrast between Mead's work and the more highly valued scientific or masculine style of ethnographic writing. Derek Freeman is the most recent in a series of male critics who have faulted Mead's work for its feminine or artistic qualities. See Mac Marshall's analysis of Freeman's rhetoric in *Margaret Mead and Samoa,* "The Wizard from Oz Meets the Wicked Witch of the East: Freeman, Mead and Ethnographic Authority," *American Ethnologist* 20 (August 1993): 604–17.

20. Mead, *Coming of Age in Samoa,* 212–13.

21. Mead, *Complete Bibliography,* 2.

22. Ibid.

23. Mead, *Coming of Age in Samoa,* 247.

24. Marcus and Fischer, *Anthropology as Cultural Critique.*

25. Margaret Mead, *Growing Up in New Guinea: A Comparative Study of Primitive Education* (New York: Morrow, 1930) and *Sex and Temperament in Three Primitive Societies* (New York: Morrow, 1935).

26. Mead was to some extent aware of the dangers of essentializing "male" and "female." Unlike contemporary feminists and anthropologists, however, she did not discuss variations of class, race, and sexuality. For example, in speaking of her attempt at generalizations, she wrote, "The problem will be whether as I write from this background those who read can keep such words as 'men,' 'women' and 'children' open-ended words that carry an echo, though not the precise detail, of these varieties of human behavior out of the knowledge of which I am attempting to communicate" (*Male and Female,* 22). Mead was the conveyor of difference, not the various individuals themselves.

27. Ibid., 22.

28. See, for example, Deborah A. Gordon's discussion in "The Politics of Ethnographic Authority: Race and Writing in the Ethnography of Margaret Mead and Zora Neale Hurston," in *Modernist Anthropology,* 146–62. Both Mead and Hurston were female students of Boas, but, as Gordon shows, their different subjectivities as white and black, as well as their different class backgrounds, contributed both to their different styles of writing and to their relationship to the academy.

29. Or fortune. Mead donated her royalties and speaker's fees to a nonprofit organization, the Institute for Intercultural Studies, that she and Bateson founded to support the work of young researchers. This is not to deny that the level of Mead's activities, especially in later life, may have been motivated by a desire, indeed even a need, for public recognition.

30. See George W. Stocking, Jr.'s discussion of Boas's advocacy role for anthropology in "Anthropology as Kulturkampf," in his *The Ethnographer's Magic and Other Essays in the History of Anthropology* (Madison: University of Wisconsin Press, 1992), 92–113.

31. Mead, *Complete Bibliography,* 2.

32. Ibid.

33. Peter M. Worsley, "Margaret Mead: Science or Science Fiction?" *Science and Society* 21 (1957): 122–34.

34. Ibid., 122.

35. Ibid.

36. Ibid., 125.

37. Ibid., 122.

38. Ibid., 123. Margaret Mead, *New Lives for Old: Cultural Transformation, Manus, 1928–1953* (New York: Morrow, 1956).

39. Worsley, "Margaret Mead," 123. See also Marianna Torgovnick's *Gone Primitive: Savage Intellects, Modern Lives* (Chicago: University of Chicago Press, 1990) for an insightful discussion of Mead's use of the primitive and its appeal to Western audiences.

40. This attitude is not surprising given that Worsley, a radical sociologist, published his critique in *Science and Society,* a journal whose articles and readership have a Marxist-socialist theoretical and/or political orientation.

41. See, for example, Sandra Gilbert and Susan M. Gubar, *The Madwoman in the Attic: The Woman Writer and the Nineteenth Century Literary Imagination* (New Haven, Conn.: Yale University Press, 1979); and Tania Modleski, *Loving with a Vengeance: Mass-Produced Fantasies for Women* (New York: Routledge, 1982).

42. Marshall, "Wizard from Oz," 605.

43. See, in particular, the new work by anthropologists and historians on childhood and children, such as Carolyn Steadman, *Landscape for a Good Woman* (New Brunswick, N.J.: Rutgers University Press, 1986); Ann Stoler, "Children on the Colonial Divide" (manuscript, n.d.); and Barrie Thorne, *Gender Play* (New Brunswick, N.J.: Rutgers University Press, 1993).

44. Mead, *Male and Female,* 57.

45. Ibid., 77. Michel Foucault and Pierre Bourdieu, for example, refer to the body as a site for the encoding of culture through the praxis of everyday life. Mead, of course, unlike Bourdieu or Foucault, did not develop her insight about "learning through the body" into more elaborate theories of cultural reproduction or the relationship between the body, power, and knowledge. See Pierre Bourdieu, *Outline of a Theory of Practice* (Cambridge,

England: Cambridge University Press, 1977), and Michel Foucault, *Discipline and Punish: The Birth of the Prison* (New York: Vintage, 1979).

46. Mead, *Letters from the Field,* 117–18.

47. Mead, *Complete Bibliography,* 2.

48. Ibid., 8.

49. Marshall Sahlins, "Views of a Culture Heroine," *New York Times Book Review,* August 26, 1984, 20.

50. See the collection of lectures and essays Mead revised for publication during World War II in the volume *And Keep Your Powder Dry* (New York: Morrow, 1942). Three collections of Mead's articles from *Redbook* magazine have been edited by Rhoda Metraux: *A Way of Seeing* (New York: McCall, 1974); *Aspects of the Present;* and *Margaret Mead: Some Personal Views* (New York: Walker, 1979).

51. Metraux, *Aspects of the Present,* 131–32.

52. Barbara Ehrenreich and Deirdre English, *For Her Own Good: 150 Years of Experts' Advice to Women* (New York: Anchor Books, 1979).

53. Metraux, *Aspects of the Present,* 140.

54. See Modleski's analysis of mass-produced fantasy literature for women and its utopian functions in *Loving with a Vengeance.*

55. Mead, *Blackberry Winter.*

56. Mead, *Complete Bibliography,* 8.

57. Few anthropologists have chosen to write biographies of other anthropologists, and fewer still have attempted to expand the genre of biography itself. As Carolyn Heilbrun notes in *Hamlet's Mother and Other Women* (New York: Ballantine, 1990), a telling exception to this statement is Mary Catherine Bateson's biography of Mead and Bateson, her parents, *With a Daughter's Eye* (New York: Morrow, 1984).

58. Richard Elman, *"A Rap on Race," New York Times Book Review,* June 27, 1971, 5.

59. Anatole Broyard, "Books of the Times," *New York Times,* May 21, 1971.

60. Mead and Baldwin, *Rap on Race,* 187.

61. Ibid., 200.

62. Gordon, "Politics of Ethnographic Authority."

63. Mead, *Complete Bibliography,* 16.

64. However, as Henricka Kucklick points out in *The Savage Within: The Social History of British Anthropology, 1885–1945* (Cambridge, England: Cambridge University Press, 1991), this was not always so. In the nineteenth century British anthropology was to a great extent oriented toward presenting its findings to a popular audience of interested laymen and amateur anthropologists. But as it developed into a full-fledged discipline in such institutions of higher education as Cambridge and Oxford universities and the London School of Economics, academic anthropologists began to retreat from these public gatherings, gradually preferring to establish their own professional associations for the exchange of ideas among peers.

65. As Andrew Ross points out in *No Respect: Intellectuals and Popular Culture* (London: Routledge, 1989), the quiz-show scandals of the late 1950s did much to discredit television in the eyes of intellectuals, who were already predisposed on class terms to distrust a medium that was so blatantly dedicated to entertainment.

66. See Nancy Lutkehaus, "'She Was *Very* Cambridge': Camilla Wedgwood and British Women Anthropologists" (*American Ethnologist* 13, no. 4 [1986]: 776–98), for a discussion of this issue with regard to British women anthropologists.

67. See Elaine Showalter, *These Modern Women* (New York: Feminist Press, 1978), on the early twentieth century and the notion of the New Woman.

68. Boas may have inadvertently helped launch Mead's popular career in ways neither of them could have anticipated at the time. Mead claims she had originally wanted to study culture contact and culture change in Samoa but had agreed to change the focus of her research to adolescent girls at Boas's request. See Mead, *Blackberry Winter.*

69. Geertz, *Works and Lives,* 111.

70. Hélène Cixous, "The Laugh of the Medusa," *Signs* 1 (Summer 1976): 875–93. Not surprisingly, the terms Cixous uses to describe *l'écriture féminine* sound similar to, albeit more celebratory than, those Geertz uses to describe Mead's writing: "Her [feminine] writing can only keep going, without ever inscribing or discerning contours. . . . Her language does not contain, it carries; it does not hold back, it makes possible . . . oral drive, anal drive, vocal drive—all these drives are our strengths and among them is the gestation drive—just like the desire to write: a desire to live self from within, a desire for the swollen belly, for language, for blood."

71. Mead's bisexuality, only revealed publicly after her death, was but one manifestation of this synthesis of masculine and feminine qualities.

72. When she talked about class and race, as in *A Rap on Race,* she did so in non-gender-specific terms, hence from a more disengaged, sociological or masculine perspective.

73. "Views of a Culture Heroine," 1. Jane Howard quotes Betty Friedan's recollection that students jokingly referred to Mead behind her back as "God the Mother," in *Margaret Mead: A Life,* 226.

10

The Ethno-
graphic Films
of Barbara G.
Myerhoff:
Anthropology,
Feminism,
and the
Politics
of Jewish
Identity

Gelya Frank

*Every tradition has some gems, the fruits of
thousands of years of practice. Now they
have come down to us, and we cannot ignore
or deny them. Even the food we eat has our
ancestors and our cultural values in it. How
can we say that we have nothing to do with
our culture? We can find ways to honor our
own tradition, and other traditions as well.*

— THICH NHAT THAN,
Touching Peace, 1992

Write for your dead. They are listening.

— ALICE WALKER

ANTHROPOLOGIST Barbara Myerhoff was a
mentor to me, I considered her my friend, and
I loved her. We met in 1979, the year after the
publication of *Number Our Days,* Myerhoff's
ethnography about aging among the very old
Yiddish-speaking Jews who were members of the
Israel Levin Senior Citizen Center in Venice, California.[1] Based on fieldwork Myerhoff began in
1972, *Number Our Days* was a gem of humanistic writing—social science for the masses,
reportage filled with subtle emotional turns and
rich intellectual play. Myerhoff's book was one
of the first full-length ethnographies to integrate
the reflexive, narrative, dialogic, processual, and
interpretative approaches that have now moved
to the center of anthropological discourse. It is

ironic—and from a feminist standpoint disheartening—that no reference to Myerhoff appears in *Writing Culture* or in *Anthropology as Cultural Critique*, the works
most cited by anthropologists and other scholars when they discuss interpretative
ethnography and experimental genres.[2] Because of that omission, Myerhoff's work
risks exclusion from the countercanon she helped invent.

In 1976 a film called *Number Our Days* was made about Myerhoff's fieldwork-
in-progress for the KCET public television network. It won an Academy Award
for Best Short Subject Documentary in 1977 and brought Barbara Myerhoff's work
further into the public eye with a story in *People* magazine.[3] The book *Number
Our Days,* published in 1978, was selected as one of the ten best social science
books for that year by the *New York Times Book Review.* Myerhoff had already
gained national attention in academic circles with her first book, *Peyote Hunt: The
Sacred Journey of the Huichol Indians,* based on her doctoral fieldwork in Mexico,
published in 1974, and nominated for a National Book Award in 1975.[4] But the
Academy Award for the film *Number Our Days* bumped Myerhoff into the category
of being a celebrity and brought her a new measure of fame that she appeared to
immensely enjoy.

The book *Number Our Days* was most likely the first full-length ethnographic
study of a Jewish community in the United States.[5] Certainly it was the best known
and most accessible to a general audience. Myerhoff began to fill a particular niche
in a growing movement among Jews in this country toward cultural and spiritual
renewal. With support from her colleague, folklorist Barbara Kirshenblatt-Gimblett,
an expert on Yiddish language and studies of cultural performances, Barbara Myerhoff became a sought-after spokesperson on Jewish topics to Jewish audiences.[6] If
you think about the Margaret Mead who collaborated for seventeen years with
Rhoda Metraux in writing a column on issues in American culture in the women's
magazine *Redbook,* then perhaps Barbara Myerhoff was on her way to becoming
something like the Jewish Margaret Mead.[7]

The central theme of Myerhoff's professional and popular contribution was the
importance of symbols, stories, and rituals in establishing and maintaining Jewish
community—and, specifically, for transforming disorder into coherence or meaning. Getting to know Barbara personally meant being affected by her quest for
meaning, the gauge of which was her ability to make intellectually challenging, emotionally resonant, and usually long-enduring relationships with others. She was enormously charismatic. Anthropologist Paul Bohannan, who became dean of social
sciences and communication at the University of Southern California (USC) during
this period, remarked about his first meeting with Barbara Myerhoff that he was prepared for someone charming but unprepared for "how totally charming" she was.

Reading *Number Our Days,* I had felt Barbara's capacity for making connections powerfully because the people whose accents, whose faces, whose emotions,
and whose history she portrayed were familiar. They were my people. And Barbara's work permitted me to perceive them in a new way, with less anguish about
their self-sacrifice in the land of opportunity. These immigrants from Eastern Europe

produced in one or two generations a professional American Jewish middle class, which Myerhoff and I both represented.[8]

Barbara perceived the lives of the Israel Levin Center members as dignified even in loneliness and poverty and as meaningful despite the many physical and social losses of old age. Her approach was a corrective to an anxious, self-critical mood in American Jewish intellectual life and popular culture. While writing this paper, I showed Myerhoff's films in a graduate course on research methods in USC's Department of Occupational Therapy. One student wrote:

> *Although most of the class seemed to agree that Myerhoff's similarity to her subjects was an asset, I found from my own personal reactions to the film that it could also be a liability. As a Jewish woman, I felt I was bringing a lot of "emotional baggage" into my viewing of the film which interfered with my ability to watch it with the mindset of a researcher. The fact that the subjects were so similar to my grandmother, who is currently dying, brought out feelings of guilt and depression that were often so distracting that I found it difficult to simply jot down notes. Furthermore, the talk about how the religion is dying elicited all of my feelings of confusion and guilt over not having been a practicing Jew and started me thinking about what I will pass on to my children in terms of their religion and heritage. This also took me away from the purpose of watching the film.*

This sort of response is not unusual for Jewish viewers. And Myerhoff would have considered such emotional and personal reflections not extraneous to the purpose of her film but exactly on target. Myerhoff used to tell a story about having shown *Number Our Days* at a conference. When the lights came up after the film, the audience was in tears.

"This is obviously very moving," the moderator announced. "So let's break for ten minutes before the next panel."

Recounting that event, Barbara remarked forcefully, "I promised myself: The next time, I won't let them get away like that. I'll make them stay and talk about it."

Myerhoff's vision of the people at the Israel Levin Center was a form of redemption through historicization. She assumed the role of a granddaughter who took time from her busy and successful life to give her "grandparents" the recognition and respect they deserved. It was one part *nachas fun kinder* (joy from the children) and the rest *dereheritz* (respect). Embedded in this filial act was the irony that as a professional Myerhoff was not exactly sacrificing her time or herself. Living life as an anthropologist in the fullest sense was Myerhoff's fundamental project, which included continuing to construct herself as an enculturated person. The old women at the Israel Levin Center understood this when they persistently inquired, "And who's with your children?"

Barbara discussed the afterlife of *Number Our Days* in two essays, "'Life Not Death in Venice': Its Second Life" and "Surviving Stories: Reflections on *Number Our Days.*"[9] A festival of Yiddish culture emphasizing the Israel Levin Center members' artwork was presented at USC in 1980, and a theatrical adaptation of *Num-*

Barbara Myerhoff with members of the Israel Levin Center, ca. 1976–1978, at a celebration after the publication of Number Our Days. *(Photograph by Bill Aron)*

ber Our Days was developed and performed at the Mark Taper Forum in Los Angeles in 1981. From 1976 to 1980 Myerhoff was full professor and chairperson of the USC Department of Anthropology. With the intellectual sympathy and enthusiastic support of her colleagues, she established the emphasis in the department on visual anthropology.[10] At first the Center for Visual Anthropology that she founded was simply a nominal unit within the department to which *Number Our Days* was credited. But Myerhoff's successes helped gain the support of the university to establish a Master of Arts degree in Visual Anthropology (MAVA), which was also the department's first graduate-level program. Courses in ethnology and anthropological theory were offered, along with ones in film production taught by faculty both in the department and in USC's large, well-equipped, and highly rated film school. MAVA has since become a leading program in visual anthropology: Its students' films have won numerous awards and prizes, including a student Academy Award nomination. The department now also offers a doctoral degree in social anthropology.

There is an old joke about the place of anthropology among the priorities of most universities: "Where is the anthropology department?" "Keep going till you find the oldest building on campus." In Barbara's day the Anthropology Department at USC was housed on the first floor of Bruce Hall, a brick walk-up with a tiny elevator, an apartment house once on the outskirts of campus that had been engulfed by the university. When I visited the main office, a drably painted room which had been someone's front parlor, it was impossible not to be drawn into the aura and excitement of the *Number Our Days* phenomenon. Open packing cases of Barbara's book were always kept near secretary Mae Horie's desk, ready to be shipped in response to the frequent phone requests for copies.

In Barbara's tiny office hung two primitive folk paintings by a member of the Israel Levin Center: one of a man in a *tallis* (prayer shawl) praying, the other of a woman blessing the Sabbath candles. (A Huichol yarn painting remained in the office but had been placed to one side.) On the lower shelf of her bookcase were several volumes of letters from people who had seen or read *Number Our Days*. The many piles of papers sometimes spilled over onto the folding director's chair covered in orange duck that sagged impossibly when, as a part-timer, I sat at Barbara's desk to type.[11]

I had the feeling that Myerhoff could not let go of her enormously successful project, nor would it let go of her. A painful issue seemed to hover in the background: that of abandoning the center's elderly just as their children had. There was a period of transition before Barbara undertook her next major project, which would be her last. Initially attracted by the influx of recent Russian Jewish immigrants to Los Angeles, Barbara began in 1981 to study the Jewish community on and around Fairfax Avenue—a north-south street in the mid-Wilshire district synonymous with the name of Cantor's kosher-style delicatessen and bakery, a Los Angeles landmark.[12] The Center for Visual Anthropology would produce a film based on the Fairfax study. Barbara initially invited Timothy Asch, the renowned ethnographic filmmaker whom she had recruited to teach at USC, to collaborate with her and Vikram Jayanti on the project.

By this point in her career, Barbara had already been influenced by certain British social anthropologists and their emphasis on institutions and social processes. She was perhaps first exposed to this approach as a graduate student in anthropology at the University of California at Los Angeles (UCLA) by her professor Hilda Kuper, who had been a student of Malinowski;[13] Myerhoff and Kuper became warm friends. Later, when she herself was a professor at USC, Myerhoff collaborated with lawyer turned social anthropologist Sally Falk Moore, then on the faculty, who had taken Max Gluckman, head of the Manchester School, as her mentor.[14] Eventually Barbara entered the exhilarating circle around Victor and Edith Turner of scholars interested in ritual and performance. (Victor Turner was editor of the series in symbolic anthropology at Cornell University Press and published Myerhoff's *Peyote Hunt* and a volume she coedited with Moore.)

Thus, for Barbara, British social anthropological influences came not merely intellectually or professionally. They were part of a social world, a network of Africanists trained by Malinowski and his students, of whom some members, like Myerhoff, were descendants of Jewish immigrants who had left Eastern Europe after the pogroms of 1881. Max Gluckman had been a friend of Hilda Kuper since they were both teenagers in southern Africa; the Kupers and the Moores were friends. Vic and Edie Turner were also old and dear friends of Hilda and Leo Kuper.

Number Our Days showed the humanistic and processual influence of Victor Turner. The film focused primarily on the meanings of shared activities and rituals through time of the community that constituted the Israel Levin Senior Citizen Center, although Barbara also relied on life histories and expositions of cultural knowledge in her informants' heads—the latter focus more in the American anthropological tradition. In the Fairfax project Barbara gravitated again to institutional and specifically religious life within the Jewish community and was fascinated by the startling array of diverse congregations located there. Finding herself at a great smorgasbord of Jewish life, Barbara intended to taste it all. But it was at this time that she began to feel tired and short of breath, and in June 1984 she learned she had lung cancer.

It was the summer of the Olympics in Los Angeles. I was visiting my friend anthropologist Rosamund Vanderburgh and her family in Owen Sound, Ontario.[15] Hilda Kuper sent me there a note written in her small, lively, and sometimes indecipherable script. After commenting on the crowds due to the summer games and on family news, Hilda continued, in characteristic measured style:

> *Yesterday Barbara Myerhoff came to see us — I begin with the good news. She drove herself and she looked as she had when I saw her two months ago. The doctors find she has lung cancer. . . . Oh my dear Gelya, it is very frightening & everyone is anguished. Yet she does not want pity; she needs support, recognition of the possibility of miracles. The film of Fairfax Jewry has been given a new focus: she is the centre, & the different groups ranging from Chassidic to Gay are in it providing their own healing powers, in addition to chemotherapy. Her friend Lyn who worked with her on* Number Our Days, *& who directed* Testament, *has taken on the directing of this project, which has received funding from Norman Lear; Barbara is excited by it, her spirit is high. I'm sorry to have had to write & tell you of the illness, but know you will want to know & write.*[16]

As Hilda indicated, the filmic component of the Fairfax project was promptly and dramatically reorganized and focused around Myerhoff herself as "the centre." The result was a film entitled *In Her Own Time*, for which the last on-screen interviews with Myerhoff were completed only two weeks before her death on January 7, 1985.[17] Barbara's initial impulse to document the diversity of Jewish life on Fairfax was checked by circumstances beyond her control.[18] *In Her Own Time* became, among other things, a vehicle for Barbara's reflections on her illness experience while studying an ultra-Orthodox sect, the Lubavitcher Hasidim, and accepting traditional forms of healing that its leaders offered.[19]

To many people, and I am one, Barbara Myerhoff's death was a stunning loss. Her personal example and her support profoundly shaped my thinking and practices as an anthropologist who is a woman and a Jew. The aspect of Barbara's work that has affected me the most is her proud assertion of an interpretative approach.

Within this approach, I have been most impressed by her use of self or "reflexivity," her emphasis on storytelling, her surprisingly fluent insights and emotional depth, and her wide-ranging appropriation of humanistic sources. Superb accounts of her intellectual and professional development and her place within wider scholarly currents have been prepared by a former student, anthropologist Riv-Ellen Prell, and by a colleague, Marc Kaminsky.[20] I hope that Barbara herself would be pleased with my offering here, in which I try to show, focusing on her films, what her ethnographic example has made possible.

Reflexive Methodology in Film: Going Native without Leaving Home

Of all the barometers capable of revealing to the historian the deeper movements of an economy, monetary phenomena are without doubt the most sensitive. But to look upon them as a symptom only is to do them less than justice: they have been, and they are, in their turn, effective causes. One might think of them as a seismograph that not only registers earth tremors, but sometimes brings them about. This amounts to saying that when we really know the history of gold as a medium of exchange — during the Middle Ages, a flood of light will be shed upon many hidden trends and connections which at present elude our understanding.

— MARC BLOCH,
"The Problem of Gold in the Middle Ages," 1969

French medieval historian Marc Bloch's statement of method in an article written in 1933 suggests something of Myerhoff's approach fifty years later in *In Her Own Time*. As Bloch pointed out, certain phenomena not only register but affect change. Tracing monetary phenomena (gold coinage and circulation) from the late Roman Empire through the twelfth century, Bloch was able to portray and explain in relatively few pages the complex changing fortunes of diverse empires, nationalities, governments, religions, and classes. Myerhoff's approach does something similar in a small-scale social context, but the phenomenon is a person, not a thing.

Anthropologists are often said to be the "instrument of research," like a seismograph that registers gross and subtle movement or a glass plate dipped in silver nitrate that records the play of light. That was Myerhoff's view of her own methodological stance in *In Her Own Time* when she commented:

I certainly didn't intend to make a film about the Orthodox per se. But they turned out to be somehow the most compelling and drew my life into theirs so deeply that they became the focus. And in a way that was kind of familiar and satisfying because that is really what anthropologists are taught to do. You study what is happening to others by understanding what is going on in yourself. And you yourself become the data gathering instrument. So that you come from a culture and step into a new one and how you respond to the new one tells you about them and about the one you came from.

This is the conventional professional view; its terminology (the person as "instrument") can be read in almost any book on ethnographic field methods. Myerhoff indeed used that approach in *Number Our Days*. The film shows her attending and documenting congregant meals at the Israel Levin Center, secular New Year's Eve dances, Friday-night Sabbath candle-lighting, and the ceremony of unveiling the monument at the grave of a member who had died the year before. She is shown interviewing the center's members along the ocean front, walking on the boardwalk with them, where they feed pigeons and stop to talk on benches. She interviews them in their homes.

But in the next film, *In Her Own Time*, Myerhoff's own life became a methodological tracer, an isotope that emitted particles of change into the environment and registered the reactions. This was a new and hastily invented method, but one that progressed to the next logical step given Myerhoff's prior work and was on the cutting edge of developments in ethnography elsewhere in the discipline.[21] When diagnosed with cancer, Myerhoff was expected to have no more than six months to live.[22] At that point she and Vikram Jayanti met with Lynne Littman. Littman agreed to take over the direction of the film only if she could move Myerhoff to the center, with her illness as the trope for constructing a coherent piece. Her move to the center allowed Myerhoff to experience and record the Hasidic community more as an insider (albeit a novice or an initiate) than would have been possible otherwise. As in Bloch's essay, a phenomenon of choice afforded a path through a complex world of relations that would otherwise have been unintelligible. This is most evident in scenes throughout the film connected with the efforts of the Lubavitcher to help Barbara recover from lung cancer. Myerhoff's own life-or-death struggle made her like a "seismograph that not only registers earth tremors but sometimes brings them about."

The film opens with Barbara's visit to the office of a physician for a second opinion to diagnose the cancer in her lungs. The physician, who wears a *yarmulke,* the traditional daily head-covering of an Orthodox man, touches his hand to his lips and then touches the *mezuzah* on the doorpost before entering the examining room.[23] My first thought on viewing the scene was of the incongruity of his act—kissing his ungloved fingers—among the antiseptic protocols of medicine. He moved forward to take Myerhoff's medical history and give her a physical examination. It is Myerhoff now who is being interviewed, her life history is being taken. She answers with a patient's requisite candor to the doctor's intimate inquiries: She had smoked, but only for a year, about a pack of cigarettes a week. She had had surgery, a hysterectomy, for a cervical carcinoma. Less anthropologist than anxious patient, Myerhoff questions the doctor in turn. The metaphor of a film within a film, and of going deeper into the self in this film than in the one before, is established with an X-ray image of Myerhoff's lungs while her physician's voice confirms the diagnosis and a *klezmer*-like horn begins softly to wail.[24]

Although Barbara did receive chemotherapy to treat her lung cancer during the filming, *In Her Own Time* focuses on her willing and grateful acceptance of various magical Jewish interventions for her healing. In several scenes connected with healing, Barbara's own life events are the focus that generates her informants' speech and actions and on which she herself offers participant observations. These include Barbara's experience of immersion in a ritual bath (*mikveh*) for purification; her ritual change of name; her receiving an official Jewish writ of divorce (*get*) from a rabbinical court; and her phrasing a letter, with help from Reb Beryl Salzman and his wife, to request a miracle from the spiritual leader of the Lubavitcher Hasidim, Reb Menachem Mendel Schneerson.

Anthropology has always had heretics and apostates, people who were trained in the discipline and then went native. My teacher, L. L. Langness, relished retelling the legend of Frank Hamilton Cushing, who went to New Mexico to study Zuni Pueblo ceremonialism.[25] Once initiated into secrets of the *kiva*, Cushing never came back. He did publish an impressive body of ethnographic material, but without divulging sacred facts. In a real sense, Barbara went native; but, as *Number Our Days* showed, the easy dichotomy between native and nonnative in late modernity was already blurring. By the 1960s international markets and mass media had created what communications guru Marshall McLuhan dubbed "the global village." Anthropologists were forced to notice that the distinction between native and nonnative was already shifting in its utility as a heuristic and becoming more a didactic device. A landmark in this trend was the publication of a collection of essays edited by Messerschmidt on issues of doing anthropology at home and with one's own ethnic group.[26] Despite being a Jew and having great charm, Barbara would probably not have been able to film a *mikveh* or a *get* in the insular world of the ultra-Orthodox had she herself not been a willing subject.

In neither of her films was Myerhoff completely native to the culture. In each there were distinct speech communities (Yiddish, classical Hebrew) to which Myerhoff did not belong. The people she studied were bilingual, or multilingual, but they spoke English to her. Yet Myerhoff did have bona fide credentials as a Jewish woman. She was a lady professor, yes, but with a nice Jewish *punim* (face), as she narrated in *Number Our Days*. Thus her subjects recognized themselves and their children in Barbara, just as she made efforts to see herself in them.[27]

In *Number Our Days*, Barbara was able to join the community by creating a role for herself by following the example of social worker Morrie Rosen, the center's director. As described by Myerhoff in the film, Rosen was sometimes father, sometimes son, always advocate for the old people. But he was not one of them. Barbara did not learn Yiddish. And while it is arguable that to do so would have enriched her study greatly, Myerhoff could never gain direct access to *shtetl* (village) life, the part of these old people's past that she emphasized as their core cultural reality. What Barbara could offer was herself as a surrogate to their assimilated families. It was impossible for her to gain entry as a participant observer into a world in which entire towns, villages, and their inhabitants in Europe had been effectively eradicated, decades after the immigration of Myerhoff's informants to America, by Hitler's genocide of the Jews.

In making her next film, *In Her Own Time,* Barbara was an appropriate and eligible candidate for incorporation into an existing role in the community. People very much like her were becoming *ba'alei teshuvah,* secular Jews who "returned" to Orthodoxy. The Lubavitcher Hasidic movement known as Chabad, an outreach directed toward nonobservant Jews, was a major force in the *ba'al teshuvah* phenomenon.[28] Thus Barbara's encounter in *In Her Own Time* with Sultana/Shoshana, a secular Jew who led her family to adopt an ultra-Orthodox lifestyle, was particularly fascinating and challenging to her. Barbara reflected on this in an on-camera interview conducted by Lynne Littman: "To tell you the truth, I can identify in that I can understand her. And probably more than anyone else I know, I feel envy because I feel that she stepped through that invisible barrier."[29]

Barbara's Romance with Hasidism: A Guide for the Perplexed

Learning that no longer starts from the Torah and leads into life, but the other way round: from life, from a world that . . . pretends to know nothing [of the Law], back to Torah. . . . All of us to whom Judaism, to whom being a Jew, has again become the pivot of our lives. . . . We all know that in being Jews we must not give up anything, not renounce anything, but lead everything back to Judaism. From the periphery back to the center; from the outside, in.

— FRANZ ROSENSWEIG,
"On Jewish Learning," 1972

Barbara Myerhoff's ignorance of the Hebrew prayers in *In Her Own Time* jumps out to me as an emblem of the religious disenfranchisement of certain Jewish women historically in Europe and the United States.[30] Furthermore, it troubles me to see how Barbara, a feminist, places herself over and over again in the position of patient and supplicant, appealing and waiting for healing and redemption to come from above and beyond—from anywhere the learned men are.[31] The scenes in which this temporal and spatial quality comes through are those concerning her own healing that come close to the end of the film and of Barbara's life.

In one scene Barbara receives a *get,* a Jewish ritual divorce. She had only recently been divorced from Lee Myerhoff, her husband of thirty years and the father of her two sons, Nick and Matt. Everyone who knew Barbara could sense that the divorce was devastating to her. Despite my own efforts to avoid thinking it, news of Barbara's divorce and the diagnosis of her cancer were linked in my mind.

Barbara's friends and associates knew that her parents had been divorced and that she had grown up without knowing her father. In an early article on reflexivity, Barbara described hers as an unhappy childhood in which books provided a "great consolation" and an "alternative world."[32] She went on to memorialize her grandmother, Sophie Mann, who taught her to press a warm penny against a frosty window in winter to make a little frame through which life in the street outside became quite fascinating. Later, she dedicated *Number Our Days* to her grandmother.[33]

Barbara Myerhoff with a professional film and sound crew as she conducts an interview at a beauty shop on Fairfax Avenue during production of In Her Own Time, *in 1984. Director Lynne Littman is seated, second from right. (Photograph by Bill Aron)*

In 1985, I attended a memorial gathering at Barbara's house organized by her close friend, writer Deena Metzger, who was appointed executor of Barbara's estate. The following day Barbara's belongings would be dismantled. In a corridor I saw a series of framed pencil sketches of figures of flappers wearing fashions of the 1920s. The drawings were signed by Barbara's mother, Florence. Barbara's friend and colleague Zandy Moore, then department chair, was standing beside me and explained that Barbara's mother had been a performer, before Barbara was born.

"She was something of a flapper herself," Zandy commented. "Played the trombone in an all-girl jazz band."

After Barbara's diagnosis of cancer, the Hasidic rabbis who had become her friends urged her to obtain a *get,* an official Jewish divorce. As Barbara narrated in the film, the purpose of the ritual was to get back her *neshuma,* her soul, from her husband. Getting back her soul was something she felt she had not yet done. Had I been asked, I would have advised Barbara by all means to go ahead with the ritual. But I felt uncomfortable with the actual event as documented in *In Her Own Time.*

As Barbara explicitly stated in her narration, "I put myself in their hands."

In the ritual the role of Barbara's husband was played by an old man, as improbable a "husband" for Barbara as anyone could be. Unlike Barbara, he needed no instructions, having played the surrogate role before. What struck me about Barbara's situation was her complete dependence on these functionaries to whom she had been escorted by her friends, the two Lubavitcher rabbis. She repeated what she was told to say during the divorce proceeding, certainly one of the most archaic enactments of patriarchal authority extant in Jewish practice. After all, it is the husband who must agree to grant a *get* to release his wife; and he may refuse to do so. The stand-in for Barbara's husband delivered the writ from on high to her waiting hands. Exaggerated care was taken so that Barbara and her "husband" did not touch. Barbara obediently followed the directions to catch the folded document, place it under her arm, and walk several paces away and back. The functionary took the document and cut through the corners.

With this act of severing, Barbara was informed that her divorce was accomplished. It was exactly the kind of symbolic enactment noted by van Gennep in his classic book on the rites of passage—the work that so emphatically influenced Victor Turner, Barbara Myerhoff, and many other students of ritual life. The functionary pronounced the formula that made Barbara, a dying woman, after a brief interim "permissible to anyone." Why did Barbara turn to these bureaucratic male guardians of Orthodoxy, who could perhaps only dimly perceive the richly developed person Barbara was, for the authority to regain her soul?[34]

Another scene documented Barbara sitting on one side of a *mechitza,* the partition that separates women from men in an Orthodox synagogue. She could only sit and peer around the *mechitza* while her friend and informant, Reb Naftali Estulin, performed a ritual to change her name and thus confuse the Angel of Death. Barbara did not understand Hebrew and so asked one of the male congregants to let her know when the rabbi reached the portion of the service in which he would pronounce her new name. She asked Reb Naftali to choose the name for her. He gave her the name "Chana Basha bas Feigi."

Barbara explained to the camera that her new name meant "all good things" as she waited for the rabbi to bestow her life-preserving name in a service from which she was physically separated and linguistically excluded. When the ceremony was completed, Barbara smiled with the dizzy happiness of a child who receives a sweet— or perhaps it was the smile of an outpatient giddy on pain-killing medication.

"I expect to feel better this afternoon," Barbara concluded.[35]

It is not difficult to see Barbara's romance with the Hasidim partly in psychoanalytic terms. Her vulnerability to a fatal disease came soon after she was divorced from her husband of thirty years and only a year after her mentor Victor Turner had died. Her desire for contact with her father had been thwarted by her mother who, to protect the child, withheld from her letters that he sent. Barbara did not meet her father until quite late in her life, and found him an ordinary man.[36] Prell writes about Barbara's tendency to value the cultural knowledge invested in women less than that invested in men—in the Huichol shaman, Ramón Silva; in the iconoclast Shmuel

Goldman in *Number Our Days;* and in Victor Turner, a most creative anthropologist gifted with a large and inclusive spirit.[37] But Barbara chose mentors, including Hilda Kuper, who were strongly involved in their marriages. With the wives of her male mentors (Lupe Silva, Rebekkah Goldman, and Edie Turner) Barbara had important, sometimes conflictual, sometimes rewarding relations, if in the shadow of the more important "father." Thus Barbara was involved always in remaking her family, bringing in the missing father and dealing with the ambivalent mother.

The central theme of *Number Our Days* was death, which Myerhoff called in her narration "the invisible protagonist in every little scene." Paradoxically, a central preoccupation of *In Her Own Time* is marriage. Barbara's interview with Nesha, an ultra-Orthodox woman who fits women for wigs, focuses on purity and impurity—and fidelity and infidelity—in marital relations. Reb Beryl Salzman delivers a lecture on the benefits of the family purity laws prohibiting contact between husbands and wives. He validates what Nesha has already confirmed—that sexual prohibitions lasting two weeks out of every month are a way of keeping physical love alive in his marriage. Shoshana/Sultana and her husband, though shown sparring over their account of early struggles about sleeping in separate beds, nevertheless remain bound together. The story of a young Russian couple, former refuseniks, is woven through the film, and their Hasidic wedding ceremony is documented.

By the time Barbara is shown having her first *mikveh* (ritual bath) to purify herself for the ceremony to change her name, it has been well established that *mikveh* is taken by women to mark the end of a menstrual period. In a voice overlay, Barbara remarks that it must be "very arousing" to go to the *mikveh* before making love with one's husband after a two-week separation. Reflections about her impending death (the ostensible theme of *In Her Own Time*) are displaced by an emphasis on love, marriage, family, and the cultural and reproductive survival they imply.

It could be said that Barbara's second film exoticized (and eroticized) the Hasidim. But concerns with survival may help explain the scene of men in shirt-sleeves with beards and *payes* (sidelocks) shoveling ritually prepared Passover *matzos* (unleavened bread) like pizzas in and out of ovens. The scene evokes laughter, partly because of the incongruity of these scholarly types in the kitchen and partly because of the background music, a *klezmer* band playing *freilich* (happy) music at a frantic pace.

In a voice overlay Barbara is heard to comment unself-consciously, "It was as if I walked into a New Guinean village in my own backyard."

What purpose does this exoticization of the Lubavitcher serve? Jews and ovens make a potent conjunction of images from the standpoint of the Holocaust, a collective memory never far from the surface in American Jews of Ashkenazic origin. There is subconscious shock value to seeing people, in a film about Jews, shoveling things into open ovens. The comical music cues instant relief: harmless-looking Jews are in command and innocent matzos (Nazis?) are the only things going in and out of the ovens. Barbara's reference to far-off New Guinea may underscore the psychological distancing required to deal with the Holocaust in this film. Closer to death herself than in *Number Our Days,* Myerhoff appears to have focused this time not on the Holocaust, which indeed brought about the demise of Hasidism in Europe, but on political and religious suppression of Jews in the then Soviet Union.

Had Barbara lived, she—like any informant—might have confirmed or discon-firmed my symbolic analysis of scenes in her film.[38] But she died two weeks after the last interview was recorded for the film. The selection and editing of scenes, music, and voice overlays were the work of director Lynne Littman and coproducer Vikram Jayanti. Thus many difficult issues concerning interpretation of the film remain.

The matzo-baking scene may represent an empathic choice made by Myerhoff's surviving colleagues. But it is also filler material salvaged from the period prior to Myerhoff's diagnosis, when a less focused film crew cruised not only the Luba-vitcher Hasidim but also the Satmar Hasidim, gays, and anonymous men and woman on the street in search of colorful footage.[39]

The preoccupation with marriage in the film could have been as much director Lynne Littman's, then experiencing a divorce, as Myerhoff's. We cannot assume Myerhoff to have been merely introspecting on her experiences or simply providing narration; she was engaged in an intense life-and-death drama with Littman and Jayanti through the filmic veil. Thus Myerhoff cannot be viewed unproblematically as a naive informant on her forays into the world of the ultra-Orthodox. She must been seen also as a visual anthropologist in a trance of deep play, reenacting one last time the role of anthropologist taking part in exotic rituals, an award-winning Ariadne adding precious weeks to her life by spinning one last tale.

Hilda Kuper had it right: Myerhoff had intended to cast the Hasidim and gays in the same film. But that is where the story begins, not ends. The Lubavitcher refused to appear in the film with gays. Just when Myerhoff was considering going head to head over the issue, most of the film shot at Beth Chayim Chadashim, the gay and les-bian synagogue of the Fairfax district, was spoiled in the lab. Was it romance, after all, or *beshert* (fate) that moved the Hasidim along with Barbara to center stage?

Before, Through, and Beyond Her Own Time: Anthropologia Pro Vita Sua

Judaism is a religion of time aiming at the sanctification of time. . . . The Sab-baths are our great cathedrals; and our Holy of Holies is a shrine that neither the Romans nor the Germans were able to burn; a shrine that even apostasy cannot easily obliterate: the Day of Atonement. . . . Jewish ritual may be charac-terized as the art of significant forms in time, as architecture of time. Most of its observances—the Sabbath, the New Moon, the festivals, the Sabbatical and the Jubilee year—depend on a certain hour of the day or season of the year.

— ABRAHAM HESCHEL,
The Sabbath, 1951

In his critique of Barbara Myerhoff's approach to narrative, Marc Kaminsky takes a postmodernist position: Myerhoff's work was limited by her commitment to meaning as "coherence" and her preference for narrative closure.[40] Kaminsky questions whether coherence and closure are possible, or even desirable, when presenting the experiences of individuals and groups. Riv-Ellen Prell suggests that Myerhoff's view of narrative was based in Redfield's dualistic model of the "Great Tradition" (written by priests, scholars, and their elite patrons) and the "Little Tradition" (narrated by the folk).[41] Most anthropologists today view Redfield's approach as glossing too heavily over the polyphony of voices. Kaminsky uses his own life history to point out contrasts of social class, politics, language, and ethnic milieu that would make his account of American Jewish culture different from that which Myerhoff created in *Number Our Days.*

Myerhoff was aware that there is a political dimension to narrative. She taught that "Little Traditions," because they are marginal, are often subversive. Her article with Deena Metzger on women's journals reflects an awareness of the historical marginalization of European women's voices because of restricted literacy and confinement to devalued genres.[42] That there can be no story of the Jewish people, only stories, is a position I associate with Barbara's thought. In a talk on ritual at a conference on "Illuminating the Unwritten Scroll: Women's Spirituality and Jewish Tradition," Myerhoff drew on the example of the Passover seder to emphasize variation and improvisation, the reframings and even the disputes that arise while performing the ritual acts (and retelling "the" story).[43] In *In Her Own Time,* one has only to notice the knowing look of amusement Barbara shares with the camera as Shoshana/Sultana and her husband assert discrepant versions of their family's turn to Orthodoxy and then struggle to smooth them into a coherent account.

Barbara did not pursue the more dialectical theories implied by her interests yet not encompassed by Redfield's "Great Tradition/Little Tradition" approach. We do not find in Myerhoff the ideas and language of Marxism and critical theory: She did not cite Gramsci on hegemonic discourse; Adorno and Benjamin were not invoked to critique the forms and functions of popular media. There was no reference to Raymond Williams or the newer, interdisciplinary iconoclasts of the cultural studies movement dealing with the implications of multiple and diverse cultural identities. She did not apply Bakhtin's concept of "heteroglossia." *Number Our Days* came during the Geertz craze, before the new anthropological fashions were out. Yet Barbara did in her ethnographies many of the things those writers only theorized about.

I find Barbara Myerhoff's work useful and relevant to the postmodern discourse on gender and ethnicity. *Number Our Days* deals with the construction and deconstruction of traditional identities. *In Her Own Time* takes the next step of showing Myerhoff's distress at her own limitations in achieving a coherent Jewish identity. She was tantalized by what appeared to her a rather strict dichotomy between secular rationalism and spiritual belief. In the film, Myerhoff states clearly the conflict between her desire for order, meaning, and coherence (that she perceived in the lifestyles of the Hasidim) and her intolerance of imposed restrictions. She also displays her desire to enjoy valued prerogatives of the Orthodox Jewish male while

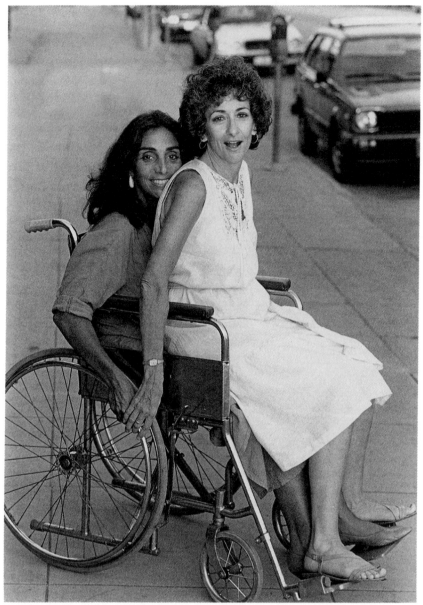

Anthropologist Barbara Myerhoff and director Lynne Littman collaborated in 1976 to make the Academy Award–winning documentary Number Our Days. *In 1984 Littman agreed to help Myerhoff complete a second ethnographic film about a Los Angeles Jewish community. The film,* In Her Own Time, *also dealt with Myerhoff's fatal lung cancer. Although Myerhoff did not require a wheelchair during her illness, Littman suggested she use one to conserve her energy during a long hot summer day of filming along Fairfax Avenue. (Photograph by Bill Aron)*

retaining her identity as a modern woman. And the film reveals Myerhoff's near failure to meet the daunting challenge set by her earlier work on aging—that of making a coherent story about herself to meet impending death.

Myerhoff's approach to these dilemmas was encapsulated in a scene at the home of Shoshana/Sultana which, incidentally, shows off her skill as a field interviewer.

Indicating a bookcase on her left, Barbara remarked, "This is the library of a profoundly questioning mind: Dostoevsky, Flaubert, Cervantes.

"And this," she continued, pointing to the bookcase on her right, "is the library of a profoundly believing mind. How do you reconcile them?"

Shoshana said there was no contradiction for her between the two kinds of knowledge.

Barbara shook her head and responded gracefully with a quote from somewhere: "When the heart is truly open there is room for No and Yes."

If Jews had saints (and some Jewish traditions have them), Barbara Myerhoff was not one. She seemed less concerned with the political implications of her work than I would have liked. I don't know that Myerhoff ever questioned the limited view of the Lubavitcher Hasidim that her film presented. It may not have concerned her that her film was great publicity for Chabad. With nearly two hundred thousand followers, Chabad, alone among the Orthodox, has launched an audacious Jewish proselytizing movement with "*mitzvah* (good deed) tanks" patrolling the Lower East Side and the Golan Heights.[44] Some Lubavitcher regarded their leader, Reb Menachem Mendel Schneerson, as the Messiah. It is reported that nearly every word of the sect's leader was taped and broadcast worldwide on the Lubavitcher satellite television network.[45] His talks on the Sabbath (when recording is forbidden) were reconstructed by scribes and faxed "to disciples at the outposts of empire the minute the sun sets."[46] This is the man to whom Barbara was filmed writing a letter to request a personal miracle.

Respectable critics of the late Rebbe called his authoritarianism cultlike, a dangerous quality in the world of Middle Eastern politics in which he more than dabbled. Although he never visited Israel, many of his followers live there, even setting up in Kfar Habad a replica of his three-story brick home in Brooklyn at 770 Eastern Parkway. More than once the Rebbe intervened and disrupted the fragile Middle East peace process. In 1992 his comment to a visiting Israeli cabinet minister on trading land for peace ("It is an abomination even to think about discussing autonomy for the Palestinians")[47] was widely reported by the Israeli press and had its intended cooling-off effect on Prime Minister Yitzhak Shamir. With friends like these, do we need enemies?

I recall a story told by Deena Metzger at the gathering of friends in 1985. The mythologist Joseph Campbell was reported to have made some anti-Semitic remarks. Barbara was said to have dismissed them. More important to her was Campbell's scholarship, which she had found inspiring not only in her youth but throughout her career. In her last, posthumously published piece, Myerhoff used Campbell's analysis of the hero's journey as the backbone of her account of her participant observations of a pilgrimage to Meron.[48]

Barbara also believed that brilliant people could be excused for arrogance. To her it was a character blemish rather than deadly sin.

Was Barbara arrogant? I don't think so. Probably her worst sin was *chutzpah* (nerve). Witness the scene in *In Her Own Time* in which she interviews Nesha the hairdresser. She plays Nesha like a fiddle—skillfully, daringly—without Nesha even knowing.

As a mentor Barbara was generous and caring. She did what mentors do: she listened to me and made me feel that my ideas were important. She invited me to present papers at conferences, introduced me to friends and colleagues, mentioned my work, wrote letters of recommendation, advised me in job interviews, and proposed my name instead of hers when she declined professional invitations. When I was disappointed not to receive a full-time position in the Department of Anthropology at USC in 1980, she took me aside to read from a confidential letter. She bolstered my self-confidence by informing me, whether it was the case or not, that people don't usually say the kinds of things my referee wrote. That talk meant a great deal to me. When subsequently I applied for an advertised position for an anthropologist in the Department of Occupational Therapy at USC, Barbara prepped me for the interview and encouraged me to mention my strong relationship with the Anthropology Department, which would offer a joint appointment, and the expectation of future collaboration.

"And don't forget to smile," Barbara prompted. "You have a beautiful smile."

No matter how fragmented and incoherent the "self" is alleged to have become in late modernity, I hope we will never outgrow our need for heroes (plural and with a small "h"), inspiring teachers, and role models. Myerhoff was one of these, not just to me but to many others.[49] She helped open a door in contemporary anthropology for things to come that we cannot yet assess. As a middle-class professional living out the liberal feminism of her time, Myerhoff positioned herself and her ideas revealingly and allowed us the privilege of accessing them. One thing is certain: the reflexive methods Myerhoff espoused and pioneered finally extended to Jewish ethnicity in the United States the same seriousness and regard that Boasian anthropology has so assiduously accorded the "Other."

According to the Bible, every fiftieth year is to be proclaimed as a Jubilee. All the laws governing the sabbatical year apply to the Jubilee, but with additional provisions. According to Leviticus (25:9–10), the fiftieth year or the Jubilee meant "liberty proclaimed throughout the land unto all its inhabitants."[50] All slaves were released and all land acquired by means other than inheritance was restored to the original owner. The custom was designed to prevent the accumulation of vast wealth in the hands of the few and the pauperization of the many. Barbara Myerhoff died in the seventh month after her illness was diagnosed, in her forty-ninth year. Numerologically I take her death to mark, for anthropology and the politics of Jewish identity in America, a completion and renewal.

Notes

The following colleagues encouraged and helped me greatly with their reminiscences about Barbara Myerhoff, their conversations about her films and work, their generously shared sources, and their detailed comments on my text: Patsy Asch, Haim Dov Beliak, Paul Bohannan, E. M. Broner, Janet Carnay, Eric Eisenberg, Faye Ginsburg, Harvey E. and Judy Goldberg, Janet Hoskins, Amy Halpern, Marc Kaminsky, Sharon Kaufman, Laurie Levin, Jane Litman, Nancy Lutkehaus, G. Alexander Moore, Riv-Ellen Prell, Andrei Simić, Marty Spiegel, Melford E. Spiro, George W. Stocking, Jr., Savina Teubal, and Raḥel Wasserfall. In addition, I am very grateful to Deena Metzger, Vikram Jayanti, and Lynne Littman, who generously took the time to talk with me in depth about Barbara in relation to this essay and whose comments I quote frequently below. Deena, Vikram, and Lynne were the people closest to Barbara and most intimately involved in the events described. As might be expected, each had his or her own interpretations of Barbara and her work, some of which conflicted with mine as well as with one another's. Also, their recollection of events varied. Not all of the conflicting interpretations could be incorporated into the body of the text, which had to go to press, but as many factual errors as possible were corrected and additional footnotes were inserted. Photographer Bill Aron, who taught visual anthropology at the University of Southern California (USC) and collaborated with Barbara, added his perspectives and graciously provided the photographs that accompany the text. Ruth Behar invited me to write this essay and motivated me to go far beyond my initial conception of the piece. I am grateful for her creative and thought-provoking suggestions at every stage of its preparation.

I would like also to acknowledge support for writing this chapter from the American Occupational Therapy Foundation in the form of a three-year grant (1992–1994) to the Department of Occupational Therapy at the University of Southern California to investigate "The Relationship of Occupation to Adaptation and Its Implications for Occupational Therapy." Although Barbara Myerhoff may have had as few as three months to live when diagnosed with lung cancer in 1984, she lived for six months while engaged in the task of completing an ethnographic film focused on her own life. Her final work demonstrates what it can mean to a person who is dying to have something worth living for.

1. Barbara Myerhoff, *Number Our Days* (New York: E. P. Dutton, 1978). Myerhoff's field-work was funded in part by a grant from the National Science Foundation, as part of a multiethnic study of aging conducted with the sponsorship of the Andrus Gerontology Center at the University of Southern California. Although we had corresponded earlier, I met Barbara in June 1979 to discuss her work in relation to my coauthored book, L. L. Langness and Gelya Frank, *Lives: An Anthropological Approach to Biography* (Novato, Calif.: Chandler and Sharp, 1981), 136–39 and 154–55. I described our meeting in "Barbara, May She Rest in Peace, But Her Spirit Be with Us Always" (paper delivered to the invited session, "In Memory of Barbara Myerhoff," at the American Anthropological Association annual meeting, Washington, D.C., December 4–8, 1985).

2. James Clifford and George E. Marcus, eds., *Writing Culture: The Poetics and Politics of Ethnography* (Berkeley: University of California Press, 1986); George E. Marcus and Michael M. J. Fischer, *Anthropology as Cultural Critique: An Experimental Moment in the Human Sciences* (Chicago: University of Chicago Press, 1986). For a critique of male bias in the works of these authors, see Frances E. Mascia-Lees, Patricia Sharpe, and Colleen Ballerino Cohen, "The Postmodernist Turn in Anthropology: Cautions from a Feminist Perspective," *Signs* 15, no. 11 (1989): 7–33. See also Catherine Lutz, "The Erasure of Women's Writing in Sociocultural Anthropology," *American Ethnologist* 17 (1990): 611–27.

3. Lynne Littman, producer and director, *Number Our Days*, 16 mm. color-sound film, 30 minutes, produced for the Public Broadcasting Corporation, 1976; Direct Cinema, Santa Monica, California (distributor). In addition to the Academy Award, the film also won the Special Jury Award for Outstanding Achievement, 20th International San Francisco Film Festival, 1976; and the Public Broadcasting Corporation Special Interest Award, 1976.

4. Barbara Myerhoff, *Peyote Hunt: The Sacred Journey of the Huichol Indians* (Ithaca, N.Y.: Cornell University Press, 1974). Myerhoff's fieldwork in the Sierra Madre of Mexico was conducted during 1965 and 1966, partly in collaboration with Peter Furst and partially funded by a Ford International and Comparative Studies Grant administered through Johannes Wilbert, Myerhoff's dissertation chair at UCLA.

5. The first full-length anthropological study of a Jewish community was Mark Zborowski and Elizabeth Herzog, *Life Is With People: The Jewish Little-Town of Eastern Europe* (New York: International Universities Press, 1952). The research was directed by Ruth Benedict at Columbia University under a grant from the U.S. Office of Naval Research; the writing of the book was subsidized by a grant from the American Jewish Committee. *Life Is With People* was a study of "culture at a distance," a composite portrait of *shtetl* life researched solely through interviews conducted in 1949. Probably the first full-length anthropological study of a Jewish community based on participant observation was Melford E. Spiro's report of his research in 1951 in Israel (*Kibbutz: Venture in Utopia* [New York: Schocken Books, 1956]).

6. Much of the foregoing account of Myerhoff's career appears in Barbara Kirshenblatt-Gimblett, "Foreword," in Barbara Myerhoff, *Remembered Lives: The Work of Ritual, Storytelling, and Growing Older,* ed. Marc Kaminsky (Ann Arbor: University of Michigan Press, 1992), xi–xiv. I have also relied on Myerhoff's professional curriculum vita from 1984.

7. Margaret Mead and Rhoda Metraux, *Aspects of the Present* (New York: William Morrow, 1980).

8. American Jews constitute 3 percent of the U.S. population. Forty percent of American Jews belong to the working class.

9. Barbara Myerhoff, "'Life Not Death in Venice': Its Second Life," in *The Anthropology of Experience,* ed. Victor Turner and Edward M. Bruner (Urbana and Chicago: University of Illinois Press, 1986), 261–87, and, with additional footnotes and remarks by the editor, in *Judaism: Viewed from Within and from Without,* ed. Harvey E. Goldberg (Albany: State University of New York Press, 1987), 143–69; reprinted in Myerhoff, *Remembered Lives,* 257–76. See also Barbara Myerhoff, "Surviving Stories: Reflections on *Number Our Days,*" in *Between Two Worlds: Ethnographic Essays on American Jewry,* ed. Jack Kugelmass (Ithaca, N.Y.: Cornell University Press, 1988). Unfinished at the time of Myerhoff's death, "Surviving Stories" was revised and completed by Marc Kaminsky; it is also included in Myerhoff, *Remembered Lives,* 277–304, and a version appeared in *Tikkun* 2, no. 5 (November/December 1987): 19–25.

10. Although neither a faculty member nor student, Vikram Jayanti was Barbara's most constant collaborator. He produced *In Her Own Time* with Lynne Littman and became the entrepreneurial force behind the 1986 Barbara Myerhoff Film Festival, a proposed annual event at USC that was intended to be a West Coast analog to the Margaret Mead Film Festival in New York. Jayanti alone raised $300,000 for the Barbara Myerhoff Film Festival—and then spent it. USC did not contribute any funds to the festival, nor did dean Paul Bohannan curtail Jayanti's expenditures, despite the urging of his boss, Chet Lieb, dean of the College of Letters and Sciences. These circumstances account for the fact that no endowment or enduring memorial to Myerhoff's contribution presently exists at the university.

11. I first taught at USC as a part-timer in the spring of 1980, filling in for Barbara while she was on release time in her course on the Life History. The following spring, I taught her class in Culture and Personality and also a class in Applied Anthropology: Health. There were not enough offices or typewriters in the department, so Barbara let me use hers.

12. In 1982 Myerhoff received a Jewish Community Foundation Grant, with Vikram Jayanti and Ira Handelman, to research "the Los Angeles Community of Fairfax" and a Sydney Stern Memorial Trust Grant, with Jayanti, to prepare a treatment for a related documen-

tary film. The following year she received a National Endowment for the Humanities Grant to research the community of Fairfax. In 1984 she received, with Jayanti, a Jewish Community Foundation Grant to produce a film on the "Culture of Fairfax." Vikram Jayanti's sister, Vimala Jayanti, an anthropologist and an Orthodox woman, participated with Barbara in the field research and writing of *Tales of Fairfax,* the anticipated book from the Fairfax project. Myerhoff also received a National Institute on Aging Grant, with Andrei Simić and Joan Weibel-Orlando, to research ethnicity and aging in the Fairfax area between 1983 and 1986. She also collaborated as second author with Elinor Lenz on the book *The Feminization of America: How Women's Values Are Changing Our Public and Private Lives* (Los Angeles: Jeremy P. Tarcher, 1985).

13. Myerhoff received a B.A. in sociology at UCLA in 1958 and an M.A. in human development from the University of Chicago in 1963, with a thesis on "Father-Daughter Incest among Delinquent Adolescent Girls." Her Ph.D. in anthropology at UCLA was awarded in 1968, with distinction, for "Deer-Maize-Peyote Symbol Complex: The Huichol Indians of Mexico." Hilda Kuper (1911–1992) is known for five decades of ethnographic work in Swaziland. She became for me, as for Barbara Myerhoff and many other students at UCLA, a wonderful mentor and beloved friend. Kuper remarked about a term paper Barbara had written—later published with W. R. Larson as "The Doctor as Culture Hero: The Routinization of Charisma" in *Human Organization* 24 (Fall 1965): 188–91—saying that it was an unmistakable mark of Barbara's talent. Barbara, in turn, found in Hilda Kuper a model for teaching that she tried to emulate:

> *I've had two teachers I completely trust. One is Hilda Kuper, with whom I studied anthropology at UCLA. And one was Shmuel, who appears in* Number Our Days. *It is so clear that teachers like this want your growth and that they are forcing you to question. It's a forcing, a forcing of patience, a reflectiveness, a kind of listening, a continual selection. It forces such a complex relationship to them and what they are saying that it goes far beyond the usual kind of teaching, the teaching that merely asserts how things are. You can never be the same after that, because it forces you to pay attention to people in a different way. That's the humanization: You can never dismiss people again, and although you may not have the time to live that way, or the energy, or the spirit, or the appetite for it, once you do it, even if once, it is a transformative experience. (quoted in Langness and Frank,* Lives, *155)*

14. Sally Falk Moore and Barbara G. Myerhoff, eds., *Symbol and Politics in Communal Ideology: Cases and Questions* (Ithaca, N.Y.: Cornell University Press, 1975), and *Secular Ritual: Forms and Meanings* (Assen, Holland: Royal Van Gorcum Press, 1977).

15. R. M. Vanderburgh, professor emeritus, University of Toronto, Mississauga, deserves mention in this volume. A student of A. I. Hallowell, Vanderburgh has been ethnographer and life historian of the Anishnabe (Ojibwe) people, focusing particularly on women at Manitoulin Island and the Cape Croker Reserve in Ontario, Canada. Vanderburgh pioneered a yet unexploited ethnographic genre by collaborating with a novelist to produce a full-length piece of ethnographic fiction based on her understanding of Nishnabe cultural history and religion, ca. 1897–1967. See Nan F. Salerno and Rosamund M. Vanderburgh, *Shaman's Daughter* (New York: Dell, 1980).

16. Hilda Kuper to Gelya Frank, letter July 26, 1984.

17. Lynne Littman, director, Vikram Jayanti and Lynne Littman, producers, *In Her Own Time,* 16 mm. color-sound film, 60 minutes; Direct Cinema, Santa Monica, California (distributor).

18. As Barbara narrated in *In Our Own Time:* "This was not the film that I started out to make. Originally, I intended to do a broad-based depiction of Jewish life in Fairfax, in L.A. I hoped for the kind of professional distance that every social scientist wants to bring to the subject. But to do anything except something that touched my own life was time I didn't have." I find Barbara's statement disingenuous. She had already made the turn to

reflexive ethnography in *Number Our Days*. This move was ratified and intensified by the Fairfax project. It is not that Barbara had lost "the kind of professional distance that every social scientist wants to bring to the subject" but that, in my opinion, she had already traveled far beyond the paradigm from which the language of "professional distance" comes. In that context, her commentary makes little sense except as a narrative device used to create an engaging story line.

19. Arthur Kleinman, *The Illness Narratives: Suffering, Healing, and the Human Condition* (New York: Basic Books, 1988).

20. Riv-Ellen Prell, "The Double Frame of Life History in the Work of Barbara Myerhoff," in her *Interpreting Women's Lives: Feminist Theory and Personal Narratives* (Bloomington: Indiana University Press, 1989), 241–58; Marc Kaminsky, "Introduction," in *Remembered Lives*, 1–97. Kaminsky is co-director, with Deena Metzger, of the Myerhoff Center at the YIVO Institute for Jewish Research in New York. Barbara's friends, performer Naomi Newman and husband Micah Taubman, initiated the formation of the Myerhoff Center soon after Barbara's death. Thus, it has been the Jewish community, rather than her university or her profession, that has coalesced to honor Myerhoff's scholarly contributions and proclaim her cultural legacy.

21. As much as a decade earlier, David MacDougall ("Beyond Observational Cinema," in *Principles of Visual Anthropology*, ed. Paul Hockings [The Hague: Mouton, 1965], 109–24) called for visual anthropologists to augment viewers' understanding of filmed realities by making visible otherwise hidden aspects of the filmic situation. He did not, however, discuss the possibility of the visual anthropologist's becoming the subject, as happened in Myerhoff's film. In written ethnographies, especially in life histories, the role of the anthropologist as autobiographer was coming into view. Among Barbara's contemporaries in symbolic anthropology experimenting with placing themselves in the text were Paul Rabinow, *Reflections on Fieldwork in Morocco* (Berkeley: University of California Press, 1977), and Vincent Crapanzano, *Tuhami: Portrait of a Moroccan* (Chicago: University of Chicago Press, 1980).

22. According to Vikram Jayanti, Barbara had six weeks to live. Deena Metzger, who accompanied Barbara to the doctor when she was given her prognosis, said she was given six months. Lynne Littman said, "I don't know if it was ever six weeks. Vikram and I took Barbara to an oncologist in Santa Barbara. I think he said three months. He was brutal." In any case, Lynne felt most definitely that Barbara "hung on" to finish the film.

23. *Mezuzah* means "doorpost." It is a small parchment scroll on which are inscribed the first two paragraphs of the *Shema* (Deut. 6:4–9; 11:13–21; R. J. Zwi Werblowsky and Geoffrey Wigoder, eds., *The Encyclopedia of the Jewish Religion* [New York: Holt, Rinehart and Winston, 1966], 261). Through an aperture in the scroll's case appears the word *shaddai*, the meaning of which is unknown. Feminists point out its possible translation and Midrashic interpretation as "breasts" (of God).

24. An X-ray image was used to similar effect some fifteen years later in the commercial film *Map of the Human Heart*, which dealt poignantly with absence of parents and the identity politics of mixed ethnicity. The haunting melody that is used in this scene and throughout *In Her Own Time*, composed for electronic synthesizer by James Horner (who wrote the score for Littman's film *Testament*), was based on a tune that was used for *davening* (prayer) in Reb Naftali's *shul* (synagogue). Mournfulness is not typical of *klezmer* music per se, a popular style enjoyed by Eastern European Jews usually performed by a small ensemble with horns and strings. It is associated with *freilach* (happy) occasions, such as weddings and other celebrations, at which furiously fast-paced music is played. In the film *Number Our Days* a saxophonist plays the *klezmer*-style 1940s swing tune "Bei Mir Bist Du Shane" at a New Year's dance. *Klezmer* music accompanies the wedding scene in *In Her Own Time*.

25. Frank Hamilton Cushing (1857–1900) is also briefly mentioned in Stanley Diamond, "Paul Radin," in *Totems and Teachers: Perspectives on the History of Anthropology*, ed. Sydel Silverman (New York: Columbia University Press, 1981), 67–100. A photograph of Cushing in Zuni dress appears in L. L. Langness, *The Study of Culture* (San Francisco: Chandler & Sharp, 1974), 43.

26. Donald A. Messerschmidt, ed., *Anthropologists at Home in North America: Methods and Issues in the Study of One's Own Society* (Cambridge, England: Cambridge University Press, 1981). See also Khalil Nakhleh, "On Being a Native Anthropologist," in *The Politics of Anthropology: From Colonialism and Sexism toward a View from Below*, ed. Gerrit Huizer and Bruce Mannheim (Paris: Mouton, 1979).

27. In *Number Our Days* Myerhoff wrote of her informant, Shmuel Goldman:

> Our shadows were exactly the same size — small, compact, heads enlarged by wiry curls. Despite the forty years that set us apart, despite our differences in sex, history, knowledge, belief and experience, we resembled each other. It could be seen that we were of the same racial stock. Shmuel had a way of reckoning all differences between us in his favor, mocking but without cruelty, yet in a way that always made me feel somewhat apologetic. I was grateful for all our similarities and read them as signs of hope in the validity of my attempt to comprehend him. (p. 42)

28. Hasidism is a religious and mystical revival movement that originated in southern Poland and the Ukraine in the eighteenth century. It spread to other parts of Eastern Europe (Poland, Rumania, Hungary) and is now found mainly in Israel and the United States. Numerous Hasidic dynasties remain, of which the Lubavitcher, founded by Rabbi Schneur Zalman of Lyady (Lubavitch) in Russia-Poland, are among the most numerous. Outreach to non-Hasidic Jews has been a unique contribution of the Rebbe, Menachem Mendel Schneerson, a Sorbonne-educated engineer born in 1902, who inherited his position of leadership in 1950 and died in 1994.

29. Lynne Littman's general criticism of my essay was its literalism, its "confusion of film and reality," which bears on my reading of this scene. She stated:

> There's no sense here of making a movie . . . which misses a level of Barbara's incredible professionalism. Barbara, when working on a movie, was an actress. She was not entering into Hasidic life as an incoming Hasid. Your perceptions are off base. . . . She was an uncanny performer and had an awareness of how quickly to make a point. She never lost sight of the point that she needed to get from her subject, yet never stayed outside. She was a scientist. Not in any way was she envious of Sultana. . . . Or, if she was, it is in the way one is envious of a ballet dancer. She didn't really want to be a ballet dancer. She wanted a miracle. But she didn't want to be Orthodox. She loved too many trafe [non-kosher] things. The fact is that she could ask for a miracle, mean it, and still know she was a scientist.

Deena Metzger similarly portrayed Barbara as a completely secular Jew yet heard Barbara's comment regarding Sultana as "absolutely true," evidence of her "wishing that she could step through to faith."

30. Charlotte Baum, Paula Hyman, and Sonya Michel, "'Woe to the Father Whose Children Are Girls': Women in the Jewish Tradition," in their *The Jewish Woman in America* (New York: New American Library, 1975), 3–16.

31. Deena Metzger, thinking back to Barbara's role in the women's community that centered around The Women's Building in Los Angeles in the 1970s, commented: "Most women at that time, even her friends, would not have called her a feminist." Lynne Littman commented: "The feminist question is not the right grid. Barbara tried to be a feminist. She was too busy. She missed the women's movement. She was producing. She was out working. She was out doing it."

32. Barbara Myerhoff and Jay Ruby, "A Crack in the Mirror: Reflexive Perspectives in Anthropology," in *Remembered Lives*, 307–40. The paper originally appeared as the "Introduction" to *A Crack in the Mirror: Reflexive Perspectives in Anthropology*, ed. Jay Ruby (Philadelphia: University of Pennsylvania Press, 1982), 1–35.

33. Myerhoff wrote:

> When I grew into the world of words, my life was dominated by a storytelling grandmother, an illiterate woman of European origin, whose passion for storytelling transformed my life. Each day she told me a different story about one of the houses on the hill behind our house. We imaginatively entered each in turn, making their stories into a commentary on our own lives. One day I wept because the kitchen window was covered with frost. I thought there would be no story since we could not see out. My grandmother laughed, warmed a penny in her palm, pressed it against the glass to make a peephole in the frost, then informed me that I had all I needed there. An opening big enough to glimpse the street outside, transformed by this frame, this tiny aperture, providing the sharpest possible focus; the ordinary scene without became a spectacle, separated from the ebb and flow of mundane life around it. It was the first time I clearly understood that something magic happened when a piece of nature was isolated and framed. It was the beginning of some comprehension of the seriousness of paying attention to a selected aspect of one's life or surroundings. (Myerhoff and Ruby, "Crack in the Mirror," 338)

34. An alternative reading of Myerhoff's position in the film and in this scene appears in Sandra Butler and Barbara Rosenblum, "In My Own Time," in their *Cancer in Two Voices* (San Francisco: spinsters book co., 1991), 51–56. Barbara Rosenblum writes: "It was a stirring sequence and the ceremony of divorce was the only place where I felt her [Barbara] fully engaged and present" (p. 53). Deena Metzger and Lynne Littman are clear about why Barbara put herself in the hands of the patriarchs. Deena argued, "Who else could do it? Was it the *only* way to get her soul back? Of course not. But it was what the tradition has to offer. If she were going to go into a Huichol ceremony, she would go into it as it was given. When you enter ritual, you enter it." The old man who played Barbara's husband's surrogate was the amusing part of it, since "from her point of view ritual is *ritual*, not literal." Similarly, Lynne asserted:

> This was not about giving herself over to male figures. We were touched that there was a kind of maleness that was so remarkable to both of us because it doesn't exist in the secular world. We were both . . . in love with Beryl. It was not pre-feminist or anti-feminist, it was appreciation. It wasn't a struggle. She participated in a ritual. . . . She repeated what she was told to say, of course. It was all like theater. A reality was set up. They moved into it and made it real. She had another text, she was also the scholar and the dying person. It was magical, authentic theater. . . . That was the most accessible, highly placed rabbi in the community. They were phenomenal old men who came together on a 90 degree afternoon. They showed such generosity. Why? Ver vays? Who knows. They came out for her. Maybe that's what makes them rabbis.

35. Lynne Littman sees this sequence in another light, as an example of Barbara's consummate skill in crafting a dramatic episode and of the smooth synchromesh of their collaboration:

> Barbara took a scene that was completely inaccessible. What she was doing was writing drama, not religion. It was uncanny how her intellect slid seamlessly into drama. She turned to me and talked to me and knew the camera would be there. That's about trusting: When I jump off the roof my partner's going to be there. A dance. We never disagreed. We were in the same movie. She and I were attached and that's what made it such fun. I didn't know how rare this was. The deal we made was this . . . I said, "When I think you are too ill to do the final interview, that's when we have to do it." And she agreed because that was the professional in her, because we needed it for the film. I needed her to do the interview because she was the anthropologist.

36. Lynne Littman says that Barbara met a man she intuitively recognized as her father in the turnstile of a pharmacy on Ventura Boulevard, not far from her home in the San Fernando Valley. Shortly thereafter she discovered that some neighbors of hers were in fact cousins. Deena Metzger recalls that when Barbara's stepfather, Norman, was dying, Deena schlepped herself to the hospital with her own two small children nearly every day because Barbara was so grieved and needed support. Even so, Deena comments, Barbara always felt an irreparable sense of tragedy and loss fostered by Barbara's mother about her father's absence.

37. Prell, "Double Frame," gives an account of Myerhoff's relationship with Ramón and Lupe Silva and points out that *Peyote Hunt* begins with a chapter entitled "Ramón and Lupe." Myerhoff (*Peyote Hunt*, 24–25) wrote in her introduction: "This work is their work [Ramón's and Lupe's] as much as mine. . . . I have tried to tell it as they told it to me, so that it shall not be forgotten." Myerhoff's relationship with *Number Our Days* informant Shmuel Goldman is also discussed at length by Prell. Myerhoff documented her difficulties with Shmuel's widow, Rebekkah, in her article "Surviving Stories," in which she recalled Rebekkah's scolding her for spending so much time with Shmuel. Myerhoff described her friendship with Victor and Edith Turner in her paper "Pilgrimage to Meron: Inner and Outer Peregrinations," an account of her 1983 pilgrimage with them to the shrine in Israel of a saint and scholar, Shimon Bar Yohai. After Barbara died, Edie Turner prepared the paper for publication in *Creativity/Anthropology*, ed. Smadar Lavie, Kirin Narayan, and Renato Rosaldo (Ithaca, N.Y.: Cornell University Press, 1993), 211–22.

38. Deena Metzger called this interpretation "way out." Lynne Littman said: "I never thought about that! They're making bread! If anything, it shows you men cook!" (Sometimes a matzo is just a matzo?) On the other hand, Vikram Jayanti offered praise: "I loved it. It's the sort of thing Barbara would come up with!"

39. The rabbi's broad-brimmed fur hat (*shtrimel*) marks the matzo bakers as Satmar Hasids, not Lubavitcher. The activity of baking matzos marks the filming as having occurred before Passover, most likely in the early spring of 1984.

40. Marc Kaminsky, "Introduction."

41. Prell, "Double Frame."

42. Barbara Myerhoff and Deena Metzger, "The Journal as Activity and Genre," in *Remembered Lives*, 341–59.

43. The two-day conference, held at USC on November 4 and 5, 1984, was organized by Rabbi Laura Geller and Rabbi Patricia Karlin-Newman and was sponsored mainly by grants from the Max and Anna Levinson Foundation and the Jewish Community Foundation of the Jewish Federation Council of Greater Los Angeles. Myerhoff shared the podium with E. M. Broner in a session on transforming Jewish ritual in which each delivered a keynote address. Broner has since published an account of feminist retellings of the Passover story over sixteen years of seders conducted by "the Seder Sisters," a group including a number of high-profile feminists (Phyllis Chesler, Letty Cottin Pogrebin, Gloria Steinem, Bella Abzug, Grace Paley, and numerous others). See E. M. Broner, *The Telling* (San Francisco: Harper, 1993).

44. Michael Spector, "The Oracle of Crown Heights," *New York Times Magazine*, March 15, 1992, 38. See also Yosef I. Abramowitz, "What Happens If the Rebbe Dies?" *Moment: The Magazine of Jewish Culture and Opinion* 18, no. 2 (April 1993): 30–39; and David Eliezrie, "Outreach Chabad Style," *Moment: The Magazine of Jewish Culture and Opinion* 18, no. 2 (April 1993): 40–42.

45. Spector, "Oracle of Crown Heights," 38.

46. Ibid.

47. Ibid.

48. David Eliezrie, "Outreach Chabad Style."

49. For a beautiful tribute to Myerhoff's influence, see Faye D. Ginsburg, "Preface," *Contested Lives: The Abortion Debate in an American Community* (Berkeley: University of California Press, 1989), ix–xi. See also R. Ruth Linden, "Prologue," *Making Stories, Making Selves: Feminist Reflections on the Holocaust* (Columbus: Ohio State University Press, 1993), 1–11.

50. Werblowsky and Wigoder, *Encyclopedia of the Jewish Religion,* 215–16.

11

Writing against the Grain: Cultural Politics of Difference in the Work of Alice Walker

Faye V. Harrison

Anthropology, Fiction, and Unequal Relations of Intellectual Production

FOR MICHAEL FISCHER postmodernism is "a general condition of multicultural life demanding new forms of inventiveness and subtlety from a fully reflexive ethnography."[1] He looks to ethnic autobiography for insights into the way culture operates in "pluralist, post-industrial, late Twentieth Century society."[2] He believes that this genre, both its form and content, can potentially revitalize and refashion ethnography as a mode of cultural criticism. I take Fischer's approach one step further to claim that ethnic/minority fiction—not just autobiography—is a salient genre that represents a rich mode of writing the cultures, cultural politics, and history of our multicultural world. I am particularly interested in what black women writers such as Alice Walker have written from the vantage point of black female cultural workers struggling against the grain of exploitative objectification and alienation from the means of intellectual production. Chandra Talpade Mohanty, Ann Russo, and Lourdes Torres assert that "questions of race, class, sexuality, colonialism, and imperialism are . . . constitutive of knowledge production in a number of disciplines (not merely ghettoized in marginal fields)."[3] If these inequalities are indeed at the heart of the postmodern/postcolonial experience, then certainly the subaltern should have something significant to contribute to contemporary social analysis.

Black feminist cultural critic Michele Wallace has noted that black women's most prolific, articulate, and concentrated intellectual production is found in creative endeavors.[4] Fiction, it appears, has served as a sanctuary offering greater freedom for critical explorations of the cultural, psychological, and historical dilemmas of the black and human experience. Fiction encodes truth claims—and alternative modes of theorizing—in a rhetoric of imagination. In some respects the concealed, coded articulations that fiction allows seem to be opaque interreferences to social science's exclusive and monopolistic claims to the verification of social/cultural knowledge and truth. Fiction resists constructs of validity and reliability that privilege elitist white male representations and explanations of the world.

Literary production is not free of racial and gender domination, however; the literary milieu is also stratified and segmented. The visibility of only a chosen few—however deserving they are—obscures the reality of the majority of black women writers, who must struggle "to speak [critically and oppositionally] from the still radically unspeakable position of 'the Other' of 'the Other'."[5] In a hegemonic scheme that attributes to blackness and femaleness the natural ability to create and to be aesthetically expressive, and that elevates a masculinist science to the most privileged and rewarded echelons, writing fiction is an acceptable behavior for some black women. Their overwhelming concentration in aesthetic and commercial entertainment arenas and their underrepresentation in literary criticism and the social sciences is a consequence of opportunities structured in racial/gender/class dominance. Anthropology's opportunity structure accommodates limited black participation in rank-and-file ethnographic production—particularly as glorified field assistants "on the cheap"—but limits positive, validating sanctions for their formulating cross-culturally testable explanations of data.[6] When radical black women write fiction or ethnography, they do so against the grain of a hegemony that peripheralizes them yet appropriates the value of their creative and critical productivity.

Alice Walker as Anthropology's Interlocutor

The experimental moment permeating anthropology can be constructive and indeed liberating, depending on how it is used and whether it is grounded in responsible worldly praxis. Although black women's fiction is not automatically subversive or counterhegemonic, some of it can provide insights into how writing culture can be both experimental and potentially liberating. As Michelle Wallace admits, black women's literature "alternately conspires with and rebels against . . . current cultural and political arrangements."[7]

Alice Walker is readily identified with feminism/womanism, civil rights, and other social-justice struggles. She is one of the token few black women who have enjoyed the esteem of the literati, yet she is one of anthropology's less visible interlocutors. This relationship with the discipline emerged most clearly at the point in her career when she searched for and rediscovered Zora Neale Hurston for herself and for the world of readers and thinkers. Walker, along with Robert Hemenway, is probably most responsible for revitalizing interest in the enigmatic and forgotten Hurston.[8] That revitalization, however, has affected and involved literary scholars more than it has anthropologists. Gwendolyn Mikell is one of the few anthropologists who has thoughtfully examined Hurston as one who was just as much an anthropologist as she was a novelist, as one whose fiction was grounded in a contextual, participatory ethnographic subjectivity, which during her lifetime had no comfortable home in American anthropology.[9] This professional homelessness is reflected in Hurston's being scorned at Columbia University for her so-called lack of rigorous techniques.

For Walker, Hurston represents a cultural ancestress, who along with Billie Holiday and Bessie Smith "form[s] a sort of unholy trinity."[10] Walker first "became aware of [her] need of" Hurston's work when she "was writing a story that required accurate material on voodoo practices among rural Southern blacks of the thirties."[11] She was sorely disappointed and insulted by the literature written by racist anthropologists and folklorists of the period, so she searched on until she came upon *Mules and Men.* When she and her rural southern relatives read and talked about the tales and "lies" Hurston reported, Walker learned from her family's reaction that the material Hurston had collected was valid. This was the beginning of her special relationship with Hurston—and, obliquely, with anthropology.

The interrelationship between the use of historical and anthropological literatures as sources for facts and ideas and the writing of culture in fictive rhetoric is salient in Walker's work, which strongly resonates with discourses in a number of scholarly disciplines, particularly anthropology. With her ancestor's blessings, Walker's fiction is ethnographic and ethnohistorical, even if not as deliberately or as self-consciously as Hurston's was.[12] An intertextual reading of Walker's short stories and novels, especially *The Temple of My Familiar,* reveals how Walker's creative inscription of culture, politics, and history—and her cultural critique of the colonial/postcolonial world-system—can be seen to be embedded within a larger interdisciplinary discourse to which anthropologists contribute.[13]

As in the case of the ethnic autobiographies that Fischer examines, Walker's literary production "parallels, mirrors, and exemplifies contemporary theories of textuality, of knowledge, and of culture."[14] Her writing is consistent with postmodernist ethnographic experiments in its deployment of a number of techniques. Key among them are bifocality or reciprocity of perspectives (that is, seeing others against a background of ourselves and ourselves against a background of others), juxtapositioning of multiple realities, interlinguistic play (such as moving from standard English to dialect [code switching] to Spanish and back to English), comparison through families of resemblance, and emphasis on dialogue and discourse.

In brief, Walker's *The Temple of My Familiar* is an intricate tale of several people's stories of past and present experiences in love and friendship relationships; in families; and in precolonial, colonial, and postcolonial contexts of gender, race, and class oppressions. The diverse stories converge in the lives of two San Francisco couples, one African American and the other mixed Latino and African American. These couples are multiply connected through work (at a college or university), an extramarital affair, a masseuse-client relationship, and their common ties to a wealthy, globe-traveling Anglo American woman. As presented, the various personal dilemmas and conflicts that the two couples (and their relatives and friends) experience are embedded in and indeed implicate the wider status quo in both national and international contexts. The characters' many narratives and conversations open windows on an historically dynamic world marked by dramatic differences as well as basic commonalities.

The novel's main characters are Carlotta, a Latin American immigrant and women's studies professor; her mother Zedé, a feather-goods seamstress and former schoolteacher who escaped political persecution in Latin America; Carlotta's husband, Arveyda, a popular African American singer and musician with the power of spiritual healing; Suwelo, a black history professor who inherits his dead greatuncle Rafe's house in Baltimore and struggles over his relationships with women; Mr. Hal, Uncle Rafe's best friend and a talented painter with the gift of delivering his wife's babies; Miss Lissie, Mr. Hal's wife, who was also a common-law wife to Uncle Rafe, with whom she, Hal, and their daughter Lulu shared a home; Fanny, Suwelo's wife/ex-wife, a former literature professor and college administrator, who must come to terms with her kinship to Africa and her relationship to Suwelo, in and out of marriage; Olivia, Fanny's mother, a nurse and lecturer on African affairs who came of age in a family of black American missionaries in Africa; Ola/Dahvid, Fanny's father, former freedom fighter and political prisoner, prominent playwright, and minister of culture in a postcolonial African nation with a white settler colonial past; Nzingha, Ola's African daughter and Fanny's half sister, who struggles to assert her womanhood and find a new place in a male-dominated postcolonial society; and Mary Ann/Mary Jane, a committed radical from a rich Anglo American family, Ola's wife-of-convenience (for the sake of her immigration status) and an art school founder and director, who in her youth helped Zedé and Carlotta find refuge in the United States and in her mature years committed herself to the people of postcolonial Africa.

Through the intersecting and at times parallel experiences and memories of these characters—as well as of their more extended networks of relatives and friends—the novel moves the reader back and forth across a long-distance itinerary linking urban and suburban neighborhoods, universities, museums, and massage parlors in San Francisco, Baltimore, and London with mountain villages, export-crop plantations, and political prisons in Latin America, and all of these with government ministries, art schools, grass-roots theaters, and rural villages in postcolonial Africa. All of the personalities, situations, and conflicts in Walker's novel are complex and multidimensional. The predicaments related to, for example, love triangles—and rectangles (Carlotta, Arveyda, and Zedé; Carlotta, Suwelo, Fanny, and Arveyda; and Hal, Lissie, and Rafe)—and to, as another example, exile (in the cases of Zedé, Mary Ann/Mary Jane, and M'Sukta, a human museum exhibit) provide poignant points of entry into and shed light on wider fields of knowledge, power, and possibility.

Walker's novel is a world cultural history from a pluralistic Third World feminist perspective. As feminist "her-story," the novel deessentializes gender as well as race and class. This novel should be seen as an integral part of the broader literature on the politics of representing gender, race, and culture history. The monolithic Third World victims reified "under Western feminist eyes" are nowhere to be found in Walker's narrative.[15] In this respect her understanding of women's multidimensional experiences concurs with those advanced by Chandra Mohanty and Ifi Amadiume, whose analyses are anchored in a critique of Western feminist constructions of the female Other.[16]

In *Temple,* Walker writes an enabling history that is designed to inform present and future struggles for the full humanization of men and women around the world. The novel is a gender- and race-sensitive complement to and friendly critique of ungendered texts such as Eric Wolf's *Europe and the People without History.*[17] Despite Michael Taussig's caustic and, in my view, not completely convincing criticism of Wolf's concern with commodities rather than with commodity fetishism, Wolf's anthropological history is a watershed that expands the stage and action in world history to include the diverse peoples anthropologists have traditionally studied.[18] Although Wolf sets new standards for the study of historicized political economy and the world-system, his contribution does not give visibility to women's historical agency. His vision and approach are necessary but not sufficient for a feminist project in culture history—a project that privileges the role of consciousness and experience in resistance and contestation.

The works that Walker challenges most forcefully are those blatantly racist and sexist Eurocentric histories that objectify or render invisible the majority of the world's peoples, both male and female. In Walker's fictive history of the world and of humanity, she emphasizes the agency of the colonized (especially the women) and of counterhegemonic Western women. She amplifies agency by focusing sequences of events and extended dialogues around the life stories and memories of several individuals and their kin and friendship networks. These parallel networks intersect at various points in historic time and extend across four continents—North and South America, Africa, and Europe—and eventually converge in the "ethnohistorical present" of contemporary northern California.

Walker explores the interrelationship among history, myth, and "the painful dream world of memory" as she weaves together myths, legends, magical realist accounts, and documentable historical reconstructions in her depiction of African, African American, (U.S.) Latino, and Latin American experiences and dilemmas. In Walker's writing myth is not history's binary opposite. For the great masters of social anthropology (key among them Bronislaw Malinowski and A. R. Radcliffe-Brown), history was absent and unknowable among "primitive" Others, whose mythical minds were functions of social structures fossilized in an ahistoric present. In *Temple,* however, myth provides an idiom and narrative form for encoding queries, recollec-

tions, and constructions of the distant and not so distant past. Suwelo, Fanny, Carlotta, and Arveya come to resolve their personal and marital crises collectively
through the reconciliation between, on one hand, the formal knowledge that they as
historians, literary scholars, and artists have attained from both within and without
"academic plantations" and, on the other hand, the experiential, mythical, magical
narratives their elders—Miss Lissie, Mr. Hal, and Zedé—transmit to them as counsel. The younger generation's rediscovery and reclaiming of the suppressed folk
knowledge of human origins, the subjugation of female humanity and deities, and
the psychological and cultural consequences of colonial and postcolonial oppression help steer them along a growth-inducing route to more decolonized and gender-
egalitarian consciousness and lifeways.

Walker spotlights and privileges black-brown intellectual discourse in her reconstruction of history, her critique of postcolonial states and their sexist, class-biased
and too-often militarized strategies of national development, and her excavations of
the deeply implanted distortions and discontinuities in the psychic and sociocultural
experiences of both the oppressed and the oppressive in unjust social orders of both
the First World and the Third World. Black and brown characters whose subjectivities have been thwarted and warped in hegemonic situations and contexts collectively come to voice by talking with each other, sharing painful memories of their
past experiences, and revealing and coming to terms with multiple and sometimes
clashing facets of self. This coming to voice, however, is not predicated on the exclusion, erasure, or negation of critical Western discourse. Third World intellectual
subjectivity is depicted as a dialogic encounter between formal knowledge producers and those who are articulate and expert in folk wisdom. Intellect and knowledge, then, are not elitist and exclusive; they are based on a collective, historicized
consciousness, in which the experience and wisdom of the folk can invoke authority
in negotiating the resolutions that the younger, formally trained intellectuals make
in their thinking and in their lives. Walker's depiction is compatible with Helán
Page's analysis, in which she demonstrates that subaltern communities can in fact
exert authority and influence outcomes in dialogic negotiations of interpretations
and meaning.[19]

Subaltern authority notwithstanding, Walker's novel highlights and accentuates the ongoing crisis of being a black or brown intellectual. Fanny, Nzingha, Ola,
Suwelo, and Carlotta grapple with, talk extensively about, and seek to understand
the dilemmas stemming from living under conditions of racist and sexist domination. As professional intellectuals they struggle to come to terms with their formal
education as a means of conquest that they must resist and overcome. This dilemma
is most acute in Nzingha's painful experience. As a small child she was taken away
from her illiterate mother, who had fought in the armed struggle that won the country its liberation but had no respected place in postcolonial society. At boarding
school and later at university in France, Nzingha underwent an enculturation that
alienated her from her mother and people. The disjuncture that schooling created

between Nzingha and her mother eventually resulted in the severance of their tie, leaving Nzingha in a painfully liminal position, for the negation of her mother and all she symbolized was not at all offset by a welcoming assimilation into the Western culture on which her education was based. After recounting the trials and tribulations of her youth, Nzingha shares this lament with her sister Fanny: "Being educated by people who despise you is also conquest."[20] However, in resistance, Nzingha, like her father, invests her educational capital in cultural projects designed to raise popular consciousness and to mobilize social forces for political and economic democratization.

Fanny, Suwelo, and Carlotta all eventually decide to leave academia for more creative vocations in music, playwriting, massage, and carpentry, where they find greater peace and freedom. This fictive solution to the crisis of the black-brown intellectual is tantamount to a strong indictment of American academia at a juncture when the conservative political backlash against multicultural and feminist subjectivities is on the rise.

Through her characters' struggles for self-knowledge, Walker illuminates the dynamic, nonessentialist, and culturally constructed nature of social identity. She, like the authors of autobiography that Fischer examines, elucidates how each generation reinvents and reinterprets race, ethnicity, gender, and class.[21] These reconstructions are based on a process of interreference between two or more cultural traditions, and they are also anchored in critiques of past and present rhetorics and ideologies of domination. The sense that social identity and self-knowledge emerge from the cross-fertilization and conflicts within cultural/class borderlands is consistent with Renato Rosaldo's remark that borders have the potential of "opening new forms of human understanding."[22] He goes on to comment that "All of us [not just the subaltern] inhabit an interdependent late-twentieth century world marked by borrowing and lending across porous national and cultural boundaries that are saturated with inequality, power, and domination."[23]

The multidimensional self (or the multiplicity of selves) is a recurrent theme in Walker's novel. This combined with her concern with the ambiguity of boundaries is most powerfully symbolized through the character of Miss Lissie, an elderly black woman who shares her memory of her innumerable reincarnated lives that span both evolutionary and historic time. Miss Lissie, having been—among other things— both male and female and both black and white in past lives, is the metaphoric embodiment of plural and collective human experiences. Furthermore, her insight into the reification of Otherness is also informed by her past life as a lion at the evolutionary juncture when humans estranged their animal familiars. She recalls that in the earliest and most peaceful days of human existence, familiars were closely associated with women and children, who interacted with animals in much the same way they interacted with other people. Eventually men forced familiars away from women's fires. This antagonistic act occurred around the time that the social foundations were laid for male domination and the carnivorous consumption patterns associated with hunting. Human society was, hence, re-created in the interests of power-hungry men, who subjugated women and killed and ate their former familiars.

The influence of multidimensional selves on racial and ethnic identity is also illuminated by Walker's techniques of bifocality and comparison through families of resemblance. Zedé and her daughter Carlotta, refugees from a repressive Latin American republic, see images of themselves in Arveyda, the African American singer/musician who marries Carlotta. Arveyda's combined Indian-Chinese-African features and kinky hair remind Zedé of her mate, a Latin American *indio* with traces of African ancestry. Fanny, an African American born of a black missionary and an African freedom fighter and playwright, is described as having an Apache-like nose. Even her native African half sister, Nzingha, has this nose, at once symbolizing political-economic parallels between native Americans and native Africans in settler colonialism and the fallacy of notions of racial purity. Interethnic fusions and similarities are mentioned throughout the novel. They reflect Walker's human-centered multiracialist sense that "when [she] look[s] at people in Iran and Cuba, they look like kin folk."[24] This view effects a penetrating critique of the very concept and historically constituted realities of "race," which severely constrain enactments of alternative selves.[25]

Walker's provocative treatment of marriage and family illuminates the tension between conjugality and blood and fictive-blood relationships.[26] She exposes the severe limitations of forms of marriage constrained by patriarchal values and explores alternative arrangements such as polyandry (such as Miss Lissie, Mr. Hal, and Suwelo's Uncle Rafe) and extended marriages in which co-couples form fictive familial units. Although such arrangements are indeed controversial, especially at a time when monogamy is advanced as a defense against the spread of AIDS, Walker's treatment of marriage and kinship resonates with the extensive literature on African and Afro-American kinship that elucidates the traditional primacy of the mother-focused consanguineal core over conjugal units, which tend not to be focal points in extended family contexts. As Niara Sudarkasa points out, the stability of extended families is not dependent on the stability or permanence of marriage. In both *The Color Purple* and *The Temple of My Familiar*, reinvented families encompass blood-kin, friends, co-lovers, and co-spouses. Fanny, for instance, had two "grandmothers"—Mama Celie and her partner/lover Mama Shug, both of whom had had intimate relations with Celie's husband, Albert. In these communalist configurations, women take the lead in establishing ties of sisterhood as an alternative to the destructive sexual rivalry that exists in situations where clandestine polygyny and its exploitation of women prevail.

The Temple of My Familiar articulates an opaque but penetrating critique of anthropological discourses that nativize and objectify Third World women. A poignant allegory of the reification of the African woman is found in M'Sukta's plight. M'Sukta, the last survivor of her annihilated people, was taken to England, where she lived in a replica of an African village at the Museum of Natural History.

FAYE V. HARRISON

She, along with the material culture, was on exhibit to demonstrate her vanished way of life and to pass on "the history of her people's ancient way of life." [27] She no longer had a home outside the colonial museum—nor outside a colonizing system of anthropological data collection, analysis, and representation.

Walker contrasts this discursive system with that adumbrated, for example, by African American missionaries, who embedded ethnographic accounts in letters and reports during the late nineteenth and early twentieth centuries. In her youth Fanny's Aunt Nettie had written letters to her sister Celie about the indigenous African societies she encountered and the oppressive impact of colonialism. [28] St. Clair Drake, in describing the hidden contributions of Africans and diasporan blacks to early ethnography, noted that the ethnographic descriptions that black missionaries wrote were generally more sympathetic and less susceptible to ethnocentric and racist biases than the standard missionary and travelogue ethnography of that time. [29] However, the latter ethnographies provided "evidence" for armchair ethnology, while the former have virtually been forgotten. Interestingly, "by the time World War I ended," black missionaries, whose antiracist and anticolonial accounts can possibly be revisited "in the files of the national Baptist conventions and the two African Methodist Episcopal Churches," "were suspected of being a subversive influence and attempts were made to reduce their numbers." [30] Drake points out that

> This was the same period when the first large foundation grants were made for a study of various African peoples using the techniques and theoretical frameworks of the infant field "functional anthropology." Needless to say, no Black graduate students were sent out by the British who administered these American donations, nor did the International African Institute — also American subsidized — offer an opportunity to any Blacks from the West Indies or the U.S.A. to participate in its research. Africans were extensively used, but as "informants." [31]

Walker's critique of anthropology is predicated on a keen awareness that alternative and oppositional perspectives and voices exist both within and outside the discipline's boundaries. After all, she is more than aware of Hurston's precarious place within professional anthropology and of her decision to write against the grain with the aid of instruments of creative writing.

Interestingly, compared with *The Color Purple*, to which it can be seen as a sequel, *Temple* has not stimulated much debate or discourse. Perhaps many people do not know exactly what to say about the book, whose content extends beyond the fictive turf black women writers have traditionally been allowed to control. Walker has defiantly left the place reserved for writers like herself; she has moved beyond the internal dynamics and conflicts within southern black life to the whole wide world and some of its most pressing contradictions—racial, sexual, class related, political economic, environmental, and intellectual.

Hers is a holistic fiction that reflects her vision of a pluralistic yet human-centered set of interlocking experiences. Her creative work boldly envisions and interprets.

The responsibility for subjecting her provocative truth claims to proof or disproof lies not in her literary project but in those discursive/intellectual realms where testing, falsification, and explanation are characteristically expected and undertaken. However, these latter realms, which include, of course, the social sciences, operate in relations of complementarity and cross-fertilization with the arts and humanities. This complementarity can be especially beneficial to the most interdisciplinary of all the social sciences—anthropology.

Subaltern Voices "Talking Back"

Alice Walker is only one of the most visible participants in a wider, more inclusive, interdisciplinary domain of subaltern intellectual production. At this experimental moment in American anthropology's trajectory, the creative and theoretical insights as well as the sociopolitical sensibilities of subaltern thinkers should not be erased. The postmodernist "fetishizing of [textual and rhetorical] form" and its sharp separation from intellectual content may be responsible in part for the near failure to engage the many substantive analyses and critiques that Third World anthropologists have produced.[32] Nonetheless, attempting, as some may be inclined, to excuse this exclusion or erasure with the claim that "groups long excluded from positions of institutional power, like women or people of color, have less concrete freedom to indulge in textual experimentation" and, therefore, are more likely to confront issues of data content in "the anthropological archive" is a smoke screen obscuring the heterogeneity of theoretical perspectives, methodological approaches, and textual strategies that people of color and white women have actually contributed to anthropological knowledge.[33] If form is to be prioritized, how can the virtual invisibility of Hurston, John Gwaltney, and interlocutors like Walker be justified?[34]

The ethnography-as-literary-text trend is one of the contexts within which subaltern voices—those of intellectuals and informants—have been rendered mute or have been appropriated as aesthetic and academic commodities in ethnographic representation and writing. In the process of redefining anthropology's critical project(s) and of reconstituting anthropological authority, we must offset the persistent pattern of relegating the work of women—and that of women of color in particular—to the discipline's periphery.

Notes

I would like to acknowledge a number of persons whose encouragement and constructive comments have been beneficial to me in the writing and rewriting of this article: Ruth Behar, Deborah Gordon, Catherine Lutz, Lucy Freibert, Estella Conwill Majozo, Deborah D'Amico, Anne Francis-Okongwu, Yvonne Jones, Angela Gilliam, Lynn Bolles, Pem Buck, and the reviewers for the longer and complete version published in "Women Writing Culture," Ruth Behar, ed., *Critique of Anthropology* 13, no. 4 (1993): 401–27. As usual, I am deeply indebted to William L. Conwill for patiently listening to my reading of the earliest draft and for subsequently offering helpful suggestions.

1. This quotation on Fischer is from James Clifford's "Introduction: Partial Truths," in *Writing Culture: The Poetics and Politics of Ethnography,* ed. James Clifford and George E. Marcus (Berkeley: University of California Press, 1986), 23. See also Michael Fischer, "Ethnicity and the Post-Modern Arts of Memory," in *Writing Culture,* 194–233.

2. Fischer, "Ethnicity and the Post-Modern Arts of Memory," 195.

3. Mohanty, Russo, and Torres, "Preface," in *Third World Women and the Politics of Feminism,* ed. Chandra Talpade Mohanty, Ann Russo, and Lourdes Torres (Bloomington: Indiana University Press, 1991), x.

4. Michele Wallace, *Invisibility Blues: From Pop to Theory* (New York: Verso, 1990), 182.

5. Ibid., 215, n. 4.

6. This expression comes from Christine Obbo's "Adventures with Fieldnotes," in *Fieldnotes: The Makings of Anthropology,* ed. Roger Sanjek (Ithaca, N.Y.: Cornell University Press, 1990), 291.

7. Wallace, *Invisibility Blues,* 250.

8. Robert E. Hemenway, *Zora Neale Hurston: A Literary Biography* (Urbana: University of Illinois Press, 1977).

9. Gwendolyn Mikell, "When Horses Talk: Reflections on Zora Neale Hurston's Haitian Anthropology," *Phylon* 43, no. 3 (1982): 218–30; "The Anthropological Imagination of Zora Neale Hurston," *Western Journal of Black Studies* 7, no. 1 (1983): 27–35; "Zora Neale Hurston," in *Women Anthropologists: A Biographical Dictionary,* ed. Ute Gacs, Aisha Khan, Jerrie McIntyre, and Ruth Weinberg (Urbana: University of Illinois Press, 1989), 160–66. Other anthropological literature concerned with Hurston as an ethnographer are John Dorst, "Reading *Mules and Men:* Toward the Death of the Ethnographer," *Cultural Anthropology* 2 (1987): 305–18; and Deborah Gordon, "The Politics of Ethnographic Authority: Race and Writing in the Ethnography of Margaret Mead and Zora Neale Hurston," in *Modernist Anthropology,* ed. Marc Manganaro (Princeton, N.J.: Princeton University Press, 1990), 146–62.

10. Alice Walker, *In Search of Our Mothers' Gardens* (San Diego and New York: Harcourt Brace Jovanovich Publishers, 1983), 91.

11. Ibid., 83. The short story to which Walker was referring is "The Revenge of Hannah Kemhuff," in her *In Love and Trouble: Stories of Black Women* (New York: Harcourt Brace Jovanovich, 1973).

12. According to literary artist Estella Conwill Majozo, black women writers have historically expanded literary genres, blurring boundaries among them, history, and the social sciences. In this respect, both Walker and Hurston are part of a broader and older tradition (personal communication).

13. Alice Walker, *The Temple of My Familiar* (New York: Pocket Books, 1989).

14. Fischer, "Ethnicity and the Post-Modern Arts of Memory," 230, n. 1.

15. Chandra Talpade Mohanty, "Under Western Eyes: Feminist Scholarship and Colonial Discourses," in *Third World Women,* 51–80.

16. Mohanty, Russo, and Torres, "Preface"; Mohanty, "Under Western Eyes"; Ifi Amadiume, *Male Daughters, Female Husbands: Gender and Sex in an African Society* (London: Zed Books Ltd., 1987).

17. Eric Wolf, *Europe and the People without History* (Berkeley: University of California Press, 1982). Walker's concern with rewriting not just black but global history is paralleled in anthropologist Gwendolyn Mikell's more narrowly delimited political economy of the Akan of Ghana, *Cocoa and Chaos in Ghana* (New York: Paragon Press, 1989). Mikell situates the rise and fall of Ghana's cocoa economy in the wider historical and

worldly context of colonial and postcolonial capitalism. A global framework, however, does not preclude her from underscoring the lived experiences and struggles of subsistence producers and cash-cropping farmers, matrilineal kinspeople, and traditional and modern bearers of power/authority at the local as well as regional and national levels. Moreover, the history, political economy, and culture that Mikell analyzes is both gender- and class-focused.

18. Michael Taussig, "History as Commodity in Some Recent American (Anthropological) Literature," *Critique of Anthropology* 9, no. 1 (1989): 7–23.

19. Helán Page, "Dialogic Principles of Interactive Learning in the Ethnographic Relationship," *Journal of Anthropological Research* 44, no. 2 (1988): 163–81.

20. Walker, *Temple of My Familiar*, 265.

21. Fischer, "Ethnicity and the Post-Modern Arts of Memory."

22. Renato Rosaldo, *Culture and Truth: The Remaking of Social Analysis* (Boston: Beacon Press, 1989 [1993]), 216.

23. Ibid., 217.

24. Walker is quoted in Fischer, "Ethnicity and the Post-Modern Arts of Memory," 213, n. 1.

25. Ibid. See anthropologist Patricia Zavella, "Reflections on Diversity among Chicanas," *Frontiers* 12, no. 2 (1991): 73–85, for a discussion of the oppressive constraints on "crossing borders" and constructing identities. Zavella's conception of Chicano/a ethnicity is grounded in her understanding of the "compounded diversity" of a set of historical experiences that has drawn on Indian, African, and European "racial" and cultural sources.

26. For an excellent analysis of this tension, see Niara Sudarkasa, "African and Afro-American Family Structure," in *Anthropology for the Nineties: Introductory Readings,* ed. Johnetta B. Cole (New York: Free Press, 1988), 182–210.

27. Walker, *Temple of My Familiar*, 233.

28. See Alice Walker, *The Color Purple* (New York: Harcourt Brace Jovanovich, 1982).

29. St. Clair Drake, "Further Reflections on Anthropology and the Black Experience," *Transforming Anthropology* 1, no. 2 (1990): 1–24.

30. Ibid., 5.

31. Ibid.

32. Clifford, "Introduction," 21, n. 2.

33. In "Introduction," 21, Clifford admits that this proposition is untenable. For just a small sample of the range of writing strategies and approaches among contemporary black women anthropologists, see A. Lynn Bolles, "Kitchens Hit by Priorities: Employed Working-Class Jamaican Women Confront the International Monetary Fund," in *Women, Men, and the International Division of Labor,* ed. June Nash and María Patricia Fernández-Kelly (Albany: State University of New York Press, 1983), 139–60; Faye V. Harrison, "Women in Jamaica's Urban Informal Economy: Insights from a Kingston Slum," *Nieuwe West-Indische Gids/New West Indian Guide* 63, nos. 3 and 4 (1988): 103–28; Gwendolyn Mikell, *Cocoa and Chaos in Ghana,* n. 36; and Leith Mullings, *Therapy, Ideology, and Social Change* (Berkeley: University of California Press, 1984). These studies are representative of historicized political economy and class analyses of households, informal economic activities, changes in kinship and stratification, and indigenous psychotherapy. For more humanistic, reflexive, interpretive approaches to intellectual history, life stories, and the performance of ethnographic scripts, see A. Lynn Bolles, "African-American Soul Force: Dance, Music and Vera Mae Green," *Sage* 3, no. 2 (1986): 32–34, and *Without Them, We Wouldn't Have Survived: Women Trade Union Leaders of the Commonwealth Caribbean* (Washington, D.C.: Howard University Press,

forthcoming); Faye V. Harrison, "'Three Women, One Struggle': Anthropology, Performance, and Pedagogy," *Transforming Anthropology* 1, no. 1 (1990): 1–9.

34. See Zora Neale Hurston, *Mules and Men* (Bloomington: Indiana University Press [1935] 1978); John L. Gwaltney, *Drylongso: A Self-Portrait of Black America* (New York: Vintage Books, 1980); Betty Lou Valentine, *Hustling and Other Hard Work: Life Styles in the Ghetto* (New York: Free Press, 1978).

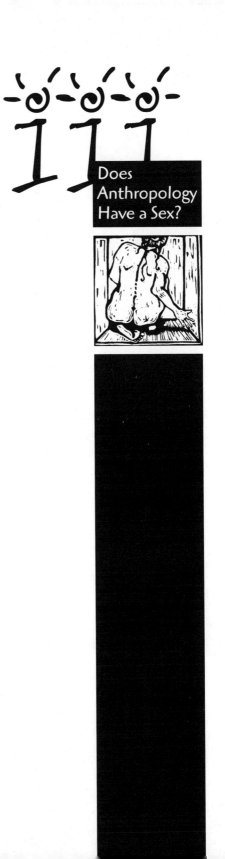

III

Does Anthropology Have a Sex?

12. The Gender of Theory

Catherine Lutz

HOW DOES gender play into the formation of the canons of anthropology? One central way is through the designation of particular works as theoretical and the masculinizing of theory. In this essay I ask how that process has worked and explore its implications for the reception of women's writing and feminist theory, with particular reference to anthropology.[1]

Why does the topic matter, given world events of the last several years? When the oil-blackened corpses of soldiers by the tens of thousands lie buried in the deserts in and around Iraq, a focus on how academics behave may simply be self-indulgent or imperial myopia. While I recognize the fact that the anthropological canon is crucial to what is taught in the university and so establishes authoritative discourse for the educated classes in this society, I believe that it is also important to look at the flaming cultural responses to Hillary Rodham Clinton, the wimp-baiting of George Bush during his tenure, and Anita Hill's televised shaming during the confirmation hearings of Clarence Thomas. The public debate over Hill and Thomas focused on whether the African American woman lied, whether her painful discourse was a fantasy. As Carole Boyce Davies asked in a talk afterward, When is a black woman given respectful attention? Not often throughout the last several centuries: certainly not as a slave, with testimony to give, but also not even when she is Yale-educated, a lawyer, conservatively dressed, politically conservative, comparatively wealthy, religious, and a professor.[2] Anita Hill's words did take center stage, but they were spotlighted with sex and race hatred.

Thus questions about gender and the anthropological canon have renewed meaning. The masculine bias of the canon exemplifies a wider process by which hegemonic discourses—especially on gender and race—are established; how "uncomfortable information" is erased from public view; how subaltern groups and their ideas are erroneously said to have achieved hegemony (often through some kind of "affirmative action") or are locked in rooms of their own. These are the processes by which the definition of such things as "the need to go to war" or "who is credible" are retained by the powerful. They have a direct bearing on how feminism(s) can be most effective, or on how the suppressing, ignoring, or "managing" of feminism in the academy and society at large can be countered.

I raise several queries about the anthropological canon and gender, each of them organized around the general question, How does a piece of anthropological writing become established as more or less valuable, and what does gender have to do with it? The explanation most to hand for the limp reception of women's writing is somewhat distinct from that for interpreting the reception of feminism(s). For at least a partial explanation of the erasure of women's writing in general, one can point to two decades of feminist research indicating that women's words, work, and selves in U.S. society have been undervalued, judged less competent, less rational, and more emotional.[3] Even when a traditional division of labor is destabilized, as it has been to some degree since World War II (as, for example, with college teaching), the perceived value, distribution, and compensation for a particular job depends more on the sex, race, and age of the worker than on the intrinsic characteristics of the job itself.[4] In domains of high culture, the process of devaluation has been well documented. Deborah Bright describes how it is overwhelmingly men who have been canonized as the geniuses of landscape photography—both the heroes of its practice and the leaders of its theorization—and she shows the effects of this masculinization on the discourse of photographic criticism. Gaye Tuchman describes the expulsion of nineteenth-century British women from the novel writing they dominated before 1840.[5] That process involved not only edging women out of possibilities for publishing their writing, but reevaluating the novel: when women wrote them, they were low-prestige cultural items. Once men dominated the field, the novel was lauded as high art.

In anthropology the same process has been identified through an examination of the canonical fate of the writing of individual women, from Ruth Benedict to Zora Neale Hurston to Elsie Clews Parson, and through general observations about the construction and marginalization of a woman's tradition of ethnographic writing.[6] Deborah Gordon has provided insights into one way the canon is formed, in anthropology as elsewhere: that is, through the creation of a distinction between art that experiments with and comments on its own form and all other types of art; the formation of a hierarchy of these two types; and the masculinization of the former,

CATHERINE LUTZ

more valorized avant-garde.[7] Women's writing in general is less cited and feminist work is marginalized, as when the *Annual Review of Anthropology* from its inception through the late 1980s failed to include more than a single review of the large corpus of critical anthropological work on gender.[8]

Feminism is obviously not simply or uniformly excluded from all academic arenas beyond women's studies. The situation in literary fields is quite different from that in political science, for example. In some fields there is still complete or nearly complete erasure;[9] in others, nodding or relativistic tolerance (with all of relativism's friendly hostility played out); and in others, anxious reworking and deflation of feminism's claims, as in the relations between feminism and postmodernism. Growing markets for feminist literature have certainly had an effect on valorizing some feminist work, as one can see in looking at recent revisions at some universities of general-education college curricula to include feminist and antiracist scholarship. The dynamics of such incorporation are complex, however. An example is the required undergraduate introductory course in social science at the University of Chicago, in which the central works presented in the "theory" semester in 1990–1991 were by Freud, Weber, Marx, Woolf, and Baldwin. The ultimately most important question is what students make of this mix of thinkers—two of whom they will soon find are not "really" social scientists, even if important intellectuals.

In general, however, the exclusion of feminism from the central canon can be explained by its identification of the politics in scholarship. It directly challenges nonfeminist scholarship rather than defining itself as simply another specialty working alongside colleagues in a neatly partitioned division of labor over the social body. For those who are committed to a view of feminism as offering more adequate accounts of the world than do prefeminist accounts, the exclusion continually surprises and has little redeeming value. From another perspective, the exclusion of feminism is predictable and perhaps necessary—required as proof of the challenge feminism can pose to business as usual in the academy and elsewhere and to retain a marginal position from which to view the center.[10]

The feminist margins have their own margins, however, with white feminism privileged over Third World feminism within the academy. When theory is gendered, then, it is simultaneously raced and classed.[11] There are historical processes by which subordinate groups are allowed access to writing and through which the general or theoretical value of their writing is assessed. Writing by white women or by women of privileged class backgrounds is no doubt read more positively by much of its audience, though particularly by people of their own race and class. What can be said about the process of theory gendering below, then, can be seen as an unstable matrix that can be used by or on behalf of white women in containing the challenge of scholarship by women of color.

Theory has acquired a gender insofar as it is more frequently associated with male writing, with women's writing more often seen as description, data, case, personal, or, as in the case of feminism, "merely" setting the record straight. To document the existence of the process of theory gendering, one can begin with a group of

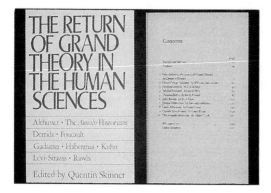

The cover and table of contents of Quentin Skinner's The Return of Grand Theory in the Human Sciences. (Photograph reprinted with the permission of Cambridge University Press)

books published in the past decade. Quentin Skinner's *The Return of Grand Theory in the Human Sciences* produces a kind of "Top Nine" list which is exclusively male and nonfeminist. There is also the hyper-hierarchical title (and unselfconscious subtitle) of *Metatheory in Social Science: Pluralisms and Subjectivities,* edited by Donald Fiske and Richard A. Shweder. While the editors claim to be examining a broad range of theoretical issues in the philosophy of science and producing a book "intended for conceptualizers in social science," eighteen of the nineteen chapters are written by men, and none of them deals with feminism or antiracist scholarship. Take *Culture and Society: Contemporary Debates,* by Jeffrey Alexander and Steven Seidman, a book whose Cambridge University Press blurb says "brings together *the* major statements by *the* leading contemporary scholars of cultural analysis on the relation between [*the* two major concepts of social science] culture and society" (emphasis added). These statements run from Adorno and Bellah through Thompson and Willis to include, in the end, twenty-six men and three women. Nineteen of the contemporary theorists whose names appear in the chapter titles of Jonathan Turner's influential fifth edition of *The Structure of Sociological Theory* are men, and feminism is missing in action. Robert Ulin's book *Understanding Cultures: Perspectives in Anthropology and Social Theory,* takes on very general questions of "epistemological problems related to understanding other cultures." In surveying work that contributes to this, Ulin comes up with a 211-item citation list, eleven of which are by women (and only two of whom appear to be feminist).[12] One might also look at syllabi in graduate orientation seminars on social theory in anthropology or in any of the social sciences for evidence of this same process.

So, what is theory? Something called "theory" is intentionally or unintentionally signaled to and consciously or unconsciously picked up by readers *as* theory. The first way this is done is through straightforward self-labeling, as in Pierre Bourdieu's *Outline of a Theory of Practice.*[13] This can have an immediate impact on how weighty a work is taken to be, as exemplified by the academic psychologist who told me that she noticed her work received much more serious attention from her peers after she inserted the word "theory" in an article title, even though that article simply continued arguments she had made in earlier papers.

The second signal is the one that allows readers to imagine that the writing describes a wide variety of instances rather than a single case. As Dorothy Smith pointed out nearly twenty years ago, theory can also be identified as a process in which statements are denuded of their origin in a writer and his or her experience or are stripped of their reference to a concrete phenomenal world of specific contexts and history.[14] Theory is generally and informally seen as consisting of more rather than less abstract statements, widely relevant or universalistic or "deeper" statements of more ultimate or timeless value than others,[15] and as statements that require more rather than less substantial intellectual "gifts" to compose. This quality enhances the authority of the speaker while, conversely, the "perception of authority diminishes in direct proportion to the speaker's proximity."[16] Thus the move to theory is involved in historical struggles over the authority of women and of minorities of both sexes to speak:[17] the seeming antihistorical character of theory is a politically conservative move, and so one more likely to be produced by or perceived in the powerful.[18]

These signals also include more abstract language, and often more academic jargon. Trinh Minh-ha notes that this kind of writing "to many men's ears . . . is synonymous with 'profound,' 'serious,' 'substantial,' 'scientific,' 'consequential,' 'thoughtful,' or 'thought-engaging.'"[19] Theory is often seen as more difficult reading than ethnography, although difficulty is an ideological notion, as has been pointed out:[20] my husband thinks childcare is difficult when he does it, easy when I do it; the work of electricians or nurses is treated as less difficult than that of administrators or doctors. The subtly critical humor in a Roslyn Chast cartoon depends on play with that notion. But the argument is also sometimes made that theory's difficulty is inevitable if it articulates thoughts not spoken before, taken for granted, or hegemonic. Theory becomes almost synonymous with the idea, the original thought. Difficult theory can have the effect—intended or unintended—of saying to some readers: "This is not for you," so it sorts readers into the privileged and the lowbrow. Through a kind of halo effect, the persevering reader of theory is elevated as she or he is shown to have the "right stuff" to understand what is being said.

One could argue that the difficulty of theory is a simple outcome of growth in the division of labor, a process that produces the specialized, technical languages of many groups of workers, including the mental workers in ever more specialized intellectual niches. Even if this were all that was at work, however, theory's maleness would still draw certain terms into the theoretical corral and make their specialized nature more imposing, difficult, and hyperrational. The difficulty of hegemony or intertextuality comes from the gendered and raced history of their users; without rejecting those terms we can nonetheless note how their masculinization as theory gives them more social force than does specialized language such as "participant observation" or "womanist," whose writers or purposes are usually seen as not theoretically oriented.

Theory's abstractness requires or creates a more active reader. Like poetry, it allows for imagination. Like a Rorschach, it allows for projection. Theoretical writing requires a reader who will take the abstract skeleton or the opaque jargon of its prose and fill it in with his/her own understanding and cases. Stated more negatively, theoretical writing is like a capitalist enterprise: it exploits or appropriates the labor of readers, who are made to do the work of instantiating, of making "real" sense of the theoretical prose. A reader may often imagine that the writer has written or said or implied all of the ideas that her or his reading has actually provided. Like the worker who does not recognize the source of the commodity's value, the reader then fetishizes the theoretical writer.[21]

Another signal for theory appears to be certain styles of citation to others' work. Theorists cite other theorists and appear to tend to cite more deeply into the academic past and to cite even more males than does the average piece of academic writing (as in the Ulin example above). Theoretical writing often has fewer citations, this dearth being a sign of the work's originality, its creativity. It can also be a sign of a patriline in the making or, rather, of the text's claim to motherless origins. Sandra Gilbert and Susan Gubar describe the more general psychodynamic process involved in masculinity and writing:

> *In patriarchal Western culture, therefore, the text's author is a father, a progenitor, a procreator, an aesthetic patriarch whose pen is an instrument of generative power like his penis. More, his pen's power, like his penis's power, is not*

just the ability to generate life but the power to create a posterity to which he lays claim . . . as the author of an enduring text the writer engages the attention of the future in exactly the same way that a king (or father) "owns" the homage of the present.[22]

Theoretical writing seems to involve issues of anxious paternity even more sharply than does writing in general. Not only does the absent citation stand as a symptom, but those theories spawn patrilineal offspring that are then posited to belong more to their father theory than to their mother data.

Finally, the signal of theory is sometimes given not so much by these more or less formal devices but via a text's positioning itself at a "choke" or origin point for a biological, social, or developmental process. As Margaret Conkey and Sarah Williams have so clearly described for human evolution stories, the person who specifies the nature of the beginning point of this process provides the limits and/or the skeleton for all accounts by others of later points in the process.[23] So, too, in psychology, researchers on infancy have competed to narrate the baby's capacities at earlier and earlier points in development.[24] That field and its canon are predominantly male (in contrast with research at later stages of child development) and are high-status fields within psychology.[25] The general relevance that this kind of work is thought to have, then, gives a kind of theoretical patina to it even if, on other grounds, it might be seen as more straightforwardly descriptive or interpretive.

How is theory evaluated relative to other kinds of writing, beyond the factors already alluded to? While there are certainly differences by academic discipline,[26] one can say generally that theory, like great art, builds on "the ideal of the artist, the narrative of genius, the cult of celebrity,"[27] all of which have been masculinized in this culture, particularly since the Romantic period.[28] Like art, theory draws from the world but is not of the world. Just as the pen and the paintbrush have been taken throughout Western history to stand for the phallus,[29] writing theory is celebrated as an art (as opposed to the craft of ethnography) and coded masculine.

To illustrate the connections between gender and genius, we can take the example of *Structures of Social Life,* by Alan Fiske. Its Free Press flyer included the following phenomenal recommendations from other academics: "he has synthesized almost everything worth synthesizing in social theory"; "comparable in scope to Marx and Freud"; "one of the most important scholarly books to be published in this decade"; "breathtaking in its comparative reach."[30] While the book may in fact represent a very important effort, the blurbs' evocation of genius is the same as that found in the notion of "grand" theory as well as in the identification of theories by the individual who wrote them, not by the movement or social context that spawned them or the subject on which they focus (see figure p. 252).

The association of genius with release from social strictures—with social license—also helps to determine the masculinity of theory. While the license allowed the professor/theoretician seems not to be of the same order as that allocated to the artist, there are the legends of Louis Althusser's criminality and of Erving Goffman's social eccentricity. If genius requires such rule-breaking, women will rarely be geniuses in a world abounding with narratives of the goodness of the domesticated (and thereby) conventional woman and of the culpability of the victims of battering, rape, or sexual harassment, women whose blame is often accomplished by portraying them as unconventional, most notably through promiscuity or failure to achieve middle-class, heterosexual, or white status. The converse of the genius of the theoretician is the silencing of the nontheoretician—the use of this linguistic convention to establish rules of listening.[31]

Theory can confront, however, cultural mythologizing of direct experience, something that plays out in anthropology through the valorization of fieldwork.[32] Among other things, that experience is seen as resistant to the dehumanization of bureaucratic, scientific, and academic routinizations to which the office worker/ theoretician is more prone. The resulting tension between the demands and value of experience and abstraction/reflection can reverberate with the tension of gender politics. The relationship between data and theory can shift as needed, Judith Okely pointed out two decades ago, and in the following way: "Where the specific is described as 'hard', scientific and objective fact, it's opposite is 'airy fairy' speculation, emotional and soft—woman's domain. In another context where fact is equated with 'vulgar empiricism' and its opposite is theory, women are seen to be the fact gatherers and men the theoreticians. . . . Whatever 'female thought' may be, it is the one which is undervalued."[33] When the question of theory is not at issue, fieldwork can be coded masculine, heroic, adventurous.[34]

Joan Gero has laid this out in archeology, called the "cowboy science" when a masculine tackling of experience is the focus. Women who do fieldwork are more often described as having done a good job of meticulously collecting material and as having tolerance for repetitive, boring work that someone else would process into theory.[35] So, too, ethnography contrasted with theory becomes descriptive science, and the plodding labor of fieldwork is necessary, even crucial. It often appears, however, that this labor is acknowledged in the same way that childcare is acknowledged—as crucial for the reproduction of society but not as particularly challenging. Even where the data/theory distinction is questioned, a hierarchy is often preserved in which concrete, specific ideas are "led" or more constrained by larger, more abstract ones.[36]

Theory can also acquire a gender through the relationship between its contents and the contexts of its production and consumption.[37] An example is found in some forms of postmodern cultural analysis. Some of the main contrasts between modernism and postmodernism as historical ideal types correspond to ideologies of gender differences (see Table 1). The association of postmodernism with consumer culture, for example, is paralleled by the popular culture assignment of the task of shopping to women (as well as its denigration, as when Blondie, Lucy, and the "Shop Till You Drop" T-shirt wearer announce their shopping behavior's comic-shameful character). Several feminist observers have noted the implicit association drawn between mass culture and the feminine, with the two linked through the

CATHERINE LUTZ

TABLE 1—*Postmodernity and gender ideologies*

Modernity	Postmodernity
Gender as Usual	
Production (man as breadwinner)	Consumption (woman as shopper)
Sharp self-other distinction (man as individualist)	Absence of self (woman as lacking ego boundaries)
Depth models (man as deep thinker, inner directed)	Surface as all there is (woman as appearance, fashion oriented, outer directed, shallow)
Universalistic (man as operating with universal principles of market)	Particularistic (woman as operating with particularistic criteria of family)
Heyday of positive science (man as objective)	Critique of science, use of reflexivity (woman as subjective)
Some wholeness (man as whole person)	Fragments (woman as a face, a breast, a womb)
Cultural hierarchy maintained (men as involved in dominance displays, competition, power brokering) (gender hierarchy intact)	Cultural hierarchy collapsed (women as noncompetitive, not interested in power) (gender hierarchy erased; equality achieved, affirmative action no longer needed)
Gender Reversals	
Mood of alienation and angst (woman as emotional)	Absence of feeling (man as emotionless, stoic)
Neurosis as model (woman's emotional disease)	Schizophrenia as model (man's cognitive disease)
Essentialism tolerated (woman as nature/born)	Essentialism rejected (man as culture/constructed)

ascription to both of passivity, emotionality, and mystifying qualities.[38] These analogies between postmodernism and the female and between modernism and the male are so numerous that one might say that postmodernism is a woman. However, given the dominance of men among its explicit or canonized practitioners, this would have to be amended to say that the postmodern is a man in woman's clothing.

In fact, the problem looks like one analyzed elsewhere in which a masculine identification with the feminine is an underlying psychocultural dynamic producing a discourse. Tania Modleski posits it in Alfred Hitchcock's films, in which men are often both threatened and fascinated by the notion of their own and women's bisexuality.[39] The violence done or threatened to women in these films—from Janet

Leigh in the *Psycho* shower scene to Grace Kelly in *Rear Window*—is the price women pay for this male ambivalence. Modleski finds in Hitchcock's movies "an oscillation between attraction to the feminine and a corresponding need to erect, sometimes brutally, a barrier to the femininity which is perceived as all-absorbing."[40] Andreas Huyssen has identified the same process in the modern novel, as when Flaubert says of his most famous heroine, "Madame Bovary, c'est moi." This identification is likely in the novelist who is situated in the "increasingly marginal position of literature and the arts in a society in which masculinity is identified with action, enterprise, and progress."[41]

So, too, with postmodernism in anthropology, a movement which, in its association with literary criticism and its antiscience reputation, is itself associated with the female. This is in contrast with the thoroughgoing masculine self-presentation of someone like Napoleon Chagnon, intrepid scientist among "the fierce people," whose account of fieldwork stresses his exploits in heroic, dangerous pursuit of the facts.[42] What Huyssen says of the novelist can also apply here, namely, that "the imaginary femininity of male authors, which often grounds their oppositional stance vis-à-vis bourgeois society, can easily go hand in hand with the exclusion of real women from the [literary] enterprise."[43] While the feminine attributes of the postmodern may appear to be simply a function of the way the postmodern, as oppositional practice, is peripheralized, one has to question why postmodernist male writers have not taken feminist writing seriously or acknowledged its role in the rise of postpositivist ethnography and theory.[44]

An example of this process is a layout in the *New York Times Magazine* in 1991. An article on the Modern Language Association conference, it includes photographs of several participants, including someone most people would identify as a postmodernist—Andrew Ross—and someone clearly identified as a feminist—Catharine Stimpson. Ross's photo, outsized and colorful (he wears an orange jacket), contrasts with the small, serious black-and-white rendition of Stimpson. Attention is drawn both in the photographs and in the text to his clothes and style, not to hers. The covertly feminine male looms large here, as he does in more academic journals.

Another theory with a special relationship to gender is, of course, feminism. Feminist theory is valued and conceptualized in different ways by its writers and main audiences. Much feminist reflection on theory has shown a skepticism about its roles, a willingness to continually press against the dualism of theory and practice, a long commitment to the notion of the intimate connection of the personal and the political, the local and the abstract, and a questioning of the universal voice behind the bird's-eye view of theory.[45] In some quarters there is a fundamental suspicion of theory and its potential effects, even as theory is seen as allowing for the imagination of connections between aspects of the world otherwise ideologically invisible.[46] Its negative effects have included the appropriation by the more privileged of theoretical contributions by lesbians and women of color and the reassignment of the latter to the job of writing "experience."[47] Katie King has concluded

CATHERINE LUTZ

that these exclusionary effects in feminism are associated with theory's increasing restriction to the "rationalist essay," the reification of theorizing (that is, all of the processes of knowledge production) into the product called theory, and the contribution of marketing pressures in feminist academic publishing. The result, according to King, is that "this term 'theory' has to be bracketed in feminist thinking now, used ironically and proudly, shamefacedly and shrewdly, gloriously and preposterously, if it is really to convey anything like what feminists are doing, in the academy and elsewhere."[48]

Outside feminist circles, feminist theory is often represented as a marked and peripheral form of the genre rather than as theory itself, much less grand theory. Judith Goldstein has made the telling point that feminism is seen—in the wider context of academia—as at best a kind of middle or middling art, taking a place in a hierarchy of cultural objects analogous to that of photography in relation to oil painting on the upper hand and velvet paintings on the lower. In Goldstein's words, "It is a middle theory, lacking the virile authenticity of the low and the aristocratic cachet of the high [whose ground in the academy she notes much postmodernism has resolutely taken up]. It is, therefore, unforgivably middlebrow, a theory associated with women, and (often) with the practical concerns of political engagement."[49] Nancy Miller gives an example of feminism's effacement from the theoretical realm altogether: a recent ad for an academic job in literature asked for applications from a "feminist or a theorist."[50]

To the extent that women are seen as less intelligent, their writing will be seen as less theoretical, no matter how they write. Evidence for the existence of this phenomenon in all areas of sociocultural life is overwhelming. Women's discourse equals description (or complaint); male discourse equals theory, the covering law. The words of women do not have the same weight as the words of men, and theoretical words are especially heavy.

Men and women may also be more or less willing or able to write in a way that is self-consciously or conventionally recognizable as theoretical. Most graduate students learn early on that they must learn to speak the language of theory, to transform personal issues into theoretical forms, to erase authorship and context. Those who come into the institution defined as a special kind of person ("a woman"; "a minority student") rather than as a universal thinker may not either cozy up to or be invited to this style as quickly. The feminist critique of traditional ideologies of science has taken on this issue squarely: by definition, theory has traditionally allowed for the erasure of the subject—both the subject who writes and the human subjects who are written about. It allows the theorist to avoid the roots of statements in real-world encounters, to speak for or appear to speak for the whole, and to speak from a transcendental vantage point.[51] These potential differences in authorial intent are less a part of my concern here, however, than are the gender relations that organize both the writing and the reading of women's work. As Dorothy Smith suggests, "The text [can be] analyzed for its characteristically textual form of participation in social relations. . . . The text enters the laboratory, so to speak, carrying the threads and shreds of the relations it is organized by and organizes," rather than simply trailing the psychology of its writer.[52]

Differences in the kinds of experiences graduate students have include the problems women encounter with some professors and peers in having their writing taken as seriously as their breasts, as well as, in some cases, their skin color or their sexual orientation. The gender of theory can also be seen as resulting from the subsumption of women's writing to the cultural demands of American femininity, which include the injunction to be concerned with how we appear before others. Women may then experience pressure to have beautiful writing, if not beautiful bodies. Are we enjoined to work on our writing as we work on our bodies and our fashions? To see our style as deficient and to treat our thinking and writing as we treat our beauty secrets,[53] even as we defensively raise the issue of Ruth Benedict's lyricism and Zora Neale Hurston's avante-garde style? Even as I find liberation in writing precisely because I send a self out into the world without a body to be measured and assessed, I am accompanied to my keyboard by the patriarchal gaze. The underlying femininity of much postmodern discourse hinges on just this: the fashion styling of the new ethnographic text. Is the power of Clifford's infamous words in *Writing Culture* their suggestion that women ethnographers are, like women everywhere, not feminine enough? Like the editorial voice of a woman's magazine, he says, "Your (writing) style does not measure up." Women's dilemma is to see the contradiction of our choices (to work or not on narrative styling because or in spite of its evocation of this injunction) but to choose nonetheless while trying to imagine and enact other possibilities.

The control of theory by men has important implications for women's obtaining and keeping academic jobs. In a recent case at an elite university that echoed many others, a woman's very strong claim for tenure was denied. One member of the department that rejected her told me that her work was fantastic, wonderful, voluminous, but, he said, ventriloquizing to his colleagues, "Some people wondered if it were theoretical enough." The valorization of a particular genre of writing as the top layer in a hierarchy of kinds of discourse has also marginalized work by gay and minority scholars and jeopardized their tenure at universities.

The struggle over the nature and value of theory is just one example of the more general process of group struggle via the canons of taste in cultural objects.[54] While taste struggles between class factions in American history have been most extensively documented, African American writers have explored the historical processes by which their community's cultural productions have been misplaced.[55] Barbara Christian notes that "for an entire century Afro-American writers . . . have protested the literary hierarchy of dominance which declares . . . when literature is great." The theoretical insights often attributed to "New Western philosophers" have roots in this African American tradition but, she says, "since we are a discredited people . . . our creations are also discredited."[56] The dismissal of a variety of cultural objects through their feminization has also been traced in many institutions, as when a pundit in the 1880s wagged that the rapidly growing magazines

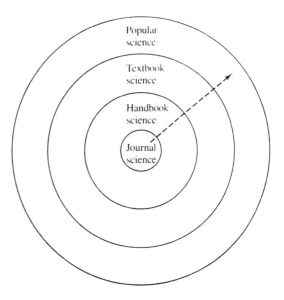

Fleck's concentric model of the development and diffusion of a scientific "fact," from Angela M. O'Rand, "Scientific Thought Style and the Construction of Gender Inequality," in Jean F. O'Barr, ed., Women and a New Academy, *© 1989. (Reprinted by permission of The University of Wisconsin Press)*

Popular science

Textbook science

Handbook science

Journal science

(appealing both to newly literate women and to a new middle class) were "ready to menstruate."

The influx of women into the academy and the perceived influx of men and women of color creates a space for the emergence of the middlebrow between the white male theorist and the uneducated masses who are his students. This is contested by the feminist and antiracist scholars whose work is placed in that category (and politically contained) by virtue of being posed as pragmatic/political/not (grand) theory. The changing demographics of the university and the publishing industry have been accompanied by a heightening of the debates and stakes involved in writing that is perceived as theoretical. One effect of the struggle for institutional space and respect may have been an inflation of theory's value even as questions are raised about the dualisms and individualism on which its existence is based.[57]

The importance and source of the masculinization of theory can be rooted in its ideological control function in society at large. This was suggested to me by the figure in Angela O'Rand's acute analysis of the role of scientific research on sex differences in cognitive abilities.[58] O'Rand shows how theoretical presuppositions, drawn from wider cultural ideologies, are continually reconfirmed through science and funneled back, with new authority, through the domains shown in the model. The central circle can be subdivided into theoretical and other academic literature, with theory at the core, or at the top of a hierarchy that extends "down to" schoolchildren's textbooks and to what Oprah Winfrey's and Phil Donahue's audiences say they believe. Theory is then clearly about the politics of all culture, not just academic culture.

Michele Wallace suggests that a central question ought not to be simply how a text signifies gender or race but what the impact of that text is, given its gendered and raced reading.[59] This means we need to know not only what floats up in a hierarchy of writing to be canonized, but what floats out of the academy via undergraduates and via space allocated to certain scholars' ideas by the mass media. To better understand how women's writing and feminism are read by their several audiences is to begin to write and intervene more effectively in cultural discussions, including the one around Anita Hill's harassment and around the Gulf War, for which gender was a central point of home-front mobilization. How we theorize details such as these is important, and we have to figure out how to be heard doing it here and far beyond the rooms of academia where our papers began.

Notes

I would like to thank Ruth Behar, Denise Coker, Carole Boyce Davies, Phoebe Ellsworth, Deborah Gordon, Faye Harrison, John MacAloon, and Marianna Torgovnick, as well as all of the participants in the "Women Writing Culture" conference, for help in thinking through gaps and problems in earlier drafts of this paper, some of which their good advice may not have erased.

1. I understand *canon* to refer not just to published work that receives special treatment and recognition in other published work but to everyday speech acts (such as lectures to peers and students, workplace discussions, and so on) in which parallel processes of evaluation occur.

2. See Nell Irvin Painter, "Hill, Thomas, and the Use of Racial Stereotype," in *Race-ing Justice, En-gendering Power: Essays on Anita Hill, Clarence Thomas, and the Construction of Social Reality,* ed. Toni Morrison (New York: Pantheon, 1992).

3. For a summary, see Bernice Lott, "The Devaluation of Women's Competence," *Journal of Social Issues* 41, no. 4 (1985): 43–60. No one, female or male, transcends these cultural notions. There is, however, a more than casual interest in the culture at large with the question of women's prejudice against women (see Dale Spender, *The Writing or the Sex? or Why You Don't Have to Read Women's Writing to Know It's No Good* [New York: Pergamon Press, 1990], 13), which seems to arise more from a need to absolve men by finding women equally guilty than from a need to understand how systems of inequality are reproduced through the actions of individuals of both sexes.

4. Ann Game and Rosemary Pringle, *Gender at Work* (Sydney: George Allen & Unwin, 1983).

5. Deborah Bright, "Of Mother Nature and Marlboro Men: An Inquiry into the Cultural Meanings of Landscape Photography," in *The Contest of Meaning: Critical Histories of Photography,* ed. Richard Bolton (Cambridge, Mass.: M.I.T. Press, 1990), 125–42; Gaye Tuchman with Nina E. Fortin, *Edging Women Out: Victorian Novelists, Publishers, and Social Change* (New Haven, Conn.: Yale University Press, 1989). See also Gladys Engel Lang and Kurt Lang, *Etched in Memory: The Building and Survival of Artistic Reputation* (Chapel Hill: University of North Carolina Press, 1990), on the effect of gender on the reputations of three hundred British and American printmakers during the late nineteenth and early twentieth centuries.

6. Barbara Babcock, "'Not in the Absolute Singular': Rereading Ruth Benedict," this volume; Deborah Gordon, "The Politics of Ethnographic Authority: Race and Writing in the Ethnography of Margaret Mead and Zora Neale Hurston," in *Modernist Anthropology: From Fieldwork to Text,* ed. Marc Manganaro (Princeton, N.J.: Princeton University Press, 1990); Lila Abu-Lughod, "Can There Be a Feminist Ethnography?" *Women and Performance* 9, no. 1 (1990): 1–24; Kamala Visweswaran, "Defining Feminist Ethnography," *Inscriptions* 3/4 (1988): 29–57.

CATHERINE LUTZ

7. Deborah Gordon, "Writing Culture, Writing Feminism: The Poetics and Politics of Experimental Ethnography," *Inscriptions* 3/4 (1988): 7–24.

8. Catherine Lutz, "The Erasure of Women's Writing in Sociocultural Anthropology," *American Ethnologist* 17 (1990): 611–25. The erasure or marginality of feminism within the academy has been often noted and theorized: see Gayatri Chakravorty Spivak, *In Other Worlds: Essays in Cultural Politics* (New York: Routledge, 1988); Sandra Morgen, "Gender and Anthropology: Introductory Essay," in her *Gender and Anthropology: Critical Reviews for Research and Teaching* (Washington, D.C.: American Anthropological Association, 1988); Kathryn B. Ward and Linda Grant, "The Feminist Critique and a Decade of Published Research in Sociology Journals," *Sociological Quarterly* 26 (1985): 139–57. The tensions between feminism and anthropology have also been usefully explored: see Marilyn Strathern, "An Awkward Relationship: The Case of Feminism and Anthropology," *Signs* 12 (1987): 276–92; and Abu-Lughod, "Can There Be a Feminist Ethnography?"

9. This process occurs for women as well, according to Abu-Lughod ("Can There Be a Feminist Ethnography?"), with their anxieties about the cultural associations of the female (as well as the risks they run of being ignored or discounted) leading to some avoidance of the "woman's tradition."

10. bell hooks, *Yearning* (Boston: South End Press, 1990). In Spivak's more complex deconstructive formulation, "pointing attention to a feminist marginality [is an attempt], not to win the center for ourselves, but to point at the irreducibility of the margin in all explanations. That would not merely reverse but displace the distinction between margin and center" (*In Other Worlds*, 107).

11. Norma Alarcon, "The Theoretical Subject(s) of *This Bridge Called My Back* and Anglo-American Feminism," in *Making Face, Making Soul: Haciendo Caras*, ed. Gloria Anzaldúa (San Francisco: Aunt Lute Foundation, 1990); Maxine Baca Zinn, Lynn Weber Cannon, Elizabeth Higginbotham, and Bonnie Thornton Dill, "The Cost of Exclusionary Practices in Women's Studies," *Signs* 11 (1986): 296–303. See also Harrison, this volume.

12. Quentin Skinner, *The Return of Grand Theory in the Human Sciences* (Cambridge, England: Cambridge University Press, 1985); Donald Fiske and Richard A. Shweder, eds., *Metatheory in Social Science: Pluralisms and Subjectivities* (Chicago: University of Chicago Press, 1986); Jeffrey Alexander and Steven Seidman, *Culture and Society: Contemporary Debates* (Cambridge, England: Cambridge University Press, 1990); Jonathan Turner, *The Structure of Sociological Theory*, 5th ed. (Belmont, Calif.: Wadsworth, 1991); Robert C. Ulin, *Understanding Cultures: Perspectives in Anthropology and Social Theory* (Austin: University of Texas Press, 1984), xi.

13. Pierre Bourdieu, *Outline of a Theory of Practice* (Cambridge, England: Cambridge University Press, 1977).

14. Dorothy Smith, "Theorizing as Ideology," in *Ethnomethodology: Selected Readings*, ed. Roy Turner (Harmondsworth, England: Penguin Books, 1974).

15. Nicolas Thomas, "Against Ethnography," *Cultural Anthropology* 6 (1991): 306–22.

16. Nancy K. Miller, *Getting Personal: Feminist Occasions and Other Autobiographical Acts* (New York: Routledge, 1991), 66.

17. Chela Sandoval, "U.S. Third World Feminism: The Theory and Method of Oppositional Consciousness in the Postmodern World," *Genders* 10 (1991).

18. Richard Ohmann, *The Politics of Letters* (Middletown, Conn.: Wesleyan University Press, 1987).

19. Trinh T. Minh-ha, *Woman, Native, Other: Writing Postcoloniality and Feminism* (Bloomington: Indiana University Press, 1989), 41. She makes the point that to other ears (which she, but not I, would characterize simply as female), this kind of writing sounds "'mascu-

line,' 'hermetic,' 'elitist,' and 'specialized,' therefore 'neutral,' 'impersonal,' 'purely mental,' 'unfeeling,' 'disengaging,' and—last but not least 'abstract'" (41).

20. Colin MacCabe, foreword to Spivak, *In Other Worlds.*

21. While all reading requires an active reader, and while I know of no studies of readers' actual interpretive work along these lines, it seems plausible that theory requires more of readers' imaginative work for the reasons I cite below. Reading groups in the humanities and social sciences that I am familiar with—premised on the value of laboring collectively to read challenging material—often focus on work or on parts of work considered theoretical.

22. Sandra Gilbert and Susan M. Gubar, *The Madwoman in the Attic: The Woman Writer and the Nineteenth-Century Literary Imagination* (New Haven, Conn.: Yale University Press, 1979), 6–7.

23. Margaret Conkey with Sarah Williams, "Original Narratives: The Political Economy of Gender in Archaeology," in *Gender at the Crossroads of Knowledge: Feminist Anthropology in the Postmodern Era,* ed. Micaela di Leonardo (Berkeley: University of California Press, 1991).

24. William Kessen, *The Rise and Fall of Development* (Worcester, Mass.: Clark University Press, 1990).

25. Women predominate in the study of child development at later ages, but that work is taken less seriously than is infancy research. Women's concentration in this area is consonant with their allotted domestic role of childcare, and they are presumably then expected to defer in some sense in their narratives to the infancy story already told by men.

26. The theoretician is valued over the empiricist everywhere from physics (see Sharon Traweek, *Beamtimes and Lifetimes: The World of High Energy Physicists* [Cambridge, Mass.: Harvard University Press, 1988]) to the humanities, where the position of philosophy as the "Queen" of its larger domain has often been asserted. Theory has played a special role in social science, where it is valorized in a somewhat different way than it appears to be in the humanities. There is a kind of mechanical rather than transcendental role assigned to theory: on the one hand, it should be a simple generator of research ideas and practices; on the other, it competes with "methodology," at times nearly deified, which is taken as key to social science's aspirations to scientific status.

27. Richard Bolton, "In the American East: Richard Avedon Incorporated," in his *Contest of Meaning,* 268; see also Griselda Pollock, "Artists Mythologies and Media: Genius, Madness and Art History," *Screen* 21, no. 3 (1980): 57.

28. Christine Battersby, *Gender and Genius: Towards a Feminist Aesthetics* (Bloomington: Indiana University Press, 1989). They are also whitened. With the exception of certain kinds of "popular" arts and celebrity, art, writing, and theory are treated as white racial patrimony; cf. hooks, *Yearning;* Barbara Christian, "The Race for Theory," *Cultural Critique* 6 (1987): 51–63.

29. Gilbert and Gubar, *Madwoman in the Attic;* Linda Nochlin, "Why Have There Been No Great Women Artists?" in her *Women, Art and Power and Other Essays* (New York: Harper and Row, [1971] 1992).

30. Alan Page Fiske, *Structures of Social Life: The Four Elementary Forms of Human Relations* (New York: Free Press, 1991). Fiske does not synthesize any of the work on gender that has been produced in the last two decades.

31. Alarcon, "Theoretical Subject(s)."

32. John Carlos Rowe, "Eye-witness: Documentary Styles in the American Representations of Vietnam," *Cultural Critique* 3 (1986): 126–50.

33. Judith Okely, "The Self and Scientism," *Journal of the Anthropological Society of Oxford* 6 (1975): 174.

34. See also Joan Gero, "Socio-Politics of Archaeology and the Woman-at-Home Ideology," *American Antiquity* 50 (1985): 342–50; and Simone de Beauvoir, *The Second Sex* (New York: Alfred A. Knopf, [1949] 1953). Bonnie Nardi, "Margaret Mead's Samoa," *Feminist Studies* 10, no. 2 (1984): 323–37, shows that Freeman's critique of Mead hinges in part on his sense of her transgression of proper gender roles: a woman daring to set out on a masculine adventure.

35. Gero, "Socio-Politics of Archaeology."

36. But see Thomas, "Against Ethnography," on ethnography's "subsumption" of theory.

37. The following three paragraphs appeared, in somewhat altered form, in "Social Contexts of Postmodern Cultural Analysis," in *Postmodern Contentions: Epochs, Politics, Space,* ed. J. P. Jones, W. Natter and T. Schatzski (New York: Guilford Publications, 1993).

38. Patrice Petro, "Mass Culture and the Feminine: The 'Place' of Television in Film Studies," *Cinema Journal* 25, no. 3 (1986): 5–21.

39. Tania Modleski, *The Women Who Knew Too Much: Hitchcock and Feminist Theory* (New York: Methuen, 1988).

40. Ibid., 42.

41. Andreas Huyssen, "Mass Culture as Woman: Modernism's Other," in *Studies in Entertainment,* ed. Tania Modleski (Bloomington: Indiana University Press, 1986), 189. Battersby's exploration in *Gender and Genius* of the history of the idea of artistic genius also demonstrates that the shifting criteria for genius have often involved a "swallowing" of those feminine qualities which have been theretofore valued.

42. Okely, "Self and Scientism."

43. Huyssen, "Mass Culture," 189.

44. James Clifford and George Marcus, *Writing Culture: The Poetics and Politics of Ethnography* (Berkeley: University of California Press, 1986); George Marcus and Michael Fischer, *Anthropology as Cultural Critique: An Experimental Moment in the Human Sciences* (Chicago: University of Chicago Press, 1986).

45. Christian, "Race for Theory"; Patricia Hill Collins, *Black Feminist Thought* (New York: Routledge, 1991); Teresa de Lauretis, "Aesthetic and Feminist Theory: Rethinking Women's Cinema," *New German Critique* 34 (1986): 154–75; Katie King, "Producing Sex, Theory, and Culture: Gay/Straight Remappings in Contemporary Feminism," in *Conflicts in Feminism,* ed. Marianna Hirsch and Evelyn Fox Keller (New York: Routledge, 1990); Miller, *Getting Personal;* Smith, "Theorizing as Ideology."

46. Christian, "Race for Theory."

47. Sandoval, "U.S. Third World Feminism"; King, "Producing Sex."

48. King, "Producing Sex," 91.

49. Judith Goldstein, "Sex, Makeup and Videotape" (paper presented at the annual meeting of the American Anthropological Association, New Orleans, 1990), 2.

50. Miller, *Getting Personal,* 41.

51. Dorothy Smith, *Texts, Facts, and Femininity: Exploring the Relations of Ruling* (London: Routledge, 1990); Lila Abu-Lughod, "Writing against Culture," in *Recapturing Anthropology,* ed. Richard Fox (Santa Fe, N. Mex.: School of American Research Press, 1991). Those, including feminists, who attempt to avoid totalizing theory do not avoid abstracting, decontextualized language or the possibility of being read as simply the newest kind of grand theorist.

52. Smith, *Texts, Facts, and Femininity,* 4.

53. See Wendy Chapkis's moving *Beauty Secrets: Women and the Politics of Appearance* (Boston: South End Press, 1986).

54. Laurence W. Levine, *Highbrow/Lowbrow: The Emergence of Cultural Hierarchy in America* (Cambridge, Mass.: Harvard University Press, 1988); Janice Radway, "The Book-of-the-Month Club and the General Reader: On the Uses of 'Serious' Fiction," *Critical Inquiry* 14 (1988): 516–38.

55. See especially Ohmann, *Politics of Letters,* on the class alliances of the theorists versus the composition teachers in English. On race, see Faye Harrison, "Introduction: An African Diaspora Perspective for Urban Anthropology," *Urban Anthropology* 17 (1988): 111–41; and Michele Wallace, *Invisibility Blues: From Pop to Theory* (New York: Verso, 1990).

56. Christian, "Race for Theory," 54. See also Faye Harrison, "Anthropology as an Agent of Transformation: Introductory Comments and Queries," in her *Decolonizing Anthropology: Moving Further toward an Anthropology for Liberation* (Washington D.C.: American Anthropological Association, 1991); and Harrison, this volume.

57. Alarcon, "Theoretical Subject(s)"; Wallace, *Invisibility Blues.*

58. Angela M. O'Rand, "Scientific Thought Style and the Construction of Gender Inequality," in *Women and a New Academy: Gender and Cultural Contexts,* ed. Jean O'Barr (Madison: University of Wisconsin Press, 1989).

59. Wallace, *Invisibility Blues,* 250.

13

Barbara
Tedlock

UNTIL RECENTLY it has been mainly women who have published experiential fieldwork materials. Where husband and wife worked in the same region, it was usually the woman who adopted the narrative mode and the man the expository one. Compare, for example, Daisy Dwyer's *Images and Self-Images: Male and Female in Morocco* with Kevin Dwyer's *Moroccan Dialogues: Anthropology in Question.* This sexual division of textual labor continues an older tradition that was established by the wives of anthropologists. Examples include D. Amaury Talbot's book on the Ibibio women of southeastern Nigeria, *Women's Mysteries of a Primitive People;* Ann Axtell Morris's two accounts of archaeological fieldwork with her husband, *Digging in Yucatan* and *Digging in the Southwest;* Mary Smith's life story of a Hausa woman, entitled *Baba of Karo;* Margery Wolf's family history, *The House of Lim;* and Elizabeth Fernea's three memoirs, *Guests of the Sheik, A View of the Nile,* and *A Street in Marrakech.* Why were these books, which were all published by trade houses rather than university presses, written, and how have they been received and read within anthropology?[1]

The archaeological writings of Ann Axtell Morris make up significant sections of her husband Earl H. Morris's technical site reports, but her best-known credited publications are her first-person accounts of fieldwork. Her first archaeological memoir, *Digging in Yucatan,* is filled with youthful enthusiasm. She introduces herself photographically as a young woman wearing a tropical helmet, necktie, jodhpurs, and knee boots and describes her writing project by saying, "I wish to tell something about those years spent in Yucatan and the things I learned there, for maybe you too would like to become one of those people who study archeology . . . following the old trails over land and sea, desert and forest, canyon and plain—a life that is hard, sometimes uncomfortable, more often laborious, but one that is far too much fun ever to be called work."[2] Her later book, *Digging in the Southwest,* which was originally published in 1933 and is still in print today, has been described as "the greatest recruiting device ever written for archaeology."[3] Unfortunately, popularizing has long been undervalued in anthropology and thus, although Ann Morris attracted a number of people into archaeology, her books are not included in the official history, or canon, of the discipline.[4]

Elizabeth Fernea, an ethnographic popularizer, characterizes herself and her rationale for writing as follows: "I am not an anthropologist. Before going to Iraq, I knew no Arabic and almost nothing of the Middle East, its religion and its culture. I have tried to set down faithfully my reactions to a new world; any inaccuracies are my own. My husband, Robert Fernea, first encouraged me to write *Guests of the Sheik.*"[5] On her initial visit to Iraq she describes spending time with the women in the harem while her husband hunts partridge with the sheik. Later she reports back to him about the harem women, but either he does not report back to her about the partridge-hunting men or she does not communicate this information to her readers. The asymmetry here is a reflection of her situation in the field, where her husband decided that she should begin visiting the women regularly and keep a journal in order to provide him with materials about women and children for his doctoral thesis. Her mandate to write was wifely, to be a helpmate to her husband.

Fernea's self-portrait in the field is also instructive. In a touching cameo, she employs the narrative figure of indirect free style, which echoes the voices of the other in dialogue with the voices of the self. By means of a kind of "dissolve," these voices are superimposed, and what would otherwise be quoted is integrated into the speech of the narrator by parentheses. As a result we hear one voice speaking within another. This second voice is not quoted, as in a dialogue, but mimed. Since mimesis flows from the intersection of alterity with primitivism, this artful miming is revealed as a powerful form of othering.[6]

The children plucked at my abayah [a one piece outer garment worn by women and men alike over their other clothing] and touched my shoes; the women would call them off, then draw near enough to touch the material of my abayah themselves. They talked loudly about me, indifferent to my presence or possible comprehension. However, I caught a few comments: my heavy shoes (horrible); my skin (white); my husband (not bad); my skirt, visible when I sat down even though I keep my abayah around me (good wool, but too short); and my cut bangs (really strange, quite awful in fact). They wondered audibly what I had on under my skirt; when they asked me outright, I pretended that I couldn't understand.[7]

Her discourse here does not seek a unified, authoritative speaking subject. The subject is split by virtue of realizing itself as both protagonist and narrator. The self sees, it sees itself seeing, it sees itself being seen, and it parodies itself. She closes with a sentimental commonplace of women's travel narratives, namely, portraying the natives as wanting to undress her in order to determine her humanity.[8]

Fernea's wifely and fieldwork roles are sketched for us again in the introduction to *Nubian Ethnographies*. In this book, consisting of reprints from earlier texts plus a new introduction, the husband-and-wife coauthors, Elizabeth and Robert Fernea, define themselves and their project in the third person. "Elizabeth Fernea was in Nubia not as an anthropologist but as a wife and mother, accompanying her anthropologist husband. She tried [and failed?] to gather material about women's and children's lives in order to understand their position within larger society."[9] While her project is to be read as a contribution to the anthropology of women, her husband's project is to be read as "an ethnography providing an overview of Nubian society and culture, the result rather than the experience of fieldwork."[10]

This same representational segmentation appeared earlier, although it was not expressly commented on by these authors, in *The Arab World*. Here, while Elizabeth Fernea narrates encounters in a topographic travel diary style—"Beirut, Lebanon," "Amman, Jordan," "Tripoli, Libya," "Et and Nubia"—Robert Fernea contributes sections with typifying authoritative commentary—"The Idea of the Family in the Middle East," "Religious Fundamentalism," "Arab Leadership." What we learn through the inscription practices of this couple is that just as a wife ethnographer is subordinate to her professional ethnographer husband, so a woman's experiential narrative ethnography provides only a "partial" view of society which is subservient to a man's "holistic" overview.[11]

If, as Claude Lévi-Strauss has suggested, anthropology is an adventure and anthropologists are adventure's bureaucrats, then anthropology may simply be another manifestation of Western corporate life. The wives of policemen, diplomats, colonial officials and colonists, soldiers and sailors, and corporate executives in Britain have been studied and often found to be incorporated into their husbands' careers.[12] If anthropology is analogous to corporate life, then the wives of anthropologists might likewise become incorporated. That this team situation, referred to as the "two-person single career," has been common is indicated by the lives of a number of anthropologists' wives.[13] In the early twentieth century Gene Meany Hodge learned both to drive a car and to type in order to deliver her ethnologist husband, Frederick Webb Hodge, to conferences and to assist him by typing his manuscripts.[14] Rosemary Firth describes her own incorporation with her husband Raymond Firth thus: "He wanted at that time to study the social economy of peasant farming somewhere in Southeast Asia, and nothing seemed more natural than that I should go along with him, to help in a general way."[15] Likewise, Chicago graduate student Rosamond Brown, after her marriage to Edward H. Spicer, was incorporated into his career. During the course of her forty-seven-year marriage to Spicer (1936–1983) she helped him professionally by collecting Yaqui field data and life histories as well as by drawing maps and taking photographs for his published ethnographies.[16]

Just how often incorporation takes place we cannot actually know, since many of the affected women are not only muted, in that their work is subsumed into the corporate body and identity of their husbands, but their presence in the field is often unacknowledged. Perhaps the most remarkable example of incorporation is the case of Carobeth Laird, the wife of linguist John Peabody Harrington. Although he never officially acknowledged her help, Carobeth materially assisted him by hand copying and typing native vocabulary, translating from Spanish, gathering plant samples, and cooking, as well as driving for both him and his informants. After several years of this unpaid labor, however, she resisted his demands and refused to turn her body into an ethnographic field site:

> He had suggested, months before, that to have the baby there [on the Tejon ranch] with an Indian woman to help would be a way to open up invaluable information, both ethnological and linguistic. But I had been absolutely adamant. I would have the child in my parents' house in San Diego, and the subject was not open to discussion. I had not before opposed him in this way and was surprised when he gave in.[17]

Other men who have benefited materially from the ethnographic and other labor of their wives mention them in their book acknowledgments or footnotes. Ruth Maslow Lewis was acknowledged by her husband, Oscar Lewis, for having collaborated with him in Tepoztlán, Mexico, "in all aspects of the field work," including administering Rorschach tests and writing "a long detailed guide for observing and recording behavioral data and for the writing of life histories."[18] More recently, Dorothea Whitten, who was a funded National Science Foundation coresearcher among the jungle Quichua in Ecuador, was described by her husband as the project cook and paramedic.[19] Surabela Blatt-Fabian, on the other hand, who was an untrained, unpaid ethnographic assistant in the Amazon, was described by her husband as an undercover operative for anthropology:

> As a couple I believe we were more readily received than if I had entered into the village alone, and my wife's presence was more crucial to the project than at first I had anticipated. Her companionship and participation in daily and ceremonial activities, and the depth in village relationships that her affinity with some of the women initiated for us, were factors that made feasible and enriched the fieldwork situation. Detailed information on the central topics of my research was often necessarily a purchased commodity. Fortunately, my wife, who had never been identified as an official investigator, was never

required to pay money for what she was told or taught, and her discussions with the women constituted another rich source of information, as well as verification of my own data.[20]

As with the Merneas, we learn of the specific usefulness of a wife in collecting data on the anthropology of women, but here, uniquely, we also learn of the underground, unauthorized, illicit nature of one woman's (how many others?) nonprofessional research. As an unpaid wife, Surabela Blatt-Fabian was able to freely gather a valuable commodity, independent information and verification for her husband's own data sets, and her undercover work was doubly unauthorized.[21] How and in which sections of the work did she contribute? Did she collect any of the myths or star lore recorded in this text? We simply won't know except, perhaps, by interviewing both husband and wife. But there are instances when time reveals the writer, as in the famous case of the French intellectual Colette. She was forced by her husband to write about her girlhood sexual experiences (the Claudine books), which he then published under his own name. Not until she was fifty did Colette publish her first novel under her own name. Then, upon her death, after a long, distinguished career as a famous author, she became the first woman in France to be accorded a state funeral.[22]

Just as in this example of writerly incorporation, a silent wife-ethnographer may undergo a metamorphosis, moving from housewife and participant informer to active, professional ethnographer. Edith Turner's emergence gave us a beautifully crafted memoir, *The Spirit and the Drum,* which captures the drama of raising a family in unfamiliar surroundings, the sexuality that animates Ndembu rites of passage, and the Turners' difficult education in patterns of African life and thought. In describing the genre of her book Edith Turner writes:

> *I would like to call it advocacy anthropology in the female style, that is, speaking on behalf of a culture as a lover or a mother. I decided to use all the observations, knowledge, and field materials that I and Victor had collected, and form them — these actual facts of fieldwork, not imaginary material — into a coherent story, adding my own blood of motherhood, as it were, to feed the embryo so that it might grow in its own true way.*[23]

Edith's vivid, joyful portrait of bodily involvement and maternal nurturing reminds me of the *jouissance* recommended as an antidote to phallogocentrism by French feminists.[24] A bit farther on, however, she paints another, more reflective and melancholy portrait of herself and Victor in Africa: "We took pencils and wrote poetry. Then we rested, almost miserable at the loneliness and freedom, the not-knowing-whither of everything."[25]

Margery Wolf reveals, in *A Thrice Told Tale,* a rather different script for the wife-ethnographer turned professional. She inscribes a conversion narrative, revealing how she changed from an incorporated wife into a professional anthropologist. In this 1992 book she publishes, for the first time, a short story entitled "The Hot Spell," written in 1960, when, as she describes herself:

> I thought of myself as the wife and assistant of an anthropologist who was on his first field trip; now, I think of myself as an anthropologist. At that time, they were notes on one more exciting event in the exotic environment in which I found myself living; now, they are an intriguing record of the ideology and social context that led residents of a small village to reach one conclusion about a member of their community rather than another. They have become data, interesting data that should be analyzed and shared with my intellectual community in the usual academic format, a book, or a journal article, rather than in the fictionalized format I had used so many years earlier.[26]

Today, as a professional ethnographer, Margery Wolf comes upon this written trace of her wife-ethnographer youth and artfully uses it to indignantly portray experimental ethnography, defined by a clutch of opportunistic postmodern males, as nothing really very new. After all, she tells us, she was writing experimentally more than thirty years ago—luckily, however, she has since come to her senses. Now she takes on the admonitory role of senior scholar advising feminists not to be led astray by postmodernism, warning that "discussing one's problems with rapport in the field or one's bouts of irritability during fieldwork or similar reflections might be good methodology to one group and good ammunition to another whose members do not wish one well."[27] From my own perspective this advice sounds like the 1950s paranoia I was raised on: "Don't stick your head out" and "Don't make waves," or else. . . . Why cannot ethnographers make the professional personal, and in so doing reach both academic and nonacademic audiences? Why should the form of ethnographic writing not be the product of a multivocal postmodern feminist discipline?

Behind-the-scenes gender negotiation between married ethnographers is revealed in Paul Stoller and Cheryl Olkes's *In Sorcery's Shadow: A Memoir of Apprenticeship among the Songhay of Niger*. Cheryl Olkes, who is "a sociologist and a veteran of Songhay country," is described as "a specialist in research methods and design."[28] Indeed, these coauthors tell us that it was she who designed the interviews and analyzed the data on the therapeutic uses of medicinal plants. But according to Paul Stoller there was another, perhaps even more important, reason for her presence in the field: "As a fellow social scientist she would add a measure of objectivity to my admittedly subjective approach to the Songhay; she could observe me as I interacted with sorcerers. As my wife, Cheryl's presence legitimized me as a normal person in Songhay eyes."[29] Not only was she present for many of the events described in the book, but we are also told that she recorded many of her observations in notebooks and that even the idea for the book and the book itself were coauthored. Ironically, given all the talk about coauthorship, the narrative was written in the first person singular masculine. It never hints at what Olkes did, saw, thought, or felt during her

BARBARA TEDLOCK

fieldwork with Stoller in Africa. And, since the photograph of "the ethnographer's office" is singular, with but one desk and one chair, we know that Cheryl was also present only through the testimony of a photograph of the couple, in African dress, in the back of the book.

This book, though jointly constructed, is a contribution to the romantic literature of the quest and outdoor adventure and travel, in which a lone heroic male undergoes a difficult initiation in an exotic setting.[30] Stoller describes himself aggressively: "I thrust myself into the discussion and asked the men why they could not organize the young man's initiation."[31] Later, after a terrifying experience in which his "lower body" became paralyzed, briefly, he confronted the female sorcerer who accomplished this magical act.

> *The previous night I had reacted to my crisis like a sorcerer and, having weathered the crisis, I had to continue to behave like a Songhay sorcerer. And so I slowly walked out of my compound in Karia. The sun was still low in the eastern sky and the air cool and dry. But I was tired and my heart pounded against my chest and I wondered what might happen when I confronted Dunguri. . . . As she closed the distance between us, I saw that she was beaming. Stopping a few feet from me, she said: "Now I know that you are a man with a pure heart." She took my left hand and placed it in hers. "You are ready. Come into my house and we shall begin to learn."[32]*

This is the sort of phallocentric male fantasy, combined with self-aggrandizement, that Carlos Castaneda employed as part of his own heroic storytelling. What is odd here is that a husband and wife together constructed this narrative out of their joint research. On the other hand, contemporary male travel writing and fiction have recently shifted away from the lone male who seeks the freedom of adventure by leaving females behind and toward the male who takes a woman with him or finds one on the quest.[33] But what did Cheryl Olkes do and learn in the field? Once again, as in the Amazonian example, the female ethnographer's field experiences are erased. If we are to believe Vincent Crapanzano, this may be inevitable:

> *Built into anthropology's project is its own subversion. Like the trickster the anthropologist risks tricking himself. Tikoloshe, the African trickster, had a giant penis which he slung over his shoulder. One day, as he was chopping wood, he accidentally (so we must assume) chopped it off. Anthropology's project, which I articulate in strong male imagery—for it has grown out of and reflects a predominantly male orientation—is governed by this subversion.[34]*

Crapanzano seems to be suggesting that the only credible ethnographic texts must conform to masculinist scripts with their underlying fear of castration—of the loss of their Lacanian phalluses as symbolic banners of culturally conferred meanings. If that is true, then future experimental ethnographies, if they wish to be compelling and avoid subversion, may once again be inscribed heroically as they were more than twenty years ago in Theron Nuñez's Mexican research. "One day, after almost fourteen months in the field, I rode my horse into the plaza and dismounted in front of the café."[35] There he heard the story of the arrest of a woman he knew for cursing a man who had told her to sweep debris out of the street. (She had refused and called the man *buey*, ox, which is an explicit reference to castration.) "Upon hearing the full story of Doña Augustina's dilemma, I remounted my horse, galloped across the cobblestone plaza, reined up sharply in front of the town hall, dismounted, and entered, my spurs jangling as I walked. . . . I was angry and arrogant."[36]

How ought women respond to strongly masculinist writing? By slipping into the imperial masculine mold, becoming social men, and creating romantic heroic tales about themselves as "honorary males"?[37] Mary Kingsley and Alexandra Tinné in Africa, as well as Gertrude Bell and Freya Stark in the Middle East, constructed their lives, or at least the representation of their lives, as much as possible in the heroic masculine manner.[38] That it is not all that difficult is demonstrated by the masses of new female questing books.[39]

Laura Bohannan (Elenore Smith Bowen), in her ethnographic novel *Return to Laughter,* portrays herself as frustrated during her initial fieldwork in Africa by being accepted as a woman among women when what she wanted was access to male knowledge concerning the social, political, economic, and religious institutions that were so important in both her own society and her chosen discipline of anthropology.

> *I should have been content, and I was — as long as I thought only in terms of enjoying myself and of feeling at home. My dissatisfaction lay wholly in the part I was being assigned. I was rapidly being absorbed in the life of the women and the children. All the magic, all the law, all the politics — over half the things professionally important to me — were in the hands of the men, and so far not one man had been willing to discuss such matters with me.*[40]

Later she portrays herself as behaving simultaneously as an honorary male and as a senior female. As she explains it, during a local wedding she was stopped by one of her women friends, who said loudly, "You must make up your mind . . . whether you wish to be an important guest or one of the senior women of the homestead. If you are an important guest, we will again lead out the bride, so you may see her. If you are one of us, you may come inside, but then you must dance with us."[41] After a moment's deliberation she made her choice and went inside, where she was taught by the women to both dance and sing. Other women anthropologists have also portrayed themselves as enjoying being in all-female groups in the field, but as feeling they might be wasting their time talking with women.[42]

Just as male ethnographers have cast their lives into heroic molds in order to project their universal import, female ethnographers may also exaggerate, mythologize, or monumentalize their own or their consultants' lives. Judith Okely, for example, reports that she found that her own stories about fieldwork with gypsies "naturally" became heroically embellished through numerous tellings and retellings to her male colleagues. "I recall spontaneously telling a university interview committee for a research award how I had been drawn into some illegal activities in the field and that I had been a character witness for a Traveler at the Old Bailey. He had been charged with attempted murder by shooting and kidnapping, although found not guilty. I was uncontrollably recounting the sensational in a highly controlled academic encounter." [43]

This masculinization of an ethnographic narrative is not at all surprising, given that professional identity, like sexual identity, is acquired through a process of language learning that constitutes the social person. During the early days of anthropology, women such as Audrey Richards and Margaret Mead may even have succeeded, to a certain degree, in achieving disciplinary equality in anthropology by becoming "surrogate" or "honorary" males. [44] Some female ethnographers claim to have had honorary male status bestowed on them during their fieldwork. However, most women trying to be men found themselves perceived as "pseudo-males," occupying neither a male role nor a female role. [45] Jean Jackson, an anthropologist working in South America, wrote home to her family and friends, "I am like a man from Mars here; I suppose I should say woman except that I am so foreign to the Bará they probably don't see much difference." [46]

That the behaviors leading to this honorary-male or pseudo-male role during fieldwork ought to be examined, modified, and perhaps rejected by feminists is suggested by Ifi Amadiume, who points out that such actions may in fact be neopatriarchal as well as neocolonialist. During ethnographic research in her own matrilineal Igbo community, when she found that an important women's council was excluded from the constitution by local male leaders, she spoke up about the unfairness of a situation that seriously diminished the status of local women. After becoming directly involved in raising the local women's consciousness of this situation, however, she decided on a self-imposed exile in England, where she says she plans to do research and use her pen in the political struggle back home. [47]

Yet women ethnographers can and often do write from a politically involved, woman-centered perspective. This movement from honorary-male ethnographer to woman-centered ethnographer is revealed in fieldwork memoirs and narrative ethnographies in the plotting, rhetoric, and texture of writing produced through a feminist consciousness. Feminist ethnographers today, though they exist within a patriarchal discipline, are practicing an antilogocentric or antiphallocentric approach to writing by speaking "otherwise," against, even outside, paternal truth, reason, and phallic desire.

Literary scholars have noted that while there has been a strong male proclivity toward elaborating their life stories in order to project a poised self-image, the image of the self projected in women's memoirs and autobiographies reveals a need to sift through their lives for explanation and understanding. [48] The female autobiographical intention is often powered by the motive to convince readers of the author's self-worth, to clarify and authenticate her self-image. Thus the self-glorification found in male memoirs is not typical of female memoirs. Instead, many women's self-image is projected by the very means used to distance or detach themselves from intimacy—namely, a variety of forms of understatement. In place of glowing narratives, women tend to write in a straightforward and objective manner about their experiences. However, they may, as Elizabeth Fernea does, also write obliquely and elliptically, using a free, indirect style.

Women may also poke fun at themselves as field-workers in order to camouflage their professional desires and will to power. As psychoanalyst Jane Flax has noted:

> My clinical experience and reading convince me that the repressed is gendered in the sense that women in our culture tend to repress distinctive aspects of the self which are bound up with autonomy and aggression. One dimension of what is repressed is women's non-object related ambition and interest in exerting various sorts of mastery: interpersonal, intellectual, or creative. Both men's and women's sense of gender and the self partially grow out of and are dependent upon the repression of women's desire and ambition. Both genders maintain an active interest in forestalling or prohibiting the return of this repressed material.[49]

Western male autobiographers, on the other hand, often shape the events of their lives into a coherent whole by means of a chronological, linear narrative, and they unify their work by concentrating on one period of their lives or one characteristic of their personalities. It is not surprising that with men socially conditioned to pursue the single goal of a successful career, we find harmony and orderliness in their autobiographies. The unidirectionality of men's lives seems somehow appropriately cast into self-assured progressive narratives. Thus, for example, we find anthropologist Kenneth Read's beatific self-portrayal of fieldwork: "Looking back now, I believe I was permanently elated most of the time I was there. At least this is the only name I can give to a state of mind in which certainty in my own abilities and discovery of myself joined with a compassion for others and a gratitude for the lessons in acceptance that they taught me."[50]

The narratives of women's lives, in contrast, are often neither chronological nor progressive but instead disconnected, fragmentary, or organized into self-sustained units rather than connecting chapters. The multidimensionality of women's socially conditioned roles seems to have encouraged a pattern of diversity when they write their autobiographies. An extreme example is the controlled chaos within Kate Millett's autobiography *Flying*, with its stream-of-consciousness and mixed chronology containing flashbacks within flashbacks, sometimes three times removed.[51] These rhetorical strategies no doubt reflect the fragmentation Millett experiences in her multiple roles as writer, teacher, filmmaker, critic, political activist, and feminist.

More recently, American feminist authors and critics have begun to weave autobiography into history and criticism, journals into analysis, and the spirit of poetry into interdisciplinary prose. This more personal writing at times even obfuscates the boundary between the author's self, the subject of the discourse, and the audience.[52]

BARBARA TEDLOCK

A number of ethnographers have also constructed their texts of fragments: letters from the field, diary extracts, musings, poems, dreams, drawings, and stories.[53] One of the most radical and successful examples of this type of experimentation is Karen McCarthy Brown's *Mama Lola: A Vodou Priestess in Brooklyn,* in which she employs four separate vocal registers: the voice of Alourdes, the vodou priestess who is the main character; the scholarly voice of Karen Brown, the ethnographer; the personal, intimate voice of Brown, as narrator and character in the tale she herself is constructing; and the mythic voice of Gede, the teller of ancestral fictional tales.[54]

The feminine narrative is also often marked by conflicts between the personal and the professional. There may be a tension between the conventional role of wife, mother, sister, or daughter and another, unconventional role that includes ambition or a vocation. Over and over again women anthropologists, be they novices or experienced researchers, reveal their uncertainty about fieldwork and about ethnographic writing. Kirin Narayan, in *Storytellers, Saints, and Scoundrels,* undermines her own ethnographic authority by not offering a romantic insider's view of an alien culture.[55] Instead, she subtly portrays the irony of an inside/outside woman who, while sitting among people with whom she grew up and with whom she felt a comfortable sense of solidarity, was partly rejected as an academic outsider listening to religious teachings for material, rather than spiritual, reasons. As her Guru, Swamiji, put it: "You're taking this on tape. You'll take this and do a business. Understand? . . . In your university you'll say, I saw this, I saw that. This is what Bhagavan is. That's why you learn this; not to understand it."[56] Narayan symbolically marks both her presence and her absence in the ethnographic scene by photographing her own handbag and empty camera case on the women's side of the room. And although we cannot see her, I am certain she is wearing a sari, like the other Indian and European women students who sit listening to their Guru. But Narayan is different from the others in that she is there not simply to participate but to observe and document the scene for herself and for an academic audience back in the United States. Her difference was underscored again when she was leaving the field and presented her tape recorder to Swamiji, who said, "I'll call this Kirin. I won't give it away. I'll listen to [devotional songs] in my room and when I go on pilgrimage." Then, according to Narayan, "He paused, and an impish smile came over his face. 'Maybe I'll tape other people's stories,' he said."[57] A delicious inversion of roles.

In *The Beautiful and the Dangerous: Encounters with the Zuni Indians,* I inscribe the invasiveness of my own camera eye in the ethnographic scene. One summer evening as my husband and I sat in a Zuni kitchen with a returned pilgrim from Kachina Village, the Land of the Dead, I suggested that I might take a picture of the pilgrim, "for history and all." The family agreed, but the first photo revealed only a gleaming-white electronic blur bouncing off his glasses, and the second, without glasses, a blank red-eyed stare. Pictures no one loved, liked, or even wanted. Instead of a loving family portrait, those photos betrayed my insistent documentary urge to freeze, store, and retrieve the authenticity of an encounter with a returned Zuni pilgrim, a classic act of ethnographic bad faith.

Also, instead of the traditional myth of rapport, I inscribe our consummate outsiderness. After Hapiya promised to make us a pair of prayer sticks so we could offer them at the upcoming summer solstice, he decided, for some reason, not to. I expressed my feelings of being shut out poetically as follows:

> *Coyotes walking the line together*
> *watching*
> *waiting for the invite in*
> *a scrap of food or a cornmeal blessing*
> *some other day*
> *some other time*
> *some other place*
> *perhaps.*[58]

Not until years later, when he was dying, did Hapiya begin to incorporate us into Zuni culture by curing us of a bad fright.

Martha Ward, in her memoir, *Nest in the Wind: Adventures in Anthropology on a Tropical Island,* undermines her own authority by noting, "I have probably imparted more wisdom to myself in recounting these events than I deserve. The written accounts, letters, field notes, and reports from this period have provided a framework, but memory and shifts in my own consciousness alter my perspectives."[59] This admittedly unreliable narrator also notes that "this book was not written for my peers or professional colleagues. It is only what John van Maanen calls 'an impressionist tale.'"[60]

Women ethnographers have confessed to not only lack of rapport, bad faith, and unprofessionalism during fieldwork but also the unpremeditatedness of their research. Barbara Bode's stated motive for doing research in Peru was to fill the void in herself created by the loss of her child. In the introduction to *No Bells to Toll: Destruction and Creation in the Andes,* she says, "I was free, awesomely free, shaken like the glacial valley I had heard about on the radio that first day in June 1970. I needed to do something extraordinary to catapult myself out of my personal tragedy. So I went to that Peruvian valley . . . and spent a year there that forever marks my life."[61] She further confesses:

> *Most often, as I had planned it, my tragedy was dwarfed by the immensity of the event and aftermath there. I dreamed survivors' dreams — that another earthquake would come, that Huascarán would "devour us all" [in an avalanche] — sometimes with fragments from my own fears and past. Early in my stay in the valley, I dreamed I wore two layers of clothes. At a certain time, I would be forced to reveal the under layer, though I feared doing so. Perhaps the under layer was my own sorrow and personal search for survival.*[62]

This is the only case I am aware of in which a personal tragedy serves as a major motive for doing anthropological fieldwork. Bode also candidly confesses uncertainty about her own ethnographic abilities: "I had doubts when I was there in the valley, doubts about seeing accurately, portraying accurately, and interpreting accurately, the fears of any anthropologist, magnified by the vastness of the Andean setting, the event and its aftermath."[63]

Female ethnographers of the reflexive sort may also reveal themselves as foolish, uncertain, and bored. Marjorie Shostak, in *Nisa: The Life and Words of a !Kung Woman*, admitted that "the impetus for collecting personal narratives, came from an overlapping but distinct set of issues: recently married, living in the field with no other outsiders, I found fieldwork much more isolating than life as I had known it before. . . . In truth, I was drawn to interviewing people because I felt lonely; I hoped, perhaps, that 'structured friendships' would allow me to share in people's lives and feel part of the community."[64]

Ruth Behar, in *Translated Woman: Crossing the Border with Esperanza's Story*, portrays her inner feelings in typographically marked sections of the text such as the following:

> *I am remembering the hurt I had felt several days before. While I was sitting in the half-open doorway reading, a boy had run past, gotten a peek at me, and yelled out with what to me sounded like venom in his voice, "Gringa!" But I don't want to tell Esperanza about this incident; it seemed very minor, even though it bothered me a great deal. So, instead, I decide to tell her about something I had noticed earlier that day.[65]*

She also reveals, in dialogue form, her extreme discomfort in collecting another woman's life story:

> *Sitting forward and looking me in the eye, Esperanza now says, "Look, comadre, why would you like me to tell you about my life since childhood?"*
> *"It seems very interesting," I reply earnestly.*
> *"Well, look. Since I was born, God only knows."*
> *Esperanza is laughing again, as are her children. I try to keep a smile on my face, but I am beginning to feel like a fool.[66]*

Behar's stated desire in writing herself into Esperanza's life story is "to show myself as a complex many-sided person, a person who is self-doubting but who has gained some intellectual tools to do her work. But I didn't want anyone to totally accept anything I've said uncritically."[67]

Behar also confesses how worried, yet relieved, she was when she realized that after nearly three years of developing relationships with other townswomen and studying what colonial women had said to their inquisitors, she had let one of her subjects take over her research. She further reveals an explicitly feminine environment for the ethnographic encounter. Instead of a lone-wolf outdoor male adventurer pitching his tent among the natives or hanging out with the guys on a ghetto street corner, we find two women seated at a kitchen table chatting into a tape recorder. The kitchen table here suggests ethnography as a form of dialogue and social solidarity.

> *In the kitchen with the mint green walls and the dark pink cracked cement floor tiles, two women sit across from one another talking, a tape recorder between them. Our chairs creak and are not very comfortable; they are cheap wicker chairs that have become worm-eaten over the years. The wobbly kitchen table, one of David's first efforts at woodworking, is covered with a plastic tablecloth imitating an embroidered design of green and purple.*[68]

This opening vignette portrays the ethnographer's husband as having constructed the table that functions as his wife's field site. As is revealed later in the book, he domesticates himself by providing childcare, freeing her to conduct research. While Ruth Behar, like the Norwegian ethnographer Marianne Gullestad in *Kitchen Table Society*, evokes her kitchen table, neither of these women is an innocent housewife whiling her time away. Gullestad works within her own ethnic group, in her own nation, even in her own home town. Behar, a Cuban American Jewish ethnographer, crosses the U.S. border into Mexico and works with a Roman Catholic mestiza marketing woman.[69]

Behar's use of "border crossing" as a central trope in her ethnography is as metaphorically fertile as it was in the autobiography of the Mexican poet and essayist Gloria Anzaldúa, *Borderlands/La Frontera*. In both books, border crossing is employed not only as a theme but also as a compositional mode through which these women can display their many selves, cultures, and countries. While it aptly reveals the mosaic pattern of their writing, it also reveals a state of what Anzaldúa calls "mental nepantilism"—from an Aztec word meaning "torn between two ways."[70] This location in between has also been explored by Pat Mora in *Nepantla: Essays from the Land in the Middle,* in which she notes that she, like Latinas all across American campuses today, lives in "the middle land between the university and the community, the Latino community, our broader civic community, and our international community."[71]

While Behar, like Anzaldúa and Mora, lives in the land in the middle, or the borderlands, her writing project is somewhat different from theirs, as she reveals in her subtitle, *Crossing the Border with Esperanza's Story.* Behar inscribes a one-way trip from Mexico into the U.S., carrying another woman's life story as an exotic import. That this is not a neocolonialist move on Behar's part is indicated by the fact that it is Esperanza herself who, because she is afraid of the ridicule from people in her home community, does not wish her life story to be published in Mexico:

> *Just as rural Mexican laborers export their bodies for labor on American soil, Esperanza has given me her story for export only. Her story, she realizes, is a kind of commodity that will have a value on the other side that it doesn't have at home. . . . She has chosen to be a literary wetback, and I am to act as her liter-*

ary broker, the border-crosser who will take her story to the other side and make it be heard in translation.[72]

Reflexive awareness of the politics of her scholarly intervention is revealed again later in the book, when she sketches herself within a classic neocolonialist scene in which a man carrying a fiesta pole asks her to take his photograph. She does so to please him, or so she thinks, but then finds that he wants five hundred pesos for the privilege of having his picture taken. When ignoring him doesn't work and he keeps demanding money, she finally pays him exactly what he wants, which "amounted to all of a quarter." She notes that the incident irritated her terribly, since she knew that the interaction inscribed a history of Westerners photographing "others," in which those others were now seizing some of the power involved in snapping their pictures.[73]

A similar combination of memoir—centering on the intertwining of the narrative of the ethnographic encounter, both in the field and in retrospect—with native autobiography as intercultural performance also structured Laurel Kendall's book *The Life and Hard Times of a Korean Shaman: Of Tales and the Telling of Tales.* Here, in a series of exchanges reproduced from memory and captured on tape, Kendall represents herself and her field assistant as sympathetic students of a woman shaman. We, as readers, join this shamanic audience as attendees to a series of autobiographical stories. With the addition of Kendall's personal and theoretical interludes, which occur in typographically marked sections throughout the book, we witness a double narrative of a female shaman actively engaging with a female ethnographer.[74]

The types of joint projects inscribed by Behar and Kendall take place at what Renato Rosaldo has called a "complex site of cultural production," where we can "study culture practices and processes of cultural mediation."[75] Furthermore, since the self recognized by feminists is multiple, while a single and unified self created through opposition to another is blocked, feminist ethnographers cannot stand outside. What feminist ethnography is currently contributing to anthropology is, as Lila Abu-Lughod has noted, "an unsettling of the boundaries that have been central to its identity as a discipline of the self studying the other."[76] In the form of borderzone cultural production currently being pioneered by feminist ethnographers we can see the future direction of ethnographic interchange and cultural inscription.

Notes

I am grateful to David Treuer for suggesting "Works and Wives" as the title for this essay.

1. Daisy Dwyer, *Images and Self-Images: Male and Female in Morocco* (New York: Columbia University Press, 1978); Kevin Dwyer, *Moroccan Dialogues: Anthropology in Question* (Baltimore: Johns Hopkins University Press, 1982); D. Amaury Talbot, *Women's Mysteries of a Primitive People: The Ibibios of Southern Nigeria* (London: Frank Cass, 1915); Ann Axtell Morris, *Digging in Yucatan* (Garden City, N.Y.: Doubleday, 1931) and *Digging in the Southwest* (Garden City, N.Y.: Doubleday, 1933); Mary Smith, *Baba of Karo: A Woman of the Moslem Hausa* (New York: Praeger, 1954); Margery Wolf, *The House of Lim: A Study of a Chinese Farm Family* (New York: Prentice-Hall, 1968); Eliza-

beth Warnock Fernea, *Guests of the Sheik: An Ethnography of an Iraqi Village* (Garden City, N.Y.: Doubleday, 1965), *A View of the Nile: The Story of an American Family in Egypt* (Garden City: Doubleday, 1970), and *A Street in Marrakech* (Garden City, N.Y.: Doubleday, 1975).

2. Morris, *Digging in Yucatan*, xvii.

3. Shelby J. Tisdale, "Women on the Periphery of the Ivory Tower," in *Hidden Scholars: Women Anthropologists and the Native American Southwest*, ed. Nancy J. Parezo (Albuquerque: University of New Mexico Press, 1993), 328. For an evaluation of Ann Axtell Morris's career see Cynthia Irwin-Williams, "Women in the Field: The Role of Women in Archaeology before 1960," in *Women of Science: Righting Her Record*, ed. G. Kass-Simon and Patricia Farnes (Bloomington: Indiana University Press, 1990), 1–41.

4. Linda Cordell, "Women Archaeologists in the Southwest," in *Hidden Scholars*, 219, argues that female archaeologists manifest different life and career patterns from female ethnographers. Since I am an ethnographer and am most familiar with the lives of female ethnographers, I concentrate on them here.

5. This quotation is from the unnumbered introduction to Elizabeth Warnock Fernea, *Guests of the Sheik: An Ethnography of an Iraqi Village* (Garden City, N.Y.: Doubleday, 1965).

6. For a discussion of mimesis, see Walter Benjamin, "Doctrine of the Similar," *New German Critique* 17 (1979): 65–69. The implication of mimesis in primitivism and alterity is discussed by Michael Taussig, *Mimesis and Alterity: A Particular History of the Senses* (New York: Routledge, 1993).

7. Fernea, *Guests of the Sheik*, 46–47.

8. This writerly commonplace has been described by Mary Louise Pratt, "Fieldwork in Common Places," in *Writing Culture: The Poetics and Politics of Ethnography*, ed. James Clifford and George E. Marcus (Berkeley: University of California Press, 1986), 27–50.

9. Elizabeth Fernea and Robert Fernea, *Nubian Ethnographies* (Prospect Heights, Ill.: Waveland, 1991), 2.

10. Ibid.

11. Elizabeth Warnock Fernea and Robert A. Fernea, *The Arab World: Personal Encounters* (Garden City, N.Y.: Doubleday, 1985).

12. For an excellent discussion of the "incorporated wife," see Hilary Callan and Shirley Ardner, *The Incorporated Wife* (London: Croom Helm, 1984).

13. See Hanna Papanek, "Men, Women, and Work: Reflections on the Two-Person Career," *American Journal of Sociology* 78, no. 4 (1973): 858–72.

14. Gene Meany Hodge, "A Brief Account of My Life and How I Met Dr. Hodge," in *Frederick Webb Hodge, Ethnologist* (book manuscript in the Bancroft Library, University of California at Berkeley, 1956), 241–43.

15. Rosemary Firth, "From Wife to Anthropologist," in *Crossing Cultural Boundaries: The Anthropological Experience*, ed. Solon T. Kimbal and James B. Watson (San Francisco: Chandler, 1972), 10–32.

16. Kathleen Mullen Sands, "Women Researchers and the Yaquis in Arizona and Sonora," in *Hidden Scholars*, 150–51.

17. Carobeth Laird, *Encounter with an Angry God: Recollections of My Life with John Peabody Harrington* (New York: Ballantine Books, 1975), 40.

18. Oscar Lewis, *Life in a Mexican Village: Tepoztlán Restudied* (Urbana: University of Illinois Press, 1951), x, xix, xx, 306n.

19. Norman E. Whitten, *Sacha Runa: Ethnicity and Adaptation of Ecuadorian Jungle Quichua* (Urbana: University of Illinois Press, 1976), 287–304.

20. Stephen Fabian, *Space-Time of the Bororo of Brazil* (Gainesville: University Press of Florida, 1992), 10.

21. I have borrowed the concept of "an undercover operative for anthropology" from Dan Rose, *Black American Street Life: South Philadelphia, 1969–71* (Philadelphia: University of Pennsylvania Press, 1987), 210. He used the phrase to describe both himself and his first wife, Karen Rose, during their joint fieldwork in Philadelphia during the late 1960s and early 1970s.

22. For more details about Colette's life, see Elaine Marks, *Colette* (New Brunswick, N.J.: Rutgers University Press, 1960); Michele Sarde, *Colette*, trans. Richard Miller (New York: Morrow, 1980); and Carolyn G. Heilbrun, *Writing a Woman's Life* (New York: Ballantine, 1988), 83–84.

23. Edith Turner, *The Spirit and the Drum: A Memoir of Africa* (Tucson: University of Arizona Press, 1987), x.

24. French feminism, of the *écriture féminine*, or the writing-of-difference type, proceeds from the psychoanalytic premises of Jacques Lacan and employs the deconstructive methods of Jacques Derrida. French feminists declare that mainstream Western philosophy is phallogocentric, and that it has been based on a systematic repression of women's experience; they share a common opponent, "masculinist" thinking. Their resistance to phallogocentrism takes place in the form of *jouissance,* that is, in the direct reexperience of the physical pleasures of infancy and of later sexuality, repressed but not obliterated by the Law of the Father, or the incest taboo. In their writings they oppose woman's bodily experience to the phallic symbolic patterns embedded in Western logic and thought. Hélène Cixous, for example, asks: "Who in me writes?" Her assumption is that the "I" is multiple and that writing is never simply "the expression of the self." For an interesting discussion of the thought of Hélène Cixous, see Verena Andermatt Conley, *Hélène Cixous: Writing the Feminine* (Lincoln: University of Nebraska Press, 1991).

25. Turner, *Spirit and the Drum,* 84.

26. Margery Wolf, *A Thrice Told Tale: Feminism, Postmodernism and Ethnographic Responsibility* (Stanford: Stanford University Press, 1992), 2–3.

27. Ibid., 138. Carolyn G. Heilbrun and Catharine R. Stimpson, in "Theories of Feminist Criticism: A Dialogue," in *Feminist Literary Criticism,* ed. Josephine Donovan (Lexington: University of Kentucky Press, 1975), 64, identified this form of "righteous, angry, and admonitory" feminist criticism as Old Testament in that it looked "for the sins and errors of the past." They contrasted it with a more disinterested mode seeking "the grace of imagination," which they compared to the New Testament. As they noted, both are necessary, for only the Jeremiahs of ideology can lead us out of the "Egypt of female servitude" to the promised land.

28. Paul Stoller and Cheryl Olkes, *In Sorcery's Shadow: A Memoir of Apprenticeship among the Songhay of Niger* (Chicago: University of Chicago Press, 1987), 199.

29. Ibid., xii–xiii.

30. For discussions of the romantic heroic quest genre of literature, see Donald J. Greiner, *Women Enter the Wilderness: Male Bonding and the American Novel of the 1980s* (Columbia: University of South Carolina Press, 1991), and Mary Louise Pratt, *Imperial Eyes: Travel Writing and Transculturation* (London: Routledge, 1992).

31. Stoller and Olkes, *In Sorcery's Shadow,* 126.

32. Ibid., 148–49.

33. This change in the inscription of male questing is described at length by Donald Greiner, *Women Enter the Wilderness,* as well as in his later book, *Women without Men: Female Bonding and the American Novel of the 1980s* (Columbia: University of South Carolina Press, 1993).

34. Vincent Crapanzano, "Introduction," in *Hermes' Dilemma and Hamlet's Desire: On the Epistemology of Interpretation* (Cambridge, Mass.: Harvard University Press, 1992), 6.

35. Theron A. Nuñez, "On Objectivity and Field Work," in *Crossing Cultural Boundaries,* 169–70.

36. Ibid.

37. For a discussion of the behavior of professional women who refused to be identified as women and became "honorary males," see Carolyn G. Heilbrun, "Non-Autobiographies of 'Privileged' Women: England and America," in *Life/Lines: Theorizing Women's Autobiography,* ed. Bella Brodzki and Celeste Schenck (Ithaca, N.Y.: Cornell University Press, 1988), 70–71.

38. For a discussion of women's travel narratives, see Julie Marcus, *A World of Difference: Islam and Gender Hierarchy in Turkey* (London: Zed, 1992), 46–48; Pratt, *Imperial Eyes,* 213–16; and Mary Morris, "Women and Journeys: Inner and Outer," in *Temperamental Journeys: Essays on the Modern Literature of Travel,* ed. Michael Kowalewski (Athens: University of Georgia Press, 1992), 30–31.

39. The recent resurgence in female adventure and questing books is perceptively discussed by Dana A. Heller, *The Feminization of Quest-Romance: Radical Departures* (Austin: University of Texas Press, 1990), and Greiner, *Women without Men.*

40. Elenore Smith Bowen, *Return to Laughter: An Anthropological Novel* (New York: Doubleday, 1954), 78.

41. Ibid., 123.

42. See, for example, Christine Hugh-Jones, *From the Milk River: Spatial and Temporal Processes in Northwest Amazonia* (Cambridge, England: Cambridge University Press, 1979), xiv; Jean Jackson, "On Trying to Be an Amazon," in *Self, Sex, and Gender in Cross-Cultural Fieldwork,* ed. Tony Larry Whitehead and Mary Ellen Conaway (Urbana: University of Illinois Press, 1986), 270; and Barbara Tedlock, *The Beautiful and the Dangerous: Encounters with the Zuni Indians* (New York: Viking, 1992), 99–100.

43. Judith Okely, "Anthropology and Autobiography: Participatory Experience and Embodied Knowledge," in *Anthropology and Autobiography,* ed. Judith Okely and Helen Callaway (New York: Routledge, 1992), 15.

44. Margaret Mead has been called "the ultimate honorary male anthropologist" (Carol A. B. Warren, *Gender Issues in Field Research* [Newbury Park, Calif.: Sage, 1988], 59). The honorary male status in anthropology has been described by Laura Nader, "From Anguish to Exultation," in *Women in the Field: Anthropological Experiences,* ed. Peggy Golde (Berkeley: University of California Press, 1970), 114; Hazel Weidman, "On Ambivalence in the Field," in *Women in the Field,* 255–56; Janet Bujra, "Women and Fieldwork," in *Women Cross-Culturally: Change and Challenge,* ed. R. Rohrlich-Leavitt (Chicago: Aldine Press, 1975); and Martha C. Ward, *Nest in the Wind: Adventures in Anthropology on a Tropical Island* (Prospect Heights, Ill.: Waveland, 1989), 96.

45. Pat Caplan, "Engendering Knowledge: The Politics of Ethnography," *Anthropology Today* 4, no. 5 (1988): 15.

46. Jackson, "On Trying to Be an Amazon," 263.

47. Ifi Amadiume, "The Mouth that Spoke a Falsehood Will Later Speak the Truth: Going Home to the Field in Eastern Nigeria," in *Gendered Fields: Women, Men and Ethnography,* ed. Diane Bell, Pat Caplan, and Wazir Jahan Karim (London: Routledge, 1992), 182–98.

48. Estelle Jelinek, "Introduction: Women's Autobiography and the Male Tradition," in *Women's Autobiography: Essays in Criticism* (Bloomington: Indiana University Press, 1980), 1–20. Margo Culley, in "What a Piece of Work is 'Woman'!" in *American Women's Autobiography: Fea(s)ts of Memory,* ed. Margo Culley (Madison: University of Wisconsin Press, 1992), 4, notes that critics who have focused on how women's autobiography is different from men's have argued that women's writing in this genre displays narrative discontinuity, exhibits a collective consciousness, and writes the Self through the Other.

49. Jane Flax, "Re-membering the Selves: Is the Repressed Gendered?" *Michigan Quarterly Review* 26 (1987): 92.

50. Kenneth E. Read, *The High Valley* (New York: Charles Scribner's Sons, 1986), 6.

51. Kate Millett, *Flying* (New York: Knopf, 1984).

52. See Diane P. Freedman, *An Alchemy of Genres: Cross-Genre Writing by American Feminist Poet-Critics* (Charlottesville: University Press of Virginia, 1992).

53. For example, see Manda Cesara, *Reflections of a Woman Anthropologist: No Hiding Place* (New York: Academic Press, 1982); Laurel Kendall, *The Life and Hard Times of a Korean Shaman: Of Tales and the Telling of Tales* (Honolulu: University of Hawaii Press, 1988); Julia Meyerson, *'Tambo: Life in an Andean Village* (Austin: University of Texas Press, 1990); C. Nadia Seremetakis, *The Last Word: Women, Death, and Divination in Inner Mani* (Chicago: University of Chicago Press, 1991); Tedlock, *Beautiful and the Dangerous;* and Ruth Behar, *Translated Woman: Crossing the Border with Esperanza's Story* (Boston: Beacon, 1993).

54. Karen McCarthy Brown, *Mama Lola: A Vodou Priestess in Brooklyn* (Berkeley: University of California Press, 1991).

55. Kirin Narayan, *Storytellers, Saints, and Scoundrels: Folk Narrative in Hindu Religious Teaching* (Philadelphia: University of Pennsylvania Press, 1989).

56. Ibid., 59.

57. Ibid., 62.

58. Tedlock, *Beautiful and the Dangerous,* 111.

59. Ward, *Nest in the Wind,* 3.

60. Ibid., 101.

61. Barbara Bode, *No Bells to Toll: Destruction and Creation in the Andes* (New York: Charles Scribner's Sons, 1989), xix.

62. Ibid.

63. Ibid.

64. Marjorie Shostak, *Nisa: The Life and Words of a !Kung Woman* (Cambridge, Mass.: Harvard University Press, 1989), 238.

65. Behar, *Translated Woman,* 250.

66. Ibid., 28.

67. Liz McMillen, "Esperanza's 'Historia'—and Ruth's: An Anthropological Study of Two Lives," *Chronicle of Higher Education,* May 5, 1993, A6–7, 12.

68. Behar, *Translated Woman,* 25.

69. Marianne Gullestad, *Kitchen Table Society: A Case Study of the Family Life and Friendships of Young Working-Class Mothers in Urban Norway* (Oslo: Universitetsforlaget, 1984.)

70. Gloria Anzaldúa, *Borderlands/La Frontera: The New Mestiza* (San Francisco: Spinsters/ Aunt Lute, 1987), 78–79.

71. Pat Mora, *Nepantla: Essays from the Land in the Middle* (Albuquerque: University of New Mexico Press, 1993), 6.

72. Behar, *Translated Woman*, 233–34.

73. For a perceptive discussion of photography and colonialism, see Irvin Schick, "Representing Middle Eastern Women: Feminism and Colonial Discourse," *Feminist Studies* 16, no. 2 (1990): 345–80.

74. Kendall, *Life and Hard Times of a Korean Shaman.*

75. Renato Rosaldo, *Culture and Truth: The Remaking of Social Analysis* (Boston: Beacon Press, 1989), 217.

76. Lila Abu-Lughod, "Can There Be a Feminist Ethnography?" *Women and Performance: A Journal of Feminist Theory* 5, no. 1 (1990): 26.

14

Ms.Represen-
tations:
Reflections
on Studying
Academic
Men

Judith
Newton
and Judith
Stacey

EXCERPT FROM an (unsuccessful) application
to the Spencer Foundation, August 1992:

*We are applying to the Spencer Foundation
for support which would enable us to complete a collaborative, cross-disciplinary investigation of the comparative impact on radical
academic men of the goals and perspectives
associated with Women's and Ethnic Studies.
Combining textual criticism with oral history
and participant-observation, our project takes
as the object of its investigation our subjects'
scholarship as well as their teaching, their collegial relations, their institutional practice and
behaviors, the development of their cultural
knowledge, the intellectual and political
milieus in which they move, and their personal lives.*

*In studying the complex ways that radical
academic males have assimilated, translated
and/or evaded critical perspectives on gender,
race, and sexual identity, our study sheds light
upon the uneven and complicated ways in
which different kinds of privileged "others"
come, and do not come, to take on knowledges and goals which in some way challenge
their own privilege. Our project focuses, that
is, on the conditions which produce "traitorous identities," a willingness to betray the traditional privileges of one's group and one's*

own position. An investigation of this kind, it seems to us, has insights of partic- ular importance to offer at the present time, when U.S. society itself is rapidly becoming racially and ethnically more diverse, when race and gender tensions are on the rise, when economic resources are shrinking (for all but the elite), when "multiculturalism" in higher education is under attack, and when affirma- tive action policies, in particular, are the subject of intense debate. As scholars invested in equality and justice, we feel that careful, ethnographic investigation of changing discourse and practice in relation to race and gender and of the processes by which such changes have taken place are key to developing further strategies for democratizing not just the academy but U.S. society as a whole. This is, for us, the central contribution our project makes to new knowledge about education.

Changing Our Story

Like most feminist scholars, during the past two decades we have spent the greater part of our intellectual energies gathering and interpreting material about women.[1] Part of this work, to be sure, involved us in studying men, but when it did so, our goal was less to understand them than to better know ourselves and other women. The current political and intellectual context has prompted us to shift this focus somewhat. First, the general backlash against feminism, multiculturalism, and affirmative action provokes stock-taking about what second-wave feminism and multiculturalism have actually accomplished. Secondly, the proliferation of various species of men's movements (from feminist, to spiritual, to antifeminist) challenges us to think about ways in which men are and want to be changing and about what feminisms have had to do with these efforts to reinvent masculinity.

More broadly, the conservative backlash against political correctness positions academic feminists, antiracist men of color, and gay academic men alongside white straight men of almost any critical intellectual stripe, attacking us all as if we were disloyal to civilization in the same way. On the other end of the political spectrum, cultural studies, the academic signifier of the 1990s, offers to embrace us under its own conceptual and institutional umbrella, while the emergence of a conservative Congress suggests a renewed need for political alliance and activism that extend well beyond the academy. Together these developments generate important ques- tions about our relationship as feminists to left-leaning and antiracist academic men and to collective political action as a whole. It seems more urgent than before to define the kinds and forms of alliances that are desirable and possible. For this rea- son, among others, we have begun to study men in a different way.

The Postmodern Fix

Studying men, however, with an eye to alliance rather than surveillance or self- knowledge raises dilemmas which even the current priorities and frameworks of academic feminism seem ill suited to handle. One formulation of the difficulties we have encountered is something we call "the postmodern fix." Mainstream academic feminism, as is well known, has undergone a series of transformations in the last fifteen years, which have opened it to new forms of dialogue and exchange. Unified categories like "women" have come into question; gender has come to be seen as multiple and various, as coconstructed with race, class, and sexual and national identity. Identity politics, as the politics of the "same," has given way, as a dominant mode of conceptualizing feminist community, to a politics involving multiple alliances, alliances across identities, alliances with those whose lives and identities are in a sense "wrong."[2] These are the transformations, often referred to as postmodern, in which we situate our own "border crossings" in this project.

Ironically, however, for all its identification with the fluid and the multiple, postmodernism has (inevitably) taken on some unifying and homogenizing functions. Postmodern as a category, for example, is often employed in order to fix the heterogeneity of theoretical and political genealogies into the grand narrative of itself. Thus the fragmentation of unitary assumptions about gender, which is often glossed as postmodern, was introduced into feminist discourse as early as the 1970s through the work of feminists of color and lesbians, who did not then identify themselves with that term.[3] Dominant forms of feminist postmodernism, moreover, seem themselves to run in some well-worn grooves. (We are familiar with these grooves. This is our fix too.) The most dominant form of postmodern feminism, for example, signifies alliance across identities and rightly privileges some alliances over others. It privileges alliance between women, most particularly now across racial and ethnic lines. As white feminists we feel, without question, that women of color are currently the "other" of most pressing concern, and on our own campus we have worked hard to build a women's studies program that is fully multicultural and that aims at mutually constructed agendas and shared power. We would raise the question, nonetheless, of whether a postmodern feminism can afford, any more than modernist feminism, to be a project for women only. Feminists of color have almost always claimed some alliance with progressive men in their own racial or ethnic communities, but for most white feminisms men (often unified as a single category) have been the most "other" of all "others." The shift within academic mainstream feminism from identity politics to politics across identities challenges us to move more fully across this divide as well, challenges feminists in general to at least investigate the possibilities of alliance with progressive men, including white men, who have signaled the desire and potential for a politics beyond their own interests.[4]

Although most academic feminists tend to assume, in good postmodern fashion, that their identities are contradictory and divided, that it is possible, for example, to be a white antiracist or a heterosexual woman of color who is antihomophobic, men are more likely to be ms.represented as somewhat fixed. (Or, like Cathy in the cartoon, feminists may complain: "Why is it the only time men really change, it's into something totally aggravating?") There is something to the complaint raised by critics of political correctness (and critics writing for the *New Criterion* intersect here with those writing for *Socialist Review*) that certain feminist categories—the Western subject, white middle-class male, dead white men—lack complexity and nuance.[5] These critics of political correctness, moreover, intersect with the mild-mannered complaint of an African American male scholar we interviewed who reported that "I get impatient with feminists who represent men of color as perpetually underdeveloped. You know—'you men can't get it right!' We need dialogue with feminists about this. Maybe we *can't* do it on your terms alone."

Postmodern feminisms assume that identities are constructed in multiple, shifting, contradictory discourses, and yet the most dominant feminist mode of writing about male others is that of confidently reading their race and gender politics, and sometimes their psychologies and characters, out of their published texts. (We should know. We have contributed to this genre.)[6] But published texts, which are peculiarly subject to the norms governing career advance—such as displays of mastery over one's own turf—may be not only partial but also misleading indices of what some male others are up to when our backs are turned. Perhaps there are more multi-layered, more "postmodern" ways of reading these academic others, with whom our intellectual, political, and social lives are often entwined.

Although most current feminisms assume the situated, partial nature of all knowledge, acknowledgment of the partiality, the limitations, the possible night blindness of one's own critique, seems almost easier to come by these days, in white feminist texts at least, when they are written from the position of the white feminist's greater power (in relation to women of color, for example) than when they are written from the position of her/our subordination (in relation to men and especially those who are white and heterosexual).[7] And here again, although we are committed to the radical revision of race and gender power relations in the academy and beyond, we have to acknowledge that there are positions which appear to present themselves as beyond criticism. (Some of them are our own, when we write with the rectitude and moral authority of subordinates, when we know we're right.) It is in the context of this fix on postmodernism that we also situate our study of radical academic men. It is in the context of this postmodern fix—and of other fixes as well—that we attempt in the following pages to think about rethinking men, that we attempt to reflect on the positions, discourses, and paradigms with which we began, which we were to encounter, and through which we sometimes moved as we began our work on this project.

But, Judy . . .

Excerpts from three responses to our first paper, which focused on white male cultural critics:

1. (A WHITE FEMINIST) "I enjoyed reading this immensely, and/but it made me slightly nervous. What I am curious and worried about is that the attention to [these guys] reproduces a celebration and authority you are trying to question

and combat. I mean, they'll love it, no? And won't it keep them center-stage despite your critique? Well, that's a basic, overall concern I have."

2. (A FEMINIST OF COLOR) "Could your focus on two white male theorists at this particular historical moment be read as a kind of displacement of the critiques feminists of color have been making about retaining gender at the center of feminist theorizing? . . . Is there also a way in which you retain 'men' as the 'other' of feminism rather than addressing the range of theoretical responses of 'other' women currently contesting and refiguring feminist epistemology?"

3. (A WHITE, PROFEMINIST MAN) "I wonder if you bend over backwards too much. You take 8 pp to get going, and some of the later text too sounds, not nagging, but very apologetic, as if you are not sure you have the right to say all this. I think we should insist that all the members of the rainbow do have a right to robust speech, and if they get it wrong then they turn around and correct themselves and go forward."

Excerpt from a taped "conversation about race and class" between bell hooks and Mary Childers:

HOOKS: It is important to remember that victimization by men has been the primary category of oppression in feminism.

CHILDERS: Though I certainly don't want to let men off the hook, it is worthwhile to look out for examples of how often an exclusive focus on male/female conflict serves as a distraction from other kinds of conflict.[8]

Tania Modleski on the dangers of a dialogic approach to writing about men:

While terms like "dialogism" . . . are commonly evoked in the rationale for these volumes it is hard to see how such a term functions as anything more than a euphemism for "dialogue"—a concept that in eliding the question of power asymmetry has rather conservative implications.[9]

A male participant in the Marxist Literary Group's Summer Institute after hearing a draft of our paper on two male cultural critics and on learning that we were planning not only to interview them but to show them the paper we were writing:

Do that and you're dead in the water.

A conversation between Judys:

JUDY: There's no end of things we can be criticized for; how about heterosexual presumption?

JUDY: Of course, we can raise all these issues overtly, but then we'll be vulnerable to the charge of having included an "inoculating critique" of our own blind spots "so as to allow business to proceed as usual."[10]

JUDY: Great! We're going to alienate everyone.

Excerpt from our risk-to-human-subjects protocol:

My co-investigator Judith Newton and I are convinced that the potential bene-
fits of this project far outweigh the small risk it poses to interviewees. Indeed,
we believe that this project may place our own scholarly output and reputations
at greater risk than that of our subjects. Fear of offending cooperating colleagues
may hamper our own critical expression, and if we do offend any subjects,
they are well-positioned to "retaliate" in print. Perhaps, Judith Newton and
I are the principal human subjects at risk in this study.

The Return of the Suppressed

Despite our desire to hear the discourse of progressive male others in a more
multivalent, less self-righteous way, our initial efforts to know these potential allies
took a familiar shape—ms.representing men's stories through critical readings of
their written texts. We did adopt, to be sure, a less sarcastic, more self-critical tone
than in our previous efforts to write about men—a tone which will inevitably sit
better with male academics than with female feminists, but which will, we are convinced, actively please no one. In spite of these cosmetic changes, however, what we
achieved in the end was a more moderate version of some familiar modes, the well-
meaning feminist report card, the gently nagging text.[11]

In keeping with our focus on cultural studies and on the politics of academic
men, we chose as subjects two well-known, white cultural studies scholars, both of
whom had written on the colonizing nature of Western discourse on "the other."
Somewhat serendipitously—we happened to see Kevin Costner's Oscar-winning
Dances with Wolves while working on our subjects' latest books—we adopted a
strategy familiar to cultural studies itself, that of reading across cultural texts and
juxtaposing high and low. We used the insights of our subjects' texts as grids through
which to read the colonizing strategies of *Dances with Wolves,* an officially anti-
imperialist film, and then employed our enhanced reading of Costner's film to investigate the ways in which our subjects reinscribe some of the same colonizing
strategies in their own anti-imperialist texts. Finally, we drew on our own insights
to read the gender politics of all three works and to suggest some relations between
their gender and racial narratives.

In the texts of Costner and of the cultural studies scholars, for example, issues
having to do with the politics of knowledge and authority are critically entertained
in relation to strategically distanced male native others. These same narratives, we
felt, might also be read as implicit, displaced responses to feminist and domestic
antiracist critique—responses that struck us as radically abstracted from overt considerations of gender politics, in particular, and as reinforcing sexual hierarchies.[12]
Our initial explanation for what seemed to us displaced responses to gender challenge was a fairly egocentric one—that feminist challenges were too threatening for

men to engage with head on. This at least is how we initially ms.represented men's stories, inevitably projecting onto them perspectives from our own.[13]

Ethnographic Encounters of the Unsettling Kind

If the major conceit of the ethnographic enterprise is its capacity to disrupt cultural prejudice, we were not to be disappointed. It did not take long before fieldwork began to complicate the analysis about male responses to gender and race challenges that we had derived from men's texts.[14] As soon as we initiated the process of conducting oral histories on male cultural critics, we elicited self-representations of the impact that feminism has had on their lives and work that are at once more deflating and more flattering than we had anticipated.[15]

ENCOUNTER I

JUDY: You know, you were living in an area that was a major center for feminism then; did you know that?

A MALE CULTURAL CRITIC: Of course!

JUDY: You knew it then?

HIM: Of course.

JUDY: Like what? Was it noticeable?

HIM [*pause*]: No. I don't think so.

JUDY: Do you have any memories?

HIM: No.

JUDY: Any personal life, any social life, things happening, incidents, soundings?

HIM: Feminism was a minimal kind of thing.

JUDY: What do you remember at all?

HIM: Nothing.

JUDY: Media stuff, or what?

HIM: Nothing, zero [*laughing*], I mean it's really, I'm going to have to say that in lieu of having, I mean if I don't have a strong memory, I mean I could probably, well let me put that, nothing, goose egg. What I'm saying is that without anything coming immediately to mind, I would have to think about it, and that tells you something.

JUDY: But that's important.

HIM: Yeah.

JUDY: This is a very important question for me. I mean it's not a criticism, it's not a question of, why didn't you?

HIM: No, it's just me, what can I say?

JUDY: But it's not just you, because it's a milieu you were part of.

HIM: Oh yeah.

JUDY: I'm not even asking how you felt about it. I just wonder how and when it entered.

ENCOUNTER 2

ANOTHER MALE CULTURAL CRITIC: New historicism is a pathetic phenomenon compared with feminism; it could only make any sense in the kind of ground that's been broken by feminism, for a lot of different reasons. So I feel good about having been pressured into having done this work. Feminism is, it seems to me, a kind of sublime model for what it is that any intellectual formation might hope to do.

JUDY: What do you mean by that?

HIM: Well, it's sublime because it's not approachable by something like deconstructionism or new historicism, since it actually, since feminism has a presence in the real world that no academic theory, whatever the game is, will have. But I think that feminism is not only having this presence in the world, including a political presence, but also to have changed both the theoretical and object landscape dramatically, and that's all that an academic can possibly hope to do. So it's the model. I don't feel rivalrous at all. At least I'm not aware of feeling rivalrous, in that I think there's plenty of room for all kinds of things . . . But in any case, I think of feminism as a vastly bigger, more important field than mine.

Our initial construction of the troubling textual silence on gender issues in many of our subjects' work (that gender critique was too threatening to handle), while not entirely discredited by our ethnographic encounters, was at least radically decentered. As a group our subjects were far from uniform in their reported responses to early feminist critique, and as individuals their sensitivity to, and practice of, gender criticism were unevenly developed. Subjects who did engage with gender issues in their published work were often already marginalized by ethnicity or sexual identity or by the employment of "feminized" discourses such as psychoanalysis. Some had been in long relationships with feminists or had had deep and often painful ties to female relatives. Still others were young enough to have had feminist teachers or at least feminist cohorts in graduate school. A younger white scholar, for example, who is now in men's studies, reports that he entered the field in part because he received "strokes" for doing gender from his feminist college teachers.

In the case of many others, however, their published work, as the area of their lives most open to public scrutiny and most crucial to their career advance, often displayed the least imprinting by critical gender knowledge. Registering the keenly competitive and hierarchical nature of academic scholarship, some subjects recorded anxieties about "losing one's edge" if they did gender criticism, while others expressed fear of not being seen as serious by other men or of being perceived as soft on feminism.

Still others mentioned fear of offending gendered and racial others as a primary motivation for excluding gender and race issues from their published work: "If I'm wrong, the person who's upset is across the table." They talked of not wanting to be a "tourist" in relation to gender issues or cited anxiety (at times justified) over being charged with appropriating and usurping ethnic and/or women's studies terrain. One prominent white culture critic, for example, recounts an incident in which he gave what he meant to be a profeminist talk on the work of Virginia Woolf, only to be met with feminist charges of encroachment, an experience which he refers to as the damned if you do, and damned if you don't conundrum.

Our subjects' teaching, however, and their academic politics were more often reflective of serious engagement with gender and racial issues. In classrooms, for example, which are more private spaces and where an audience of graduate students, in particular, is likely to insist on hearing the perspectives of a full range of historically marginalized groups, critical perspectives on gender are more likely to be included by both white men and men of color. As one African American male scholar explained:

> I had two T.A.'s who were feminists in every sense of the word, T.A.'s of color. It's a course that I've taught on "The Black Experience," and we got into quite a few discussions about the question of gender and its relationship to difference and multiculturalism, and all these kinds of issues. And again, having to confront the deep ways in which a kind of masculinity fits in my own way of seeing the world and having it challenged, and expanded and elaborated upon by these graduate students has been very helpful. It's been frustrating and contentious at times, but it's also been incredibly helpful in terms of confronting just what I was talking about, how do you make it become an active part of one's work without taking it over, without being a tourist, without trying to speak for, from a place that you really can't.

To some degree, then, our confident assumption that silence on gender issues in our subject's scholarship might be ascribed to gender threat came to seem to us ideological. Specifically, it began to seem a product, at least in part, of our continuing immersion in early white feminist understandings of the world, understandings forged in a period of revolutionary fervor and in a period of (understandably egocentric) anger and disbelief that what was world shaking to us was not passionately cathected by our male comrades.[16] These were not the only assumptions, however, that our ethnographic encounters were to challenge. Our initial construction of the political and methodological difficulties that our project posed had been deeply and consciously informed by later discourses as well, most particularly by contemporary feminist/postmodernist understandings about the politics and dynamics of knowing "others." Our excursions into the "field" were also to complicate and decenter these understandings.

Colonization Revisited

The governing premise of most current critical discourse on ethnographic authority, for example, is that ethnographers inescapably exercise and exploit textual and social authority over the people they study, people who characteristically occupy subordinate social positions. Astute critique and self-critique of the colonizing impulses, practices, and effects of ethnography dominate this literature. Much feminist discussion of ethnographic practice has been preoccupied with fieldwork and rhetorical strategies that attempt to disrupt these asymmetrical authority relations, presuming, reasonably enough, that most of the "others" of feminist ethnographic research are less powerful women and/or, occasionally, subordinated men.[17]

Our first move in relation to these formulations was to see our own project as a replication in reverse of the usual script. As women studying men, that is, we were, in ethnographic parlance, "studying up," at least in relationship to the men who are white and heterosexual, while our political goals committed us to try to "study across" as well. Although, as white, heterosexual, academic women, we share with the majority of our subjects diverse forms of privilege, most of them are more privileged still. Not only do they occupy the dominant gender position, but most are prodigious achievers with fame, status, and ready access to print and to institutional and cultural authority worldwide. Thus the inequalities between researchers and researched sometimes seem pronounced, even in some instances in which our gender "handicap" is offset by our racial or sexual privileges or by our status as representatives of institutionalized feminism. Yet the culture wars and our own politics also position our research subjects with us against threatening defenders of traditional privilege inside the academy and beyond. We too, after all, are "tenured radicals."[18] Thus, from an at least partially subordinate location, we are studying "dominants" who are also potential, and desired, allies—men whose capacity for, and commitment to, "traitorous" gender identities we seek to investigate and foster. Our paradoxical location we felt posed ethical, political, social, and emotional challenges rarely encountered by, indeed often the inverse of those that have troubled, many feminist or other postmodern ethnographers.

We were, we reflected, in little danger of colonizing most of our subjects. Spared the temptation of humanist illusions about "giving voice to the voiceless," we could evade the snares of Western feminist ethnographic romanticism.[19] The subjects we are studying are masters of representation, consummate storytellers, often sophisticated ethnographers themselves. Their rhetorical expertise enables them to generate ethnographic "data" even more self-serving and difficult to decode than that generally produced by less self-conscious narrators. What is more, their facility with and access to academic and print media assure that they can command more than "equal time" to respond to any "ms.representations" of their narratives or work on our part they find offensive. As our "risk to human subjects" protocol joked, fear of such retaliatory maneuvers well might inhibit our legitimate, critical impulses and expression.

Indeed, there seemed a significant risk that some of these informants would colonize their ethnographers! Our very choice of male cultural critics as subjects, as several feminist colleagues warned, might reinforce the colonization of the ethnographers and other women by recentering the very male authority we seek to challenge and revise. Our political commitment to potential alliance—the "studying across" component of our project—intensified the danger by fostering a dialogic approach which, as Tania Modleski points out, easily elides questions of power—the "studying up" dimension here. In avoiding the mode of the feminist report card, the scold, nag, or meter maid, we saw ourselves as flirting with our own domestication.

Ethnographic empathy, we concluded, compounded by conventional heterosexual gender codes, magnified these hazards and threw our dialogic pretensions into question. Ethnographic research necessitates a capacity for, indeed a flirtation with, "going native"—occupying the cultural and emotional space of "the other." As heterosexual women, we uneasily observed, we were all too practiced in the conventional forms such flirtation takes with men—empathic listening, conversational and social deference, drawing men out, decoding their moods, words, and silences, encouraging, reassuring, and pleasing them—the myriad tactics of feminine social sensitivity, solicitousness, and seduction.

Fieldwork, we felt compelled to confess, had begun to mimic, perhaps to parody, heterosexual dating conventions and to erect surprising constraints on our capacity for critical analyses of the lives and the texts of our subjects. Having initiated a series of intensive, often intimate, often pleasurable, conversations with our male informants (who were sometimes also friends), we found ourselves genuinely worried about later wounding or offending even the less known and more powerful figures. Betrayal, abandonment, and guilt are endemic to ethnographic research, as one of us has discussed elsewhere,[20] but here their symbolic loadings and effects were overburdened and distorted by heterosexual cultural codes. Intriguingly, our anxiety over broken relationships and the guilt and regret we might experience by publicly "betraying" male subjects seemed far more inhibiting than did any concerns about public, academic forms of reprisal.

The social anxiety we began to experience was not simply a symptom of feminine paranoia. Almost all of the oral histories we had conducted indicated male vulnerability to feminist critique and female judgment. In the words of one cultural critic, whose work has engaged deeply and powerfully with feminist theory: "I feel more on the line when I foreground gender than when I write in any other voice. From direct and indirect experience, I feel scrutinized, held accountable by feminists. I worry about becoming a target of their hostility or ridicule. Of course, these feelings articulate with old issues like a desire for female approval, which, I suspect, drove my very interest in gender analysis to begin with." His accounts of the "skittishness" he feels about assuming a feminist voice are echoed in almost all of the narratives, by men who have and those who have not braved the effort. "I've always been afraid, I was very nervous about teaching that feminist theory class," confided one who has. "I'm afraid to talk about feminism; that's where the PC policing is done," declared one who has not. And while a third claimed that his published work had received so much feminist criticism that he has "developed a thick skin," the rhetoric he employed—"See, that's where I got busted, not only for excluding but also for including" women's texts—hinted, to us, of a less callused epidermis.

Moreover, our earliest forays into this ethnographic terrain provoked evidence that despite our most cautious use of fieldwork "data," some informants will prove easy to offend. For example, we sent an early conference version of this paper to the anonymous cultural critic who narrates his minimal early awareness of feminism in the first excerpt from interview transcripts above. We had, we thought, employed this data at our own expense, to expose the feminist narcissism implicit in our preethnographic male "displacement" thesis. The postcard we received back from our "dialogic subject," while good-naturedly ironic, suggests that he read our use of his words differently:

Dear Judy,

As our late President, a star, said, "Where's the rest of me?" Ginny loved the use you made of me—I was less enamored, but I do understand the value of good material in a pinch. Speaking as a victim, I think you should familiarize yourself with the literature on what you can and can't get from interviews.

By return post we hastened to reassure our "victim" of our benevolent intentions, displaying some deference by requesting more specific remedial reading suggestions.

In a second, more ethically confusing example, we interviewed two men after we had already drafted a paper we meant to be both appreciative and critical of their published work and then tried to honor our dialogic commitments by providing each an opportunity to respond to a prepublication copy of the text-based critique. While one claimed to have read our paper "with enormous pleasure and interest," and then to wonder if, "maybe I've been snookered," the other prefaced his lengthy, far less enthusiastic reactions to our readings of his work with the acknowledgment that "it would take a while, and several readings, to get beyond a 'reactive,' defensive response. That's where I'd like to be, but as you'll see, I'm not there yet." Our response, a cross between apology and debate, promised to make editorial changes in our paper.

Such experiences left us uncertain whether to read the kinds of self-censorship we began to find ourselves practicing as signs of political maturity or as capitulation. Might we be succumbing to the seductive dangers of overidentifying with a male elite cultural vanguard who possess the power, again in hallowed heterosexual tradition, to confer on us vicarious cultural capital? We hoped it was "too soon to start worrying yet," as a character from To Kill a Mockingbird might say, but we remained uneasily aware that our project had the capacity to foster our own traitorous gender identities as well as those of our often-ingratiating, male "subjects."

Weapons of the Weak

A second set of reflections promoted by current theorizing about ethnographic power relations had to do with the somewhat neglected topic of the powers available to the weak. Although feminist/postmodernist theory emphasizes the power of the dominant, we were conscious that not all the structural or cultural advantages of our project were stacked against us. While we encountered many unusual dilemmas in conducting ethnographic work on somewhat more powerful others, at the same time we found ourselves enjoying a number of unanticipated resources, spontaneously deploying various "weapons of the weak."[21] Our research, for example, struck us as exploiting certain heterosexual conventions that worked to our advantage. The somewhat suspect pleasure in our ethnographic encounters that fueled our interest in this project, we thought, must attract the cooperation of our male interlocutors as well. There was, for example, the seductiveness of the intimate interview situation in which a rapt, female audience of one or two attended appreciatively to the male subjects' every word. "There's an erotic side to this," one of our more forthcoming research subjects acknowledged, "that we aren't talking about, that I'm sure is going to be true of almost all men that are involved in this issue. . . . That's one of the reasons it's fun to talk to you, and a lot comes out."

We were, we realized, also asking men to engage in "rapport talk," the kind of private, intimate conversation about people, relationships, and emotions, that most men, according to Deborah Tannen, find difficult and in which most women excel. Although sociolinguists find that "masculine" forms of "report talk" characterize most "mixed" gender conversations, we called on our male informants to talk more like women.[22] This was difficult for some, who displayed obvious signs of reticence, but we benefited from decades of practice in facilitating and decoding such male locutions and often enjoyed the power of a superior facility in this oratorical genre. At the same time, asking men to serve as our "informants" on their intellectual work and politics exploits masculine facility with "report talk," as it appeals to both their didactic and chivalrous impulses.

Courtly etiquette, moreover, seemed to collude with the political climate in left-liberal circles, which still gives moral privileges to women as subordinates, to foster male participation in our project. Indeed, one informant predicted that men would be willing to talk to us "out of not narcissism, but duty." This same weapon of the weak, we felt, might also shield our eventual ms.representations from suffering retribution in kind. Men might feel reluctant to "hit" women in public (or so we hoped), and leftist men might afford feminists special purchase to speak without being retaliated against in print. What is more, in some respects our project seemed to empower us to invert certain courtship rituals. Without waiting for Sadie Hawkins Day, we could take the initiative, deciding on whom we wished to bestow our ethnographic attentions and whether or not to call again.

We were surprised, moreover, by the level of receptivity to our ethnographic overtures. Although several men evinced an initial skittishness, we had a 100 percent "accept" rate for the interviews we requested. Most of the cultural critics we approached appeared enthusiastic, eager, at times explicitly grateful, to be asked. A few even volunteered to "subject" themselves to our interrogations before we dared to ask. Their eagerness to cooperate with our project appeared to overwhelm whatever legitimate anxieties they must have had about subjecting themselves to forms of manipulation, violation, and betrayal that are inherent in ethnographic research and to the ms.representations of their work and lives we would inevitably commit. We had imagined that the ethnographic sophistication of our desired informants would render them exceptionally wary of assuming the position of ethnographic subject.

Speaking with the "Enemy"

Although these critical reflections on the politics and power relations that our project involved had been carefully derived from current feminist and postmodernist models of knowing "others," they did not sit well with us in several ways. First of all, the consistent focus of these models on unequal power prompted us to categorize our subjects primarily as "more powerful others," an identification that intersected with the lingering influence of early white feminisms to cast our publicly confessed interest in alliance in a negative or at least suspect light. In the language of some early feminist positions, "more powerful others," especially white "more powerful others," often translated as "the enemy." In relation to "the enemy" our more correct, and familiar, position as white feminists was not to fraternize, to experience pleasure (unless it was the pleasure of critique), or to seek alliance but to engage in rigorous and often righteous criticism.[23]

Our dutiful focus on unequal power, overlaid once again with the lingering influence of some early white feminist discourse, also prompted us to reduce the heterosexual energies, which so clearly suffused our encounters, to their strategic uses. For despite the fact that neither of us had ever ceased speaking with (or sleeping with) "the enemy," the hold of early feminist discourses had prompted us to some public reticence about both. Working both consciously and unconsciously within these conceptual parameters, we found ourselves dutifully assessing the heterosexual pleasures of many interviews for their tendency to contaminate us further (by suggesting that we actually enjoyed consorting with "the enemy," by suggesting that we had engaged in this work out of pleasure rather than mere duty) or for their defensive usefulness in providing us with "weapons of the weak."

Our work and alliances with feminist women, of course (and now our interviews with the same), have always been suffused with pleasures of many sorts—sisterly bonding, passionate friendship, erotic frisson, and the various pleasures of shared meals, shared gossip, and shared jokes. We suspect, moreover, that successful political alliances are as rooted in personal bonds and mutual pleasures as in agreements over ideologies and goals. Still, confessing in print to our enjoyment of heterosexual energies in our interviews with actual or potential male allies, whether our subjects were white men or men of color, gay or heterosexual, alternatively prompted us to engage in good-girl queasiness and bad-girl posturing and flouting. (We were not equally positioned in this dialectic. One of us finds bad-girl posturing more congenial than does the other.)

As we continued to conduct interviews, we found ourselves constructing our encounters very differently in private than in our public talks (or in early drafts of this paper). While unequal power relations clearly informed our ethnographic encounters, our desire to study across, to be open, to take the position of potential allies set up an uneasy tension with our official focus on unequal power. This tension, moreover, was significantly augmented by the collegiality and self-critical spirit displayed by many of our subjects, not to mention the eagerness with which many regarded themselves as seeking alliance too. Although there is no discounting the possibility that we are the ones "being snookered," most of our subjects appeared to treat the interviews as opportunities to respond seriously to feminist criticism in ways that might restore their political credibility and build bridges to feminist colleagues. Indeed, one subject began his interview by directly expressing appreciation for the collegial commitments he read in our first work:

> There were really important gestures made in the paper, I thought, that I found very heartening, of moving beyond the feminist response to white male scholarship of the late 70s and 80s . . . without forgoing the notion of critique, but sort of changing the mode and the tone of the critique. And I thought, as some of us who've been through some of the wars, I found that very encouraging. Very. . . . At the same time it was significant to me that the gestures being made were coming from feminists.

Alliance among "Others"

Our ethnographic encounters have suggested in several different ways that a focus on unequal power, while essential in an ongoing way, is not a sufficient lens through which to explore our relation to "others," most particularly in an age when feminism and postmodernism also call for alliance, and alliance specifically across old relations of unequal power. As Wendy Brown asks, "What if it were possible to incite a slight shift in the character of political expression and political claims common to much politicized identity? What if we sought to supplant the language of 'I am'—with its defensive closure on identity, its insistence on the fixity of position, its equation of social with moral positioning—with the language of reflexive 'wanting'?"[24]

Perhaps, without forgoing the concepts of " 'position' and 'history' as that which makes the speaking subject intelligible and locatable,"[25] without forgoing our memory of past wounds and our critical apprehension of continuing wrongs, without refusing to give "discredit where discredit is due," we might shift our focus somewhat to include an exploration of shared desires and potential projects.[26] Perhaps, we might forgo somewhat the practice of wounded memory in order to take the risk of more forgetting and letting go. Perhaps, too, we might consciously enlarge our critical apparatus for "knowing" "others" to include, and validate, the possible intersection of unequal power with alliance, comradeship, likeness, pleasure, and desire. Age and our ethnographic encounters, at least, have made us more aware of how continuing conflict, recurring wounds, and missed opportunities are not the sole productions of the more powerful.

We began our project with an unexamined sense of rectitude in respect to the male others who have served most white feminist scholars, perhaps too facilely, as the generalized objects of our suspicion. We are beginning to feel that the rectitude of this particular, and privileged, subordinate (we do not generalize our analysis of ourselves as white, middle-class, heterosexual feminists to differently and more radically subordinated groups) can make essentializing impulses even more difficult to perceive and forgo than does the different rectitude of politically committed dominants.[27] We believe there is some truth to the presumption that the potential for knowledge of the subordinate is structurally superior to that of the dominant, but like every truth, it is only partial. When ms.representing these partially dominant others, those at least with whom political alliance seems possible, white feminists would do well to resist the self-indulgent snares of this partial truth. Reflexive restraint, at least, seems our best hope if we are to transcend the postmodern fix and build critical alliances, with women and men of color and with progressive white men too, alliances potent enough to survive and subvert the new world disorder.

Notes

We wish to thank Ruth Behar, Debbie Gordon, Barbara Laslett, Michael Rogin, Debby Rosenfelt, and Patricia Turner for their comments on earlier drafts. After we had titled this essay and presented versions of it publicly we learned that feminist graduate students in the Department of English at the University of California, Berkeley, had used *Ms.representations* as the title for a parody of the journal *Representations* which they issued informally in 1991.

1. Judith Levine, *My Enemy, My Love: Women, Men and the Dilemmas of Gender* (New York: Doubleday, 1992), 235, suggests that from 1971 until the mid-1980s "discussion of men virtually disappeared" in feminist journalism and women's studies. Levine's account is impressionistic, but we date our own focus on women and our immersion in communities of women from the late 1970s.

2. See Gloria Anzaldúa, *Making Face, Making Soul: Haciendo Caras: Creative and Critical Perspectives by Women of Color* (San Francisco: Aunt Lute Foundation, 1990); bell hooks, *Yearning: Race, Gender and Cultural Politics* (Boston: South End Press, 1990); Sandra Harding, *Whose Science? Whose Knowledge? Thinking from Women's Lives* (Ithaca, N.Y.: Cornell University Press, 1991).

3. We are not the only feminists who read the genealogy of postmodernist feminism this way. See Meaghan Morris, *The Pirate's Fiancé: Feminism, Reading, Postmodernism* (London: Verso, 1988); Lila Abu-Lughod, *Writing Women's Worlds: Bedouin Stories*

(Berkeley: University of California Press, 1993); Chandra Mohanty, "On Race and Voice: Challenges for Liberal Education in the 1990s," *Cultural Critique*, Winter 1990, 179–208.

4. For compatible initiatives see Harding, *Whose Science?* 274; bell hooks and Cornel West, *Breaking Bread: Insurgent Black Intellectual Life* (Boston: South End Press, 1991); Elazar Barkan, "Fin de Siècle Cultural Studies," *Tikkun* 8, no. 4 (July/August 1993): 49–51, 92–93; Stanley Aronowitz, *The Politics of Identity: Class, Culture, Social Movements* (New York: Routledge, 1992).

5. For a left-wing critique of political correctness on the left, see Barbara Epstein, " 'Political Correctness' and Collective Powerlessness," *Socialist Review* 21, nos. 3–4 (July-December 1991): 13–35. Levine suggests that the construction of essentialist stereotypes about men had its roots in the expectations, disappointments, terror, and rage of intimate relationships. Women's ambivalence about men, therefore, our manhating and manloving, predated the second wave of the women's movement, where it intersected with and complicated feminist analysis. See Levine, *My Enemy*, 6, 14, 227, 396.

6. See, for example, Judith Newton, "Historicisms New and Old: 'Charles Dickens' Encounters Marxism, Feminism, and 'West Coast Foucault,' " *Feminist Studies* 16 (Summer 1990): 449–70; and Judith Stacey and Linda Collins, "Salvation or Emancipation? Reflections on the Wright/Burawoy Exchange," *Berkeley Journal of Sociology* 34 (1989): 51–56. While there is nothing inherent in textual criticism that necessitates this move, neither is there anything in this method to impede it. Ethnographic and oral history methods are more apt to complicate such a critical strategy.

7. A feminist historian interviewed by Susan Krieger acknowledges this dynamic:

> *Although men had initially brought my use of 'we' to my attention, by responding to it as exclusive, it was easier for me to see it as a problem when the issue was raised about exclusion of ethnic minority women. Ethnic minority women are the center of the work, and that exclusion was both more hidden from me and more troubling. The response of the men mostly made me mad. Considering the ethnic minority women's issue made me want to change things.*

Here we are quoting not the historian directly but Krieger's textually experimental, paraphrased retelling of the interview in *Social Science and the Self: Personal Essays on an Art Form* (New Brunswick, N.J.: Rutgers University Press, 1991): 197–98.

8. Marcy Childers and bell hooks, "A Conversation about Race and Class," in *Conflicts in Feminism*, ed. Marianne Hirsch and Evelyn Fox Keller (New York: Routledge, 1990), 63.

9. Tania Modleski, *Feminism without Women: Culture and Criticism in a "Postfeminist" Age* (New York: Routledge, 1991), 6.

10. Ibid.

11. Morris, *Pirate's Fiancé*, discusses the feminist dilemma of the nagging text. We see these modes as retaining some usefulness in feminist work. Certainly feminist politics should continue to employ many genres. Our goal in this particular ethnographic, alliance-focused project, however, was to move beyond these familiar modes for the reasons we detail.

12. Our subjects engaged with race more than with gender in these instances, although the raced "others" in question were distant in time or space.

13. Our larger project deals with discourses of gender and race in the work and lives of men of color as well as of white men. In the course of working on this project, however, it was our assumptions about gender and about white men that came to seem to us the most obviously skewed. (There is no assurance, of course, that our initial assumptions about race will prove to be any less vulnerable.) This paper focuses on gender discourses, largely—though not entirely—as they appear in the work and narratives of liberal and

radical white men. Subsequent papers will focus on race in relation to gender discourse and on the comparative study of white men and men of color.

14. We do not wish to suggest, of course, that ethnographic work is free of distortion, but ethnographic work, especially when combined with the textual, can range over a larger number of sites than can the purely textual. The "in-your-face" nature of ethnographic investigation, in particular, has the potential to unsettle assumptions in a way that purely textual work may not.

15. At this writing we have conducted in-depth interviews with thirty left-identified male scholars in the humanities and social sciences. Almost all of these subjects do interdisciplinary work in cultural criticism. Each initial interview has been two to three hours long, and in several cases we have conducted follow-up interviews of similar length. We prepare for each interview by reading selectively from the subject's work. In addition, we have conducted numerous ethnographic "field trips" to the many conferences and institutes frequented by our subjects and, not incidentally, by ourselves. A fuller reading of these initial interviews in relation to the theme of what Sandra Harding calls "traitorous identities" will be the subject of our next paper.

16. The assumption here that gender critique ought to have had dramatic "impact" on our white male colleagues, at least, seems to be a reflex of our race, class, and sex positions. That is, as white, middle-class, heterosexual women, feminist discourse, the "discovery" that we were subordinated too, came to us as an earth-shaking revelation. The feminists of color to whom we have talked do not report the same sudden discovery of their gender subordination. Their entries into gender critique seem to have had longer, more gradual histories.

17. Thus Kristina Minister, "A Feminist Frame for the Oral History Interview," in *Women's Words: The Feminist Practice of Oral History,* ed. Sherna Gluck and Daphne Patai (New York: Routledge, 1991), 27–41, suggests how a feminist oral history frame may nurture and assist in the interpretation of stories by women for women. Feminists experimenting with fieldwork and textual strategies include Behar, *Translated Woman: Crossing the Border with Esperanza's Story* (Boston: Beacon, 1933); Abu-Lughod, *Writing Women's Worlds;* Trinh Minh-ha, *Woman, Native, Other: Writing, Postcoloniality and Feminism* (Bloomington: Indiana University Press, 1989); Karen McCarthy Brown, *Mama Lola: A Vodou Priestess in Brooklyn* (Berkeley: University of California Press, 1991); Dorinne Kondo, *Crafting Selves: Power, Gender and Discourses of Identity in a Japanese Workplace* (Chicago: University of Chicago Press, 1990); and Judith Stacey, *Brave New Families: Stories of Domestic Upheaval in Late Twentieth Century America* (New York: Basic Books, 1990). Feminist critiques of ethnographic practice include Kamala Visweswaran, "Defining Feminist Ethnography," *Inscriptions* 3/4 (1988): 27–46; and Deborah Gordon, "Writing Culture, Writing Feminism: The Poetics and Politics of Experimental Ethnography," *I.B.D.* (1988): 7–24; Judith Stacey, "Can There Be a Feminist Ethnography?" *Women's Studies International Forum* 11 (January 1988): 163–82; Lila Abu-Lughod, "Can There Be a Feminist Ethnography?" *Women and Performance* 5, no. 1 (1990): 7–27.

18. Here we make ironic use of the title of a reactionary polemic against "political correctness" that targeted feminists along with other forms of cultural studies. See Roger Kimball, *Tenured Radicals: How Politics Has Corrupted Our Higher Education* (New York: Harper & Row, 1990).

19. For feminist critiques of the pitfalls of Western feminist humanism, see Gordon, "Writing Culture"; Vicky Kirby, "Comment on Mascia-Lees et al.," *Signs* 16, no. 2 (Winter 1991): 394–400; and Aihwa Ong, "Colonialism and Modernity: Feminist Re-Presentations of Women in Non-Western Societies," *Inscriptions* 3/4 (1988): 79–93. Marnia Lazreg blends a critique of Western feminist imperialism with a defense of a humanist stance in "Feminism and Difference: The Perils of Writing as a Woman on Women in Algeria,"

Feminist Studies 14, no. 1 (Spring 1988): 81–107. Likewise, Abu-Lughod, *Writing Women's Worlds,* proposes adopting a "tactical humanism," and Nancy Scheper-Hughes defends the limited humanism of a "good-enough ethnography" in *Death without Weeping: The Violence of Everyday Life in Brazil* (Berkeley: University of California Press, 1992).

20. Stacey, "Can There Be a Feminist Ethnography?"

21. The term is particularly identified with peasant studies. See James Scott, *Weapons of the Weak* (New Haven, Conn.: Yale University Press, 1985).

22. See Deborah Tannen, *You Just Don't Understand: Women and Men in Conversation* (New York: William Morrow, 1990), esp. chap. 3, "'Put Down That Paper and Talk to Me!' Rapport-talk and Report-talk," and 236–37. Minister, on the other hand, makes the somewhat contrary claim that "the standard oral history frame—topic selection determined by interviewer questions, one person talking at a time, the narrator 'taking the floor' with referential language that keeps within the boundaries of selected topics," imposes a more masculine rhetorical form on women. See her "Feminist Frame," 35.

23. Noting that the women interested in theory or postcolonial discourse have been more willing to overlook the sexism and racism of white male thinkers whose work is deemed "important" than they have the sexism of black male thinkers, bell hooks, *Yearning,* 66, calls for "complex critical responses to writing by men even if it is sexist."

24. Wendy Brown, "Wounded Attachments: Late Modern Oppositional Political Formations," *Political Theory* (May 1993): 390–410.

25. Ibid., 407.

26. Levine, *My Enemy,* 397.

27. We wish to underscore our awareness that the particular strategy we are adopting as white, middle-class, heterosexual feminists in relation to progressive men who are potentially allies is not necessarily appropriate for others in different relations of domination and subordination. All such relations have specific histories and developments for which we would not presume to generalize these reflections.

15

"Man's Darkest Hours": Maleness, Travel, and Anthropology

Laurent Dubois

Thinking our limits we can perhaps glimpse the possibility of our redemption.

—IAIN CHAMBERS,
Migrancy, Culture, Identity, 1994

Invocations

I WROTE in my journal:

> *The mystical piece of anthropology, the quest of it, the common experience of estrangement, of homesickness, homelessness, homeness: there's the invisible core of what we do, the place we'll always have to come home to, no matter what.*

Leiris's Ghost

I was at the garage getting an oil change, reading the *Condé Nast Traveler,* when I came across a fashion spread under the title "The Man Who Kept His Cool." [1] "The raffish, turbaned figure on the far left is not a Hollywood creation, although he looks like one," it read, pointing to a series of black-and-white pictures of a French man with a mustache and, sometimes, a turban. It is Henri de Monfreid, we learn: an "adventurer" who "first sought fortune in pearls, weapons, and opium on the wild coast of East Africa" and writer who "became an icon for the French." Recovered from the archives, his "cool figure" is the articulated inspiration for the next pages, in which a young French model graces the landscapes of Zanzibar, fitted with Yves Saint Laurent or Yohji Yamamoto shoes, shorts, and shirts. We see him standing on the mast of a small boat, above a group of African men in the shadows on the deck. A few pages later "Our Henri de Monfreid" is seen on the same page, though not in the same picture, as an unnamed African woman. We learn that "It is said that Monfreid 'married' a local woman. Inspired by this, our beauty wears a pleated and embroidered silk gandoura and a heavy Arabic-style necklace, both by Callaghan." The sexual and cultural politics of colonialism (why "marriage" in quotes?) are pictured in terms of style and the romance of travel.

The celebration of a colonial adventurer through an appropriation of his style and his "cool" scared me enough about this discipline of anthropology where people go on trips, clothed in the fashions of "ancestors" (in order to bring back pictures), that I was inspired to steal the old and torn magazine from the waiting room and bring it home with me.

I keep it next to another kind of story about traveling to Africa: Michel Leiris's *Afrique Fantôme*. Leiris's book is also about imaginary and real encounters—sexual, artistic, intellectual—with Africa and Africans. It, too, was inspired by a set of romantic visions of how travel could transform and redeem a man. Leiris, though, did not keep his cool. An artist involved in the surrealist movement in Paris, Leiris became directly involved in the ethnographic Mission Dakar-Djibouti and so in a project that had greatly affected surrealist thought and action: ethnography. Advised by his analyst to get out of the city, he sought deliverance as he embarked with others on a journey across the French colonial empire of Africa. This journey, and the writing of the ethnographic diary called *Afrique Fantôme* through which I participate in it, seem to me to be crucial events for any understanding of the ethnographic project because of the way this text mines some of the deep but ignored dreams and desires that propel that project. Leiris's diary illustrates Michel Butor's phrase that (within a certain European tradition of traveling and of representations of travel) "to travel is to write . . . and to write is to travel."[2] Particularly, it illustrates how the process of travel, sought out as a release from constricting traditions and ways of life—as a release from the *pre*-scribed—is inevitably pre-scribed as well as inscribed in a tradition of travel writing of which anthropology is a part.[3]

Leiris wrote, "I'd rather be possessed than study possessed people, have carnal knowledge of a 'zarine,' rather than scientifically know all about her. For me, abstract knowledge will never be anything but second best." Yet, as James Clifford notes:

L'Afrique Fantôme *portrays the surrealist ethnographer enmeshed in writing— himself through the others. Toward the end of an intense period of research on* zar *possession in Ethiopia, a sacrifice is made especially for Leiris. His journal records that he tasted the blood of the animal but did not perform the* gourri, *the dance of the possessed. We see him seated among the* zar *adepts, the room*

thick with incense, sweat, and perfume. His head is smeared with butter, and—
as required by ritual—the dead animal's entrails are coiled around his brow. He
does not, however, interrupt his note taking.[4]

Throughout *Afrique Fantôme* we see Leiris trapped in the continually disappointing epiphanies of travel: seeking escape from Europe and from himself, only to
find himself inexorably present, again, in Africa. Leiris wrote of his "disappointment as an uncomfortable Occidental who had madly hoped that this long voyage . . .
and the experience of true contacts, through scientific observation, with their inhabitants would make of him a new man, more open and cured of his obsessions." In
Africa, he wrote, "I found many things, but not deliverance."[5] Leiris later wrote
that *Afrique Fantôme* was

> *a document about how a thirty-year-old European, impassioned by what had*
> *not yet been called "Negritude" and pushed to travel to then-faraway lands*
> *because that signified not only an ordeal but also a kind of lived poetry and*
> *"dépaysement," felt as he crossed pre–World War II black Africa from west to*
> *east, surprised—naively—that he could not escape himself,* realizing that the
> all-too-personal reasons that had propelled him to rip himself away from his
> friends made it impossible, from the start, for it to happen any other way.[6]

In his diary Leiris manages to expose the fragility and ambivalence of this
motion that provides conditions of possibility for anthropology.[7] Throughout the
text Leiris struggles with the colonial situation and the absurdity and immorality of
what he is engaged in (such as collecting artifacts through advanced techniques like
hiding them in umbrellas) without, however, finding any way out of this situation—
other than production of a brilliant text that exposes and explores the ambivalence
and paradoxes inherent in the ethnographic project and in the male visions and
dreams of travel and redemption that prop it up.[8]

Leiris's text has inspired me to ask myself some questions about my own experiences of training and travel. The conditions in which Leiris traveled are in many
ways different from those in which I have traveled or will ever travel; but there may
not be such difference as I might like to believe. As Michael Kowalewski has suggested in his writing on travel, "The vestiges of imperialism continue to linger: less
in the narrow sense of militant jingoism or explicit advocacy for annexing new territory than in a more ingrained and nebulous confidence about being culturally and
racially superior."[9] Many of the basic premises and processes that help create the
particular experience of white, male, privileged travel are part of a continuing tradition which emerged and became articulated in colonial times through the travel
writing and anthropological works of that time.[10]

Through a doubled exploration that moves between theoretical discussions and
autobiography, I trace the outlines of a white, male tradition of travel which, while
it has become universalized in much anthropological discourse, actually has a set of
very specific characteristics and modes of transmission. I speak about this tradition
as one wrapped up within it, appreciating its possibilities but increasingly wary of

naturalizing them as fundamental experiences. The questions I explore here have been raised as I have read travel narratives written in ways and voices different from those that initially attracted me to this discipline. Various texts, experiences, and friends have jolted me into seeing my own experience as rooted in my identity—which I can start by describing as white, suburban, middle-class, and male. The particular comfort that I, unlike many others, feel within the intellectual environment of anthropology is due in part to the fact that the anthropological ancestors often invoked in classrooms are, for me, just that. The discourse set up by these figures of course influences all of us involved in this project, wherever we come from; but there are various conscious and self-conscious privileges and privilegings that come out of my identity and its "normality" with relation to the identities of most of the writers we read.[11]

Standing behind this essay is the ghost of a much larger project that would seek to craft a more gendered understanding of male social theory by thinking about certain texts in terms of sexuality, desire, and the different meanings and articulations of rebellion against the home culture. The essays by Catherine Lutz and Barbara Tedlock in this volume make important contributions to understanding the gendering of both ethnographic writing and theoretical work in anthropology. I am curious about how blindness to this gendering of anthropology is reproduced in the present despite the sense of difference and rebellion from older texts often exuded by contemporary critique. It seems vital to me to appreciate the ways in which the anthropologists we critique today imagined themselves as going against the grain of their time—as escaping—in ways not always so distant from our own romancing of travel and ethnography. My particular preoccupation with this has to do with my position as a white male graduate student in anthropology. I wonder whether the travels I have embarked on, and the work I hope to produce, are not in some way already inscribed so deeply that I may not be able to direct them. Has my story already been written?

Awakenings

Summer 1987. Deep Springs Valley, California:

It was out in that desert valley that I first felt this thirst. A friend and I got separated from each other out in the rocky hills, in the afternoon sun. He had the water. I wandered for hours searching for him, worried that he was hurt, before finally heading down the hill towards the ranch and its reservoir. I jumped in the water with my clothes on and choked as I drank. My friend was at the ranch when I got there, eating a Danish and drinking Kool-aid.

Julian Steward was once a student at Deep Springs College too, when there were still Paiute villages nearby. Wandering in the valley, speaking with the last old people who still lived in those villages, he started his work as an anthropologist. In the archives of the school, among pictures well preserved by the dry air, I found his face: eighteen and smiling—out in the sun, walking in the sagebrush. There was

Julian Steward (seated in front row, in blackface) with other students at a Deep Springs College costume party, mid-1920s. (Photograph courtesy of Deep Springs College archive)

another picture further in the pile; it was a costume party, and the twenty male students had all dressed up to celebrate. They were sheiks, ghosts, monsters. Kneeling in front of them all was Julian Steward, wearing the same clothes as in the other picture, smoking a pipe, wearing blackface.

Maleness, Travel, and Anthropology

Why do men become anthropologists? What are they looking for in it? What am I? I want to gesture toward a more gendered understanding, on the part of male anthropologists, of what we study, of how, and of why. To produce a shifting in the methodology and language of ethnological research requires not only the opening up of a space for feminist voices, but also a closing down and a reinterpretation of the spaces available to male voices within the field. How are these spaces constructed? How are male students, like myself, socialized into those spaces? How are these spaces created, not only according to intellectual projects but also according to male sexualities and male desires?[12] What is the relationship between some of this society's larger "male" narratives, invented characters, adventure stories, and so forth and the project that men have invented in the field of anthropology? Finally, how strongly constructed are these spaces? How do they shape male students in conscious and unconscious ways? Is it possible for men to create and write a new type of anthropology? To begin to answer this it is necessary to ask a question I often find myself pondering in classrooms and lectures these days—the question Bruce Chatwin asked in the title of his last book, *What Am I Doing Here?*

If I could trace my presence in this discipline back to one particular place, it would be sitting in front of my house on spring afternoons, when I started reading *Granta* magazine: travel stories, short stories, photo essays from all around the world. Those stories were more than news: they pulsated from the page, they were lives coming through to me, and they made me want to go.

Maybe more than anyone, it was Bruce Chatwin who made me thirst for travel. I first read a chapter from his book *The Songlines*[13] in *Granta*: a chapter called "From the Notebooks"—an amazing collection of short anecdotes, quotations, and ruminations collected through many years of wandering, mostly in North Africa and Central Australia. They were notes about Chatwin's obsession: nomadism. They were autobiographical and anthropological at the same moment, all the way through, because in his travels he sought people who were chronic wanderers in order to better understand, or perhaps to justify, his own state as a chronic wanderer. In his texts these two very different things bleed together: living as nomads (which in his view is a more spiritual and healthy way of living) and living as a twentieth-century European traveler/adventurer. He first began to travel because his job as an expert on art authenticity at Sotheby's made him temporarily blind. His doctor suggested long horizons. Chatwin suggested the Sahara, and the doctor wrote a prescription: for Africa. His escape—and his argument for the naturalness of nomadism—were breathtaking to me as a sixteen-year-old, searching, in the suburbs.

Those days of reading were also days for running. I wanted to get out; I was sure that my neighborhood wasn't real, was too sheltered, was, finally, insane because it caused suffering it ignored. I knew my school was insane: knew it on those days in May, smelling the air outside, daydreaming, watching those long minutes stretching out as the traffic moved in and out and around the big white office buildings nearby. Kids spent the nights looking for escape in drugs and drinking and driving fast down three a.m. roads. Those nights some of us gathered, and got drunk from the fact that in our wealthy neighborhoods we were danger, that we couldn't gather anywhere without the cops coming along; in our own suburbs, we, the children, were always suspect when we gathered in the parks at night or walked the streets in groups. They were waiting for us to break the glass, and we took them up on it, breaking windows in the schools, hitting the street signs with baseball bats, running from police, escaping once more and laughing about it in our basements, only to realize an hour later, when the adrenaline had stopped pumping, that nothing had changed.

I might go into the city, stay out all night, or kiss in the parks which on some nights radiated with sex, but I always came home. We came home again and again;

there was no escape from that home. And home had been built twenty years before on farmland; those streets and jobs and shopping malls had all been invented not too long before I was born, planned out just right, and something was closing in on me in that home.

I searched for advice as to how to avoid the settled futures I saw lurking around me. I wanted to escape, to see another reality; I wanted to be able to come back and tell stories of other places, and to understand and criticize this place better. It was a continuity with the nausea I felt in school, the push that made me leave, midday, and travel into the city with friends, the push that took me down to the river, to sit on the rocks and watch the water instead of waiting through another day of school—running now and running later, they were salvations.

It was the promise of this salvation that I thought I saw in the study of anthropology in college a few years later, where I imagined I could make a life out of running and out of the learning that comes from running. But as I have begun to travel through anthropology, I have found that the freedom of travel is not a free space; I do not escape the strictures of the suburbs and of the mindset that made them by going far away. Although I have traveled as I had dreamed, for a long time, of doing and I have found myself doing exactly what I thought an ethnographer was supposed to do, I felt discomfort in that place and doubt about the real value of bringing it back here, back home.

A Healer

January 1992. Guadeloupe:

I met a man who healed people from his hospital room. He had a thrombosis in his leg, so he could barely walk, but he still did what he had done before his sickness: he was a doctor—a quimboiseur, a Gadézafé—meaning "the one who can see into the beyond." He grew plants in his room, and made his medicines there, and people from the town, knowing of his reputation, often came to see him when they were sick—especially when they knew they had something the hospital itself probably couldn't treat, or see at all.

A lot of what he'd learned—many of the books he'd read to learn about the world and the plants he used—came from the United States. When I told him I was from there, he told me, "There are some very powerful people up there. I knew someone who ordered a potion from a magazine in the United States. When he got it, he didn't send the money he owed them; he just kept the potion. It was sitting on his night table, and a spirit came down and took the potion back to America."

Those days, in my sleep, people came to me in the hot afternoons; and I would say "It's nice to see you again," and sleep for a long time, deeply. I told him that.

"If you dream of someone, then all you have to do is turn around, and put your head where your feet were, and they will dream of you. You'll see, you turn around and they dream of you. I used to do this, and I would see the woman I dreamed about and she would tell me 'I dreamed about you last night.'"

LAURENT DUBOIS

Jean Valquin was old, and when, during the last few days of my stay, I started telling him that I might come back in June, he told me he might not be around then.

"Death comes to everyone. Sometimes you just stay stuck in your sleep."

"And what will happen then?"

"When you die, your breath leaves you, but it has a life of its own, that is what we call a 'spirit.' Your spirit keeps living after you're dead. The living know they're going to die, but the dead don't know they're dead. There's an invisible world they live in. They might be right next to us—we wouldn't know it. They don't eat, they don't drink."

"But they talk?"

"They talk."

"And can you hear them?"

"You have to know how."

"How do you learn?"

"You read books, you learn."

"What books do you read?"

"You have to go to the library, and you ask them there, read what they have there."

I asked him if I could take his picture. He said that people can use pictures to put a spell on you. But he let me take one. The film didn't come out.

Now I keep thinking about him, as I saw him last, drying out leaves for medicines in front of his hospital room, and I want to go back, and I want to learn more from him; and then, in part, I want him to keep his knowledge away from me. I don't know what I would do with it—I would write it down, I would make an article from it, I would take his picture—I would turn this friendship into something else; sometimes, I don't want to. Sometimes, I want to leave it alone, keep it there, stop asking so many questions, stop writing—just like he told me to—asking me: What are you writing? Stop writing and listen to me.

Travel Notes

Like the model in the Henri de Monfreid fashion spread, Rudyard Kipling's Kim, that consummate adolescent, loves to dress up and pretend he is not a white boy; he travels with an old spiritual seeker and teacher across India, playing along, learning, and taking what he can for himself while also spying for the British forces.[14] The character of General Creighton, a colonial official and ethnographer who has no problems reconciling these two identities, could be seen as the figure of the anthropologist in the text. But Kim also represents a crucial aspect of the ethnographic project. He seeks, and mostly finds, a kind of invisibility through dressing, acting, and speaking like the "natives." Kim is often portrayed, in fact, as knowing more about the "natives" than they do. All of this is only possible, of course, because of his whiteness. His privilege becomes clear at certain points in the text; it is implicit throughout the work because only a white person could play that role in the "Great game." As with Huck Finn, who also travels with an older companion, it is ultimately Kim that we hear about most; it is his shoes we are encouraged to wiggle our toes in.

I remember reading *Huckleberry Finn,* the classic statement of the desire to "light out," in high school. I read the book and wanted to be on that river. I told my teacher that if we had really read the text and paid attention to it we would not have come to class, we would have skipped, knowing that "You can learn better on the streets." What I didn't see then was that the key point was exactly that we were reading, in a high-school English class, a book about a white boy running away from school. At just the moment I thought I was rejecting tradition—and finding support for this rejection in the works I was reading—I was in fact being inducted into a deep and structured tradition of male dreaming and male visions, of European exploration and adventure, a tradition in which I would eventually become intellectually and critically involved through anthropology. As explored in Toni Morrison's *Playing in the Dark,* the narrative of Huck Finn sets up racial relationships which, while enrobed in a story of escape, are also entrapped.[15] In learning, in school, about this tradition of particular escapes, the power of flight was tamed somehow, redefined, and the story I thought I was making for myself became something with a long and repetitive history. At the heart of what I wanted to run from were texts about that very act of running; I couldn't escape, because the ways of escaping were already defined, from right in the heart of what I thought I was escaping.

I thought I was rebelling against my father when, at sixteen, I drove across the country with a friend. (He did not tell me I should not go—it was I who invented his disapproval.) But on that trip I began to remember that, in my house, there were pictures of that same trip, pictures from when I was a little kid. Six months after arriving here from Belgium, carrying me as a three-week-old child, my family went on a road trip; we drove, seeking, seeing. And my father inherited from his grandfather; the land my father sold in Belgium last year, after my grandfather's death, was land my grandfather had bought long ago so he could park his trailer there. With my father, I have seen pictures of the early days, when my grandfather was one of the first people to own a camper; they traveled all over Europe, driving, seeking, seeing. Those pictures are our mythology: of grandfather and his trailer, the whole family piled in and tugged along by the old Mercedes. These dreams are older than I am.

But this history—and its ramifications—doesn't stop there. Because these stories of my father and grandfather tie me into a much bigger history of a peculiarly destructive brand of nomadism called colonialism. For the wealth of that country I came from and this country I have come to was amassed through travel, "adventure," through trips that transformed the tripped-to. Bruce Chatwin did not need to travel to Africa to find a traditional nomadic culture: he came from one. Not coincidentally using the same group that obsessed Chatwin as an example, Michel Butor writes that "for the Australian aborigine to move in what appears to us a desert is, in fact, to move within his own history."[16] We could paraphrase this, and say: "For the European male to move into what may appear as 'uncharted' territory is, in

LAURENT DUBOIS

fact, to move within his own history." "Western man has been wandering the world over ever since the great voyages of discovery beginning in the fifteenth century," writes Rockwell Gray, perhaps unwittingly describing the parameters of this particular "history" of travel which is defined around men, in terms of the "greatness" of exploration.[17] It is a history of a nomadism that seeks to erase its own tracks in dangerous ways.

In the classroom we have become used to talking about colonialism and its nefarious influences on our way of thinking and on our discipline; often, however, some kind of radical break is theorized between then and now. What seems more realistic, more honest, and especially important as a path for those of us who have inherited a certain comfort in the discipline through the benefit of gender and race, is to realize the deep continuities that link us not only to colonial categories of knowledge and methodologies but also to colonial desires, dreams, visions, and rebellion. I wonder how deeply, and invisibly, some of the insidious problems that one can clearly see, at certain moments, in traditional anthropological theory really imbue not only the theory but also the fantasms and visions that propel the search itself. How deep does it run? I now see that my desires for flight, which I always assumed came from myself, from those days in high school, are part of a much bigger and much more problematic tradition than I imagined. The dialectic I clearly experienced through my own travels—coming back from Costa Rica and understanding more closely what it was about this place I hated, coming back from Romania and understanding exactly how lucky I am here—is linked to a much more troubled dialectic of colonial history through which the identities of the dominant classes are formed through a kind of bizarre love-hate ballet of rebellion and racism. How much of what goes on in my mind, how much of my desires, do I understand? To what extent—and in what ways—is it to preserve the core motion of travel within anthropology while getting rid of a colonialist penchant for taking power—through photographs, through the repetition of other's stories—over other people? Is it possible to think this way and still hold on to anthropology?

Things Carried

August 1992. Home:

Coming home this time was strangely familiar; I'd pictured it in my mind so much during the time I was away—or maybe it had pictured me, since it was at strange times, when I wasn't even thinking of this place, that home hallucinated and insinuated its way into me. Not special things—just home, a friend's house, driving with the windows open, the blinking lights on the radio towers, the sound of cicadas—things I hadn't known I was seeing before; the familiar, that which told me what home was, where it was, that I was there.

The low, wet air of the ex-swamp of Washington, D.C., feels different after months high up, near the sun, in the dry Andes. And though it's comfortable here, back home, at night I still dream my way to the mountains of Ecuador, and I'm still traveling, meeting people, and writing down their addresses so that, when I wake up, I can write to them.

Am I back? From here, I go back there, and I'm surprised waking up in this room, in this city, with these dreams — of there — instead of those dreams of here.

What did I carry back with me? It was heavy, and it still is, weighing on me, these stories I want to tell in order to make sense of the trip, stories and graffiti poems I learned by heart, words and words and pictures etched in my head, pictures I didn't take with a camera because that felt like some sort of sacrilege, days and days of sun absorbed into my skin, sun that still keeps me warm when I remember it; and we will see if it survives this winter of a return to school. I carry stories and a desire to tell, but really, most of all, I carried myself back into a home that is more home.

What did I find here? A place in which to tell these stories, the place that propelled me to go find those stories, this place which survives on stories of those other places, this me that survives leaving and coming back.

The Mythology of Whiteness

It has been years since I sat in front of my house reading Bruce Chatwin's words; when I came back from this last of my trips that came out, somehow, of those words, I found a new issue of *Granta* waiting for me, and in it new selections from the notebooks of Bruce Chatwin, plus a piece about him by Paul Theroux.[18] Both of these chipped away at my image of Chatwin, especially the observation by Theroux that he was a great talker and a bad listener. I remembered an earlier interview at Chatwin's home, over a dinner his wife had prepared.[19] She never spoke once during the interview (as it was printed), and when the interviewer, describing the relatively bourgeois English surrounding (country home, fire, lots of meat to eat), asked him if this was home, Chatwin responded that no, it wasn't home, that it never would be, adding that this attitude drove his wife crazy. Nowhere else in all the work of his that I know is she present. Who was his wife? Why did they not wander together? Could that have been part of the story, or was it necessarily about a lone man traveling, seeking?

§

I still believe in travel. I believe in it as a moment of liminality which holds great promise. The reason I was drawn to the narratives of Chatwin—and the reasons I still find promise in my present and future travels—is because, despite everything, they still contain the potential for transformation. Travel provides a possibility for an intellectual uprooting, for deterritorialization that can be channeled into the fight against the xenophobia and racism that are on the rise in the United States and Europe. Travel—like the migrations which so many of us, in very different ways, have experienced—join us with what Homi Bhabha calls "gatherings of exiles and emigrés and refugees, gatherings on the edge of 'foreign' cultures . . . gathering in the half life, half-light of foreign tongues . . . gathering the past in a ritual of revival;

gathering the present."[20] As Iain Chambers explored evocatively in *Migrancy, Culture, Identity,* the fact of contemporary migrancy and nomadism constantly challenges, through our daily experience, a confidence in a unitary, occidental mode of interpretation and forces us instead to engage with the historical and cultural contingencies of interpretation and representation.[21] As Europe and the United States veer increasingly toward a historically unconscious violence and xenophobia, the appreciation of migrancy and métissage as processes deeply embedded within our cultures can provide a foundation for a reaction against these tendencies.

But in exploring the possibilities for action that can emerge from the defamiliarizing experience of travel, it is crucial to avoid falling into what Gayatri Spivak calls the "masculine radicalism that renders the place of the investigator transparent."[22] Michel Butor has written of the "Mythology of Whiteness" desired by the traveler who "wishes to be a kind of invisible intruder, without weight, without tainting effect: a sort of phantom who leaves no trace, like the man who wants to walk in snow without leaving footprints."[23] The search for an untainted world that constantly recedes before the seeker is a crucial trope in Lévi-Strauss's classic *Tristes Tropiques.*[24] The traveler, seeking that which is outside what is known, finds that all landscapes are inscribed, or even scarred, with a previous presence that anticipates theirs. There can be no travel outside the historical and cultural relationships that arise out of colonial histories; the places toward which one goes, seeking escape, have already been written upon.[25]

Escape from one's own past through travel is impossible also because journeys are rarely initiated—especially in ethnographic projects—without being constructed in advance. Butor defines the "Round-Trip" as a journey that emanates from a place of origin where "we are truly settled. We depart, but leave behind our possessions, our roots; we keep our rights. It is well understood from the beginning that we will return."[26] "Keeping our rights" in the context of travel has to do, within the particular tradition of anthropology, with the assumption that a text will emerge from the journey. Frameworks are set up so that the encounters which occur in travel are almost preinterpreted. The place toward which we travel—the supposed source of our knowledge (in anthropology, the process of fieldwork)—is constructed, theorized, limited, and defined before it is ever experienced. This construction is in some ways hidden by the truism that the process of fieldwork is an escape from one's own position. As Susan Sontag writes: "Anthropology conquers the estranging function of the intellect by institutionalizing it. For the anthropologist, the world is professionally divided into 'home' and 'out there,' the domestic and the exotic, the urban academic world and the tropics. The anthropologist is not simply a neutral observer. He is a man in control of, and even consciously exploiting, his own intellectual alienation."[27]

Anthropology profits from the feeling of homelessness incited by travel and intellectual engagement with the "other"; but the anthropologist is at home in an institution that, even if it centers itself on a process of alienation from institutions, still functions as an institution. Its paradoxical nature is the source of its power; by institutionalizing a supposedly homeless state, it creates a sort of home through which experiences of other places are interpreted. This "homeless" state, however, is very different from the mass of travels that go on each day among refugees, immigrants, migrant workers; "for the homeless wanderer, the semantic value of 'home' differed profoundly from its connotation for those of us who have the choice to depart and return," writes Rockwell Gray.[28] As Winifred Woodhull points out, "It is essential to underline what is specific to the situation of 'real immigrants.' . . . In this way the slogan 'we are all immigrants' can bring together real and figurative immigrants *without collapsing the differences between them,* and can thus figure as an effective collectivity."[29]

Within the complicated "collectivity" of travel writing, the works of women writers tell very different stories—often, as in anthropology, at the cost of exclusion on various levels. The power of a certain mode of travel, and fieldwork, is made clear by the need many women writers have found for "disguise." Mary Morris has suggested that: "As a woman, I travel differently than a man. I believe most women do. When I read the classic travel memoirs, I am amazed at how many times women traveled in difficult parts of the world disguised as men."[30] An example of this explicit "dressing-up" can be found in the wanderings of Isabelle Eberhardt, a "woman who repudiated Europe and its civilization, converted to Islam, dressed as a man, assumed male identity, and roamed the Sahara."[31] This disguising, made necessary by male violence, could also be read as a metaphor of what has happened in the tradition of travel writing which has been formed by male voices: a certain kind of experience has come to be defined as travel of the kind that grants the authority to write about it; writing in an entirely different way is difficult when the tropes and styles set up within the tradition of travel writing as it exists. But the struggles of women to write differently about travel have forced the rethinking of the work of travel, and of fieldwork, and about the ways they are represented.[32]

As I work on my own writing, I wonder: How can I write my story in a different way? For now, my answer is simply to assert that the space I occupy does not allow me to see over mountains and around corners; my position, and the travels it allows for me, does not bring me outside of myself. I will always, no matter where I live, be coming from that suburb I grew up in, and returning to that home of sorts; realizing this opens up for me new forms of narration that can revel in the fluid communication between memory, imagination, and experience that defines travel. The more I understand the connections and contingencies of my observations, the more I can participate in the creation of something necessary and as yet unseen.

Paradise

July 1992. Ecuador:

Alex signs with a triangle, which has made him famous: you can say "You know, the graffitis with the triangle" and everyone will have read one, will have taken it in one day on the way to work. Since he started using this symbol, many artists have begun signing their poems: with a teary eye, with a bird, with different symbols. Alex has studied sociology in Quito and Cuba but really he is a poet, and poetry is what he writes on the walls.

It is not "just" politics, or, perhaps, it is a truer politics: the incitement to dreaming, to reinventing oneself and language and the right to communicate, to reinventing the purposes of the walls, capped with broken glass, that are meant to keep the poor out, or keep the rich in. These walls become the canvases, saying: "It's not envy, it's hunger," pinching "Remember the time you almost caught me," smiling "I don't know why, but this wall holds a strange attraction." "Craziness is an art that few understand."

It is the last night in Ecuador for Alberto, who is going to study in the States, and Alex and Alberto, who have been painting together in the last months, have one last graffiti to paint. We spend the night drinking and singing with a big group of friends, and slowly everyone goes home until there are just us three and the can of black paint. Outside, the streets are empty and quiet, a few taxis going by, the police mostly at home, the private guards mostly snoring. As one of the graffitis puts it: "1:30, the city sleeps, the police keep guard on our insane dreams." We drive and search for the wall, talking: we will see each other in the States, maybe, or on other wanderings, for all these things are somehow connected now, what I am searching for there, what they are searching for here.

The wall is perfect, clean white, newly painted, and the two jump out while I stay in the car (scared). They write, enacting what they're painting:

Busques no más el paraíso. Ayer, lo quemé.

Search no more for paradise. Yesterday, I burned it.

Notes

I am grateful for the helpful criticism I received from friends, especially Ruth Behar, Katharine Brophy, Deborah Gordon, Javier Morillo-Alicea, Setrag Manoukian, and David Treuer.

1. Nicolas Bruant, "The Man Who Kept His Cool," *Condé Nast Traveler,* May 1991, 136–43.

2. Michel Butor, "Travel and Writing," in *Temperamental Journeys: Essays on the Modern Literature of Travel,* ed. Michael Kowalewski (Athens: University of Georgia Press, 1992), 55.

3. A number of works have raised the issue of the literary and inescapably written methodology used in the inscription of ethnographies, and of ethnographers' lives within and through these ethnographies. See, especially, James Clifford's *The Predicament of Culture* (Cambridge, Mass.: Harvard University Press, 1988); and James Clifford and George E. Marcus, eds., *Writing Culture: The Poetics and Politics of Ethnography* (Berkeley: University of California Press, 1986), 309–18. These explorations show how, despite a profound ambivalence and "scientific" distrust of such things, an inescapable series of romantic and visionary ideas of travel remains in and imbues entire bodies of anthropological work. See Clifford Geertz, *Works and Lives* (Stanford: Stanford University Press, 1988) and *The Interpretation of Cultures* (New York: Basic Books, 1973)—particularly "The Cerebral Savage"—for an interesting exploration of the traces of traditions of travel writing, and the erasure of those traces, in the work of Bronislaw Malinowski and Claude

Lévi-Strauss. All of these works have in common a generalized underrepresentation of women's voices, which are often simply absorbed into a discussion of men's work. For me these writers outline a particular white, male tradition of travel, and it is important to keep in mind the limits of that tradition, limits I am trying to highlight rather than reproduce.

4. Clifford, *Predicament of Culture,* 168–69. In a book called *Inside the L.A. Riots* (Los Angeles: Institute for Alternative Journalism, 1992), a picture was published from a demonstration at the Los Angeles Police Department headquarters that began the rebellion. In it, a fire rages. Nearby are three men: two have their fists raised and are shouting something while the third, a journalist, is writing in his notebook, looking down, a few feet from the fire.

5. Michel Leiris, *Afrique Fantôme* (Paris: Editions Gallimard, 1934), 7 (my translation).

6. Ibid., 14 (my translation; my italics).

7. Michael Taussig writes in *The Nervous System* (London: Routledge, 1992):

> *Anthropology was always a homesickening enterprise. To the (not necessarily unhappy) travail of the sojourns abroad with their vivid flashes of (generally unrecorded) homely memories, one has to add the very logic of its project to connect far away with home in ways that the folk back home could understand. . . . To that you have to add that once home, the anthropologist is likely to become homesick for that home away from home where being a stranger conferred certain powers. And so, home multiplies its temptations no less than it becomes a little sickening, and a fellow such as myself, sitting at home in Sydney, Australia, can find strange if temporary relief by journeying "home" to the cane fields and forests of southwestern Colombia by dint of the activity of writing about them—drawing into the noose of the real by means of the snare of the text. What makes this noose of the real effective, so it seems to me, is precisely the way by which the ambivalence of this fellow's homesickness recruits, through a process of mimetic magic, the presence of that other home. That this is a rather shady business propping up, among other things, High Theory, I hope to make clearer.*

8. See Richard Price and Sally Price's recent work *Equatoria* (New York: Routledge, 1992) for an interesting exploration of these issues which uses, as one of its many sources, Leiris's text.

9. Michael Kowalewski, "Introduction," in *Temperamental Journeys,* 11.

10. Mary Louise Pratt, *Imperial Eyes: Travel Writing and Transculturation* (London: Routledge, 1992), provides a wonderful articulation of this issue and inspired much of my thinking here.

11. Clearly, this privilege has everything to do with the comfort with which I can write this and seek out a kind of "traitorous identity" (see the piece by Judith Newton and Judith Stacey in this volume) in order to attack some of the very processes which allow me to speak as I do.

12. The question of male sexuality is not a particular or separate question from all the other things I explore here; rather, I see images of travel, of the exotic, as well as images of return and recounting as all enmeshed within sexuality and desire; what we are seeking and how we search for it are very deeply defined by our sexuality. A heterosexual discourse is also privileged in most travel writing and ethnographic work, and it is this particular discourse that I address here.

13. Bruce Chatwin, *The Songlines* (New York: Penguin, 1987).

14. Rudyard Kipling, *Kim,* ed. Edward Said (New York: Penguin, 1989).

15. Toni Morrison, *Playing in the Dark: Whiteness and the Literary Imagination* (Cambridge, Mass.: Harvard University Press, 1992).

LAURENT DUBOIS

16. Butor, "Travel and Writing," 58.

17. Rockwell Gray, "Travel," in *Temperamental Journeys,* 37.

18. Paul Theroux, "Chatwin Revisited," *Granta* 44 (Summer 1993): 213–22; and Bruce Chatwin, "The Road to Ouidah," *Granta* 44 (Summer 1993): 222–34.

19. Michael Ignatieff, "An Interview with Bruce Chatwin," *Granta* 21 (Spring 1987): 21–38.

20. Quoted in Winifred Woodhull, "Exile," *Yale French Studies* 82, no. 1 (1993): 9.

21. Iain Chambers, *Migrancy, Culture, Identity* (London: Routledge, 1994).

22. Gayatri Chakravorty Spivak, "Can the Subaltern Speak?" in *Marxism and the Interpretation of Cultures,* ed. Cary Nelson and Lawrence Grossberg (Chicago: University of Illinois Press, 1988), 295.

23. Butor, "Travel and Writing," 68.

24. Claude Lévi-Strauss, *Tristes Tropiques* (Paris: Plon, 1955).

25. This obsession with marking (like dogs peeing on a tree) is carried even in the most "empty" of locales; Butor ("Travel and Writing," 63) writes: "The first thing that Americans do upon walking on the moon is to raise a flag, and no one even dreams of being surprised."

26. Butor, "Travel and Writing," 59.

27. Susan Sontag, "The Anthropologist as Hero," in her *Against Interpretation, and Other Essays* (New York: Farrar, Straus, and Giroux, 1966), 74.

28. Gray, "Travel," 48.

29. Woodhull, "Exile," 11.

30. Mary Morris, "Women and Journeys," in *Temperamental Journeys,* 31.

31. Hedi Abdel-Jaouad, "Isabelle Eberhardt: Portrait of the Artist as a Young Nomad," *Yale French Studies* 83, no. 2 (1993): 93.

32. For example, only recently reprinted, Mary Seacole's *Wonderful Adventures of Mrs. Seacole in Many Lands* (New York: Oxford University Press, 1988) provides a fascinating nineteenth-century imperial travel account told by a Jamaican Creole woman; the text struggles to tell a different kind of story, alternatively antiracist and solidly imperialist, through and within the tropes of the dominant forms of male travel writing. A series of twentieth-century women's works on Haiti have challenged the tradition of (mostly male) exotic and racist writing about the island. Maya Deren, a dancer who traveled to Haiti in the 1950s, wrote a book (*Divine Horsemen* [New York: Documentext, 1953]) that is remarkably attentive to issues about the politics of ethnographic representation that were not raised by male writers until much later, for which she was criticized at the time by the anthropologist Alfred Metraux, *Voodoo in Haiti* (New York: Schocken Books, 1959), 21, as being "an excellent observer" but "burdened with pseudo-scientific considerations which reduce its value." Amy Wilentz, *The Rainy Season* (New York: Touchstone, 1989), and Karen McCarthy Brown, *Mama Lola: A Vodou Priestess in Brooklyn* (Berkeley: University of California Press, 1991), are two more recent texts about Haiti which, while written within traditions and institutions of journalism and anthropology still dominated by men, variously provide different kinds of visions from many of the male texts about the Haitians, whose representation has been so metaphorically important for so long.

16
Writing Lesbian Ethnography

Ellen Lewin

WHAT IS lesbian ethnography? Is it an ethnography that focuses on lesbians as the population under study? Or should it refer to the work of ethnographers we know to be lesbian, work that inspires us to ask how this source of social difference may have influenced the questions lesbians ask, their experience carrying out fieldwork, and the interpretations they favor in their written scholarship? Ethnographies that focus on homosexual behavior or identity are certainly not numerous;[1] it has been even rarer for lesbian or gay anthropologists to reveal their identities or to reflect on whether or how sexual identity has influenced their professional activities.[2] Even though discussions of homosexuality have recently become common in the political arena and in some popular media, being public as a lesbian or gay man in the academy rarely accelerates one's career.[3]

In Jim Wafer's thoughtful attempt to define "gay ethnography," he concludes that "a gay ethnography would be one in which the identity of the ethnographer as a lesbian or as a gay man is an explicit and integral part of the text" and notes that few ethnographies meet this criterion.[4] While any work done by a lesbian or gay researcher might, in Wafer's terms, benefit from such candor, Wafer himself only considers the sort of writing he has done on a culture that includes significant homosexual dimensions.[5] The idea that being gay or lesbian might somehow shape one's creative energies is not new, but in anthropology we seem to expect the impact of sexual orientation to be directly reflected in choice of subject matter or theoretical specialization.[6]

Lesbians and gay men have, of course, been writing ethnographies throughout the history of anthropology, though only recently have any felt comfortable revealing their identities or reflecting on how being lesbian or gay might have affected their conduct as anthropologists.[7] Speculation about such matters is not limited by the ethnographer's willingness to be publicly identified as a homosexual. Margaret Caffrey's biography of Ruth Benedict, for instance, indicates a relationship between Benedict's concern with difference and deviance and her lesbianism, though she suggests that Benedict's hearing impairment also profoundly shaped her sense of isolation and estrangement from others in her social world.[8] If fascination with otherness and difference were the only way to identify lesbian and gay anthropologists, however, we would probably have to question the sexual orientation of virtually all practitioners of the field.

More commonly, those who write about lesbians (or gay men) expose themselves to assumptions about their own sexuality. Like those who launched the anthropology of women some twenty-five years ago, ethnographers who focus on homosexuality or sexual difference are seen as acting on some sort of personal, and probably also political, mandate to make members of their own group more visible and to moderate the biases that seem to derive from Western cultures' phobic attitudes toward same-sex erotic expression.

With some exceptions, these assumptions are not unreasonable.[9] Taking a similar approach to feminist anthropologists at the start of the Second Wave, some lesbian (and gay) anthropologists have responded to the call for a more balanced view of homosexual behavior and identity and have set themselves the task of setting the ethnographic record straight, so to speak, in an area that has been characterized, for the most part, either by profound ignorance or, more likely, by total invisibility. Many clearly are involved in what Barbara DuBois, writing about women's studies, called "passionate scholarship," a kind of research stance that would abandon the quest for "objectivity" and instead "reject the dichotomies between science and the maker of science, between observation and experience."[10]

Early in the development of feminist scholarship, researchers began to define feminist methodology in terms of its adoption of goals and methods that would distinguish it from male-centered approaches that either objectified women or rendered them invisible.[11] Central to this concern as it came to be applied to anthropology was a questioning of the image of the ethnographer as a "professional stranger"[12] and the assumption that the best fieldwork must be undertaken in remote and preferably geographically distant locations.[13] Unlike the traditional focus on methods for bridging the assumed distance between the "natives" and the anthropologist through participant observation, feminist anthropology, along with feminist sociology, defined the appropriate focus of research as women and assumed that because feminist anthropologists would almost certainly be women themselves, the distance between observer and observed would be reduced.[14]

This assumption grew directly from the feminist theory of the period, which tended to define women and their problems in a universalized, highly dichotomized language that depended on the notion, earlier developed by Simone de Beauvoir, that gender transcended national, historical, and cultural boundaries and that women were everywhere the subject of patriarchal oppression.[15] Feminist scholars influential in creating the anthropology of women and the wider field of women's studies tended to characterize the task at hand as the dual one of breaking through women's invisibility in traditional ethnography and confronting the issue of objectivity and commitment in research. To work with women meant to work with "one's own," to be able to apply personal knowledge to the situation of those who had not yet been heard. Thus the problems of objectification that plagued masculinist social science could be resolved by feminism. Such techniques as interviewing, in the words of Ann Oakley, would simply be "a contradiction in terms." [16]

Lesbian ethnographers working on lesbian and gay topics have tended to be strongly influenced by the same assumptions. In particular, the notion that work on "one's own group" was needed to address the long-standing invisibility of that group was bolstered by the related notion that a gay or lesbian investigator would benefit from a sort of insider status that would avoid problems of objectification and exoticization. The apparent inability of traditional anthropology to consider sexual variation as other than a bizarre curiosity speaks to the parallel phenomenon of a "heterosexual assumption" in Western societies, that is, the assumption that heterosexuality is natural and universal and that it requires neither explanation nor theorizing.[17] Homosexuality, on the other hand, becomes visible under these intellectual conditions only when specifically revealed, and it tends to be seen as an aberration that requires some sort of situational explanation.

Probably the first full-length ethnographic study to confront issues of identity and personal experience undertaken by a lesbian scholar was Susan Krieger's 1983 study of a midwestern lesbian community, *The Mirror Dance*. In the preface to the book Krieger, a sociologist, speaks of having been a member of the community she later wrote about and of having only conducted formal interviews toward the end of the year she spent in the town where this community was located. She explains that writing the book was difficult for her, largely because she had been a member of the community and could not easily transform herself into a distant analyst.

> *I found that it was not a simple matter to move from my experience of intimate involvement with the community to a sociological analysis of that experience. I spent a year alternatively picking up and putting down my interview notes before I learned that, in order to progress, I had to confront the ambivalence of my personal feelings toward the community in which I had lived and done my research. The process of exploring my own experience led me ultimately to see that feelings similar to my own were important in the accounts of the*

ELLEN LEWIN

women I had interviewed and enabled me to use those feelings to guide my larger analysis.[18]

Reflecting her intimate involvement in the community and her continuing concern with the status of her membership in it, Krieger's account of its social dynamics focuses on the community's efforts to define and enforce its boundaries. She looks in particular detail at how gossip shapes women's notions of their position in the community, at the centrality of the couple as a basic social unit, and at how political activity and lesbian bars also help form the boundaries of community membership. Tellingly, discussions of "work" and "families, friends, and straight society" are placed in chapters titled "The Outside World, I and II." While vital aspects of women's lives, Krieger's treatment suggests that, to the extent that these elements of "the outside world" are located beyond the boundaries of the lesbian community, they have only peripheral effects on identity.

Kath Weston's groundbreaking study of lesbian and gay kinship, *Families We Choose,* speaks frankly not only of how being gay legitimized her work to potential informants and helped her gain access to people she wanted to interview but also of how being a lesbian specifically shaped the way she spent her time during her San Francisco fieldwork. On one level, knowing that she was a lesbian meant that informants did not feel they needed to dispel antigay stereotypes or to give her basic information about homosexuality; rather, they felt comfortable speaking of subjects that aroused some controversy within gay and lesbian circles, such as sadomasochism or drag queens.

More significant for Weston as a researcher were the effects of shared identity on how she conducted research, particularly in terms of the efforts she had to make to render the familiar sufficiently strange so that she could ask informants to explain their own cultural assumptions. Not surprisingly, she often felt as though she were asking them to talk about things that were as obvious to them as they were to her.

> *Early in the research my daily routine was structured by decisions about what to record. Everything around me seemed fair game for notes: one day I was living a social reality, the next day I was supposed to document it. Unlike anthropologists who have returned from the field to write ethnographies that contain accounts of reaching "their" island or village, I saw no possibility of framing an arrival scene to represent the inauguration of my fieldwork, except perhaps by drawing on the novelty of the first friend who asked (with a sidelong glance), "Are you taking notes on this?"*[19]

Weston's difficulties working in her "own" culture recall recent work by other "native anthropologists." José Limón, for example, has described similar dilemmas while doing fieldwork in a South Texas community not unlike his own hometown. While out for an evening of drinking and dancing with a group of informants, he observes himself maneuvering between participation and observation and worries about whether describing this scene will reinforce pejorative stereotypes of Mexican

Americans.[20] And Emiko Ohnuki-Tierney speaks of how the native anthropologist must struggle to distance herself from the culture in order to ask questions but must also allow herself to benefit from her intimate understanding of its nuances. "Native anthropologists," she tells us, "have easy access to not only the intellectual dimensions but also to the emotive and sensory dimensions of these behaviors."[21] Other anthropologists who have worked in their own cultures, or in cultures closely related to those which they consider their own, have noted similar difficulties.[22]

But are studies of lesbians by lesbian scholars necessarily plagued only by dilemmas of overlapping identity? Feminist anthropologists, despite their early conviction that shared femaleness would give ethnographic studies of women by women an authenticity and authority not present in studies of women done by men, later followed other feminist theorists and came to question the degree to which identity of gender erased or minimized other sources of difference. This recognition eventually grew into an insistent, and still unresolved, questioning of the use of terms like *woman* and *gender* to characterize qualities that transcend culture and a corresponding suspicion that use of these terms may reinforce the very dichotomization feminist scholarship presumably seeks to erase or undermine.[23]

While academic gender studies have moved away from their earlier reliance on fixed definitions of masculinity and femininity, popular discussion of homosexuality continues to elaborate rigid notions of sexual orientation as a core identity determined, either wholly or in part, by still poorly specified hereditary factors. The extensive media coverage of recent and highly speculative neurological and genetic studies tends to assert that these studies prove that homosexuality is "natural" or genetically determined and therefore neither morally reprehensible nor the "fault" of one's parents or other early influences.[24] But however effective these approaches may be in engendering tolerance of and sympathy for homosexuals among the general public, they require a classification of sexuality based only on the sex of one's preferred partner—same or opposite—a scheme that fails to consider many other variables in how sexual desire is manifested and that blurs the meanings people give to sexual behavior in particular cultural contexts. The polarized images of sexual orientation these theories generate have been reflected in recent discussions of gays and lesbians in the military as well as in debates over the need for civil rights legislation to protect homosexual citizens. Asserting that homosexuality is a source of difference between people, these theories propose sexual orientation as a method of classification that eliminates the need to understand behavior on any other basis.

Despite these influential popular trends, recent ethnographic writing by lesbians, following theoretical debates in feminist scholarship, has begun to consider the ways in which our differences from the lesbians we study—differences of class, age, nationality, ideology, cultural background, or race, or the differences drawn from our status as investigators—may mean that these lesbians are not necessarily "our own," at least not in the sense that our identities and experiences share some centrally defining sameness. Even residence in the same local area or community may not entail shared identity in every instance, though such shared identity may be a dimension of particular situations. These understandings are crucially aided by a growing focus in lesbian ethnography on the permeability of both communities and identities and on our expanding awareness of the instability of identity, particularly in complex cultural settings. Even the act of writing about lesbians from our own communities poses a difference between the ethnographer and the informant, no matter how participatory her research technique; in most instances, other differences arise even as we put ourselves into the research picture. An examination of recent ethnographic writing on lesbian populations by lesbian investigators will not only show that ethnic, racial, and generational difference can be more salient dimensions of these research situations than sameness based on shared lesbian identity but also will suggest that the definition of lesbian ethnography is at least as illusive as trying to arrive at a satisfactory understanding of feminist ethnography.

Over thirteen years of ethnohistorical research on the working-class lesbian community of Buffalo, New York, Elizabeth Kennedy and Madeline Davis struggled with their relationship to the narrators whose accounts form the basis of their 1993 book, *Boots of Leather, Slippers of Gold.* Early in the book Kennedy and Davis discuss the kinds of dilemmas they faced both as current members of the community and as researchers attempting to capture the flavor of lesbian life in Buffalo during the 1930s, 1940s, and 1950s, periods critical to the formation of lesbian community in the United States.

They began by interviewing some of their friends, women who initially doubted that their stories might be worth telling. Although Kennedy and Davis were not part of the community of the 1940s and 1950s, they explain that they are members of "the same general community in which our narrators now function today and our paths invariably interconnect, depending on age, friendship groups, class, race, ethnicity, and culture."[25] Their community involvement helped them to locate women willing to participate in the study but also limited them, in that members of groups with which they had little direct contact were less willing to become narrators. For example, through the initial group of narrators they gained access to white women and to black and Indian women who had socialized together in the lesbian community of the 1950s. But finding black women whose circles in the 1950s had been exclusively black proved to be far more difficult, for their definition of the boundaries of their community was clearly different from that of Kennedy and Davis. Similarly, finding "fem" narrators was far more difficult than locating "butches" willing to tell their stories.[26] It seemed that fems sometimes left the community, went straight, or became butch; they also seemed to have less sturdy ties within the community and more fragile friendship links apart from their relationships with butch lovers. Thus the initial requirement Kennedy and Davis maintained for selecting narrators, that the women still be members of the community, did not take full account of the transitory nature of the lesbian community they were studying. And their observation that it was difficult to recruit narrators who saw themselves as different from Kennedy and Davis, on the basis of some social or cultural category, points to the limitations of defining the lesbian community as a closed system, in terms of either interaction or meaning.

While belonging to the community generally let them ease their way into the narrators' confidence, Kennedy and Davis are candid in relating the difficulties their closeness to the narrators generated.

> The main drawback to researching a community where we carried on our social lives was that we could not make a clear separation between work and personal life, placing tremendous demands on our moral character to meet high ethical standards for research. We felt — rightly or wrongly — the need to be models of respectability and sensitivity in order to convince people that we were trustworthy and that the project was worthy of their participation. We also had to manage our personal lives carefully so that we did not inadvertently become involved in community tensions and rifts, thereby limiting our access to those who might help us find narrators. It was also essential to guard against using the research to personal advantage in our social lives. As we collected oral histories, moreover, we came to know a great deal about the lives of members of the community; yet because we had guaranteed our narrators confidentiality, we had to develop a discipline for digesting information without using it or sharing it directly in our lives. And when narrators who were not held to our standards as researchers might use an interview to vent a grievance or manipulate one of us, we had to learn to ignore it.[27]

While some of these issues are persistent problems for all anthropologists, the implications for Kennedy and Davis's personal lives clearly go beyond the consequences most ethnographers must consider. Kennedy and Davis knew they would continue to live in this community and to socialize with at least some of the narrators. Their most delicate negotiation had to do with achieving a balance in representing positive and negative aspects of community history. Narrators' accounts sometimes emphasized the pain they had experienced as members of a despised minority; at other times their stories focused on the good times they had together, on fun, romance, and their success in maintaining a lesbian community in a hostile environment. The researchers were aware that their methods tended to draw on a limited pool of narrators—those who mentally and physically survived the rough gay life of the 1940s and 1950s, those whose relationships to the community were sufficiently positive for them to wish to discuss it, and those who were white and more rebellious, largely because they were the easiest to contact. Black and upwardly mobile (that is, more closeted) white lesbians were less available and hence less central players in the history constructed by the narrators.[28]

Kennedy and Davis's meticulous description of their methods raises a number of provocative questions about lesbian ethnography. Insider status is revealed to be unstable, yet the collection of ethnohistorical data is driven by assumptions, by both the researchers and the narrators, of what it means to be lesbian. Variables based on race, ethnicity, and class, by helping to define social networks, had a significant impact on who was interviewed. But beyond these factors, the authors speculate that only those lesbians who had positive memories of community life were inclined to participate in the study; these variables not only defined the pool of narrators but also tended to shape the narrators' accounts of their experience. Kennedy and Davis's common membership in the lesbian community of Buffalo both enriches their access to and understanding of its history and helps construct a definition of and boundaries for the community. Although they have not shared the specific memories of their narrators, they are able to convey the assumptions and meanings—the culture—of that community in a way that preserves its integrity, celebrates its strength, and relates its struggles to more recent developments.

Issues of similarity and difference are played out in a different way in Sabine Lang's account of the difficulties she faced trying to carry out research among Native American "two-spirited" women.[29] Lang, a young German anthropologist whose previous work on the *berdache* was based on archival research, came to the United States to conduct her first real fieldwork and to extend her documentary, largely historical analysis of gender variance among Native American groups through participant observation among contemporary women who defined themselves as lesbian, or "two-spirited." As a lesbian, Lang expected that she would be welcomed into the groups she planned to visit, or at least that the women would have little reason to doubt her motives for working with them, though she was also aware, from extensive reading on lesbians of color in the United States, that race and racism were persistent issues in North America.

But no amount of prior reading could have prepared Lang for the indifference and even hostility she faced when she began to attend ceremonies held by Native American lesbians and attempted to schedule interviews with "manly females." It seemed clear to her that race and nationality were far more salient indicators of identity to these women, and to other Native Americans she met, than was sexual orientation—or sexual orientation pulled out of context. At best, she felt that some of the groups she visited tolerated her presence; at worst, she felt excluded and disliked. She concluded that only luck and individual personality could account for the successes she experienced in the field when someone to whom she happened to be introduced and with whom she happened to get along happened to introduce her to someone who was willing to be interviewed. She also discovered that the remaining "two-spirited" people on reservations tend to be sheltered and protected by their families, making them almost unapproachable by outsiders. In other words, Lang learned that the construction she placed on her own sexual orientation had little meaning in the Native American settings where she attempted her research; for her purposes, no concept of lesbian or gender variance bridged the cultural gulf between herself and her informants.

In a different context, Esther Newton's recent paper on the erotics of fieldwork suggests that her own identity and that of informants cannot be assumed to be the same, even when the researcher is an active participant in the same community she is studying.[30] In a highly nuanced approach to the politics of "studying one's own," Newton scrutinizes the idea of the "romance of anthropology," asking whether this is only a manner of speaking or whether there is an "erotic equation" in fieldwork. After reviewing the few allusions to erotic adventures to be found in the anthropological literature, nearly all by men (both heterosexual and homosexual), she identifies her own inclination to work on gay topics as a gay woman anthropologist as having more to do with her own political and cultural identity than with eroticism. But she also recognizes an emotional component and erotic dimension in her fieldwork, particularly when she began to work on an ethnohistory of Cherry Grove, a gay beach resort outside New York City where she had spent several summers.

Newton's account focuses on the relationship she had with her "best informant," Kay, an elegant elderly woman with a legendary reputation as a seductress, on whom she developed an instant crush. At her first meeting with Kay, Newton's fieldnotes report that her "heart quite turned over." The intensity of flirtatious energy that passed between anthropologist and informant became the inspiration for the research, though they tacitly agreed, largely because of Kay's frail health, that a physical relationship was out of the question. Newton remains aware that their relationship is that of informant and researcher: Kay talks about herself but does not ask about Newton; Kay's allure is enhanced by her ability to give life to memories of the early days in the Grove that Newton is trying to document. Her fieldnotes emphasize the importance of Kay's contribution to the research:

> The more I think about Kay allowing herself to be seduced in the girl's school the more her life connection to the history I am helping to construct excites me. Kay's beauty and presence would have made me crazy in her younger days, but I wonder if — because she was a party girl rather than an intellectual — I could have loved her deeply. But now, instead of having ideas she embodies ideas.[31]

Kay's death from a heart attack marked the end of an era for many Cherry Grove residents, and for Newton it signaled the time to end her fieldwork. Her research was importantly shaped by the intensity of her bond with Kay and their mutual attraction. Yet it is clear that the relationship with Kay was an artifact of the fieldwork experience and that it was strengthened by the distance between researcher and informant rather than by their similarities as lesbians.

Questions of identity, motivation, and loyalty were important components of my own decision to undertake research on lesbian mothers in the late 1970s. At the time, considerable attention was being directed toward lesbian mothers' problems with child custody and particularly their vulnerability to custody challenges from former husbands. Lesbian mothers generally lost their children in such cases because the courts tended to view lesbianism and motherhood as inherently contradictory. Because my earlier work had focused on motherhood and questioned the causal relationship between motherhood and women's secondary social status, I felt that I would be well equipped to shift my attention to motherhood in what I viewed as my own community—lesbians in the San Francisco Bay area.[32]

While I had expected to find that lesbian mothers would reveal many of the same concerns and problems faced by heterosexual single mothers of similar social and economic status, I could not have predicted the degree to which motherhood would prove to supersede and overwhelm other sources of identity. Lesbian mothers spoke of feeling distant from friends who did not have children and of being drawn to other women, regardless of sexual orientation, who were also mothers. One mother told me:

> There's a difference between people who have children and people who don't have children. People who don't have children, to my way of thinking, are very selfish. . . . They needn't consider anyone other than themselves. They can do exactly what they want to do at any given time. And though I admire that, it's not possible for me to do that and I guess for that reason most of my friends are single mothers, because it's hard for me to coordinate my needs and my time with someone who's in a completely different head set. . . . I just prefer being with people who have some sense of what it's like to be me, and I understand where they are too.[33]

As my project progressed, I found myself becoming increasingly conscious of the difference between my lesbian mother informants and myself. While identifying myself as a lesbian sometimes meant that women were more willing to be interviewed, my status as a nonmother—what many of my informants called "single"—did little to enhance rapport during the interviews. Some mothers simply assumed that I must be a mother and were quite surprised when I revealed that I was not. Why, then, was I interested in mothers? What personal conflict was I trying to resolve? Now that I had talked to so many lesbian mothers, had I not decided to become one, too? My hasty explanations about wanting to contribute something to the community seemed lame; my intellectual concerns with the place of motherhood in feminist theory were even less compelling to those for whom motherhood is anything but theoretical.

Noticing that the lesbian mothers I worked with seemed to be distancing me from their central concerns, I also became aware, as I completed my research, that I tended to withdraw from continuing interaction with mothers. Not only did I begin to understand that being a lesbian is not the same sort of identity for a mother as for a nonmother, but I also came to see my identity as a lesbian as having assumed a particular guise in that it informed and motivated my intellectual interests. "Lesbian" for me became not only the identity that defined my erotic preferences and the source of my alienation from many (but not all) aspects of mainstream culture, but also a critical stance, the angle from which I regarded my own experience and that of other people: a set of ironies and incongruities, perhaps, but not my only personal identity.[34]

While bringing together seemingly contradictory identities as lesbians and mothers challenged traditional constraints on who may be a mother, lesbian mothers constructed motherhood in a way that validated and intensified the long-standing division of women into mothers and nonmothers.[35] Doing research, on the other hand, made my identity as an anthropologist seem a more central determinant of "who I was" than did being a lesbian or even a nonmother. As a researcher, I could allow my nonmother status to shift into the background; it did not matter "who" I was, as long as I could do a good interview and come up with a reasonable interpretation of lesbian motherhood in American culture.

Can there be a "lesbian ethnography," and, more to the point, can lesbian ethnography exist only as the product of research by "native anthropologists" among "their own"? The varying experiences of lesbian anthropologists working in gay or lesbian communities have underscored the shifting significance of lesbian identity in the field; its inconsistencies in the research context are, of course, no more noteworthy than is its changing significance in ordinary experience. None of us is always first and foremost lesbian, any more than we are defined exclusively by ethnicity, race, age, or profession. Ethnographic research presents yet another context for defining identity, within which being lesbian is expressed with particular self-consciousness, rarely just as it would be in ordinary circumstances.

This exploration of lesbian identity and ethnography raises broader questions about the mechanisms whereby any ethnographer, gay or straight, native or outsider, conceptualizes a personal identity and determines to what degree it resonates with the culture under investigation. I would agree with Jim Wafer that the measure of a "gay ethnography" is its commitment to make explicit how the researcher's sexual orientation frames the work, but I would resist the implication that homosexuality necessarily does this, or that its meaning in the field can readily be pinned down in the ethnography. A lesbian ethnography informed by feminism offers us an opportunity to reduce the distance between ethnographer and subject and to provide the basis for a level of intimacy not readily achievable by the nonlesbian investigator working with a lesbian population. But it cannot overcome fundamental differences that still emerge between ethnographer and subject simply because of the nature of the enterprise. As ethnographers we can all strive to examine ourselves as candidly as possible, but our descriptions themselves are the product of a part of our intellectual identities that cannot help but cast a shadow on all the other dimensions that make up our vision of our selves.

Notes

This paper grows out of work done with William Leap in editing our forthcoming collection, *Out in the Field: Anthropologists Reflect on Fieldwork, Writing, and Representation* (Urbana: University of Illinois Press, in press), and I wish to acknowledge his many contributions and those of Liz Goodman to the ideas I have developed in this essay. I also wish to thank Deborah Gordon and Ruth Behar for their thoughtful comments on an earlier draft of the paper and for their useful suggestions for revisions.

1. But see, for example, Evelyn Blackwood, ed., *Anthropology and Homosexual Behavior* (New York: Haworth Press, 1986); Gilbert Herdt, *Guardians of the Flutes: Idioms of Masculinity* (New York: Columbia University Press, 1987); Gilbert Herdt, ed., *Gay Culture in America* (Boston: Beacon Press, 1992); Serena Nanda, *Neither Man nor Woman:*

The Hijiras of India (Belmont, Calif.: Wadsworth, 1990); Esther Newton, *Mother Camp: Female Impersonators in America* (Englewood Cliffs, N.J.: Prentice-Hall, 1972); Esther Newton, *Cherry Grove, Fire Island: Sixty Years in America's First Gay and Lesbian Town* (Boston: Beacon Press, 1993); Kenneth E. Read, *Other Voices: The Style of a Homosexual Tavern* (Novato, Calif.: Chandler and Sharp, 1980); Will Roscoe, *The Zuni Man-Woman* (Albuquerque: University of New Mexico Press, 1991); Kath Weston, *Families We Choose: Lesbians, Gays, Kinship* (New York: Columbia University Press, 1991); Walter Williams, *The Spirit and the Flesh: Sexual Diversity in American Indian Culture* (Boston: Beacon Press, 1986).

2. It should not be necessary to mention that we never see parallel inquiries into the influence of heterosexuality on the work of scholars or artists.

3. Esther Newton's eloquent personal account of her experience of homophobia in academia ("Academe's Homophobia: It Damages Careers and Ruins Lives," *Chronicle of Higher Education,* March 11, 1987, 104) is only one example of the kind of discrimination faced by gay and lesbian anthropologists, as well as by scholars in other fields.

4. Jim Wafer, "Out of the Closet and into Print: Sexual Identity in the Textual Field," in *Out in the Field.*

5. Jim Wafer, *The Taste of Blood: Spirit Possession in Brazilian Candomblé* (Philadelphia: University of Pennsylvania Press, 1991).

6. Discussions of this issue have been extensive in such fields as music, where there are heated debates about the influence of, for example, Schubert's or Tchaikovsky's homosexuality on the abstract musical elements of their work.

7. Lewin and Leap, *Out in the Field.*

8. Margaret M. Caffrey, *Ruth Benedict: Stranger in This Land* (Austin: University of Texas Press, 1989).

9. The first book-length ethnographic study of a lesbian "community" was written by Deborah Wolf, a nonlesbian researcher (*The Lesbian Community* [Berkeley: University of California Press, 1979]). As Weston points out in her review article on lesbian/gay ethnography ("Lesbian/Gay Studies in the House of Anthropology," *Annual Review of Anthropology* 22 [1993]: 339–67), Wolf had considerable difficulty producing a reputable study, particularly because she confused the population of radical feminist lesbians she studied in San Francisco with the totality of lesbian culture.

10. Barbara DuBois, "Passionate Scholarship: Notes on Values, Knowing and Method in Feminist Social Science," in *Theories of Women's Studies,* ed. Gloria Bowles and Renata D. Klein (London: Routledge & Kegan Paul, 1983), 112.

11. See Edward Ardener, "Belief and the Problem of Women," in *Perceiving Women,* ed. Shirley Ardener (London: Malaby Press, 1975), 1–27, for a classic statement of the need for such rethinking. Also see a number of the essays that appeared in Rayna R. Reiter, ed., *Toward an Anthropology of Women* (New York: Monthly Review Press, 1975), particularly Sally Slocum's now classic "Woman the Gatherer," 36–50.

12. Michael H. Agar, *The Professional Stranger: An Informal Introduction to Ethnography* (New York: Academic Press, 1980).

13. These approaches owed much to earlier efforts by African American anthropologists to question the expectation that they ought not to conduct research in Africa because they would lack objectivity about members of their own race (Delmos Jones, "Toward a Native Anthropology," *Human Organization* 29 [1970]: 251–59). At about the same time, some anthropologists began to pioneer research in American cultures, though the discipline remains ambivalent about whether work conducted in one's own language close to home can really qualify as anthropology. These studies have been followed by more recent discussions of otherness and orientalism popularized by the postmodern wing

of the discipline. See Frances E. Mascia-Lees, Patricia Sharpe, and Colleen Ballerino Cohen, "The Postmodernist Turn in Anthropology: Cautions from a Feminist Perspective," *Signs* 15, no. 1 (1989): 7–33, for an illuminating discussion of the relationship between feminist scholarship and calls for anthropology to reconstitute its relationship to its "object."

14. See, for example, Helen Roberts, ed., *Doing Feminist Research* (London: Routledge & Kegan Paul, 1981), for some typical approaches from sociology. See also Michelle Z. Rosaldo and Louise Lamphere, eds., *Woman, Culture and Society* (Stanford: Stanford University Press, 1974), and Reiter, *Toward an Anthropology of Women*, for early and influential contributions to the anthropology of women that reflected an implicit assumption that feminist concerns would motivate the formation of this new field and that women would most likely do the work. Peggy Golde's early collection of reminiscences by women anthropologists, *Women in the Field: Anthropological Experiences* (Chicago: Aldine, 1970), while not explicitly inspired by the feminist agenda, revealed assumptions about women as a distinct subset of anthropologists and suggested certain regularities in our experience of fieldwork.

15. A number of classic contributions to the early anthropology of women, particularly some of the essays in Rosaldo and Lamphere, *Woman, Culture and Society,* depend on this approach. See, for example, Nancy Chodorow, "Family Structure and Feminine Personality," 43–66; Sherry B. Ortner, "Is Female to Male as Nature Is to Culture?" 67–87; and Michelle Z. Rosaldo, "Woman, Culture, and Society: A Theoretical Overview," 17–42. But despite the common assumption that all of the work done in this period was based on a notion of universal gender subordination, much of the early anthropology of women was concerned instead with accounting for instances of discontinuities between gender and status and with teasing out how gender and other possible sources of inequality, such as race, class, and caste, intersected and how women might manipulate gender to advance particular social and cultural goals. See, for example, in Rosaldo and Lamphere, *Woman, Culture and Society:* Jane Fishburne Collier, "Women in Politics," 89–96; Carol P. Hoffer, "Madame Yoko: Ruler of the Kpa Mende Confederacy," 173–88; Karen Sacks, "Engels Revisited: Women, the Organization of Production, and Private Property," 207–22; and Carol B. Stack, "Sex Roles and Survival Strategies in an Urban Black Community," 113–28; also Denise Paulme, ed., *Women of Tropical Africa* (Berkeley: University of California Press, 1963); Margery Wolf, *Women and the Family in Rural Taiwan* (Stanford: Stanford University Press, 1972) and "Chinese Women: Old Skills in a New Context," in Rosaldo and Lamphere, *Woman, Culture and Society,* 157–72.

16. Ann Oakley, "Interviewing Women: A Contradiction in Terms," in *Doing Feminist Research,* 30–61.

17. See Evelyn Blackwood, "Breaking the Mirror: The Construction of Lesbianism and the Anthropological Discourse on Homosexuality," in *Anthropology and Homosexual Behavior,* 1–17.

18. Susan Krieger, *The Mirror Dance: Identity in a Women's Community* (Philadelphia: Temple University Press, 1983), ix.

19. Weston, *Families We Choose,* 14.

20. José Limón, "Representation, Ethnicity, and the Precursory Ethnography: Notes of a Native Anthropologist," in *Recapturing Anthropology: Working in the Present,* ed. Richard G. Fox (Santa Fe, N. Mex.: School of American Research Press, 1991), 129.

21. Emiko Ohnuki-Tierney, "'Native' Anthropologists," *American Ethnologist* 11, no. 3 (1984): 585.

22. See, for example, Soraya Altorki and Camillia Fawzi El-Solh, eds., *Arab Women in the Field: Studying Your Own Society* (Syracuse, N.Y.: Syracuse University Press, 1988).

23. These perspectives, articulated by academics and writers from a variety of backgrounds, have been particularly clearly developed by feminists seeking greater recognition of the experience of women of color and women from non-Western cultures in formulating theory. See, for example, Patricia Hill Collins, *Black Feminist Thought: Knowledge, Consciousness, and the Politics of Empowerment* (New York: Routledge, 1991); Chandra Talpade Mohanty, Ann Russo, and Lourdes Torres, eds., *Third World Women and the Politics of Feminism* (Bloomington: Indiana University Press, 1991); see also Judith Butler, *Gender Trouble: Feminism and the Subversion of Identity* (New York: Routledge, 1990).

24. Recent media coverage of studies that seek to demonstrate a biological or genetic explanation for the occurrence of homosexuality includes articles in such publications as *Atlantic Monthly* (Chandler Burr, "Homosexuality and Biology," March 1993, 47–65) and *Newsweek* (David Gelman, with Donna Foote, Todd Barrett, and Mary Talbot, "Born or Bred?" February 24, 1992, 46–53). Among the works now receiving significant popular attention are the work of Simon LeVay (*The Sexual Brain* [Cambridge, Mass.: MIT Press, 1993]), whose studies of the hypothalamus glands of presumably gay and straight men started the current wave of biological speculation, and a recent study by geneticist Dean Hamer and others ("A Linkage between DNA Markers on the X-Chromosome and Male Sexual Orientation," *Science,* July 16, 1993, 321–27).

25. Elizabeth Lapovsky Kennedy and Madeline D. Davis, *Boots of Leather, Slippers of Gold: The History of a Lesbian Community* (New York: Routledge, 1993), 18.

26. Kennedy and Davis (ibid.) describe the use of the terms *fem* (or femme) and *butch* in the lesbian community to refer to the system of contrasting gender roles whereby some women (the butches) projected a relatively masculine image through dress and mannerisms and other women (the fems) presented a more stereotypically feminine appearance. In the community they studied, butch/fem roles were a somewhat inflexible dimension of social-sexual organization, indicating, among other things, which women were possible sexual partners for which other women.

27. Ibid., 18.

28. Ibid., 24–25.

29. Sabine Lang, "Travelling Women: Doing a Fieldwork Project on Gender Variance and Homosexuality among North American Indians," in *Out in the Field.*

30. Esther Newton, "My Best Informant's Dress: The Erotic Equation in Fieldwork," *Cultural Anthropology* 8, no. 1 (1993): 3–23.

31. Ibid., 14, emphasis in original.

32. Ellen Lewin, *Lesbian Mothers: Accounts of Gender in American Culture* (Ithaca, N.Y.: Cornell University Press, 1993).

33. Ibid., 118.

34. See Newton, *Mother Camp,* 104ff. on *camp.*

35. See Ellen Lewin, "On the Outside Looking In: The Politics of Lesbian Motherhood," in *Conceiving the New World Order: The Global Politics of Reproduction,* ed. Faye D. Ginsburg and Rayna Rapp (Berkeley: University of California Press, 1995), 103–21, for a more extensive discussion of this point.

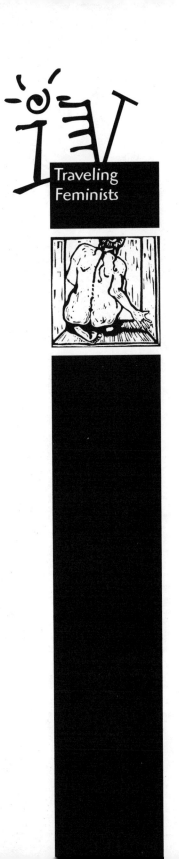

Traveling
Feminists

17

A Tale
of Two
Pregnancies

Lila
Abu-Lughod

ENTERING MY twenty-fourth week. Heartburn woke me up this morning, and I turned to my favorite of the three pregnancy guidebooks I keep near my bed—the one organized around anxieties. In the section titled "Heartburn and Indigestion," sandwiched between "Losing Your Figure" and "Food Aversions and Cravings," I read: "It's nearly impossible to have an indigestion-free nine months; it's just one of the less pleasant facts of pregnancy."

I closed my eyes. This was, I thought, what my friend Kareema must have felt.[1] She was the mother of eleven whom I'd seen through two pregnancies in the 1980s. Like all but one of her others, her last pregnancy, at an age closer to my current age than I liked to imagine, had proceeded without the benefit of medical care. She had suffered terrible indigestion, and I remembered those many evenings when, by the light of a kerosene lantern, I had prepared her the fizzy orange drink she swore relieved the pain: effervescent tablets of vitamin C purchased at the local pharmacy, dissolved in a glass of water.

In those days I understood little about what Kareema and the other Awlad 'Ali Bedouin women I lived with in Egypt were experiencing. Caught up in my own world and my research, first in my mid-twenties and later in my thirties, I claimed to be, and was, very interested in women's experiences. But I barely noticed anything about their pregnancies except protruding bellies artfully hidden by large red belts. The women worked hard, lifting heavy cooking pots, carrying their other children on their backs, washing clothes, and walking long distances to visit friends and relatives. Pregnancy hardly seemed to interfere. At the end, with the help of a local midwife, their mothers, or their mothers-in-law, these women suddenly produced infants who, by the time I would see them, were lovingly swaddled and lying close to them. Or so it seemed. Except that every older woman who told me her life story mentioned a miscarriage or a stillbirth.

My pregnancy, in contrast, was the ultimate late-capitalist U.S. achievement: assisted by the most recent advances in reproductive technology, monitored from egg production to fetal heartbeats with the help of ultrasound and hormonal analysis, and expensive. I was one of the fortunate women in her late thirties for whom in vitro fertilization had succeeded on the first try. I began the pregnancy with a mix of scientific knowledge, common sense, and holistic medical advice: warned by my books about pre-eclampsia, prevented from carrying heavy objects by my husband, pampering myself by lying down to allow blood to flow to my placenta, counting my calcium milligrams, balancing my green and yellow vegetables, and studying with some despair the undecipherable diagrams that promise to guide pregnant women through proper exercise regimens.

If I had not known Kareema and the other women in Egypt who had shared their lives with me, I would not have been able to shake my head and laugh at myself for the fuss I was making. I also might not have felt so lucky. My personal experience of the pregnancy was shaped by the double (or hybrid, in Kirin Narayan's view) life I lived as an anthropologist.[2] I moved between the world of "home" in the United States, with my network of friends and family and the resources of feminist scholarship on reproduction to help me think about the facts of life, and "the field" in Egypt, where I was surrounded by women who became pregnant, gave birth, lived with children, and talked to me and to each other about why things sometimes went wrong. I looked to both places for help in understanding what was happening to me, just as I had sought this pregnancy in both places.

Searching for Children

Living in what is known as the Western Desert of Egypt, with only a substandard clinic not close enough for easy access, the Bedouin women I knew could not take advantage of the superb doctors and excellent hospital facilities available in Egypt's major cities, Cairo and Alexandria. They gave each other advice, told stories about their pregnancies and those of others, and complained—of headaches, fevers, aches, swelling. That did not stop them from feeling sorry for me, their anthropologist friend, still childless long after their own daughters, who had kept me company on the long winter evenings of my first stay in the late 1970s, had married and given birth to one, two, sometimes three children.

Even though I did not yet want children, they sympathetically told me stories about women who were "searching for children" too. They explained the theory of "blocking"—how conception could be blocked by a sudden fright, by being confronted with someone who has come back from a funeral, or by a donkey who has just given birth. They scared me by offering to take me to healers to have a string sewn through my back or an amulet made. They told me how a second fright could undo a blockage, or how bathing on successive Fridays with water in which a gold necklace had been soaked might counteract a different kind of blockage.

I eagerly scribbled all this in my notebooks; mostly it was material for my book on Bedouin women's stories. I wondered, occasionally, how these notions about flows and blockages fit with our medical narratives about hormones, eggs, sperm, and fallopian tubes. I had long been skeptical of images of how our bodies worked that relied on biological entities whose existence I had to take on faith. Emily Martin's analysis of the mechanical metaphors and bizarre implications of these scientific stories about women's bodies had confirmed my own ambivalence.[3]

Later, when I was back in Egypt in 1990 with my husband, I felt it was time to get pregnant. I did not yet know there was a serious problem, but other friends were generous with remedies for infertility. After appointments with the quiet and serious doctor at the Cairo Motherhood Center—where the equipment was sterilized, the sheets clean and white, the ultrasound machine shiny, and the receipts computer-generated—I would fly south to the palm-draped village in Upper Egypt where my husband and I were then doing research. My new friend Zaynab, mother of five children conceived on annual visits of her migrant husband, took time from her busy schedule of working her small fields, collecting fodder for her animals, and pressing land claims against her paternal relatives to try to help me.

Zaynab knew of three treatments. First she took me to the ruins of the Pharaonic temple that dominated the small hamlet in which her mud-brick house stood. Calling out to the local guard that we were just going to the well, she saw to it that he waved us on, ignoring the fact that we had no entrance tickets. She took me around the temple and then down some steep steps to a pool of stagnant water. "It is good to bathe with this water," she said. Anticipating my modesty, she had brought with her an empty tin container. "You can do it back at the hotel," she explained as she filled the can with the water.

When we came out of the cool, dark shaft she steered me away from the entrance to the temple. "You have to leave by a different path from the one you used to enter," she said. Later, another old village woman told my husband that Zaynab should have had another woman there, hiding above the shaft, to drop a stone into the water just when I was looking in. This would have frightened me. Although they lived hundreds of miles from the Bedouin and shared little of their way of life, these village women seemed to be working with the same theory of blocking: a second fright undoes the effect of a first, and leaving by a different route literally opens up, or unblocks, a path to conception and birth.[4]

The next time I came to the village, still not pregnant, Zaynab decided to take me to the Coptic monastery nearby. "It's good," this Muslim woman explained, "to look at those Christian priests with their beards." When we had been admitted by a gentle nun, Zaynab whispered in the hush of the monastery, "Just look at the beautiful things, the velvet curtains, the pictures. The older things are, the better."

Next we went to the monastery's cemetery. Zaynab kept calling out for someone. She seemed agitated and finally hailed a young boy who was riding by on his donkey. "Where is your father?" she asked. "Go get him. Tell them there's a woman here who wants him." Eventually a burly man with a huge grey mustache appeared. He was the undertaker. He led me around the cemetery, explaining so much that I couldn't tell if this was a guided tour meant for a tourist or something special to induce pregnancy.

I realized that he knew why I was there when he took me to a cloth-draped coffin, its cover half on, empty inside. He instructed me to take off my shoes and step back and forth over the casket seven times, using my right foot first each time. Later he took me down to some dusty vaults. Reaching inside, he tore a strip of green cloth off the top of another unused coffin. Zaynab had gone off. "Wrap it under your breasts and bathe three times with it," he said conspiratorially. "But don't tell the woman you're with about this."

Then he told me to climb into the vault. I started in but jumped back in fear as a lizard darted out. Scolding me for being afraid when he was there, he then instructed me to tear another strip of cloth from the cover of the empty coffin in the far corner. He wadded this up and told me to stuff it inside me when I had sex with my husband.

Just then Zaynab returned and reminded him that it was important for me to see the well. So we all walked on. With a key he opened a small structure housing a very old brick well. He told me to look down until I could see my own eye. It was a long way down and there was very little water at the bottom. He explained that the monastery had an electric pump for irrigation and that tanks of water were brought in from the pipeline for drinking. Zaynab and I finally left, she apologetically giving him a small sum (all I had brought with me), he saying he hoped God would grant me what I wanted.

A few weeks later Zaynab decided, with some encouragement from me, that she should take me to visit the local Muslim woman curer. This was an old woman who had married and had five children, spent years in Cairo, and returned to her father's village when her husband died. Her father, himself a religious figure with powers of healing, had appointed her his successor, and she was now famous throughout the area. It was rumored that people came from as far away as Kuwait to seek her help. I had heard about her and was curious.

We waited until the heat of the day had passed and then set off to her hamlet. In her courtyard we saw other women leaving. The healer herself sat in a dark room, a small and wrinkled blind woman with her knees drawn up and her feet tucked neatly under her black dress. Women with children in their laps sat waiting their turn to speak to her. After listening to them, she would talk quickly in a kind of rhyme while deftly winding green thread into small objects they were to take with them. When our turn came, Zaynab first discussed her land dispute. Then she explained my problem and answered questions for me. The old curer prescribed a concoction that my husband was to drink. Zaynab and I pressed some money into her hand and then walked home.

In the end the recipe was too complicated. I didn't know where to get many of the ingredients. I didn't even know what these spices and powders were. Their Arabic names meant nothing to me. And though surely I could have arranged to put the bowl of liquid out on the balcony to catch the starlight, as instructed, where would we get the glowing rod to douse in it, in our Cairo apartment?

The problem, of course, was that my husband and I didn't believe it would work. I had half-heartedly bathed with the water from the Pharaonic temple, wary enough of the dead insects floating in it not to splash sensitive parts of my body— the very parts that were supposed to receive this healing treatment. I had also dutifully stepped over the coffins in the Christian cemetery, feeling silly and hypocritical, but I never wrapped the cloth strips around my chest or stuffed them inside me. Oddly, though, I still have the strips of cloth in my dresser drawer, somehow unable to bring myself to simply throw them away. I also don't quite know what to do with an old amulet I acquired from my Bedouin friends. I had wanted to see what was inside and had even photographed the contents. But then I could not help being awed by people's insistence that amulets were powerful and should never touch the ground or be thrown away. In matters mysterious, like religion and reproduction, one finds oneself uncertain enough about the truth to be half willing to "go native."

Inside and Outside the Body

When I returned home after a year in Egypt, I entered that new world that has become familiar to so many women of my generation and class in the U.S.—the world of laparoscopies, tubal adhesions, endometriosis, amniocentesis, and other such unpronounceables; the world of busy doctors in white coats who inspect and prod and shine lights at parts of you that you cannot see; the world of procedures that, they inform you absentmindedly, might cause slight cramping. I finally was allowed to graduate into the world of IVF, as in vitro fertilization is known. I joined well-dressed women with bags under their eyes who spent the early morning hours waiting their turn to have blood drawn from bruised veins and to lie back in darkened rooms with their legs in stirrups so their ovaries could be scanned on grainy black-and-white screens.

It was a world of sitting by the phone, waiting for your daily instructions. Of injections that quickly cured you of any squeamishness about large hypodermic needles. Sometimes, as you expertly drew from the small vials the correct dosages of Pergonal or Metrodin, or later, progesterone in a viscous base of sesame oil, you wondered if someone watching outside the apartment window might take you for a drug addict. This was, after all, New York.

"Our goal is to make you pregnant," the doctor had explained in our first visit. "Our success rates are the highest in the city. We average about thirty-three percent per three-month cycle." This kind of talk leads to a world of uneasy comparison. You look around the waiting room and wonder who will make the statistics. The woman next to you tells you she has fifteen eggs; yesterday you'd been told that you had five but that one was bigger than the others. "What does that mean?" you ask the busy doctor. "We'll see how they come along. If the others don't catch up, we'll have to cancel the cycle." You beg those little ones to grow.

Another woman tells you that this is her third try; last time she had to be hospitalized for ovarian enlargement. The next day someone tells you about her friend who had so many eggs she froze some. She became pregnant and had twins. Then her husband was killed in a car accident. Now she wants to thaw her other eggs and have another child by him. A tough young woman in blue jeans cheerfully jokes with the nurses as they take her blood. She's been coming for a year. You listen in dismay as another recounts how she got pregnant after four tries and then lost her triplets. She and her husband couldn't stand the strain, so they took a break for two years. You also look around at some of the women and think they're just too old.

All these women are surely bringing down the percentages. You think, with some secret pleasure, that this means your own odds as a first-timer are that much better. You keep talking to your friend and colleague, the one who told you about this clinic and who became pregnant on the first try. She barely seems to remember the anger and frustration you feel, or the uncertainty. She encourages you and tells you what will happen next. You compare notes about the waiting-room experience and tell her what an interesting anthropological study it would make, if only you didn't feel so much hostility to the money-making production line the clinic creates that all you want to do is escape—as soon as you no longer need their services so helplessly.

Retrieval is the clinical term for the procedure of removing your ripe eggs from the ovary to be fertilized outside your body. You go to the hospital for this, feeling perfectly healthy and afraid that when you wake up you won't be anymore. After being kept waiting, as usual, you are walked in your oversized nonskid slippers down corridors, into elevators, and then into an operating room. The room looks familiar from the slide show the nurse gave a few weeks earlier, and you feel less resentful at that two hours wasted in a session of elementary talk about IVF. (The session protects the IVF program by covering in simple language the complex material contained in the pile of consent forms you must sign.) The lights in the room are bright. It's a little cold. An intravenous feeder is put in your wrist, and the nurses talk to you reassuringly. You disappear. You wake up in the recovery room, people groaning all around you, some quite frightening with tubes in their noses. You want to get away but are too groggy to move.

As we were leaving the hospital, my husband and I bumped into one of the doctors. She asked how it had gone. I said no one had told us. Surprised, she went off to telephone the lab. She gave us the first good news: they had retrieved six eggs. She insisted that someone must have come to tell me in the recovery room but I had forgotten. I didn't believe her.

Then we waited for the telephone call our typed instructions said would come as soon as they knew the results. Five eggs had fertilized. One more success. As Sarah Franklin, one of the few feminist anthropologists to study IVF, has noted, the cultural narrative of conception has been rewritten by the infertility specialists so that conception is no longer the natural result of intercourse but a scientific and technological achievement. The road to pregnancy is a complex obstacle course in which hurdles are overcome, one by one.[5]

The next step was what they call "the transfer"—from dish to womb. Back at the hospital, I sat on a simple wooden bench with the same women who had been in the surgical waiting room on the day of the retrieval. Everyone was a little nervous, but cheerful. This part wasn't supposed to hurt. To pass the time we chatted. One of the women asked if I remembered the blonde woman who had been there with us three days earlier. Yes. "Well," she whispered, "her husband was in there for an hour and a half and couldn't do it. So they had to rush me ahead of her in line for the retrieval." We giggled in a mixture of relief that our husbands had performed efficiently and embarrassment at the others' humiliation.

Finally, my turn. I entered the familiar operating room and climbed onto the table. The doctor was joking with the embryologist in the adjoining room. It had been a long day. Suddenly I saw something come into focus on the elevated television screen to my right. My name was typed on the screen, and there were my four fertilized eggs. The fifth, the doctor explained, had disintegrated. An assistant printed out the image on two polaroid snapshots, a general view and a close-up. I had imagined test-tube babies as little fetuses in jars, but these were just cells, clusters of overlapping circles sitting in a petri dish, like illustrations from a biology textbook.

The transfer only took a minute, with some joking about not dropping the catheter as the embryologist rushed from the lab to the table. I was moved onto a trolley and wheeled out, like the women who went before me, clutching my polaroids.

Abandoned together in a small, otherwise empty ward, we made conversation. One woman's companion helped us exchange our "baby pictures," all we might get for the $8,000 we had had to pay up front (I was counting the days until my insurance company would reimburse me; most of the women had no insurance coverage for IVF). The doctor had told us we could leave after fifteen minutes, but we all insisted on staying for forty-five—superstitious that if we stood up our precious embryos might slide out. One by one, we gingerly climbed out of bed and dressed. I took a taxi home, not wanting to risk the subway.

The month during which I underwent IVF was also the month in which the copyedited manuscript of my book on Bedouin women's stories arrived in the mail.[6] I read over the chapter called "Reproduction," written before I'd entered that strange world of reproductive technology. I could have longed for the more natural character of these women's experiences of becoming pregnant and having babies. I could have viewed pregnancy as an alienation of my body by the medical establishment. But I thought of Donna Haraway, the feminist historian of science, who keeps insisting that it is dangerous for feminists, nostalgic for an organic wholeness, to condemn and reject science and technology. Such associations of the natural with the feminine have been essential to women's confinements to the body and the home; and such rejections of science leave it in the hands of others who may not have women's interests at heart.[7] In the late twentieth century the boundaries between inside and outside our bodies are more fluid. Are glasses to be rejected because they are not our natural eyes? So what if for two days a petri dish served as my fallopian tubes?

Still, I refused to believe the nurse who telephoned twelve days later to say my blood test was positive. I thought the IVF staff would fudge the results so they could publish articles in the medical journals and claim to be the best clinic in the city. Then they'd accuse you, the incompetent female body, of having lost the baby. I didn't believe I was pregnant until two weeks later, when I saw, on that familiar black-and-white television screen, the image of those tiny sacs, each with a twinkling star in it. Fetal heartbeats. Multiple gestation, as they call it in the business.

Kareema, on the other hand, knew the other signs of pregnancy. Her period stopped. She began to feel sick. She threw up. She felt fatigued. She couldn't bear to smoke. Some women have cravings; others have aversions to certain foods. Some Bedouin women claim to have aversions to their husbands.

My menstrual cycle had been suppressed by drugs, and it was too early for the other signs. I was dependent on the ultrasound scanner for my knowledge of pregnancy. I recalled Rosalind Petchesky's classic work on fetal imaging and the politics of reproduction. Rather than condemning, along with other feminists, the panoptic gaze the ultrasound technologies afford the male medical establishment or even the disembodiment of the fetus from the mother, demoted to a mere environment for this rights-bearing entity, she drew attention to the possibility that women might experience this technology positively. "How different women," she wrote, "see fetal images depends on the context of the looking and the relationship of the viewer to the image and what it signifies."[8] I couldn't help finding it reassuring to see on the screen to my right what was supposed to be inside me. I was so unsure of my babies that I worried about their having disappeared if I didn't see them every two weeks or so.

Communities of Women

Now, months later, when I have heartburn and the amazement of feeling the babies move in a part of me that had never even existed before, I feel closer to Kareema. The belly I rub with almond oil and look down at is here, not on the screen. It looks the way Kareema's did. My pregnancy book had told me I'd first feel the babies' movements as butterflies or fish swimming around, but the book was wrong. It was a definite thumping—like a heartbeat in the wrong place. I wondered what else the book might be wrong about and instead tried to remember every detail of what the Bedouin women had said and done. How would I cope when the babies came? I tried to remember how these women had managed. How had they breast-fed? It had all seemed so natural and easy. How had they coped at night? I don't remember Kareema's babies crying. I realized I hadn't paid much attention to things that now mattered enormously to me. I also understood now that Kareema had probably been feeling that same thumping inside her as she kindly told me folktales to record for my book.

When you are pregnant for the first time, you suddenly see other women you know in a different light. My mother began to tell stories about her pregnancies, and I loved seeing her soften as she reminisced about how exquisite it was to hold an infant. My mother-in-law seemed remarkable for having had seven children. I asked my sister about her experience of giving birth alone in India. She said she had never read a book on the subject and had no idea what was going on. My friends with children began to seem more important. I felt I was crossing a threshold I hadn't noticed before.

This experience of recognizing a commonality among women led me to think back to an article I had begun writing five years earlier about the possibilities for feminist ethnography.[9] I had argued that women ethnographers who studied women unsettled the central divide between Self and Other on which anthropology usually rested. This was not because of any essential, cross-cultural sameness of women but because feminist anthropologists had to recognize that womanhood was only a partial identity. In the abstract language of academic life I wrote, "By working with the assumption of difference in sameness, of a self that participates in multiple identifications, and an other that is also partially the self, we might be moving beyond the impasse of the fixed self/other or subject/object divide."[10] I also noted, however, that there was often a perceived kinship, albeit limited, between women anthropologists and their women subjects that made seeking knowledge of their situations more of a political project that had implications for "home." The kinship Zaynab and other women in Egypt felt for me was apparent in their sisterly concerns about my childless state and their efforts to help me. My feelings for them had led me both to friendships there and to explorations in my anthropological work back home about ways to represent them that might make the complexity of their lives and individual personalities—forms of complexity we recognize in the Self, not the Other—more apparent.

What I did not explore then was another process that could occur: that one's own constructions of personal experience would be shaped by knowledge of these women's lives and even by particular women one had come to know.[11] In being pregnant, I was finding that the cultural resources I had at my disposal to think about what I was experiencing and to fill in gaps in my knowledge of an uncertain terrain included both those from "home" and those from "the field," often juxtaposed. From "home" I had my own family background, the biomedical discourse with which so many white middle-class women feel comfortable, feminist critiques of this same discourse as well as of the popular cultural representations in media and books, and a patchy familiarity with women who had given birth.[12] From Kareema and the other women I knew in Egypt I had notebooks full of beliefs about reproduction, stories about reproduction, and, most important of all, years' worth of vivid memories of an everyday world rich in pregnancies, births, and children. I now thought and felt with all these resources.

As I begin to gain confidence that the pregnancy really will last, I have started to worry about the birth. I sometimes skip ahead to the later chapters of my pregnancy books and frighten myself with those glossy photographs that seem to have nothing to do with the reassuring text about positions, helpers, and water births. I look at my husband and wonder about my new dependency—will he mop my brow as they show husbands doing in the photographs, will he comfort me, will he find the birth disgusting, will he help me? When I dare look beyond the birth, I am excited. My husband, always more optimistic than I am, reminds me that this is a new adventure for us. When he compliments me for being so brave I swell with pride.

Yet when I think ahead to the days and weeks just after the birth, I envy Kareema. Like most professional women I have good friends, but they don't live nearby. My family too is scattered. My sister, whom I saw every day for more than a month because she gave me my injections, won't be around. I look forward to the new intimacy with my husband, and I'm counting on him; but I've been warned about the strains. As an academic I think of books as companions, but will they really give me the advice I need? So much is unknown: I don't know how long I'll be in the hospital; whether I'll have a caesarian section; who will deliver me; whether the babies will be in incubators.

When Kareema gave birth, as usual the women in her community dropped everything to come help. She had her baby in the room she likes best for this—a warm room away from the rest of the house. Her cousin and her best friend, women she has known nearly all her life, were there to hold her. Along with some other women and all her children, they stayed with her for a week, busily cooking, doing her laundry for her, and talking. They had all been through this experience. They knew she would be there when it was their turn. They joked and gossiped and told stories late into the night. They made her soothing teas. No men came near, and few demands were made on them. It was a sort of holiday. Kareema's only responsibility was to rest, to nurse and change her new infant, and to receive her women visitors, who came bringing chickens, eggs, bars of soap, and little handsewn dresses.

At my wedding four years ago, I missed my Bedouin friends. To bring them in, I recited some songs they would have sung to celebrate my wedding had they been there. It will be harder to find a substitute for the busy companionship they provide to the mother of a newborn. They say a new mother should not be left alone. I expect I will be, from time to time. They say she is vulnerable. We call it postpartum depression. Perhaps I'll wear my Bedouin silver bracelet. They say it is good for a new mother to wear silver; it protects her.

Notes

I am grateful to the women like Kareema and Zaynab in Egypt who taught me about infertility, among other things. A fellowship from the National Endowment for the Humanities through the American Research Center in Egypt enabled me to come to know Zaynab in

1990. Since 1978 I have had generous support for my research among the Awlad ʿAli Bedouin; my most recent extended stay with Kareema and her family was made possible by a Fulbright award. Ruth Behar's insightful suggestions made the essay richer.

1. All the names used in this essay are pseudonyms.

2. In a sensitive and sensible rethinking of the misnomer of "native" or "indigenous" anthropologist, Kirin Narayan has drawn attention to the complex and shifting identifications all anthropologists have and has proposed hybridity as a more appropriate characterization of anthropologists' identities. She has also suggested that their texts should embody the enactment of that hybridity. See Kirin Narayan, "How Native Is a 'Native' Anthropologist?" *American Anthropologist* 95 (1993): 671–86.

3. Emily Martin, *The Woman in the Body: A Cultural Analysis of Reproduction* (Boston: Beacon Press, 1987).

4. For more on Awlad ʿAli theories of infertility, see Lila Abu-Lughod, *Writing Women's Worlds: Bedouin Stories* (Berkeley: University of California Press, 1993), chap. 3. See also Marcia Inhorn, *Quest for Conception: Gender, Infertility, and Egyptian Medical Traditions* (Philadelphia: University of Pennsylvania Press, 1994), especially its rich descriptions of Egyptian infertility treatments.

5. Sarah Franklin, "Making Sense of Missed Conceptions: Anthropological Perspectives on Unexplained Infertility," in *Changing Human Reproduction,* ed. Meg Stacey (London: Sage Publications, 1992), 75–91; and "Postmodern Procreation: A Cultural Account of Assisted Reproduction," in *Conceiving the New World Order: The Global Politics of Reproduction,* ed. Faye D. Ginsburg and Rayna Rapp (Berkeley: University of California Press, 1995), 323–45.

6. Abu-Lughod, *Writing Women's Worlds.*

7. Among the articles in which Donna Haraway makes this sort of argument, "A Cyborg Manifesto," in her *Simians, Cyborgs, and Women* (New York: Routledge, 1991), 149–81, is probably the most powerful.

8. Rosalind Pollack Petchesky, "Fetal Images: The Power of Visual Culture in the Politics of Reproduction," *Feminist Studies* 13, no. 2 (Summer 1987): 280.

9. Lila Abu-Lughod, "Can There Be a Feminist Ethnography?" *Women and Performance* 5, no. 1 (1990): 7–27.

10. Ibid., 25.

11. It is difficult for anthropologists to reflect on the ways their sense of self or their experience of life events might have been shaped by the people and ideas encountered in the field. It can be done, however, as exemplified by Dorinne Kondo, "Dissolution and Reconstitution of Self: Implications for Anthropological Epistemology," *Cultural Anthropology* 1 (1986): 74–88; Renato Rosaldo, "Introduction: Grief and a Headhunter's Rage," in his *Culture and Truth* (Boston: Beacon Press, 1989), 1–21; and Paul Riesman, *Freedom in Fulani Life: An Introspective Ethnography* (Chicago: University of Chicago Press, 1977).

12. This greater acceptance by middle-class women of the biomedical discourse on reproduction is documented by Martin, *Woman in the Body,* and by Rayna Rapp, "Constructing Amniocentesis: Maternal and Medical Discourses," in *Uncertain Terms: Negotiating Gender in American Culture,* ed. Faye Ginsburg and Anna Lowenhaupt Tsing (Boston: Beacon Press, 1990), 28–42.

18

Women Out of China: Traveling Tales and Traveling Theories in Postcolonial Feminism

Aihwa Ong

The instabilities of the categories "Chinese" and "women" are multiplied by their juxtaposition, allowing for questions such as: Who are Chinese women? What do they tell us about "China"? What do they tell us about "woman" and "women"? What does it mean when China [scholars] study them as one entity? . . . Basically, how have the stories of Chinese women been told "internationally"?

— REY CHOW,
"Violence in the Other Country," 1991

Writing Chinese Women Out of Context

STORIES ABOUT Chinese women disseminated in the West have recently enjoyed an extraordinary reception. Perhaps, for Western readers, the satisfaction of these stories derives from their depiction of Chinese women fleeing an unremittingly oppressive society into full emancipation in the West.[1] For instance, after a harrowing story of her youth in socialist China, Jung Chang departs for England: "As I left China farther and farther behind, I looked out of the window and saw a great universe beyond the plane's silver wing. I took one more glance over my past life, then turned to the future. I was eager to embrace the world."[2] Compared with China, the West is "the world": the universe of expansion—of space, freedom, and self.

As an expatriate Chinese woman myself, I seek to problematize that notion of flight to the West as the point of female liberation by retelling stories of other Chinese women which express a more muddled, contradictory, and ongoing struggle of emancipation in diaspora. As Rey Chow's epigraph indicates, identity for Chinese women has become even more unstable as labor migrations, frequent travel, and political flight all reconfigure the links between place and identity. Given these conditions, immigrant Chinese women must be understood outside categories conventionally associated with the cultural, national, and geographical spaces of ancestral China. By presenting my own life alongside the stories of two other emigrant Chinese women, I hope to capture the specific diasporic articulations James Clifford calls "traveling-in-dwelling, dwelling-in-traveling."[3] By attending to the specific circuits of travel—of the anthropologist, the expatriate student, the working-class woman—we reveal how the everyday consciousness and practices of diaspora women are caught up in struggles between different cultures and socioideological points of view. The women who tell their stories here talk about travels not only away from a home country but also away from their home culture and about finding themselves unevenly assimilated into the host society. As a traveling theorist myself, I am acutely attuned to the unstable and varied meanings of Chineseness that have to be dealt with in the anthropological literature by retelling alternate stories that express the vexed reworking of Chinese women's identity internationally.

Locations and Identities

The figure of the multiply inscribed diaspora subject—whether anthropologist or informant—poses interesting questions for feminist anthropology and the writing of culture. I hesitate to support the claim that Third World scholars in the West are, as opposed to their locally born colleagues, in any way more inherently inclined to reject hegemonic discourses constructing cultural differences. For every Salman Rushdie there must be a V. S. Naipaul in the world of postcolonial writing. My approach is not to assert positionality as a kind of privileged nativism in the anti-hegemonic representation of difference[4] but to argue that the expatriate anthropologist, and informants, are multiply inscribed subjects who cannot be contained by essentialized terms like "Chinese women." Teresa de Lauretis has noted that the gendered subject is "simultaneously a racial, ethnic, and class-determined subject."[5] This subject occupies different subject positions at different moments, and she cannot be determined by any single discursive apparatus. The stories below are intended to present a multifaceted view of how traveling "Chinese" women become variously decentered from their cultural bearings and, in the United States, seek different forms of accommodations with the host society and distances from their ancestral cultures. In studying the culture of traveling subjects, there is "the whole question of identity as a politics rather than an inheritance."[6] For women in diaspora, there is a range of possible commitments—to family, to one's ethnic or class groups, to a gender identity, and even to different parts of the world—but also the tensions among them that continually destabilize any one hegemonic position.

§

I present my own story here to highlight the dynamics of being an overseas Chinese in America rather than being American Chinese. Although considered culturally "impure," marginalized, and incomplete, such an identity for me becomes a positive strategy of being in the world today.

I was born in what was colonial Malaya, into a family that traces its origins both to South China and to the Malacca Straits Chinese world. My upbringing, though predominantly Straits Chinese, was multicultural, and we spoke different Chinese dialects, English, and Malay under the waning hegemony of the British Empire. I was educated in an Irish convent, and the alchemy of Irish Catholicism and local Chinese culture encouraged the development of smart and outspoken girls. We lived among different Chinese groups, Indians, Eurasians, and Malays. I went to college in New York City and now teach at a California campus. My parents remain in Malaysia, while my siblings live in Singapore, Sydney, Hong Kong, Princeton, and New York. My work and family take me to Southeast Asia every year, and my life is lived simultaneously in the West and in Asia. Locations, movements, and displacements, not a fixed positionality, are vital forces of my life.

A few years ago, after the birth of my first child, I became naturalized as an American. Although motherhood is now linked to citizenship, it does not thereby tie my body inexorably to the United States, nor my subjectivity to an Asian American identity. I am only comfortable in between the spaces of Asian, American, and Chineseness; I cannot be fully at home in any one of them. I thus cling to the raft of "overseas Chinese" as a way to express my position as one that always maintains a detached and skeptical attitude toward the singular claims of race, ethnicity, culture, nationhood. In a similar vein, Abdul JanMohammed uses the term "specular border intellectual" to describe certain expatriate intellectuals (like Edward Said) who operate effectively in two or more cultures but refuse to be subjected to the allegiances tied to a single home country; they attempt to achieve freedom from the "conflation of identity and location."[7] Such border intellectuals experience "homelessness-as-home" in the sense of using their interstitial cultural space as a vantage point from which to define other political possibilities.[8]

Languages also produce in-between consciousness of differences. The literary theorist Mikhail Bakhtin calls this state *heteroglossia,* which refers to the struggle among different socioideological perspectives that are embedded in language as "dialects."[9] The socioideological points of view represented by my varied uses of Chinese dialects, Malay, and English continually keep me conscious of imposed hegemonic views embodied in any single language, including the "dialects" of Chinese culture, of academic feminism, and of ethnic studies.[10] I try to bring this multiple positioning and multilingual sensibility to my work among different Asian groups in Southeast Asia and in North America.[11] Below, I present other Chinese women's stories of travel to the West, in the belief that their testimonies produce an alternate stream of theorizing about diasporic gender consciousness.

Writing Their Stories

Lately, a subfield of feminist discourse has expressed doubts as to the legitimacy and advisability of writing about other, less privileged women. This topic is broached with some honesty but also much confusion between personal and wider social responsibilities. Warned about the (unintended) reproduction of colonial domination in academic writing, feminists have defined the representation of less privileged and non-Western women as a question of negotiating trust and avoiding betrayal. To what extent do these ethnographic anxieties reflect our (emotional) fears of relationships (the subject of anthropological inquiry, after all) and our pessimism about the possibilities of exchanges that will benefit both sides? Indeed, given the academic, professional, and commercial competition tied to writing, even well-meaning feminists cannot deny that however much they may try to make the writer-informant relationship more equitable, they will probably gain more from the encounter in terms of their careers than will the informants. Judith Stacey and Susan Geiger regret that the inequality of the ethnographer-informant relationship is such that the researcher-writer can sometimes even profit from informants' tragedies and thus from the betrayal of their own egalitarian ideology.[12] It seems especially unethical when Third World women's stories become the means for Western feminists to participate in different translinguistic forums, thus extending their academic authority to transnational contexts.

Given such concerns about betrayal, what claims do we have left to write the stories of people less privileged than we? I believe that these concerns, though valid, are nevertheless blind to the complex and unexpected ways in which power can work. There is a tendency to consider the subjects' power as totally defined by the ethnographer, while their words are given little weight because they are represented and rescripted by the ethnographer. However, if one considers power as a decentralized, shifting, and productive force, animated in networks of relations rather than possessed by individuals, then ethnographic subjects can exercise power in the production of ethnographic knowledges.[13] After all, the ethnographer-informant relationship is enacted and portrayed in different fields of power—the informant's home, the native community, the ethnographer's academic worlds of (Western) universities, scholarly forums, journals and published works, national and international scholarly meetings. While we do not deny our use of informants' stories for our own purposes, we can also choose to introduce their perspectives into rarefied realms of theory-making.

How informants treat ethnographers, what they demand and withhold, is part of the process whereby they persuade us to provide "a point of access" to cultural conversations in metropolitan centers.[14] In recounting their stories of setbacks, courage, resourcefulness, and inventiveness, feminists help challenge and destabilize the truth-claims of Western cultural knowledges. Indeed, writing the stories of marginalized populations is one way of throwing all authoritative systems "back to first base so that their claims may be re-evaluated."[15] By presenting informants' stories, we help marginal groups intervene in global narratives by putting into circulation alternative circuits of discursive power. Given our privileges, there is greater betrayal in allowing our personal doubts to stand in the way of representing their claims, interests, and perspectives. The greater betrayal lies in refusing to recognize informants as active cultural producers in their own right, whose voices insist on being heard and can make a difference in the way we think about their lives. The most critical point is not that we reap material and social benefits from their stories but that we help to disseminate their views and that we do so without betraying their political interests as narrators of their own lives.

A less visible but more critical problem in representation deals with whether we can truly represent less privileged others. Gayatri Spivak argues that the authentic feelings of the subaltern once named will be misrepresented, because of the multiple mediations of more powerful groups and institutions, both local and global. In phallocentric writing subalterns have been named, given a unified subjecthood, and spoken on behalf of, and they are thus misrepresented in their true situation as dislocated and hybrid subjects.[16] In struggling against that form of misrepresentation, Spivak calls on women to "win back the position of the questioning subject," especially on behalf of the larger female constituency. Privileged women must "unlearn one's privilege": "So that, not only does one become able to listen to that other constituency, but one learns to speak in such a way that one will be taken seriously by that other constituency."[17] The question then is how, through our mediation, we can learn to listen well and to convey our informants' stories without political betrayal.

Telling and Listening

A postcolonial position alone does not guarantee that we can or will convey the truth. The question is how, despite and because of our relation to power, informants will decide to trust our authority with their truth. Indeed, trust does not automatically spring forth because the informants and I are the embodiment of Chinese women. As part of a larger project on cultural citizenship as experienced by new Asian immigrants in California, I had contacted Chinese immigrant women through service agencies in San Francisco.[18] My status as a Chinese female professor did not persuade all of the women to yield their stories. Many had considered themselves forced, by desperate family circumstances, to seek help at the agencies. They feared further exposure to shame by talking to me.

Others were fired more by anger than by shame to share their experiences of growing up in Asia, of emigrant life, and of discrimination in the United States. My being Malaysian as well as Chinese was invisible to them, since they were seeking identification with that part of me that is "Chinese" and which they hoped they could tap for emotional and political support. Indeed, they were not wrong to do so, for a major part of my being Chinese is the sense of being formed by the history of the great Chinese diaspora following the Opium Wars (1839–1860), when Britain imposed its will on China and much of Asia. Although many different local factors have stimulated Chinese emigration since then, and although Western cultural hegemony has replaced Western imperialism in the late twentieth century, our diasporic (and postcolonial) histories must be seen as confrontation, engagement, and mutual seduction between the Chinese and the West.[19] Thus the crosscutting histories of Chinese diaspora and postcolonialism, despite our very different and particular experiences of Chinese and Western cultures, create at the global level one strand of identification as "Chinese in the West."

Diaspora has caused one to question key assumptions about one's "own" culture, while relocation to the West impels a resistance to Western constructions of one's Third World identity. Our shared condition is finding ourselves often at odds with Chinese patriarchy and resisting Western domination at the same time. Thus, being postcolonial means not only challenging different forms of colonial domination in the home country and abroad but also radical questioning of certainties tied to culture, race, and nation. This betwixt-and-between state is the spiritual condition of postcoloniality, and it impels a desire to change both our home cultures and Western construction of Third World women. My informants' perception of my sharing a similar political goal created the initial opening to their confidences.

It is this sense of shared marginalization in Chinese culture and history and in Western society that creates an ethnographic situation different from that of an ethnographer from a privileged Western country who descends into a village in some Third World country. Our sense of having been shaped by the history of Western imperialism and diaspora out of China and by being Chinese women in the West made possible a situation of telling and listening. This lessening of the personal and pedagogical distance between the ethnographer and the informant allows an intimacy that nurtures trust and increases the informants' power to influence the ethnographic product. Bakhtin notes that in heteroglossia, double-voiced discourse speaks of two different intentions—the intention of the speaking subject and the refracted intention of the writer. These two voices are dialogically interrelated, and they are internalized dialogically.[20] A postcolonial, culturally hybrid ethnography would pursue this kind of situated, shifting, many-voiced conversation that deals with many lives, and many places, and in which anthropological knowledge is always subject to qualification and challenge by those outside it.

Life stories, I believe, are an especially powerful mechanism to convey authentic experiences and relationships between self and others.[21] Life stories have been defined as testimonials, a "process of struggling towards a particular consciousness," that both reinterpret and remake the world.[22] Many women's stories are pregnant with the condition of family embeddedness and with the different ways they negotiate the claims of family, marital, and sexual relations.[23] Here the stories of diasporic Chinese women can convey authentic concerns that challenge any prefigured definitions of their identity and reality. Even when they choose to tell their stories, there are non-disclosures, and this dialectic of telling and silences depends on the informants' sense of the ethnographer's capacity to understand sympathetically and intellectually.

Among those who spoke to me are Ming Zhang and Christine Chu (pseudonyms), two women who had recently separated from their husbands. Ming Zhang, from an elite Beijing family, recently arrived in the United States to pursue higher education. Christine Chu, a working-class woman, left Hong Kong when her husband joined his parents in San Francisco. Because of their education, both Ming and Christine are in a better power position to articulate their concerns than are subalterns. Nevertheless, both women are still embedded in the immigrant Chinese community and, as recent Asian female immigrants, are dominated culturally, socially, and politically. As educated Chinese women, they understand that writing can be both a betrayal of their interests and a strategy of power. They chose to speak out because they recognize their social weakness and wish to change the conditions of their existence and isolation. They wish to define themselves in their own ways and also to resist the expert knowledge of the ethnographer. Although I do not thereby claim some spurious political solidarity through the sharing of tales, I believe I am using their stories as they desired, to qualify Western images of Chinese women and to provide a glimpse of their complex subjectivity in negotiating family relationships in a trans-cultural context. Our common frame of reference in the Chinese diaspora and my sympathy with their desire to change stereotypical Western perceptions of Chinese immigrant women help ensure that at least some of their tone and truth-claims have survived in my retelling.

Border Crossing: Two Early-Middle-Aged Chinese Women

Ming Zhang and Christine Chu, both early-middle-aged, look back to their recent emigration and dislocation for meaning with which to plan their future. They are both voluntary and involuntary participants in the latest wave of Chinese diaspora, a global phenomenon in which male participants have received overwhelming academic and media attention,[24] while female Chinese emigrants have been virtually sidetracked or only discussed in novelistic forms.[25] There is a common perception that migrant Chinese women depend on connections with male immigrants to enter the United States. Scant attention has been given to the importance of Chinese women as the creators and embodiment of critical connections through marriage and motherhood that have made border crossing possible for generations of Chinese immigrants.

For decades after the Chinese Exclusion Act was passed in 1882, villages in South China depended on their daughters to marry American Chinese men in order to create a legitimate channel for the eventual emigration of entire families. This process intensified after the 1965 immigration law allowed family unification. Many Chinese male immigrants, unable to find women in American Chinatowns willing to marry them, have participated in mail-order bride schemes organized in Guangdong villages. Local matchmakers send photographs of prospective brides to Chinatown bachelors. Because overseas Chinese men are considered great catches in the villages, they have the pick of the most beautiful girls. In many cases there is a big age difference between the middle-aged Chinatown cooks and workers, on the one hand, and their attractive teenaged brides, on the other. According to Chinatown social workers, after the young women have spent a few years in the United States, the differences in age, education, and personal aspirations sometimes create severe marital problems. Also since the 1960s, increasing numbers of women from China have arrived in the United States on student visas and have thus acquired another role as the first link in chains of green-card seekers.[26] Chinese emigrant women are often expected to be the preservers of home traditions as well as the vehicles for family emigration and continuity in the West.[27] However, conflicts can erupt not only between personal desires and cultural norms but also between the interests of the husband's family and those of the wife's family. Chinese women in diaspora are thus in a liminal position to tell stories of family strategies, emigration, marital breakups, and "uterine family" formation abroad.[28] As survivors of emigration and marital breakup, Ming and Christine are perhaps more willing than their peers are to break the cultural taboo on family revelation, because they saw themselves in the process of breaking constraints imposed by home cultural norms. Separately, they spoke to me in a mixture of English and Chinese (Mandarin or Cantonese), a hybrid language to express their mixed emotions and culturally tangled lives. Their stories of emigration, loss, vulnerability, and desire express an evolving hybrid subjectivity and changing moral agency rather than simply emancipation.

Speaking the Unspeakable in the Home Culture

I spoke to Ming in a refuge near her workplace after she had left her husband. We met on a Saturday morning, and she was tired, still in her bathrobe after a late night working as a waitress. She patiently told me her story.

Ming is a Beijing graduate student who first met her husband at college. "You can say it was love; you can say we were from the same background, or *men dang hu dui* ['matching doors and windows']."[29] A whole cultural principle is summed up in that sentence: if women and men are socially matched in marriage, other things, like personal desire, will coincide as well. Very soon, however, Ming found that her status as wife did not match her self-esteem. In the climate of market reform, her husband became a manager in a business and began to order people around: "He gave commands to me; he wanted everybody to obey him." They started arguing, and they discovered that they had different interests and wanted different lives. He allowed her to go to the United States as a computer science student in a Midwest college because he hoped to follow her later and become an American. When he arrived a year later he started hitting her and did not want her to complete her Ph.D. program. She criticizes the conspiracy of silence around marital abuse.

Before I never talked about this, I felt shame. But not now. The face is not important; I just can't bear his values. In Beijing, according to the law, men and women have the same rights, but the culture . . . a lot of men think they have the right to beat their wives. Almost everyone does not want to talk about marital problems; we don't want to lose face. Maybe it's Chinese culture. . . . In the city the situation is better [than in the countryside]. Women get education, they know their rights. Some women have complained, and gotten divorced from their husbands. Among young educated women, some have begun to choose to be single. It is not that difficult to support oneself; all the women have jobs.

Christine told her story in the lounge of a community center. Smartly dressed, she was waiting for a singles' evening arranged by a Chinatown church. Her appearance belies her story of self-sacrifice for her family. She was born in Toishan, in the Pearl River Delta in Guandong Province, which for generations has been exporting families to the United States. She grew up in a working-class environment after her family moved to Hong Kong. After graduating from a Christian high school, where she was named Christine by her teachers, she planned to work for a few years before settling down.

But my mother was not thinking like that. She wanted me to marry immediately, because she is a Toishan yan [Toishan native] who always want girls to marry someone so as to go to the United States. It was a bad custom for Toishan women. They were not educated, and they always thought that the girls should not receive education, but should marry instead and go to the United States so that the relatives can come to the U.S. too. Most of the women would find a matchmaker to get their girls married off to men going to the U.S., to places just like the Chinatown here [in San Francisco]. Toishan emigrants who cannot find girls to marry in the U.S. go back to Toishan to obtain a mail-order bride so that they would not create a problem for their families [by remaining single]. My mother had someone introduce me to my husband. I was not even twenty-one years old, but my mother herself was married at eighteen, so to her I was getting old. Even though I was already helping to support the family, this was not what she wanted. She wanted a future in the U.S.; just like selling a girl [to obtain that goal]! Now that I am older, I can understand why she did that. But I was really mad with her for several years, because I thought she was selling me, because all she wanted was a future for the boys, but she did not care about my future.[30]

In telling their stories, Ming and Christine focus on how, as daughters and wives, they negotiated family claims, which were closely tied to strategies of emigration. Ming bargained with her husband to help him get a green card if he allowed her to pursue her studies in the United States. In contrast, Christine was pushed into marriage in order to gain entry into the country. She sees Chinese women as part of the conspiracy that uses and abuses daughters to favor sons and to obtain entry into the United States. Her mother did not consider her personal desires and wishes and practically sold her into marriage in order to secure conditions for the eventual emigration of her entire family to the United States. Their breaking of cultural taboos represents a breaking of constraints imposed by hegemonic constructions of themselves. In struggling to give voice to an alternate morality, they express the conflict between their personal desires and cultural expectations. This conflict, and its resolution, compel both women to criticize their home cultures without totally rejecting their Chinese identity.

Marital Abuse and Isolation in the New Country

Ironically, in different ways both women, as wives in the land of the free, have experienced greater abuse and social isolation than they expected. Christine's in-laws sponsored their emigration to the United States, where they all lived in the apartment building her in-laws had bought in San Francisco's Chinatown. In the United States, Christine's husband began to feel extremely insecure about their discrepant educational achievements: he never graduated from high school and worked as a cook, whereas she was a high-school graduate who had worked in a Western company in Hong Kong. He controlled his insecurity about his "American" face by confining his wife in the apartment—and by beating her.

In his mind, a woman should stay at home. He was very old-fashioned, just like his mother. They were very old-fashioned. They thought that a woman's place is at home, not at work. The woman should serve the in-laws, the husband, the children. In other words, the woman had no place at all at home, just like a servant. When I was new here, I had no friends, no relatives, they were all in Hong Kong. I thought I had to do what [my in-laws] wanted me to do; who could I turn to for help? I was living in the same building, had to cook for the in-laws in another apartment. There was a lot of contact between son and parents and the husband was manipulated by the mother. He did what his mother wanted. It was real hard; I've lost all my friends, they were in Hong Kong. I felt like a stranger, a loner and I had no support at all. Whatever they wanted me to do, I had to obey them. I felt like a slave but what could I do?

Christine paints a picture of greater oppression as a wife in the United States than as a daughter in Hong Kong. Her husband and his family treated her like a servant and a slave, while her mother-in-law is described as the oppressor behind the scenes and her husband as an insecure and weak man. Emigration had only intensified her loneliness as a married woman.

Ming went through a similar period of marital abuse and isolation after her husband arrived in Los Angeles as the business agent for a Chinese company.

I went to L.A. to help him be familiar with the environment. I was not excited to see him. We have had few connections. Over the past two years, he had been very busy; he only sent two letters and made an occasional phone call. In L.A.

he often hit me. The beating started about four years ago. . . . He used to hit me on the face; but now he has a gun. Now that he is an American, he has bought a gun. . . . Maybe his girlfriend [in China] treated him very nice, so he hit me. He just wanted me to stay in L.A. to be his assistant. His English was very poor and he can't handle it [on his own]. He [also] wanted me to get a green card; if I got one, he would get one automatically. He has applied to a Los Angeles college for his girlfriend. But he treated me so bad.

For both Ming and Christine, emigration created conditions for greater abuse by their husbands.[31] Family life became more unbearable as their husbands gained more power over them in the United States because they were separated from family and friends. Christine's husband's power was reinforced by his mother's interference in their marriage, while Ming's husband's personal power was increased by acquiring a gun, which she sees as an American symbol of masculinity. Given their intense isolation from the wider society, both women in different ways became tools to serve the needs of emigrant families. Christine had to perform housework for two households, while Ming helped her husband with language difficulties, getting a green card, and everyday problems of living in Los Angeles.

Postemigration Divorce

Although isolation and dislocation in the new country initially made both women victims of marital abuse, they gradually resisted and eventually decided to break away from their domestic situations.[32] Elspeth Probyn uses the term "locale" to indicate "the lived contradictions of place and event." The home as locale is intersected by the lived domestic situation and the subjective desire for the ideal family.[33] The family is often a place where women find the pleasures of home life (cooking dinner) contradicted by their everyday behavior which unintentionally reproduces patriarchal rule. For women, the immigrant Chinese family becomes homes, where subjective desires are suppressed by patriarchal power. The ideological and domestic regulation of the daughter-in-law and wife increased after emigration, as the family found itself detached from the larger home society and relatively isolated from the host society. Ironically, this separation from the mother community also incites desires for subjective freedom as the old rules of society are no longer enforced outside the family. The desires of unhappy wives become individuated from the ideological construction of the Chinese family and community, and there is less pressure to hold things together when the marriage deteriorates. As the contradictions between their domestic situation and their personal desires become intolerable, divorce, once totally out of the question, increasingly becomes a possibility. In emigration, the ground constructing the practices of locale ("home") began to fall away. Ming talks about the event that precipitated her divorce: "I found a letter from his girlfriend in his suitcase. He did some wrong things. You know that Chinese men think that males and females have different rights. That he has the right to do that." However, it was a Chinese man who helped her plot her escape:

AIHWA ONG

One day just after my husband hit me, the friend came to the apartment. He saw my bruises and asked my husband what happened. And he said I fell down in the bathroom, but clearly the guy didn't believe him. A few days later he called up when my husband was not home and asked what happened. I needed to confide in someone, and so I told him about the situation. He just told me that in America, the law will protect the woman. He suggested that I find a lawyer to help me with the situation.

Through a newspaper advertisement Ming found a Chinese lawyer who asked for only a small fee.

He suggested that if I could not stop him from abusing me, I should find another place to live. . . . He said if I tell the police, at most my husband would be restrained but he will try to come back. Now my husband is more familiar about housing, the car, and can take care of himself. He is thirty-four years old. In May I made the decision to leave him. I could not bear the treatment, it was too often, I couldn't bear it. In the evening, he went to the club to do exercise. I left him a letter, telling him why I was leaving. I went to the Greyhound station and took the bus. In the morning I arrived in San Francisco, and my male cousin came to the station and sent me to the woman's shelter. I did not want my husband to find me at my cousin's place. I stayed at the shelter for a few days until I found this job [in a Chinese restaurant in the suburbs]. I just wanted to support myself. It's a very hard job, each day I work ten or eleven hours, from opening to closing. After the customers leave, I must clean up. . . . The boss offered me this room, and board. I left with nothing, just some clothes, so this job is very useful.

Thus a network of Asian American connections helped Ming to map her escape and plot her new life as an independent woman. Chinese men—her friend, her lawyer, and her cousin—directed her to personal and institutional resources that helped her escape her husband and find her own way in American society. It is not clear whether Asian women at the shelter helped Ming rethink her marital conflict as one between her personal desires and cultural constraints, but Ming appeared to me to be a woman who kept her own counsel.

For Christine, the mother of two young boys, leaving her husband was a more torturous and protracted affair. Ironically, her husband used to discipline her by forcing her to leave their home, until she finally left for good:

He was doing everything he wanted with me. If I did not want to obey, he would kick me out of the apartment and said don't you ever come back again. He just kicked you, hit you on the face, to show that he was a big man, he has control of you, that kind of thing. So for years I stayed in the apartment and did not know what to do.

Christine and her husband bought a house in a nearby city with her savings and with contributions from his father, as an investment for her family of origin when they eventually arrived in the United States. Fearing she was giving too much to her relatives, her husband decided to sell the house. When she protested, he threatened to divorce her.

At that time I did not think divorce was right. I was also conservative, you know. I thought that a woman should marry and stay forever, happy or not, with the same man. I knew many families that were unhappy. That's the problem with Chinese families. For newcomer husbands and wives, if they have the same lack of education when they come here and they just work in Chinatown or in the factory, they will not have a big gap between them. In my case there was a gap in education, in jobs. Once I came here, I started to learn about women's rights, equal opportunities. At work, I turn on the radio, look at the TV, I hear about all this. And I think, why do I have to be submissive, why am I being abused? Why can't I go out and work and support myself? Feel good about myself? So I was ready to change. On the other hand he was not willing to change. He just thinks, "Tai nan yan juyi" ["The big man is in charge"]. He just thinks that he is the head, he is superior and he can control everybody and they have to be submissive, especially the women, otherwise he would be insecure.

In time, despite her isolation, Christine was getting ideas from American society that provided ideological support for resisting her husband's control. As the mother of schoolboys she explored the wider world of Chinatown and discovered a church that provided marriage counseling services.[34]

Somehow I persuaded my husband to come for counseling. He changed a little bit. He allowed me to work. I found a job at the Department of Social Services. I was able to persuade his mother [to let me work], because I know that he listened to her. . . . Then he became insecure again. He had a pretty good job at the Strafford Hotel where he was an American cook; he had good benefits and pay. However he did not feel secure at all and he wanted me to quit.

Christine's husband suspected that she was working to send money to her family (she wasn't) and stopped giving her a monthly allowance. He also began to itemize the household expenses. He stopped her from seeing the friends she made through her children's school. He again threatened to divorce her. "After one year of counseling, he changed a little bit, but still we had a big gap. . . . He no longer beat me, but somehow we could not get back together, there was so much difference. I wanted to go to school, to further my education, and he said 'No!!'"

Christine tried harder to make the marriage work. Using her savings, she helped her husband open a bookstore and managed it on evenings and weekends. A month later she overheard her mother-in-law telling her husband, "Now that your wife is working in the bookstore, she is going to control. A woman's place is in the home. If you don't control the bookstore, she is going to look down on you." Soon her husband told her that he wanted her to stop working and that he would sell the bookstore.

I thought I was doing a good job helping him in his career, but he did not like it. All the time his mother was doing things to him; he was so stupid. . . . So it's the same thing again and again. First we had the house and he wanted to sell it. Now we have a bookstore and he wants to close it down. So I thought that was the end of it. I could not put up with it. I felt I have given him enough chances, and what did I get in return? I decided to divorce him. And it was my decision. It was hard, as a Chinese woman. Americans get divorced differently from us. But as a Chinese woman it was a difficult choice, because I felt I have contributed too much, but I have gotten back nothing. And what I got was pain, and I saw no future.

By this time Christine had made some American female friends, including her former supervisor. They helped to raise her consciousness about women's rights and supported her decision to divorce. Although this was a radical move for someone brought up with Chinese cultural values, Christine still considered herself acting like a Chinese woman who has been forced to break off an abusive marriage, not like American women who she presumes are ready to divorce for more trivial reasons. With her new sophistication as a city employee, Christine planned her divorce.

It was a shock to him. First, I went to the attorney's office; I told him my plans. I told him that on a certain day, I would leave. The next morning, I wanted him to serve the papers. I had rented an apartment beforehand. I left with my children, but did not take anything. But I had good friends who gave me emotional support and some old furniture. So I was able to get by. Financially I was independent.

As Ming and Christine broke away from their marriages, their participation in locales other than home enabled them to read domination differently and to remake their agency. They drew on different kinds of external resources—the women's shelter, the marriage counseling at the church, and the support of friends and professional helpers—to resist family control and the notion that a woman's place is (only) in the home. In different ways, the movement between different contexts enabled them to remap and transform the meaning and locale of home itself.[35]

Making a Home of One's Own, in Diaspora

After Christine and Ming decided to leave their husbands, they found themselves in a stronger bargaining position, and they also found bitter satisfaction in making their husbands take an unaccustomed conciliatory posture. Although neither woman returned to her spouse, they revealed ambivalent feelings about their single status and about both Chinese and American cultures.

While Ming waited for her divorce to be processed, she occasionally talked to her husband on the phone, but she refused to tell him where she was.

A few days ago my husband said, "I can't agree to a divorce; you must come back." I want a divorce. I think it's better for us, both of us. I don't want to go back. . . . California law requires a six-month stay before one can file for a divorce. The lawyer says if your husband doesn't get a lawyer to contest the divorce, it won't be too expensive. I hope he won't do so, so that both of us can save time and money.

Ming wants to save money so that she can return to her graduate studies:

I plan to return to the university in the Midwest, where there are lots of Chinese students. We live together in a house. In the department we take the same courses, we study together. So I have spent a lot more time with Chinese friends than with American friends. So I have not been changed very much in America. [However], here in America I learned that to be married one should be happy. If a couple is not matched, and cannot be happy living together, they should go their separate ways.

Although Ming now embraces the American notion that one has the right to marital happiness, her decision to divorce must be seen not as a rejection of Chinese culture but as a reworking of her relation to Chinese tradition in a way that allows for cultural criticism and even the breaking of taboos: "Before the Tiananmen incident, I wanted to return to China because my parents and friends are still in Beijing. . . . If the situation in China has changed [after I get my degree], I will probably return to China." Thus, despite her unhappy marriage and her American education, Ming sees her identity in continuity with Chinese tradition and rooted in China itself.

Christine, in contrast, comes through her divorce extremely critical of Chinese family values but not yet able to free herself totally from them.

Looking back, I should have left my husband earlier. I lost my freedom in America. I feared for the future if I could not support myself. Later, when the pain was bigger than the fear, I felt I had to go. My husband told the counselor he did not want a divorce, he wanted me back. His mother said, "I knew I was wrong, I should not have tried to separate them, and bad-mouth her. If she comes back, I would move so that they can have their own family life." But that was too late. I have made up my mind. So we were quite bitter in court. She wanted him to claim the children, he wanted to claim all my savings. . . . He said for the sake of the children I should come back, but I said that the children were happier because there were no more arguments at home. Besides, they were doing better in school. Of course they had some emotional problems as children in a single-parent family, but their grades were better. His mother wanted grandsons, to carry on the family name. They wanted custody of the children but the court awarded them to me. I was the one who took care of them, taught them, cared for them when they were sick.

It is interesting that Christine sees America as the place where she lost her freedom and, after a long struggle, gained it back by using American institutions to help her divorce her husband. Laughing with both scorn and relief, she continues: "He has visitation rights. . . . He finally said he was wrong, he wanted me to be his partner again. I said 'No need!' I feel happy now, I have no need to go back to the old habits!'"

However, her new life continues to be burdened by obligations, this time from her family of origin. Although she helps to realize her mother's plan of family emigration, she remains resentful of and ambivalent about the Chinese insistence on safeguarding the male family line.

> In 1983, I had become a citizen. Then I sponsored two brothers and a sister to come here. I financially supported them, had them live in my house for two months, cooked for them. I do collect a small rent from them, because I have a big mortgage. I would say that as new immigrants they always have problems — language problems, culture shock. They have to adjust to all kinds of things, social etiquette, find a good job, dealing with discrimination in the workplace, communication problems, financial problems.

When asked whether they appreciated what she has done for them despite what she has been through, Christine replies:

> The older brother understood a bit, but not the younger one. So if I want to get emotional appreciation from them, I would be rather disappointed. This despite the fact that I petitioned for them, and told them that I had married in order to help them get to the United States. Before, my mother did not want to come because perhaps she fears I am still angry at her for marrying me off to get my brothers to the U.S. Now she wants to come too, and I have to start petitioning again. My father is now in a senior citizen home. I cannot support everybody forever. I mean I've got to think of myself, and my two kids. I sacrificed my life, my marriage for them. I petitioned for them, and now I think they should be on their own. I tell myself I will not do that again. It's enough. I have to think of myself now. It's time for myself.

Christine's first son is in college, and the younger one will be going soon. Most of her friends are white Americans at work. She is starting to date:

> I don't like Chinese men anymore. I guess it is because of my bad experiences with my husband. In my mind I just think that most Chinese men are tai nan yan juyi; they just think that they are superior. They look down on you, and they suppress you. And I hate that. So I don't want to socialize with Chinese men. Sometimes I find it easier to get along with Caucasians. I don't know why . . . maybe, I'm, I'm Westernized. Maybe.

Christine worries, however, that her Cantonese accent will be an obstacle in forming long-lasting relations with white men. Furthermore, as a company president's assistant, she has been told that she needs to erase her accent in order to be promoted.[36] To improve her chances in both areas, she is taking speech classes so that she will sound more American.

Christine continues to be ambivalent about both Chinese and American cultures. She admits that American society is discriminatory toward Asians, and she finds herself defending Chinese culture. Despite her disappointment in Chinese men, she boasts that her sons are bright because they have "Chinese genes." Although she finally feels free to be her own person in America and to make time for her own self, Christine finds that she has to make herself over by muting her cultural identity and changing her accent in order to be accepted by mainstream society.

Conclusion: Political Decentering & Postcolonial Feminism

Ming's and Christine's narratives express an emerging agency as immigrant women, as well as a critical commentary on overseas Chinese communities. Their stories reveal moral ambivalences about emigration and Chinese family strategies, but also newfound strength in the self-willing of a changing identity. Looking over their lives in different locales, they articulate a transnational, translational subjectivity that has developed through the mediation and dissolution of boundaries. Both autobiographical accounts span the transition from cultural criticism to the reinvention of ethnic identity across a series of locales.[37] For Ming, emigration and marital breakup have problematized her relationship to her "home culture," but she considers herself anchored in the community of overseas Chinese students in the United States and in her family in Beijing. In other words, she sees herself as a Chinese in America, as part of an expatriate community. In contrast, Christine, more affected by American middle-class aspirations and feminism, seeks to remake her identity by defining a private self and her own place in America. This private interest and place—to be spent acquiring cultural capital like standard speech, piano playing, Catholicism, a college degree—are to help her ambivalent exploration as a Chinese American.

By contrasting these tales of emigration, cultural criticism, marriage, and self-transformation I strip away comfortable Western pronouncements about Chinese culture and Chinese women. The decolonization of anthropology goes beyond recognizing that cultures are differently practiced outside their original geographical homes.[38] Part of that deconstruction of culture is attending to the different forms of postcoloniality in the former colonial societies. Another dimension of postcolonialism is the larger global project of Third World peoples to change the way we as global subjects rethink and reimagine the world. Anthropology needs to reflect the postcolonial situations whereby we increasingly live inside, outside, and through the East-West divisions.

Autobiographical accounts of diasporic women similarly challenge feminist theories of postcolonial women as victims. Much recent feminist work has dwelled on postcolonialism as a particular conjunction of victimization for women in diaspora. Feminists of color, for instance, frequently talk about the postcolonial situation of Third World women in terms of the numerous axes of domination along lines of gender, class, race, and nationality. Their intentions are clearly antihegemonic, to expose and critique more precisely the multinational and multiple contexts of gender oppression and resistance. These theoretical formulations come alive only in actual narratives, when Third World women explore the varied meanings of postcolonialism in different geopolitical sites. Our ethnographic authority derives not so much from our position and embodiment as postcolonial analysts as from recognition of an interreferencing sensibility that we share with less privileged postcolonial women. This common ground of a decentered cultural/political relationship to the West can foster a more equitable kind of listening and retelling.

Ackbar Abbas notes that "Postcoloniality begins when subjects cease to feel that they need to apologize for their lives just because they differ from more centrally placed others."[39] A first step toward hearing these views is to recognize that postcolonial agency expresses the defeats and also the resourcefulness and creativity that are frequently engendered in the margins of society.[40] Changes engendered by emigration, marriage, divorce, and children leaving home make women reflect on their lives, and their reflections are deepened by the daily negotiations of cultural, national, and linguistic borders. Such examined lives bred in the liminal spaces between cultures and societies represent new imaginations about power and about the self, the kind of self-knowledges that can modify metropolitan theories of postcolonialism as multiple victimization. Feminists can become a channel for the voices of postcolonial women, thus creating greater opportunities for them to interrupt and intervene in metropolitan circuits of gender and cultural theory. Ordinary women telling their own stories inter-nationally—in the double sense of talking about border-crossing lives and the transnational dissemination of tales—should form a counterpoint to hegemonic narratives.

As fellow immigrants and refugees, postcolonial feminists can help create conditions for a transnational "intermingling of subjectivities" in different sites of struggle.[41] If, as Gayatri Spivak maintains, the real critic is interested "in being vigilant," then postcolonial feminists must recognize and learn from the restless vigilance and transgressions of ordinary border-crossing women.[42] Ming's and Christine's lives in different ways suggest the evolution of a critical consciousness that deflects the singular claims of culture, race, and nation. Similarly, diasporic feminists (and we should all be somewhat mobile to be vigilant) should develop a denationalized and deterritorialized set of critical practices.[43] These would have to deal with the tough questions of gender oppression not only in that "other place" (the Third World, the West, capitalism, the white race, and so forth) but also in one's own family, community, culture, religion, race, and nation.

This denationalization of feminist ethnography creates a special challenge to Western anthropology and feminism. If "feminism seeks to be the paradigmatic political discourse of postmodernism," it must stop being "blind to the geopolitical implications of its own program" that is tied to First World privileges and declining Western hegemony.[44] The narratives of postcolonial women describe a political decentering that will be necessary in Western knowledge as it allows itself to be redefined by discourses from the geopolitical margins. Deterritorialized feminist subjectivity presupposes a dynamic process of disowning places that come with overly determined claims and reowning them according to different (radical democratic) interests. This dialectic of disowning and reowning, of critical agency shifting between transnational sites of power, expresses a deliberate cultivation of a mobile consciousness. Such postcolonial/postmodern feminisms create conditions for crosscutting coalitions that challenge totalizing discourses in the name of culture, race, ethnicity, and nation.

Margaret Mead once said that everyone is an immigrant in the twentieth century. Perhaps everyone will be a postcolonist in the next. People living outside contexts of former societies, cultures, and self-understandings may become the norm in the changing geopolitical conditions of hegemony. By allying themselves to postcolonial movements, postmodern feminists will be among the most astute participants and observers of shifting global powers and emerging forms of "cultural struggles" in our brave, new, mobile, multinationalized worlds.[45]

Notes

I am grateful to Ming Zhang, Christine Chu, and other women for telling me their stories and allowing them to appear in print. Debbie Gordon and Ruth Behar made useful suggestions on an earlier draft.

1. See Amy Tan, *The Joy Luck Club* (New York: G. P. Putnam's Sons, 1989) and *The Kitchen God's Wife* (New York: G. P. Putnam's Sons, 1992); and Jung Chang, *Wild Swans: Three Daughters of China* (London: Flamingo, 1993). Sau-ling Wong has written a critical assessment of the relationship between Amy Tan's novels and their predominantly white female readership. See Wong, "Sugar Sisterhood: Situating the Amy Tan Phenomenon" (paper presented at the "After Orientalism" Conference, University of California, Berkeley, April 24–25, 1992).

2. Chang, *Wild Swans,* 671.

3. James Clifford, "Traveling Cultures," in *Cultural Studies,* ed. Lawrence Grossberg, Cary Nelson, and Paula A. Treichler (New York: Routledge, 1992), 108.

4. See Kirin Narayan, "How Native Is a 'Native' Anthropologist?" *American Anthropologist* 95 (1993): 671–86, for an extended and sensitive reconsideration of "halfie anthropology" by exploring native anthropologists' "multiplex identity," which may have many strands of identification available for, or withdrawn from, alignment with particular groups. She concludes by observing that ultimately "the process of doing fieldwork involves getting to know a range of people and listening closely to what they say" (679).

5. Teresa de Lauretis, *Technologies of Gender: Essays on Theory, Film, and Fiction* (Bloomington: Indiana University Press, 1987), 137.

6. Clifford, "Traveling Cultures." See also Stuart Hall, "Cultural Identity and Diaspora," in *Identity, Community, Culture, Difference,* ed. Jonathan Rutherford (London: Lawrence & Wishart, 1990), 222–37.

7. Abdul JanMohammed, "Worldliness-without-World, Homelessness-as-Home: Toward a Definition of the Specular Border Intellectual," in *Edward Said: A Critical Reader,* ed. Michael Sprinker (Oxford: Blackwell, 1992), 97.

8. See Edward Said, "Traveling Theory," in his *The World, the Text, and the Critic* (Cambridge, Mass.: Harvard University Press, 1993). In fact, Said first introduced the notion of

traveling theories as theories that are transformed by their use and position in new contexts of reception (226–27). For other perspectives, see the *Inscriptions* issue "Traveling Theories and Traveling Theorists," especially the essays by Lata Mani, "Multiple Mediations: Feminist Scholarship in the Age of Multinational Reception," *Inscriptions* 5 (1989): 1–24, and Mary E. John, "Postcolonial Feminists in the Western Intellectual Field: Anthropologists and Native Informants?" *Inscriptions* 5 (1989): 49–74, which discuss how postcolonial feminist politics is shaped by a politics of location that raises the vexing question of accountability to audiences in home cultures and in Western feminism.

9. Mikhail M. Bakhtin, "Discourse in the Novel," in *The Dialogic Imagination*, ed. M. Holquist (Austin: University of Texas Press, 1981), 259–422.

10. In ethnic studies the tendency is to make pedagogical claims of a Chinese American identity and to ignore the other ways of being Chinese in America that go beyond claiming a rightful citizenship in the United States. Michael M. J. Fischer, "Ethnicity and the Post-Modern Arts of Memory," in *Writing Culture: The Poetics and Politics of Ethnography*, ed. James Clifford and George Marcus (Berkeley: University of California Press, 1986), 196, contrasts the two ways of being Chinese. On the basis of reading Chinese American literary writing, he says that "Being Chinese-American exists only as an exploratory project, a matter of finding a voice and a style." Is this the only way of being Chinese American? Furthermore, does Fischer mean to imply that such an exploration of identity is absent among those who consider themselves "Chinese in America"? For further consideration of this point, see Aihwa Ong, "On the Edge of Empires: Flexible Citizenship among Chinese in Diaspora," *Positions* 1 (1993/1994): 745–88.

11. See Aihwa Ong, *Spirits of Resistance and Capitalist Discipline: Factory Women in Malaysia* (Albany: State University of New York Press, 1987), "Limits to Cultural Accumulation: Chinese Capitalists on the American Pacific Rim," *Annals of the New York Academy of Sciences* 645 (1992): 125–45, "On the Edge of Empires," "Making the Biopolitical Subject: Khmer Immigrants, Refugee Medicine and Cultural Citizenship in California," *Social Science and Medicine*, forthcoming, and Aihwa Ong and Michael G. Peletz, eds., *Bewitching Women, Pious Men: Contested Genders and Body Politics in Postcolonial Southeast Asia* (Berkeley: University of California Press, 1995).

12. Judith Stacey, "Can There Be a Feminist Ethnography?" in Sherna B. Gluck and Daphne Patai, eds., *Women's Words: The Feminist Practice of Oral History* (New York: Routledge, 1991), 111–19; Susan N. Geiger, "Women's Life Histories: Method and Content," *Signs* 11 (1986): 335–51.

13. Michel Foucault, "Truth and Power," in his *Power/Knowledge* (New York: Pantheon Books, 1980).

14. Chicago Cultural Studies Group (CCSG), "Critical Multiculturalism," *Critical Inquiry* 18 (1992): 542.

15. Alan Sinfield, *Literature, Politics and Culture in Postwar Britain* (Berkeley: University of California Press, 1989), 24. Indeed, stories are not merely appropriated by the ethnographer, in circulation they also "transmit power: they are structured into the social order and the criteria of plausibility define or seem to define, the scope of feasible political change" (25).

16. Gayatry Chakravorty Spivak, "Can the Subaltern Speak?" in *Marxism and the Interpretation of Culture*, ed. Cary Nelson and Lawrence Grossberg (Urbana: University of Illinois Press, 1988), 271–316.

17. Gayatry Chakravorty Spivak, *The Post-Colonial Critic: Interviews, Strategies, Dialogues*, ed. Sarah Harasym (New York: Routledge, 1990), 42.

18. In this project I explore the ways in which state agents and immigrants mutually though unequally create what it means to be an ethnic minority in the United States. In order to

capture the diversity of Asian immigrant experiences in the San Francisco Bay Area, I sought subjects through a number of leads. I met subjects through corporations, business meetings, political gatherings, refugee clinics, self-help groups, women's shelters, real estate agencies, and low-income housing. I also tapped personal networks for contacts.

19. See Ong, "On the Edge of Empires," where I discuss in greater detail the mutual though unequal construction of Chineseness as Chinese professionals and investors now operate widely in the Western world.

20. Bakhtin, "Discourse in the Novel," 324.

21. For a different perspective, see Caren Kaplan, "Resisting Autobiography: Out-law Genres and Transnational Feminist Subjects," in *De/Colonizing the Subject: The Politics of Gender in Women's Autobiography,* ed. Sidonie Smith and Julia Watson (Minneapolis: University of Minnesota Press, 1992), 115–38. Kaplan maintains that Third World women's experiences cannot be authentically accessed through autobiographies, a Western practice. Local people have home-grown theories ("out-law genres") like psychobiography and testimony, which challenge the structures of patriarchy, capitalism, and colonial discourse. It is not necessary to make autobiography thereby an out-law genre for non-Western peoples, since their life stories need not be narrowly defined in Western terms as the stories of unified subjects.

22. CCSG, "Critical Multiculturalism," 534.

23. Susan Geiger, "Women's Life Histories," 348.

24. See, for example, Ronald Takaki, *Strangers from a Different Shore: A History of Asian Americans* (New York, Boston: Little, Brown & Co., 1989); Lynn Pan, *Sons of the Yellow Emperor: A History of the Chinese Diaspora* (Boston: Little, Brown, 1990).

25. As Sylvia Yanagisako, "Transforming Orientalism: Gender, Nationality and Class in Asian American Studies," in *Naturalizing Power,* ed. S. Yanagisako and C. Delaney (Stanford: Stanford University Press, 1993), has noted, this focus on male Chinese immigrant experiences also characterizes the academic histories of Asian Americans, such as Takaki, *Strangers from a Different Shore.* Until recently the subject of diasporic Chinese has been marked by a division of gender interest in academic writing, which tends to privilege male experiences. See "The Living Tree: The Changing Meaning of Being Chinese Today," *Daedalus* (Spring 1991), and literary writings, which privilege female voices (Jade Snow Wong, *Fifth Chinese Daughter* [New York: Harper & Brothers, 1945]; Maxine Hong Kingston, *The Woman Warrior: Memoirs of a Childhood among Ghosts* [New York: Random House, 1975]; Tan, *Joy Luck Club* and *Kitchen God's Wife;* Chang, *Wild Swans*). This sexual division of representation in academic and literary voices reflects an ethnic and peculiarly American construction of Asian American identity. For an ethnographic analysis of upper-class male and female emigrant strategies from Hong Kong, see Ong, "Limits to Cultural Accumulation" and "On the Edge of Empires."

26. Despite the booming economy in coastal Guandong and Fujian provinces, many poor villagers in South China are still caught up in the dream of making their fortune in the United States, and many seek speedy and illegal ways to enter the country. The recent influx of illegal Chinese boat people is a graphic example of the tenacity of the labor-exporting tradition. There is a new method of gaining illegal entry into the United States: As more overseas Chinese return to China, there is a profitable crime in stealing American passports, which can be sold for thousands of dollars to would-be immigrants.

27. See Yanagisako, "Transforming Orientalism."

28. This phrase was coined by Margery Wolf, *Women and Family in Rural Taiwan* (Stanford: Stanford University Press, 1967).

29. This phrase is in Mandarin. This saying represents a recent reversal of the marriage situation during the Great Proletarian Cultural Revolution (1962–1976), when state ideology

encouraged urban students and professionals to marry people with peasant or worker backgrounds. The replacement of proletarian revolution with Confucian values is one of the many forces adding to the confusion and conflict surrounding marriage and prestige.

30. Christine's words are in Cantonese.

31. These stories of marital abuse are Ming's and Christine's and should not in any way be generalized as a norm in American Chinese communities.

32. Numerous informants and Chinatown social workers have told me that divorce after emigration is frequent among all classes of Chinese immigrants. However, there are no statistics to indicate the extent of the phenomenon, which tends to contradict the ideological construction of Chinese family unity.

33. Elspeth Probyn, "Travels in the Postmodern: Making Sense of the Local," in *Feminism/Postmodernism,* ed. L. J. Nicholson (New York: Routledge, 1990), 182, 179–80.

34. Since the late nineteenth century, church groups have played a major role in mediating between Chinese immigrant women and men in disagreements over sexuality, marriage, and family life. See Peggy Pascoe, "Gender Systems in Conflict: The Marriages of Mission-Educated Chinese American Women, 1847–1939," in *Unequal Sisters,* ed. Ellen C. DuBois and Vicki L. Ruiz (New York: Routledge, 1990); and Lucie Cheng Hirata, "Free, Indentured, Enslaved: Chinese Prostitutes in Nineteenth Century America," *Signs* 5 (1979): 3–29. At the turn of the century, white mission women saw themselves as engaged in "rescue work," saving Chinese women and girls from prostitution and directing them toward "companionate marriages" (Pascoe, "Gender Systems in Conflict"). The mission interventions created situations in which Chinese immigrant women were subjected to the dictates of white morality but which also allowed Chinese women some leverage in combating male power in the Chinese immigrant community. Today most Chinatown mission services in the areas of sex, marriage, and morality are limited to counseling, although singles parties are held on church premises to provide a context for Chinese men and women to meet potential marriage partners. Christine has found that the single Chinese men she met through these gatherings were socially inferior to her expectations of a husband.

35. Chandra T. Mohanty, "Feminist Encounters: Locating the Politics of Experience," *Copyright* 1 (1987): 42, inspires this interpretation: "Movement between cultures, languages, and complex configurations of meaning and power have always been the territory of the colonized. . . . It is this process, this reterritorialization through struggle that allows me a paradoxical continuity of self, mapping and transforming my political location. It suggests a particular notion of political agency, since my location forces and enables specific modes of reading and knowing the dominant."

36. A newspaper report notes that increasing numbers of immigrants from Asian and Latin American countries are seeking help at "speech-evaluation clinics" because of ridicule and prejudice against their accents. Asian Americans are especially vulnerable to discrimination in the workplace because of their accents (*New York Times,* February 3, 1993, A12).

37. See Fischer, "Ethnicity"; and Lisa Lowe, "Heterogeneity, Hybridity, Multiplicity: Marking Asian American Differences," *Diaspora* 1 (1991): 24–44.

38. Akil Gupta and James Ferguson, "Beyond 'Culture': Space, Identity, and the Politics of Difference," *Cultural Anthropology* 7 (1992): 6–23.

39. Ackbar Abbas, "The Last Emporium: Verse and Cultural Space," *Positions* 1 (1993): 16.

40. See Aihwa Ong, "The Gender and Labor Politics of Postmodernity," *Annual Review of Anthropology* 21 (1990): 279–309; and Ong and Peletz, *Bewitching Women, Pious Men.*

41. Mayfair M. H. Yang, *Gifts, Favors, and Banquets: The Art of Social Relationships in China* (Ithaca, N.Y.: Cornell University Press, 1994).

42. Quoted in Probyn, "Travels in the Postmodern, " 186.

43. Shu-mei Shih, "Asian Women and Border Crossing: Towards a Paradigm for a Diasporic Subjectivity" (unpublished manuscript, 1993).

44. Laura Kipnis, "Feminism: The Political Conscience of Postmodernism?" in *Universal Abandon? The Politics of Postmodernism,* ed. Andrew Ross (Minneapolis: University of Minnesota Press, 1988), 160, 162.

45. Ong, "Gender and Labor Politics of Postmodernity."

19

Border Work:
Feminist
Ethnography
and the
Dissemination
of Literacy

Deborah A.
Gordon

IN 1991, on completing my Ph.D. thesis, I came across a letter from Peggy Sanday. Sanday, who published her earliest work on the status of women in *Woman, Culture and Society,* had answered a letter I had written to feminist anthropologists in the initial stages of my research. I wanted to understand the traffic in academia and politics from 1967 to 1975 and the intermeshing of social activism and technical debates among a cohort of feminist anthropologists in the late 1960s. I asked a number of feminist anthropologists to reflect on how feminism had affected their professional practice and on how anthropology had shaped their feminism. Although Sanday wrote the longest response to my request, I put her letter away, being vaguely put off by the fact that it did not "fit" the type of textual experimentation I was looking for. Rereading her letter, I was dismayed that I had dismissed her words so lightly:

> *I am now working on a book that begins with an ethnography of an incident that occurred at Penn in Feb. 1982. One of my students alleged that she was raped by 6–8 fraternity brothers after a party. I am writing on that incident as a lens for looking at male dominance on college campuses, particularly date and the group rape by fraternity brothers. The person who influenced me was my student.*

When she told me about the incident, I felt that it was essential to go to bat for her. I was also influenced by my own work on rape that taught me that rape is publicly condemned only where it is publicly aired. I convinced the student that rather than hide the incident it was important to fight it openly on campus. I am writing the book with a male journalist who wrote a very important story about the incident in the Philadelphia Inquirer *Sunday magazine. Because he wrote the story with feminist eyes he did a lot to swing the climate that makes incidents like the one at Penn quite common. It will be an ethnography of sexuality. In this book, anthropology will definitely contribute to a political effort on my part to change American understanding of sexual abuse and use of young women. I consider this book to be extremely important from an action standpoint.*[1]

I dismissed the letter not only because I could not locate Sanday's project within a framework of experimentation but also because of the subject matter. By 1991, action-oriented research seemed academically dated. Sanday published the results of her research in *Fraternity Gang Rape,* a study of fraternities, rape, and masculinity among white college men.[2] Using interviews with college students and university administrators as well as written accounts by students, Sanday and a team of student researchers accessed the "sexual subculture that encourages and supports rape." *Fraternity Gang Rape* mixes different types of analysis—sociological, social psychological, legal, and culturally symbolic. Sanday's book has not made it into the canon of experimental ethnography, nor does it fit with the turn toward fiction, genre-mixing, and autobiography that anthropologists have exploited in the search for a feminist ethnography. It is also not likely to reach a broad feminist audience, for it is difficult to read. Detailed descriptions of fraternity initiation rituals, of turning young men into "brothers," disturb the academic penchant for interesting writing that is not too emotionally disturbing. Judge Lois Forer, who overrode the University of Pennsylvania's refusal to prosecute the rape of Sanday's student, wrote the book's foreword. While feminists clearly support the full use of the law to stop sexual violence against women, there is a more general mistrust of feminist alignments with the regulative power of the state. In addition, despite tenacious efforts to make college campuses habitable and equally supportive for women students, the fear that ethnography might expose university negligence threatens distorted notions of academic freedom that many men and women still hold.[3] Indeed, Judge Forer's foreword to *Fraternity Gang Rape* functions as a shield for the institutional radicalness of this account by demanding that university officials enforce rape laws. Sanday's odd proximity to genre shifts in feminist anthropology serves less as a model and more as a point of departure for exploring ethnographic form and social change.

Feminist Ethnography and Social Action

Sanday's phrase "from an action standpoint" provides a critical perspective on the emergence of recent attempts by feminist social scientists to carve "feminist

DEBORAH A. GORDON

ethnography out of the literary turn in anthropology." [4] *Fraternity Gang Rape* locates ethnography where ethnographers live, that is, in the halls of academe. A recent wave of feminist anthropology "at home" responds to new-right political and intellectual agendas of the 1980s that carried particular consequences for women. [5] Yet Sanday's study of gang rape in fraternities is more than an ethnography at home. It registers the unstable character of ethnographic form. This timely ethnography serves as a counterpoint to a potential hardening of "experimental" ethnography. I consider the problematic nature of ethnographic form not simply within its present literary moment but also within a growing cultural hostility toward higher education and especially academic research on the part of citizens outside universities, regents of public systems, and the media. When academic research and publication are under intense public scrutiny, we need to articulate why and how feminist research matters. Poor journalism and sensationalized editorials exploit middle-class frustration and encourage a public content with mass illiteracy. It seems necessary for feminists, who are only too aware of the gender and race barriers to publication, to counter myths that publishing necessitates abandoning students for the archives and the library. Defining and supporting women's research and publication in the face of budget crises must be a priority for feminist faculty members, particularly those with tenure.

Of all feminist academics, feminist ethnographers may be uniquely suited to articulate the "public" as an essentially contested category. As the meanings surrounding culture shift from bounded, timeless objects to heterogeneous codes, ethnography may be a growing political resource in battles over the public interest, if only to underline that there is no such thing as "the public" in the singular. Consider, for example, how both conservative and liberal politicians distinguish the public from the immigrants and the homeless. California's Proposition 187 is only the most dramatic sign of widespread anti-immigrant sentiment in which liberal Democrats and Republicans are allied. The urge to exploit demographic shifts and xenophobia motivated people in Florida and Washington to pursue similar legislation, to support border enforcement. In a new twist on a long discursive history of Malthusian practice in the West, newspapers fuel middle-class blaming of these "populations" for its decline. Feminist ethnography might counter the racism and class hostility that seeks to punish immigrants and those left homeless by discovering field sites in immigration and welfare offices, government agencies, and on literal borders.

As part of the anthropological turn toward "home" in the 1980s, feminist anthropologists moved away from more traditional area studies to study the symbolism and practices surrounding reproductive technologies, abortion politics, medical and legal discourse, and gay and lesbian communities. While the ethnography produced by this wave of scholarship has been particularly rich, we need feminist fieldwork in the United States that participates in political activist and advocacy-oriented research. Interdisciplinary dialogue with oral historians who work within a disciplinary tradition of public advocacy might pull feminist anthropology at home toward grittier intellectual alliances such as with community educators and activists. [6]

Locating feminist ethnography at the crossroads of anthropology at home and advocacy-oriented oral history speaks to what may turn out to be the critical political terrain for feminism in the 1990s—women's literacy. Access to formal education and literacy among white women and people of color in the United States has always been unevenly distributed. During a period of deep economic change fueled by deindustrialization and global corporate capitalism, access to formal education increasingly determines material reality for women.[7] Recent research on the economic status of women in the United States suggests an intensified earnings gap between white women and women of color.[8] Given present conditions, which include dynamics of multinational capitalism, limited access for some women to low-paid service-sector jobs, poor labor conditions at home and abroad in industry, and federal, state, and city budget crises, contests over and for literacy become directly political.

Testifying before the Senate Committee on Labor and Human Resources, economists Heidi Hartmann and Roberta Spalter-Roth have argued that a dominant trend in the workplace has been the deterioration of relationships between workers and employers. But deteriorating labor conditions, particularly the growth of involuntary part-time and low-wage work, have affected women more than men. The preliminary results of Hartmann and Spalter-Roth's 1991 study suggest that the factors contributing most to increasing earnings of both African American and white mothers were, above all, higher education, followed by full-time employment, work experience, and union membership.[9] Without making the mistake of expecting education to solve the problem of global economic restructuring, Hartmann and Spalter-Roth's policy prescriptions make women's access to higher education a priority.

If we consider policy research alongside the growing awareness that differences among women are substantive not superficial, feminist ethnography as literacy work becomes a compelling model of politically grounded research that does not reduce intellectual acts to political acts or vice versa. Critical literacy creates new notions of women writing culture to fit patterns of global migration under multinational capitalism. Resisting assimilationist logic, Latino scholars have retheorized knowledge, identity, and citizenship by affirming the process whereby disenfranchised groups assert their own sense of human, legal, and social rights.[10] During a period of increased immigrant-bashing, especially in the wake of the North American Free Trade Agreement, feminist ethnographers may be uniquely suited to address the racist fantasy that holds immigrants responsible for adverse economic conditions such as downsizing. Feminist ethnography as a practice of critical literacy situates ethnographic writing within these daily life struggles of women who are pulled away from their homes and toward the United States.[11]

In the wake of collections such as *Writing Culture,* anthropologists have exploited the conceptual slipperiness of the term *ethnographic writing.* The pull toward writing as individual authorship has encouraged critics to take individual ethnographies to be the main unit of analysis in the critique of ethnographic representation. In turn, the political aim of decolonized knowledge has rested on individual writing experiments. The hope of challenging that larger, weightier sense of social inscription gets funneled through publishing practices, which are based in the ideologies of authorship as unique, individual expression.

How will feminist ethnographers negotiate the conceptual ambiguity surrounding ethnographic writing? In considering the political connection of ethnography to knowledge, one must have a sense of the political terrain on which objects such as ethnographic canons and cultural authority are built. In a compelling analysis of the antidisciplinary character of anthropology's present moment, George Marcus argues that the rhetoric of canon formation obscures the fact that cultural authority rests more on oral modes of communication, such as corridor talk, than on print media.[12] Marcus's ordering of the oral as the authoritative form of communication and print as secondary downplays their mutual dependency. His argument for more ethnographically based studies of the production of knowledge, however, nicely dovetails with a feminist ethnography that charts global capitalism's impact on women's literacy. Without ethnography among women, it is difficult to know what literacy means to women who negotiate different cultural practices and political dynamics.[13] Where literacy work politically focuses Marcus's call for accounts of cultural migrations is in its pursuit of women's own effort to define citizenship in cultural rather than legal terms. Feminist literacy work recognizes that reading and writing may have radically different meanings for those groups that have historically struggled for literacy rather than taken it for granted.[14]

Literacy Work and Feminist Ethnography

Research based on literacy work already functions to make feminist research travel between academic offices and community-based classrooms. The El Barrio project exemplifies this mobile research. In the heart of New York City, this community-based program of action research initiated by the Center for Puerto Rican Studies (El Centro de Estudios Puertorriqueños) at Hunter College ran from 1985 until 1989. In 1985 the center initiated a Spanish-language adult literacy program in the Puerto Rican community of East Harlem. Researchers at Hunter created the project to study educational patterns in a community with a high rate of high-school dropouts. Directed by Rosa Torruellas in collaboration with Pedro Pedraza, an instructional and counseling staff, students, and a board of directors, the project eventually included the oral historians Ana Juarbe and Rina Benmayor. Torruellas, Benmayor, and Juarbe participated in classes on a regular basis, collecting life-histories that contributed to curriculum development. Most of the women who participated in the El Barrio project were female heads of households with sole responsibility for childrearing. Most had extensive experience dealing with the loss of jobs brought by deindustrialization combined with the indignities of the welfare system and grossly inadequate social services. The neighborhood women had no access to formal education, and the project's primary goal was to "promote empowerment through native-language literacy training and education of Spanish-speaking adults."[15]

The greatest achievement of the El Barrio project was its making of feminist ethnography a partner in women's evolving sense of entitlement. Literacy work took place beyond the classroom as the women formed a culture of support in their daily lives. The participants in the program referred to it as their "second family," attesting to both their significant emotional investment in the term *family* and their ability to subvert its patriarchal meaning. As the women learned to read and write, they challenged power dynamics that structured family relations and were able to continue their education without risking the isolation that so often accompanies women's withdrawal from taking care of men and children. During a period of great gender and class instabilities, women whose identities have rested on their roles as mothers, wives, and family members need a sustained social community in order to exercise choice in a range of political circumstances. The research of the El Barrio project participated in the political empowerment of women through the institutionalization of social alternatives to families that emerged out of the classroom.[16] In the El Barrio project, literacy work became a lifestyle of resistance forged by the women participants, with researchers and tutors acting as guides and interpreters.

The centerpiece of the El Barrio project, one critical in any discussion of feminist ethnography, is research that attempts to redistribute educational privilege. That redistribution is centered in teaching critical rather than functional literacy. Critical literacy assumes that disempowered communities need forms of knowledge to negotiate and change the inequities that keep them disadvantaged. The pedagogical commitments in critical literacy work urge the subversion of power between literate and "illiterate" women. An important contributing factor to redistributing power through critical literacy in the project was the willingness to continually redefine oral history and ethnography based on their pedagogical values. Initially, they were part of a long-term and extensive oral history project on Puerto Rican immigrants in New York. When they joined the literacy project oral history became part of the teaching of literacy skills. In addition, the researchers also moved from doing oral history to utilizing "classroom ethnography." Their detailed notes and their observations on what occurred in the classroom aided the teaching process. Class assignments intersected oral histories through tutors' request that women participants write autobiographies. Life histories were collected by teaching women participants to write in a way that changed their sense of self and led to collective empowerment. For example, as women reinterpreted their lives through the life-history process, they became more willing to resist welfare workers. Rather than seeing themselves negatively in the ugly mirror the state holds up to them, these women came to realize that, as citizens, they had a right to welfare. Their perception of welfare as a political right grew from their articulation of fulfilling gendered and cultural responsibilities in their labor as mothers and wage laborers. More recently, the oral historians assessed how classroom processes interact with students' domestic lives. Their fieldwork shifted to visiting students' homes and accompanying them on their rounds. Like many anthropologists, they worked in distinct spaces in which informants acted out different identities. By pushing beyond oral-history collecting to an interdisciplinary practice of classroom ethnography, combined with interviewing in spaces outside the classroom, the Hunter College researchers tracked the shifts in identity that are critical to the women's expressed sense that they can act on their own behalf despite the humiliations of the welfare system.

From the perspective of traditional patterns of career and research development in the discipline, the practice of classroom ethnography and the use of oral history as the material of critical literacy violate anthropology's traditional romanticism and exoticism. The "work" of classroom ethnography is not prestigious, because it does not involve travel to geographic regions that compose departmental hirings, curricula, and reputations. Because prestigious university departments with long-standing traditions of sending graduate students abroad are well funded, they are able to attract faculty and students who are insisting on new, unorthodox definitions of the "field." A crucial example of this process of reconstituting the field is the attempt to theorize and describe processes such as cultural diasporas. As "home" becomes a problematic site of identity construction in the wake of mass migrations, anthropologists increasingly study the neighborhoods in which they grew up or the immigrant communities that border many urban universities. Calling classroom ethnography "fieldwork" assumes that the process of literacy is immanently a site of cultural politics, a "site" for participating in what Arjun Appadurai designated as ethnoscapes: "As groups migrate, regroup in new locations, reconstruct their histories, and reconfigure their ethnic 'projects,' the *ethno* in ethnography takes on a slippery, nonlocalized quality, to which the descriptive practices of anthropology respond."[17]

As ethnic and cultural groups lose their spatial rootings as a result of tourism, migration, and warfare, human mobility and patterns of forced travel become obvious anthropological objects. Critical literacy projects that are enmeshed in the traffic of immigration are important places where the reconfiguration of ethnicity occurs. How women reconstruct gender identity through immigration, through guest work in foreign countries, and through becoming refugees must be a crucial area of feminist ethnography. The "feminism" of feminist ethnography will carry greater political weight if it is grounded in social change as a collective project. Critical literacy projects are ideal sites for further ethnographic experiments with advocacy work. Critical literacy involves commitment to classroom dynamics, tutoring, and staffing the program so that the self-redefinition that frequently accompanies education is shared. The sharing goes in two directions as researchers gain theoretical insights into social life. In the case of the El Barrio project, researchers noted how the gendered nature of class relations became increasingly clearer as they listened to participants' reconstruction of their identities in their life stories. A heightened sense that class must be understood as carved with the knife of gender became one of the lessons the women students provided. Carefully monitored engagement with the women participants over time suggested that intersecting relations of race, gender, class, and culture shift with the gains of writing and reading. Researchers and women students are not equal partners in this collective learning process, but in the face of that inequality they do reshape each other's intellectual skill.

The El Barrio project promotes reciprocity and mutual gains among community members and researchers, but its idealism does not work through a language of coauthorship. The idiom of empowerment present in the publications of the El Barrio research team does not offer images of dispersing ethnographic authority through shared authorship but evokes collective action. Ironically, the actual writing practice of the project includes joint authorship, use of quotations by the women participants, and extensive space for the women's autobiographies. The latter calls up the discourse of leftist women working in urban projects to ameliorate poverty in the 1960s, the same women who would come to participate in women's liberation activism.[18] The relatively greater emphasis on community rather than on authority emerges from ethnic identity among an immigrant group that values cultural practices in deep tension with the dominant, nativist, Anglo-American, Puritan myths of individualism. The language of community, however, does not draw static and impenetrable lines between insiders and outsiders but rather signifies political struggle for material resources. In Rina Benmayor's words, the project converges on the "common bonds of interests and solidarity" shared by the neighborhood women in the project and the oral historians serving their desire to read and write. The "identity politics" of the project thus move toward a goal—acquisition by the women of the ability to act on their own behalf. It is clear from the project's publications that researchers do not believe that community interests don't have to be created, yet they also recognize the motivating character of the belief in the promise of common interests in making claims on the state and in enabling new subjectivity. The project's reports suggest that these women use the term *community* to signify an ongoing process of cultural reinvention that is deeply political. Cultural affirmation works through and with the construction of community interests. For these women the shared desire to be able to read and, especially, to write has motivated them to claim citizenship on the basis of positive cultural expression rather than assimilation.

Theoretical insights also include the realization that race and gender are not the sole categories through which communities are articulated in the United States. Here the El Centro researchers' care in attending to participants' language reveals the importance of the category "uneducated" to the women in the literacy program. According to Benmayor, an important bond among participants is their stigmatized identity as uneducated. She argues that it is this stigma that motivates women to take part in a process of countering the dominant definitions of women on welfare as either lazy or products of a culture of poverty. At a time in which the once-discredited notion that poverty is a result of behavioral deviance has reemerged in government policy and popular imagination, these women's collective identification with the category "uneducated" does not so much signal their enactment of the regulative power of state disciplining of "populations" as it moves them to write so that they may attain dignity, formal education, and jobs.

Given what appears to be the upward mobility of at least some of the women who went through the program, can literacy work such as in the El Barrio project

DEBORAH A. GORDON

merely be celebrated and used as a model for feminist ethnography in other sites of transnational cultures? What political dilemmas are eclipsed by an optimistic claim that literacy can be the site of collective empowerment? One trenchant response to characteristically North American naïveté based on voluntarism suggests that attempts to empower others hide patronizing inequities. A critical moment in the debate over anthropology's debt to colonial "benevolence" appeared in the infamous *Signs* exchange between Frances Mascia-Lees et al. and Vicki Kirby. In a dramatic critique of the literary turn in anthropology, Mascia-Lees et al. argued that applied anthropology might be more appropriate for feminists in the discipline than engagement with textual theory and criticism. In a reply, Kirby warned of the dangers of misunderstanding "alterity, assuming that this space of negation is something we should work to overcome, an unfairness to be redressed rather than an enduring structural asymmetry with constitutive force." [19] Applying Kirby's insistence on the force of asymmetry to the action-oriented life-history and classroom ethnography of the El Barrio project highlights the limits of pragmatic politics, even among women who have a shared purpose in tying ethnicity to citizenship. In fully entering the dilemmas of action-oriented research, however, we confront the need for less permanent and fixed concepts of asymmetry. We need to understand social processes in a manner that does not flatten all research between relatively privileged women and disenfranchised women into images of well-intentioned but naive ethnographers who cannot think about the structures within which they work.

To not caricature feminist ethnographers, a nonreductive theory of agency must be central to any assessment of specific research projects. In a post-Foucauldian and post-Lacanian theoretical moment, agency emerges as the negotiation of the regulative fictions in which subjectivity is an effect, not a cause, of social order. [20] Feminist social theory has greatly benefited from Foucault's productive and dispersed view of power. Yet even Foucault's impact on new feminist theories of identity and agency seems overly bound up with legal rhetoric. The language of order, restraint, regulation, and management dominates in an attempt to hold on to power. As Judith Butler so nicely puts it, "Neither power nor discourse are rendered anew at every moment; they are not as weightless as the utopics of radical resignification might imply." [21] At the same time, the contingencies of participants in specific fieldwork sites make clear the need for low-level generalizations about agency within asymmetrical relations among women. Although Kirby corrects the relative ease with which Mascia-Lees et al. claim that feminists are one with their politics, fully certain and in control of their enactment and meaning, theorizing action-oriented or advocacy research must grasp the texture of struggle for shared understanding that accompanies self-conscious efforts for collective empowerment of those marginalized in capitalist economies. Context-specific judgments as to which kinds of social, economic, and political privilege can be changed by literacy projects and which need more massive challenges to the welfare system, corporate practices, and global political alliances must be foregrounded in feminist theory.

Gayatri Spivak has offered one ethical model for assessing how women respond to and enact a politics of translation, which is highly suggestive for feminist literacy work. In her view, translation offers an opportunity to discover the trace of the other in the self. How one responds to that trace determines one's accountability to another's language. Because feminist ethnography is always bound up with situations of translation, the politics of its form lie in the conditions of both its production—including its modes of travel, and technologies of listening, recording, and writing—and its dissemination. There are important parallels between literary translation and the translation of ethnography, but also specific circumstances that give life to ethical dilemmas and their potential resolution. For example, Spivak's meditation on translation concerns her position as a postcolonial Indian woman, working in the American academy and translating contemporary literary work in Bengali, her native language. As she reminds us, Bengali divides into class dialects that suggest social layers which cry out for attention in translation.

The El Barrio researchers present a quite different situation of translation. Like Spivak, the researchers are fluent in the language of the women they work with in constructing histories. Class distinctions in language use are less centrally noted than in Spivak's discussion. The fieldwork situation allows for dialogue between the Hunter researchers and women students, which centers more on the women's expressed struggle and pleasure in learning to write. The differences between Spivak's and the El Barrio researchers' attention to language speaks to disciplinary, methodological, geographical, historical, and ethnic locations. In addition, the El Barrio researchers' ability to speak intimately with these women may be the result of the relatively long history of neighborhood relations between the Center for Puerto Rican Studies at Hunter and East Harlem. They may also emerge from who pays for and/or publishes the translation. In the case of the El Barrio researchers, it is the Center for Puerto Rican Studies that funds publication of their reports.

Given the ways in which languages carry social divisions and given the political complexities of research, how might one know whether one has actually learned another's tongue? Spivak suggests two tests of solidarity with women whose native tongue differs from one's own. The first is whether one can converse about intimate matters in the other's language. The second is whether one is capable "of distinguishing between good and bad writing by women, resistant and conformist writing by women." [22] In Spivak's ethics, one has to be able and willing to judge the quality of writing within its local scene. Does it make sense to draw parallels between the translator and the translated and between the researcher/teacher and studied/student in literacy projects? Are Spivak's ethical guidelines appropriate to the literacy work of the El Barrio project? The researcher and teacher of literacy is obliged to learn her students' language not simply to communicate but to enter the delicate process of leading and being led, which involves change. In the pedagogy of critical literacy is an especially intimate experience, because its pleasures and frustrations go to the core of women's shifting conception of self and community. The researchers

DEBORAH A. GORDON

include quotations from women attesting to their growing sense of deserving education, a good life, and support from family members to pursue their education. Spivak's second ethical test of translation concerns translators' ability to distinguish good writing from bad writing. While Spivak's focus is the politics of literacy translation, attention to student writing demands the same kind of nonpatronizing and nonracist stance of teachers.[23]

The ethnographic form of the El Barrio project's writings registers that process of being led into and deeply learning another's language that subverts individual authorship. The students' building of support networks nicely parallels the team authorship of the project's publications.[24] Paperbound reports to its funding sources circulate out of El Centro for little money. One such report is "Responses to Poverty among Puerto Rican Women: Identity, Community, and Cultural Citizenship." Rich description of the interplay between structural, cultural, and symbolic processes juxtaposed with women's life stories reveals the collective character of authorship when literacy is defined as a mode of constructing new subjectivities for disenfranchised communities.

In discussing how the women students led them to understand the role literacy played in their gender identities as well as their sense of citizenship, the authors call up their status as witnesses rather than as sympathetic observers, writers, or guides. This report suggests another figure in the history of anthropology, the participant witness rather than observer. Carrying a host of conflicting associations, including informant, litigant, function of the Holy Ghost, and spectator, a witness is less an observer than a teller—that is, one who translates what s/he sees and hears for an audience. The notion of the litigant calls up the courtroom as scene of performing the law with all of its theatricality, finesse, and savvy. As an informant, the witness purposely informs or tells, with all of the potential for betrayal implied. Yet witnessing in the context of the Americas also brings to mind the long-standing indigenous tradition of personal testimony, with the witness calling up a broken humanity to redeem it. Characteristically American traditions of African American preachers, Latin American human-rights activists, and advocates for the poor continually reinvent stories of redemption through suffering to challenge social injustice. The El Barrio project's classroom pedagogy relied heavily on personal testimony, in which women literally altered their life possibilities through witnessing their lives and those of other women. In participant witnessing, the lines between ethnographer and informant blur as each hears the other in a way that encourages self-representation. By portraying themselves as more closely akin to participants witnessing change than to classroom observers, the oral historians mark the instabilities of power dynamics in the project.

The El Barrio project researchers thus must be viewed as students and actors in literacy politics and not simply as instruments of state power. The careful qualifying of their research by continual insistence that they are not "insiders" in the Puerto Rican women's community despite the fact that they include second-generation

Puerto Rican women who grew up in the neighborhood attests to the limits of social policy work. Spivak nicely designates the state's hold on political meaning as "global social work." In the face of a difficult political situation, cultural differences became the imaginative basis for U.S. citizenship rather than legal categories that enforce homogenization. Researchers' "complicity" with the actual economic realities of global, postindustrial conditions is inevitable—but no more so than library research, close readings, or any other disciplinary method. One of Spivak's and Kirby's points in their cautionary tales about women's cross-cultural research is that of the depth and endurance of Western feminism's complicity with the history of colonialism. My impression of anthropology is that as it has come to terms with its colonial legacy, it has designated applied anthropology, advocacy, and action-oriented research as entirely politically dirty compared with the more theoretically informed self-reflexive field account. Low rungs on the ladder of the disciplinary reward systems, advocacy-oriented fieldwork and applied anthropology are too obviously caught up in government and global aid bureaucracies that are laden with anthropology's complicity with colonial ventures.[25] Yet these kinds of anthropology and their specific ethnographic forms need to be rethought for feminist purposes. Precisely because so much Western feminism has enacted the colonial logic of either saving non-Western women from themselves or their men or turning them into curious, quaint relics through government or missionary work, applied or advocacy anthropology needs not to be abandoned but to be reconstructed.

The El Barrio project provides a beginning sense of what that reconstruction might look like. One central fact of this project is the researchers' up-front acknowledgment of the inequalities of their undertaking. Instead of essentializing ethnicity and claiming the space of the Puerto Rican community of East Harlem, they opt instead for what I would call the equalizing of power relations. Equalizing is a process, uncertain and ongoing. Equalizing inequality through research in this popular education project could not take place without the historical involvement of El Centro de Estudios Puertorriqueños in the immigration of Puerto Ricans to New York City after World War II. More importantly, the commitment of El Centro to the immigrant neighborhood built research that has not so much completely subordinated individual, academic achievement to community goals but has struggled for reciprocity between professional and neighborhood agendas. The neighborhood women participate in the project to learn to read and write Spanish. In 1989 the project's center, Casita María, made a transition from being managed by Hunter College to self-management by the neighborhood. This goal of community management was central to the education project from its beginning. Because researchers had responsibilities for directing or coordinating the literacy project, they agreed to perform multiple roles and fulfill multiple demands. Structuring literacy projects so that researchers are an integral part of the daily work of the center avoids a division of labor that would separate them from the hands-on running of the program, including classroom activities. Especially given that the El Barrio project implemented community leadership and self-management of the project, this kind of feminist ethnography highlights the achievements of accountability to those studied, to the neighborhood, and to a vision of public life that is peopled by more than taxpayers. Equalizing strategies in feminist ethnography appear to come both from an experimental flexibility in method that continually shifts over time and from researchers' willingness to help run the project.

There is a distinction between claiming equality and working to equalize that is not merely semantic. In the former, the image of giving voice to the disempowered suggests a troubling "matronization" of women who have not benefited from affirmative action policies and professional employment.[26] Building equalizing strategies connotes participation in an uneven process that considers how power and resources are redistributed. The intellectual pleasures of research and writing get disseminated beyond the academy by widening education's scope. Feminist academics need to institutionally defend and promote ethnographic projects that involve research teams and jointly authored publications. Academic feminists, especially those with tenure and in positions of relative institutional strength, must not simply legitimate this type of research even in universities that are not located in urban centers such as New York City, but treat it as serious theoretical, epistemological, and ethical material for considering what "counts" as feminist ethnography. Overprivileging one kind of cultural anthropology as the sole arena for an ethnographic politics that interrogates neocolonialism, inequality, and knowledge runs the risk of containing critical insight within very limited circles.

Deconstructing the border between oral history and ethnography introduces new feminist networks that reach out in two directions: toward other scholars and toward creating new kinds of intellectual communities. I am not arguing that feminists should rally around some naive politics that is stripped of ethnographic form, writing, or rhetoric. This is not a call for the "real" struggle over and against the mere "literary." On the contrary, the feminist ethnographic work I have examined rejects false distinctions between practice and writing, but it does so less through a focus on representing the experiencing individual than through grappling with the politics of academic research and writing. Although there are significant differences between ethnography and oral history, recent reflection on power in feminist fieldwork suggests a need for further dialogue among historians, anthropologists, and sociologists who work with interview and participant-observation methods.[27] If ethnography is the process and product of cultural translation, feminist ethnography brings the dilemmas and limits of that exercise into an interdisciplinary feminist dialogue. In the 1980s the rhetoric of coalition politics within academic feminism often belied half-hearted attempts at crossing lines of race, class, culture, and sexuality. Literacy work provides one limited avenue for forming coalitions among women that situate the utopian impulse of dispersing ethnographic authority within a class-conscious politics. Donna Haraway has argued that information is our ontology, as being collapses into textualization in a world no longer captured by the traditionally Marxian sense of labor but by an "informatics of domination."[28] Clearly, much of a woman's life experience in a world structured by information will turn on the types of literacy and access to formal education she has. Feminist ethnography as critical literacy gives a "politics" of ethnographic writing some weight. It deeply socializes the meaning of ethnographic form. Questions of ethnographic form, then, move beyond the staging of voices and textual authority to modes of description that change who reads and who writes, for what purposes and with what effects.

Conclusion

We have seen how Sanday's words, "from an action point of view," fit into the border between oral history and ethnography, community organizing and academic research, ethnicity and gender. Feminist anthropology is undergoing a transformation as ethnography becomes an object of reflection not only for poststructuralist critics and historians but also for women ethnographers who are struggling to account for their relations with women in postcolonial conditions. The critique of ethnographic authority has compelled feminist anthropologists to account differently for how they come to know or not know women living outside Western feminist demands. Fieldwork and research in "homes" that are woven with cultural and political conflict expand feminism to encompass more than the usual media lineup of reproductive rights, affirmative action, the glass ceiling, the mommy track, and sexual harassment. Action-oriented research is not a panacea. Research similar to that generated by the Center for Puerto Rican Studies at Hunter may only be realistically possible among people who are culturally familiar enough with each other's backgrounds to warrant the type of trust that supports literacy projects. Finally, advocacy-oriented research is more physically dangerous and politically impossible for anthropologists in some geographical regions and under certain political circumstances (such as military dictatorship and occupation) than in others.

It seems fitting to end not on a celebratory note but with caution. The advantages of locating feminist ethnography in politicized textual experimentation are obvious. Feminist ethnographic efforts to alter textual voice, representation, and style in their widest and most radical senses move the profession in a way that makes daily work of anthropology accountable to feminism. Shifts in genre conventions to action, however complicated and nonessential its meaning has become after the decentering of the subject, will increasingly need to be theorized if feminist ethnography wants to accept challenges to its own authority. I purposely keep open what the politics of representation means. I continue to ask what kind of change makes what kind of difference to whom. And I ask these questions very much from within, not from outside, anthropology's "textual turn." We have no choice but to think in these "old-fashioned" terms if women's lives are to be of value. The question for feminist ethnography must be how to situate writing culture within those sometimes imaginary, sometimes real, communities we call women's movements while not reifying politics.

D E B O R A H   A .   G O R D O N

Notes

A previous version of this essay appeared in "Women Writing Culture," Ruth Behar, ed., *Critique of Anthropology* 13, no. 4 (1993): 429–43. A longer and different version was presented at the School of American Research in Santa Fe, New Mexico, in March 1994. I would like to thank the school for inviting me to give a colloquium on feminist ethnography and the following resident scholars who participated in it: John Forrest, Mary Hancock, Jon Ingimundarson, Jennie Joe, Toby Lazarowitz, Kirin Narayan, James Snead, and Henry Wright.

1. Peggy Sanday, personal correspondence, January 1985.

2. Peggy Sanday, *Fraternity Gang Rape: Sex, Brotherhood, and Privilege on Campus* (New York: New York University Press, 1992).

3. Lois Forer, one of the earliest women judges to serve on the Pennsylvania Court of Common Pleas, practices her politics by writing popular books on legal commentary. Her latest, *Unequal Protection: Women, Children, and the Elderly in Court* (New York: Norton, 1991), examines injustices in the legal system wrought by the "reasonable standard" and "neutrality" doctrine of the law.

4. On feminist ethnography, see Kamala Visweswaran, *Fictions of Feminist Ethnography* (Minneapolis: University of Minnesota Press, 1994); Ruth Behar, *Translated Woman: Crossing the Border with Esperanza's Story* (Boston: Beacon, 1993); Lila Abu-Lughod, *Writing Women's Worlds* (Berkeley: University of California Press, 1993).

5. See Emily Martin, *The Woman in the Body: A Cultural Analysis of Reproduction* (Boston: Beacon Press, 1987); Faye Ginsburg, *Contested Lives: The Abortion Debate in an American Community* (Berkeley: University of California Press, 1989); Faye Ginsburg and Anna Tsing, eds., *Uncertain Terms: Negotiating Gender in American Culture* (Boston: Beacon Press, 1990); Judith Stacey, *Brave New Families* (New York: Basic Books, 1990).

6. I am not suggesting that feminist anthropologists have not built these types of alliances in their practice. Many have. Rather, I am arguing that on balance much feminist anthropology is too narrowly scholastic despite its rich encounters with cultural politics over the past ten years. On participant observation in political activism, see Gail Lardsman, "Negotiating Work and Motherhood," *American Anthropologist* 97, no. 1 (1995): 33–40.

7. On the politics of literacy, see Marcella Ballara, *Women and Literacy* (London: Zed Books, 1992); Jennifer Horsman, *Something in My Mind besides the Everyday: Women and Literacy* (Toronto: Women's Press, 1990); Peter Freebody and Anthony R. Welch, eds., *Knowledge, Culture and Power: International Perspectives on Literacy* (Pittsburgh, Pa.: University of Pittsburgh, 1993); David Archer and Patrick Costello, *Literacy and Power: The Latin American Background* (London: Earthscan, 1990); Colin Lankshear and Peter L. McLaren, eds., *Critical Literacy: Politics, Praxis and the Postmodern* (Albany: State University of New York Press, 1993).

8. See Teresa Amott, *Caught in the Crisis: Women and the U.S. Economy Today* (New York: Monthly Review Press, 1993).

9. See Heidi Hartmann and Roberta Spalter-Roth, "Improving Women's Status in the Workforce: The Family Issue of the Future," Testimony on Women and the Workplace: Looking toward the Future, Hearings of the Subcommittee on Employment and Productivity, Committee on Labor and Human Resources, U.S. Senate, July 18, 1991, Washington, D.C.: Institute for Women's Policy Research.

10. See C. E. Walsh, ed., *Literacy as Praxis: Culture, Language and Pedagogy* (Norwood, N.J.: Ablex Press 1990), particularly Rosa M. Torruellas, R. Benmayor, A. Goris, and A. Juarbe, "Affirming Cultural Citizenship in the Puerto Rican Community: The El Barrio Popular Education Program."

11. On immigrant-bashing as the most recent distraction from the economic crisis in the United States, see David Bacon, "World Conditions: The Anti-Immigrant Backlash," *Z Magazine* 6, no. 12 (December 1993): 19–21; and Elizabeth Martinez, "Latino Politics: Scapegoating Immigrants," *Z Magazine* 6, no. 12 (December 1993): 22–27.

12. George E. Marcus, "A Broad(er) Side to the Canon; Being a Partial Account of a Year of Travel among Textual Communities in the Realm of Humanities Centers, and Including a Collection of Artificial Curiosities," in *Rereading Cultural Anthropology,* ed. George E. Marcus (Durham, N.C.: Duke University Press, 1992), 103–23.

13. They might also create greater disciplinary balance in interdisciplinary dialogue at a time in which the humanities have placed the social sciences somewhat on the defensive. In a 1992 talk, Barrie Thorne offers an impressionistic sense that a gap between theories and methods in the social sciences and those in the humanities now shapes feminist scholarship. Thorne grapples with the need for new dialogue across a division of labor between the poststructuralist and semiotic developments in the humanities and the relatively more empirical, Marxist-oriented work of the critical social sciences. Reacting to the perceived exclusions of feminist poststructuralist work, Thorne suggests that interdisciplinary feminist theory should work against unspoken, untheorized disciplinary biases. Interdisciplinarity ought to provide work that forms bridges among academics and between the academy and community activists. See Barrie Thorne, "The Metamorphosis of Feminist Theory" (talk presented at the University of California, Santa Cruz, April 1992).

14. Each semester I watch women students fall in love with ideas that they get from reading books. Their relationships break up, their children become less central to their lives, they grow bored with friends who are not intellectuals, and they talk of passionate attachment to certain texts and authors. They voice their hunger and attachment not so much to feminism (although clearly that is central to their consciousness) as to theory or ideas. The women are not of a class whose parents raised them to anticipate earning advanced degrees. They are starting to shift the gears of their lives toward graduate school, and they are entering into a love affair with intellectual work. These women are not caught up in world literary events such as the Salman Rushdie controversy. Neither are they ordinary people, figures of the duped masses. They demonstrate the kind of passion that comes with literal reading and writing, which the women in the El Barrio project also voiced. It is this passion for the written word that I think Marcus does not adequately appreciate in his insistence on the primacy of oral culture in academia.

15. Rina Benmayor, "Testimony, Action Research, and Empowerment: Puerto Rican Women and Popular Education," in *Women's Words: The Feminist Practice of Oral History,* ed. Sherna Berger Gluck and Daphne Patai (New York: Routledge Press, 1991), 159.

16. Judith Stacey's account of born-again Christian networks in Silicon Valley, California (*Brave New Families* [New York: Basic Books, 1990]), makes a similar argument by showing how families are being reconstructed in the wake of socioeconomic changes and alterations in gender ideology. Through the El Barrio project women gain support that is idealized in family ideology.

17. See Arjun Appadurai, "Global Ethnoscapes: Notes and Queries for a Transnational Anthropology," in *Recapturing Anthropology: Working in the Present,* ed. Richard G. Fox (Santa Fe, N. Mex.: School of American Research, 1991), 191–210. On "homework" as a kind of fieldwork "in reverse," see Kamala Visweswaran, *Fictions of Feminist Ethnography,* 101–4.

18. See Sara Evans, *Personal Politics: The Roots of Women's Liberation in the Civil Rights Movement and the New Left* (New York: Random House, 1979).

19. See Vicki Kirby, "Comment on Mascia-Lees, Sharpe, and Cohen's 'The Postmodernist Turn in Anthropology: Cautions from a Feminist Perspective,'" *Signs* 16, no. 1 (1991): 398.

20. Through a brilliant examination of materializations of the body, Judith Butler theorizes gender after Foucault and Lacan. See her *Bodies That Matter: On the Discursive Limits of "Sex"* (New York: Routledge, 1993) for an extended statement on the nature of the "social," after distinctions between discourse and practice, bodies and meaning, and the law and its discontents, are deconstructed. In a related vein, see Elspeth Probyn, *Sexing the Self: Gendered Positions in Cultural Studies* (New York: Routledge, 1993); and Teresa de Lauretis, *Technologies of Gender: Essays on Theory, Film and Fiction* (Bloomington: Indiana University Press, 1987), for analyses of technologies of identity.

21. Butler, *Bodies That Matter*, 224.

22. Ibid., 186.

23. One lacuna in the writings of the El Barrio project oral historians is whether students and teachers disagreed over "good" writing.

24. Thus far the oral historians of the El Barrio project have produced the following working papers published by the Centro de Estudios Puertorriqueños: Rina Benmayor, Ana Juarbe, Celia Alvarez, and Beatriz Vazquez, "Stories to Live By: Continuity and Change in Three Generations of Puerto Rican Women," and Rina Benmayor, Rosa M. Torruellas, and Ana L. Juarbe, "Responses to Poverty among Puerto Rican Women: Identity, Community, and Cultural Citizenship." See also Rina Benmayor, "Testimony and Empowerment in Community-Based Research."

25. This is what Mascia-Lees et al. understand and Kirby misses. These compelling critiques of this moment in anthropology ought to be considered as offering competing theoretical and political strengths.

26. On the dynamics between maids and the women who employ them, see Judith Rollins, *Between Women: Domestics and Their Employers* (Philadelphia: Temple University Press, 1985), 155–203. On white middle-class women's management of poor or socially disadvantaged women in social work, see Linda Gordon, *Heroes of Their Own Lives: The Politics and History of Family Violence* (New York: Viking Books, 1988). On the dynamics of matronization among white women and Native Americans of the Southwest, see Deborah A. Gordon, "Among Women: Gender and Ethnographic Authority in the Southwest," in *Hidden Scholars: Women Anthropologists and Native Americans of the Southwest*, ed. Nancy Parezo (Albuquerque: University of New Mexico Press, 1993), 129–45.

27. See Gluck and Patai, *Women's Words*.

28. See Donna Haraway, "A Cyborg Manifesto: Science, Technology and Socialist Feminism in the Late Twentieth Century," in her *Simians, Cyborgs, and Women: The Reinvention of Nature* (New York: Routledge, 1991), 161–69.

20

In Dialogue?
Reading
Across
Minority
Discourses

Paulla Ebron
and Anna
Lowenhaupt
Tsing

PERHAPS THE most exciting interdisciplinary
development in the last two decades of academic
writing has been the creation of a diverse range
of theoretical approaches with which to think
seriously about the perspectives of the politically
subordinated and the culturally marginalized.
Feminists, colonial discourse analysts, and U.S.
and European minority scholars have been particularly active here. We have exposed the political
biases of intellectual frameworks once regarded
as neutral and omniscient, and we have shown the
vitality of the emergent traditions that marginalized peoples have created in recognition of their
exclusions. Yet the strength of this scholarship—
its attention to the processes of marginalization,
and thus the relationship between margin and
center—has also become a limitation: there is
very little dialogue between one marginalized
position and any other. We build alliances with a
rhetoric of solidarity, but we have few tools with
which to create critical and reflexive conversations that recognize our differences as well as our
common stakes. When intellectual and political
tensions arise, advocates of each marginal group
remain insensitive to the challenges of others. Our
essay enters this gap to begin the process of building theoretical tools for dialogue. As "women
writing culture," we are particularly concerned to
move beyond understandings of culture that have
confined women inside cultural communities.

Our topic is that emergent U.S. coalition subject called "people of color." "People of color" names a tension as well as a hope. Scholars working on issues of race in the United States have done important work in tracing out a field broad enough to include a full range of nonwhite peoples and traditions. Yet when hostilities among people of color outside the academy break out, scholars hardly know how to address them. The collaboration that led to this article had its source during a period in which black-Asian hostilities were particularly obvious. In 1991 a Korean shop-keeper in Los Angeles shot a black teenager in the back, and, after a trial for the killing, she received three years probation. Many African Americans believed that this light sentence reflected American disregard for African American lives. A few months later, Koreans and blacks fought each other in the Los Angeles uprising. Korean Americans felt devalued by the lack of police protection for their businesses. Although the news media sponsored a variety of discussions of black-Asian relations, there was little recognition of the contradictory logics of marginalization each group employed. Indeed, much of what the "experts" said (such as, only Asian families have values; only black families fight racism) exacerbated these contradictions. Even the well intended rarely moved beyond platitudes about interracial harmony. Our collaboration has aimed to create other possibilities for mutual respect.

Although we focus our argument on dialogue across racial lines in the United States, we believe our approach is important for rethinking the full range of topics involving exclusions of gender, class, race, ethnicity, and national status. Whether one is speaking of the political fights that divide feminists ("antiviolence" versus "prosex," for example), or the intellectual tensions that divide U.S. "people of color" and Third World "diasporic postcolonials," there has been little precedent among scholars for doing anything other than restating the forms of marginalization with which one side or the other is most familiar—as if attempting to bully one's way to the moral high ground of "most oppressed."[1] In this practice, other marginalized groups are collapsed into the dominant center because they do not share the particular form of marginalization about which one is writing. Instead, we advocate an intellectual practice capable of recognizing forms of marginalization that are not shared—but that are nonetheless debilitating and challenging to those who experience them. This practice involves critical readings and reflections across lines of group identity.

Community Stories

In this essay we interpret African American and Chinese American narratives of identity, as found in recent works of fiction, across racial lines. We read fiction— together with genre-blurring imaginative memoirs and personal essays—as cultural analysts, not as literary critics. Rather than looking at textual strategies for producing meaning, we are interested here in the socially constructed reading and discussion practices through which racially marked fiction becomes part of the cultural production of race in the United States. We have come to our understandings of these reading and discussion practices through an admittedly unsystematic process of participant observation, as teachers, students, colleagues, advisors, activists, community members, readers, and listeners-in to conversations about race and ethnicity, particularly those occurring in and around universities.[2] In the course of our attention to these discussions, we turned to fiction and semiautobiographical narratives because we found them to be important in contemporary U.S. constructions of race.

As anthropologists we are concerned with the making of culture. Yet this is a task with many contenders; anthropologists have no privileged role. It is essential for anthropologists to attend to the debates and public contests over "culture" in which we are participants, but not alone. Indeed, in the past twenty years, speakers and writers other than social scientists have assumed dominant positions in shaping U.S. public understandings of culture. In the 1970s the public may have been reading Carol Stack's *All Our Kin* and Elliot Liebow's *Tally's Corner* to learn about U.S. communities of color; today they are more likely to be reading Toni Morrison or Amy Tan.[3] (As a friend told one of us, "Everything I know about Chinese culture I learned from *The Joy Luck Club*.")[4] Novels and memoirs by people of color have obtained a wide cross-racial readership. Furthermore, such works are often required reading in college courses in ethnic studies, women's studies, cultural studies, anthropology, literature, and more. Their inclusion in college teaching has not only spread their readership but also given such works an easily visible role in the multicultural debates over U.S. racial policy.

Our discussion of novels and the reading practices associated with them enters a long history of dialogue between minority novelists and social scientists in the United States. This dialogue has fostered recognition that both minority fiction and factual writing are imaginative projects that tell politically charged stories about race and culture. Zora Neale Hurston, of course, studied with anthropologist Franz Boas; her "ethnographic" depictions of rural black culture in the South drew from anthropological concerns with the still-vibrant vitality of almost-encompassed cultural worlds.[5] Yet this was only one moment in a conversation about minority status that has known sharp shifts and turns through the twentieth century. In the 1930s New Deal programs supported both creative and social science writing about the struggles and crises of "little people" in the United States; anthropologist Mary Orgel has argued that conventions of naturalist ethnography as well as literature were forged in those New Deal refigurings of American populist nationalism.[6] African American novelist Richard Wright was particularly active in forging ties with social scientists.[7] Influenced by the Chicago school of urban sociology (which included Robert Park, St. Claire Drake, and Louis Wirth), he transformed the earlier romance with rural folk culture to show the social problems of the urban poor. In concert with sociological concern to show the dehumanization of individuals in an oppressive society, Wright—and the series of "naturalist" black writers he inspired—showed how racism and poverty broke the spirits of black men and women.[8] By the 1960s, however, writers began to show how those same damaged individuals could rebuild their pride and reassemble their social networks. Inspired by the civil rights movement and anticolonial struggles around the world, both creative writers and social scientists began to show the building of respect-inspiring communities.

The challenge of representing minority communities has led, since the 1960s, to particular trends and dilemmas of representation. First, black models began to inspire conventions of writing for other U.S. minorities. Asian American writing was shaped as a field at this time through dialogue with the African American legacy. In some cases, personal associations across color lines helped to shape new "minority" styles; thus, for example, African American Ishmael Reed and Chinese American Frank Chin pioneered new critical standards together, even as each wrote about "his" people.[9] In this period, themes of community building became the shared base of minority writing. Second, the rising appreciation of authenticity and intimacy in accounts of social process have increasingly privileged novels by those imagined as insiders as the most telling descriptions of minority communities. By the 1970s, white writers about minority struggles were losing their dominance; minority audiences were impatient with external views. Third, the conditions of community building began to change. In the 1960s, the claim for the autonomy of minority communities formed a statement within a global struggle for the political self-determination of the once-colonized, exploited, and enslaved. By the 1980s, the notion of a global movement had begun to fade. Yet the importance of representing community building only grew, as racism came to be understood as an issue of community representation. Social science descriptions of minority communities became entangled in charges of exoticizing or even silencing; first-person narratives, in contrast, could be interpreted as creating "voices" for communities, as attention turned to the right to speak. Then, too, the representation of community has become particularly charged *among* those imagined as insiders, as issues of gender and genre have come to the fore. The challenges we address in this paper are particular to this moment. On the one hand, similar concerns about community dominate the foreground of varied minority groups' writing; on the other hand, it has become increasingly difficult to discuss the connections among these varied minority communities.

We use the term *community* to reference a U.S. folk notion. Communities are formed in contemporary literary works in part by the creation of dichotomous *outsider* and *insider* reading strategies. To the extent the works are seen as about defining race, they also define outsiders and insiders. (Particular readers pick or combine these reading positions for a variety of reasons, in which their own racial or ethnic identity is only one factor.) Outsiders read these works to learn about the group described and to pick out universal "American" or human themes. Insiders trace an allegorical narrative of identity with which to reimagine the specificity of their own racial challenges.[10] They chart the protagonist's story, not so much to emulate it as to see how it highlights and addresses group dilemmas. The protagonist becomes an allegorical figure of struggle and hope for his or her racial or ethnic community. When students and critics argue that these literary works give particular peoples a voice, they are referring to these reading practices. These readings depend on the common U.S. assumption that nonwhite race and non-European ethnicity adhere to persons as dispositions or *identities;* through identity, each individual makes himself or herself an allegorical figure in relation to a marked social group. Cultural critics are often contemptuous of interpretive strategies in which insider readers pick out characters and events with whose truth they identify; but it is these popular readings that are the object of our analysis. Literary works have become important in the process of consolidating publicly recognized racial and ethnic identities. Because our project explores racial representations, we are most concerned here with reading these literary works as narratives of identity. To stimulate dialogue among alternative minority perspectives, we investigate currents of interpretation rather than the construction of particular texts.

In placing African American and Chinese American literature in dialogue, we look for their divergent and conflicting understandings of racism and community building. Our cross-racial reading diverges from most recent scholarly strategies for analyzing relations among communities of color, in which minority traditions are assumed to be autonomous and parallel units of culture. Perhaps the most common model for connecting varied people of color as a coalition subject is the anthology. There are many ways to read anthologies; but the currently prevalent reading practice on U.S. college campuses is to read the collected essays as voices from communities imagined as separate and equivalent and lined up like towels on a clothesline. Such a lineup makes it very difficult for differently positioned minority communities to engage in dialogue. We need to imagine more creative weavings between these so-called communities.

Such weavings begin with careful thinking about the relationships among minority groups. Most such thinking so far, even that which carefully criticizes the notion of autonomous cultural communities, stresses similarities among racial groups or else their complementarity in racist thinking. One sophisticated attempt to chart similarities among marginalized groups is seen in JanMohammed and Lloyd's promotion of the term *minority discourse;* divergent subordinate groups, they argue, face related challenges in their literary expression.[11] We respect and draw from their work but are concerned to also explore the nature of overlap and incompatibilities between particular minority discourses. And, while attending to the multifaceted nature of racism, we also move beyond the assumption that all its forms are part of a predetermined master plan of domination. Homi Bhabha's discussion of stereotypes, for example, usefully focuses on the repetitive structure of racism. He writes:

> As a form of splitting and multiple belief, the "stereotype" requires, for its successful signification, a continual and repetitive chain of other stereotypes. This is the process by which the metaphoric "masking" is inscribed on a lack which must then be concealed, that gives the stereotype both its fixity and its phantasmatic quality — the same old *stories of the Negro's animality, the Coolie's*

inscrutability or the stupidity of the Irish which must be told (compulsively) again and afresh, and is differently gratifying and terrifying each time.[12]

There is some truth to the interconnection between varied forms of racism. But taken to this extreme, this position reduces every form of discrimination to an expression of the same static and essentially psychological profile. To imagine all forms of racism as features of an unerring and ahistorical structural logic denies the existence of separate histories of discrimination and struggle. In contrast to Bhabha's attempt to make the familiar more familiar, we look for unexpected cross talk.

One piece of cross talk with which we begin lies in our social units. Unlike African Americans, many Asian Americans do not identify themselves by race but by Asian national or ethnic origin. The identities and dilemmas imagined by Asian Americans are as often those of component, ethnic units as of the larger—and often problematic—racial coalition. Because our project investigates popular readings, we have chosen to stick closely to folk boundaries concerning narratives of identity; in this spirit, we limit our discussion here to Chinese Americans. (This limitation is not intended to work against the coalition of Asian Americans; it seems necessary only for the particular project at hand.)[13] We are aware that a Chinese-black dialogue begins from asymmetrical assumptions about the making of social categories. This awareness is at the heart of our strategy.

Men's Stories

It is impossible to begin a discussion about U.S. minority identities and communities without talking about gender. Individuals take on minority identities as gendered identities; race and gender are defined together in the stories that define and represent race. Contemporary narratives of racial and ethnic identity are gendered narratives.

Furthermore, recent discussion of race has been marked by gender-segregated arguments for just what "of color" might mean. Since the 1970s there has been growing self-consciousness among people of color about the divergence between male and female traditions of literary and critical writing. A number of outspoken male critics blame this on the influence of a white-dominated feminism; otherwise, they argue, gender would be irrelevant, and women would support their men who are fighting for the rights of unified communities.[14] Their words harbor contradictions. Gender is already relevant as long as representatives of communities are expected to be male.

Since anticolonial struggles after World War II filled the world with supposedly independent nations, every marked community must recall the model of the nation to attest to its political rights. In this sense, minority nationalism refers not just to one specific radical tendency but also to the most effective cultural grounds on which any disadvantaged group can proclaim itself a political community. In this sense, too, fictional narratives of community identity are always in dialogue with national models. And if, as Benedict Anderson suggests, the nation as internationally imagined is a fraternity of men's ties, even these domestic nationalisms are men's affairs.[15] In the space that the national model has carved out, men create communities and represent them to others. Men lead by showing themselves to be masculine, active subjects who have the power and respect to speak for their wives and children. This is how they show themselves politically equal to other men, both within and between national communities. Men of color in the United States are pressed into engagement in a struggle to show themselves leaders of the kinds of communities that have gained international political legitimacy.[16]

In the literary works we read, male stories of identity create the figure of the African American or Chinese American man who can build and redeem a community. Here we are less interested in the gender of particular authors and more in the gender of claims for representing a community. Women authors can write a man's story and vice versa; we postpone the question of how feminist and male-identified authors may differentially inflect male stories.[17] In the global cultural economy of fraternal nations, men's narratives are those in which individual achievements can stand for nation building.

When we first began this collaboration, we thought that African American and Chinese American men struggled with paired racist images—the two poles of a single spectrum of stereotypes. In such images African American men are overmasculinized studs, while Chinese American men are feminized nerds. Are these not two sides of the same racist coin—perhaps the mindless body and the bodyless mind? Yet as we have continued to read through the narratives that plot men's dilemmas, we have increasingly seen the noncoincidence of two separate frameworks of exclusion. In these narratives, black men fight a racism that makes them struggle over and over across the line between nature and culture. Black men must fight to be considered human, not savage, dangerous animals; they work within the "Fear of a Black Planet."[18] To show themselves leaders, black men must thus worry about control: control over themselves and control over their women and children. They are objects of violence; they become agents of violence in their quest to obtain human status. To lead a community they need to lead women and children; the most frightening specter, perhaps, is the unprotected and unruly black woman who cannot be led, for she symbolizes his powerlessness. A 1992 story in *Essence* is full of black men's descriptions of their humiliation at remembering racist objectifications aimed toward them in front of women, thus proving their inabilities to protect, to lead.[19] Black men fight an imagined inability to be fathers—and thus to claim their own fathers—because they are considered unable to support and control a paternal family, the building block of community.

At the turn of the century, Chinese men in the United States worked against related forms of racial discrimination; it is sobering to remember that Chinese men have also been seen by whites as dangerous animals and savage rapists. As Sky Lee reminds us in her novel *The Disappearing Moon Cafe*, Chinese houseboys in the

Pacific Northwest were once feared by the white community as potential desecrators of white womanhood.[20] Like black men, they could be lynched. More recently, however, a different set of dilemmas has seemed more pressing: dilemmas that emerge from the imagined line between tradition and modernity.[21] Chinese men fight the fact that they are representatives of a backward nation. Unlike African Americans, who are imagined without history, Chinese Americans are imagined with too much history. They must struggle to become effective individual actors in a regime of modernity that defines the traditional as outside, ineffective, already having lost the game. As carriers of tradition, they are seen as feminine. They cannot portray themselves as sexual subjects, subjects through desire. Confronted by the specter of the white woman, the object of modern desire, they appear impotent. Although they have no problem imagining controlling their wives and children, Chinese American men are still blocked from being, and claiming, effective fathers. They are blocked by their inability to have active, modern identities. They are haunted by the powerlessness of a martial arts, which, as tradition, has always already been lost.

Let us turn to some specific texts. Contemporary black men's stories refer continually back to Richard Wright's *Native Son,* a story of how racist stereotypes of the Bad Nigger were internalized by one "native son."[22] Bigger Thomas, the protagonist, slowly becomes the beastlike monster racism imagines; he kills accidentally, but by the end of the novel he is ready to say: "But what I killed for I *am!* It must've been pretty deep in me to make me kill!"[23] In post-1960s community building, this story of the making of the black man as animal must be turned around; the black man as leader must be redeemed.

The narrative of the black man as community leader is perhaps clearest in the stories real black male leaders tell about themselves. Both *The Autobiography of Malcolm X* and Eldridge Cleaver's *Soul on Ice* tell of the rise of a man from beastlike abjection into full control as a cultural leader and a man.[24] Cleaver was a rapist; Malcolm was a numbers runner; both were frustrated, angry, and stuck in prison. Through Islam and then black militancy, each moves beyond weak black fathers (Malcolm's promiscuous Elijah Muhammad, Cleaver's homosexual James Baldwin). Each becomes a man capable of leading, and controlling, a community.

For both Cleaver and Malcolm X, to lead a community means to protect women and children. A more recent articulation of this theme shows black men's frustration in trying to control the terms of sexual access to black women (for example, Trey Ellis's *Platitudes* or Spike Lee's *She's Got to Have It).*[25] But perhaps a striking image from Toni Morrison's *Beloved* makes the point most sharply: Halle, the husband of the female protagonist, loses his sanity when he helplessly watches two white boys sexually assault his wife. "Not a one of them years of Saturdays, Sundays, and nighttime extra ever touched him. But whatever he saw go on in that barn that day broke him like a twig," says his friend Paul D.[26] Without the right to claim and protect his woman, he cannot be a self-respecting human being. He loses his claim on culture, manhood, life.

The challenges are different in Chinese American men's stories. As Frank Chin argues, dominant white representations made Chinese Americans "lovable for being a race of sissies."[27] Maxine Hong Kingston begins *China Men* with a striking mythical image that sets the stage not only for her book but also for the general problem; she tells of a Chinese man who crossed the ocean and found himself transformed into a woman.[28] *China Men* goes on to tell the stories of somewhat less mythical Chinese men as they are humiliated and challenged by the anti-Chinese racism of the United States. They are allowed no women to control and protect; instead, they find *themselves* treated as women: they become outsiders, suspicious strangers; they lose their names and their prerogatives as members of a community. Treated with contempt, they are forced to wash laundry, which they think of as washing menstrual blood.[29]

Other Chinese American men's stories bring up a key confrontation in which emasculating sexual humiliation occurs: Chinese American men's sexuality is denied and destroyed by white women, who stand as symbols of U.S. modernity. In Louis Chu's *Eat a Bowl of Tea*, the young man Ben Loy becomes impotent after seeing white prostitutes; he is unable to consummate his marriage.[30] In Gish Jen's *Typical American*, the immigrant protagonist loses all his strength to act after a foolish, doomed attempt to court a white secretary.[31] How could the white woman ever see him as a man? In Gus Lee's *China Boy*, the hero, a young boy, is emasculated by his white stepmother.[32] She attacks him, he believes, the minute she realizes he does not speak standard English; to stand up to her, he must learn to fight like a (Western) man. Such themes cross the Pacific, defining Chinese vulnerability. Sau-ling Wong writes of Chinese immigrant fiction in which immigrant men's stories are tales of coping with desexualization in the face of modernized, Americanized Chinese American women; for these immigrants, Chinese American women stand in for their white counterparts.[33] The man from a traditional society, these protagonists fear, is not equipped with the sexual agency required for success in the modern Western world.[34]

Nature and culture, tradition and modernity: the two frameworks cut across each other. Racial categorizations hold both in place; physical appearance keeps both African American and Chinese American men in their sway. Certainly, too, there are other overlaps and convergences. Yet the specificity of each framework makes it difficult for each to imagine alliances with the other. It is easy, for example, for Chinese American men to see black men as just another part of that violent modern America that uniformly confronts their vulnerabilities. Lee's *China Boy* offers an explicit case: the young Chinese hero is taunted and tortured by black toughs on the streets; in order to stand up to his fearful white stepmother, the specter of the modern, he must first prove his manhood by challenging his black peers.

This identification of violent manhood with effective modern subjectivity is also the grounds for interracial alliance in this novel. Lee's hero learns to box, and thus to be a man, in a multiracial YMCA. There can be no martial arts for this young American; it is the legitimate modern sport of boxing that can save him by showing him the doors to freedom of opportunity. It is promising to find an African American story that looks in the other direction. In Charles Johnson's short story "China," a middle-aged black post office worker is ready to submit to the unfairness of a life in which hard work leads only to an early demise until he discovers Chinese martial arts.[35] The black man has no problem with modernity; what he believes he needs is discipline and control. In the story, martial arts training becomes a program for the man's return to a fully human pride. Indeed, the story recalls a moment of imagined alliance between black and Asian men in the United States during and after the Vietnam War, when the unexpected effectiveness of unarmed fighting arts and guerrilla warfare, both associated with Asians, inspired a cohort of black men.[36] Boxing and martial arts become an equal trade between the stories; each can represent what the other needs. Yet Lee's black fighter remains a tough; Johnson's Chinese fighter remains inscrutable. Neither story shows any gesture toward the other's perspective.

The gender and sexual specificities of African and Chinese men's dilemmas also make it difficult for either to recognize the struggles for self-respect, identity, and community of women of the same groups. The sisters of Lee's hero assimilate without problems; the wife of Johnson's hero looks on with awe at the self-development of her husband. Yet other women—fictional characters and authors—have more independent narratives. It is to these we now turn.

Women's Stories

Figures of African and Chinese American women are also crafted in stories of identity and community, but the conditions of this crafting are neither the same as nor symmetrical to those of male figures. Figures of men of color represent their communities through their terrors and struggles; in contrast, women of color are told in stories about how groups of women strategize to build community-like ties *despite* the absence of powerful male representatives. Again, we are talking about gendered narratives, not authors. Powerful expectations for male-represented nations shape a world in which narratives of the identities and communities of women of color are fragmented, incomplete, and unstable because they cannot aspire to the imagined closure of a masculine national perspective. Yet these figures cannot cut their ties to this problematic national community; unlike white people who masquerade as communally unmarked speakers, women of color—even as fictional figures—must conjure a speaking community, that is, a nation, to create a space from which to speak.

The comparatively weak standing of men of color in the United States due to racism haunts the stories of women of color. The distinctive and creative solution found by a number of African American and Chinese American women writers, for which they have been justly acclaimed, has been to write into being strong female worlds that sustain rich affective cultures despite the problem of absent patriarchs. This is neither an easy nor an automatic solution. It has challenged the prerogatives of male authors and protagonists to determine what counts as community. It has opened opportunities for women who never thought they could speak or write. Yet it does not, of course, create an ideal world, as some eager reviewers have maintained. One way to see the mix of challenge to, maneuver within, and acceptance of assumptions about race, culture, and gender is in the divergent courses of recent Chinese American and African American women's fiction.

What do the film *Dim Sum* and the books *Woman Warrior, The Joy Luck Club,* and *The Kitchen God's Wife* have in common?[37] Each tells the promise of mother-to-daughter cultural transmission. Chinese culture is, in its own ideals, a father-to-son arrangement. But North American Chinese fathers have not always been appropriately positioned to transmit culture. They have had to forge a present with "paper" fathers (fictive kin acquired to enter the United States), uncertain immigration status, and demeaning employment; this has not been advantageous ground for arranging a vision of patrilineal cultural continuity.[38] It is in this context that women's stories show the possibility of mothers and daughters who pick up the task of narrating the past and creating a pathway into the future. This task is difficult and full of ambivalence. Not only do the women have to work their way around Chinese patriarchal and patrilineal conventions, they also have to make the best of racist and sexist limitations in their U.S. setting. Each of the stories listed above is full of the tensions of female tellings of a male-dominated world. The mothers, never properly trained to transmit Chinese culture, conjure a fragmented, dreamlike, and self-exoticizing world. The daughters don't always want to hear mixed-up maternal tales, particularly tales of female submission. The daughters resent both the authority and awkwardness of their mothers' tellings; and they are not sure they want the responsibility for retelling these stories. At the end, however, each story tentatively confirms the possibility of female cultural transmission in a racist world.

In *The Women of Brewster Place, The Color Purple,* and the film *Daughters of the Dust,* we see quite different kinds of female-female ties; the women forge a cultural community through a horizontally extended network rather than an intergenerational chain.[39] Toni Morrison's novels at first appear to be a contrast, in that a number of them focus on mother-daughter ties, but, like the other works we have listed, they show incorporative female bonding rather than cultural transmission.[40] All of these stories depict a racist world in which women must maneuver through poverty and violence to hold on to socially organized and culturally promising lives. They cannot rely on the support of fathers, husbands, lovers, or sons because men are vulnerable to racist violence and incarceration, unpredictably employed, and caught up in their own masculine insecurities. Women must forge extraconjugal networks to survive. This is not easy, for the violence and poverty of daily life splits women apart. Mothers kill their daughters out of love (*Beloved*). Homophobia breaks up neighborhood spirit (*The Women of Brewster Place*). Sisters sustain only distant memories (*The Color Purple*). Petty morality causes some women to shun others (*Daughters of the Dust*). But sometimes love, struggle, spirituality, and magic work to gather up and move beyond everyday disappointments. The image at the end of *The Women of Brewster Place* is telling of the hope in many of these stories: the community of women, forgetting for the moment the dangerous future and the terrible past, together tear down a wall that blocks in their neighborhood. The possibility of incorporative nurturant female ties that continue and expand despite the pain of racist violence is confirmed. In this vision, women become founders and centers of communities that can hope to survive.

To a certain extent, the differences between these two visions of female community reflect divergent class agendas. The Chinese Americans represented in these works build ladders of intergenerational cultural transmission as part of an agenda of upward mobility and at least aspiring middle-class status. In contrast, the African Americans in the novels mentioned above are managing poverty through extended networks of neighbors and kin. These fictive class agendas correspond in part to the economic situation of Chinese Americans and African Americans. Throughout this century, some Chinese Americans have been able to gather the capital to start small businesses; a younger generation of educated and professional children, as well as more well-off immigrants, have risen farther still in class and social status. In contrast, despite individual gains, in the main the barriers against African American economic and social mobility have been increasingly strengthened. However, we also want to emphasize that the narratives of identity we are discussing are imaginative visions for building communities rather than compilations of realistic detail. There are class divisions within each group as well as between them. Furthermore, the African American authors of these novels may have a higher class status than do the characters they depict. The Chinese American authors may have faced rather more racism than they bother to portray. There is room here for other conversations.

What conversations might draw African American and Chinese American versions of community into dialogue? Feminist discussions of women of color often treat the fictional works we have been discussing as if they were self-evidently similar. Both traditions of writing are considered feminist triumphs. We do not disagree. Yet the most striking feature shared by these African American and Chinese American versions of community may be their compliance with a problematic gender agenda. Both depict women's ties to each other as producing inward-looking, domestic communities. It is ironic that black women in particular have pioneered criticisms to feminist models that show only women's domestic ties; black women have rarely had the privilege of staying at home.[41] Again it is clear that these domestic fictional communities are intended not as full descriptions of women's lives but as visions of what counts for community building. Nor are these domestic visions apolitical; they are politically charged constructions of home. This is the famed "kitchen table" of mutual support among women of color.[42] It shows women's abilities to build enduring social ties with each other. Yet the inward focus downplays women's experience with work and activism to show women coping despite their public exclusions.[43]

An inward-looking focus reproduces notions of separate, autonomous communities—the very notions that make cross-racial dialogue difficult. The parallel with the use of the "domestic" in anthropology seems relevant. The dichotomy between "domestic" and "politico-jural" grew up in anthropology with analytical commitments to understanding the social structure of closed, self-reproducing social groups;[44] each sphere played a role in social reproduction. The 1970s feminist project of connecting women and female dilemmas with the "domestic" half of this dichotomy was in a sense only a note on this larger anthropological agenda.[45] Stories by women of color similarly show a commitment to closed, self-reproducing communities. This is the national model that allows claims of political autonomy; in a sense, despite their rejections of male superiority, women's domestic stories complement men's leadership. The model of separate nationlike communities still pushes women inside.

Furthermore, with increasing success, female authors of color take more responsibility for representations of community; they begin to determine what counts as continuity and vitality. Perhaps the strength of these calls is due in part to their appeal within hegemonic standards: the fragmented and nostalgic depictions of community produced by women of color correspond in some ways to the expected status of communities of color in dominant U.S. understandings. (Minority male authors worry that their work will not sell because their leadership expectations offend white readers.) In this context, it becomes particularly urgent for women writers and readers to reexamine our complicities with as well as our refusals of dominant frameworks.

The building of communal boundaries reflects in part a necessary defense against white racism; but it also builds silences in other directions. When we began this project, we expected that the main obstacle to dialogue among women of color would be stereotypes that mimicked dominant racist interpretations of the other. Instead, we found silence.[46] We could find no fictional communities that included both African American and Chinese American women, even in minor roles. Sometimes such roles are hinted at, but they are never directly labeled. From these marginal examples, it seemed that each was incorporated, through silence, into the other's vision of dominant society. In this Chinese American vision, blacks are just another kind of "typical American." In this African American vision, Chinese Americans are just another kind of white person. This effect is produced by defining minority communities only in relation to their dominant Others. Unfortunately, we think this effect can be just as problematic for dialogue as can derogatory stereotypes.

The problem emerges more clearly as one looks at the ways in which African American and Chinese American writing has been appropriated into a multicultural feminism. A comparison of feminist readings of Maxine Hong Kingston's *Woman Warrior* and Toni Morrison's *Beloved* can illustrate this. Each of these books has been celebrated as a key feminist text—and as a milestone of creativity for Chinese American and African American women, respectively. Yet sometimes feminist celebrations can reproduce and extend technologies of exclusion for other groups.

Feminist readings forge an alliance between insider and outsider women; they highlight the courage of key female figures in terms that resonate with dominant, white understandings of female struggles. Lest this seem to be a distinctive criticism of feminism, we hasten to add that all insider narratives are forged on these terms: To seem convincing, powerful, and worldly, an insider narrative must tap the legitimacy of at least some corner of a dominant discourse. Insider and outsider reading strategies are always interdependent and formed in conversation. Yet different insider narratives may tap different pieces of dominant discourse. It is in this process of differential appropriations that assertion of strength by one marginalized group ignores or humiliates another marginalized group.

Kingston's "woman warrior" has been celebrated as the brave daughter, the woman who refuses to be silent. Feminists celebrate her as a trickster, a border crosser, a clever chameleon of multiple identities. She embodies an oxymoron; she is a woman who speaks as a woman. She emerges within patriarchal discipline but somehow, improbably, breaks with its feminine silences. She demands to speak as a subject but refuses disciplinary individuation, mixes fact and fantasy, and insists on the complexity of the articulated "I."[47]

Yet have African American feminists not argued that escape from silence is a white women's preoccupation? Feminine silence is part of the machinery of civilization; black women have been denied its disciplines. Black women are said to be noisy and unruly, not frightened and still. Allegorical black daughters do not fight patriarchal silencing, but, from the first, witness "talking back" as a means to cultivate social resources.[48] The woman warrior thus appears as another exclusionary device against black women's concerns.[49]

In contrast, Toni Morrison's *Beloved* has been said to have "opened the space for *maternal* narrative in feminist fiction."[50] *Beloved* tells of the ambiguity of the maternal; it is violent and cruel as well as caring and accepting despite all costs. The female protagonist kills her baby daughter rather than see her returned to slavery; the pain, horror, and responsibility of this loving maternal action haunt the woman for the rest of her life. The story humanizes understandings of slavery by showing its terrible effects on loving mothers.[51] Yet to humanize means to bring in familiar, dominant frameworks. The all-incorporating nurturance of the mother creates a figure of hope for white feminists as well as black; she represents the possibility of love in a damaged world.[52]

At a recent conference on African American women, a number of scholars argued that Toni Morrison's novel *Beloved* exemplifies the maternal semiotic—Julia Kristeva's prelinguistic borderless domain that proceeds, sits beside, and challenges phallic authority.[53] In keeping with Kristeva's ideas, *Beloved* describes the boundless power of mother-child ties to mix memory, violence, magic, and love. Yet this discourse on maternal love is an alien and alienating one for Chinese American women, and, indeed, it is a discourse that is used to define their exclusion from modernity. It is no accident that Kristeva developed her theory of identity in self-conscious contradistinction to what she calls the Chinese. In *About Chinese Women*, Kristeva creates an exotic China that defines through reversal the discourse of the West, the Enlightenment, modernity.[54] Love, the caring-without-cause counterpart and challenge to paternal power, is a requirement for the modern subject; it is what is said to be lacking for those held by the bounds of tradition. Chinese and Chinese American women stand outside the discourse on modern subjectivity.[55] Morrison's embrace of the discourse on nurturant maternal love, the very quality that allows white critics to canonize her as a genius speaking to universal themes, excludes Chinese Americans as speaking subjects within the conversation.

In Dialogue

Our analysis of this contrast is partial and tentative. It is clear that interpretations of these novels are in constant flux. Recently, King-kok Cheung has rejected white feminists' appropriations of the speaking daughter of *The Woman Warrior* by arguing that silence is often powerful and provocative; it is a racist exclusion to see silence as only that which should be overcome.[56] Similarly, a number of black critics have argued against white feminist universalizations of the black maternal. Black women, they argue, have a culturally distinctive relationship to their mothers; unlike white women, black women receive the power of authorship from their mothers.[57] The continual appearance of contestations such as these calls for open and dynamic discussion across borders. Furthermore, the black-Chinese contrasts we find are not particularly "true" ones; they are contrasts in stories and perspectives that may not sit easily with the accumulation of lives. Thus even as we draw contrasts, we stress their limited and ephemeral quality. Our goal is not to solidify difference but to foster possibilities for alliance.

The first step in moving beyond mutual exclusions is to address each other directly. Thus we begin with attention to the divergent frameworks of racist exclusion and antiracist struggle that have been brought forward by readers and writers of particular communities of color. Only by attention to these differences can we create the possibilities of coalition-building dialogue. This kind of dialogue challenges the neat boundaries of nationlike models of community building; despite the power and legitimacy of such models, we argue that exciting political possibilities for both women and men of color can be opened up by crossing the boundaries in dialogue.

We are suggesting a model for the analysis of marginalization that does not imagine exclusion through the history of just one particular margin. Because each group's status negotiations have a different history, attention to the relationships among marginalized groups draws attention to varied forms of exclusion as well as to the diverse strategic compromises, comparative privileges, and creative reworkings that accompany each group's struggles against marginal status. Rather than locating all forms of racism in a unitary psychology or logic of the privileged, we look for the ways in which specific understandings of race—including those of both dominant and subordinate groups—intertwine, overlap, and diverge. From these histories we hope to glimpse not just cross-racial misunderstandings but also the possibilities for mutual respect.

As our anxieties here about reinvoking racial stereotypes suggest, frameworks that stress cultural difference are dangerous as well as insightful. In recent years a number of scholars have criticized the mapping of difference as colonizing and exoticizing.[58] From an imagined stand of neutrality, Western scholars too often draw differences as signs of exclusion; depictions of cultural specificity become forms of entrapment that bar those so named from participation in high places. Our project works to use difference in another (that is, an Other) way. Instead of pretending to exclude power from our readings of culture, we begin with the inextricability of power and knowledge. Arguing that minority narratives of identity gain their appeal within the challenges of racism, we compare projects of self-definition and struggle, as these expose the conditions of racial exclusion, rather than offer static and essential contrasts. We redefine culture to look for strategic moments of self-expression within politically charged histories. This involves sensitive immersion in the dilemmas of marginalization as experienced from particular margins. From there we can shape a dialogue that shows the courage as well as the necessary complicities of each culture-making project. In this way we hope to both tap and transform "the master's tools." (Our reference here is to Audre Lorde's generative article, "The Master's Tools Will Never Dismantle the Master's House,"[59] which opened the discussion of respectful attention to difference that we extend in this essay.)

This is a project of special appeal for and challenge to women readers and writers. We have argued that women are those who cannot straightforwardly represent nationlike communities. Indeed, the awkwardness of women's representational authority was brought home to us again recently when black male writers refused to celebrate Toni Morrison's Nobel prize in literature as a black achievement. (After one black male writer after another dismissed Morrison's writing, novelist John Williams summed up the reaction: "I guess all the guys are pissed and the ladies like it.")[60] In this context, women of color have become particularly aware of men's complicities in hegemonic masculinist agendas, at the same time as we recognize the forms of racism that encourage this solution. Scholars such as E. Francis White and Sylvia Yanagisako have shown the importance of sympathetic but critical feminist readings of minority nationalisms.[61] Their readings, which show the intertwining not only of gender and race but also of struggle and often unself-conscious compromise, lead directly into our project of dialogue across minority discourses. As we remember the tentativeness of women's culture-writing, we see our stakes in border-crossing dialogue.

Our emphasis on moving beyond an analysis that imagines closed, parallel communities of color recalls the criticisms that have been made for a number of years about ethnographic descriptions of cultures as bounded and autonomous. Critics have called for attention to the regional-to-global political, economic, and cultural context of the local social groups anthropologists once studied as isolated societies. Most of these calls have pushed for better understandings of the ties between First World and Third World cultures, between colonizer and colonized, between researchers and researched. Once the second term in each of these dichotomies was studied alone; now attention has turned to the interaction between the terms. Our critique accepts this move but pushes farther. Those once considered objects of research are now also researchers and writers. Yet so much of our talk of refocusing knowledge brings into perspective only the forms of discrimination we each know best. If we want to move toward better, richer understandings of culture and community, we cannot stop at enhancing dialogue with our imagined dominant group. It is time for dialogue across margins.

Notes

An earlier version of this paper was presented at the symposium on "Border Crossings" at the 1992 annual meeting of the American Anthropological Association. We are grateful to Claudia Casteneda and Brenda Rao for comments that helped us prepare our presentation. Ruth Behar, Deborah Gordon, Karen Ho, Barbara Ige, Saba Mahmood, Renato Rosaldo, and Carolyn Martin Shaw offered comments that helped us revise our paper for this essay.

1. An off-beat and therefore useful introduction to the feminist debate mentioned here can be found in Carla Freccero, "Notes of a Post–Sex Wars Theorizer," in *Conflicts in Feminism*, ed. Marianne Hirsch and Evelyn Fox Keller (New York: Routledge, 1990), 305–25. A discussion of the theoretical differences dividing U.S. minority scholars and Third World postcolonial critics can be found in the introduction to Anna Tsing, *In the Realm of the Diamond Queen* (Princeton, N.J.: Princeton University Press, 1993). Smadar Lavie's work on the possibilities for collaboration between Arab Jews and Palestinians in Israel ("Blow-ups in the Border Zones: Third World Israeli Authors' Groping for Home," *New Formation* 18 [1984]: 106) is an exciting exception to our generalization about lack of attention to dialogue among marginalized groups; her work forms an important contribution to such a project.

2. In this paper, we use the terms *race* and *ethnicity* as U.S. folk categories that divide people by physical appearance and cultural commitments, respectively. They are not synonymous, yet they overlap and blend in defining the groups (African Americans and Chinese Americans) about which we are most concerned here. Sometimes we remind the reader of the existence of these two competing frameworks by using both terms; otherwise, we just use one, hopefully the more relevant, to refer to the communal divisions we discuss.

3. It is perhaps for this reason that a number of minority literary critics have become sympathetic to ethnographic readings of these novels. Patricia Lin, for example, argues that Maxine Hong Kingston's work should be read as polyphonic ethnography because it offers multiple, clashing versions of reality ("Clashing Constructs of Reality: Reading Maxine Hong Kingston's *Tripmaster Monkey: His Fake Book* as Indigenous Ethnography," in *Reading the Literatures of Asian America*, ed. Shirley Geok-lin Lim and Amy Ling [Philadelphia: Temple University Press, 1992], 333–48); Sau-ling Wong, following Clifford Geertz's usage, calls literature "the 'thickest description' possible of a people's life" (*Reading Asian American Literature: From Necessity to Extravagance* [Princeton, N.J.: Princeton University Press, 1993], 39). Similarly, Bernard Bell reads African American literature as "thick description" (*The Afro-American Novel and Its Tradition* [Amherst: University of Massachusetts Press, 1987], xiii) and calls on anthropologists such as Sidney Mintz for his understanding of black culture.

4. Carol Stack, *All Our Kin* (New York: Harper and Row, 1974); Elliot Liebow, *Tally's Corner* (Boston: Little, Brown, 1967); Amy Tan, *The Joy Luck Club* (New York: Putnam, 1989).

5. Deborah Gordon, "Politics of Ethnographic Authority: Race Writing in the Ethnography of Margaret Mead and Zora Neale Hurston," in *Modernist Anthropology: From Fieldwork to Text*, ed. Marc Manganaro (Princeton, N.J.: Princeton University Press, 1990), 146–62.

6. Mary Orgel, "American Culture and American Cultural Anthropology during the 1930s" (M.A. thesis, University of Massachusetts, 1992).

7. Carla Cappetti, *Writing Chicago: Modernism, Ethnography, and the Novel* (New York: Columbia University Press, 1993).

8. Bell, *Afro-American Novel,* chap. 5.

9. See, for example, Frank Chin, "Come All Ye Asian American Writers of the Real and the Fake," in *The Big Aiiieeeeee!* ed. Jeffery Chan, Paul Chan, Frank Chin, Lawson Inada, and Shawn Wong (New York: Meridian, 1991), 1–93; Steve Chapple, "Writing and Fighting: Ishmael Reed," *Image* 14 (June 1987); Ishmael Reed, *Reckless Eyeballing* (New York: St. Martin's Press, 1986).

10. In "Being the Subject and the Object: Reading African American Women's Novels" (in *Changing Subjects: The Making of Feminist Literary Criticism,* ed. Gayle Greene and Coppelia Kahn [New York: Routledge, 1993], 195–200), Barbara Christian uses her own reading experience to illuminate "insider" reading strategies that highlight allegorical narratives of identity.

11. Abdul JanMohammed and David Lloyd, "Introduction: Toward a Theory of Minority Discourse: What Is to Be Done?" in their *The Nature and Context of Minority Discourse* (New York: Oxford University Press, 1990), 1–16.

12. Homi Bhabha, "Difference, Discrimination and the Discourse of Colonialism," in *The Politics of Theory,* ed. Francis Barker, Peter Hulme, Margaret Iverson, and Diane Loxley (Colchester, England: University of Essex, 1983), 204, emphasis in original.

13. A number of scholars have tried to push beyond ethnic and national-origin divisions to promote the more inclusive and politically incisive category "Asian American" in the study of minority literatures. But there are still pitfalls, most notably discussing mainly one ethnic tradition and calling it "Asian American." One recent attempt that works hard to avoid this problem is Sau-ling Wong's *Reading Asian American Literature.* We respect this difficult move, but, in this paper, we take a more ethnographically cautious "ethnic" tack.

14. See the references in note 9, as well as King-kok Cheung, "*The Woman Warrior* versus *The Chinaman Pacific:* Must a Chinese American Critic Choose Between Feminism and Heroism?" in *Conflicts in Feminism,* 234–51; Barbara Smith, "Toward a Black Feminist Criticism," *Conditions: Two* 1, no. 2 (October 1977): 42–47. Trey Ellis's novel *Platitudes* (New York: Vintage, 1988) spoofs male and female styles in recent African American writing from a masculinist perspective. Maxine Hong Kingston teases her Chinese American male critics in *Tripmaster Monkey* (New York: Vintage, 1990).

15. Benedict Anderson, *Imagined Communities: Reflections on the Origin and Spread of Nationalism* (London: Verso, 1983).

16. A discussion of this issue as it relates to African American performance arts can be found in Paulla Ebron, "Rapping between Men: Performing Gender," *Radical America* 23, no. 4 (1991): 23–27.

17. The question of how male versus female authors tell gendered stories has been central to much feminist literary criticism, including that about minority literatures in the United States. We would not go along with those claims that make the gender-status of the author the determinant feature in how gender is depicted in the text; however, there certainly have been male versus female traditions of telling. For example, some critics have argued, with much support, that male authors who wrote before feminists raised the importance of gender rarely offered sympathetic and nuanced female narratives. Thus Ruth Hsiao argues convincingly that Chinese American author Louis Chu was unable to draw an insightful portrait of the female protagonist in his pioneering novel *Eat a Bowl of Tea* (Seattle: University of Washington Press, 1979). Nor were the male authors who followed him: "For all their criticism of patriarchy, the male writers perpetuate the patriarchy-centered world, in which the woman is a polemical tool to reinforce the emasculation of Asian males" (Hsiao "Facing the Incurable: Patriarchy in *Eat a Bowl of Tea,*" in *Reading the Literatures of Asian America,* 161). In contrast, Chinese American women writers, such as Maxine Hong Kingston and Gish Jen, have worked hard to construct complex portraits of the dilemmas of Chinese American men. However, these por-

traits still tend to differ from those being constructed by male authors; perhaps they are less interested in having a renaturalized masculine agency win out in the end. Donald Goellnicht argues that Maxine Hong Kingston's *China Men* (New York: Vintage, 1980) is "an act of revenge on the father," for, despite its basically sympathetic account, "the father has no voice" ("Tang Ao in America: Male Subject Positions in *China Men*," in *Reading the Literatures of Asian America*, 205).

18. This is the title of a rap recording by the popular African American raptivists Public Enemy.

19. Charles Jamison, Jr., "Racism: The Hurt That Men Won't Name," *Essence*, November 1992, 62ff.

20. Sky Lee, *The Disappearing Moon Cafe* (Seattle: Seal Press, 1991).

21. Various competing frameworks of racism and cultural marginalization have defined Chinese American status at every period of history. It is only useful to a certain point to suggest a historical shift. Notions of "Yellow Peril" reminiscent of the 1890s return to exclude immigrants in the 1990s. However, we argue that the framework most responsible for the emasculation of Chinese American men is the tradition/modernity dichotomy. And since this is the dilemma highlighted in so many Chinese American men's stories, it seems important to focus on this framework here.

22. Richard Wright, *Native Son* (New York: Perennial Classic, 1966 [1940]). Bell, *Afro-American Novel*, 159, develops the concept of the Bad Nigger on which our interpretation draws.

23. Wright, *Native Son*, 391–92.

24. Malcolm X with Alex Haley, *The Autobiography of Malcolm X* (New York: Grove, 1965); Eldridge Cleaver, *Soul on Ice* (New York: McGraw-Hill, 1967).

25. Ellis, *Platitudes*; Spike Lee (director), *She's Got to Have It* (Island Visual Arts, 1986).

26. Toni Morrison, *Beloved* (New York: Plume, 1987), 68.

27. Frank Chin and Jeffrey Paul Chan, "Racist Love," in *Seeing through Shuck*, ed. Richard Kostlanetz (New York: Ballantine, 1972), 66.

28. Kingston, *China Men*.

29. Goellnicht, "Tang Ao in America."

30. Chu, *Eat a Bowl of Tea*.

31. Gish Jen, *Typical American* (Boston: Houghton Mifflin, 1991).

32. Gus Lee, *China Boy* (New York: Dutton, 1991).

33. Sau-ling Wong, "Ethnicizing Gender: An Exploration of Sexuality as Sign in Chinese Immigrant Literature," in *Reading the Literatures of Asian America*, 111–29. Even in China, this story is powerful; Zhang Xianliang's popular protest novel *Half of Man Is Woman* (trans. Martha Avery [New York: Viking, 1988]) allegorizes the problem of China in the contemporary world as a problem of male sexual impotence. The strength of such an allegory depends on international understandings about the "emasculated" position of China, although for Zhang, the source of emasculation is the Communist state rather than tradition. Indeed, the possibilities for conflating the overbearing state and overbearing tradition are clear in a number of recent Chinese films, such as *Raise the Red Lantern*. Such Chinese stories draw from earlier twentieth-century literary work to genderize Chinese predicaments facing the "modern" West.

34. Wong ("Ethnicizing Gender") describes the process in which such exclusionary frameworks are internalized by individuals as "ethnicizing gender."

35. Charles Johnson, "China," in *Breaking Ice: An Anthology of Contemporary African-American Fiction*, ed. Terry McMillan (New York: Penguin, 1990), 369–85.

36. Martial arts was a key feature of 1960s Black Nationalism, which emphasized control and discipline as necessary for personal and political transformation. The "Swahili" term *yangumi* was used to Africanize Asian martial arts.

37. Wayne Wang (director), *Dim Sum* (Pacific Arts Video, 1987); Maxine Hong Kingston, *The Woman Warrior: Memoirs of a Girlhood among Ghosts* (New York: Random House, 1975); Amy Tan, *The Joy Luck Club* and *The Kitchen God's Wife* (New York: Putnam, 1991).

38. In an interview about her book *China Men,* Maxine Hong Kingston speaks to her sense of men's gendered inability to transmit history: "In fact, I wrote the characters so that the women have memories and the men don't have memories. They don't remember anything. The character of my father, for example, has no memory. He has no stories of the past. . . . He is so busy making up the present, which he has to build, that he has no time for continuity with the past" (Rabinowitz, cited in Goellnicht, "Tang Ao in America," 202). Faye Ng's novel *Bone* (New York: Hyperion, 1993) also takes up the difficulties of Chinese American fathers in building intergenerational continuity. Ng's father character is unhappy that he has never been able to return the bones of his "paper father" to China; as a sailor with uncertain employment, he also cannot offer his daughters the life he wants to give them. Unlike the books discussed in the main text, Ng's daughter character does not turn to her mother for a sense of ethnic continuity. Instead, her hope is in the fragile, tentative, but present-engaging ties of conjugal affection.

39. Gloria Naylor, *The Women of Brewster Place* (New York: Penguin Books, 1983); Alice Walker, *The Color Purple* (New York: Harcourt, Brace, Jovanovich, 1982); Julie Dash (director), *Daughters of the Dust* (Kino Video, 1992).

40. Morrison, *Beloved, Sula* (New York: New American Library, 1973), and *The Bluest Eye* (New York: Washington Square Press, 1970). Carolyn Martin Shaw (personal communication) points out that mother-daughter relationships in novels of black female identity are often about the hope of discontinuity across generations; mothers and daughters both try to make the new generation different from the old. Grandmothers, in contrast, sometimes symbolize the also-present hope of cultural transmission. We have found that, in contrast to U.S. blacks, immigrant Caribbean mothers, like Chinese American mothers, are portrayed as believing they can be the transmitters of cultural authority. See, for example, Audre Lorde, *Zami, A New Spelling of My Name* (Trumansburg, N.Y.: Crossing Press, 1982); Paule Marshall, *Brown Girl, Brownstones* (Old Westbury, N.Y.: Feminist Press, 1981); Latoya Hunter, *Diary of Latoya Hunter: My First Year in Junior High* (New York: Crown Books, 1992).

41. Bonnie Dill, "Race, Class, and Gender: Prospects for an All-Inclusive Sisterhood," *Feminist Studies* 9 (1983): 131–50.

42. Barbara Smith, ed., *Home Girls: A Black Feminist Anthology* (New York: Kitchen Table—Women of Color Press, 1983).

43. This is not to say that it would necessarily be helpful to incorporate more men into the stories or, as two recent novels set in cafes have done, to move the kitchen table out into the male-dominated city square. Both Gloria Naylor's *Bailey's Cafe* (New York: Harcourt Brace Jovanovich, 1992) and Lee's *Disappearing Moon Cafe* try to tell more than women's stories. Each cafe is owned by a man whose stories help hold it together. Encompassed by the story of men, the women who serve, eat, or count money at these tables have lost their power: they are perverse, cruel, ruined, sad. Ishmael Reed says Naylor "has transcended the cliché-ridden gender-bashing tracts of the nineteen-eighties" (Naylor, cover blurb). What he means, perhaps, is that women are taking the blows.

   The similarities between Naylor's and Lee's novels accompany an equally important divergence. Naylor's African American cafe seats every neighborhood worker, drunk, or whore in a slice in time. Lee's Chinese Canadian cafe offers a story of three generations. This contrast in what is meant by the term *community* is similar to that of the other novels and memoirs we have mentioned: Chinese American communities are portrayed as intergenerational ladders; African American communities are imagined as support networks for taking one challenge at a time.

44. Meyer Fortes, "Introduction," in *The Developmental Cycle in Domestic Groups,* ed. Jack Goody (Cambridge, England: Cambridge University Press, 1958).

45. Sylvia Yanagisako, "Mixed Metaphors: Native and Anthropological Models of Gender and Kinship Domains," in *Gender and Kinship: Essays toward a Unified Analysis,* ed. Jane Collier and Sylvia Yanagisako (Stanford: Stanford University Press, 1987), 86–118.

46. This is not to deny racism against other nonwhite groups among both Chinese Americans and African Americans. We claim only that in the classic stories that have become established as voices for women of color, there have been few references to women of other colors. Gloria Anzaldúa ("En Rapport, In Opposition: Cobrando cuentas a las nuestras," in her *Making Faces, Making Soul/Haciendo Caras* [San Francisco: Aunt Lute, 1990], 142–48) and Virginia Harris and Trinity Ordona ("Developing Unity among Women of Color: Crossing the Barriers of Internalized Racism and Cross-Racial Hostility," in *Making Faces,* 304–16) introduce some of the other issues that have hampered activist alliances among women of color.

47. Lee Quinby, "The Subject of Memoirs: The Woman Warrior's Technology of Ideographic Selfhood," in *De/Colonizing the Subject: The Politics of Gender in Women's Autobiography,* ed. Sidone Smith and Julia Watson (Minneapolis: University of Minnesota Press, 1992), 297–320; King-kok Cheung, " 'Don't Tell': Imposed Silences in *The Color Purple* and *The Woman Warrior,*" in *Reading the Literatures of Asian America,* 163–89; Trinh Minh-ha, *Woman, Native, Other: Writing Postcoloniality and Feminism* (Bloomington: Indiana University Press, 1989); Bettina Aptheker, *Tapestries of Life: Women's Work, Women's Consciousness, and the Meaning of Daily Experience* (Amherst: University of Massachusetts Press, 1989), 130–35.

48. bell hooks, *Talking Back: Thinking Feminist, Thinking Black* (Boston: South End Press, 1989).

49. King-kok Cheung (" 'Don't Tell' ") argues that the question of women speaking out is central not just to *The Woman Warrior* but also to Alice Walker's *The Color Purple.* Yet, in our reading, Walker's heroine faces not so much a limitation of language as a limitation of social ties and purposeful action. Her struggle is to reach past isolation; Kingston's heroine is not isolated but tongue-tied.

50. Marianne Hirsch, "Maternal Narratives: 'Cruel Enough to Stop the Blood,' " in *Reading Black, Reading Feminist: A Critical Anthology,* ed. Henry Louis Gates, Jr. (New York: Meridian Books, 1990), 415–30, emphasis ours.

51. Lucie Futz, "Images of Motherhood in Toni Morrison's *Beloved,*" in *Double Stitch: Black Women Write about Mothers and Daughters,* ed. Patricia Bell-Scott et al. (Boston: Beacon Press, 1991), 32–41.

52. As one literary analyst has argued, Toni Morrison "doesn't care how the family is organized as long as it is motivated by love" (Denise Heinze, *The Dilemma of "Double-Consciousness": Toni Morrison's Novels* [Athens: University of Georgia Press, 1993], 57). Our point is to mark the ease with which critics have been able to naturalize Morrison's notion of love—a conceptual site of alliance between African American and white women.

53. This was the conference on "Psychoanalysis and African American Women" held at the University of California, Santa Cruz, in 1992. Neither of us was able to attend the conference; however, we read drafts and heard summaries and comments from a number of those who did attend. Julia Kristeva's notion of the semiotic is explored in much of her

work; Kelly Oliver (*Reading Kristeva: Unraveling the Double-bind* [Bloomington: Indiana University Press, 1993]) attempts a balanced summary.

54. Julia Kristeva, *About Chinese Women* (London: M. Boyers, 1977).

55. One way of reading Chinese American daughters' stories is as attempts to come to terms with the fact that their mothers care about them without expressing the forms of all-accepting maternal love considered ideal by white—and black—American society. ("[I]n our family 'proud' is as close as we get to saying 'love,'" says the daughter character in Tan's *The Kitchen God's Wife*, 11, thus setting up the story of a difficult mother-daughter reconciliation.) Yet the film version of *The Joy Luck Club*, made, as we understand it, with the full cooperation of Amy Tan, appears to make nonsense of this generalization. The film excised everything from the novel that concerned cultural transmission and the anxieties of maintaining Chinese identity in the United States; these are the issues that gave the mothers in the novel authority. Instead of a story about Chineseness, the film is a sentimental paean to mother-daughter love despite obstacles: a true "American story." Perhaps it is the equivalent of Bill Cosby's black television family: an assertion that Chinese Americans have precisely those "universal" white qualities that they have been expected least to have. Indeed, one might argue that themes have been borrowed from *Beloved* and represented in a greeting-card version: An abortion in the book becomes infanticide in the film; women are haunted by maternal contradictions rather than guided by maternal duties.

56. King-kok Cheung, *Articulate Silences: Hisaye Yamamoto, Maxine Hong Kingston, Joy Kogawa* (Ithaca, N.Y.: Cornell University Press, 1993).

57. Alice Walker, *In Search of Our Mothers' Gardens: Womanist Prose* (San Diego: Harcourt Brace Jovanovich, 1983); Patricia Bell-Scott et al., eds., *Double Stitch*.

58. See, for example, Edward Said, *Orientalism* (New York: Pantheon Books, 1978); James Clifford and George E. Marcus, eds., *Writing Culture: The Poetics and Politics of Ethnography* (Berkeley: University of California Press, 1986).

59. Audre Lorde, in *Sister Outsider: Essays and Speeches* (Trumansburg, N.Y.: Crossing Press, 1984), 110–13.

60. David Streitfeld, "Toni Morrison Wins the Nobel for Literature," *San Francisco Chronicle,* October 8, 1993, A19.

61. E. Francis White, "Africa on My Mind: Gender Counter Discourse and African-American Nationalism," *Journal of Women's History* 2, no. 1 (1990): 73–97; Sylvia Yanagisako, "Transforming Orientalism: Gender, Kinship, Nationality, and Class in Asian American Studies," in *Naturalizing Power,* ed. Carol Delaney and Sylvia Yanagisako (New York: Routledge, 1995), 275–98; see also Cheung, "*The Woman Warrior.*"

21

Border Poets: Translating by Dialogues

Smadar Lavie

I. Amira Hess

the black hand's palm
the black woman's voice
the old black woman's face,
afraid of a man

don't touch me — if you do
ragged weary Yemenis will gather inside me
in screaming want, trying to move their home's walls,
their dwelling caves, and fly here by magic carpet
I fight off Yemen, the desert south
and the rod of wrath — stay away
because — why me?

and I'm a room of my own body
gasping for breath inside my own turf,
let no strange man come touch me
to taste my skin. A wandering Jew
comes up to my oasis — cool water purifies —
as if immersed in white, I am shined
he polishes away my charcoal and Yemenis

I flee to the caves
and weep the seven days
and ten nights, then put on eye make-up
downing tears and pain
leaving only a void to be orphaned from me too
then I catch ringing laughter
from petals of flowers
and shake myself all over
to get my second wind

— AMIRA HESS,
translated from Hebrew by Helene Knox
and Smadar Lavie

"I WAS THINKING, what's a Mizrahi woman?[1] Nothing. Maybe I always dreamed of being white, but kept killing the white woman in me. Now the white woman is dead, because I'm aware of who I am. When I wanted to be white, I managed to be white in the world, but was still black under my skin. Now I know I could never have been white in world, because black is more than my color. It's my essence. My thinking. My feelings. It's my history of home in Iraq."

So said Amira Hess, an Israeli poet who writes in Hebrew though her mother tongue is Arabic. I have long studied subaltern identities as conjunctures,[2] so I was amazed to hear her talk about identity as essence. The essence, however, was not in the color. It was in the thinking, the feelings, and the history of the colonized home. Does Hess use essentialism as a strategy for racial mobilization?[3] Apparently not. In her many interviews with the Israeli media, she always refuses to be labeled an "ethnic poet," saying that "the stigma of one's country of origin might mean that the poetry would not be appreciated for its intrinsic merits."[4] Because she insists on being considered a universal poet, Hess, who is about fifty years old, has finally been accepted as a talented rising star by the Israeli literary establishment. But at what cost to her?

"We were so together then, in Baghdad," she continued, agitated. "Nostalgic as it sounds, we were family. But here, suddenly you had to be an individual. An ego. I had to camouflage the East in me, my roots. The day I arrived here, I buried my mother and father alive. Every day I killed them again. Now I want to die, because I killed such beautiful people in me, the most beautiful people I knew. And not just to create my poetic self, either. It was a matter of everyday survival in Israel. You know, they passed on so much Auschwitz gas to us. Though it was not really to Westernize us. Anyway, as an upper-class Iraqi, I already had a lot of London in me."

The literary establishment perceives Hess's evocation of the East not as an expression of her political agency but as Jewish mysticism. In the context of Israeli literature in the Jewish nation-state, Jewish mysticism is not an experience of specificity but a universal value. Hess plays along with this misinterpretation in order to continue being published and winning national awards from the Israeli government. "You know, Smadar, you are the first one to really see that I'm not writing mysticism. You are more aware than I am of my poetry as politics. So let's talk about my self-hate."

Until that moment of our conversation, the Western-trained anthropologist[5] had been quite comfortable in Hess's sleek living room. It felt so spacious—white-washed walls, off-white sofa, other Danish minimalist furniture, abstract art. The house, in the Beit Hekerem neighborhood of Jerusalem, is near the Knesset, the Israeli national museum, and the old campus of the Hebrew University. Hess's neighbors include professors, Knesset members, and international media bureau chiefs. The anthropologist was also pleased to note that Hess referred to herself as a black woman, thus cracking open the Israeli academic model of melting-pot-style ethnicity, by foregrounding that model in the discourse on race.

"Self-hate," I echoed. Memories hit me, connecting my own body to Israel. My

Yemeni mom forbidding me to get any darker at the beach with my Ashkenazi girl-friends. How I got away with it because my Ashkenazi dad said it was OK. Struggling with high school desperation to wedge my Arab hips into slim Levi's. My trophy first boyfriend, a blond kibbutznik in an elite commando unit, begging me to go on a starvation diet but also to tan even darker so we could make a chess board with our bodies in bed.

"Self-hate," she echoed me. "I was born Amira, but when I was eight and we entered Israel, they said my name was Arabic and changed it to Leah, from my full name, Amira Leoni 'Ainatshi. So I lost my name. I lost my home. And when I turned into an Israeli woman I couldn't have a womb. Your womb is where your home is. But my body was full of grief. I tried so hard not to be. I clowned around so people would love me."

She suddenly clutched her arms around her body and burst into tears. "Erotica!" she said spitefully. "The critics, all Ashkenazi men. For them, the East is a woman and I'm just a sex queen, a femme fatale."

Sobs.

"I've been married twenty years to a German, a Hess. He's my second husband. But I've never found a space inside him or alongside him. I love him very much. He lets me be that Western individual, a poet. I don't have to work for a living any more."

She took a deep breath.

"My first husband, he was Iraqi. I was only a lab technician then. My family wouldn't let me aspire to anything more—I had to start working young. My first husband was a castrated male. A robot. Israel castrated him. He dominated me because he was so dominated. He hemmed me in, but I was inside him. I didn't write poetry in those days. Now I write, but I still have no womb. Even with two daughters, one black, one white. No home. I just have a hole—a black one."

"Your critics certainly see you as a hole," I remarked, "a woman, but not a black one."[6] Out of my bag I pulled copies of all the articles on her work, gleaned from the exhaustive archives of the Hebrew Authors Association, and read aloud to her. "Listen to this: 'Wild erotic poetry.'"[7]

She nodded wryly.

"Here's the scholarly version: 'Modernist meter for ecstatic, oracular poetry full of pathos . . . in a mystical sexual framework. . . . The denouement, corresponding to the sexual discharge, is shaped in the poem as an elegiac-tragic epilogue where the woman grieves over the dualism in the world, which she keeps seeking to transcend in the sexual act of male/female unity.'"[8]

She cracked up.

"Wait," I said, shuffling papers. "There's more. 'Amira Hess, with her cryptic utterances, no logic or syntax . . . just mysticism.'[9] Or this: 'She arouses my sympathy for exoticism.'[10] Or here it is again: 'Bursting in a colorful storm, connecting tradition and modernity.'"[11]

She rose abruptly, dumping her chubby, tan lapdog to the floor. Reaching across me to the end table, she grasped my copy of her first book, *And a Moon Drips Madness.*[12] "Well," she said, "decide for yourself," and began to read aloud in a monotone.

> I, Amira,
> Salima's daughter . . .
> ask the reader's forgiveness
> if my face doesn't match
> the stories
> I was sent to tell . . .
> I can't come to touch
> this despised East
> I refuse to remember my parents' home
> my mother's face an owl's
> weeping on the ruins
> my father's a cabbage — God
> did not save him.
> And yet I said
> the West — no fables like caressing breezes
> the West in a white shroud, cooked until charred
> I'll catch East hitting West
> in stormy rhythms . . .
> Amira Hess calls Amira Bar-Haim . . .
> they talk now, compare notes
> heart pounds, hand trembles
> they are both dead
> how will they settle it[13]

She laid the open book down and said, "This came out in '84. My second book was in '87, and I wrote it to play along with the critics' line that it was just mysticism, except for . . ." She grabbed my copy of her second book, her red fingernails trembling as she nervously flipped pages. "Listen."

> Suddenly I'll glance at my book
> confused . . .
> and I'll write
> pleading for words to come
> like they did before[14]

She choked up. "But nobody noticed this patch. After my second book, I just couldn't write. I couldn't bear to keep pleasing them like that. Then I did write, but didn't dare publish it. I can't afford to get labeled an ethnic poet. I started publishing again only last year [1991]. Baghdad was in ruins and the newspapers said all the new Ethiopian immigrants smelled and had AIDS. I couldn't stand it and had to write."

I asked, "Have you considered publishing in *Nogah* or *'Iton Aher?*"[15]

"Are you kidding?! *Nogah* is a bunch of Ashkenazi elitists. They'd translate some American Jewish woman poet before they'd take my stuff—I have an [Arab] accent. They're the ones who have defined feminism—I'm not in it and don't want to be. As for *'Iton Aher,* they're too militant. If I appeared there, I'd never appear anywhere else. Besides, how could all my female body imagery help the Mizrahi cause?"

II. Siham Da'oud

I LOVE IN WHITE INK
at evening, who knows what day or time
from my brow bursts a memory
smuggled from jail to jail
scattered like my land's windwisps
my breath under my embroidered scarf
fleeing in white ink
in smuggled folksongs
of his color — don't ask — like grapes, like wine
and when snow fell from my face
I wanted to tell him good-bye.
I searched, aspired to his height
took a walk to dry the
storm in my throat
all my words have been detained
maybe written in white ink

I reviewed Arab history
found no dream to borrow
again shook myself all over:
how do you keep turning into a lie
so that my throat remains detained
in the airports of the universe
I long for my land's windwisps —
always departing, I leave love at addresses
that can't even be looked for
and in your beautiful eyes
and again
I wanted to draw the disfigured faces
you bear
the tortured homeland infiltrated me
between wisps
and birdwings
but I — I have only my skin

and a dream in white ink
and eyes as big as Mt. Carmel

all that was between us —
my full height
and days passing
on Palestine time —
maybe in your true form you are beautiful
maybe
but I'm just a tear, wet
on my mother's scarf, fed up with its color
its noncolor
a dried tear on the scarf
so I'm telling you all
I'm giving myself up to fruiting and multiplying
I know the truth
and love the words stitched on my old scarf
ready to pounce day and night

and love my land's windwisps
and babies in Beirut and Sakhnin
and I love my storm birthing
and the pomegranate bursting

— SIHAM DA'OUD,
I Love in White Ink, 1981, translated from Hebrew
by Helene Knox and Smadar Lavie

Amira Hess, though self-identifying as a woman of color, affiliates herself with neither Israeli feminism nor Mizrahi activism. She is therefore able to publish in Israel's top literary periodicals. The Palestinian poet Siham Da'oud, in contrast, as a non-Jewish citizen of the Jewish state of Israel, does not have the paradoxical luxury of choosing in-betweenness as the road to fame.[16] She grew up in the sixties in the only Palestinian family in a Jewish neighborhood of Ramla, until 1948 a thriving Palestinian metropolis. She started publishing at sixteen in the literary supplement of the Arabic-language *al-Ittihad,* the daily newspaper of the Israeli Community Party. This was then the only non-Zionist outlet for Palestinian intellectuals. After graduating from high school, she moved by herself to Tel Aviv, an unheard-of act for a Palestinian woman even now. For about the last twenty years she has been living independently in Haifa. She writes in Arabic, but her only collection of poems, *I Love in White Ink,*[17] is in a Hebrew translation by Sasson Somekh, an Iraqi Jewish professor of Arabic at Tel Aviv University.[18]

In May 1992 I sent Da'oud, on official letterhead of the University of California at Davis, a letter similar to the ones I sent all of the other authors in this study. I introduced myself and the research in some detail, because I was acutely aware I was "studying up,"[19] and asked for cooperation from intellectuals even busier than I was. Da'oud is the only Palestinian woman citizen of Israel who is an established writer. Moreover, in the only two interviews she has given the Israeli press,[20] the Ashkenazi woman journalists could not drop the subject of her marital status as a single woman who chose creativity over family, in the accurate belief that in the current state of Palestinian patriarchy, she could not have both. "I am an Arab in a Jewish society and a woman in an Arab society," she told them. "I live between two cultures and two languages."[21]

When I arrived in Israel I called Da'oud, and she was very excited about meeting me. I was surprised to hear her completely de-Semitized Sabra Hebrew accent[22] and mentioned it, which she took as a compliment—though she made no comment on my using the same accent. On the appointed August day I arrived at her office at the *Dar Arabesque* publishing house, in the Palestinian section of Haifa. Glued to her Macintosh, she was willfully oblivious to the foot traffic near her desk in the large, open room. I recognized her from her picture in the newspaper, so I walked over and introduced myself. She stood up and said, "*You're* the one? You don't look like a professor at all."

"What do you think a professor *should* look like?" I inquired, noting how young she looked in her jeans, white shirt, and wireframe John Lennon glasses typical of the Ashkenazi leftist intelligentsia.[23] "I'm only two years younger than you are."

Stumped, she looked uncertain, then offered to make me a cup of coffee. Having returned with it, she took out her appointment book and stared at it intently. "We weren't scheduled to meet today," she announced.

I looked at my book and said, "I have it right here, 4 P.M. today. Here I am."

"Well, I'm busy now. We'll have to reschedule. Call me Friday."

I couldn't believe it. I had just driven all the way from Tel Aviv in drenching heat to see her. I was sure she was wrong, but it was clear she didn't want to talk to me. Out of politeness, I apologized profusely and took my leave. On my way out I ran into the brother of an old college pal. We hugged and chatted cheerfully in Arabic. Da'oud looked up from her Mac in amazement. As I write this now, I wonder if that was because it was so rare in her circles to see Palestinian and Mizrahi intellectuals engaged in everyday conversation devoid of politics, instead of talking to each other through the Ashkenazi liberal left.

At the appointed hour on Friday, I called. I got an answering machine, but when Da'oud heard my voice she picked up the phone.

"I thought it would be your secretary calling," she said.

"I wanted to speak to you personally," I responded warmly. "I think your poetry is brilliant and I want to talk to you about it. I don't agree with the critics who say you just write the Community party line. I've read the interviews you gave, and quoting your own images, I wonder how it feels to always be the only woman in the room who is there because *you* chose to be, not because some man in your family chose to be. How do you live your everyday life when you are, as you say, 'an Arab in a Jewish society and a woman in an Arab society'?"

"So you do have a secretary."

After she probed some more about the technical details of my professional life, she said, "I just don't have time to meet with you. Go ahead and ask me your most crucial questions now."

"OK. What have you published since *I Love in White Ink,* and where? I'd like to get copies."

An ominous silence ensued. Then, groping for words, she said, "Well, you know, some of my poems have been published in Hebrew, thanks to some Palestinian writer friends of mine, men who write in both Arabic and Hebrew and are well connected. They would ask me to print out a copy for them, then they'd translate it and get it into print."[24]

§

"She didn't know what to do with you," a Palestinian feminist activist, Kamla,[25] explained to me in San Francisco two months later. The city was shrouded in chilly ocean fog. We were huddled in my car late at night, parked across the street from the Mission police station waiting for her traveling companion, a Peace Now kibbutznik.[26] They were on a tour of U.S. campuses organized by the Progressive Zionist Caucus, to show American youth that Palestinians and Israelis, if they were women, could actually sit down together and engage in dialogue.

"I didn't know what to do with you either, when you walked into my office three months ago. I'm not used to seeing dark women in positions of power. Though your letter looked impeccable, when I actually saw you I didn't think you could be a professor. You just didn't match your stationery."

Kamla paused a long time, watching a lone car swish by, piercing the fog with tubes of light. Then the words came as if she were chewing Galilean stones.

"You know, the trouble is, we Arab women, Jewish or not, can talk to Ashkenazi women, but not to each other. We know they have the money, the funding, the grants, the contacts with the American liberal Jewish community. If we ask nicely, they might let something trickle down to us, as long as it is for feminism and has nothing to do with Palestinian nationalism. Even so, we Palestinian women get more that way than you Mizrahi women do. It's easier for Jews to admit they colonize non-Jews, than other Jews. And it's just as hard for us Palestinians to admit we have anything in common with any Jews, even if they're Arab."[27]

She paused again. "You know, here I can be the feminist I am. Back home I'm only a woman. I can speak out as a Palestinian activist, but not as a feminist Palestinian activist. The very few outspoken feminists have had threats on their lives."

A siren revved up, and a police car leapt out of the parking lot.

"Theoretically, we Palestinian women have two choices. One is to put ourselves first and be feminists, but we balk at allying ourselves with the Israeli feminists, who are Ashkenazi Zionists, even though they support us financially and we have to keep good relations with them. And the feminist activists in the West Bank are from the aristocracy. For them, even with our Ph.D.'s, we are peasants, because our aristocracy left in 1948. The other choice is to ally ourselves with our men and fight for Palestinian nationalism. But even in a Palestinian state, there will still be battered wives, prostitutes, and daughters killed if they lose their virginity before marriage."

Long pause. Suddenly more loud sirens shrieked, and police cars sped off.

"And besides, we are Israeli citizens. I'm not going to leave my home in my native village and move to the West Bank where there's a Palestinian state, even though the Israeli government will try to get me to do it."

She stared out the car window, then spoke slowly, meditatively, sadly.

"And as for Siham Da'oud, even if she was finally convinced you were a professor, she still wouldn't want to talk to you, because your line of questions would make her face the contradictions in her life. She's so talented. It's too bad she found it impossible to ally herself with any other feminists. She's sacrificed so much in her life just to get free of Arab patriarchy. But she felt she had to go with the guys, and eventually they shut her up. I don't think she even writes anymore."

My mind drifted to Da'oud's poetry and her two interviews with the Israeli media. The journalists who interviewed her could not understand who the male figure in her poems was, and they tried to pin down which ex-boyfriend it might be. They asked her where in her poetry was Palestine, the feminine homeland, the motherland. But she answered that her love was for Palestine the man.[28]

Yes, I thought, but she's ambivalent, frustrated by the man/homeland who demands that she enact traditional womanhood and bear children for the nation rather than enact her own creativity.

> how do you keep turning into a lie
> so that my throat remains detained
> in the airports of the universe
> I long for my land's windwisps —
> always departing, I leave love at addresses
> that can't even be looked for
> and in your beautiful eyes. . . .
> So I'm telling you all
> I'm giving myself up to fruiting and multiplying.[29]

III. Na'im 'Araidi

BACK TO THE VILLAGE
Back to the village
Where I found how to cry my first cry
Back to the mountain
Where nature's so full
The walls bear no art
Back in my home, of stones

My fathers hacked from rock
Back to myself—
And that was why I came.

Back to the village.
For I dreamed of the difficult birth
Of za'atar spices, fading
From my poet's word-hoard
And the far harder birth
Of wheatsheaves from stony soil,
For I dreamed of the birth of love.

Back to the village
Where in my last round
I was a graperoot
In the good ground
Until that wind rose
And scattered me far and gathered me here
As a penitent.
O, my dream number 32
Here, the paths no longer here
And houses layered up like the tower of Babel
O, this heavy dream of mine—
No sprout from your root will bear!

Poverty's children, where are they now,
Torn autumn leaves?
Where is my village that was,
Those named paths
Now asphalt roads?

O little village, you're a
Township. Tamed.
Back to the village
Where dog barks died a slow death
And the dovecote's a tower of neon.
All those peasants I wanted to sing with—
Stanzas of hay to the nightingale's song—
Laborers, throats thick with smoke.
Where are they all, who were, and are gone?

O, my heavy dream
I came back to the village
To flee the city and all its ways

But arrived
As if coming from one exile
To another.

—NAʿIM ʿARAIDI,
"Back to the Village," 1985, translated from Hebrew
by Helene Knox and Smadar Lavie

We were talking about Elik, the prototypical literary protagonist of the Sabra. Elik, the tall, blond, blue-eyed, square-jawed, broad-shouldered neo-Adam, who rose unengendered, unbegotten, from the sea. Elik, the mythical Ashkenazi who lacks any diasporic genealogy.[30]

"I am the wife of Elik," declared Naʿim ʿAraidi, as his wife served us food. We were sitting in the vast living room of his ancestral house in the Galilean mountain village of Meghar. "How do I feel? Castrated. I want you to understand. This Israeli mutation of the West is very seductive, and I am in love with it. That means, I am ambivalent, because I'm not accepted on my own terms. How's the kabob?"

I nodded approvingly. "The dinner's great," ʿAraidi reassured his wife.

"They imposed on me the specificity of writing about the Druze village. Such specificity might liberate someone like Rushdie or Ben-Jalloun from writing humanistic universalistic prose, but for me it is a complete castration. Because in Israeli literature, universalist humanism, that is, Zionism, is what gets you canonized. But my imposed specificity at least gives me the power to get published. I'm a border-zone author, mediating between Arab and European."

He took a bite of hummous and another chunk of kabob and kept talking, matter-of-factly, with his mouth full.

"Once I thought that if I joined the left, I could be cosmopolitan. But my cosmopolitan words became impotent as I gradually figured out how their women were taking me as an exotic jock. The left raped me."

His words were measured, even as his face struggled to contain his pain.

"So I married a Druze woman. I tried to make a home out of the fence I'm sitting on. In my home, I am the Arab patriarch." He leaned over and put his arm around his wife, hugging her to him. Her eyes widened and her body stiffened, but she was silent. The anthropologist was quite surprised by this public display of affection.

"My loneliness is so Israeli, and my family warmth is so Druze. Having a large family is my guerrilla warfare against being inscribed as a castrated Arab Other, even among the demands of my professional life in the West. I live in a third space.[31] I am not the masculine East. I'm not the masculine West. I'm not the feminine East. I'm not the feminine West. I'm in flux."

IV. Bracha Serri

THE MAID
I went to the movies.
A lady saw me and said,

"Why not work for me?
I need a maid."

I took my son for a walk.
They called me a nanny.
The kid was a doll,
But his mommy looked funny.

I did volunteer work.
They offered me a job.
"Poor thing," they clucked.
"She must be unemployed."

I taught a class. They said,
"Where is her director?"
"She's just a guest," they said,
When I came as school inspector.

"New tenant," they assumed,
As I showed off my own home.
"New typist," they presumed,
As I typed my new poem.

—BRACHA SERRI,
"The Maid," 1983, translated from Hebrew
by Helene Knox and Smadar Lavie

"The Maid" is a poem from Serri's first book, *Seventy Wandering Poems*.[32] She not only paid for the publication of that book, she also typed the text and did the graphic design herself. Unlike Hess, Serri does not shroud her politics with mystical imagery. Her poems map not only the racialization of the borderzone but also its gendered construction. They deal with her Yemeni experience in Israel. "I am the dark woman," she says.

She cleverly situated her second book of poems in the context of the Ashkenazi Zionist left's protest movement against the Lebanon War and Israel's attempts to suppress the Intifada, so it was published by Breirot, a respectable, though fringe, press.[33]

"But I think your assumption is right. In hindsight, I think I did try to hide the Mizrahi militancy of my early poems among the rhymes and meters," she said, cupping her hands around steaming hot chocolate one fall 1990 midnight in my Berkeley office. "And the critics just dismissed it as folk art. They said I write testimonials, not literature. I couldn't establish a real dialogue around my work in Israel, because of that famous first short story, the one I was so embarrassed to publish I used a pseudonym. People thought the rape of a Yemeni bride on the wedding night of her arranged marriage was just erotic titillation. The feminists liked it, but they didn't want me to talk about the ethnic thing. Too divisive, they said. The Mizrahi male intellectuals said my feminism was divisive. They claimed I was serving the Ashkenazi men by giving them ammunition to attack our men's masculinity even more. So in 1988 I finally sentenced myself to exile. If I'd stayed another day in Israel, I would have gone crazy. It's one thing for an American woman of color to weave between and among racist feminists and sexist minority revolutionaries in the U.S.— there's a spacious borderzone here. But in Israel the resources are so limited. The networks are so tight. And the Arab-Israeli conflict sharpens the edges so you get cut and bleed.

"Before I finally left, I tried everything. I tried the best I could to build bridges. I went with the men, but as soon as I mentioned sexism, they retaliated. I threw myself in the [Ashkenazi] feminist movement, and gritted my teeth so long at all the racism. Finally I confronted them with it, and they hurt me even more than the men by using their whole upper-class network to blackball me from jobs, grants, anything."

As I transcribe Serri's words, I realize I too am in exile so I can write. I have known for a decade that Israeli academia would never give a job to anyone of my color and gender, not to mention my political positionality. But talking to Serri, I realize I am here not just for a job, but for survival. To keep my voice. But what has it cost me? The house I grew up in. My grandmother's Shabbat foods. The smell of citrus in the spring. Turning the radio on to all my favorite folksongs. Always having someone in the extended family to help me care for my son, so I would have time to write. But the patriarchy would not let me write—especially what I write. And I lost my language—I cannot write this in Hebrew. No one would publish it.[34] The authors I study had to learn Hebrew because no one would publish them in Arabic. They bear the burden of representation for their communities, but they cannot express themselves in the languages of those communities. Despite my U.S. academic privilege, I who have chosen to bear the burden of representation for these writers cannot do so even in the tongue they had to adopt—my native language.

"I still can't go back to Jerusalem," Serri continued. "The pain is too raw. Here in Berkeley I discovered that Israel was my exile from Yemen. I just couldn't breathe there. I kept getting asthma attacks. It tore me apart, the way I was ignored and dismissed by both. Here I am a nobody. I babysit and give massages, but I can breathe. I write and write and write."

§

Two years later Serri ordered me, "You stay here and battle free-floating academic theory! *I* am going home."

It was Saturday, 24 October 1992. Serri was packing her bags and fixing up her apartment for her big going-away party that night. "After four years in exile," she said, "I have finally learned how to fight on all fronts at once, and live to tell of it."

The air smelled fresh from the first autumn rain that morning, rain that had washed away the summer dusts.

"I have to publish all the stuff I've written in Berkeley, and it has to be in Israel, and in Hebrew. This time I'll have answers no matter what they say. If they say I write testimonials, I'll say, so what? Rigoberta Menchú does it. If they say my work is just folkloric storytelling, I'll say, isn't that the latest postmodernist style?" And she ticked off a string of formidable comebacks.

"I'm even going to buy my Jerusalem apartment from my landlord, so I finally have a home. Well—Israel will never be a home, but it'll be home base."

Notes

1. Arab Jews, often called *Sephardim*, prefer the term *Mizrahim* (Orientals, in Hebrew) for political mobilization. *Mizrahi* is the adjectival form of Mizrahim. This point is further elaborated in Smadar Lavie, "Blow-Ups in the Borderzones: Third World Israeli Authors' Gropings for Home," *New Formations* 18 (1992): 84–106, and in Shlomo Swirski, *Israel: The Oriental Majority* (London: Zed Brooks, 1984).

   The dialogues in this essay are translated from Hebrew by me, Smadar Lavie, and are between the poets and myself. They are a part of a larger project in progress, a book on Third World Israeli authors. The book discusses the lives and words of authors whose mother tongue is Arabic but who write and publish Hebrew prose and poetry and translate. Another layer of translation through dialogue, discussing the technical elements of the poetry translation on which Helene Knox and I collaborate, is discussed in Helene Knox and Smadar Lavie, "Translating by Dialogue: Tracing the Politics of Metonymy" (n.d.). I have also translated poetry written in English by U.S. women of color, such as Janice Gould or Cheryl L. West, into Hebrew (see *KLAF Hazak* 12 [1994]: 46–47; or *Nogah: A Feminist Magazine* 26 [1993]: 45; both in Hebrew). I also lectured on the relevance of works by U.S. feminist theorists of color, such as Gloria Anzaldúa, Norma Alarcon, Chela Sandoval, bell hooks, and Trinh Minh-Ha, among others, to a joint meeting of the Tel Aviv Mizrahi Feminist Forum, the Lesbian Feminist Form (which published *KLAF Hazak*), and the mainly Ashkenazi organization of Women for Political Prisoners. The lecture was a cultural translation of sorts. See also my interview by Ya'el Ben Zvi, "Dialoguing the Zone in-between Darkness and Whiteness," *KLAF Hazak* 9 (1993): 30–40 (in Hebrew).

2. See, for example, Smadar Lavie, *The Poetics of Military Occupation: Mzeina Allegories of Bedouin Identity under Israeli and Egyptian Rule* (Berkeley: University of California Press, 1990); or The Hajj, Smadar Lavie, and Forest Rouse, "Notes on the Fantastic Journey of the Hajj, His Anthropologist, and Her American Passport," *American Ethnologist* 20, no. 2 (1993): 363–84; or Lavie, "Blow-Ups."

3. This point is discussed theoretically in Angela McRobbie, "Strategies of Vigilance: An Interview with Gayatri Chakravorty Spivak," *Block* 10 (1985): 5–9.

4. See Tovi Soffer, "She Comes Galloping, *Yedi'ot Aharonot,* May 25, 1988, in Modern Times Section. See also Diana Lam, "Roots Have No Revival," *'Al Hamishmar,* February 1, 1985. Both articles are in Hebrew.

5. I discuss in detail my textual method of writing in the split authorial voice, "the anthropologist" and "I," in Lavie, *Poetics,* 37–38.

6. In Hebrew the word woman, or *nekeva,* is derived from the word *nekev,* or hole.

7. "Salvation for Copulating Souls," *Ha'olam Haze,* February 6, 1985, Book Review Section (in Hebrew).

8. Avidav Lipsker, "The Language and Style of the Mystic Poem: A Reading of the Poem 'And from the Height of My Bed I'm a Woman' by Amira Hess," *'Alei Sadeh* 24: (1986): 181, 184, 186 (in Hebrew).

9. Shmuel Shetel, "The Pain of Her Love to the Dead Father and the Living Lover," *Ma'ariv,* May 29, 1987, Literary Supplement (in Hebrew).

10. Eyal Meged, "Poetry to the End," *Ha'aretz,* April 30, 1987, Literary Supplement (in Hebrew).

11. "The Storm and the Outburst," *Ma'ariv,* March 13, 1987, Book Review Section (in Hebrew).

12. Amira Hess, *And a Moon Drips Madness* (Tel Aviv: 'Am 'Oved, 1984; in Hebrew).

13. Ibid., 7–10. Translated from Hebrew by Helene Knox and Smadar Lavie.

14. Amira Hess, from an untitled poem in *Two Horses on the Light Line* (Tel Aviv: 'Am 'Oved, 1987), 40. Translated from Hebrew by Helene Knox and Smadar Lavie.

15. *Nogah* (*Venus*), the magazine for the Israeli feminist movement; *'Iton Aher* (*An Other Newspaper*), the quarterly that publishes militant Mizrahi intellectuals.

16. For discussion of in-betweenness as a strategy of minority discourse, see Nahum Chandler, "The Signification of the Autobiographical in the Work of W. E. B. DuBois," in *Displacement, Diaspora, and Geographies of Identity,* ed. Smadar Lavie and Ted Swedenburg (Durham, N.C.: Duke University Press, forthcoming); or Smadar Lavie and Ted Swedenburg, "Between and among the Boundaries of Culture: Bridging Text and Lived Experience in the Third Timespace," *Cultural Studies* (in press).

17. Siham Da'oud, *I Love in White Ink* (Tel Aviv: Sifriyat Po'alim, 1981; in Hebrew).

18. Another collection of her work was published in Arabic in Beirut, but without her permission and in violation of copyright law. Because some of the text has been altered, Siham Da'oud has dissociated herself from this collection. See "Small Country, I'm Getting Closer," *Ma'ariv,* April 30, 1981, Book Review Section (in Hebrew).

19. This concept was coined by Laura Nader in "Up the Anthropologist—Perspectives Gained from Studying Up," in *Reinventing Anthropology,* ed. Dell Hymes (New York: Pantheon, 1972), 284–311.

20. See Ronit Lantin, "To Be an Arab Poet in Israel," *Siman Kri'a,* 1980; and Yonah Hadari-Ramaj, "I'm Ready to Be Naive to Be an Optimist," *Yedi'ot Aharonot,* June 3, 1988, Literary Supplement. Both articles are in Hebrew.

21. Hadari-Ramaj, "I'm Ready."

22. For discussion of the process of the de-Semitization of Hebrew due to the Ashkenzai hegemony of Israeli culture, see Ella Shohat, *Israeli Cinema: East/West and the Politics of Representation* (Austin: University of Texas Press, 1989), 54–55.

23. For discussion of Israeli yuppie leftist style of dress and interior design, see Smadar Lavie, "Locating a Home on the Border: Third World Israelis, Minor Literature, and the Racial Formations of Zionism," in *Displacement.*

24. After I returned to the United States in the fall of 1992, I sent one of Da'oud's friends a translation of *I Love in White Ink* and my book, even though the friend asked only for the book. Da'oud was pleased with the translation, and she read it in an international poetry conference that took place in Jerusalem. The next summer Da'oud met with me for a generous six hours and apologized about the scheduling "mixup" of the previous summer.

25. At her request, I have changed her name to this pseudonym.

26. Both Peace Now and the Kibbutz are social movements that are almost purely Ashkenazi.

27. Ted Swedenburg and I have commented on the possibilities that theoretical concepts such as hybridity offer for building minority coalitions based on overlapping fragments. In "Between and among" we argue that

> One of the most intractable problems for creating such bridges is the history of the White Left practice, which misperceives the minorities' tactical syncretized articulations as a business-as-usual avant garde free-floating fragmentation. Despite the poststructuralist collapse of the humanistic enterprise in theory, in practice, the White Left

still wants to privilege itself with the humanistic role of interlocutor between the various minorities. This filter remains a bottleneck to the free flow of dialogue minorities need in order to sort out their historical commonalities and differences. The White Left could best contribute to the inter-minority dialogue by getting out of the way and becoming an active listener rather than a patronizing participant.

The case of the Mizrahi and Palestinian feminists' communicating via the Ashkenazi liberal feminists is an excellent illumination of this point, where "the master's house" cannot be dismantled with "the master's tools" (see Audre Lorde, "The Master's Tools Will Never Dismantle the Master's House," in *Sister Outside: Essays and Speeches by Audre Lorde* [Freedom, Calif.: Crossing Press, 1984], 110–13). Yet Diana Jeater ("Roast Beef and Reggae Music: The Passing of Whiteness," *New Formations* 18 [1992]: 107–21) suggests that considerable work, both academic and activist, needs to be done in order for progressive whites to participate in the dismantling project. Whiteness as a category needs to be interrogated so that the hybridity built into the category "whiteness" is brought to the surface of both social relations and the analytical discourse about them. Instead of borrowing/exploring/putting on/exoticizing the trappings of other ethnicities, progressive whites need to radicalize and deprivilege their own (Lavie and Swedenburg, "Between and among"; see also Ruth Frankenburg, *White Women, Race Matters* [Minneapolis: University of Minnesota Press, 1993]).

28. Lantin, "To Be an Arab Poet."

29. Da'oud, *I Love in White Ink.*

30. For further discussion on the prototypical Sabra, see Shohat, *Israeli Cinema,* 253. See also Swirski, *Israel;* Ammiel Alcalay, *After Jews and Arabs: Remaking Levantine Culture* (Minneapolis: University of Minnesota Press, 1993); or Michael Selzer, *The Aryanization of the Jewish State* (New York: Black Star, 1967).

31. When I asked, 'Araidi said he was unfamiliar with the current theoretizations of "the third space" (see, for example Homi Bhabha, "The Third Space: Interview with Homi Bhabha," in *Identity: Community, Culture, Difference,* ed. Jonathan Rutherford [London: Lawrence and Wishart, 1990], 207–21; or Trinh Minh-Ha, "The Third Scenario: No Light No Shade," in *When the Moon Waxes Red* [New York: Routledge, 1991], 155–236). For 'Araidi, as for Bhabha or Trinh, living in such a borderzone is a postcolonial authorial privilege. Unlike Bhabha or Trinh, however, because he is a Druze in a Jewish, Zionist nation-state, this third space is also where he lives his daily life dangerously, because it is the racial borderline of neocolonialism.

32. Bracha Serri, *Seventy Wandering Poems* (Jerusalem: author's self-publication, 1983; in Hebrew).

33. Bracha Serri, *Red Heifer* (Tel Aviv: Breirot, 1990; in Hebrew).

34. I have tried a few times to apply for jobs in Israeli academic institutions and to publish Hebrew translations of my English articles in Israeli scholarly periodicals. According to Mizrahi activist and political philosopher Asher 'Idan (personal communication), 98.2 percent of Israeli tenure-track and tenured faculty are Ashkenazi. Of the remainder, 1.2 percent are Mizrahim and 0.6 percent are Palestinian-Israelis. Only 16 percent of the tenure-track and tenured faculty are women, and since their racial/ethnic origins are a nonissue, one might assume that the vast majority of them are Ashkenazi (see Eli Nahmias, "No Discrimination, yet No Equality," *Davar* [in Hebrew; I have no date for the article, which was mailed to me in the fall of 1994]). The Israeli citizenry, on the other hand, is 26 percent Ashkenazi, 54 percent Mizrahi, and 20 percent Palestinian-Israeli (see Lavie, "Blow-Ups"; and Swirski, *Israel*). Anti-Zionism has recently become the latest fad among the Ashkenazi male progressives of Israeli academia. Yet none of these scholars interrogates the gendered and racialized construction of Zionism. Given my gender and race, however, and my deconstruction of the race/gender intersection built into the patriarchal structure of Zionism, I have received nothing but rejections.

Conclusion:
Culture Writ-
ing Women:
Inscribing
Feminist
Anthro-
pology

Deborah A.
Gordon

*You say there are no words to describe this
time, you say it does not exist. But remember.
Make an effort to remember. Or, failing that,
invent.*

— MONIQUE WITTIG,
Les Guérillères, 1973

WHILE THE title of this volume, *Women Writing Culture,* accentuates women as writers of culture, its reverse emphasizes cultural inscription.
Inscription highlights the way culture produces
individuals, authors, with a sexed identity. It is
in tacking back and forth between the sense
of women as writers and the cultural inscription
of women that this volume eschews the notion of
writing as individual effort and essence. Technologies, demands, and contexts all create "the
writer," with a recognizable identity and signa-
ture. Writing is about history coursing its way
through us. The women in this volume process
words more than take up pens, and they do so
within an academic culture. Neither artisan's
cooperative nor knowledge factory is an accurate
description of the contemporary university.
Rather, universities are increasingly like supply-
and-distribution centers, a service-oriented economy's dream of higher education.

Anyone who still imagines that the university
is an ivory tower does not live in it. Evan Watkins sends a chilling warning of a future in which

writing will be determined by an entrepreneurial, corporately managed university. That future is already here. From its beginning, the political culture of Reaganism targeted the reconstruction of schools as the culmination of its vision. The Reagan and Bush administrations and research pundits proposed educational reform centered on "school culture" as they slowly, steadily cut federal funding for education. The Clinton administration's Goals 2000 continues the Republican administrations' assumption that what students know and value is a direct result of educational organization, curriculum, and instruction. Taxpayers, administrators, and legislators now think of school as an insular unit in which the "relevant measure of appropriateness and efficiency could then be read off from the student 'product' generated." As Watkins reminds readers, in the nineteenth century public educators proposed schools as levers for transforming the rest of society. Whatever work you were certified to do, education was "assumed capable of getting you there." We now face a radical reform agenda that openly disconnects and removes education from other social territories. Increasingly, we market a student-product, and students emerge from a university available to be taken up by "employers, political parties, cultural groups, and so on, if the quality of the product is approved."[1]

Welcome to a world in which intellectual expertise may increasingly be defined by consumer "needs." This is a world that assumes a fundamental tension between teaching and research and privileges the former over the latter. We have the mass media to thank for a barrage of newspaper reports since 1993 on professors who abandon undergraduates for the library, helping to create a populist antiprofessorial protest.[2] Watkins predicts that pressures from both parents and students to ensure a marketable education are likely to give administrators greater control over the "permissible boundaries of expertise." In the process, new barriers to faculty research and writing may be erected.[3] Stricter and more regularized tenure- and promotion-review procedures may well penalize scholarship "whose 'payoff' is not immediately obvious." Radical thought does not sell as it did in the 1960s, those years that stamped academia with a culture of dissent. So we fight for its existence in the midst of increased hostility to knowledge that is noninstrumental. It is no small contradiction that just at the moment when women are receiving more Ph.D.'s and entering tenure-track positions they are caught in a crisis that curbs their writing. Mary Shelley's adage, "Invention, it must be humbly admitted, does not consist in creating out of void, but out of chaos," is fitting for the mundane pressures that situate this volume.[4]

In the belly of this beast, however, lies a central irony. Despite the trend toward corporate management of universities, oppositional research is traveling along an alternative route. Cultural studies, queer theory, science and technology studies, anthropology at home, and mass-media studies all intrude into social sectors. These proliferating fields mock the maximization of product quality and attractiveness as education's goal by adhering to an older model of the university.[5] In the process, cultural studies have increasingly taken over ethnography and forced anthropologists to travel to the very places where right-wing educators, activists, and legislators have been hard at work, the spaces of daily life. Anthropology no longer looks like anthropology when its noncertified colleagues claim to be doing fieldwork at Star Trek conventions and among virtual-reality communities and sex workers.

Feminist anthropology has not been immune to the transdisciplinization of ethnography. Accomplished field-workers have become feminist critics and theorists who travel back and forth between audiences. It was Marilyn Strathern who first pointed out the "awkward relationship" of feminism and experimentalism in anthropology in a *Signs* article. Since then, *Critique of Anthropology* and the *Anthropological Quarterly* have taken up this theme in special issues. Feminist theorists who are not anthropologists now move in anthropological circles, facing a shared crisis in the politics of representation among women. Feminist ethnography is the orphan of this exchange.[6] Without a disciplinary home, it signifies a crisis in feminism, fieldwork, writing, and ethnography. Within this interdisciplinary wild zone I want to step into a particularly troubled zone of contention, that of feminism and experimental ethnography.

Why did feminists not experiment with the genre of ethnographic writing or produce debates over textual theory? Feminist responses to this question have ranged widely. Some have contended that women have also written experimental ethnographies, but their literary and political creativity has gone unrecognized.[7] Others have expressed skepticism. Frances Mascia-Lees et al. argue that experimental ethnography's "politics by other means" inflates its real-world effect or, more cynically, expresses careerism masking as academic radicalism. Underscoring the dangers to changing the academy, the authors privilege the theoretical, epistemological, and institutional superiority of feminism over the more slippery reforms of textual innovation.[8] In response, Vicki Kirby, an Australian feminist theorist, has raised the curious question of why U.S. feminists in the social sciences have resisted poststructuralist insights. Without entirely advocating textual experimentalism, she finds an "anti-theory" parochialism among feminist social scientists who curiously reject what they do not seriously read.[9] Feminism and postmodernism in anthropology are not unified identities, she suggests. Finally, Lila Abu-Lughod speculates that feminists did not experiment with textual form because they were trying to establish academic legitimacy.[10] Unlike the wives of many well-known and prominent male anthropologists who could write novelistic accounts of experiences among foreign people and cultures, feminist anthropologists did not want to jeopardize their incipient professionalism. In the feminist appropriation of *Writing Culture*, attention to the political significance of metaphor, textual voice, and narrative now makes us aware of feminist anthropology as a literary genre. Having a literary history of feminist anthropology requires letting go of the reductionism of the "conventional" realist and "experimental" ethnography.

Feminists have not questioned this distinction because experimentalism is a loaded term for intellectuals in the United States. In North American culture the term is particularly rich in political meaning. It bears all the love of iconoclasm so near and dear to the Anglo, Protestant, entrepreneurial, dominant culture. In an immigrant nation that has historically demanded and fueled assimilationist dreams, breaking from tradition, imagining one can forget the past, is an American obsession. Fascination with the new, desire to be associated with innovation or to be on the cutting edge, is the frontier philosophy. With it critics have pasted an indigenous overlay on imported European products such as continental theory and criticism. In politics, experimentalism connotes democracy, innovation, and freedom, and in the arts it carries positivist associations of being in an avant-garde. These indigenous meanings cast an aura over the textual turn in anthropology, making it difficult to resist, despite the weaknesses surrounding its treatment of feminist theory and women's writing in anthropology.

In addition to the "American" rhetoric of experimentation, however, there are professional reasons for the appeal to feminists of the question of writing experimentally. Systematic, disciplined attention to ethnographic form engendered by the idea of textual experimentation has enabled feminist anthropologists to increasingly write "first" mixed-genre ethnographies. A number of feminist ethnographies interweave autobiography, ethnography, and memoir to reflect on Western feminist desire, location, and knowledge. It is not entirely clear whether feminist experimental ethnography will simply solidify into another genre or become something more mobile and open to redefinition. Indeed, one unintended consequence of the experimental turn in anthropology may have been to nail the lid on the coffin of professional writing that has historically been even less prestigious than has the biography or the life history. Other forms of writing culture, such as library-research-based dissertations, human-rights organizations' reports, and certain forms of applied anthropology disappear in the conceptual privileging of ethnographic voice as the location of a politics of representation. Subsequently, original ways of conceiving experimental ethnography may be lost if feminist ethnography simply means more academic books rather than material dispersion of authorship. Feminist experimentalism with ethnography will be impoverished without sustained reflection on how to mix sociological, political-economic, and historical analysis as well as policy recommendations such that women historically excluded from higher education gain from its material resources.

While the future of feminist anthropology remains unclear, one thing is certain. The distinction between conventional and experimental writing in anthropology has permitted feminists to misread their past. Funneling the history of feminist anthropology through a loose version of that distinction, the rich texture of literary practices, epistemological dilemmas, and forms of self-reflexivity that have characterized feminist anthropology since its birth in the 1970s have been flattened. For all of the previously mentioned explanations of feminism's "absent" experimentalism miss the social density that produced feminist anthropology. A cohort of feminist anthropologists who began writing during the 1970s has not followed the same generic route, specifically the quasi-autobiographical mode, that their male peers followed. After receiving tenure from major universities and establishing substantial professional reputations, the founding generation of feminist anthropologists continues to publish what, from within the ideology of experimentalism, appear to be conventional ethnographies and essays. This earlier generation did not write experimental ethnographies but, instead, published essays that interpreted women's status cross-culturally, not because they were less professionally rebellious than their male peers, but because they were institutionalizing a different kind of radical anthropology. They were not more textually conservative; nor was their research more politically grounded or superior. It is also tempting to imagine a second generation of feminist anthropologists who identify with being writers more than social scientists. Reacting against the establishment of feminist social science, they may be reconceiving academic writing as part of their own disciplinary authority. While there is probably some truth to the fact that a younger generation finds the identity of writer compelling, this view obscures the social thickness of experimentalism as well as the literary history of feminist anthropology. Feminist anthropology needs another past, one that is predicated neither on lack nor simply on the claim that women have also experimented with textual form. Instead, we need to relativize experimentalism by looking at the textuality of feminist anthropology itself.

Despite the fact that feminist anthropologists have not had their own theoretical debates about the textual nature of ethnography, feminist anthropology from its origins has been preoccupied with issues of anthropological representation. The form that concern took, however, was not grounded in the ethnography but in a hybrid genre, the feminist essay. Reading, redefining, and eventually muting the polemic of women's liberation writing, the anthropology of women of the 1970s radicalized the expository essay. A traffic in popular and academic theorizing during the early 1970s situates the dominance of this genre that women used to design a new object of study, "women's status." If the feminist version of the essay could speak to us, how might it tell its biography? It would have to mention the torrid affair between women's liberation and a leftist counterculture that experimented with communal living, children's liberation, self-help, group marriage, sexology, voluntary poverty, and a barter economy. The women's liberation movement occurred at a time of cultural immersion in the imagery of socialist revolutions, armed guerrilla resistance, and a Third World that was coming onto the stage of history. Its beginnings are ones of contact—not simply literal travel to countries such as Vietnam, Cuba, and areas of Latin America but also desire, projection, and appropriation. Without imagining Vietnam, an anthropology acutely aware of its indebtedness to imperial practices would not have existed. Its illegitimate daughter, the cross-cultural study of women, would not have been born either.

That transformation from anticolonial to feminist anthropology occurred in the work of radical women such as Kathleen Gough. In 1968 her controversial and internationally debated essay, "New Proposals for Anthropologists," appeared in the December issue of *Current Anthropology*. The article insisted on the need for empirical fieldwork on socialist revolutions to fulfill the anthropological study of imperialism. Just four years later Gough participated in a growing debate on the origins of the family. Eleanor Leacock brought Engels out of cold-war mothballs, introducing the 1972 reprint of *The Origin of the Family, Private Property, and the State*. Yet before the reprinting the underground press, especially regionally based countercultural newspapers, explored group marriage and the extended family as alternatives to capitalism's nuclear unit. Feminist anthropology of this period owed as much to reflections on experimentation with communal living as it did to the ethnographic record.[11] Rhetorically, it often followed the lead of broadsides, poetry, and critical essays that graduate students and journalists wrote in creating a radical intellectual life. Quickly written and circulated essays were an important literary backdrop to early feminist anthropology. The swiftness of writing, its polemic vigor, owed much to the mimeograph machine rather than to the university press book.

If feminist anthropology owed its literary existence to radical countercultural media, its immediate rhetorical context was the exchange in consciousness raising and the training of a cohort of women. Consciousness-raising and study groups were crucial sites of feminist theory, which was not, in the early 1970s, the academic genre or speciality it is today. From one perspective, theory could be understood to be multigeneric, taking form in poetry and fiction as well as nonfiction. Its multiplicity, however, was dominated by the manifesto-essay. This was a period in which women's liberationists were reacting not so much against the academy as against university-based new-left organizations such as Students for a Democratic Society. Feminists proposed consciousness raising to counter the debilitating effects of the new left's refusal to permit women to participate in writing position papers and theoretical analyses. In Pamela Allen's widely circulated statement "Free Space," collective personal testimony was only one stage in the process of abstract theorizing and analysis. Feminists used autobiographical revelation and personal testimony because they associated these forms with Third World revolutions, especially the socialist revolution in China. Seeking to create "speech," much as the Chinese practice of "speaking bitterness" supposedly resocialized peasants, women's liberationists were preoccupied with voice per se as a means for developing analytical skills. The proliferation of small, quasi-academic groups, including consciousness raising and study groups, resulted in a range of manifesto-essays in around 1970.

Women's-liberation essays emerged from the self-consciously theatrical and media-conscious antiwar movement, and they aimed to move people to action. All radical academic research had to negotiate the flamboyant new-left style that imprinted itself on intellectual life in America in the 1960s. Radical journalism in the explosion of underground newspapers charged expository essays with militancy. The earliest feminist anthropology was published not in academic collections but in the spate of trade anthologies that disseminated documents from the women's liberation movement. Coming into print around 1970, anthologies such as *Sisterhood Is Powerful*, *The New Woman*, and *Woman in a Sexist Society* reprinted Beverly Jones's "The Dynamics of Marriage and Motherhood," Marge Piercy's "The Grand Coolie Damn," and Roxanne Dunbar's "Female Liberation as the Basis for Sexual Revolution." These essays had circulated around the country either in mimeographed form or in underground newspapers such as *Rat, Ram-*

parts, *Leviathan,* and *The Voice of the Women's Liberation Movement.* After they were included in anthologies they were used as texts in early feminist anthropology courses. Robin Morgan's career as a child actress, member of the yippies (whose guerrilla theatrics and philosophy of "act first, analyze later," were renowned), poet, writer, and editor at *Rat* situates her opening declaration to *Sisterhood Is Powerful:* "This book is an action."

Morgan's anthology was the publishing outlet for Karen Sacks's doctoral research. Sacks participated in women's liberation groups in Ann Arbor, Michigan, where she was a Ph.D. student in anthropology. In her first teaching position, at Oakland University, she published her essay in *Sisterhood Is Powerful,* "Social Bases for Sexual Equality: A Comparative View." Her doctoral research was based not on fieldwork but on an examination of forms of social organization that encouraged sexual equality between women and men. Sacks, a Marxist feminist, participated in the growing dialogue over the nature of women's subordination under capitalism. While others had pointed to consumerism as the culprit, Sacks insisted that it was capitalism's need to "superexploit working women" and put them in competition with men that "kept both sexes down."[12] She turned to the ethnographic record on the Mbuti and Iroquois to claim that women needed a reorganization of work to be emancipated. In a statement that nicely captures the push-pull between the expository essay and radical polemic, she proclaimed: "Once we end exploitation, what are the conditions necessary to end our oppression? Looking at Mbuti and Iroquois societies suggests that we need a complete reorganization of 'work,' a radically different kind of division of labor. If they can do it, so can we."[13]

By 1974 and 1975, when the classic companionate volumes, *Woman, Culture and Society* and *Toward an Anthropology of Women,* came out, the polemic edge had been muted. The militant tone of earlier years was particularly subdued in Michelle Rosaldo and Louise Lamphere's introduction to *Woman, Culture and Society,* published by Stanford University Press. Instead of beginning with a demand or declaration, they began with the interrogative, "Why is Woman 'The Other'? *Are* women universally the 'second sex'?"[14] Even in *Toward an Anthropology of Women,* published by the more radical press, Monthly Review, a rhetorical shift occurred in Gayle Rubin's classic essay "The Traffic in Women." Rubin both enacted and mocked Sacks's optimistic appropriation of the "Other" for feminist purposes. Noting that answers given to the question of the nature and genesis of women's subordination would "determine our visions of the future," she went on to half-joke: "If the world historical defeat of women occurred at the hands of an armed patriarchal revolt, then it is time for Amazon guerrillas to start training in the Adirondacks."[15]

Nancy Chodorow, whose earliest work was published just one year after Sacks's, presents a slightly different version of the infusion of women's liberation into anthropology. Before she published *The Reproduction of Mothering* in 1978, Chodorow depended heavily on a cross-cultural framework to show the relativity of North American gender socialization patterns. She had majored in anthropology as an undergraduate at Radcliffe College and spent a year in Harvard's social relations program before transferring to sociology at Brandeis University.[16] Like Sacks, she published her initial research in a trade anthology, but unlike Sacks she chose the more scholastic anthology *Woman in a Sexist Society,* edited by Vivian Gornick and Barbara Moran. Gornick's and Moran's political and academic backgrounds were different from Morgan's, whose political style came from the yippies and her work as an activist poet. Gornick was a staff writer for the *Village Voice.* She had taught English at Hunter College, at the City University of New York, and at the State University of New York at Stonybrook. Co-editor Barbara Moran was an editor of *Woman's Day* magazine, where she had written on women's rights. Their introduction to the volume began with a cooler but nonetheless politicized statement: "The political nature of woman's condition has only rarely been recognized and never fully understood."[17] Chodorow's essay was a cross-cultural examination of male and female socialization that drew as much on the Six Cultures Study by the Whitings, on George Murdock's and Roy D'Andrade's data on the division of labor by sex, and on Margaret Mead's studies of sex and temperament as it did on psychoanalytic theory. Like Sacks, Chodorow's graduate school research was not based on fieldwork but was heavily influenced by theorizing in the women's liberation movement. In graduate school she participated in a reading group that explored mother-daughter relationships. While most members were "psychologically sophisticated," as she put it, and were familiar with therapy, she stressed that the group was primarily a study group.[18]

Chodorow's mother-daughter group met in Cambridge, Massachusetts, and was part of the landscape of consciousness-raising groups in which feminist anthropologists in New York City also participated. Sherry Ortner, a contributor to *Woman, Culture and Society,* participated in the Ruth Benedict collective, a consciousness-raising group composed of women anthropologists in New York City. Ortner also went to meetings of MF-III, one of three Marxist-feminist study groups in the city. Anthropologists and writers met together in these study groups, attesting to the variegated intellectual support system that bonded women in academia to a wider culture of the mind.[19]

There is one final reason why feminist anthropologists did not create an anthropology of women, at least initially, through ethnographies. Historical timing was also involved, in that many of the founding cohort who did fieldwork-based dissertations went to the field before the eruption of women's-liberation activism. Ortner, for example, returned from the field in 1968. Rosaldo came back to Cambridge, Massachusetts, where she had attended graduate school at Harvard University, only to meet with a dynamic center of women's-liberation-movement writing.[20] Because a first generation of feminist anthropologists went to the field in the mid-1960s, before the birth of women's liberation, their fieldwork was not centered in feminist questions. As they entered the women's movement they reacted to collectively constructed, transdisciplinary and transacademic questions. Cautiously, they used the Human Relations Area Files and the existing ethnographic record for infusing activist-oriented theory with greater anthropological rigor. Their graduate training gave them the intellectual tools to address conflicts among feminists over monogamy, housework, childrearing. Everything from primate studies to evolutionary stories about the origins of women's subordination in history to cross-cultural comparative data was fair game as they tried to determine whether women were, in fact, universally the second sex. Around the mid-1970s feminists produced essays that were "ethnographic" but not ethnographies. Their range included essays that focused on one culture, on two in a comparative analysis such as Sacks's, or, like Chodorow's, on the ethnographic record of a number of societies. Alongside these ethnographic essays were social theoretical essays like Rubin's classic. "The Traffic in Women" wore its ethnographic data lightly, because it was subordinated to the bringing together of Marx, Freud, and Lévi-Strauss in a critique of marriage. Instead of thinking "ethnography" versus the "essay," we have to imagine instead the value of the "ethnographic" within a particular moment in intellectual history.

In her introduction to *Toward an Anthropology of Women* Rayna Rapp proposed an *"anthropology* of women" but not a "women's" ethnography. Rapp's comments signaled a nascent opening for ethnographic research by women about women, but she was not interested in ethnography per se. Rather, she self-reflexively explored two related sets of epistemological questions—What is male dominance? How do we know when we see it? And how do we explain its origins when the concept itself is so hazy? Rapp confidently asserted, "We need new studies that will focus on women; it cannot be otherwise because of the double bias which has trivialized and misinterpreted female roles for so long."[21] This incipient "ethnography among women" is a world apart from a self-consciously feminist ethnography. The question that both Judith Stacey and Lila Abu-Lughod raised in 1988—Can there be a feminist ethnography?—could not have been asked during the 1970s. The posing of a distinctly feminist ethnography rather than an anthropology of women makes sense only in a context in which ethnography has become separated from anthropology.[22] To read either that separation or the distinction between experimental and conventional ethnography back into the past desocializes genres.

The heterogeneous traffic of genres suggests they mutate in moments of social crisis. Fredric Jameson has argued that genres are "essentially literary institutions, or social contracts between a writer and specific public, whose function is to specify the proper use of a particular cultural artifact."[23] If we think of genres as commodities rather than as contracts, however, we are obliged to see that exchange is central to their existence. Arjun Appadurai instead suggests that "commodities like persons have social lives." Treating them as alive demands embracing the fetishism of the social life of things. Commodification then becomes the site of economic value, neither entirely subjective nor objective.[24] If commodities are always in motion, and if commodification is a stage within a history of exchange, temporality subverts any absolute law of self-interest in the circulation of commodities.[25] Appadurai lays out a methodological terrain which is neither sociology nor literary criticism but the cultural study of objects that stresses their sensuous texture. His image of commodification breathes theoretical air into the stiltedness of the dichotomy between conventional and experimental writing in ethnography. To understand why feminists did not write experimental ethnographies one has to stand in the traffic of academic research and political passion to grasp the forms, uses, and trajectories of genres.

If we can call feminist anthropology a genre, clearly it has changed over time from a bastard form of the expository essay into feminist ethnography. However tempting it might be to understand this shift as a transition from a radical to a conservative university genre or from a white-dominated feminist anthropology to a race- and power-sensitive ethnographic practice, neither tragedy nor romance captures its history. Ironies emerge when one recognizes the growing conservatism of academic life and the spaces engendered within that conservatism. The expanded use of computers, the demise of a counterculture based on voluntary poverty, administrative pressures for research publication in disciplinary, refereed journals, regents' and legislatures' attempts to micromanage public universities, the re-establishment of authoritative mentoring, and a tightened job market all situate the multigenre nature of this volume. For feminist anthropologists who must meet the professional demand to write ethnographies, textual experimentation has transformed the "personal is political" into a new form of academic capital. As university presses experience greater pressure to sell books and as a competitive job market drives up publication rates, anthropologists can now become writers. Any lingering ideology of individual experimentation mystifies the scene of exchange that writes us as much as we write it.

During a period in which information technology has expanded and television plays an even greater role in the construction of politics, social action has become, largely, the manipulation of signifiers. If the distant past of *Women Writing Culture* can be heard in *Woman, Culture and Society* and *Toward an Anthropology of Women*, its more recent predecessors are *This Bridge Called My Back* and *Making Face, Making Soul*. It is true that African Americans, Chicanos, and immigrant groups in the United States have long stressed the importance of writing and literacy in battling political subordination. The linguistic skill that marks the discourse of women of color also feeds off a culture dominated by electronic media. Lessons in countering the media's tendency to trivialize any political activities left of center abound. The cross-genre rewriting of feminist theory by women of color sustained a vibrant intellectual production other than the "star system" of the U.S. academy of the 1980s. Creating radical intellectual life within the hypercapitalist marketplace of academic publishing, *Making Face, Making Soul* owes its existence to Aunt Lute Press in San Francisco, California. This alternative press publishes and distributes books "that have the educational potential to change and expand social realities."[26] The collection, edited by Gloria Anzaldúa, came from her search for materials for a reader for a course at the University of California, Santa Cruz, on U.S. women of color. By 1990 a new infusion of consciousness raising into academia was marked by the wrenching labor of excavating racism. That excavation has reconfigured feminism, stung its academic commodification, and made it again accountable to a wide range of intellectuals, artists, poets, and writers. Like Anzaldúa, whose course spawned additional writing for the volume from students, we seek to publish the work of students as well as already-established faculty.

In a world of fast-paced intellectual exchange we deny at our peril that we are all within the high-speed, entrepreneurial world of academic fashion. Learning from the practice of multicultural feminism, we nonetheless bring forward a volume characterized by collaboration, cooperative dissent, and negotiating politically charged relationships between faculty and students, women of color and white women, anthropologists and critics, and those altering academic prose and those using it to advance feminist arguments. *Women Writing Culture* peoples academia with bodies, voices, processed texts, and conversations that work against the easy slide into despair that facing the hyperconsumerism of the halls of academe invites. Echoing the past, we bring back into circulation the possibility of an academic culture in which women write not simply for their own "old-girls'" networks but also for a wider readership. We hope to continue transdisciplinary debate for a broadly defined intelligentsia. The brief account of feminist anthropology presented here socializes the ethnographic.[27] Whether we write with pens or type on keyboards, history possesses us as much as we create it. And the past gently mocks us in all its cacophony.

Notes

I would like to thank Ruth Behar for reading an earlier draft of this essay. I would also like to acknowledge the following people at Wichita State University, Center for Women's Studies, who read the final draft: Jan Afrank, Shelley Endsley, Kim Hinkson, Marilyn Klaus, and Laura Rotremal.

1. Evan Watkins, *Throwaways: Work Culture and Consumer Education* (Stanford: Stanford University Press, 1993), 199.

2. See Louis Freedberg, "UC Berkeley Debates Teaching vs. Research," *San Francisco Chronicle*, December 26, 1993, 1, 13; William M. Honan, "Report Says Colleges Are Failing to Educate," *New York Times*, December 5, 1993, 46; William M. Honan, "New Pressures on the University," *New York Times*, special section, "Education Life," January 9, 1994, 16–18.

3. See Watkins, *Throwaways*, 200.

4. See Mary Shelley, *Frankenstein* (New York: Bantam Books, 1981), xxiv.

5. See Watkins, *Throwaways*, 202.

6. Marilyn Strathern, "An Awkward Relationship: The Case of Feminism and Anthropology," *Signs* 12, no. 2 (Winter 1987): 276–92. On feminist ethnography as border crossing, see Ruth Behar, *Translated Woman: Crossing the Border with Esperanza's Story* (Boston: Beacon Press, 1993). On writing against culture, see Lila Abu-Lughod, *Writing Women's Worlds* (Berkeley: University of California Press, 1993). On feminist ethnography as betrayal, see Kamala Visweswaran, "The Betrayal: An Analysis in Three Acts" in her *Fictions of Feminist Ethnography* (Minneapolis: University of Minnesota Press, 1994), 40–59; and Judith Stacey, "Can There Be a Feminist Ethnography?" *Women's Studies International Forum* 11, no. 1 (1988): 21–27.

7. See, for example, Kamala Visweswaran, "Defining Feminist Ethnography," *Inscriptions* 3/4 (1988): 27–44.

8. See Frances Mascia-Lees, Patricia Sharpe, and Colleen Ballerino Cohen, "The Postmodernist Turn in Anthropology: Cautions from a Feminist Perspective," *Signs* 15 (Autumn 1989): 7–33. Wonder over whether a focus on ethnographic rhetoric really captures the ethical and political dimensions of ethnographic work, including fieldwork, can be heard as well in Stacey, "Can There Be a Feminist Ethnography?"

9. Vicki Kirby, "Feminisms and Postmodernisms: Anthropology and the Management of Difference," *Anthropological Quarterly* 66 (July 1993): 127.

10. See Lila Abu-Lughod, "Can There Be a Feminist Ethnography?" *Women and Performance: A Journal of Feminist Theory* 5 (1990): 7–27.

11. The literature on group marriage and family in the underground press is extensive. For a sampling, see Allen Ginsberg, Timothy Leary, Gary Snyder, and Alan Watts, "Changes," *San Francisco Oracle*, February 1967, reprinted in *Notes from the New Underground*, ed. Jesse Kornbluth, (New York: Viking Press, 1968), 155–59; Engels's classic was first published in 1942, went out of print during the McCarthy era, and was brought back into print with a foreword by Eleanor Leacock in 1972. Kathleen Gough's essay, "The Origin of the Family," *Journal of Marriage and the Family* 33 (1971): 760–71, was reprinted in *Toward an Anthropology of Women*, ed. Rayna R. Reiter (New York: Monthly Review Press, 1975), 33–76.

12. Karen Sacks, "The Social Bases for Sexual Equality: A Comparative View," in *Sisterhood Is Powerful*, ed. Robin Morgan (New York: Random House, 1970), 455.

13. Ibid.

14. Michelle Zimbalist Rosaldo and Louise Lamphere, "Introduction," in their edited work *Woman, Culture and Society* (Stanford: Stanford University Press, 1974), 1.

15. Gayle Rubin, "The Traffic in Women," in *Toward an Anthropology of Women*, 158.

16. See Nancy Chodorow, *Feminism and Psychoanalytic Theory* (New Haven, Conn.: Yale University Press, 1990), 2, for a discussion of her intellectual biography.

17. Vivian Gornick and Barbara K. Moran, "Introduction," in their edited volume *Woman in Sexist Society* (New York: Basic Books, 1971), xv.

18. Nancy Chodorow, personal interview, March 1985.

19. Sherry Ortner, personal interview, Oct. 1991.

20. Renato Rosaldo, personal interview, June 1990.

21. Rayna R. Reiter, "Introduction," *Toward an Anthropology of Women*, 16.

22. This separation of anthropology and ethnography was largely accomplished through both the continued institutional labor of George Marcus and James Clifford, editors of *Writing Culture*, and Marcus's inaugural editorship of the journal *Cultural Anthropology* in 1986. Clifford sat on the editorial board of the *American Ethnologist* from 1985 to 1989. In addition, Marcus and Clifford initiated a publication series with the University of Wisconsin Press aimed at giving graduate students a venue for publishing experimental ethnographies. As a result of their efforts, anthropologists now struggle over the meaning of a discipline that has fractured in new and exciting ways as a result of spinoffs from the intellectual openings of experimental ethnography. See, for example, Richard Fox, *Recapturing Anthropology* (Albuquerque, N. Mex.: School of American Research Press, 1991). See, as well, George E. Marcus, ed., *Perilous States: Conversations on Culture, Politics, and Nation* (Chicago: University of Chicago Press, 1993); and Nicholas B. Dirks, Geoff Eley, and Sherry B. Ortner, eds., *Culture/Power/History* (Princeton, N.J.: Princeton University Press, 1993).

23. On genres as social contracts, see Fredric Jameson, *The Political Unconscious: Narrative as a Socially Symbolic Act* (Ithaca, N.Y.: Cornell University Press, 1981), 106.

24. See Arjun Appadurai, "Introduction: Commodities and the Politics of Value," in his edited collection *The Social Life of Things: Commodities in Cultural Perspective* (Cambridge, England: Cambridge University Press, 1986), 3–63.

25. I have drawn on Arjun Appadurai's analysis in his *The Social Life of Things*, particularly his reading of Bourdieu's critique of "objectivist" treatments of social action (see ibid., 12).

26. This quotation is taken from the press's promotional statement in the back of Gloria Anzaldúa, ed., *Making Face, Making Soul: Hacienda Caras* (San Francisco: Aunt Lute Foundation, 1990).

27. In a book manuscript, "A Troubled Border: Feminism and the Textual Turn in Anthropology," I explore the relationship of feminist anthropology and experimental ethnography in greater depth.

Notes on
Contributors

LILA ABU-LUGHOD teaches anthropology at New York University. Her most
recent book is *Writing Women's Worlds: Bedouin Stories*. She is currently doing
research on Egyptian television and the politics of gender and community.

BARBARA A. BABCOCK is regents professor and director of the program in comparative cultural and literary studies at the University of Arizona. Her publications include *Daughters of the Desert: Women Anthropologists and the Native
American Southwest, 1880–1980* and *Pueblo Mothers and Children: Essays by
Elsie Clews Parsons, 1915–1924*.

RUTH BEHAR is professor of anthropology at the University of Michigan, where
she is also affiliated with the programs in Latina/Latino studies and women's
studies. She is the author of *Translated Woman: Crossing the Border with Esperanza's Story* and the editor of *Bridges to Cuba*. She is at work on a memoir.

SALLY COLE is associate professor in the Department of Sociology and Anthropology at Concordia University, Montreal, Canada. She is the author of *Women
of the Praia: Work and Lives in a Portuguese Coastal Community* and is at
work on a book about the life and writing of Ruth Landes.

LAURENT DUBOIS is a graduate student in the program in anthropology and history at the University of Michigan. He is currently doing historical research on
racial ideology, emancipation, and citizenship during the French Revolution. His
ethnographic work focuses on the healing practices of Caribbean migrants in
Paris.

PAULLA EBRON teaches in the Department of Anthropology at Stanford
University.

JANET L. FINN is assistant professor of social work at the University of Montana,
Missoula, Montana. Her recent publications include "Contested Caring:
Women's Roles in Foster Family Care," *Affilia: Journal of Women and Social
Work*.

GELYA FRANK is associate professor in the occupational therapy and anthropology departments at the University of Southern California. She is co-author, with
L. L. Langness, of *Lives: An Anthropological Approach to Biography*.

DEBORAH A. GORDON is assistant professor of women's studies at the Center for Women's Studies, Wichita State University. She is currently completing a book, *A Troubled Border: Feminism and the Literary Turn in Anthropology*. Her most recent publication is "Feminism and Cultural Studies," *Feminist Studies*.

FAYE V. HARRISON is associate professor of anthropology at the University of Tennessee–Knoxville and co-chairs the International Union of Anthropological and Ethnological Sciences' Commission on Women. She edited *Decolonizing Anthropology* and has written on the cultural politics and political economy of African American and Caribbean life.

GRACIELA HERNÁNDEZ is a doctoral student in the program in American culture at the University of Michigan. She recently published her essay "Multiple Mediations in Zora Neale Hurston's *Mules and Men*" in *Critique of Anthropology* and is writing her dissertation on Chicana/o religion, spirituality, and healing.

DORINNE KONDO holds the MacArthur chair in women's studies and anthropology at Pomona College. She is the author of *Crafting Selves: Power, Gender and Discourses of Identity in a Japanese Workplace* and has acted as a dramaturge for the world premiere of Anna Deavere Smith's acclaimed *Twilight: Los Angeles 1992*, a play based on the uprisings in Los Angeles.

LOUISE LAMPHERE is professor of anthropology at the University of New Mexico. She is the author of *Sunbelt Working Mothers: Reconciling Family and Factory*, co-authored with Patricia Zavella, Felipe Gonzales, and Peter B. Evans.

SMADAR LAVIE is associate professor of anthropology and critical theory at the University of California, Davis. She is the author of *The Poetics of Military Occupation: Mzeina Allegories under Israeli and Egyptian Rule* and co-editor of *Creativity/Anthropology*.

ELLEN LEWIN is an affiliated scholar at the Institute for Research on Women and Gender, Stanford University, and lecturer in anthropology at the University of California, Santa Cruz. She is the author of *Lesbian Mothers: Accounts of Gender in American Culture*.

NANCY C. LUTKEHAUS is associate professor of anthropology and an affiliated faculty member in the program for the study of women and men in society at the University of Southern California. She is the author of *Zaria's Fire: Engendered Moments in Ethnography*.

CATHERINE LUTZ is associate professor in the Department of Anthropology at the University of North Carolina, Chapel Hill. She is the author, with Jane Collins, of *Reading National Geographic*.

KIRIN NARAYAN teaches anthropology at the University of Wisconsin at Madison. She is the author of *Storytellers, Saints, and Scoundrels*, an ethnography, and *Love, Stars, and All That*, a novel.

JUDITH NEWTON is professor of women's studies at the University of California, Davis. She has just published *Starting Over: Feminism and the Politics of Cultural Critique* and is presently at work on an ethnographic study of academic male cultural critics.

AIHWA ONG is associate professor of anthropology at the University of California, Berkeley. She is the author of *Spirits of Resistance and Capitalist Discipline: Factory Women in Malaysia* and the co-editor of *Bewitching Women, Pious Men: Gender and Body Politics in Southeast Asia.*

JUDITH STACEY is professor of sociology and women's studies at the University of California, Davis. She has published widely on feminist family politics, theory, and methods, and is the author of *Brave New Families: Stories of Domestic Upheaval in Late 20th Century America.*

BARBARA TEDLOCK is editor-in-chief of the *American Anthropologist* and professor of anthropology at the State University of New York at Buffalo. Her most recent book is *The Beautiful and the Dangerous: Encounters with the Zuni Indians.*

ANNA LOWENHAUPT TSING teaches anthropology at the University of California, Santa Cruz. She is the author of *In the Realm of the Diamond Queen: Marginality in an Out-of-the-Way Place* and the editor, with Faye Ginsburg, of *Uncertain Terms: Negotiating Gender in American Culture.*

Index

Dominant discourses: on African Americans, 156, 234; establishment of, 250–62; on heterosexuality, 324; male travel writing as, 321n32; and minority writing, 10, 140–44, 156–57, 234, 239, 402–3, 413–15, 422, 424; on Native Americans, 131–32, 140–41; and traveling subjects, 351–52; universalizing, 253, 258, 422, 424

Dorst, John, 161

Drake, St. Claire, 241

Druze, 422

Dubisch, Jill, 178

DuBois, Barbara, 323

Dubois, Laurent, 16

DuPlessis, Rachel Blau, 15

Eberhardt, Isabelle, 318

Ebron, Paulla, 6, 20

Education, 190–91, 356; broadening scope of, 378, 385; under market economy, 429; and Native American assimilation policy, 132–36, 141–42, 145n17. *See also* Universities

Eggan, Dorothy, 120

Egypt, 339–43

El Barrio literacy project, 377–85

Emigration, strategies of, 358, 366

Engels, Friedrich, 433

Eroticism, 299, 307, 330, 414; and the exotic, 178

Ethnicity: and critical literacy work, 379–80; essentialized, 50, 63–64, 156, 351, 352, 413, 424; in fieldwork, 384; Jewish, 224; and minority discourse, 233, 235, 391; and poetry, 413, 423–24; reinvention of, 366; as U.S. folk category, 406n2

Ethnographer-informant relation, 4, 41, 75–77, 80, 161, 280, 330; ethics of, 67, 81; and power, 136–40, 291, 296–97, 353–55

Ethnographic authority, 145n5, 168, 195, 269, 277–78; vs. Boasian polyphonic style, 93; destabilized by personal experience, 80–81, 151, 156, 161, 192, 253; in feminist anthropology, 15, 326; feminist critique of, 16, 296; politics of, 377, 385, 386; of Third World women, 367

Ethnography: Boasian, and empiricism, 88–89, 92–95, 108, 117, 129n106, 196; as dialogue, 38, 46, 92–95, 170, 198–200, 280, 291, 297; early, contribution of blacks to, 241; and fiction, 133, 140–44, 189, 193, 235, 272, 274;

formulated in 1920s, 92; gay, 322; heroic style in, 273–75; at home, 215, 375; lesbian, 322–23; male bias in, 96; naturalist, 168, 392; and personal experience, 37–39, 80–81, 92–94, 135–40, 155–56, 168–81, 235, 267–81, 322–32, 340, 347, 349n11; separation from anthropology, 385, 430–31, 437, 440n22; as text, 3–4, 10–11, 105, 119, 167, 242, 381; and travel, 16, 168, 176, 306–19; vs. theory, 256; and surrealism, 307; women's tradition of, marginalized, 2, 4, 9, 17–20, 78, 94, 166, 175–81, 250–51. *See also* Feminist ethnography

Evans-Pritchard, E. E., 188, 193, 194

Exile, 8, 66, 82

Exoticism: in anthropology, 1–2, 78, 168, 171, 178, 219–20, 333n13, 379, 404; avoiding, 324; and minority writing, 50, 156, 413–15, 423–24; and travel, 307, 320n12

Experimentalism: as academic capital, 438; in ethnography, 4–5, 151, 156–62, 169–81, 186, 192, 198–201, 208, 224, 234, 235, 242, 273, 374; and feminist ethnography, 14, 272, 386, 431–33; masculinized, 250–51

Family: African and African American, 240; Chinese, 357–66; Native American, 132, 135–39, 141; Parson's early work on, 87–91; in reflexive ethnography, 66–74, 78–81; as "women's issue," 190–91, 194, 197, 201

Father, 3, 15, 65–73, 79–82, 137, 138, 215, 218–19, 254–55, 314, 396–97, 400

Female ties, in African American narratives, 400–401

Femaleness, 260, 326; and nature, 98, 346; and poetry and aesthetic expression, 122, 188, 190–94, 201–2, 234

Feminism: African American, 149–50; backlash against, 288; and colonialism, 353, 384; critique of, by women of color, 3, 6, 289, 291, 402–4, 438; and experimentalism, 5, 431–33; French, 201, 271, 283n24; Israeli, Ashkenazi-dominated, 416, 419–20; and Marxism, 180, 435; and minority discourse, 237, 335n23, 390–91, 438; multicultural, 402; in 1910s, 85, 88–89, 107; in 1920s, 88; in the academy, 250–62, 287–302, 352; and politics of scholar-

ship, 251; and study of men, 287–302;
and technology, 345–46; and theory,
258–59; Western, 235, 366–67, 386;
white, 251, 295–302, 395, 402–4; and
women's movement of 1800s, 88

Feminist anthropology, 15, 192; early,
methodology of, 13, 323–24; and
ethnographic authority, 326; and public
advocacy, 375; postcolonial, 386; and
women's liberation movement, 433–36;
and writing, 432–37

Feminist ethnography: accountability in,
385; and anthropology of women, 437;
attempts to define, 14–15, 327, 347,
374–75, 385–86, 437; denationalization of, 367–68; and experimentalism,
386, 431–33; and feminist theory, 430;
and lesbian ethnography, 323–24; and
literacy work, 376–85; potential of,
281, 375; and romanticism, 79, 296;
and social action, 374–78; and translation, 72, 382–83

Feminist theory: and anthropology, 249;
and asymmetrical relations among
women, 79, 258, 381–82; and consciousness raising groups, 89–90, 96,
434, 436; early, universalizing style of,
79, 87–91, 96–98, 324, 334n15; as
marked, 259; postcolonial, 366; rewritten by women of color, 289, 291, 438

Fernea, Elizabeth, 268–69, 276

Fetal imaging, 346

Fiction, 33–48; and cultural production of
race, 391–92; and ethnography, 133,
140–44, 189, 193, 235, 272, 274; as
theorizing, 234

Fieldwork, 88–89, 92–94, 110–12,
169–73, 256, 267–81, 296–97,
317–18; fetishism of, 110, 129n106;
and native anthropologist, 138; and
writing, 35–36, 44, 190, 195–96

Finn, Janet, 18

Firth, Rosemary, 269–70

Fischer, Michael, 191, 369n10

Flax, Jane, 276

Folklore, 137, 155, 157; scholarship,
Benedict's contributions to, 112–13

Foreman, P. Gabrielle, 150–51

Forer, Judge Lois, 374

Fortune, Reo, 127n75

Foucault, Michel, 99, 381

Frank, Gelya, 19

Franklin, Sarah, 345

Fraternity Gang Rape, 374–75

Frazer, Gertrude, 176

Freeman, Derek, 202n8, 203n19, 265n34

Freyre, Gilberto, 173

Fundora, Yolanda, 1–2

Geertz, Clifford, 79, 117, 124n9, 128n88,
190, 195, 201, 221

Geiger, Susan, 353

Gender: barriers to publication, 250, 375;
and canon formation, 249–62; and
class, 379; codes, heterosexual, 79,
296–300; and community, 401; and
dominant discourse, 250; fragmenting
of unitary views of, 289; and genius,
255–56; marginalizing research on,
175–81, 251; and minority discourse,
141, 142, 157, 291, 391; and minority
identities, 395, 399; and nationalism,
420–23; of postmodernism, 256–58;
and power relations, 78–79, 290,
297–300; of the repressed, 276; and
theory, 249–62; as transcendent category, 324, 326; variance, Native American, 329

Gendered narratives, 267–76, 306–19,
395, 399, 407n17

Genres, as commodities, 437

Gero, Joan, 256

Gilbert, Sandra, 15, 254

Gilman, Charlotte Perkins, 12, 89

Goddard, Pliny, 88–89, 92, 193

Goellnicht, Donald, 408n17

Going native, 213, 215, 297, 343

Golde, Peggy, 334n14

Goldenweiser, Alexander, 108–9, 114, 174

Goldfrank, Esther, 111, 112, 120

Goldstein, Judith, 259

Gonzalez, Jovita, 19

Gordon, Deborah, 5, 12, 14, 15, 21, 153–
54, 164n25, 200, 250

Gornick, Vivian, 436

Gough, Kathleen, 433

Gray, Rockwell, 315, 318

Green, Rayna, 180

Guangdong Province (China), 357, 358

Gubar, Susan, 15, 254

Gullestad, Marianne, 280

Gwaltney, John, 242

Haddon, A. C., 188, 194

Haiti, 321n32

Handler, Richard, 126n56

Haraway, Donna, 124n6, 128n91, 345–
46, 385–86

Harrison, Faye, 11, 12, 19, 143

Healers, 169, 342–43

Hegemonic discourses, hegemonic position. *See* Dominant discourses
Heilbrun, Carolyn, 205n57, 283n27
Hemenway, Robert E., 151–54, 235
Hernández, Graciela, 18
Herskovitz, Melville, 117, 176–79
Hess, Amira, 412–17
Heteroglossia, 221, 352, 355
Heterosexual assumption, 159, 324
Hieb, Lois, 87
Higher education. *See* Universities
Hill, Anita, 51, 249
Hitchcock, Alfred, 257–58
Hodge, Gene Meany, 269
Home, 22, 311–12, 315–15; and the field, 40, 77, 81, 317–18, 320n7, 340, 343, 347; as fieldwork site, 325, 333n13, 375; as locale, 360, 363
Homophobia, 323; in academia, 322, 333n3
Homosexuality, 175–77; popular discussion of, 326
hooks, bell, 8, 19, 150, 291
Horney, Karen, 114–15
Hsiao, Ruth, 407n17
Huckleberry Finn, 314
Hurston, Zora Neale, 18–19, 143, 174, 235, 242, 260, 392; and the academy, 152–54; critical reception of, 148–51, 162; erasure of, 150; life and works, 151–55; literary strategies of, 156; *Mules and Men,* 155–61; patrons and mentors of, 153–55
Huyssen, Andreas, 258
Hybrid identity, 8, 45, 142–43, 340, 352, 357, 417–18

Identity, 309, 393; Chinese, 351, 352, 355, 359; Chinese American, 369n10; of dominant classes, 315; enactment of, in theater, 50, 63–64; fixed or essentialized vs. shifting or multiple views of, 22, 39, 50, 63–64, 155–60, 239, 280–81, 289, 301–2, 327, 347, 352, 366, 413, 424; group, reading across lines of, 391; lesbian, 329–31; minority, in U.S., 369n18; motherhood as, 331–32; and personal experience, 324, 332; and place, 351–53; sexed, 161, 429; shared, and research, 325–27; traitorous, 287, 296, 299, 320n11. *See also* Community; Ethnicity; Gender; Narratives of identity; Race; Sexual orientation
Imperialism, anthropological study of, 433
In vitro fertilization, 343–46

Incorporation of wife, by husband ethnographer, 269–72
Inequality: in fieldwork, 280, 353–54, 384; gender, 79, 90–91, 96–98, 106–7, 180, 299–302. *See also* Asymmetrical relations; Dominant discourses; Marginalized groups
Infertility: Awlad 'Ali theories of, 341–43, 349n4; and medical technology, 343–46
Inscription, cultural, 429
Insider and outsider reading strategies, 393
Insider narratives, and dominant discourse, 402–3
Insider status, 19, 37–39, 150, 161, 277, 324, 326–28
Invisibility, 61, 96, 237, 242, 313, 323–24
Irony, 106, 119, 122, 124n9
Israeli literary establishment: and Mizrahi poets, 413, 423–25; and Palestinian poets, 417–22

Jackson, Jean, 275
Jackson, Walter, 176
Jameson, Fredric, 437
JanMohammed, Abdul, 352, 394
Jayanti, Vikram, 211, 214, 220
Jewish community, U.S., 208–24; Orthodox, 213–23
Johnson, Charles, 399
Juarbe, Ana, 377

Kaminsky, Marc, 213, 220–21
Kaplan, Caren, 370n21
Kendall, Laurel, 281
Kennedy, Elizabeth, 327–29
King, Katie, 259–60
Kingston, Maxine Hong, 398, 402–4, 406n3, 407n17, 409n38
Kipling, Rudyard, 313
Kirby, Vicki, 381
Kirshenblatt-Gimblett, Barbara, 208
Kluckhohn, Clyde, 114, 120
Kondo, Dorinne, 20–21
Koreans and African Americans, in Los Angeles, 391
Kowaleski, Michael, 308
Krieger, Susan, 303n7, 324–25
Kroeber, Alfred, 125n28; and Benedict, 110–11, 114; and Parsons, 88–89, 92
Kucklick, Henricka, 205n64
Kuper, Hilda, 211–12, 219, 220

Labor conditions, deterioration of, 376
Lacan, Jacques, 99, 283n24
Laird, Carobeth, 270

tributions to U.S. anthropology, 95; peripheral in academy, 95; president of American Ethnological Society, 85, 94; and women anthropologists, 95–96

Parsons, Talcott, 99

Participation and observation, 23, 33–48, 50, 93, 170–71, 178, 277, 325, 383

Patriarchy, 15, 66, 73, 121; Chinese, 355, 360, 365; in Cuba, 81; Jewish, 218; in minority writing, 399, 400, 407n17; Palestinian, 418, 422; Western, 254, 260

Patrons and minority writers, 137, 139–40, 153–55

Patterns of culture, 109, 116–21

Pels, Peter, 11

People of color: alliances among, 52–53, 63–64, 391; writing by, 8, 140–44, 155–60, 392

Personal experience: and ethnography, 37–39, 80–81, 92–94, 135–40, 151, 155–62, 168–81, 192, 267–81, 322–32, 340, 347, 349n11; vs. theory, 37–39, 41, 253. See also Self-reflexivity

Personal testimony, 383, 434. See also Life history; Life stories; Self-reflexivity; Testimonials

Petchesky, Rosalind, 346

Photography, 186–87, 277, 281, 306–7, 313, 315

Picotte, Agnes, 145n8

Place and identity, 351–53

Poetry, 106, 113, 117, 120, 122, 189, 198, 202, 319, 412–25; as politics, 413, 434

Political correctness, critics of, 288–90

Postcoloniality, 354–55, 366–67, 386

Postmodernism, 3, 51, 220, 221, 333n13, 431; anticipated by Benedict and Mead, 105, 121–23, 192, 198; and feminism, 251, 272, 289–90, 301–2, 381; and modernism, gender of, 256–58, 260

Power, Foucaultian view of, in feminist theory, 381

Pratt, Mary Louise, 4, 320n10

Pregnancy, 339–48

Prell, Riv-Ellen, 213, 218, 221

Privilege, 66, 142, 287, 296, 308–9, 313

Proby, Elspeth, 360

Psychology: developmental, 115; and gender, 255; and psycholanalysis, Benedict's influence on, 113–15, 154

Public: as contested category, 375; as male, 98

Public advocacy, and feminist anthropology, 375

Publishing, 108, 140, 259, 261, 290, 296, 375, 413–16, 422–25, 434–35

Pueblo fieldwork: of Benedict, 110–12; of Parsons, 89, 92–94

Puerto Rican women, and critical literacy work, 377–85

Quintana, Santiago, 111–12

Race, 50, 198–200; and barriers to publication, 375; and dominant discourse, 174, 250; vs. ethnicity, 413; and insider ethnography, 327; and minority discourse, 240, 391, 393–94; power relations, 290; vs. sexuality, 329; singular claims of, 352; and theory, 168–76, 250–62; as U.S. folk category, 406n2

Racism, 171–74, 250, 316–17, 396–97; and feminism, 438–39

Radcliffe-Brown, A. R., 37, 117, 237

Ramazanoglu, Caroline, 179

Ramos, Artur, 178

Rape, 373–74

Rapp, Rayna, 98, 437

Read, Kenneth, 276

Reading: meaning of, for marginalized groups, 377, 388n14; strategies, and construction of race, 393

Reaganism, 430

Reed, Ishmael, 393, 409n43

Reichard, Gladys, 92–95, 109

Reiter, Rayna R. See Rapp, Rayna

Representations, 152; historically contingent, 317; of less privileged others, 354; of patriarchy, 407n17

Representations of identity, 49–52, 424; by dominant group, 50, 131–32, 140–41, 370n25; politics of, 3, 62–63, 155, 162, 386, 431

Repressed, as gendered, 276

Reproduction: medical narratives of, 341, 345; politics of, 346; technology, 340–46

Rich, Adrienne, 5, 13

Rodríguez, Richard, 72

Rosaldo, Michelle, 86, 96–98, 435, 436

Rosaldo, Renato, 239, 281

Rose, Dan, 283n21

Rosenberg, Rosalind, 90, 92

Rubin, Gayle, 435

Russo, Ann, 233

Sacks, Karen, 98, 435

Said, Edward, 352, 368n8

Sanday, Peggy, 373–75

Sapir, Edward, and Benedict, 3, 105, 110, 113–16, 118–19, 189, 198

Self and Other, 7, 14, 19, 22, 67, 178, 224, 268, 285n48, 333n13, 347

Self-reflexivity, 4, 151, 155–62, 192, 196, 233, 271–81; examples of, 65–82, 306–19, 330–32, 339–48, 352–53; in feminist research, 149, 432; in lesbian ethnography, 322–32; as shadow biography, 66; in visual anthropology, 213–24. *See also* Personal experience

Serri, Bracha, 422–25

Service agencies, 354. *See also* Welfare

Sexual orientation, 323; as core identity, 326; as culturally defined, 329; heterosexual, 79, 159, 289–302, 324

Shaw, Carolyn Martin, 409n40

Shelley, Mary, 430

Shostak, Marjorie, 79, 279

Silence, 13, 71, 82, 150, 175, 256, 295, 356, 357, 402

Silverman, Sydel, 182

Sisterhood Is Powerful, 435

Smith, Dorothy, 253, 259

Social action, and feminist ethnography, 287–302, 374–77

Sontag, Susan, 317

Spengler, Oswald, 118–19

Spivak, Gayatri, 263n10, 317, 354, 367, 382

Stacey, Judith, 5, 14, 21, 353, 388n16, 437

Stack, Carol B., 149

Steward, Julian, 309–10

Stillbirth, 340

Stimpson, Catharine, 258, 283n27

Stocking, George, 128n103, 130n123

Stoller, Paul, 272–73

Strathern, Marilyn, 14, 431

Studying up, 296–97

Subaltern, 44, 234, 250, 354, 356; authority, 238

Sudarkasa, Niara, 240

Tan, Amy, 368n1, 411n55

Tannen, Deborah, 299

Taussig, Michael, 237, 320n7

Tedlock, Barbara, 16, 277–78

Television, 187–88, 201

Testimonials, 249, 355, 370n21

The Masses, 88, 91

Theater, 7, 49–64; as site for enacting identity, 50, 63–64

Theory, 10, 182, 320n7; "difficulty" of, 253–54; feminist reflection on, 258; fiction as, 234; male, 309; masculinizing

of, 14, 249–60; vs. practice, 37–39, 41, 253, 258; process of defining, 252–55. *See also* Feminist theory

Theroux, Paul, 316

This Bridge Called My Back, 3, 6–7, 15, 438

Thompson, Stith, 112–13

Thorne, Barrie, 388n13

Torres, Lourdes, 233

Torruellas, Rosa, 377

Toward an Anthropology of Women, 14, 333n11, 334n14, 435, 437, 438

Tradition: Chinese emigrant women, as preservers of, 357, 364, 400, 403; and modernity, in Chinese American male narratives, 397–99

Traitorous identities, 287, 296, 299, 320n11

Translation: cultural, 199; in Israel, 412–25; politics of, 72, 281, 382–83

Travel, 2, 10, 316, 351–52; narratives, 168, 176, 269, 273, 306–19; white, male tradition of, 308–11, 314, 317, 320n12, 321n32; women writers and, 16, 318

Trinh Minh-ha, 253

Tsing, Anna Lowenhaupt, 6, 20, 23

Tuchman, Gaye, 250

Tumaka, Nick, 111

Turner, Edith, 211–12, 219, 271

Turner, Victor, 118, 211–12, 218, 219

Underhill, Ruth, 93–94, 110, 115

Universal gender subordination, 91, 97–98, 334n15. *See also* Feminist theory

Universalism. *See* Dominant discourse

Universities, 353, 374; as "academic plantations," 238; anthropology in, 210; and consumerism, 80, 429–31, 438–39; democratizing, 11, 288; and education as conquest, 239; elitism in, 7, 200; feminism in, 96, 99–100, 250; hierarchical nature of, 8, 66, 295; homophobia in, 322, 333n3; hostility towards, 9, 100, 375, 430; sexual and racial harrassment in, 51–53; unequal access to, 376, 377, 386; women in, 33–48, 52–53, 78, 95–100, 109–10, 177, 179, 200, 224, 260–61

Vanderburgh, Rosamund, 212, 227n15

Vincent, Joan, 11

Visual anthropology, 210; and reflexivity, 213–24

Visweswaran, Kamala, 14, 151

Voice, 50, 134, 137, 149, 161, 241–42, 268, 296, 309, 310, 318, 354, 359, 385, 394, 432, 434; double, 105, 122; polyphonic, 93, 221

Wafer, Jim, 184n26, 322, 332
Walker, Alice, 13, 19–20, 400, 410n49; as anthropology's interlocutor, 234–42; *Temple of My Familiar* (novel), as cultural critique, 235–41
Wallace, Michele, 150, 234
Watkins, Evan, 429–30
Weapons of the weak, 299
Welfare system, indignities of, 377–80
West, as site of female liberation, 350–51, 364, 366
Western corporate life, 269–70
Western domination, 355
Weston, Kath, 325, 333n9
White, E. Francis, 405
White, Leslie, 95, 99
Whitten, Dorothea, 270
Wilentz, Amy, 321n32
William, Sarah, 255
Witness, ethnographer as, 383
Wittig, Monique, 429
Wolf, Deborah, 333n9
Wolf, Diane L., 150
Wolf, Eric, 175, 237
Wolf, Margery, 271–72
Woman, as transcendent category, 326
Woman, Culture and Society, 5, 14, 86, 90, 96–98, 334n14, 373, 435, 438
Woman in a Sexist Society, 436
Womanhood, as partial identity, 91, 347
Women: anthropologists, 2, 17–20, 121, 179, 334n14; anthropologists, writing styles of, 267–81; as daughters, 15, 65–68, 70–73, 78–82, 179, 358; communities of, 346; experiences of, 142, 339–40; as "honorary males," 17, 274–75; as mothers, 98; and mothers-in-law, 359–62; political empowerment of, 378; roles available to, 6, 106–7, 159–60, 177; as spiritual leaders,

168–72, 177; stories of, 166, 340–41; viewed as nontheoretical, 259; white, 142, 251; as wives, 73, 267–81, 316, 358–60; work and working conditions of, 106–7, 137, 376, 377
Women of color: alliances among, 51–52, 63–64; and feminism, 3, 6, 289, 291, 402–4, 438; and identity narratives, 50, 399; poets, in Israel, 412–25; writers, 399–405; writers, and feminism, 251, 258, 401, 438; writers, Native American, 132–44; writers, as representing community, 402, 405
Women's liberation movement, 194, 380, 433; and cross cultural studies, 435–36
Women's work, devaluation of, 250–62
Women's writing, 2; marginalized, 78, 181, 221, 242, 249–62; and men, 5–6; quilting as trope for, 118; style, vs. masculinist, 188, 190–94, 201–2
Wong, Nellie, 7
Wong, Sau-Ling, 368n1, 406n3
Woodhull, Winifred, 318
Woolf, Virginia, 1, 4, 17, 119–21
Worsley, Peter M., 193–94, 201
Wright, Richard, 397; and Chicago school of urban sociology, 392
Writing, 66–69, 107–8, 188–202, 307–8, 313, 429; against culture, 167–68, 181; the cost of, 80; cross-genre, 276–77; ethnography, as, 105, 119; about father, 70–71; gendered traditions of, 250–62, 267–76, 306–19, 395; meaning of, for marginalized people, 7, 15, 132–33, 135, 152, 377, 388n14; pleasure of, 188–89, 196; and theorizing, 188–90. *See also* Women's writing
Writing Culture, 3–6, 8, 11–12, 14, 15, 19, 23, 45, 208, 260, 319n3, 376; feminist appropriation of, 431

Yanagisako, Sylvia, 370n25, 405

Zavella, Patricia, 244n25
Zhang Xianliang, 408n33

Designer:	Seventeenth Street Studios
Compositor:	G&S Typesetters, Inc.
Text:	9/13 Sabon
Display:	Highlander and Chilipepper
Printer:	BookCrafters
Binder:	BookCrafters